Letters of H. P. Lovecraft

LETTERS TO E. HOFFMANN PRICE
AND RICHARD F. SEARIGHT

E. Hoffmnn Price

H. P. LOVECRAFT

LETTERS TO
E. HOFFMANN PRICE AND
RICHARD F. SEARIGHT

EDITED BY DAVID E. SCHULTZ AND S. T. JOSHI

Hippocampus Press

New York

Published by Hippocampus Press
P.O. Box 641, New York, NY 10156.
www.hippocampuspress.com

Cover design and Hippocampus Press logo by Anastasia Damianakos. Cover production by Barbara Briggs Silbert.

First Edition
1 3 5 7 9 8 6 4 2

ISBN 978-1-61498-335-4

Contents

Introduction

Edgar Hoffmann Price became one of the more significant colleagues and correspondents of H. P. Lovecraft during the 1930s; but given their antipodally differing temperaments and outlooks, especially in regard to their own literary work, it is a wonder that they became colleagues at all. They would not have encountered each other had not Robert E. Howard, who had known Price for some years, urged his friend to meet with Lovecraft as the latter was visiting New Orleans in 1932. Howard himself did not have the funds to make the visit from his home in Cross Plains, Texas. Price met Lovecraft on 12 June, and thereafter a substantial correspondence developed, interspersed with an additional meeting in Providence.

Price was born on 3 July 1898 in Fowler, California. After joining the Fifteenth Cavalry in 1917, he served extensively in World War I, seeing action in the Philippines, the Mexican border, and France, thereby earning him the sobriquet "Trooper." He graduated from West Point in 1923, and soon thereafter he began writing while employed at Union Carbide, first in Newark, New Jersey, then in New Orleans. His first published story was the non-weird "Triangle with Variations" (*Droll Stories,* June 1924), but soon he turned his attention to weird, adventure, Oriental, and occult fiction, publishing "The Rajah's Gift" in *Weird Tales* (January 1925). His fine story "The Stranger from Kurdistan" (*Weird Tales,* July 1925) is likely to have slightly influenced Lovecraft's "The Horror at Red Hook" (written 1–2 August 1925), whose protagonist, Thomas Malone, "could not help recalling that Kurdistan is the land of the Yezidis, last survivors of the Persian devil-worshippers" (*CF* 1.489). About a year later, Price himself wrote a letter to Farnsworth Wright, the editor of *Weird Tales,* published in the letter column ("The Eyrie"), flamboyantly praising Lovecraft's early tales: "To paraphrase the Moslem, *There is but one Lovecraft, and the unnamable is his God.*"[1] Less positively, Lovecraft in early 1927 suggests that Price was acting as a kind of informal editorial adviser to Farnsworth Wright: "after due deliberation & grave consultation with E. Hoffmann Price, Wright has very properly rejected my 'Strange High House in the Mist,' as not sufficiently clear for the acute minds of his highly intelligent readers."[2]

In 1931 Lovecraft heard from Robert E. Howard that Price and his fellow-writer W. Kirk Mashburn were planning an anthology that would include

---

1. For the entire letter, see S. T. Joshi, ed., *A Weird Writer in Our Midst: Early Criticism of H. P. Lovecraft* (New York: Hippocampus Press, 2010), 66.
2. HPL to Donald Wandrei, [2 August 1927]; *Letters with Donald and Howard Wandrei and to Emil Petaja* (New York: Hippocampus Press, 2019), 140.

"Pickman's Model," but this came to nothing and Lovecraft evidently did not hear from Price directly on the matter. The next year Price and an agent named August Lenniger conceived of another anthology that would include "The Picture in the House," but this too came to nothing.

The meeting with Lovecraft in New Orleans lasted an unprecedented twenty-five and a half hours, during which Price treated Lovecraft to "a big pot of chili con carne, one of my bachelor apartment staples,"[3] and discussed everything under the sun. Lovecraft was clearly impressed with Price's wide-ranging interests and talents, writing to J. Vernon Shea upon his return to Providence:

> Price is a remarkable chap—a West-Pointer, war veteran, Arabic student, connoisseur of Oriental rugs, amateur fencing-master, mathematician, dilettante coppersmith & iron worker, chess-champion, pianist, & what not! He is dark & trim of figure, not very tall, & with a small black moustache. He talks fluently & incessantly, & might be thought a bore by some—although I like to hear him rattling on.[4]

Only a few months earlier, in May, Price had lost his job with Union Carbide, and so he plunged into the task of becoming a full-time freelance writer. In the process, he calculatedly geared his literary material toward specific pulp markets in the weird, detective, adventure, and other genres; he even wrote stories for the "spicy" pulps. This cold-blooded approach to writing as a purely money-making operation engendered lengthy disputes with Lovecraft, who had long maintained that any sincere literary work must be pure "self-expression" written without consideration of markets, remuneration, or even a chosen readership. Lovecraft did grudgingly acknowledge that the kind of hackwork Price was producing was a legitimate business, but he asserted that it had nothing at all to do with genuine literature.

One specific literary project brought the two writers into an unusually close association. As early as their meeting in New Orleans, Price had "suggested a sequel to account for Randolph Carter's doings after his disappearance."[5] The reference is to Lovecraft's story "The Silver Key" (written 1926; published in *Weird Tales*, January 1929). It was an odd story for Price to have become enamored with, since it was not so much a weird tale as a philosophical allegory—one that Wright had rejected upon first submission and only

3. EHP, "The Sage of College Street" (1937), in S. T. Joshi and David E. Schultz, ed., *Ave atque Vale: Reminiscences of H. P. Lovecraft* (West Warwick, RI: Necronomicon Press, 2018), 353.

4. HPL to J. Vernon Shea, 13 October 1932; *Letters to J. Vernon Shea, Carl F. Strauch, and Lee McBride White* (New York: Hippocampus Press, 2016), 101.

5. Price, "The Man Who Was Lovecraft" (1949), in Peter Cannon, ed., *Lovecraft Remembered* (Sauk City, WI: Arkham House, 1998), 291.

reluctantly accepted later when Lovecraft refused to send him anything else until he did so. But the sequel Price wrote in late August, "The Lord of Illusion,"[6] is very much along the lines of his own pulp writing, full of implausible action and jettisoning entirely the delicate philosophical ambiance that makes Lovecraft's story distinctive. It is unsurprising that, when Price asked Lovecraft to look over his draft and revise it, the latter noted with tactful understatement, "It'll be a ticklish job."

Price hoped that Lovecraft could get to revising the tale in short order; after all, he had produced his own draft in only two days.[7] But Lovecraft was at the time overwhelmed with his professional revision work along with his always extensive correspondence. By March 1933 he had managed to write seven and a half pages of a new draft, and he finally finished the job the next month, retitling the story "Through the Gates of the Silver Key." He sent the handwritten draft to Price, who typed it up and added some marginal notes questioning some passages in the text. The authors must have resolved these points, and Price presumably prepared a new typescript and sent it in to Farnsworth Wright on 19 June. But Wright rejected the story on 17 August, writing to Lovecraft:

> I have carefully read THROUGH THE GATES OF THE SILVER KEY and am almost overwhelmed by the colossal scope of the story. It is cyclopean in its daring and titanic in its execution. . . .
>
> But I am afraid to offer it to our readers. Many there would be . . . who would go into raptures of esthetic delight while reading the story; but just as certainly there would be a great many—probably a clear majority—of our readers who would be unable to wade through it. These would find the descriptions and discussions of polydimensional space poison to their enjoyment of the tale. . . .
>
> . . . I assure you that never have I turned down a story with more regret than in this case.[8]

But, true to his contrary ways, Wright later reconsidered his decision and accepted the story in November; it appeared in *Weird Tales* for July 1934. It proved to be Lovecraft's only collaborative tale published professionally in his lifetime.[9] The tale was not well received by the readership; the young Hen-

---

6. First published in *Crypt of Cthulhu* No. 10 (1982): 47–56; rpt. in Robert M. Price, ed., *Tales of the Lovecraft Mythos* (Minneapolis, MN: Fedogan & Bremer, 1992).
7. EHP to HPL, 10 October 1932; ms., JHL.
8. Farnsworth Wright to HPL, 17 August 1933; ms., JHL; see Appendix.
9. Three collaborative early stories, "The Green Meadow," "The Crawling Chaos," and "Poetry and the Gods" (the first two with W. V. Jackson, the third with Anna Helen Crofts), appeared only in the amateur press. "In the Walls of Eryx," written with Kenneth Sterling, was published posthumously.

ry Kuttner wrote harshly: "Lovecraft at one time could supply a good ending, but now he is getting trite as hell. It is a bad example of a forced surprize [*sic*] ending that he has on that story."[10] Price later urged Lovecraft to collaborate on yet another adventure featuring Randolph Carter, but Lovecraft begged off.

Price has created some confusion regarding "Through the Gates of the Silver Key" by writing that "I estimated that he [Lovecraft] had left unchanged fewer than fifty of my original words."[11] In fact, Lovecraft has largely preserved the overall framework of Price's story as well as the mathematical formulations that are meant to account for Carter's ability to go back and forth in time. What Lovecraft did agree to eliminate, in accordance with Price's handwritten marginalia on the original typescript, was the various theosophical terms that he had included in his handwritten draft. Although Lovecraft had mentioned theosophy as early as "The Call of Cthulhu" (1926), he evidently did not know much about it; so when in early 1933 Price presented Lovecraft with a broad outline of theosophy, Lovecraft seemed taken with it—at least in terms of its potential use in weird fiction. Writing to Clark Ashton Smith, he noted:

> By the way—Price has dug up another cycle of actual folklore involving an allegedly primordial thing called "The Book of Dyzan," [*sic*] which is supposed to contain all sorts of secrets of the Elder World before the sinking of Kusha (Atlantis) and Shâlmali (Lemuria). It is kept at the Holy City of Shamballah, & is regarded as the oldest book in the world—its language being *Senzar* (ancestor of Sanscrit), which was brought to earth 18,000,000 years ago by the Lords of Venus. I don't know where E. Hoffmann got hold of this stuff, but it sounds damn good.[12]

In fact, Madame Blavatsky, the founder of theosophy, was herself the author of the *Book of Dzyan*, which she attempted to maintain was an ancient text. In the end, Lovecraft did not use theosophical elements in his later fiction.

Price visited Lovecraft in June–July 1933, about a month after the latter moved into his final residence, 66 College Street. He had come in an automobile that Lovecraft named Juggernaut, and drove his friend to various sites in southern Rhode Island that he had never seen before. Along with Lovecraft's new friend Harry K. Brobst, who had come to Providence in 1932, Price and Lovecraft concocted another pot of spicy chili. During an all-night session, they mercilessly dissected a story that Brobst's friend Carl Ferdinand Strauch had sent to Lovecraft. It is not surprising that Strauch ceased corresponding with Lovecraft soon afterward.

---

10. "The Eyrie," *WT* (September 1934); in A *Weird Writer in Our Midst* 77.
11. "The Man Who Was Lovecraft," *Lovecraft Remembered* 291.
12. HPL to CAS, [c. 10 February 1934]; *DS* 404.

This was Price's last meeting with Lovecraft. Now well established in Redwood City, California, Price continued to churn out formula stories for the pulps. Many of these stories, both during and after Lovecraft's lifetime, focused on certain recurring characters, including Ismeddin (featured in "The Stranger from Kurdistan" and more than a dozen other stories), Pierre d'Artois (an occult detective), and others. He continued his peregrinations by automobile, visiting Robert E. Howard in Texas and Clark Ashton Smith in California. (In later years, when meeting new acquaintances, Price would shake hands and announce that the recipient was shaking hands with the only hand to have touched Lovecraft, Howard, and Smith.) When Howard committed suicide in 1936, Price wrote a brief obituary for *Weird Tales.*

Price's pulp writing largely came to an end in the early 1950s. By this time, however, he had already begun writing articles about his relations with Lovecraft. This work had begun even in Lovecraft's lifetime: in 1936 he wrote the whimsical piece "The Sage of College Street" and sent it to his friend to look over; Lovecraft made some minor suggestions for revision. The piece was published in the *Amateur Correspondent* (May–June 1937). An ampler memoir, "Howard Phillips Lovecraft," appeared in the *Acolyte* (Fall 1944); this was extensively revised as "The Man Who Was Lovecraft," which appeared in the Lovecraft miscellany volume *Something about Cats and Other Pieces* (Arkham House, 1949). Several other memoirs and articles appeared in the 1970s.

Price made little effort to gather his vast array of short fiction into books, but August Derleth brought out the collection *Strange Gateways* from Arkham House in 1967. The small press Carcosa published an immense collection, *Far Lands, Other Days,* in 1975, containing a wide array of Price's pulp fiction. Around this time Price resumed the writing of fiction, publishing several novel-length tales of Oriental adventure (*The Devil Wives of Li Fong,* 1979; *The Jade Enchantress,* 1982), along with a four-volume series of science fiction novels (1980–87), among other work.

Following Price's death on 18 June 1988, Arkham House belatedly published *Book of the Dead: Friends of Yesteryear: Fictioneers & Others* (2001), a collection of his memoirs of the many friends and colleagues he had known over the decades, including Lovecraft, Jack Williamson, Edmond Hamilton, Farnsworth Wright, Clark Ashton Smith, Robert E. Howard, Seabury Quinn, and many others. Several of these articles were first published in the 1940s, some of them appearing in W. Paul Cook's amateur journal, the *Ghost.*

Price was married three times. He married his first wife, Helen, in 1928; they divorced in 1931. He married Wanda in 1934; they divorced in 1945; he married Loriena in 1959. He had two children, Theresa and Dan.

Lovecraft clearly valued Price as an associate and a personal friend, for all the divergences in their outlooks on life and literature. Price's voluminous letters and postcards were among the relatively few that he preserved among his far-flung correspondents. The sheer volume of this material, far eclipsing in wordage the surviving letters of Lovecraft, has made it unfeasible to publish it here, but the editors have drawn upon it to clarify otherwise obscure passages in Lovecraft's side of the correspondence.

Richard Franklyn Searight was born on 13 June 1902 in Manistee, Michigan. His parents, Benjamin Franklyn and Fidelia Taylor (Ellis) Searight, were traveling actors; when his parents were on the road, Richard was raised by his grandfather, Dr. Ellsworth Stiles Ellis, and his wife, Mary Edna (Clapp) Ellis. At some point in Richard's youth, his parents divorced, and his father later married Jeanne L. Crane.

It was at his grandfather's house, with its extensive library, that Searight began reading voraciously among the classics of world literature—a form of self-instruction that took the place of a college education. Indeed, instead of finishing high school, Searight left home at sixteen to study music at the American Conservatory in Chicago; but the two years he spent there (1918– 19) did not lead to a career in music.

Searight became a telegraph operator in 1920, working in various cities in Michigan. In 1923 he settled in Detroit, working for the *Detroit News,* General Motors, and Chrysler. During his spare time he began experimenting with writing, achieving an early success with the collaborative story "The Brain in the Jar," written with Norman E. Hamerstrom. It appeared in the November 1924 issue of *Weird Tales.* Lovecraft, when he came in touch with Searight in 1933, professed to have enjoyed the "vivid" story when it was first published. It was reprinted in the June 1936 issue.

Searight did not attempt any further fictional work until the early 1930s. Instead, he devoted his life to his career as a telegrapher (which he maintained until 1942) and to starting a family. He married Dorothy Harriet Carpenter on 28 July 1925. A daughter, Marjorie Doris Searight, was born on 3 October 1930. A son, Franklyn Searight, was born on 5 August 1935.

Searight achieved some success in writing at this time, landing a poem and a story in *Wonder Stories,* but other tales were rejected. While in Chicago, Searight met with Farnsworth Wright, who urged him to get in touch with Lovecraft and make use of his revisory services. In August 1933 Searight wrote to Lovecraft, seeking advice and soliciting his professional assistance. In his reply (31 August 1933), Lovecraft wrote at length about the two rejected stories ("The Formula" and "Rays of Madness"), and, even more valuably to the Lovecraft scholar, presented a formal chart of his rates for revision. It can be seen from this that he probably undercharged his clients, since his highest rate for revision (i.e., ghostwriting, or a complete draft based only upon the client's synopsis) came to only $2.50 per page; and given that Lovecraft often devoted far more time than he should have on such work, his income from revision was relatively meager.

In the end, Lovecraft did not enter into a professional relationship with

Searight, since he maintained that the "shortcomings [in Searight's stories] are matters of subject-matter rather than technique." But a warm correspondence sprang up, continuing all the way up to Lovecraft's death. Their letters chiefly discussed weird fiction, including current markets in the field, but also extended to other areas of common interest.

In one instance Lovecraft is thought to have lent some revisory assistance to Searight, but a close examination of the documentary evidence proves that this is not the case. Searight sent "The Sealed Casket" to Lovecraft in January 1934; it contained an epigraph from an imaginary volume that Searight had created, the Eltdown Shards—a prehistoric document presumably analogous to Lovecraft's Pnakotic Manuscripts. Lovecraft acknowledged in his letter of 15 January 1934 that "it is unqualifiedly the best thing you have done so far," and also admitted to changing only a single word in the epigraph.[13] It is evident that the story did not undergo any revision by Lovecraft, for Searight immediately sent it to Farnsworth Wright. It was initially rejected, but in March 1934 Lovecraft congratulates his correspondent on the acceptance of the story. It took a long time achieving print, appearing in *Weird Tales* for March 1935.

Lovecraft, however, was taken with the idea of the Eltdown Shards. He first cited them in "The Shadow out of Time" (1934–35), and they are a fairly significant plot element in Lovecraft's contribution to the round-robin tale "The Challenge from Beyond" (*Fantasy Magazine*, September 1935). In this tale, Lovecraft borrows the background information on the Eltdown Shards that Searight had provided in the tale "The Warder of Knowledge." Although Lovecraft did not read that tale until November 1935, he presumably learned the details of the Eltdown Shards from Searight when the latter first mentioned the story in January 1935. The Shards are also mentioned in passing in Lovecraft's revision of William Lumley's "The Diary of Alonzo Typer." "The Warder of Knowledge" was not published until many years after Searight's death.

Searight published only a few other stories and poems during the 1930s. He was apparently discouraged by his lack of success in landing his work in professional markets. In 1942, he changed careers and became a bookkeeper, working for several companies in the Detroit area.[14] He later became a self-employed public accountant, retaining that position until his death on 19 August 1975.

Following his death, his son Franklyn made significant efforts to perpetuate his father's literary legacy. He assembled two volumes of Searight's weird fiction (published by Necronomicon Press in 1992 and 1996) and also published Searight's historical novel about the Copper Country region of north-

---

13. HPL supplies the full text of the epigraph in a letter to CAS [June 1935] (*DS* 606). It was not published when the story appeared in *WT*.

14. Searight had taken accounting classes through the International Correspondence Schools in 1929. HPL himself had taken some chemistry courses offered by this school in 1909.

ern Michigan, *Wild Empire* (1994), which was written in the late 1930s and early 1940s. Franklyn himself, who died in late 2020, wrote several notable Lovecraftian novels and tales.

Richard F. Searight cannot truly be considered a "disciple" of Lovecraft, given the relative paucity of his actual literary work; at the same time, he is considerably more than a mere "fan" along the lines of F. Lee Baldwin or William F. Anger. Because he had interests well outside the field of weird fiction, the letters are more variegated in subject-matter than those to other young correspondents of the 1930s; and Lovecraft provides numerous insights into his own activities and literary practices, making the letters a mine of valuable information for the biographer and critic.

—S. T. JOSHI
DAVID E. SCHULTZ

A Note on the Texts

The texts of Lovecraft letters derive from manuscript, although the manuscripts are scattered (and incomplete). The letters to E. Hoffmann Price are primarily held by the John Hay Library of Brown University. One was among August Derleth's papers at Place of Hawks. Various postcards and letters, probably given to fans as being inconsequential items, have been seen, but many more are missing.

The letters to Richard F. Searight are privately held save for two that inexplicably wound up at the John Hay Library. Arkham House's edition of Lovecraft's *Selected Letters* misattributes two of the three letters to Searight as being to "Arthur F. Sechrist" [*sic*][15] even though in all three Lovecraft addressed him as "Ar-Eph-Ess" (i.e., R. F. S.).

Acknowledgements: The editors wish to thank the late Franklyn Searight and the John Hay Library of Brown University for providing copies of the texts of Lovecraft's letters to Richard F. Searight. Mr. Searight provided information for some of the notes to the letters to his father. We are especially grateful to Alexander Kreitner, who shared his transcriptions of E. Hoffmann Price's letters to Lovecraft (held at the John Hay Library) and for providing information about Price's life and work. The editors also wish to thank Martin Andersson, Stefan Dziemianowicz, Kenneth W. Faig, Jr., Sam Gafford, Ken Johnson, Will Murray, Jesper Myrfors, and J.-M. Rajala.

---

15. HPL's correspondent was Edward Lloyd Sechrist. No letters to Sechrist survive.

Abbreviations

CAS	Clark Ashton Smith
EHP	E. Hoffmann Price
JHL	John Hay Library, Brown University
HPL	H. P. Lovecraft
RFS	Richard F. Searight
RHB	R. H. Barlow

DS	*Dawnward Spire, Lonely Hill* (2017)
FF	*Fantasy Fan*
LL	*Lovecraft's Library*, rev. ed. (2017)
SL	*Selected Letters* (1965–76; 5 vols.)
WT	*Weird Tales*

Epithets for Friends and Associates

Abba 'l'nhap Longh	Frank Belknap Long
Abdul Alhazred	H. P. Lovecraft
Al-Tarah-P'lan	EHP's Terraplane automobile
An-Ghah	Fred Anger
Adib al Klin, the Dervish	Otis Adelbert Kline
Auguste-Guillaume, Comte d'Erlette	August W. Derleth
Ar-E'ch-Bei / R H B	R. H. Barlow
Ar-Eph-Es	Richard F. Searight
Averoigne	Auburn, California
Barlovius	R. H. Barlow
Belknap	Frank Belknap Long
C A S	Clark Ashton Smith
Canevin [cane wine, or rum]	Henry S. Whitehead
C L M	C. L. Moore
Conan (the Reaver)	Robert E. Howard
Dinh-El-Wandrei	Donald Wandrei
E'ch-Pi-El / H P L	H. P. Lovecraft
E H P	E. Hoffmann Price
Emir Lhen-Eighur	August Lenniger
Eph-Li	F. Lee Baldwin
Farny	Farnsworth Wright
Hill-Billy	William Crawford
H. S.	Henry S. Whitehead
Hu'd-s'un [and variants]	EHP's Hudson automobile
Hugo the Rat	Hugo Gernsback
Don Jaime Ferdinando / J F M	James F. Morton
Juggernaut / Jug	EHP's 1928 Model A Ford
Khono-Vhah	Willis Conover, Jr.
King Pharnaces	Farnsworth Wright
Klarkash-Ton	Clark Ashton Smith
Leedle Shoolie	Julius Schwartz
Lhen-Eighur, Soldan of Philistia	August Lenniger
Little Augie	August W. Derleth
Lwi-Sees-Mith of O-Khlan	Louis C. Smith of Oakland
Malik Taus/Tawus	E. Hoffmann Price
Mortonius	James F. Morton
Old Dolph	Adolphe de Castro
Pharaoh Phon-Suth	Farnsworth Wright
Potli-K'heh [and variants]	Potlicker (EHP's cat)
R E H	Robert E. Howard

Rhi-Mhel	Duane Rimel
Satrap Pharnabozus [and variants] /	
Pharnaces /Pharney	Farnsworth Wright
Single-Plot Hamilton	Edmond Hamilton
Soldan Ab'd 'el Klin	Otis Adelbert Kline
Sonny	Frank Belknap Long
Sultan Malik / Malik Taus	E. Hoffmann Price
Tarah-P'lan / Terry	EHP's Terraplane automobile
Two-Gun Bob	Robert E. Howard

`

Letters to E. Hoffmann Price

[1]   [ALS, JHL]

Opening of the First Jornada[1]—
Year of the Hegira 1351[2]
[3 October 1932]

Abdul Alhazred to Malik Tawus,[3] Salutations & Protection from Eblis[4]—

Aië! Aië! The wrath of the preadamite sultans hath been upon me, keeping me in such a turmoil of labour as hath seldom beset me. Sore & heavy have I paid for the truancy of eclipsing, Canadianising, & guest-harbouring![5] As soon as I bade Dinh-El-Wandrei a reluctant adieu I plunged at once into the limitless primal chaos of my accumulated work—&, Allah rescue me, I'm still there, up to the thickest part of my beard! Bismillah![6] Shaïtan![7] And then some!

Incidentally—it was indeed Wandrei who saluted you on the card. He thought it would be a shame to address so profound a sage in the prosaic Anglo-Roman alphabet, hence (like me when I inscribed one of the cards we sent from the Rue Royale in far-off Bayonne)[8] he dragged out the only exotic alphabet he knows. But he went me one better by taking up an *obsolete* letter . . . . . did you notice the *digamma* he used to take the place of "W"?[9] Since his name is etymologically German, he figured out that the W ought historically to have a somewhat V-ish sound, & thought the lost digamma would fill the bill better than anything else. If I had been rendering the name I'd have taken the W at Anglicised phonetic face value & written Ουἀνδρει. Alas for us ignorami[10] who have to putter around with hackneyed Hellenism (which any fraternity house can sport on its doorplate) when real adepts can sling off Arabic, pre-Amharic, & Thibetan without batting an eyelash!

Wandrei (the young idiot!) chucked his instructor's job at the U. of Minn. this June & decided to try a year of unbroken literary endeavour. He is staying in New York to be near publishers, & spent a week in Providence—which he has always liked since his first visit in 1927. I was surely glad to see him, & we held many a session of congenial discussion both indoors & out—though none lasted quite 25½ hours![11] He is going to try, like you, to grind out a large quantity of material for popular markets—though (like Derleth) maintaining his own sincere aesthetic effort as a thing inviolate & apart. By the way—did I tell you that Derleth has won a *three-star* (Roll of Honour) mention for one of his stories ("Old Ladies", in *The Midland*) & a two-star mention for another, in Edward J. O'Brien's "Best Short Stories of 1932"?[12] I told you that kid had a side unknown to W.T.!

Wandrei was the second of my season's visitors, for no sooner had I arrived home from Quebec than I was called upon to greet a very promising

young poet from Allentown, Pa.—Carl F. Strauch. I shewed him the antiquities & arcana of the town, & in particular the famous Harris Collection of
American Poetry (greatest in the world) in the John Hay Library of Brown
University. He has a professional interest in libraries, being Asst. Librarian of
Muhlenburg College in Allentown. Well, anyway, you can see how little time I
had for work, &—consequently—how hard I have since had to labour in
compensation.

To other troubles add the need of a new fountain pen. I have the devil's
own time getting suited; for I need not only a very easy point, but an abnor-
mally free flow—since my speed of writing makes any ordinary feed run short
of ink. Also, I get fatigued if I have to press hard on the paper, so that I want
a sort of hair-trigger touch. So far I haven't got what I want. Against my better judgment I took this damn stub because the feed was so commendably
generous—but you can see what it does to my already bad-enough cacogra-
phy! Tomorrow I'm going to see if I can get the point changed without disturbing the admittedly ideal feed. I need as good a pen as I can get, for it
takes the burden of all my scribbling. You are aware of my detestation of the
typewriter. And now to more important things.

Needless to say, I perused your Randolph Carter sequel[13] with the keenest interest, pleasure, & appreciation. You certainly have a splendid conception there, & I profoundly hope we can get it into publishable shape sooner
or later. It would be unfair to the idea to try to handle it now—amidst my
desperate rush of previous work—but before long I trust I can give it the leisurely consideration it deserves. Of course, in the end I may have to echo
your confession of being buffaloed—but I'll have a try first. Just now I can
hardly predict what I'll try to do—but I fancy the changes may (if you don't
mind) be quite considerable. In the first place, the style ought perhaps to be
less unlike that of "The Silver Key." Secondly, in describing Carter's exit from
the world of reality the fact that he has returned to a boyhood stage ought to
be allowed for. This is mentioned in "The Silver Key." Third—the transition,
& the entrance to the world of illusion, ought to be *infinitely subtilised.* There
must be no abrupt entry to a tangible & describable vault inside the hill, but
rather a vague atomic filtration into a world hardly describable in terms of
matter. The Presence ought to be less conclusively anthropomorphic, & there
ought to be much less prosaic clear-cutness about the interchange of speech
or thought betwixt Carter & the Presence. Whether we had better introduce
any new elements connected with Carter's exposure to forbidden gulfs of cosmic geometry remains to be seen. The action as you have it ought certainly to
be preserved in essentials. And right here two problems come up. First—how
to get the ideas to the reader without introducing the element of concrete-
sounding dialogue—a jarring note in connexion with vague trans-spatial
abysses & nebulosities—& second, how to avoid the impression of lecture-
room didacticism. Hell, but it'll be a tough nut to crack! I admit that I may

not be equal to it, but when I get the leisure I'll do what I can. At the end, I think we might possibly devise a more vivid way of introducing the returned Randolph Carter—providing preparation for it, of course, at the opening. I don't know yet just what I want to do on this point—but I'll let instinct guide me when the time comes. It'll be a ticklish job—that's why I don't want to attempt it till I can give it undivided attention under favourable conditions. But let me repeat how much I enjoyed reading the tale. It was a delight to see the dimensional principle so adroitly handled—brought to a focus, as it were—& there is vast cleverness in the way you have Carter return. Even if we can't fix it up for publication it will certainly not have been written in vain.

By the way—I think I told you that my latest story—"The Dreams in the Witch House" is a dimensional one, linking this theme to that of the Salem (& Arkham) witchcraft, but that Derleth's very adverse criticism had caused me to suppress it. Since then both Klarkash-Ton & Wandrei—yes, & Bernard Dwyer, also—have read it & reported favourably on it, & I now have half a mind to send it to Wright before many months pass.

I read with vast appreciation & tantalisation the specimen pages of the new Bayonne–Balkis–Ismeddin–d'Artois[14] tale, & feel certain it will be a notable item. Good luck with it! Sorry "Pale Hands" didn't land. What was the weird that landed—"Satan's Prayer Rug"? Hope the 17,000-worder developed without serious trouble. Your massed wordage is certainly impressive, & I surely hope that the proportion of sales may steadily rise now that the hoodoo is cracked. Better to have things started than to have occasion for the satire!

I'll see "Around the World in 80 Minutes"[15] if I get the chance. I have seen brief cinema shots of Cambodian dancers, & can well imagine the weird effect of a more systematic presentation, including the sound of the instruments. One's fancy tends to link these cryptic ceremonials with lost & immemorial rites of forgotten cultures—of which Angkor was the least & latest.

You certainly would have enjoyed the total eclipse, for the spectacle was inexpressibly weird & suggestive of other-planetary phenomena. The Montreal–Quebec trip, too, would undoubtedly have interested you. To me it was especially significant because I had so lately been in the Southern part of New-France. From the land which Iberville & Bienville founded, I jumped to the land where they were born. The ties with Louisiana are many. For example—Marquis de Vandreuil, after his governorship at New Orleans, became governor of all New-France at Quebec & saw the French power perish as Wolfe achieved his victory in 1759. Later on he accepted the change, & lived on at Montreal as a loyal British subject. As I said on my cards, French institutions linger on in Quebec Province to an extent unheard-of in Louisiana. The province is officially bi-lingual, so that dual signs like

NE STATIONNEZ PAS		ARRETE DE TRAMWAYS
NO PARKING	or	CAR STOP

are everywhere met with. Even in the towns (except Montreal, where instruction in both languages is compulsory in the public schools) there are many Frenchmen who speak no English. The treaty of 1763 & the Quebec Act of 1774 safeguarded the French in the possession of their hereditary institutions. A considerable Anglo-Saxon population settled in the province after 1763—& especially after 1783, when vast numbers of loyalists left the revolted thirteen colonies—so that the towns in the southern part have English names. However, the tenacious & prolific French have regained ground in recent years—overrunning the English sections & filtering down into New England. Right here in Rhode Island we have towns as dominantly French as any in Quebec—towns like Woonsocket & West Warwick. Montreal is more British than Quebec, & does not seem at all foreign except in the French section east of St. Lawrence Blvd., where the street & shop signs are in French. The newer French houses there are not like the Creole houses of New Orleans, but follow a pattern peculiarly Canadian—with winding outside staircases to save room inside. Some of the very oldest houses, though, are rather like the smaller, older houses in the Vieux Carré. It is a highly attractive city, well set off by the towering slope of Mt Royal, which rises in its midst. The ancient part is that closest to the southern waterfront. Montreal would seem much like any high-grade American city but for the profusion of horse-drawn vehicles. I explored it thoroughly, & also visited the celebrated Lachine Rapids. But I was glad to get to old Quebec at last, for there is nothing to equal that on the American continent. As in 1930 I revelled in the atmosphere of massed antiquity—fortress-crowned cliff, city walls, frowning citadel, silver belfries, narrow, winding hill streets, tangles of red-tiled roofs, centuried facades & doorways, &c. &c.—& I also took a 'bus excursion around the neighbouring Isle of Orleans, where (as I fancy I wrote you) the old French countryside remains in a primitive, unspoiled state, just as when Wolfe's army landed in 1759. There were endless brick farmhouses with curved eaves, wind & water mills, wayside shrines, & quaint white villages clustering around ancient silver-steepled parish churches. Nothing but French is spoken, & the rustic population live where their ancestors have lived for over 200 years. They are extremely provincial, & many are said to visit even Quebec only rarely. I hated to go home—& when passing through Boston eased the transition by making a side-trip to ancient Marblehead. (The "Kingsport" of my tales.)

And so it goes. I hope I can eventually develop your splendid Carter sequel in a manner worthy of the clever idea—& meanwhile I have the honour to be

Yrs in the brotherhood of the djinns & afrits,

—Abdul Alhazred

P.S. That composer who set my Yuggothian fungi to music wants me to collaborate with him on a fantastic opera in verse.[16] I think it's too big an order for one absolutely without experience in dramatic technique.

Notes

1. An arduous, usually one-day, journey across a stretch of desert.

2. A *hejira* is a journey, especially one undertaken to escape from a dangerous situation. In 622, the prophet Muhammad fled his native city, Mecca, to escape persecution from those who rejected his message. The hejira in year 1351 of the Islamic calendar began Saturday 7 May 1932. HPL alludes to the fact that he was writing in the course of a long journey he himself was on at the time.

3. In the Yazidi religion, Melek Taus (among other spellings) is a benevolent angel—the Peacock Angel or Peacock King—who has redeemed himself from his fall, becoming a demiurge who created the cosmos from the Cosmic egg.

4. The Islamic equivalent of Satan, cast out of heaven by God after he refused to prostrate himself before Adam.

5. In August, HPL had gone to Boston to see the solar eclipse, then to Montreal and Quebec on an excursion, returning to Providence through Salem and Marblehead.

6. "In the name of Allah," the first word of the Qur'an. An invocation Muslims use at the beginning of any undertaking.

7. Shayṭān is the term for the figure of Satan or a devil in Islamic theology and mythology.

8. HPL and EHP had sent a picture postcard showing Royal Street, New Orleans, on 15 June 1932 to Wandrei. Wandrei visited HPL in Providence from 13 to 20 September 1932. EHP had been stationed in Bayonne, France, during World War I, hence HPL's allusion to it here.

9. The digamma (Ϝ ϝ) is a letter that was already archaic by the 5th century B.C.E. in Greece. It approximates to the *w* sound.

10. A (presumably humorous) false plural of *ignoramus,* which in Latin is a verb meaning "we do not know"; hence, by extension, an ignorant person.

11. HPL told correspondents that he and EHP had a 25½-hour session of conversation when the two met in New Orleans on 12–13 June 1932, after Robert E. Howard learned that HPL would be in the city where EHP currently lived and urged them to get together.

12. "Old Ladies," *Midland* 19, No. 1 (January–February 1932): 5–9; rewritten and incorporated into *Evening in Spring* in the section "Take Arms!" "Nella," *Pagany* 3, No. 1 (Winter 1932): 134–39. "Old Ladies" in fact received a two-star rating and "Nella" a one-star rating in Edward J. O'Brien's *The Best Short Stories of 1932* (New York: Dodd, Mead, 1932), 336.

13. "The Lord of Illusion," EHP's sequel to HPL's "The Silver Key," expanded and thoroughly rewritten by HPL as "Through the Gates of the Silver Key."

14. Pierre d'Artois was an occult detective who appeared in several of EHP's stories. HPL refers to "The Return of Balkis," which EHP mentions in a letter to him of September 1932. Since EHP only vaguely alludes to the plot, HPL is guessing what characters appear in the story, which actually features Pierre d'Artois and takes place in Bayonne with Balkis as a character. Ismeddin is not in it.

15. *Around the World in 80 Minutes with Douglas Fairbanks* (United Artists, 1931), di-

rected by Douglas Fairbanks and Victor Fleming; starring Fairbanks, Victor Fleming, and Duke Kahanamoku. The film recounts Fairbanks's tour of Asia.

16. Harold S. Farnese (1885–1945) set "Mirage" and "The Elder Pharos" (*WT,* February/March 1931) to music. He requested that HPL write a libretto for a proposed musical drama in one act set on Yuggoth to be called *Fen River,* but HPL demurred, and the piece probably was never composed.

[2]   [ANS, JHL]¹

[Postmarked Providence, R.I.,
10 October 1932]

Welcome back to the old town! I see you're in the American section this time. Wish I were in your latitude among the palms & live-oaks right now. It's beastly cold today—although last Sunday was so mild that I took an antiquarian trip to Salem & Marblehead—old Arkham & Kingsport. ¶ Sorry to learn of the ironic fate of poor Tarbis,² & hope she'll fare better with King Pharnaces. Hell, no—I haven't mentioned giving any advice in connexion with its formulation. S.T. will be missed by those who seemed to have a chance of making it regularly—Smith, Whitehead, Howard, &c. To me personally the matter is more or less academic. Sorry Pale Hands hasn't landed yet—but I'm sure Balkis must stand a good chance. Congratulations on the detective tale & novelette sold. By the way—somebody tells me that Oriental is changing its name to The Magic Carpet & will be issued monthly. That ought to be good news for you. ¶ Am still thinking of Randolph Carter's final fate, & hoping I can get around to the job of collaboration when present pressure lets up. If I can't do anything effective, I may call in the aid of Klarkash-Ton—who says you've mentioned his possible assistance. He has just done a splendid ending for Beckford's unfinished Vathek episode.³ ¶ I see in the papers that the French Market is definitely doomed. A damn shame, when all it needs is fumigation! ¶ Well—Allah & the Prophet attend thee!

ܠܠ܂ܐܨܙܐ

Notes

1. *Front:* Moonlight on the Mississippi River, New Orleans, La.
2. HPL had read "Tarbis of the Lake" in New Orleans and made suggestions for revision. The editor of *Strange Tales of Mystery and Terror* wanted to use the story but had just announced that it was ceasing publication with the January 1933 issue, after publishing only 7 issues.
3. CAS, "The Third Episode of Vathek" (with William Beckford), *Leaves* No. 1 (Summer 1937): 1–24.

[3]   [ALS, JHL]

Octr 20[,] 1932

Dear Malik:—

Congratulations on the acceptance of Balkis! In general, your commercial fortunes are beginning to justify the predictions which I made many months ago. Your percentage of sales is undoubtedly very high considering the recency of your entrance to the general quantity-production field, & there is every reason to believe that they will continue to mount—unless you chuck the whole game & go to join the Bolsheviki! Your Old Man of the Mountains plot sounds promising in the extreme, & I trust you may have no trouble in selling it.[1]

As for your Russian prospect—it certainly would be an experience to remember, & a potential source of literary material; especially if your field of labour were to be Turkestan . . . . the Golden Road to Samarcand. But much prose & dreariness would undoubtedly be mixed with the adventure, so that one ought not to embark without due reflection.

About Derleth—I'm going to mail you a copy of *Pagany* with his "Five Alone"[2]—& possibly (that is, if I can find it!) one of the *Midland* with his "Old Ladies"—three-starred by E. J. O'Brien in the Best Short Stories of 1932. Keep these as long as you like—though I'd like to see them again eventually. You will see in these things a writer absolutely alien to the facile little hack who grinds out minor W.T. junk. There is nothing in common betwixt Derleth A & Derleth B—no point of contact in their mental worlds—& yet one brain houses them both . . . . artist & business-man, standing back to back & never speaking! The real Derleth's source is in writers like Proust, & other evokers of wistful reminiscence who symbolise universal things in particular memories. Nearly all the gang agree that the kid will go far in literature—probably farther than any of the rest. All the others—including myself, god damn it, despite my best efforts to keep clear of the taint—are more or less influenced by the cheap & tawdry methods & moods of commercial writing. Derleth can stoop to hack work, & yet keep his real side intact as a sincere artist. I don't see how he does it—but he does. You'll see what I mean when you get the stuff I'm sending. All of which reminds me that I've lately purchased E. J. O'Brien's "Dance of the Machines"—a splendid exposé of the vulgar shallowness, insincerity, & worthlessness of American commercial fiction under the false-standarded conditions of the present. If you haven't read this, & would like to, I'd be glad to lend it to you. Other recent purchases of mine (at an alluring remainder sale) are Huysmans' "A Rebours" & Perutz's "Master of the Day of Judgment."

As for my "Dreams in the Witch-House"—Derleth didn't say it was *unsalable;* in fact, he rather thought it *would* sell.[3] He said it was a *poor story,* which is an entirely different & much more lamentably important thing. I'm not sure that I wish it to appear before something is done to it. On the other hand,

Smith & Wandrei liked it, & Dwyer's opinion was more favourable than otherwise. The best thing to do is to wait a while & see how it strikes me on a fresh reading. I think I need a long fallow period during which to purge my mind of the popular-fiction formula—for I can't carry water on both shoulders as Derleth can. The story before the "Witch-House"—"The Shadow over Innsmouth"—has also been unfavourably received; & all my work, past & present, has recently had a very revealing analysis from a reader whose wide attainments well qualify him to render an opinion.[4] Undeniably, I have allowed the popular forms to infect my work more than I have realised; so that it is always deficient in the subtlety & fineness of mood-drawing which marks anything even approaching real literature. Of course, I have no guarantee that I could write real literature under even the most favourable conditions—but at least I can try to rid myself of conspicuous handicaps. I'm not so much influenced by what I do in a revisory way.

Apropos of nothing—*couldn't* you substitute your improved version of the detective tale for the one recently accepted? It seems to me that I've made changes in accepted MSS. & had them incorporated. The editor might be glad of the substitution. I'd certainly try it!

About Randolph Carter—as I said before, I hope you're in no hurry, because the thing must be done under reposeful conditions if at all. I may flop miserably—but if I feel myself flopping too badly I'll send the whole works on to Klarkash-Ton, High-Priest of Tsathoggua,[5] & see what a third hand can do. What I'll send you first (god help you, my son!) will not be a carbon but a vilely scrawled rough draught in my worse-than-Amharic cursive (& cursed!) script—because I hate typing too damn badly to do it for nothing. There'll be no typing for Grandpa till the whole thing is settled. Just one session—no more!

As for your all-rights cheque—I don't know whether you were wise or not in taking it as it was . . . . provided the change to a 1st N.A. would not have endangered the acceptance. I am reminded of this by the letter which has just come from London, stating that an editor wants to buy British periodical rights to my "Erich Zann" in "Creeps by Night." This will make the third sale since W.T. took it—the fourth in all. First—after W.T.—the cheque from the John Day Co.—$25.00—& then the cheque from Curtis Brown—$10.00—for the British edition of the anthology. Now, if this extra sale materialises, there will be 6 or 7 guineas ($30.00 or $35.00 minus British taxes &c) more—& all for one very short story. In general you ought to place the inscription "First North American Serial Rights Only" at the head of all your MS. I note that an increasing number of writers do this regularly.

As for the astute & businesslike Mr. Lenniger[6]—I told you long ago that he wouldn't have any use for anything of mine. No commercialist has any sympathy with anything which tries to be honest literature—& it is unconsciously & involuntarily listening to this breed of cattle (with their demand for "explanations" which ruin the real power of any tale) which has spoiled me, perhaps permanently, for writing decent material. L's letter is very typical of the species—they don't like "unpleasant" things, & they want all their weird writers to be "pleasant & entertaining" . . . .

I really think that, as I said before, nothing of mine properly belongs in an anthology edited by a person like Lenniger. The best thing to do would be to leave me out altogether—waiting for better times, when it might be thought possible to float a collection of other than machine-made conventionalities. Commercial writing & I have absolutely nothing in common. If there is any tale of mine which such as Mr. Lenniger would like, it is one of those which I have repudiated & would not have reprinted under any circumstances.

However—I'll leave to you any decision which may be out of Lenniger's hands. Pickman's Model is not my best tale by a long shot—but L. would not even consider what is really my best story—"The Colour Out of Space", three-starred by E. J. O'Brien in 1928. That has never been in an anthology—which reminds me that after all it might be best to exclude items which have appeared in other books. Of my stuff, the following have been reprinted in anthologies:

> Horror at Red Hook
> Erich Zann
> Rats in Walls
> Cthulhu
> Pickman

Lenniger seems to have some mechanical or small-tradesman notion about *length*, which excludes most of my later things. If he wants a brief sketch of only a few paragraphs, he'd probably like "The Terrible Old Man"—which isn't much good. "The Cats of Ulthar" is short & really good as compared with most of my efforts. Probably he wouldn't like that. "The Picture in the House" was one or two starred by O'Brien in 1924—but it isn't cheerful. I give it up. I can't deal with Lenniger's kind, & really think I'd better be counted out if he is to be the arbiter & standard-fixer. Here is a list of my attempts to date[7]—a list which may never be extended—& if you recall anything on that list which you'd like, just speak up & it's yours—except for the few (say White Ship, Tree, From Beyond, Iranon, Sarnath, Celephais [*sic*], Herb. West, Outsider, Hypnos, Hound, He, & perhaps the two latest) which I think are too far below a reasonable standard. "Dagon" has a good idea, but would need re-writing. I really haven't much use for any of my junk except Erich Zann & The Colour Out of Space. I've a damned good mind to say the Colour or nothing—which of course, under Lennigerian auspices, means no Abdul represented. But you can look the list over & make what you can of it. This commercial racket is outside my line. "In the Vault" isn't a very good story. It's not quite bad enough to be repudiated, but I'd hate to be represented by it. If the enclosed list (which please return, since I use it in connexion with loans to others) & the accompanying comments aren't sufficient for guiding purposes, let me know, & I'll send any eligible story you may name. Or if you take my advice, you'll drop the idea of including anyone so incompatible with the hard guy in whose hand the business destinies of the venture rest.

Tarbis's rejection is quite typical of Satrap Pharnabazus—the fellow has just sent back one of Klarkash-Ton's finest phantasies on the ground that his herd of jackasses wouldn't like its poetic atmosphere![8] It must be terrible to have so little subtlety & insight that every undiagrammed story leaves one in a quandary. Well—maybe there'll be another weird magazine some day which will hail Tarbis as the find of the century & give it first place & cover design! Caprice & prejudice are paramount in the decisions of the editorial fraternity.

My latest revisory job[9] comes so near to pure fictional ghost-writing that I am up against all the plot-devising problems of my bygone auctorial days. There is a horrible wax-work museum in London whose half-mad proprietor claims that not all the nameless monstrosities displayed therein are artificial. Dogs are horribly sacrificed to an entity which is not on display. A man spends the night locked in with the objects . . . . . Dear me, if this ever gets to professional hands, I fear they'll find it shockingly unpleasant & depressing!

Just received Derleth's new serious novelette—"Farway House".[10] Looks like damn good stuff.

And so it goes. Eblis & Tsathoggua be with thee on the 100,000-word a day programme![11] Yr obeisant slave ज़ गरटट यतस्व

Notes

1. EHP's story "Unfit for Command," a war story, states: "Sahipa, the old man of the mountains, was almost a sultan." The story was not published until 1941.

2. "Five Alone," *Pagany* 3, No. 3 (Summer 1932): 14–44. Included in *Place of Hawks*.

3. HPL would not submit the story, but August Derleth did so surreptitiously. See EHP 11.

4. Frank Belknap Long, Jr., August Derleth, and Clark Ashton Smith all had reservations about the story.

5. CAS introduced Tsathoggua in the story "The Tale of Satampra Zeiros" (1929).

6. Lenniger was evaluating stories that EHP and his associate W. Kirk Mashburn, Jr. (1900–1968) had gathered for a proposed anthology of weird fiction. About "Pickman's Model" he wrote: "I am not keen on Pickman's Model [. . .] This does not seem properly explained; it is rather unpleasant instead of entertaining, and there isn't anything very outstanding about it. In connection with this I might suggest that it ought to be decided between Mr. Lovecraft and Mr. Wyers which one of them is going to submit a story dealing with an artist. I[ ]do not feel it would be wise to include two such stories in the same collection. They carry basically similar themes. Of the two, Pickman's Model is perhaps the best as a weird tale, but on the other hand I feel that its plot doesn't quite warrant the word length. If Mr. Lovecraft has a better length that he would like to substitute I feel it would be good to do so. [¶] But on

Pickman's Model I again leave it to the discretion of the author and yourself whether such a substitution should be made." Quoted in a letter by EHP to HPL, n.d. (TLS, JHL). Renier Wyers had had only two stories in *WT* at this time. The story referred to is "The Finishing Touches" (*WT*, June/July 1931).

7. The list is nonextant; but see HPL to Robert Bloch, 22 April 1933, which contains a list of 46 stories (plus "Through the Gates of the Silver Key," written in the interim).

8. Wright rejected "The Seed from the Sepulcher" because "it seems too long drawn out" (21 October 1932; ms., JHL).

9. "The Horror in the Museum" by Hazel Heald.

10. In Derleth's *Place of Hawks*.

11. In his letter of 31 October 1932, EHP wrote: "The probable 100,000 word total planned for 1933 will . . . enable [me] to make modest grocery & rent expense."

[4]   [ALS, JHL]

Subterrene Mosque of Eblis
Night of the Darting Flames
[Postmarked 18 November 1932]

Dear Malik:—

Do as you will with the junk I sent—that is, take or leave what you will. But no mutilation! I note your epistle to the Philistine Lhen-Eighur, & hope that *re-typing* reference isn't to be taken too literally. Although it means the loss of a lending copy, I'd any day rather sacrifice one of the MSS. already sent that [*sic*] go through the goddam hell of typing it over. Ugh! But if necessary, I suppose I could try it—or get somebody else to do it. It's a hard world! But possibly the super-Babbitt will veto any item of mine so vigorously that I'll be saved all worry anyhow! Glad you agree with O'Brien (& myself) about "The Colour Out of Space". Ed ignored me this year, although the rival annual—O. Henry Memorial Prize Stories—gave my "Strange High House in the Mist" a first-class rating, & my "In the Vault" a second-class rating.[1] That's nothing to get conceited about, though, since the standard of the O. Henry thing is not nearly so genuinely artistic as O'Brien's. By the way—O'Brien has just written Derleth that he will three-star "Five Alone" in 1933. He seems to be quite interested in the kid—& it's really stretching a point to admit an obvious novelette like "Five Alone" to short story classification. Oh, yes—about my 46 titles, only 31 have been professionally published. The two long novelettes— "Kadath" & "Charles Dexter Ward"—have never been even typed (god, how I hate that damned machine!), & besides myself no living soul but Donald Wandrei (while on a visit here in 1927) has ever read them. Some time I may look them over, see if they're worth revising, & if so try to persuade somebody to type the final result.

Congratulations on "Lord of the Fourth Axis"! I am truly anxious to see the amended & de-actionised final product, & hope Satrap Pharnabazus will not be too tardy about getting it into print. The pages of the carbon that I saw (representing, I assume, parts retained in the ultimate version) aroused my expectations most keenly.

As for the youthful Auguste-Guillaume, Comte d'Erlette—I thought "Old Ladies" & "Five Alone" would give you a new slant on the kid! In merit the two seem to me about equivalent—for, as you'll recall, I am not very enthusiastic about the plot or story element in a piece of writing. What I want is *substance*—the colour of life. As you see, O'Brien likes these things so well that he has three-starred both. I don't think the non-escape of the rebellious daughter is at all unlifelike. People do get bound & paralysed like that—helpless in the face of a family feeling which overshadows everything else. One sees it often amongst the ancient New England stock. It is, of course, lamentably unwholesome, & we may thank the modern age for removing much of the basis of this type of psychosis. As to further Derlethiana—if you're game to pay the postage on some 190 pages of thin onion-skin second sheets, I'll send you (for later return to Derleth) the kid's real masterpiece—"Evening in Spring"—when he sends me the new & revised version he is just finishing. If that isn't a real work of art I'll never utter a critical opinion again! As for the financial side—*Pagany, The Midland,* & other high-grade experimental magazines of this type do not pay for contributions at all. It is a matter of art, not of business. Their standards are very high, & Derleth bombarded them for six years before they would accept anything of his. Look at the tables of contents & see the type of author that contributes. Derleth's *business* is writing cheap junk for W.T. & the pulp detective magazines, plus working in a canning factory at odd seasons. That is one thing. His *literary* work—the effort of a sensitive personality to live fully & satisfyingly through adequate & finely-modelled self-expression—is something altogether different. One's *business* is only a disagreeable means to an end. Disinterested self-expression is *life itself*—the thing in order to enjoy which we undergo the loathsome process of commercial endeavour. It is an end in itself—not a means toward anything else. If we're paid for it, that's just so much 'velvet', as the Babbitts say.

I note your reasoning on the subject of the revision of stories already accepted, but can't quite concur with all its points. The wish to change a tale which an editor has approved is by no means a reflection on his judgment. The tale, as taken, was good—but there may be a way of making it still better. The editor would, we may assume, have himself thought the new version better if he had seen it. In sending it you could make that point quite clear—confidently expecting the editor to like the new version still more than he liked the original fairly-good version. Surely it is a generally recognised thing that there are degrees of merit among soundly meritorious items. As for the all-rights business—I dare say you know best about that. I'm no business-man—in fact, I am conspicuously lacking in all that pertains to the commercial mood & psychology.

I am hoping to get at Randolph Carter before many more weeks fly past—but hades, what a turmoil of work I am in! Have been too tied to the house to get any kind of a view of the autumn foliage this year. Haven't seen *The Magic Carpet*, but must try to get hold of the issue with your Ismeddin story.[2] As a matter of fact, I haven't had a chance to look at the last three issues of W.T. or the final issue of S.T. I shall skim them through before long—though I can't bother with the serials.

Your acceptance record is certainly what I call darned enviable. Starting in around June, gaining sales momentum as your work has penetrated the proper channels, & now beginning to reap results—being likewise wiser in the matter of editorial requirements & methods of revision . . . . . . what more could you expect in five months? Just as I said, it would have been fantastic to suppose that frequent sales could begin right away. Practice, & the discovery of market needs & openings, is the logical fruit of the first half-year—& you have had even more than that! From now on you will be working with a much clearer idea of the whole field & its problems, & sales may reasonably be expected to be more frequent. There could be no question of the sincerity of those who predicted your success at the game. All the evidence was in favour. On the one hand your repeatedly-demonstrated gift for vivid & effective writing—which one had only to turn to a W.T. file to see illustrated—& on the other hand your skill in the conscious manipulation of elements to achieve carefully calculated results, as shewn in all your activities both literary & otherwise. Given these two factors, what other result was possible? And the case of Klarkash-Ton formed a highly significant precedent. As for your present feeling of burned-outness—I'm sure you don't need to mind that. With your summer & autumn's record of wordage behind you, you certainly need a breathing-spell! As for agents—it is certainly odd that the rigidly practical & action-loving Emir Lhen-Eighur has such a poor sales record as compared with the hustling Soldan[3] Ab'd 'el Klin! It looks as though the latter were the better scouter—or persuader—or both—of the two!

Since beginning this letter I've been out (3:15–4:15 a.m.) trying to get a sight of the widely advertised Leonid meteors, but with woefully meagre results. In the first place there's a beastly fog over everything, plus a moon only 3 days past full which blots most faint objects from the sky. Secondly—I profoundly suspect that this shower is proving a fizzle like the long-awaited one of 1899. I'll see in tomorrow's papers what observers in fog-free regions report. I walked nearly a quarter of a mile to find a semi-rustic oasis with no electric lights & a good eastern horizon, but in an hour's time saw only 5 meteors—of which not more than two were really bright. I ought to get my money back at the box-office! I may try again tomorrow night if the weather is half-way decent—but after that there'll be no hope.

And so it goes. Beatitudes of Yog-Sothoth upon thee!

Notes

1. See under Blanche Colton Williams in Bibliography.
2. "Ismeddin and the Holy Carpet" (January 1933).
3. The ruler of an Islamic country.

[5]   [ALS, JHL]

Novr 26[, 1932]

Dear Malik:—

Allah reward thee, Delight of the Prophet & Protector of the Poor! May the Peris of Paradise[1] be kind to one who spares an old man the pains of toil at the Eblis-Engine of Franguistan! May all thine ancestors feast with the Preadamite Sultans, & may all thy sons become the Caliphs of opulent empires beyond the East! Well—in a way I shan't mind the appearance of the "Picture", for that is the first tale to mention the name of *Arkham*, to which I have since referred so often. Architectural note: if anywhere in the description of the old house you come upon the word *fanlight*, please change it to *transom*. Possibly, though, I had made the change in the MS. you have. I know more about colonial architecture than I did in 1920, when I produced this specimen. Again—an old man's blessings for your lifting of a grievous burthen!

As for Auguste-Guillaume, Comte d'Erlette—I have duly commended him to send to 1416 Josephine[2] the necromantic revivification story you mention—"In the Left Wing"—which he wrote in collaboration with Mark R. Schorer . . . . although such "collaboration" is usually 99.8% Little Augie, 0.2% Schorer. It appeared in W.T. for *June*. I've also asked him to furnish alternative suggestions. I imagine he'll be very glad to contribute. By the way— "The Captain is Afraid"[3] *didn't* receive the O. Henry mention expected, after all. Very odd. A.W. was told that it would be listed, but when the annual appeared, it was not among those present. That annual is very slipshod & meaningless in its policy. As a matter of fact, this tale was a mere pot-boiler not worth mentioning—though "The Sheraton Mirror", "The Panelled Room",[4] & others certainly deserved a listing. About "Five Alone"—remember that people differ in their capacity for shaking off hereditary or habitual environments. Cases like that described are by no means unusual in old, cohesive, & locally attached families—especially in the country. As an urban instance look at the case of the eccentric Wendels of New York.[5] Derleth has tried Harpers & equivalent high-grade media, but such magazines are fearsomely [*sic*] difficult to break into. The best step *toward* the Harper level is entrance into the select but unremunerative magazines like *Pagany, Trend, Contempo, Midland, Story, Frontier*, &c. It is there—never in the "pulps"—that real literary reputations are built up. Serious & high-grade magazines usually prefer material which has some close & vital relationship to the life, thought, & feeling of the day, or to the soil & traditions of the American scene. Derleth is beginning to make the grade because of his saturation in the traditional colour of rural Wisconsin life. Howard could do the same with his Texas background if he would give time & energy to a pruning of romantic & conventional tendencies. Anyhow— here's wishing you luck in your submission of "Pale Hands" to Harpers.

The extracts from "Satan's Garden" or "The Hand of Hassan"[6] read most promisingly & alluringly, & I surely think this tale ought to be a success. I note what you say on right-reservations, revision of accepted material, &c., & don't doubt but that you are well-advised. On the whole, I think you have every reason to be satisfied with your professional programme to date. Hope "Prayer for My Enemy" duly lands & repays you for the labour & postage. That was certainly quick work! The 23,500-worder sounds like great stuff, & I hope it can see print without having to submit to any amputations destructive of its colour & characterisation. But don't work too hard. Too high a pressure sometimes defeats its own ends. Take a few more days off with the zebras, tigers, camels, rocs, unicorns, & centaurs of Audubon Park!

As for the proper channel of genuine self-expression on your part—in the last analysis, that is something which only you can discover, through ex- periments in all the lines which appeal to you. The things to write of seriously are the things which seem to you of such haunting & persistent interest (ei- ther as actualities or as symbols of conditions, trends, aspirations, & instincts) that you cannot feel easy until you have them down on paper in one way or another. When you've decided what those things are, you will be inwardly compelled to write of them with artistic truth, regardless of demands—truth, that is, to the images & conceptions as they stand in your mind. It may well be that your natural channel is one involving violent adventure—a thing sym- bolising for you the escape & dominance toward which everyone reaches. It is perfectly possible for artistic fiction to hinge upon events of physical con- flict—provided those events are realistically rather than conventionally han- dled, & provided they occupy a suitable & convincing place in the lives, emotions, & characters of the persons involved. So long as the events are se- riously drawn as parts of the general life-stream, with their true proportional relationship to wider events clearly indicated, they can indeed form the subject- matter of genuine art. And the same—in general principle—goes very largely for the weird. Serious weird art is distinctly possible—although relatively few (certainly not myself, alas!) ever achieve it. The genuine artist in the weird is trying to crystallise in at least semi-tangible form one of several typical & in- definite moods unquestionably natural to human beings, & in some individu- als very profound, permanent, & intense . . . . moods involving the habitual lure & terror & imagination-stirring qualities of the unknown or half-known, the burning curiosity of the active mind concerning the fathomless abysses of inaccessible space which press in on us from every side, & the instinctive revolt of the restless ego against the galling limitations of time, space, & natural law. When a writer succeeds in translating these nebulous urges into symbols which in some way satisfy the imagination—symbols which adroitly suggest actual glimpses into forbidden dimensions, actual happenings following the myth-patterns of human fancy, actual voyages of thought or body into the nameless deeps of tantalising space, & actual evasions, frustrations, or violations of the commonly accepted laws of the cosmos—then he is a true artist in every sense of the word. He has produced genuine literature by accomplishing a sincere emotional catharsis. As for the literature of actual life—one's ability to write that depends wholly upon one's real interest in & sympathy with people as a whole. Derleth has it—I haven't. The author of genuine human literature must be able to see a vast significance tantamount to cosmic symbolism in the daily acts & thoughts & struggles of people—& he must know these acts & thoughts & struggles well enough, & first-handedly enough, to write of them with fulness, vividness, & accuracy. This sense of virtual cosmic importance in what people do & think & feel—whether or not such acts, thoughts, & feelings are romantic or adventurous—is the crucial thing which makes a real, all-around delineator of life. A reasonable period of testing will show you whether you have or haven't it. You say (in a mood like that which makes Derleth's environment-bound characters seem unconvincing to you) that you have no problems—that you dispose of such things by the Gordian-knot method. Well & good—but surely you realise that vast numbers of people cannot do that. If you have the stuff of the life-delineator in you, you will be so curious about these other types of people that you can't be satisfied till you have studied the unfamiliar emotions & conditions & problems which beset them, & have imaginatively stepped into their personalities for a while & seen life through *their* eyes, not yours. This urge & ability to become, as it were, totally different people (in thought, speech, feelings, outlook, & all else) in quick succession, is the distinguishing quality of the really substantial fictionist. Look how Derleth does it—he, a husky young egotist of 23, can for a time *actually be*, in a psychological sense, a wistful, faded old lady of 85, with all the natural thoughts, prejudices, feelings, perspectives, fears, prides, mental mannerisms, & speech-tricks of such an old lady. Or he can be an elderly doctor—or a small boy—or a half-demented young mother—in every case understanding & entering into the type so fully that, for the moment, his interests & outlook & difficulties & idiom are *those of the character,* with the corresponding qualities of August William Derleth quite forgotten. He can get the pathetic—or savage—or cold—or humorous—or ardent—or whatever it is—mood with perfect authenticity *for the time being,* no matter what his own moods tend to be, because he temporarily enters into the characters & sees what *they* (not Derleth) see & feels what *they* feel. It is mimicry on a grand scale. He can duplicate the mood because he knows objectively (& thence, by virtue of the right sort of imagination, subjectively) the natural factors creating it in each case. But of course not everybody can do that. I can't—& recognising my limitations, I soft-pedal the elaborate delineation of dissimilar characters. Long can't either—& *not* recognising his limitations he reels off page after page of alleged characterisation in which all the figures, from savants & demigods to bootblacks & charwomen, think & feel & act & talk exactly like little duplicate Belknaps! Love-stuff, of course, should be handled just like any of the other elements in the dull daily grind—as one realistic incident among others, without any special kind of treatment other than perfect truth to psychology & observed events. All *feigned* emotions like "romance" & "glamour" are cheap & inartistic. Dreiser is the boy to study when it comes to dealing with life—he or Balzac or Zola or de Maupassant. But only diligent & repeated experiment, & searching self-analysis, can enable anyone to discover his own natural field. Go to it, Son—& here's hoping it'll turn out to be the weird.

¶ I'm still looking forward to the time when I can tackle my old friend Randolph Carter again. ¶ Suppose you've heard the melancholy news, bulletined by Whitehead, that *Astounding* is to follow *Strange* into the ultimate darkness.[7]

Yrs in doleful beard-pulling—

𒀭 𒐊 𒀀 𒍝 𒌋

P.S. Have just seen an advertisement of—& article by—your hard-boiled industrial aide Lenniger in the Writer's Digest.

[P.P.S. on envelope:] Damnation! Just got the bad news. Whitehead died last Wednesday.[8] I knew he was in bad health, but never suspected it was getting as acute as all that. He wrote breezily & optimistically—& without any mention of his illness—as late as Nov. 14—less than a fortnight ago. This news really gives one a damnable jolt—he was such a splendid chap in every way—brilliant, generous, attractive, learned, courageous, & everything else admirable. It'll be a frightful blow to his father—now 84—though perhaps he was prepared for the outcome more than we were.

Notes

1. In Persian and Armenian, the peris are exquisite, winged fairy-like spirits ranking between angels and evil spirits.
2. EHP's address in New Orleans.
3. "The Captain Is Afraid" (*WT,* October 1931).
4. "The Sheraton Mirror" (*WT,* September 1932). "The Panelled Room," *Westminster Magazine* 22, No. 3 (Autumn 1933): 35–45; rpt. *Leaves* No. 1 (Summer 1937): 65–70.
5. In the early 20th century, John G. Wendel II (d. 1914) and his six sisters were perhaps the most powerful landlords in New York City, a dynasty with more than 150 properties in Manhattan worth over $1 billion in today's dollars. He was referred to as

"the hermit" and "the recluse," and the lot of them were known as the "weird Wendels." They all lived in seclusion at Fifth Avenue and 39th Street.
6. "The Hand of Hassan" is a chapter of "Satan's Garden." See EHP 6n12. EHP re-
used the title for a story.
7. *Astounding Stories* was founded in 1930 by the Clayton Publishing Co., but ceased
publication with the March 1933 issue. It was then bought by Street & Smith and resumed publication in October.
8. Henry S. Whitehead died on 23 November 1932 in Dunedin, Florida.

[6]   [ALS, JHL]

Decr. 7, 1932

Dear Malik:—

Certainly, no more universally depressing news has lately spread
through the group than that of the passing of good old "Canevin."[1] Everyone—
Howard, Long, Dwyer, Derleth, &c.—concurs in the general regret & sense
of shock; & I even received a letter from Harry Bates, who held H S in particular esteem. The jolt to me was especially acute because I had received a
breezy & optimistic note from "Padré" [*sic*] as recently as November 14th, in
which no mention whatever was made of health. Last winter he had said that
the doctors were getting at the root of his case, & that steady though gradual
improvement was now to be looked for. I doubt if he himself realised what
was coming, for his final letter was full of plans & forecasts. I answered that
letter quite promptly—on Friday, Nov. 18. It probably did not get collected
until Saturday the 19th—hence reaching Dunedin on Tuesday the 22nd—the
very day before the end. I do not know whether it was ever opened & read—
possibly it was if the last chapter of the illness was sudden & unforeseen.

Your own appreciation of H S was amply recognised & appreciated in
turn. He often spoke of you & your work with admiration, & mentioned his
pleasure at the brisk & lively "Trooper" letters.[2] Now that the cutting down
of "The Tree Man"[3] by its author is impossible, I strongly hope you can persuade your Philistine tyrant to use it exactly as it is—for it would be vandalism to refer the job to some second person. I had not realised how strongly
he was supporting the venture—20 copies is quite an order for a non-dealer!

I have been an outspoken Whitehead admirer ever since I read his first
story—"Sea Change"—in W.T.[4] That tale attracted my especial attention because it anticipated an idea of my own—although using it in a way vastly different from that which I had planned.[5] When the West Indian material began
to appear my enthusiasm was doubled; for I could sense the realism of the
background & feel a convincingness in the tales which most pulp material
lacks. And of course I likewise appreciated the charm & erudition of the writing itself—a pleasing relief from the dominant crudeness & illiterateness of
popular magazine stuff. I did not come into correspondence with H S till

1930, when Bernard Dwyer (who had previously made his epistolary acquaintance) lent me some of his unpublished MSS. with instructions to return them to the author. In effecting this return, I naturally added a word expressive of my appreciation—both of the immediate specimens & of Canevinian work in general—& from that nucleus a correspondence of instant congeniality arose. The more I heard from Whitehead the better I liked him, & I appreciated it keenly when he invited me down to Dunedin for a stay of indefinite duration. I was not able to get there till May⁶—but when I did arrive I found H S even more fascinating in person than in letters. It is doubtful if any other host ever reached quite his level of cordiality, thoughtfulness, & generosity over a period exceeding a fortnight. I really had, for his sake, to be careful what books or other possessions of his I openly admired; for like some open-handed Eastern prince he would insist on presenting me with whatever seemed to arouse my enthusiasm.* He compelled me to consider his wardrobe my own (for his physique was almost identical with mine), & there still hangs in my clothespress one of the white tropical suits he lent me—& finally insisted that I retain permanently as a souvenir. As I glance at my curio shelf I see a long mottled snake in a jar, & reflect how good old Canevin caught & killed it with his own hands—thinking I might like a sample of Dunedin's lurking horrors. He was not afraid of the devil himself, & the seizure of that noxious wriggler was highly typical of him. The astonishing versatility & multiplicity of attractive qualities which he possessed sound almost fabulous to one who did not know him in person. He was the idol of the local population both young & old, & the centre of an adoring group of small boys about 10 or 11 years old, who thought there was nobody on this planet quite as great—as playmate, story-teller, adviser, leader, & instructor—as their Padre. The snuffing out of such a beloved & useful character is surely a flagrant example of the cosmos's typical wastefulness.

I don't know whether Wright has heard the bad news or not—but acting on your suggestion, I have prepared a two-page obituary & sent it on with the suggestion that some of its contents be drawn upon for a notice in the Eyrie.⁷ Certainly, a regular contributor of H S's standing & merit ought to receive far more than a perfunctory elegy in the pages which he did so much to redeem from dulness & ineptitude.

Whitehead's best work is among the finest weird writing of the present time, & it is a pity that plans for book publication of a collection of his stories fell through. His leisurely style greatly enhanced the lifelike convincingness of what he had to say—giving the reader a vivid understanding of the chosen scene & stratum of life, & leading up imperceptibly to the one point of departure from reality. These stories illustrate admirably the precept I always try to

---

*example of generosity. He said last July that if he'd known I was going to be in New Orleans, he'd have insisted on my making a side-trip to Dunedin at his expense.

impress on weird beginners—to avoid all extravagance, freakish or capricious motivation, redundancy of marvels, & the like, & to follow absolute realism except for the *single* violation of natural law which has been chosen as a subject. Of all H S's stories, I think "Passing of a God" was indisputably the best. "The Black Beast", "The Tree Man," "Cassius", "The Great Circle",[8] & others also rank very high. There were many minor pot-boilers, of course—as there are among everyone's writings. He had a splendid tale under way called "The Bruise",[9] which (at my suggestion) involved the lost & fabulous Pacific continent of Mu.[10] I am wondering whether it was ever finished. His latest idea was a series of tales about a sinister & decadent New England town called "Chadbourne"—like my "Arkham"—of which the first was accepted by Wright. The second was taken by Bates for *Astounding*, but returned when the magazine blew up. There was a third—not altogether supernatural, & involving a Congregational minister—which I don't think has been submitted anywhere as yet.[11] Derleth wonders who will administer Canevin's literary affairs, & send out such MSS. as have a reasonable chance of placement.

I'm glad the typing of the "Picture" (for which, once more, a score of grateful & grovelling obeisances!!) had its compensating aspects. I, myself, hate *copying* above all things. Without the zest of original composition the boredom becomes intolerable, & the rhythmical nature of the process tends to get me sleepy. All this besides the nerve-strain, headache, & backache which I inevitably get from extended typing. Thanks for looking the text over for *fanlight*. I believe the word occurred only once—& very possibly it has been corrected. Wait—let me look at the MS. you returned . . . . Yep—I *had* made the change! Nothing for you to do—& I hope you haven't spent any time on the quest.

I note with close attention your recommendations regarding manuscript transmission, & believe I shall avail myself of the express company's charity in future! It surely looks like a profitable racket—your envelope came through in six days (recd. Dec. 6, 10 a.m.) & in good condition . . . . & presumably with far less cost to you than the postal system would have imposed.

Congratulations on "Pale Hands"! Most certainly I remember it—the suspicious absinthe-hound—the strangling in vain—the fatally too late information—the remorseful surrender— This bird Kline may have his limitations as a creative artist, but he surely is a great little salesman! He's beating Lhen-Eighur, Soldan of Philistia, at his own game! It must indeed be encouraging to have your favourite placed. Now I hope that Tarbis—in some form or other—will land somewhere. My prayers to Tsathoggua, Yog-Sothoth, Shub-Niggurath, Nug, & Yeb, descend with nighted eloquence to plead success for "Satan's Garden." The table of contents is surely appetising enough—especially "Monsters of the Pool"![12] And I hope that the revised detective tales, as well as the new one mentioned in your post[s]cript, may all reach their goal, & haul in an aureate harvest.

By this time you will have received "In the Left Wing" from young Auguste-Guillaume, Comte d'Erlette, together with "The House in the Magnolias",[13] a *zombi* tale laid in your own region, & "The Thing that Walked on the Wind." He knows all about Lhen-Eighur & his philistinism, hence thought it would be of no use to send anything as serious as "The Panelled Room" or "The Sheraton Mirror." Of all these tales I myself prefer "The Thing that Walked on the Wind"[14]—though Little Augie professes not to have much use for it himself. When he sends me "Evening in Spring" I'll pass it on by express as suggested. I'll prepay on my end, & you'd better prepay on yours, since the kid is unusually short of cash this month, & finds his ordinary postal expenses very burdensome. If, though, the young rascal sends it to *me* collect, I'll recommend your treating him likewise!

As for the genuine literature of self-expression—the best is the most unconscious. Just write what you really like best when you get the chance, & you'll probably hit on the real stuff before you know it, if you haven't already. After all, art is pretty much independent of subject matter in the last analysis. It is a *mood*—& it manifests itself in subtle choices of language, imagery, & suggestion as involuntary as they are imperative. Almost any kind of a theme can become genuine literature when handled by an artist in a creative mood. I would say that all the early tales you cite—Dreamer of Atlanaat, &c.—have a very considerable & enviable art element in them. So will others to come. In between will appear the pattern jobs. That's the way with Klarkash-Ton, who had to take to pot-boiling against his will. He turns out a half-dozen routine jobs—& then suddenly speaks in his own voice & writes a great story. One doesn't want to be thinking of philosophy or philosophic values. That—or anything like didacticism or conscious abstraction—spoils art.

Regarding realism & character-drawing—as I said before, that is not the only form of truly artistic literature, hence no one need waste time deploring a lack of aptitude in this direction. There are other ways of expressing moods & emotions. Relatively few persons have the power of imaginatively entering into characters radically dissimilar from themselves, but many can command a reasonable variety of literary types by personifying different aspects of their own character. All of us are more or less complex, so that our personalities have more than one side. If we are reasonably clever we can make as many different characters out of ourselves as there are sides to our personalities—taking in each case the isolated essence & filling out the rest of the character with fictitious material as different as possible from anything either in our own lives or in any other characters we may have manufactured from other sides of ourselves. Thus Ismeddin & d'Artois are clearly different sides of yourself, properly differentiated, filled out, & backgrounded. Ismeddin has your Orientalism & love of dashing arbitrary boundaries aside. Pierre, on the other hand, represents your love of logic & calculation—the mathematician in you. Of course the representation is not as clear & bald as all that—but you can undoubtedly appreciate the principle. Another mode of deriving varied characters is that of simple & accurate observation. Often we may be neither fertile in imagining alien motives & manners nor apt in personifying different sides of ourselves; yet may be able to record varied characters through our clear perception & faithful memory of the way other people whom we have actually known act & seem to think & feel. When we are of this type it is obligatory for us to possess a wide acquaintance among a great variety of people of all classes, in order that we may have an ample reservoir on which to draw. We are then able to populate a story not only with a character drawn from ourselves (although that will naturally be the strongest & most vivid one, since we can never know anybody else as well as we know ourselves), but with other characters drawn from those whom we have studied. Often this method is combined with the ability to draw different characters from different sides of the same personality—an ability which can occasionally be applied to other personalities as well as to our own. In such a case a relatively small circle of acquaintances can be made to furnish a wide array of fictional characters. The worst of all ways to devise characters is to borrow or adapt them from other authors' literary figures. That is fatal to realism. No literary figure is perfect, for distortion creeps into all adaptation; & when we try to adapt something which is itself adapted the imperfection is disastrously multiplied. Keep to a policy of first-hand transcription from life if you would create living characters.

I was vastly interested in your vivid account of that enviable problem-conquering quality of yours, & wish I could borrow enough of such psychology to make me sure of fifteen weekly dinars! But I really don't see why the possession of such strength needs to make one unable to understand—objectively speaking—the opposite types who lack it. Surely you have plenty of opportunities to see around you, & to study in some detail, many kinds of persons whose reactions to life are altogether different from your own. Take good old H S, for example. Gerald Canevin is a frank projection, on a slightly exaggerated & re-shaded plan, of himself—but where did he get his accurate, workable comprehension of the subtle, complex, primitive, & highly distinctive psychology of West Indian niggers? Nothing could be more unlike himself than the fawning, secretive, shifty, dependent blacks he drew—yet he drew them, & how!! The answer is that he observed & studied the types at first hand; watched their acts & deduced their motives, & finally became able to comprehend their psychology even though it scarcely touched his own at any point. You have a good start toward doing the same thing, as your Landon & the Pale Hands[15] fellow illustrate. Get rid of the idea that people differently motivated from yourself are incomprehensible beings past all accurate delineation!

However, as you yourself have suggested, & as I have said before, it certainly isn't necessary to draw every possible human type in order to produce literature of a certain kind—especially *weird* literature. In many sorts of literature—weird most of all—the *real* protagonists of the drama are *phenomena, & not people at all;* hence if we strike the proper atmosphere & unfold the chosen events in the most vivid possible fashion, we do not need to rely very heavily on the delineation of subtleties of human character. It will be sufficient if our human figures do not act in too improbable & inconsistent a fashion. They must be accurate enough not to spoil the realism of the picture—but beyond that we can afford to let them remain lightly sketched. It is another branch of art whose chief ingredient is the complete portrayal of human nature. And more—certain types of events do not call for more than a limited number of human types, so that we may often 'get by' splendidly in specialised fictional branches with a limited cast of characters which would seem grotesquely one-sided to an universal artist like Shakespeare or Balzac. Who would claim, for example, that Two-Gun Bob of Texas needs to understand the psychology of elderly New England school-teachers in order to write about Valusia, primal Africa, or Roman Britain? No—there's no use in pausing to envy or imitate the other guy. The way to achieve art is to be oneself & forget all about it. Just set down what's inside you clamouring to get out—or what tantalises you in dreams & seems to defy your power to crystallise it & pin it down.

Oysters? No thanks, if it's all the same to you! But your recent feat was surely a formidable & notable one.[16] These allegedly edible mollusca are as popular in Rhode-Island as in New-Orleans, & honest fellows engaged in the industry often hold contests of speed & skill not only in oyster-opening but in oyster-eating—the waterfronts of Providence, Newport, & other places having their rugged champions in such lines. You ought to come up & put these pikers in their place! ¶ Your petroleum coke sounds interesting. I'd try it if I didn't have gas to fall back on (plus the regular steam), & if my fireplace weren't filled up & concealed by a table. ¶ Maqusoud of Kashan surely was quite an old boy![17] ¶ I surely hope Wright will print some suitable paragraph regarding weird literature's loss. ¶ Blessings of the Prophet, & of the Elder Ones, upon you.

Notes

1. HPL used this name in reference to Whitehead because Whitehead wrote numerous stories featuring Gerald Canevin, a resident of the Virgin Islands who becomes involved in numerous supernatural adventures.
2. EHP was a trooper in the 15th U.S. regular cavalry in the Philippines and France during World War I.
3. "The Tree-Man" (*WT*, February–March 1931); rpt. *Leaves* No. 2 (1938): 120–32.
4. February 1925. Three other stories by Whitehead appeared previously in *WT*.
5. "Sea Change" tells the story of a man who has some medical condition (possibly a thyroid deficiency) that turns him into a "monster" unless he takes drugs to counter-

act it. The idea may dimly anticipate HPL's depiction of Wilbur Whateley in "The Dunwich Horror."

6. HPL visited with Whitehead at his home in Dunedin at his home in Dunedin c. 21 May through 5 June 1931.

7. The piece was considerably abridged as "In Memoriam: Henry S. Whitehead."

8. "Passing of a God" (*WT*, January 1931); "The Black Beast" (*Adventure*, 15 July 1931); "Cassius" (*Strange Tales of Mystery and Terror*, November 1931); "The Great Circle" (*Strange Tales of Mystery and Terror*, June 1932).

9. Published as "Bothon," *Amazing Stories* 20, No. 5 (August 1946): 122–41.

10. "The Bruise" had been rejected by *WT*, and HPL apparently provided a detailed synopsis in which he recast the story as one in which the protagonist relives his past life as a resident of the sunken continent of Mu. It does not appear that HPL contributed any actual prose to the story.

11. "The Chadbourne Episode" (*WT*, February 1933). The other two stories are unidentified and presumably are nonextant.

12. HPL means "chapter heading" within a novelette: "1—Invisible Scourge; 2—La Dorada; 3—The Hand of Hassan; 4—Shirkuh Makes Magic; 5—Ibrahim Khan; 6—Satan's Garden; 7—A Left Handed Kurd; 8—Monsters of the Pool; 9—D'Artois is Envious" (EHP to HPL, 28 November 1932; TLS, JHL).

13. "The House in the Magnolias" (*Strange Tales of Mystery and Terror*, June 1932); with Marc Schorer.

14. "The Thing That Walked on the Wind" (*Strange Tales of Mystery and Terror*, January 1933).

15. Landon is a character in "The Infidel's Daughter." The "Pale Hands" fellow is Davis Lawton.

16. EHP had told HPL he opened oysters using a screwdriver.

17. The name Maqsud of Kashan is inscribed in the famous Persian Ardabil Carpet (1539/40). Maqsud was probably a court official charged with producing the carpet. By referring to himself as a slave, he may have presented himself as a humble servant.

[7]   [ALS, JHL]

10 Barnes St.,

Providence, R.I.,

Dec. 20, 1932

Dear Malik:—

Help! Don't shoot! I surrender! *Zemargad* is in neither the Necronomicon nor in von Junzt's *Unaussprechlichen* [*sic*] *Kulten*, unless perchance it be in that passage (Nec. xii, 58—p. 984) in Naacal hieroglyphics, whose fullest purport I was never able to unravel. The Yashish passage in von Junzt (footnote, p. 751, ed. 1839)—⨤ ⦂ ∩ ᵚ ⌅⸴ ⌇ ◪⅄⦂⅂ ● ▽ᵚ ᵙ⸴ ▱ ⦠⅄⇂ ⅔∩ ▽, etc—hints at a vague, ultra-dimensional realm of nameless horror best transliterated as *H'mar;* but the resemblance of this word to *Zemargad* is too strained to be other than fortuitous. Nor is the doubtful allusion to *Khad* in the Book of Eibon any real clue. The Pnakotic Manuscripts mention the subterrene gulf of

Zim, but all scholars from de Galimatias & zu Dumkopf[1] onward have agreed that this is really a reference to the Vaults of *Zin,* so well known to all students of Alhazred & von Junzt. No—there's no use in concealing plain ignorance; & I must flatly admit that I never heard the name *Zemargad* before, & that the volumes in my library are unanimous in failing to solve the mystery. You might ask our friend Klarkash-Ton, whose Oriental attainments dwarf mine into nonexistence, but I fear this problem will prove a tough nut to crack. The literature of Lilith is, it seems to me, very scanty; although a profound student of Judaica could probably get at sources unknown to the laity. If Smith can't get at this matter himself, there is just the barest possibility that his correspondent, the somewhat well-known Benjamin de Casseres,[2] might have data. He is a scion of a very ancient & scholarly Jewish line—a lineal descendant, by the way, of Spinoza's sister—& his esoteric tastes would suggest a fair degree of familiarity with ancestral lore. But anyhow, C A S looks like the best bet as a starter. Thanks, incidentally, for those two sheets of delvings. They'll come in splendidly some time when I want to throw a new kind of bluff of arcane erudition. I did some looking up anent Lilith in 1925, when I wrote "The Horror at Red Hook"—but with characteristic negligence I have forgotten where I found the little I did.[3] In that story, if you will look closely, you will find a hint of the Lilith-jealousy which you are about to employ as a theme. This motif is not as yet badly hackneyed, & deserves some attention from modern weirdists. The roughly parallel Aryan legends of cloud & swan maidens, Maras, &c., could also be used to advantage. A friend of mine—C. M. Eddy—did write a swan-maiden story, but never succeeded in getting it published. By the way—the statement that *Ahrimanes*—the *Persian* devil—is Lilith's son, leads me to wonder if *Persian* mythology be not a good avenue through which to look for *Zemargad.* The more I think of this, the likelier it looks. Better trot down to the repository of wisdom on Lee Circle[4] & see if you can't scare up something in that line. I'd do the same myself if I weren't so damnably rushed to death—but at present I'm engulfed in a frightful maelstrom—a sizeable travel brochure to type,[5] & 21 letters (some of them long aesthetic, scientific, & philosophic arguments) to answer!

Getting around to yours of the 12th—I'm glad H S had a chance to do his own abridgement of "The Tree Man", for it would have been barbarous to let a philistine like Lenniger tamper with it. As you say, good old Canevin's willingness to alter a MS. which is capable of alteration is typical of his hearty & generous nature—although I think you do a little unconscious injustice to those who are unwilling to have certain MSS. monkeyed with. Some stories are so interdependent in their parts, & so inextricably tied up with a certain proportioning, that they wouldn't be worth a damn if mangled to suit some pachydermatous mob-caterer who knows & cares nothing for genuine quality; & when this is the case my respect goes to the chap who insists that they appear as written or not at all. This has nothing to do with work which *is* capable of change without injury, & is not in the least connected with that flighty & long-haired sort of "temperament" which I despise as much as you do. Often one knows that a MS. isn't much good, but forbids change lest it be made still worse. You can generally tell the sensible sort of fastidiousness—the sort which springs from a real respect for aesthetic integrity & an unwillingness to violate it—from the affected sort, by noting the reactions of the person in question outside the immediate field of MS. text. When the textual fastidiousness proceeds from mere caprice & pose, those qualities will usually appear in other departments of life. In general, I think a writer's attitude toward his own work depends largely upon how much of himself is involved in it. When a man is overflowing with talents, & has many holds on life besides that of self-expression, he can afford to take his writing lightly. On the contrary, if he be only mediocre in other activities, his writing will naturally loom large in his emotions. It forms in such a case the man's only hold on life—his only measure of personality—& he will consequently tend to feel that all his right to live is somehow bound up in integrity of expression. All his eggs are in one basket, as it were. Violations of his best efforts & of the principles behind them will appear to him like violations of his inmost personality & standards—like breaches of honour or infractions against good taste. And why not? . . . . for they are indeed violations of what he most respects. You tend—as your reactions toward Derleth's serious stories illustrate—not to sympathise vividly with the type of person whose life is of the imagination rather than of the external world, & with whom imponderables count more than do visible acts & phenomena. Accordingly you are probably apt to be a little more severe than is necessary toward those whose scruples & sensitivenesses spring from such a psychological constitution. As a matter of fact, there is room in life & literature for both types—the sensitive dreamer & the man of action. Civilisation would be pretty one-sided & sterile if both did not exist in something like even proportions. In some cultures, of course, there is indeed a disconcerting lack of balance in one direction or the other—too many dreamers, for instance, in India, & too few in America. But in general I think the ideal attitude for both the dreamer & the doer to hold toward his opposite is one of 'live & let live'. I always try to be fair toward the value of doers, even though my own instinctive sympathies are on the side of the dreamers. Indeed—no one could have a higher respect for the accomplishments of doers than I have. All I really despise in that line is the material profit motive when carried beyond the stage where it is linked with the maintenance of good living conditions. But on the other hand, I hate a posing & self-conscious "aesthete" who thinks that the possession of artistic sensitiveness or the pursuit of artistic activities sets him off from the rest of mankind & justifies a separate mode of dress & barbering, & a separate code of manners. It's about an even thing which I hate the more—a languishing pseudo-Paderewski in a Windsor tie, or a "practical" clod who doesn't care what he does so long as he is paid for it.

Neither type, at its respective extreme, has to my mind a proper conception of what the aesthetic principle & its normal relation to life really are.

I haven't heard from Wright, but I trust your hints will incline him toward the publication of an elegiac word in the Eyrie. It ought to be dignified & unsigned—including the essential facts & giving a brief glimpse of H S's unusual personality. What I sent was merely source-material for Wright to handle & paraphrase as he wishes. Klarkash-Ton was tremendously shocked to hear the bad news—his admiration for the Canevin tales having been particularly keen & deeply-seated. I hope that Whitehead's family will keep his MSS. & files in good order, so that an ample posthumous story-collection can some day be facilitated.[6]

I duly note the expressing information. Derleth won't be sending me the long MS. till after new-year's, so that it will probably come your way around mid-January. As for his anthology tale—"In the Left Wing" probably has the most ghoulish touch, though Derleth thought the cheer-loving Lhen-Eighur would prefer "The House in the Magnolias" on account of the happy ending.

Kline's silence about the lodging-place of "Pale Hands" is surely curious. Hope it isn't because the market is an excessively humble one! Perhaps it is such a de luxe market that he wants to give you a pleasantly paralysing surprise when the time comes. As for *Magic Carpet*—possibly, but the Oriental element in P.H. is so tenuous & subsidiary that it would be straining matters a bit to place it in an avowed repository of Eastern tales. Congratulations, by the way, concerning "Satan's Garden." Wright's generosity about the matter of marketing is certainly notable in the extreme—he undoubtedly does take the laurel wreath for honour & liberal terms, as editors go. Hope he'll take Tarbis in the end.

By the way, the reactions of that editor to "Prayer for my Enemy" & "The [*sic*] Silver Peacock" certainly were curious! Evidently the fellow doesn't really know what he wants.

I note with great interest your elucidation of the psychological sources of Ismeddin, d'Artois, &c. It is of course impossible to refer every one of an author's characters to one particular facet of his personality. There is always a vast amount of overlapping, adaptation, &c.—which in a really good author gives each different creation a distinctive nature of its own. I shall look for Balkis around the first of March. As for cover designs—with the usual "artistic" staff, the omission is often a greater favour than the providing would be. I've never been given a cover design, & have never wasted any briny tears about the matter. The most truly imaginative illustrator W T ever had was Rankin[7]—though he sometimes lapsed, through pure carelessness, into painful mediocrity . . . . . . not that he could be worse than most of the stories!

When you come to Providence—as I certainly hope you will before going amongst the savage bolsheviki to be frozen or murdered—I'll be sure to have the oyster champions marshalled in an impressive troop betwixt the archers & the kettle-drummers. The matter of handicaps deserves sober consideration, & I'm sure a waffle-iron would rate highly even in a region accustomed to the use of automobile-wrenches, book-ends, electric necktie-pressers, postal scales, & other random household accessories. But if you become R.I. champion, please list yourself as of Louisiana. I'd hate to have a Moscow red the champeen of these Plantations!

As for that proposed move[8]—it certainly would be picturesque & far from unprofitable, & I wish you luck with it until something better & less exilic turns up. Those vacations are what look good to me! Don't forget the Samarcand, Khamil, & Lhasa[9] postcards. But when I think of what a Moscow *winter* must be, I add a prayer to my congrats. If I were there, I'd have to do—albeit on a less dramatic scale—what Napoleon did. A matter of greater envy with me is Matamoras! Would that I were in Mexico or the West Indies right now! Last week I couldn't go out at all—down to 15°, 10°, & even zero for 3 or 4 days. ¶ Good luck with the new work, & hope the tobacco fast brings good results. I could never find the fabled charm of the weed—but every man to his taste. ¶ And so it goes. Again let me thank you for the recherché data, & express my humiliation & regret at not being able to straighten out the Zemargad riddle. ¶ With salaams

Notes

1. The term *galimatias* first appears in Sir Thomas Urquhart's 1653 translation of the essays of Montaigne, referring to gibberish or meaningless talk. It is analogous to the English word *gallimaufry*, also derived from the French. *Dumkopf* is German for a stupid person ("blockhead").

2. Benjamin De Casseres (1873–1945), American journalist, critic, essayist, and poet.

3. HPL noted to CAS that he found most of the occult information used in "The Horror at Red Hook" in the *Encyclopaedia Britannica* (see *DS* 84).

4. I.e., the public library in New Orleans.

5. HPL had just ghostwritten "European Glimpses" for his ex-wife, Sonia H. Greene.

6. This did not occur until Arkham House published *Jumbee and Other Uncanny Tales* (1944) and *West India Lights* (1946).

7. Hugh Doak Rankin (1878–1956), early illustrator for *WT* (1927–36).

8. EHP had an offer to move to Moscow to work for the All-Union Welding and Oxygen Trust.

9. EHP had joked that he would spend the "roubles" he earned in Moscow on vacations to Samarkand, Bokhara, and Tiflis and send postcards from there. HPL added Khamil and Lhasa to that list.

[8]   [ALS, JHL]

Caverns of Khaf[1]—
Jany. 12, 1933

Dear Malik:—

The pages from "The Daughter of the Dancer"[2] certainly look alluring & promising enough, & I feel certain that the tale will fare well editorially. Klarkash-Ton confesses himself as grossly ignorant as I concerning Zemargad, but let us hope that some informed person may turn up somewhere. C A S agrees with my final idea that the term comes from *Persian* lore, despite its occurrence in Semitic legend. Such borrowings were by no means uncommon in antiquity & the middle ages.

As for the discussion of one's attitude toward one's writings—of course the whole matter is too complex for any snap verdict. There is the whole matter of point of view to start with. You say that 'we write to sell'—whereas it is my cardinal principle *not* to write for any such purpose. For cash I will do anything honourable *except* write original fiction. That one field, with me, has to be reserved for sincerely disinterested effort, because (a) it is the one channel of real expression which I possess, & (b) because experience has shewn me that I cannot dabble in pulp cheapness without hopelessly ruining anything I have to say. If I had the ready facility of Derleth & others, it would be a different story—but each separate individual has his own peculiar problems, & hasty generalisations are always misleading.

It would be academic, of course, to say that a considerable number of stories seriously written could not be abridged without harm. On the other hand, it would be equally erroneous to say that the *kind* of abridgment & change ordinarily suggested by cheap editors could be accomplished without harm. I have more impatience with the pliant hack always ready to bow to the caprice of a low-grade rabble-caterer, than I have with the stubborn & serious writer who holds abstract quality paramount. If one must err in either direction, I prefer erring on the side of artistic integrity, however hollow & repugnant that admittedly overworked term may sound to many.

As for "dominating one's medium"—that is a very intricate & relative matter. Naturally, no artistic result is ever produced (save in rare instances like "Kubla Khan"[3]) without a certain amount of conscious intellectual direction of the emotional & imaginative impulses seeking an outlet. The calculative mind of the artist always has some authority—in determining the given product. But after all, it is invariably the unconscious image-forming which gives the work its real vitality & differentiates it from mere photography & mechanism; so that we cannot impose conscious criticism on our efforts beyond certain limits without seriously impairing the strength & spirit of the result. The question is—what are those limits? Probably they differ with different persons, though it is to be noted that those authors whose habitual methods are most conscious & intellectual are generally weakest in the creation of a convincing atmosphere. In most cases they "dominate their medium" at the expense of what that medium has to convey. I am not enough of an egotist to care for the empty sensation of domination. My one aim is to have my result as intrinsically good as it can be made, & it is immaterial to me how much or how little my conscious intellect may have contributed toward that result. I think that art is always greater than any man . . . . . a fact, despite the somewhat platitudinous sound of the assertion when unqualified by explanation. I am not interested in domination, but I am interested in authentic self-expression.

But I see your point of view, & would not for a moment confound it with Philistinism. Our differences are a matter of basic forms of imagination, whereby expression has a somewhat different meaning in point of media. Externals cannot move my imagination as they can yours, & I have not your satisfaction in victory over obstacles. My only concern is to pin down adequately for my own future reference & enjoyment some fancy which my imagination half-conceives—& incidentally (as an abstract satisfaction) to do the pinning in the most effective possible manner. That I never succeed to any extent is another matter, scarcely relevant to the point at issue. Certainly, I have always succeeded *less* the more I have conceded to external or material demands.

Probably you are right in saying that some reluctance to change work is due to indolence—but oddly enough, I have a certain respect for that form of indolence. To begin with, I do not very seriously reprehend any sort of laziness. All work is really vain, & the lazy man is often wisest in the long run. In the case of an author—it may be that a tale of his could by hard work be changed without loss of quality. But the chances are that it could *not* thus be *improved*—so that the painful labour of change would be expended to no intrinsically worthy end. A writer who might be willing to sweat & strain endlessly if he thought he was achieving *better work* thereby, might very justly be unwilling to put an equal amount of painful labour into a task *not* leading toward improvement, but merely helping to suit the cheap taste of an insensitive & mob-pandering editorial upstart. If it was a case of earning food & shelter, he might very legitimately prefer to put this extra energy into some other job less degradingly connected with his serious work. Of course, there are some tremendously facile persons for whom the alteration of a story does not involve any headache-breeding travail. It may be quite practicable for them to revise their work to order, since that process does not drain away any energy needed for worthier efforts. But not everyone is of this fortunate sort, & it is hardly fair for the lucky ones to lay down general rules & standards to which the hapless plodders cannot practicably conform. In my attitude toward auctorial indolence, I suppose I really reveal a certain amount of personal bias. Undeniably, I have a contempt for any performance of *hard work* when the object is not *intrinsic excellence* . . . . . . or else survival on decent terms. And I have an unconquerable tendency to demand a certain *separation* of excellence-work & survival-work . . . . . . seemingly illogical, & yet perhaps not without an obscure justification based on the tendency of survival-efforts to cut into excellence-efforts & vice-versa. What I really want is *any* kind of a non-literary job paying $15.00 per week or more—plus enough unworried leisure to write with excellence as a sole object, & with no thought of audience or professional markets.

I fancy you get my idea. I have *no prejudice at all* against the alteration of work *when the object is actual improvement*. Indeed, a good share of my stuff represents the result of repeated revisions. Some are better able to improve their work by change than are others, & I would recommend that each separate writer consult his own ability in deciding whether a certain case of alteration would be for the better or for the worse. When a mediocre writer knows he has done his best in a certain direction, & feels that further change would be disastrous, the sensible thing for him to do (if quality be his supreme concern) is to set his foot down & refuse to make a mess of the little he has achieved. That is often my own position regarding efforts of mine. Right here the extreme difference in our sympathies becomes manifest. You exalt the artist at the expense of his work, whereas I consider the work the most important thing about the artist. Your picture of the artist 'refusing to worship his work' & buckling down to 'master' it has only a limited appeal to me. Certainly, an artist ought not to be satisfied till he has done his best, so that he ought not to consider his work inviolate until it represents his maximum effort; but once it *has* become the best he can do, the only proper course for him is to let it alone. If his cold consciousness insists on giving such work another shape—"asserting mastery", as you would phrase it—the new shape is generally attained at the expense of the work's vitality, so that the "mastery" is a very hollow thing. I'm looking for *excellence of product*—not any cheap & empty "mastery." I never think of *myself* when trying to capture a mood or idea, since I'm too busy with the mood or idea itself. So far as the creative process is concerned, the work must be everything & the worker nothing. However—I do not fail to concede that the author of extremely vigorous mentality is usually able to impose conscious modification on his work more successfully than the author of more languid cerebration. The important thing is for each individual author to learn his own limitations & base his policy sensibly upon them.

Possibly I have made myself clearer than before. My attitude, as you see, is based upon a frank dislike of professional writing as a pursuit for persons anxious to approach actual literary expression. I think that literary aspirants ought to follow paying jobs outside literature & its fake penumbra, & keep their writing free from commercial objects. Later on, when they have achieved great perfection, they may or may not be able to sell their things, but that ought not to enter into their heads. They have a full-time job in pursuing excellence for its own sake. As for the business of supplying artificial formula-writing to the various commercial media catering to herd tastes—that is an honest enough trade, but in my opinion more proper for clever craftsmen having no real urge toward self-expression than for persons who really have something definite to say. As a concrete illustration I refer you to Putnams' rejection of my collected tales for book-form publication in 1931. They said that the stuff reflected the cheap standards of the popular professional magazines, & upon analysis & reflection I had to admit that they were right. In spite of my conscious defiance of the cheap Philistine ideal, I have become insidiously tainted with it to some degree merely through seeing so much of W.T. & knowing its demands so well. I'd have been a lot better off if I'd never tried placing stuff in the damn thing. Of course, I might not have been any good anyhow—but at least I wouldn't have been quite so rotten.

And so Little Sunshine Lhen-Eighur likes Klarkash-Ton's "Yoh Vombis"![4] Well—for once he's picked a good story in spite of himself! That has a genuine power, & it gave me a real kick both in its present form & in an earlier version which I saw in MS. If Whitehead Sr. has charge of good old Canevin's files I hope he'll give Wright a chance to see all the unpublished MSS. There are two more Chadbourne stories—one accepted by Bates & sent back after *Strange* & *Astounding* blew up, & one which does not seem to have been submitted anywhere. And then there is a tale which was (at my suggestion) to involve the fabulous sunken continent of Mu—though this may not have been finished.

Congratulations on the weaving of "Pale Hands" into the *Magic Carpet!*[5] I must get a look at the magazine in its renamed & metamorphosed form. And let me reiterate my postcard congratulations regarding "Tarbis", which I am eager to read in its final form. I wonder if the added explanations cover that point about the mode of survival (without local comment or wonder) of Tarbis which I told you I thought needed a bit more elucidation? Yes—you had mentioned that Tarbis was an early work revived. It must be rather a satisfaction to realise that your first professionally submitted effort has sold at last!

Your work on "The Silver Peacock" certainly sounds arduous enough, & I hope exceedingly that the bird may find a profitable perch. As for serious efforts—of course it wouldn't do for you to follow the same line that Derleth follows, for he is himself & you are yourself. It's the job of each separate author to write what's in *him*, not what's in somebody else. Other fields of life & other types of character arouse your greatest interest & urge for depiction, & your status as an artist will depend on how faithfully & vividly you depict them. Merit does not hinge on choice of subject, but upon the fulness & vitality with which any chosen subject is presented. You certainly don't lack for material suited to yourself, & when you've completed your explorations of Muscovy, Siberia, Thibet, Turkestan, & the unknown plateau of Leng, you'll surely be full enough of colour & ideas waiting to burst forth as serious literary portrayal. You have the right idea when you resolve to present a *man* before you begin to lay stress on his sabre-slashings. *Action* is of value only when correlated with life, & that correlation cannot be established except through giving the action significance by humanising the actors & limiting the scope to what normally occurs in life. Mere gestures without meaning don't make literature.

Right now yours of the 9th blew in. Glad to hear that my Sekhmet[6] card found an appreciative recipient! That corridor of seated lion-headed colossi[7] has always fascinated me—indeed, I have often thought it represents the actual feel & spirit of nighted, immemorial Khem better than any other one exhibit in the country. I surely wish you *would* give the thing a fictional writeup—you could do it justice, & my cat-loving soul would applaud the result. Good luck with the "Daughter"—if Satrap Pharnabazus doesn't take it he certainly deserves to be deposed! Of the two openings I vastly prefer the non-conversational—which renews my wish to get a sight of old Bayonne some day. Ah, me—I've never been even in Bayonne, New Jersey—although I've seen it across the straits from Staten Island! Kohut[8] is indeed a fascinating author to quote from . . . . . . I'd hate to meet Agrat-bat-Mahlat[9] after dark unless I had both Cthulhu & Yog-Sothoth on the job to act as bodyguard! Yes—even to Azathoth in Central Chaos wind my prayers for the success of the "Daughter". *Iä—nasht—ktha—ytho—rliu!*[10]

The magazine market is surely a pathetic mess—but may the daemons keep King Pharnaces' dominions above the vortex! No—I don't think the defunct Fiction House could be the "new" chain mentioned by Kline, since some of its titles (like *Ace-High*) have been familiar sounds on my ears for many twelvemonths.[11] Bates told Wandrei he was not looking for a job, but was planning to spend the next year writing a play—& yet something tells me he wouldn't turn a good offer down if one hove in sight! I'll let you know if I hear of any such connexion on his part.

I don't worry about the anthologies. If O. Henry skipped me in '31 he made up for it in '32 with one 1st class & one 2nd class citation. So far as I can see, the selective principles of such things are almost as capricious as editors' minds—though O'Brien's intentions are always to be respected. His is the better volume—even though he hasn't mentioned me since '29.[12] Yes— some day let us hope that Oswald Marmaduke de Marigny[13] may shew these upstarts their place!

As for Soviet Russia—I can't excuse its unnecessary demolition of those traditional folkways which give to normal life so much of its illusion of direction & purpose. All this wreckage is perpetrated in the name of *equality*, which is after all a very meaningless, mathematical thing. I agree that existing systems— essentially plutocratic oligarchy—are unadapted to the problems of a mechanised future, but I don't think that such a fanatical overturn is needed in order to restore the ability of willing workers to be sure of a decent livelihood. What will have to come will doubtless be allied to *socialism*, but that's a long way from the *communism* which destroys half the zest of life to cater to a mere theoretical ideal. Undoubtedly many individual features of the Soviet organisation are worth borrowing & adapting to the different conditions of the western world, but the system as a whole seems to me to be a good thing to keep out of one's own country. The follies of American life are numerous enough, but one can escape from them by leading a retired existence. On the other hand, Russia's follies appear to be so obtrusively forced on every individual that escape is almost impossible. I'll be interested to hear how you like the land of the Soviets after you've had a first-hand taste of it—although your position as a foreign expert will probably give you certain advantages over the natives. You'll have to use observation & imagination to picture the life of the actual Soviet subject. I'd give Little Belknap about 12 hours in Russia before his writing to Papa to come & get him out. The young scamp has never known what it is to live without an almost oppressive battery of material luxuries—& he looks upon a Truly Warner hat[14] or a servantless home as a grotesque curiosity. His present sale of his library is only to raise spending-money for cigarettes, cravats, & moustachelet-wax. But just the same, he feels "cramped & inhibited" by the "bourgeois American scene" (which has never exerted any pressure on him that I've been able to detect!), & is all for the glorious freedom of Marx & Lenin . . . . . . until he reads some glib book on the other side of the question. As for you—I really think you will get a great deal out of the exotic, cosmopolitan, & socially unsettled atmosphere of Russia if you don't expect too much in a material way. Derleth says he has heard of experts in Russia being paid in forms of currency or certificate which prove valueless—though I suppose young Carr[15] could help in steering you clear of official gold-bricks. It certainly would be inspiring to behold the glittering minarets of Samarcand, & stand on the borders of primal Asian mystery!

As for our friend Randolph Carter—just as I said before, I am anxiously awaiting a period free & unworried enough to let me tackle him in proper fashion. All the autumn & winter so far, the pressure of various events has been quite devastating; but I am hoping to get things somewhat under control within a month at least. Then I shall take a whack at Brother Randolph—& if I feel that I'm not doing him justice, shall turn my attempt (together with your original) over to Klarkash-Ton as formerly suggested. But I fancy I won't need to call in further aid—we'll see when the time comes. You'll certainly see the result before you set sail for the shadowy steppes of distant Muscovy!

By the way—a gift this Christmas provides my library with its most cherished single accession of recent years—nothing less than that apex of all Gothic fiction, Maturin's "Melmoth, the Wanderer". It is in 3 volumes—the reprint of 1892, which constitutes the last edition so far as I know. This edition—long out of print—usually sells for about $10.00 when obtainable at all, & I've often been on the point of purchasing it—though always lacking the cash when the opportunity was present. Another thing I'm getting (from the Union Library Assn. as a remainder for 79¢) is E. R. Eddison's fascinating phantasy "The Worm Ouroboros", which I perused with an almost enchanted appreciation six years ago. It is to my mind the most ethereally potent piece of work since Dunsany's best days, & I'd have bought it on its appearance but for the original price of 3 bucks. Klarkash-Ton (who had never read it before) discovered it as a remainder, & tipped me off about it. He is quite transported by it. I hope the supply isn't sold out—I sent in my 79¢ only a couple of days ago, & am watching the mails with anxiety. If you like, I'll lend it to you when (or if) it comes. Which reminds me that Derleth says he has just shipped "Evening in Spring" by express. I'll forward it to you as soon as I've digested it. If it's anything like the early version I read, you can't fail to be impressed by its promise—& by its intrinsic merit, too.

By the way—Wandrei is just finishing a psychological novel[16] which portrays a man at the moment of making a supremely important decision, & goes back to explore all of the different major chains of thought & feeling & experience which collectively determine the decision. It looks like a very substantial thing for a first serious novel—though of course there's no telling whether or not it can be placed until the attempt is actually made. I doubt its acceptance in these uncertain times. But what I admire is Wandrei's refusal to cater to any editorial prejudice or mob caprice. He is writing this to express himself—& he refuses to aim at any goal other than abstract & disinterested excellence. Long advises him to put in something sensational to catch the rabble's fancy—but he steadfastly refuses to alter the lifelike proportioning of any of the ingredients. That's what I call the right attitude—the kid is an artist in spirit, whatever may be the fate of this particular early product. Of course I hardly need point out that nothing in his serious writing resembles the more or less frankly commercial material which he has in W.T.

And so it goes. I had commendably mild weather for my holiday break in hibernation, & the temperature is still far from savage hereabouts—yet I none the less envy you your presence below the 30th parallel. It won't be like that in Moscow! If I ever seek exotic climes my choice will be the West Indies or East Indies or Africa or Brazil or India.

Best wishes for 1933, & may Allah, Agrat-bat-Mabhat, Cthulhu, Tsathoggua, & Yog-Sothoth all be on thy side. ¶ Thy obeisant Slave—

ﭑﺵ 211(ﻣﺮ111(ﺿﻤ1 211ﺿ1 ﻣ)16.

[P.S. on envelope:] Just got your card. Congratulations on the detective sale! Hamlin Daly[17] must be quite a bird—& Otis Adelbert surely knows the art of salesmanship! He seems to be putting it all over Sunshine Lhen-Eighur! Guess I'll order a dozen copies of the forthcoming Art & Science of the Detective Story—though I fear it would take more than that to make me turn out salable specimens!

Notes

1. HPL typically spells this *Kaf.* Mount Qaf is a mountain in Middle Eastern mythology. EHP mentions Kaf in "A Jest and a Vengeance." After EHP moved to Redwood City, CA, in 1935, he and HPL referred to his place at Mt. Kaf.

2. Published as "Queen of the Lilin." EHP elsewhere mentioned it to HPL as being renamed "Queen of Zemargad," and later began to refer to it by its final name without explanation.

3. Alluding to the poem (1797) by Samuel Taylor Coleridge, who composed it one night following an opium-influenced dream after reading a work describing Xanadu, the summer palace of Kublai Khan, Emperor of China. Upon waking, Coleridge set about writing lines of verse that came to him from the dream until he was interrupted. The poem could not be completed according to its original 200- to 300-line plan, as the interruption caused him to forget the lines.

4. CAS, "The Vaults of Yoh-Vombis" (*WT,* May 1932).

5. *Oriental Stories* (1930–1932) was renamed *The Magic Carpet Magazine* (1933–1934).

6. In Egyptian mythology, a warrior goddess and also goddess of healing.

7. In Assyro-Babylonian ecclesiastical art, the great lion-headed colossi serving as guardians to the temples and palaces seem to symbolize Nergal, a deity worshipped throughout Mesopotamia but with the main seat of worship at Cuthah.

8. Alexander Kohut (1842–1894), rabbi, Orientalist, co-founder of the Jewish Theological Seminary of New York, and professor of Talmudic methodology.

9. A demon in Jewish mythology, mentioned by EHP in a letter of mid-December 1932. The name means "Agrat, daughter of Mahlat."

10. *Iä,* the exclamation to address Shub-Niggurath; *Nasht,* a priest in *The Dream-Quest of Unknown Kadath* (a word from HPL's dreams); *ktha—ytho,* a variant of Cthulhu; *rliu,* a variant of R'lyeh.

11. The second publisher of *Ace-High* was Dell Publishing.

12. O'Brien gave "The Dunwich Horror" a three-star rating and "The Silver Key" a one-star rating in *The Best Short Stories of 1929.*

13. A cat at EHP's garage in Pawhuska.

14. The hatter Albert J. "Truly" Warner was known for marketing men's hats with names; e.g., the Larchmont, the Hereafter, etc.

15. Robert Spencer Carr (1909–1994), American writer of weird, fantasy, and science fiction who achieved celebrity with the best-selling society novel *The Rampant Age* (1928), adapted into a film in 1930. He "turned from books to business & became a power in the Soviet's American trading corporation" (HPL to August Derleth, late December 1932; *ES* 532).

16. *Invisible Sun.*

17. A pseudonym of EHP, used to avoid confusion with a story Lenniger was handling for EHP under his name.

[9]   [ALS, JHL]

[11 February 1933]

Dear Malik:—

Yours duly received—& abundant congratulations upon your acclamation by the *Magic Carpet* public.[1] I must get hold of the recent issue & scan the fanfare!

The other day I had a letter from Harry Bates—now in Clearwater, Fla. writing a play, & in touch with Whitehead's father & friends—which sheds light on the details of H S's passing.

It seems that during the autumn H S's cousin from the North was replaced by the bright little "cracker" boy C. J. Fletcher (whom he had had before) as secretary & general factotum.[2] On the Sunday before his death—Nov. 20—he complained of a "general malaise"—*not* connected with his stomach. His friend Miss Starr[3] (a middle-aged gentlewoman who, during my 1931 visit, lent him the use of her car) was rather worried, & told young Fletcher to watch him carefully & telephone her if anything alarming developed. Late that night the boy heard a thud—as of a fall—in Whitehead's room, & found H S in a queer & disturbing condition—partly deprived of speech. He telephoned Miss Starr, & she went over—finding H S semi-conscious. She then telephoned Dr. Mease (prop. of the local sanitarium, & H S's regular physician), who came at once & sent for two other doctors. They diagnosed the case as concussion of the brain caused by a fall. Before morning old Mr. Whitehead was notified & rushed up from St. Petersburg. H S was still semi-conscious, recognised his father, raised an arm, smiled, & said "My daddy." Those were his last words. From then until the end the doctors kept him under opiates. Fletcher, Dr. Mease, Miss Starr, Mr. Whitehead, & others were on hand & awake most of the time. Death came early on the morning of Wednesday the 23d. It is clear that H S never had a chance to read my reply to his last letter.

H S was feeling *unusually well* until Sunday, Nov. 20th, hence I doubt if the old gastric trouble was really the direct cause of death. To me it looks like a malignly tragic *accident*—the fall in the night; which, though doubtless caused by the general weakness resulting from the old trouble, might easily have not occurred. It seems that shortly before his death H S had had all his books & household effects shipped down from the north, where for years they had been in storage. He had also just built a new sun porch on the roof of his new home in Pasadena Drive. It is tragic that he could not have lived to enjoy these things.

Old Mr. Whitehead[4] (age 85), Bates says, is visibly failing under the shock—although he carries on with outward cheerfulness—the old Canevin stamina. He is quite deaf, & of late his eyes have been developing cataracts. H S's body has been placed temporarily in a St. Petersburg mausoleum, & Mr. Whitehead plans later to unite the family dust by having Mrs. Whitehead's[5] remains brought south & arranging for three graves (including his own) side by side in the St. Petersburg cemetery—father, mother, & only child. Thus good old Canevin will rest under the semi-tropical sun he loved so well, & beside the parents to whom he was so warmly & undeviatingly devoted.

Damn that pen! I'll try a change. I fear I'll never settle the pen problem, though one step is achieved by casting economy to the four winds & using Sheaffer's ink instead of the dime-a-bottle products hitherto employed. It's a tough game. A flexible coarse pen like this makes a hellishly awkward script—but if I use a stiffer pen like the above, & get a neater script, the scratchy nervousness & early fatigue of the process are liabilities to be reckoned with. This afternoon I'm going to try to change the stiff pen for a smoother one—though I guess I'll have to return to the pencil of my early childhood before I'm through.

Good luck with "Queen of Zemargad"—which I really think is a better title than its predecessor. Wright ought to take it—if he doesn't, try him again later. I hope to hear more of the new weird effort—& trust that meanwhile the detective material may prove a decided fiscal asset. Incidentally—I must surely get a copy of Tarbis when it comes out.

As for our literario-aesthetic controversy—if such it was—I fancy the real object, that of making the actual position of each debater clear to the other, has been very largely accomplished. After all, each person always keeps right on thinking & doing the same as before, whatever arguments fill the air—but it is something to understand the diversity of processes & psychological habits involved.

Your radio plans sound ambitious & potentially auriferous indeed, & I certainly hope they'll go through. Damn the luck which makes my aunt's radio (the only one at my constant disposal) unable to get any New Orleans stations.[6] It's curious, too—for she can get San Antonio, Texas, which is much farther off. As for Providence stations—of which there are three—WJAR, WEAN, & WPRO—I don't know of any which uses plays for local advertising features. WJAR (The Outlet Co.—department store) & WEAN (Shepard Co.—dept. store) handle no entertainment features except what come over the nation-wide networks; local features being confined to news flashes, speeches, & plain advertising for the respective stores themselves & for no others. WPRO (Cherry & Webb—women's clothiers) do have many local features, but I do not recall seeing any advertising plays listed among them. You might enquire, though. Another neighbouring station using local features is WSAR, over the state line in Fall River, Mass. I don't know much about their programmes. From now on, I shall keep more track of the daily programmes listed, & see if I see anything in your line.

Don't hurry about Sekhmet. We'll see which job is turned out first—that or my Silver Key collaboration. But old Sekky is a great subject when you get around to it.[7]

As for "Melmoth, the Wanderer"—which was written in 1820 by the Irish clergyman Charles Robert Maturin—when I call it the apex of *Gothic* fiction I use the adjective to describe that early phase of weird writing— including Horace Walpole, Clara Reeve, Ann Radcliffe, Matthew G. Lewis, Maturin,[8] &c.—to which it most peculiarly belongs. The term "Gothic tale" is primarily applied to these early novels (1780–1820, for the most part) in which the action centres around an ancient castle (or its equivalent), & in which certain stock character types & situations tend to appear. They were naive & crude as compared with the later weird forms evolved by Poe & perfected by Machen & Blackwood, yet many of their elements are carried over subconsciously or otherwise into contemporary work. I have an excellent history of this genre—"The Tale of Terror", by Prof. Edith Birkhead, which I'll be glad to lend you if you'd care to see it, & there is a still better history which I don't own—"The Haunted Castle", by Eino Railo. Try the public library. I also define the Gothic school in some detail in my article "Supernatural Horror in Literature"—published in 1927 in an amateur magazine. Didn't I ever send you this? If not, I must lend you a copy—my last duplicate having been given away some time ago. Other Gothic tales I possess are Walpole's "Castle of Otranto", Miss Reeve's "Old English Baron," & Mrs. Radcliffe's "Mysteries of Udolpho."

Under separate cover I am sending "The Worm Ouroboros", which I am confident you will find quite unlike anything you ever read before. Long, Klarkash-Ton, & I are enthusiastic over it. Read it at your leisure—no hurry so long as it comes back safely in the end.

You make me quite homesick when you mention the Orleans[9]—good old Lucas Carliss, the host who gave me a room & bath for one buck per! And yet this afternoon the mercury stands at 50° outdoors—up here in sub-arctic New England! The trouble is that it can't last. Even now dire reports of a coming drop fill the air.

That Russian travel magazine must be alluring—& yet, in view of the ruthless uprooting of all traditions, folkways, & reasons for civilised living in Russia proper, it seems a bit ironic for the bolsheviks to be advertising the alluring old customs & traditions of the Caucasus! I can't see the virtues of bolshevism—even though I realise that great changes in the economic system will have to take place. To fancy that nothing but a destructive upheaval, artificial equalitarianism, & tyrannical dictatorship like Russia's will lead out of the existing impasse, seems to me damned naive & dogmatic in view of the infinite number of possible compromises & gradual evolutionary trends.

Later—Feby. 11

Hades! Took the stiff pen down to the shop, but they couldn't give me a flexible point. Must send to the Parker works. What is worse, they've had to take my half-decent Waterman, too, so that the flexible point can be used as a guide to what I want. ¡Caramba! So here is poor old Grandpa with nothing but a service pen lent by the shop. And this sort of thing for over a week . . . . after which the new Parker point will probably be *wrong*. That's life. But this service pen is pretty good—better than most of my own have been lately. That's always the way—everybody can get a good pen but me! ¶ That 50° weather didn't last. Beastly cold spell, followed by the season's first considerable snow. It doesn't look much like Louisiana hereabouts today! However— it's well above 20°—my deadline. Couldn't go out at all Thursday & Friday, for it got down to 10°. ¶ Best wishes—& hope Derleth's story reached you safely. I don't think he's in a hurry for it. Yr obt Servt— אלּיﬠﬞﬡﬢ

Notes

1. See EHP to HPL, 3 February 1933 (TLS, JHL): "purely as a news item, and to one who knows how little a boast of that kind is worth, artistically. ISMEDDIN & THE HOLY CARPET walked away from a field headed by H. Bedford-Jones."
2. "Dr. Henry S. Whitehead Passes Away: Funeral of Noted Author And Clergyman to be Friday," *Dunedin Times* (25 November 1932): 1. "C. J. Fletcher has been living with Dr. Whitehead, who enjoy[ed] the companionship of boys."
3. Mary Isabella Starr.
4. Henry Hedden Whitehead (1846–1937), a Civil War veteran.
5. Mary S. Whitehead (1857–1919). The Whiteheads were interred at Royal Palm South Cemetery in Saint Petersburg.
6. EHP had mentioned failing to sell radio dramatizations to "The First Nighter Program," a radio program presenting original plays, specializing in romantic comedies. He suggested he might be able to a sell a series of thirteen detective shorts to WWL in New Orleans as part of a quarterly advertising contract. He sold his dramatization of "The Bride of the Peacock."
7. EHP's idea became "The Cat Goddess."
8. HPL addresses all these authors in "Supernatural Horror in Literature."
9. The hotel at 728 St. Charles St. at which HPL stayed when he visited New Orleans.

[10]   [ALS, JHL]

[15 February 1933]

Dear Malik:—

I thought le Comte d'Erlette's opus would give you quite a reaction! What the kid has done is to get at those subtle, unheeded impressions which we take for granted when they come, but which really contain so much of the universal that they pack a tremendous symbolic wallop when they crop out in later years. It's no easy job to single out such things & serve them up in such a way that they evoke parallel personal impressions in the minds of myriad readers—but I think M. Auguste-Guillaume has done it . . . . just as Marcel Proust did it. And that is art. D'Erlette has mastered the mechanism, as it were, of the experience-savouring & experience-recalling processes—he knows the right things to select, & the right way & tempo in which to put them across. The reader, swept into the rhythm of these processes, finds that rhythm eventually at work in his own head—utilising his own experience-material instead of the author's. My own nature & childhood differ diametrically from d'Erlette's, & yet his methods cause the early years & their impressions to come back vividly to me. I, though, find the nature sections—or in general, the sections devoted to broad impersonal impressions of landscape, architecture, atmospheric effects, &c.—far more vivid than those dealing with personalities & human relationships. This, because I have always been tremendously sensitive to the *general visual scene*—external, objective, mysterious, & full of potential cosmic suggestion—while relatively indifferent to people. I can never feel the poignancy of human affairs as keenly as I can feel the poignancy of dim vistas suggesting wonders of time, space, & the unknown on a stupendous & non-human scale—so that some of Steve's effusiveness & sentimentality about people seems to me like downright slobbering.[1] However, I know opposite types well enough to appreciate the skill & fidelity of all d'Erlette's delineations—& consequently to admire the artistry inherent in them. The little rascal certainly has the real stuff! The rural side gets under my skin because I always *knew* the ancient fields & hills & groves even though a city dweller. The house where I was born & grew up (about a mile southeast of 10 Barnes) was near the edge of the built-up streets when I was very small, & it was only a stone's throw to the rolling, stone-walled meadows, trim white farmhouses, rambling barns & byres, gnarled old orchards, dim twilight woods, & ravine-pierced river-bluffs of primitive colonial New-England. Like d'Erlette, I wandered fascinatedly through that mystical, flower-fragrant elder world & formed all sorts of imaginative impressions from it—but there the resemblance ends. For while he was an *intrinsic* naturalist like Wordsworth—sensuously content with the visible & unexplained beauty around him—I was the exact opposite; a confirmed & inveterate *associationist* who constantly linked the lovely countryside with everything in the past which folklore & reading had brought to me. I peopled the landscape with the gods, fauns, & dryads of antique Hellas, or with the castles & witch-cottages of fairy lore— or else dreamed them back into their own past & lived fancifully in bygone centuries. I twisted all reality to conform to what I had been reading—often making Old England's gnarled oaks out of New England's maples, & so on. Today the built-up city has swallowed a great part of my childhood countryside—though some of the choicest bits are providentially saved by being parts of the Metropolitan Park System. Thus I can still wander along the ancient wooded river-bank (as I do, with black bag full of reading & writing matter, each pleasant summer afternoon) & find nothing changed since my earliest infancy. Like d'Erlette, I was also sensitive to the mystery-fraught streets & huddled roofs of the town, & often took rambles in unfamiliar sections for the sake of bizarre atmospheric & architectural effects—ancient gables & chimneys under varied conditions of light & mist, &c. I always sought the *oldest* sections, where centuries of continuous life had left the most deposits, & thus formed my lifelong love for colonial houses & vistas—Vieux Carré stuff. This, of course, d'Erlette could never get in his village—although he would probably have been rhapsodic about Old Providence. Good old Providence—there is no other town quite like it! Though a centre of hundreds of thousands, it has kept an archaic, village-like quality which will never die, & which was even more marked in my youth than now. The town lies at the head of the bay, with the flat business section stretching westward on largely "made" land whilst the residence district climbs an almost perpendicular & incredibly picturesque hill just east of the shore line. The steepness of this hill (on whose crest I now dwell) has defied the spread of commerce & change, so that it narrow lanes, ancient steeples, rows of fanlighted doorways & railed double flights of steps, huddled gables, courtyard archways, walled gardens, occasional bits of actual grass-grown lane & farmyard, & countless other details, remain to a surprising extent as they were in the middle 18th century—before most of the houses in New Orleans' Vieux Carré were built. There is a 1761 colony-house,[2] a 1770 college edifice,[3] a 1769 schoolhouse,[4] a 1763 newspaper office,[5] a 1775 church,[6] a 1773 market house,[7] & so on . . . & so on . . . . And up to a recent time (curse the vandalism which destroyed the best part of it as recently as *1929*) the ancient waterfront with slant-roofed brick warehouses[8] & lanes of gambrel-roofed shops & pillared taverns was virtually the same as in the days of the African-Caribbean "triangular trade" (rum, niggers, & molasses) & the great East-India brigs. Then, too, from most points along the hill crest there is a breath-taking view of the outspread roofs & spires & domes of the westward-stretching lower town—a view reaching even to the dim violet hills of the country beyond . . . . the country whence many of my ancestors came. At sunset this vista is past description—the marble dome of the State House, the Gothic tower of St. Patrick's, & the distant spires of Federal Hill against the flaming, mysterious west—& then the cryptic twilight, with the violet of the far hills creeping eastward to engulf the whole drowsy valley, & little specks of light leaping out one by one till the expanded sea of roofs is one titanic constellation . . . . . . great stuff! And even more magical now that we have tall buildings (15, 16, 26 stories) to light up & suggest enchanted cliff cities of Dunsanian mystery. Good old Providence! The glamourous 18th century part begins at the original shore street at the foot of the precipice & climbs just over the top—with a few tongues reaching beyond the crest & inland along the gently-downward-sloping plateau. Adjacent to this are the early-, mid-, & later Victorian layers. 10 Barnes, alas, is Victorian—but it's only three houses from the ancient section, which begins with a 200-year-old white farmhouse[9] (old farmhouses imbedded in the heart of the engulfing city—like the Windtfelt house at 1st & Prytania or the Delord–Sarpy plantation house at Camp & Howard in New Orleans—are a distinctive Providence feature) still situate in the midst of its picket-fenced old-fashioned garden. Just around the corner is the splendid brick Halsey mansion built in 1801 & reputed to be *haunted*,[10] while my whole walk down town (zigzagging along the precipice & traversing an old-world street which is partly a flight of steps)[11] extends through Georgian byways & past centuried steeples & courtyards & belfries. My birthplace—at the edge of the town in the 90's—is of course in a solidly Victorian neighbourhood[12]—which made the strongly contrasted ancient hill section doubly fascinating to me in infancy. There was even a kind of faint, subtle *terror* mixed with the fascination, as if the ancient hill represented something obscurely *underlying & eternal,* whilst the newer sections represented a kind of flimsy dream out of which one might easily awake. I *still* get the sensation at times. The hill & its centuried gables seemed to me one with the ancient fields & farms & forests that stretched eastward to the river.

Pardon the rambling—but that's the way "Evening in Spring" sets one off. I also felt that kinship with *ancestors,* rather than the generation just preceding, which d'Erlette points out. My maternal grandfather—born in 1833—& his generation seemed much closer to me than the generation of my parents, uncles, & aunts, born around the '60's; while my forbears in the *18th century* (periwigged Devonshire squires & rural Anglican vicars on my father's side, & New-England planters on my mother's side) seemed closest of all. That sense of immediate personal kinship with the 18th century—its costume, architecture, literary style, thought, &c—has never left me or even diminished. It's that which sends me rambling around the country looking for Vieux Carrés & Charlestons & Natchezes & Salems & Annapolises & Quebecs!

Well—I tried once to put my imaginative reactions to Old Providence into a story, but don't think I succeeded very well. It was a 150-page novelette—"The Case of Charles Dexter Ward" (whose imaginary home was the old haunted Halsey mansion around the corner from here)[13]—which I wrote in the winter of 1926–27, but which I could never get the energy to type. Today little Barlow has offered to type it for me in exchange for the MS., but I'm not sure that it's good enough to save. I must trot it out & look it over.

Getting back to the theme—I don't believe the residue of "Evening in Spring" will disappoint you. It's solid material—& if I'm any prophet, young Comte d'Erlette will be one of the solid & recognised writers of the next decade.

Glad the verse pamphlet[14] proved of interest. I guess I'll send along another copy (I have more than I know what to do with), so that you can make that loan to your friend a gift. Keeping free of stock expressions is certainly a baffling job for many!

What you say of your new tale, & of the Pushkara–Plaksha–Kusha–Shâlmali–Mt. Meru–Sanzar–Dzyan–Shamballah myth-cycle[15] which you have dug up, interests me to fever heat; & I am tempted to overwhelm you with questions as to the source, provenance, general bearing, & bibliography of all this unknown legendry. Where did you find it? How can one get hold of it? What nation or region developed it? Why isn't it mentioned in ordinary works on comparative folklore? What—if any—special cult (like the theosophists, who have concocted a picturesque tradition of Atlanteo-Lemurian elder world stuff, well summarised in a book by W. Scott-Elliott)[16] cherishes it? For gawd's sake, yes—send along those notes, & I'm sure that Klarkash-Ton, High-Priest of Tsathoggua, would (unless he knows about the cycle in question) appreciate them as keenly as I. Incidentally—Klarkash-Ton tells me that his Semitic oracle de Casseres [*sic*] never heard of Zemargad. Tough luck! But the hint so strongly appeals to High-Priest Klarkash that he is going to use the name *Zemargad*—in conjunction with more synthetic nomenclature—in his new & hellish conception, "The Infernal Star."[17] Meanwhile, as I said before, I'm quite on edge about that Dzyan–Shamballah stuff. The cosmic scope of it— Lords of Venus, & all that—sounds so especially & emphatically in my line!

As for astrology—since I have always been a devotee of the real science of *astronomy*, which takes all the ground from under the unreal & merely apparent celestial arrangements on which astrological predictions are based, I have had too great a contempt for the art to take much interest in it—except when refuting its puerile claims. Back in 1914 I conducted a heavy newspaper campaign against a local defender of astrology,[18] & in 1926 I read quite a few astrological books (since largely forgotten) in order to ghost-write a thorough & systematic exposé of the fake science for no less notable a client than the late Houdini.[19] That comprises the sum of my astrological knowledge—the casting of horoscopes never having been included among my ambitions. If I ever employ any astrological lore in stories, I shall most gratefully call on you for realistic detail.

Your whirl of activity, as usual, is quite breath-taking to contemplate. I surely wish you luck with the radio sketches, since they ought to afford an admirable professional boost. Yes—send along a detectatiff tale some time— I'll wager you'd have an ingenious twist or two which would triumph over the pattern prescribed by conventional editors! Hope Otis Adelbert is right in his prediction concerning the novelettes—have you cast their horoscopes?

Oh, by the way—harking back to ancient legendry & pseudo-legendry— have you ever seen the books on *Mu* written by old Col. Churchward[20]—who claims to have had secrets revealed by old Himalayan priests while in India, & to have seen strange metal tablets in the primal Naacal language which tell the tragic history of the lost Pacific continent? At my suggestion Whitehead was going to incorporate this legendry into one of his tales, & he even sent for one of the Churchward books last summer. I've never seen the books, but have read fairly indicative reviews of them. Its' [*sic*] not certain whether the old boy is off his nut or whether some Hindoo priests really fed him full of fantastic ancient hooey. Speaking of a lost Pacific continent—it certainly *is* likely that a good deal of land—whether a large mass or many islands—has subsided in the Pacific. The legends of the natives teem with allusions to such a subsidence. I've just been reading an unpublished MS. on Tahitian folklore by a friend of mine who has lived on that island,[21] & one of the passages—from a myth called "The Wars of Tané"—is highly significant. Get this:

> ". . . . At one time he [Matai, God of Wind & Storm] was so wrathful that a great part of Mother Earth was submerged, & much of the dry land disappeared forever. These are the names of those who submerged so much of the earth: Terrible-Rain, Long-Continued-Rain, Fierce-Hail-Storms, Mist, Heavy-Dew, & Light-Dew, & these together left projecting only small parts of the Earth above the sea."[22]

A good book to get in connexion with Pacific mysteries is Prof. J. Macmillan Brown's "Riddle of the Pacific"—which I've never been able to lay my hands on. I am fascinated by such things as the Easter Island images (I've seen those in the Smithsonian) & the cyclopean masonry at Ponape & Nan-Matal.

Still waiting for the results of pen-exchanging. *This* is a new dime pen from Woolworth's. Splendid point so far, but feed N.G. As usual, I'm dipping. A cold wave with heavy snow has come & gone. Now ensues a period of gradual melting. I surely envy you amidst the palms of the near-tropics!

Best wishes—

Notes

1. Referring to the autobiographical character Stephen Grendon in Derleth's novel *Evening in Spring*. It was not published until 1941.
2. The Old State House (1762), 150 Benefit Street. Rhode Island declared its independence from England in the Providence Colony House two months before the Declaration of Independence.
3. University Hall, "The College Edifice"—the original, and for fifty years the only, building at Brown University.
4. Now called the Old Brick School House (c. 1769), 21 Meeting Street.
5. The John Carter House (1772), 21 Meeting Street. The *Providence Gazette and Country Journal* (est. 1762) was published by William Goddard in a shop marked by the sign of Shakespear's Head on North Main Street. Carter joined the paper in 1767 and by 1768 was sole proprietor. He and his wife moved the business into the house they built on Meeting Street.
6. The First Baptist Meeting House, 75 North Main Street.
7. On Market Square.
8. HPL refers to the destruction of early 19th-century warehouses on South Water Street in late 1929, inspiring him to write the poem "The East India Brick Row."

9. The Jenckes–Pratt House (c. 1775), 133 North Prospect Street at Barnes Street (northeast corner), the "little white farmhouse" HPL mentions in *The Case of Charles Dexter Ward.*

10. The Halsey house at 140 Prospect Street in Providence is the residence of Charles Dexter Ward in *The Case of Charles Dexter Ward* (1927), although HPL renumbered it to 100 Prospect.

11. Twenty granite steps were constructed in the late 18th century to connect Meeting Street and Congdon Street, not far from HPL's residence.

12. The house purchased in 1881 by his grandfather, Whipple Van Buren Phillips (1833–1904) at 454 Angell Street, a rambling three-story structure that HPL adored and in later years yearned to reclaim. Phillips, a wealthy industrialist, established the Owyhee Land and Irrigation Company in Idaho. He provided strong guidance to HPL in the absence of HPL's father. Upon the death of Phillips, HPL and his mother had to move to humbler quarters. The house was torn down in 1961.

13. The Thomas Lloyd Halsey House (c. 1800; c. 1825), 140 Prospect Street. See HPL to August Derleth (10 December 1931): "In the 1850's this fine old brick house was actually feared by the ignorant" (*ES* 422n).

14. I.e., *Further Criticism of Poetry.* See "Notes on Verse Technique" in the Bibliography.

15. EHP's story is "The Devil's Crypt." In letters to others on the subject, HPL mentioned the following writers and titles suggested by EHP: Annie Besant (1847–1933), *The Pedigree of Man* (London: Theosophical Publishing Society, 1904); Madame Helena Petrovna Blavatsky (1831–1891), *The Secret Doctrine* (London: Theosophical Publishing Co., 1888); C. W. Leadbeater (1847–1934), *The Inner Life* (Chicago: Rajput Press, 1911–12; 2 vols.); W. Scott-Elliot (1849–1919), *The Story of Atlantis and The Lost Lemuria* (London: Theosophical Publishing Society, 1925); and A. P. Sinnett (1840–1921), *Esoteric Buddhism* (Boston: Houghton, Mifflin, 1898). In Hindu mythology Pushkara was the brother of Nala, to whom Nala lost his kingdom and his possessions in gambling Pushkara. Plaksha is one of the seven dwipas (continents) into which the Hindus divided the earth. Kusha was a Chandravamsha king. Shâlmali–Mount Meru is the sacred five-peaked mountain of Hindu, Jain, and Buddhist cosmology. Sanzar is the mythical language in which *The Book of Dzyan* was allegedly written. The book is a reputedly ancient text of Tibetan origin that formed the basis for *The Secret Doctrine* (1888) by Blavatsky, one of the foundational works of the theosophical movement. Shamballah is, in Tibetan Buddhist tradition, a mythical kingdom.

16. Probably Scott-Elliot's *The Story of Atlantis and The Lost Lemuria* (see n. 15). It is a combined edition of two books, *The Story of Atlantis* (1914) and *The Lost Lemuria* (1904); HPL read it c. June 1926 and cited it in "The Call of Cthulhu."

17. Unfinished, existing only as a fragment.

18. J[oachim] F[riedrich] Hartmann (1848–1930), who published several articles on astrology in the [Providence] *Evening News* beginning with "Astrology and the European War" (4 September 1914). HPL not only wrote rebuttals of these articles but also satirized Hartmann in lampoons published under the pseudonym "Isaac Bickerstaffe, Jun." The entire exchange is included in *CE* 3.

19. HPL and C. M. Eddy, Jr. began work on *The Cancer of Superstition,* but ceased following the death of Houdini that year.

20. Col. James Churchward (1852–1936), *The Lost Continent of Mu* (1926), *The Children of Mu* (1931), *The Sacred Symbols of Mu* (1933), *Cosmic Forces of Mu* (1934).

21. HPL's friend, the amateur journalist and apiarist Edward Lloyd Sechrist (1873–1953), lived for a time in Papeete, Tahiti. The ms. in question is unknown, but Sechrist published an article, "The Shadow Folk: A Tahitian Legend," in *Asia* (April 1921).

22. Sir George Grey, *Polynesian Mythology* (London: John Murray, 1855), 8 (paraphrased).

[11]   [ALS, JHL]

𝐄̠𝐀̣ 𝐐̠ 𝐙̣ 𝐄𝐄 𝐎 𝐧

[Postmarked 2 March 1933]

Dear Malik:—

I have assimilated with proper awe the sundry bulletins of success which have come from the Peacock Throne, & hereby extend my massed congratulations. It is curious how well Kline & Lhen-Eighur supplement each other by covering different fields—& I am certainly glad you got hold of the pair of them. That detective-writing course sounds interesting, & I have already recommended it to one client. However—not everyone can succeed as well as yourself, even with the best instruction; for it takes a certain kind of ability to transform precepts into results. Speaking of detective stuff—the other day I saw in a window quite a reminder of my youth, in the form of a *Nick Carter Magazine*. I thought poor old Nick had slipped to oblivion a generation ago![1]

And now—amusingly enough—let me record a faint, miniature echo of your Chant of Acceptances. I think I told you last year that I had written a tale called "The Dreams in the Witch-House", which combined a Salem witchcraft aftermath with some modern dimensional aberrations. Recalling Wright's cool reception of my best story,[2] I did not bother to send this thing to W.T., but in the course of time lent the MS. to Derleth for perusal & copying. By accident, M. le Comte mentioned the tale to Wright—who thereupon asked to see it. When he had read it, Satrap Pharnabazus decided to purchase it, & accordingly dropped me a line to that effect. Although the tale really does not satisfy me, I am letting him have it for $140—less than I'd have received in 1929.[3] But I am *not* allowing any radio rights—for I certainly would not wish any tale of mine to be ruined by transposition to an inane & altogether unsuitable medium, & cheapened by the tame hokum which always accompanies radio & cinematic "horrors."[4] Of course, if any large sum were involved, I might overcome my scruples—but I doubt if there ever would be. Indeed—I doubt if any tale of mine would really be in any danger of radio use, since so little of the plot element, action, or conversation enters in.

By the way—your fame as a critic is spreading so rapidly that my friend & correspondent Bernard Austin Dwyer, Box 43, West Shokan, N.Y. (a longtime admirer of your work) is going to impose on you to the extent of asking you to read a story of his & tell him what you think of it. It is circulating among certain select members of the gang, & will come to you from Klarkash-Ton—for eventual mailing back to the author. Dwyer is frankly more or less of a beginner, but I think he has great promise. He is a young Irish giant of your own age.

Thanks prodigiously for the loan of the Shamballah dope—which I have copied in condensed form & sent along to Klarkash-Ton[5] for ultimate Barlovian delivery. Young Barlow will certainly be moved to ecstasy by the permanent possession of such a complete story-background by a master. I have taken down the names of the Besant–Blavatsky–Leadbeater books, & hope I'll have time to look them up some day. I rather thought that this material sounded like theosophical dope. Now the question is—where in hell does it come from? Some of it is certainly just as much of a modern synthetic concoction as my Cthulhuism & Yog-Sothothery, for a 19th century historical, scientific, & geographical consciousness hangs over the whole orderly system. On the other hand, scraps of actual Oriental folklore may well be woven into this synthetic fabric. Do you know anything about the sources of theosophical legendry, as estimated by the best & most conservative authorities? I suppose considerable is derived from the Hindoos. I shall probably use this stuff as an allusion-background sooner or later, if I ever get around to writing any stories again. By the way—if *Shamballah* is supposed to exist still in the Gobi, how is one supposed to get there? Do theosophists claim to have visited it?

Klarkash-Ton says he is about to publish in a booklet[6]—at his own expense, to sell for 25¢ a copy—six of his best tales, all rejected by King Pharnaces. I've read most of the proposed contents in MS. at various times, & can attest that the brochure will be a damned good buy.

What you relate of the 'psychic detonation'[7] incident to the completion of the Shamballah story interests me exceedingly. If that amount of sincere explosive energy went into the tale, I'll wager the result is something pretty close to authentic art—even if the subject-matter was more or less tinctured with wholesale slaughter of the Cross Plains variety.[8] Strong & genuine emotion dictates its own language & rhythms & imagery, & these generally have a strength & beauty impossible of duplication in artificial or calculative work. Sorry the process proved so nervously devastating—but no doubt the result was worth the exhaustion. I shall assuredly be on the lookout for the story—& if Wright rejects it I shall burn my W.T. file & call upon the Grand Caliph to excommunicate the wretch!

I envy you the genial sun that beats down upon the dust of the Herati gate[9] & fills the days of the city with vernal sportiveness! Up here in Hyperborea or Plaksha, where the frore blasts sweep down from the glacial crevasses of Mt. Meru, the ground is white with the residuum of a snowfall—tho' I rejoice to say the deposit is melting off with reasonable celerity. It is encouraging to write March instead of February as a date—& to think that the aequinox will be crossed in 18 days.

Glad you're succumbing to the unique & haunting charm of "Ouroboros". There is nothing else quite like it—even by the same author. It weaves its own atmosphere, & lays down its own laws of reality. At first one tends to rebel at the laying of the scene in *Mercury* without any attempt to depict conditions peculiar to that planet & alien to the earth (if we except the rather whimsical *horns* of the population), but gradually we come to accept or forget the gesture—taking the whole thing in the spirit of an enthralling fireside tale. Indeed, there is much of the quality of the fireside tale about it—its naivete, absence of Cabellian[10] snickers, & subordination of the obtrusive social satire which spoils the charm of so many kindred phantasies. Take your own time about finishing the volume. I'm so rushed I couldn't get at it for months if it were here. But I do intend to reread it sooner or later—I have forgotten just enough detail to derive a fresh sense of adventure from the process.

Likewise there's no hurry about the finishing & forwarding of Comte d'Erlette's opus. I shewed M. le Comte your remarks on the opening pages, & he was so pleased that he made a copy of them. Your reaction was of exactly the type he aims to excite in the reader, hence he felt he had received a testimonial of the novel's success.

No, I never heard of *Avichi*, the 8th & nethermost hell.[11] I must make an effort to qualify for it, lest my eschatological future be spent in the company of no more distinguished scoundrels than Eblis's commonplace train. How does one crash the gate—by performing the 49th rite of ultimate blasphemy against Tsathoggua, by opening the lid of the unhumanly carven chest in the nameless temple of Leng, or by setting one's soul to catch the black & forbidden radiations from the 7th or Gnothic galaxy? And is it part of the theosophical cycle, or a more personal product of the Peacock Throne of Bayonne? I blush for my ignorance of some of the cosmos's choicest arcana!

Another bit of ignorance. I don't think I've ever tasted East Indian curry—a delicacy so universal in Bayonne that you even feed it to the dogs around the city gate. But if it's what I think it is, I'd like it—for as you know from my response to chili con carne, I'm all for high seasonings. I suppose the Hindoos go in for that kind of thing because they have a genial climate plus a lack of that refrigeration which makes unseasoned meats dependable. I believe Worcestershire sauce (a favourite with me) is based on some sort of East Indian recipe, is it not?

I note the "The Return of Balkis" in the new W.T., & believe I'll knock off a few minutes to lap it up before concluding this epistle. As I think I've said, I haven't had time to read a W.T. through since September, although I've dipped in to give individual stories by congenial fellow-gangsters the once-over.

Later—3 p.m.

Have read "Balkis", & am glancing apprehensively behind me for signs of *It*. Nggrrh . . . . Yog-Sothoth! Good, vivid stuff, although to my mind it doesn't really strike its stride till the Thing appears at the barred window—p. 449. Prior to that the style is too hurried & skeletonic to convey the atmosphere of pseudo-reality. It is somehow mechanical & conventional—the various marvellous conditions & exciting events are more or less laconically & prosaically set down without the *subtle emotional preparation* necessary to make them convincing. The reader tends to say "here are some statements of impossible things" instead of "God! have these things happened on a sane planet?" Always excepting the potent allusions to Bayonne's nighted crypts & immemorial secrets. But, as I have implied, these limitations seem to me to recede after p. 449. You handle the Thing magnificently, & your description of Graf Istavan's chants & rites is moving & satisfying. There is also genuine tensity & pathos in the final sacrifice of the dervish Noureddin. A good story—& I'm sure you realise that my observations on the beginning do not mean that that beginning is below the standard average of W.T. fiction. Its relative flatness is merely in contrast to the Malik standard in its most ideal form. Hope this tale gets a good response from the readers. It ought to, since they literally slaver over Quinn, who uses the same medium. Now I shall be on the watch for "Queen of the Lilin" & other glimpses of the abyss. By the way—while I had W.T. in my hands I also glanced through Klarkash-Ton's "Ice Daemon",[12] which strikes me as being pretty good.

And so it goes. Now to get some stuff on this desk cleaned up & hike down town to send off a fat MS. before the express office closes. New fountain pen point no good. It's a great life!

Blessings of the Prophet—**А Б Д Ь Л А ЛКАЗРЕ҃я**,[13]

Notes

1. Nick Carter first appeared as a dime novel private detective in 1886 and then in various other formats, such as the *Nick Carter Detective Magazine* (1933f.).

2. HPL means *At the Mountains of Madness*, although in his letter of 20 October 1932 he calls "The Colour out of Space" his best story.

3. Wright paid HPL $240 for "The Dunwich Horror" (17,500 words) in 1929 (about 1.37 cents a word); the $140 for "The Dreams in the Witch House" (14,700 words) amounts to just under 1 cent a word.

4. See HPL to Farnsworth Wright (16 February 1933) in "Letters to Farnsworth Wright."

5. See HPL to CAS (early March 1933); *DS* 409.

6. *The Double Shadow and Other Fantasies.*

7. EHP was referring to his story "Gray Sphinx."

8. Alluding to the adventure fiction of Robert E. Howard.

9. The gateway to the Afghanistan city of Kandahar. EHP mentions it in his fiction.

10. HPL alludes to the aristocratic, whimsical, profane fantasies of James Branch Cabell (1879–1958), well regarded by the likes of such contemporaries as H. L. Mencken, Sinclair Lewis, and Edmund Wilson but disdained by HPL.

11. In Buddhism, Avīci or Avichi is the lowest level of the Naraka or "hell" realm, into which the dead who have committed grave misdeeds may be reborn.

12. "The Ice Demon" (*WT,* April 1933).

13. A rendering of "Abdul Alhazred" in Cyrillic characters.

[12] [ANS, privately held][1]

[Postmarked Providence, R.I., 11 March 1933]

I think you can safely shoot all the works to Dwyer, who is a man of sense & eager above all things to discover & master his defects. What he wants, however, is to produce really artistic work—the element of salability being secondary, though naturally he wouldn't mind a cheque now & then from the Emperor Wright. I think an expert & impersonal analysis of "Flash"[2] would increase rather than decrease his admiring opinion of you—subconscious as well as conscious. ¶ I imagined that the sketchy nature of Balkis's opening was intentional—or Wright-induced—indeed, I believe you said something about the matter a few months ago. Yes—I'd be interested to hear the reasons to which you refer. ¶ Am simply swamped with work this past week. A special research job took me to Hartford last week.[3] Not a very interesting town, although I revelled in the ancient houses of its still-quaint suburbs Farmington & Wethersfield.[4] ¶ Best wishes—& don't be afraid to tell Dwyer what's what.

Peace of Allah upon thee!

Notes

1. *Front:* View from State Capitol, Hartford, Conn.

2. A circulation list for the story exists at JHL (but not the story). EHP is not among the reviewers listed.

3. The project was to edit a history of Dartmouth College by Leon Burr Richardson.

4. It was on this occasion that HPL met his ex-wife, Sonia H. Greene, for the last time.

[13]   [ALS, JHL]

Cold, Sleety, & with a
slush of new-fallen but
melting snow on the ground—
but the First Day of Spring!
[Postmarked 24 March 1933]

Dear Malik:—

Your welcome epistle found me in the same turmoil of piled-up work which I mentioned on my card—& which is only now beginning to subside through the completion of the second of the jobs involved. Meanwhile, however, the card has given you assurance of Dwyer's complete & amiable receptiveness so far as candid criticism is concerned. As I said—he is out to *learn*, & doesn't care how he accomplishes it so long as he does accomplish it. I've criticised him enough myself to realise how well he takes corrections & admonitions of every kind. You will, I can assure you, find him highly grateful for any precepts you transmit—& not a whit less a Malik-fan thereby.

Just before the recent avalanche of work I tackled the Silver Key sequel, & produced 7½ pages of collaborated text—setting the scene at a meeting of Carter's executors in New Orleans & carrying the Stranger's narrative as far as Carter's entrance to the inner cave & figurative application of the Key to the vague suggestion of a door at the farther end. In these pages I have, I think, ironed out all the discrepancies betwixt the sequel & the original story, & paved the way for the adequately motivated development of the rest. You may complain that I've been rather ruthless in making changes—but the great necessity was to reconcile the thing with what *cannot* be altered because of being in print. And anyway, you have a subsequent chance to remove anything which you don't like. The later parts—involving mathematical concepts &c—will adhere more closely to your plan—although with your permission I may give Carter's ultra-dimensional experiences a more abstract & nebulous cast than in your MS. We shall see. I plan to continue as soon as I can get enough time to give the matter the unhurried attention it deserves.

Yes—I can certainly use that $140 when it gets my way! Satrap Pharnabazus says the "Witch House" will be in the issue out July 1st—dated July, since a slowing-up process (May out Apr. 15, June out June 1) is to bring actual & nominal dates into coalescence at last. He also plans to reprint "The Festival" sometime during the coming months. As for trying more stuff on W.T.—the trouble with catering to the cheap public is that it actually injures my ability to write decent stuff. Some can get away with it—accomodating their style to the herd for the nonce & then returning to serious effort—but I haven't that degree of cleverness & adaptability. Of course, many seriously intended tales might by chance strike King Pharnaces in the right way—& I would certainly send him any which I thought might be of this kind. Moreover—in case of a future clear demonstration of failure to produce serious work . . . . a demonstration that I absolutely lack the capacity to achieve authentic artistic expression . . . . I dare say I might in the course of time lapse back into the habit of grinding out tales suited to my own grade of appreciation—whatever that is—which (like my existing earlier attempts) might occasionally find a place in Pharaoh Phon-Suth's polite & elegant repository. I am not blind to the fact that I may be wholly unsuited to the writing of really substantial material—but I want to give myself a chance, free from the deleterious influence of cheap models, before accepting such a verdict as final. During the past year I have written nothing at all, so heavy have been the other demands on my time & energy. I appreciate very powerfully, by the way, your flattering exhortations to renewed composition. If I do start in again shortly, it will undoubtedly be due very largely to such encouragement.

Good luck with your Kurdish propaganda! I'm sure you'll successfully put the rascals over as the supreme villain-material of the century . . . . . & in later years you will feel a creator's pride as you behold the atmosphere & properties of old Kurdistan employed as standard material on every hand! That imaginative impulse you received from the casual juvenile reading of lines about *Afrasiab* in an advertisement is a good example of the vista-awaking & association-forming power of apparently trivial stimuli. It has a double interest for me, insomuch as it closely parallels a youthful mystery of my own, also involving the name of *Afrasiab*.[1] You doubtless recall the closing passage of Poe's "Premature Burial"—where, after an allusion to *Carathis* which baffled me till I had read "Vathek",[2] there occurs the tenebrous final simile:

> ". . . but, like the Demons in whose company Afrasiab made his voyage down the Oxus, they must sleep, or they will devour us—they must be suffered to slumber, or we perish."

Now that image of Afrasiab sailing down the mysterious Oxus (a cryptic stream whose imaginative associations always fascinated me) on an accursed vessel full of sleeping daemons—ineffable nighted things—held for me a macabre terror of peculiar intensity; a terror all the acuter because I could not trace the allusion to any source. I wove all sorts of hideously fanciful images about that voyage, & made obscure references to it in many of my juvenile tales. At first, the name of *Carathis* was woven into the mystery, but that faded when I found it in "Vathek". Afrasiab & his daemons remained the tough nut, & for a while I thought they must be derived from some version of the Arabian Nights more ample than any I had seen. Only after years did I find out somehow that Afrasiab came from Firdousi's great Persian epic[3]—some article or commentary on which no doubt fell into Poe's resourceful hands. (He was a great boy for second-hand erudition, ransacking the scholarly notes to "Vathek", "Lalla Rookh",[4] &c.) But I have not yet succeeded in finding any translation of the Shah-Namah,[5] hence am still ignorant of Afrasiab's frightful adventure with the daemons. I must look up more material from Sir Wm. Jones[6] some day.

Klarkash-Ton appreciated your theosophical data immensely—much being new to him despite his familiarity with the Sinnett book & others you recommended. He shares with you the opinion that much of this legendry is actually traditional in the east, & gives an interesting alternative version of *Shamballah*—here appearing as "an invisible, supra-material place, occupied by the demiurges of our planet, who, themselves, are the perfected humanity of the last evolutionary series of rounds." He never, however, heard of the "Book of Dzyan" before.[7] The lore he has read says much of *invisible planets*[8] whose substance is not exactly material in our sense. Obviously there is a great field here for anyone with the persistence to wade through the requisite books. I wonder, by the way, how all this dovetails with the "Mu" lore of Col. Churchward, who claims that Himalayan priests still harbour records of the infinite past—written in *Naacal*, the primal language of mankind? And so *Avichi* belongs to the same cycle! It certainly sounds alluring, & I'd welcome further explanatory notes—although of course I can't tell how or when I'd use it literarily. Oh, yes—if I try to make Avichi I'll leave you a full set of notes. Many of the blasphemies taught by the priests of Yog-Sothoth & Tsathoggua would undoubtedly be useful.

Your explanation of the inward nature of *curry* is surely a tantalisation of the palate![9] I must sample this gift of the Djinns, in all its perfection, either at the Peacock Throne or in the Citadel of Holy Shamballah, before I make the final incantation precipitating me into Avichi. In the interim, if I can find any 15¢ cans (what's the make?) I shall make this one of my regular dietary items in place of Campbell's soups & Heinz's beans & spaghetti. We shall see . . . . but I won't make the mistake of confounding any base commercial imitation with the real thing, as prepared according to the precepts in the Book of Dzyan.

And now—Eblis take it—I must turn to the indignities of hateful labour. Looks like a beastly fortnight ahead—I think a dull novel is headed my way for revision, & I'm too broke to turn down the job.

Yrs in the praise of Allah the Compassionate—

♀ ☽ ♯ ♬ ♪ ≈ 8 ♂ △ ⅓

Later—March 22

Didn't get this in the mail, & now yrs. of the 19th from old Mobile is at hand. Hope the buoyancy of the flight was nowhere deflated. After New Orleans the antiquities of Mobile may seem a bit tame, yet the place has a haunting charm for all that.[10] The dense live-oak shade of Bienville Sq. is quite a contrast to sun-baked Jackson Sq.—& you possibly noticed the fine wrought-iron work on certain of the houses, especially along Government St. between Franklin & Royal. The old Barton Academy on Government between Lawrence & Cedar is a good specimen of the American classic period, & the strange old Church St. cemetery farther out along Government (turn to left down Scott for entrance) has some ancient & picturesque graves including that of Don Miguel Eslava, Treasurer under the Spanish regime. But the atmosphere of the whole place is more important than any details. The waterfront—especially around the foot of Government St—is highly picturesque, while the sleepy residence streets with their overshadowing live-oaks & occasional galleried houses have an inexhaustible charm. N.O. influence is perceptible in the architecture, though there are no patios. The fires of 1827 & 1839 destroyed most of the oldest houses. The oldest surviving structure is the modern-looking business block at the S.W. corner of Royal & St. Michael Sts—built as an inn in 1804, & marking the scene of Lafayette's entertainment in 1825. I suppose you are familiar with Mobile history—French fort nearby founded 1702, moved to present site 1711, region transferred to England 1763, conquered by Spaniards (taking advantage of Am. Rev) 1779, ceded to U.S. by Spain after dispute 1798. It is, as you say, historically older than New Orleans. I found it a very pleasant place in my brief stay.

I know Dwyer will find your criticism immensely helpful, & that he will feel himself profoundly your debtor. I'll ask him to let me see those 7 closely typed pages—for I'm sure they form a powerful & absorbing bit of analysis. Congratulations on your double—& forthcoming triple—representation in the magazines![11] That's getting pretty close to big business!

As for my criticism of the Balkis opening—I said at the outset that I realised the intentional nature of the skeletonic style, & that my remarks could not be taken as a business-man's criticism of a purely business job. I am not qualified to pass upon popular commercial technique—so that I suppose I really had no right to venture an opinion . . . . . that opinion being irrelevant to the commercial problem at issue. My random jottings were merely a layman's reaction to the story *as a story*. There was *not a touch of the academic* in what I said. I merely intimated that the beginning of the tale seemed more like a 'synopsis of preceding chapters' (from the story point of view—apart from business) than like those chapters themselves, & that I didn't begin to feel a sense of interest & reality till the Nameless Thing made its appearance. There's nothing "academic" in this. I simply couldn't get interested in a bald succession of flat statements whose astonishing content was belied by the casual, cheerful atmosphere. I read on because I knew that an E H P story *must* contain something good farther along . . . . but had it been a stranger's tale my interest might not have taken me to the place where the *real story* gets under way. I think, moreover, that almost any lover of Blackwood, Poe, Machen, & Dunsany would tend to drop a story if after 2 or 3 paragraphs it threatened to be just another trivial, substanceless congeries of colourless & laconic statements in the manner of Kline, Quinn-at-his-worst, & the pulpists generally. I know that I leave about ¾ of W.T. unread for precisely that reason. Nothing academic— but who the hell (aside from the Neanderthaloid what-is-its that form 0.8 of the Eyrie slobberers) could get a feeling of *interest* out of a statistical table of *assertions* with no tone-colour, emotional preparation, or menacing atmosphere to remove these assertions from the mere index or chapter-heading class? What is there to give any sense of life—any sense that something besides a cool catalogue of impossible, irrelevant, gratuitous, & doubtfully interesting assertions is being presented—when a tale opens, in effect, like this?[12]

> "Sacrebleu!" cried de Grandin, "the ghost, it is here! Name of a little blue pig, Friend Trowbridge!"
> It was night in the old house.
> In the corner was a bit of mist shaped like a decomposed corpse with dripping eye-sockets. De Grandin fired at it, but it did not cease its advance.
> They grappled.
> [5 column-inches of tussle—Formula B1796341-m]
> "Friend Trowbridge," cried the victorious Frenchman, "this is almost uncanny. It is the spirit of a very evil being who lived on the continent of Shalmali 900,000 years ago. Not for many years have I seen such a thing. We must oppose it. But first, let us have some coffee prepared by your so-excellent Nora, after which we will enlist the aid of brave Sergeant Costello."

And so on—ad infinitum . . . ad somnum. However, remember that this has nothing to do with the commercial process of popular-formula manufacture. Flat or not, if this is what the editors believe the herd want, it is obviously the correct thing for quantity production—& all criticism from the standpoint of really interesting & effective narration (according to adult standards) is patently irrelevant & uncalled for. The only thing is that it's a pity to see good story material made ineffective in this way for the readers who would appreciate it most in its proper form. Someone ought to go over the cheap magazines & pick out story-germs which have been ruined by popular treatment; then getting the author's permission & *actually writing the stories.*

The trouble is that editors have a very myopic vision & absolutely no regard for excellence as such. They note certain preferences on the part of that mob, & proceed to cater to those without even enquiring whether a better grade of writing could be put over without alienating the mob. It is my belief that if they would ascend two or three notches in the scale of excellence, they would lose far fewer of their beloved truck-drivers & elevator boys than the number of literate readers (now totally repelled by the prevailing insufferable crap) they would gain. Thus a less grovelling policy would actually benefit them materially. Actually, cheap readers don't resent a half-literate story nearly as much as literate readers resent a typical formula product. However—this applies only to special groups like weird & scientifiction where no higher-grade magazines exist. Cheap *general* magazines have nothing to gain by improvement, since the literate general reader has magazines of his own, & would not have any occasion to purchase the pulp product.

As to whether the atmosphere of an "action" story could be made less inadequate without great expansion—I think it could, by a suitably trained & gifted craftsman. What is needed so cryingly is *emotional preparation* for the incredible events delineated, & this might conceivably be achieved in brief compass through a very discriminating use of words & rhythms & details in setting the scene & establishing the relationship of the characters to it. It would not take paragraphs of description to remove the common & *absolutely fatal effect of cheerful casualness in describing tensely tragic or horrible things.* But of course, this kind of brief adequacy could not be achieved in slapdash haste. It would take time & thought & real conscientiousness—a genuine natural zeal for intrinsic quality apart from all other considerations. And all that might be held to form a poor business policy. Moreover—in certain cases greater length might indeed be necessary. One never can tell. Each separate story dictates its own circumstances. It may be added, that *weird* or in general *strange* fiction undoubtedly suffers more than any other kind though devitalisation to the "action" state. This is because the presentation of incredible material depends absolutely on the fancy-cajoling or semi-hypnotising process which nothing but plentiful & convincing atmosphere can set in motion. A *non-strange* "action" story is not nearly such a self-defeating paradox as a story which tries to be strange & 'actionated' at the same time.

But don't take any of my remarks seriously. Really, two separate fields are involved. I am constitutionally unfitted to regard the creation of imaginative material as a business. All that I know how to do is to strive after excellence (little though I may be able to attain) for its own sake. Editors & public are not in the picture. When it comes to commercial efforts, revision presents an altogether different proposition . . . & I handle as little commercially intended fiction as possible. Yet I'm not by any means condemning the business of popular fiction. It is merely a field into which I am emotionally unable to enter, & whose psychology I can never fully grasp. I ought not to express opinions on it. ¶ Well—I'll dry up at last!

Yrs in the Peace of Avichi— (𓀀𓃭𓈖𓏏𓆣)

[P.S. on envelope:] Just had a present of Disraeli's "Alroy", which I've never read. Looks rich in Oriental colour—would you like to borrow it? Cabalistic stuff, & all that.[13]

Notes

1. Cf. "The Nameless City": "I repeated queer extracts, and muttered of Afrasiab and the daemons that floated with him down the Oxus" (*CF* 1.237). HPL was 30 when he wrote the story in 1921.
2. The celebrated Gothic novel (1786) by William Beckford.

3. Abu 'l-Qasim Firdowsi Tusi (940?–1020) was a Persian poet and the author of *Shahnameh* ("Book of Kings"), the national epic of Greater Iran and the world's longest epic poem created by a single poet.

4. *Lalla Rookh* (1817) is a long poem by Thomas Moore, set in Persia. Moore himself wrote an introduction and extensive notes to the poem. HPL cribbed *Zinge* from it for his commonplace book (entry 2).

5. See RFS 20n13.

6. Sir William Jones (1746–1794), Anglo-Welsh philologist, scholar of ancient India, known particularly for his proposition of the existence of a relationship among European and Indian languages, known later as Indo-European languages.

7. EHP got his information about the *Book of Dzyan*, a reputedly ancient text of Tibetan origin, from Madame Blavatsky's *The Secret Doctrine*.

8. In Vedic astrology, invisible planets are also called shadowy or shadowed. Their importance relates to the way they can radiate their authority as effectively as the other celestial bodies that can be seen. In ancient Hindu astrology Rahu and Ketu are named invisible planets who mythically "swallow" the Sun and Moon initiating solar or lunar eclipses. At the time of this letter, HPL made the following notation in his *Commonplace Book* (entry 201): "Planets form'd of invisible matter."

9. See Appendix.

10. HPL visited Mobile, AL, on 19 June 1932, after his visit to New Orleans.

11. By "double" HPL refers to EHP's publishing "Assassin's Gallery" in *All Detective Magazine* (April 1933; as by "Hamlin Daly") and "Silver Peacock" in the May 1933 issue (as by E Hoffmann Price). "Forthcoming triple" refers to "The Word of Bentley" (*WT*, May 1933), "The Forgotten of Allah" (*Magic Carpet Magazine*, July 1933), and "Silver Peacock," which were on the stands almost simultaneously.

12. HPL is parodying the stories of Seabury Quinn featuring the psychic detective Jules de Grandin.

13. Disraeli's *The Wondrous Tale of Alroy* (1833) is a novel or romance set in the Middle East in the 12th century. Its only weird element is the possibly supernatural powers of a ring possessed by Alroy, a Jewish prince.

[14] [ALS, JHL]

April 6, 1933

Dear Malik:—

Ecce! At last! Gawd, what a job! I suppose you'll be disappointed, but this is really the best I can do. Of course, this is only a first draught in the largest sense. If I've raised hell with your idea, just slash & alter it to fit, & let me see the result. Or send it to Klarkash-Ton & make a triangular affair of it. Anyhow, I done me dooty!

Although I never feel bound to follow my own first ideas, I have actually done just about what I said I thought needed doing last September. First, the facts, character of Carter, & general tone had to be reconciled with "The Silver Key". Re-read the latter (which I reënclose) & see why certain changes had to be made. Second, the supernatural or scientifictional machinery had to be straightened out in order to explain the marvellous Ancient Ones &c. These things can't exist materially in the Massachusetts hills. My idea is to have the First Gate (accessible with Silver Key alone) open on an extension of the *earth only* in all dimensions, while the Ultimate Gate (accessible only through the Ancient Ones plus the Silver Key) bring one to a sort of space-focus where *everything in infinity* converges to oneness. This may not mean anything, seriously & mathematically considered, but it ought to pass muster in weird fiction. Anyway, it's the only reasonable means of getting around the problem inherent in the story as first sketched. This illustrates my belief that collaboration is *exactly twice as hard as original writing*. Creation is easy. It accomplishes itself. But to make all your events square with a previously existing plot—that is what I call *work!*

Point Three concerns the problem of getting rid of the *schoolroom effect* inherent in the detailed development of the conic section theory of the cosmos. Clearly, a short story cannot devote practically a quarter of its length to academic dialectics—& this sort of thing ruins the fantastic atmosphere anyway. My solution—aside from expanding the whole tale so that this phase will occupy a smaller place (it really *can't* be a major climax . . . . it simply isn't of the stuff of fictional climaxes)—is to *condense & de-technicalise* the geometrical part, yet with as little sacrifice of essential content as possible. I leave it to you how well or how badly I've done it. If I've violated any important laws of mathematics, I'll leave it to you to set things right. But actually, I don't think the mathematical side is of paramount importance—since it involves paradox anyway. For example—the idea of the members of a family line being all facets of the same ultimate entity is a bit tenuous when one considers the facts of descent. Suppose a cousin & I have a grandfather in common. Of whom—the cousin or myself or both—is that grandfather another facet? Is the cousin another facet of myself? Remotely, almost all the members of a race have some unknown ancestor in common. Is, then, a whole race—or perhaps all mankind—a multivariated projection of a single archetype? In the story I have merely dodged this issue—but I bring it up to shew that we cannot really expect 100% plausibility or serious science in this kind of phantasy. In my original S. K. I didn't bother about science at all—it was simply a study in mood. But do what you like about this phase.

The fourth point concerns the ending. I cannot get away from the idea of a certain anticlimax in having a mere *limited & terrestrial* mutation come out of this *prodigiously cosmic* story. Decidedly, Carter's journey ought to be somewhere *inconceivably remote* in time & space. Also—since he is sent on it by an omnipotent BEING, there ought to be no flaw (as the parchment-forgetting would imply) in the transmission. Let the loss of the parchment cover something else—preferably conditions of return. I have tried to solve this detail with care. Incidentally—your original climax about an incomplete time-transition would be excellent to use in another story with suitable preparatory framework.

Point five, as brought up last September, concerns *story value*. Clearly, the *fictionally big moment* of the tale is the *revelation in the room at New Orleans*, yet this is not sufficiently prepared for. Not enough is made of the setting, & the revelation is not, as it dramatically ought to be, the flowering of a gradual & well-proportioned growth. There ought to be a sort of anchoring of the reader's mind & interest in the New Orleans room, so that the climax—when it comes—will *mean more*. It can mean more only if the scene & characters are vivid in the mind of the reader. Accordingly I have laid the New Orleans foundation with much care, & have tried not to let the long Randolph Carter narrative wholly run away with it. I have let the bizarre room & its increasing tension be mentioned from time to time, & have thrown out threads (like the cosmic, coffin-shaped clock from Shamballah) which later figure in the climax. Then I have provided for a definite *scene* with climax-building events immediately preceding the final crash, so that the latter will appear to be the logical outcome of the whole tale, & a constituent part of an homogeneous fabric. Formerly, this crash had a suspicion of the extraneous in it, because it did not contribute to what was originally the major effect. The original story was primarily a tale of cosmic space. The collaboration is primarily a tale of a strange happening in New Orleans. Also contributing toward the climax is a heightened account of the Carter adventures just preceding the return to earth, & on earth up to the time of the estate conference itself. Furthermore—I have thought it advantageous to strengthen the climax itself by adding incidents, bringing in the actual Silver Key, and changing the atmosphere of whimsicality to one of horror.

Now as for the style. "The Silver Key" was a symbolic, dreamy, quasi-poetic study of a mood—representing the final phase of my Dunsany-influenced period. It was not only non-intellectual but *anti-intellectual*, hence stood poles away from your dominantly intellectual cosmic study. How can the two be reconciled? Only compromise can turn the trick. It would be impossible to embody your subject-matter in a tale with the exact mood & style of "The Silver Key", hence I did not try to imitate that. I say "imitate" because I myself have grown away from that light, half-playful Dunsany style in the years since '26. I could not write the S.K. today. But on the other hand, the style required moving *toward* the S.K. tone in order to avoid a rupture of homogeneity. The romantic-adventure atmosphere, & the touches of pure didactic atmosphere, had to be supplanted by an atmosphere of vague soberness & directness, with a basically rhythmical prose as devoid as possible of stock romantic & scientific language, & with the tension of a dream hovering over everything. This, however, allowed the retention of many long passages in virtually your own language—for all of your flights of cosmic fancy were really superb. As a definite example of what I think the necessary *blurring of sharp outlines*, compare the two versions of the scene with the Ancient Ones on their pedestals.

Regarding length—the scope of the theme demanded what amounts to quasi-novelette form. As I said, the whole thing had to be expanded so that the schoolroom part might shrink to more modest proportions. The keynote must—so far as the Carter story is concerned—be one of breathless plunging from gulf to gulf—adventure & emotional turmoil—rather than one of static ideas. I have tried to let the moods of the cosmic plunging develop adequately, & to avoid the hurried, afterthought-like suggestion of extraneousness in the original Alamut episode. If shortening is necessary, I'd suggest that it be applied to the more abstract in-the-gulf parts. The thing *could* be shortened. In case of a radical shortening you could omit the Ancient Ones, & let Carter come directly to grips with the lost-identity sensation & with **IT**. Only one gate is really necessary. In preparing the opening, I have tried to make it acceptable to those who remember the S.K., & yet to let the tale be complete for those who have not seen or don't recall its predecessor.

Well—here it is, & do as you like with it. I fear it is not much of a commercial proposition—& you can let it lie dormant, without bothering to continue revision or to type it, if you choose. I hope I haven't let you down too badly. As I warned you, I'm a rotten hand at collaboration—but at least I've done my poor best. It occurs to me that this sequel leaves room for at least one more sequel . . . . . though Heaven forbid the dragging of poor Carter through a Tarzan-like series of forced adventures! I shall, of course, be intensely interested in what you do with the MS., & if I can give more help, pray let me know.

Your cards of 24th & 29th ult. duly received. Congratulations on the repeated successes, & especially on your advent to the Munsey group. Let me know when the picture & autobiography appear—I want both for my files.[1] I never made this group. In 1924 Robert H. Davis[2] *almost* took my "Rats in the Walls" for *Argosy*, but decided it was too morbid & horrible for his milk-fed circle of cheerful innocents. Like the Emir Lhen-Eighur, he loves the sunshine!

Actual spring seems to be getting around at last—that is, one or two days have been fit for outdoor walking though not for sitting. However, I've been too damned busy to take advantage of them. I'll be glad when it's warm enough to take my work outdoors. During the summer I may—in fact almost certainly will—have to move to cheaper quarters. Going to see if I can cut all my expenses, including rent, down to **10** bucks per week. Quite a feat, if you ask me! ¶ Blessings of the Prophet—& pardon the mediocrity of the enclosed. Yr obt Servt

Notes

1. "In the Dark Room" and an autobiographical sketch.
2. Robert H[obart] Davis (1869–1942), American journalist, editor, dramatist, and photographer. Editor of Munsey's magazines from 1904 to 1925, columnist for the *New York Sun* from 1925 to 1942.

[15]   [ALS, JHL]
66 College St.,
Providence, R.I.,
May 30, 1933
Dear Malik:—
In the name of Eblis, hail! Your presence in the Eastern Caliphate shall be kept as quiet as it can be in view of my mention—prior to your warning—of your incipient move to several correspondents. These correspondents—Derleth, Dwyer, Cook, & one or two others—are not in especially close touch with those in the metropolitan zone, & I don't imagine the news will spread to any extent embarrassing to yourself. Pray accept my sympathy anent the Ford. The incident confirms my thankfulness that I have never experimented with this new-fangled invention of Shaitan,[1] but have let the motor-coach companies serve as my magic carpet. Here's wishing you a happy financial recovery . . . . . on with the novelette! And may the convalescence be brief!

And now curiosity assails me. Where is Wantagh, N.Y.?[2] I have searched maps & lists in vain, hence cannot place you any more definitely than somewhere betwixt Fisher's Island (beyond Long Island, & just a stone's throw from Rhode Island's southwestern tip) & the Great Lakes! I gather, however, that Manhattan will be your point of departure for realms farther east. Whilst there—if you must rigorously limit your visits—I'd advise you to choose Frank B. Long Jr. (230 W. 97th St.) as the most typical Lord of the Abyss to call upon.

Meanwhile ancient Providence, brooding over its centuried & nighted secrets, continues to beckon. As for transportation—at the moment I don't know of any rail excursions, but let me point out that my own life-saving standby of latter years . . . . the Allah-created motor coach . . . . can probably underquote any ordinary excursion rate of the obsolescent iron horse. There is great competition on the N.Y.–Prov.–Boston run—New England, Greyhound, & other lines covering the same stretch—hence the rate-war is perpetual & often miraculously beneficial to the impecunious traveller. The fare betwixt N.Y. & Providence fluctuates; but has never been over *$3.00* in recent years, & is often down to $2.00. The New England Transportation Co. (subsidiary of the N Y N H & H—get your ticket at the Penn. Terminal next the Pennsylvania Station) is likely to be cheaper than the Greyhound. I would advise this mode of travel by all means. The route (whether the Shore Line through New London or the inland route) is much more attractive scenically than the rail route, & the running time does not exceed that of the trains by more than two hours. Let me know the coach line you are taking, & the hour of your scheduled arrival, & I will be on hand with the archers & kettle-drums to give you a suitable reception at the city gates. While you are here I can save you tavern bills by extending the shelter of my new & more capacious quarters. I have just picked up a camp cot in order to enable me to lodge an occasional guest. While I'm no good at Arabian or French Drip Coffee, there's an excellent Waldorf Lunch at the foot of the hill, which may be considered as an annex of my encampment . . . . . . & a worthy analogue of our friend Gluck's in New Orleans. And we have a Thompson's not inferior to that in St. Charles St.! I think you'll find many points of interest in Old Providence. Our steep hill (on which I now dwell) is a kind of Vieux Carré— & my present abode is an architectural treat in itself. My throne-room is at the opposite end of the house from my aunt's sleeping quarters, so that we can hold 25½ hour sessions without disturbing anybody.

The moving was accomplished at last—though I can assure you that the rearranging of 2000 books was no afternoon's sport! I had to get 4 new book-cases (small ones, to superimpose on others) in order to adapt my collection to this new setting, since at #10 I depended considerably on built-in alcove shelves. I also got a cabinet to file pamphlets in. Now that I am settled, the place looks delectably homelike—as if I had dwelt here for years. I leave to your imagination the fascination I feel in inhabiting, for the first time in my life, the sort of ancient house I have always longed for. It is really ironic that *economy & retrenchment* should have produced such a result! To enter through a carved colonial doorway & sit beside a Georgian mantel gazing out of small-paned windows over a sea of centuried roofs & foliage is an experience almost dreamlike—it is so like a museum that I half-expect some guard to turn up & boot me out at 5 o'clock closing time! The present moment is merely a breath-ing-spell between my own moving & the job (beginning Thursday) of helping my aunt move in. At present, the apartment presents the anomalous aspect of having 2 rooms completely settled & the rest absolutely bare. The fact that I now have 2 rooms all my own—with kitchen facilities elsewhere & an attic to overflow into—enables me to enjoy a much more tasteful layout than at #10, where I had only one room & alcove. I don't have to crowd things so—& of course the graceful Georgian proportions & woodwork help. My furniture is plain enough—& includes old pieces enough—to blend well with the room, & several especially traditional objects like a full-mounted globe (with old-fashioned wooden horizon) & an old bust of Milton (in the family for nearly a century) carry out the archaic atmosphere in an admirable way. The ancient mantel is very appropriately decked with an old wooden clock, brass candle-sticks, & venerable vases—& above it I have hung a marine view painted by my mother & now re-framed in suitably Georgian fashion.

I've forgotten just how much I have told you about the house. It is yellow & wooden, & stands on the crest of the ancient hill in a quaint grassy court just off the precipitous slope of College St.—behind & next to the John Hay Library of Brown University, about half a mile south of 10 Barnes. The fine colonial doorway is like my bookplate come to life, though of a slightly later period (circa 1800), with side lights & fan carving instead of a fanlight. In the rear & on the western side is a picturesque, village-like garden at a higher level than the front of the house. The upper flat taken by my aunt & myself contains five rooms besides bath & kitchenette nook on the main (2nd) floor, plus 2 attic storerooms—one of which is so attractive that I wish I could have it for an extra den! My quarters—a large study & a small adjoining bedroom—are on the south side, with my working desk under a west window affording a splendid view of the lower town's outspread roofs & of the mystical sunsets that flame behind them. The interior is as fascinating as the exterior—with colonial mantels, fireplaces, & chimney cupboards, curving Georgian staircase, wide floor-boards, old-fashioned latches, small-paned windows, six-panel doors, rear wing with floor at a different level, (3 steps down) quaint attic stairs, &c. Steam heat & hot water are piped in from the adjacent college library, the house being owned by the university.

I hope your eastward & northward trip was not, despite the Ford, wholly devoid of pleasant impressions. I envy you the sight of St. Augustine & Savannah. Did you see Charleston? Probably not—for if you had, I don't believe you could ever have dragged yourself away so soon! No doubt the hangar of the Interstellar Patrol[3] afforded some interesting conversations. I trust your present environment is congenial & conducive to literary labours.

Glad you received the notes on the Silver Key MS., & that you find my suggestions acceptable. As for the charcoal question—it's only a minor detail, & I don't care how it's managed as long as it allows the tripods to emit dense, engulfing fumes, & to continue emitting them for a considerable time after the frightened departure of the old nigger. Here's hoping King Pharnaces may view our joint labours with a kindly eye—though there's no use in harbouring undue expectations.

Klarkash-Ton's brochure of fantastic tales is almost ready now. He has prepared a descriptive circular which ought to aid in the sale—I think I'll offer to distribute 50 copies or so among my various correspondents. The price, as you are aware, is only 25¢—phenomenally reasonable for a volume of six stories. Which reminds me that W. Paul Cook has at last found the unbound edition of my "Shunned House", & is about to give it to Walter J. Coates (editor of *Driftwind*) for binding & distribution.[4] Coates may insert a small advertisement of it in W.T.

After a late spring, there has been a bit of decent weather hereabouts, with temperatures up to 84° & 86°. However—I've been too badly engulfed in the moving business to make many open-air trips. Just now it is cold & rainy again. I doubt if I can spare the cash for any long trip this year, though early in July I may attend the convention of the Natl. Amateur Press Assn. in New York City. On that occasion I shall try to get as far south of the metropolis as possible on a side-trip—to Philadelphia, Washington, or possibly Richmond if my luck is good. Late in the summer there may be another of those cheap Quebec excursions. If so, I shall endeavour to take it.[5] I hope you will not be deprived altogether of the pleasures of travel this summer. When you are here, we must see something of the surrounding countryside & neighbouring villages—& must also inspect quaint & ancient Newport, 30 miles south of here down Narragansett Bay. We must also, if possible, get to the Boston zone & take in Salem & Marblehead (Arkham & Kingsport). The fare from here to Boston is $1.00 each way on the 'bus, & when we get there another dollar bill apiece will see us all around—owing to the "ride-all-day-for-a-dollar" passes sold on the street railway system covering the north-of-Boston region. We might even be able to work in Newburyport on the same dollar—if we start early enough. Good lodgings in Boston can be had for $1.25 per night at a very neat place (resembling the Y M C A) near Copley Sq. called "Technology Chambers". The Y itself is a bit too far out Huntington Ave. to be convenient. Boston itself is worth a casual glance—Beacon Hill is its Vieux Carré—but I have an idea that you are already acquainted with the city proper. All this, however, is merely suggestion. Possibly the extra trip wouldn't fit at all in your schedules. But try old Providence anyhow—& give it as liberal a time-allowance as you can. I hope you can work the old Ford off for a generous price on some other victim—using the ill-gotten proceeds for judicious coach-travel!

All my weird books are assembled in one group now—except such as belong to sets of standard authors. By actual measurement this class covers a little over 17 feet of shelf space—a rather surprising increase over the conditions of a decade ago, when I had very few weird items besides Poe, Dunsany, the Arabian nights, & a few bizarre novels. Of my real favourites, I am weakest in the Blackwood class—having only "John Silence" & "Jimbo" besides "The Willows" in an anthology. I want to pick up "Incredible Adventures", "The Centaur", "The Lost Valley", & possibly "Julius LeVallon."[6] Machen & M. R. James are pretty well represented now. I guess I told you that Cook gave me a copy of Maturin's old Gothic novel "Melmoth" last Christmas. Not such a bad library—but I wouldn't want the job of rearranging it every week!

Best wishes, & hope to see you.

Blessings of the djinns upon thee!

P.S. Sorry to say my new quarters haven't a single Oriental rug!

Notes

1. The figure of Satan or a devil in Islamic theology and mythology.
2. Wantagh is a hamlet in the town of Hempstead, Long Island. HPL had visited Hempstead in July 1925.
3. HPL refers to a series of seven stories by Edmond Hamilton, published in *WT* between 1928 and 1930. Apparently EHP visited Hamilton at his home.
4. W. Paul Cook printed sheets of *The Shunned House* in 1928—about 250 copies—but never bound or distributed them. Coates's plan also came to naught, as did R. H. Barlow's (see EHP 32). The sheets ultimately arrived at Arkham House, which bound and sold the book in 1961.
5. HPL first visited Quebec in September 1930.
6. HPL acquired *Julius LeVallon* in September and *The Lost Valley and Other Stories* in 1936. He had "The Willows" in Lynch's *The Best Ghost Stories*. HPL may or may not have had a copy of *Incredible Adventures* (see note on *LL* 107).

[16] [ALS][1]

[Postmarked Providence, R.I.,

9 June 1933]

Keep me posted on your programme. Around July 1st & afterward I may be in N. Y. City attending a convention,[2] but I guess we can make the chronology & geography come out all right with a little care. Congratulations on your current work! By the way—why bothering about copying the Silver Key? The *carbon* is all corrected, & it would be easy to switch it to Wright from its present rounds. He knows me well enough not to insist on ceremony. No—I haven't heard anything about payments delayed by the bank holiday . . . . tho' nearly everyone complains of delay of some sort. Just had a circular from the Am. Fiction Guild (to which I do *not* belong) with considerable data about the recent Clayton difficulties. ¶ Glad your toil is reasonably punctuated by diversion—but I haven't yet figured out where Wantagh is. Your bulletin, though, informs me that it has a *beach*. I'll start a new search along the seacoast. ¶ My aunt is now getting settled at #66, & the place is beginning to look ineffably homelike. You must have a look at it! Weather gloriously warm for the past few days, (90° yesterday) so I've been unusually active. Have taken several walks up to 15 miles in length. ¶ New W. T. isn't bad. Klarkash-Ton's "Genius Loci" is a high spot. ¶ Well—keep the bulletins!
Peace of the Prophet—

[*On front:*] My new abode is older than this edifice—& today I doubt if N. O. [?coul]d beat Providence for temperature! I note that Two-Gun Bob has chosen a story motto from your immortal works [?].[3]

Notes

1. *Front:* Napoleon Bonaparte House, New Orleans, La.
2. The N.A.P.A. convention of 3–5 July 1933. HPL did not attend it.
3. Howard's "Black Colossus" (*WT,* June 1933) contains the following line from EHP's "The Girl from Samarcand": "The Night of Power, when Fate stalked through the corridors of the world like a colossus just risen from an age-old throne of granite——".

[17]   [ALS, JHL]

Thursday
[6 July 1933]

Dear Malik:—

Hope you had a good drive to the Sleepy Hollow country.[1] Chilly & showery here—I didn't do much of anything Tuesday.

My aunt came home yesterday, & finds it much pleasanter than at the hospital.[2] The nurse has moved into the living-room, so that the house lacks the neatness it has hitherto had. But of course my own personal quarters are intact.

Now that I can't shut myself in the kitchen with the stove, I've laid in some oil & am using the heater which I haven't used in 6 years. It goes finely, so that I am now writing at my own desk in perfect comfort. In 2 hours it has burnt only about ⅓ or ¼ of a 10¢ (nearly a gallon) filling. I got this oil at a filling station at the foot of the hill, but will later have the Socony wagon call. By the way—speaking of filling stations—how is Old Jug? Give him my regards!

Have been digging up lore of the ancient Narragansett Country which we visited, & incidentally found the enclosed treatise on shore dinners, which may interest you. Keep it if it would form a really apposite item for your files—I have one more copy.

Bismillah—

Notes

1. At the time EHP was staying in Irvington, NY (where Washington Irving lived), with a friend, Dr. Paul Kyle (1857–1935), founder of a military academy.
2. On 14 June, Annie Gamwell had broken her right ankle while descending the stairs to answer the doorbell.

[18]　[ALS, JHL]

July 19, 1933

Hail, Malik!:—

Thanks enormously for the pleasing portrait—which I am at once putting into circulation amongst sundry devotees of Eblis who have long been curious regarding the aspect of True Greatness. I can't see that you've changed any since January '29—tho' in that same period I've aged like the very devil.

Congrats on the Balkis remittance! That ought to mean that I'll get at least half of my Witch-House dough before the year is out. Wright said that W.T. was in fair shape, tho' the Magic Carpet is less solid.

Brobst was over again Monday, & is coming again tomorrow or Friday night—bringing some gifted acquaintances from Allentown who are visiting in the city. He once more expressed his admiration of the Sultan of the Juggernaut[1]—whose wholesome extravertedness, he added, is refreshingly unusual among literary folk. His full name & present address are Harry Brobst, 305 Blackstone Blvd., Providence, R.I. Business & residence coincide—this address being the hospital to which Old Jug twice delivered him. I don't know his mother's address in Allentown—at which he is to be reached during the first two weeks in August, when he has a vacation. In October he goes to Boston for a year's training at the Boston City Hospital. He'll be glad, I am sure, to help boost the Malik stock with Satrap PHARNABAZUS (or Pharabozus if you choose—why not adopt an automatic evolution-product? Thus new languages are born!)

Do as you like about the Silver Key—it doesn't matter a damn whom King Pharnaces corresponds with. Hope Libation for the Dead will find a resting-place after all. My prayers are added to all the others intoned on & over Satan's Prayer-Rug—& considering what a star customer of Frank Winfield Woolworth I am (socks, ties, collars, stationery, electric fixtures, garden tools, hardware, leather goods, shoe blacking, ornaments, & what the hell not . . . . did you know that Frank is selling *postal scales* now for 20¢?), such a prayer ought not to be without avail. May the results thereof lead to a curry ceremony on one of the tomb-tops in Providence's ancient hill graveyard, & a black mass in the dankly overgrown inner courtyard of the South County Glebe!

Hope your recalcitrant plot will consent to take form before long, & that the resultant murders & riots may be such as to knock all editors cold. Speaking of slaughter—I've just had a tremendously interesting letter of *19 closely typed pages* (equivalent to a 38-page double-spaced MS) from our friend Two-Gun Bob of Cross Plains,[2] in which he explains his philosophy of life in a more understandable way than he ever did before. A most remarkable character—I envy you the conversations you will have with him when Old Jug gets around his way.

Enclosed is a letter from young Strauch—author of the tale we pulled to pieces during that memorable all-night session[3]—which shows that he is able to take criticism sensibly even when it is brutally candid. I thought you'd be interested to see his reaction to our joint verdicts—which I presented to him with very little varnish or soothing-syrup. A bright & promising kid for all his 1890-ish foibles!

"E Hoffmann Price at the wheel of Juggernaut, 1933."
August Derleth Papers, Wisconsin Historical Society

Enclosed also is some South County stuff which will probably interest you after your sight of that tradition-haunted realm. You might let me see that version of the Robinson tale again—tho' there's absolutely no hurry. Note that the identity of our urbane & accomplished host seems to be established.

Thanks abundantly for the mystical curry formula. I'll certainly have some adept prepare a brazier full before long, to offer up to the gods of Shalmali & Shamballah.

Aunt still sits up each afternoon—& the cast ought to come off in not much more than a week. Had two very congenial visitors yesterday—each about a handful. Tiger kittens—eyes just open!

Peace upon thee—

P.S. That N.Y. convention I couldn't get to put something over on me behind my back—saddled me with the chairmanship of the Critical Bureau!

Notes

1. The name HPL gave EHP's 1928 Ford Model A, in recognition of his interest in the folklore of India. EHP arrived in Providence by car on 30 June and stayed four days. A *juggernaut* is a force regarded as mercilessly destructive and unstoppable; an allegorical reference to the Hindu temple cars of Jagannath Temple in Puri, reputed to crush devotees under their wheels.
2. See *A Means to Freedom,* letter 82 (15 June 1933).
3. See HPL to Carl Ferdinand Strauch, 13 July 1933: "Glad the returned MS. & critical notes safely reached you—& that the ruthless carping of the Terrible Three did not seem too savage & sadistic after due digestion" (*Letters to J. Vernon Shea . . .* 349).

[19]   [ANS, nonextant]

[Postmarked Onset, Mass.,
25? July 1933]

[20]   [ALS, JHL]

Wooded River-Bank
July 28, 1933

Mighty Malik:—

Doubtless you have the card from Belknap & me telling of the conjunction of Pious Companions[1] at Onset. The nurse was very good about staying in the two afternoons I was gone. Enclosed is a map illustrating the modest extent of our wanderings in Pater Longus' 1932 Essex Juggernaut.[2] The Cape Cod terrain is for the most part very picturesque—the old village of Sandwich (which suggests Kingston in spots) being my favourite point. The one thing against us was the weather—chilly, with rainy spells. But a compensating factor was the marvellous kitten at the joint where we stayed. Most of the time was spent in controversial discussion, at which young Long excels. You will discover this latter fact for yourself if you can get to see him at 230 W. 97th St., as I hope you can. I am warning him not to disseminate information regarding your continued stay in the East. On Monday next I expect to welcome to these Plantations the guy whom I mentioned so frequently to you—James Ferdinand Morton, curator of the Paterson (N.J.) Museum & grandson of the author of "My Country, 'Tis of Thee."[3] You'll probably get a card from us—for he is a man of honour, to be trusted with the secret of your hiding-place. If you're in the N Y zone when he gets back from his fortnight of Novanglian travel, you certainly ought to look him up—I'll guarantee that his conversation would amply reward your pains!

Congratulations on your discoveries regarding the secret emotions & latent potentialities of Old Jug! Before you're through, you may find that you bought an enchanted chariot or (l.c.) magic carpet in disguise; so that instead of chucking it into the abyss you'll be unwilling to sell at any price! I felt certain a month ago that Jug's rugged exterior concealed a staunch & noble heart! Now let us hope that long-delayed cheques may begin to pour in, so that you & Jug can amble along in this direction once more. The amount of interesting material in R.I. which you *haven't* seen is still appallingly vast. Think of Newport, Bristol, Warren, & Maxfield's Ice Cream![4] In going to Newport we might take the boat & give Old Jug a well-earned rest. After all, steamship competition is developing; & the good old Sagamore is now down to a straight half-dollar for the round trip. In Newport you can see the town houses of those South County planters whose estates you have already beheld.

As for Watervliet Arsenal[5]—I rather fear that such a place sounds more like N Y State than Mass. At least, I don't know of any such place in the old Bay Province. The name is Dutch—& *Watervliet* has in latter years been employed to designate the town (N. of Albany) formerly known as West Troy, N.Y. But wherever this place is, I surely hope that you can manage to get around to Providence's ancient hill again.

Best wishes to Harrison P. Steele in his quandary.[6] You surely are resourceful in thinking up situations derived from the material details of the machine age! Glad you have found such a potent stimulus in Turkish Coffee! That plus curry ought to make you able to dim the memory of the lamented Edgar Wallace.[7] Best wishes for the timely completion of the novelette!

Long & I talked much about the possibilities of hack writing—he has an idea that some of the advertised plot-mixing devices (graphs, plot robots,[8] &c) would help him to 'click', & intends to send for something of the sort. That kid's eternal optimism after 9 years of striving is something to admire! But actually—these plot things might help a certain type of person . . . mine, for example. With a plot doped out in advance, a hack construction job would automatically become a piece of revision or ghost-writing.

I envy you your Florida winter. Perhaps I shall settle there some day—though the loss of stone walls & white steeples would be a hell of a wrench. I know that living is extremely cheap there—it was remarkably so even in 1931. My aunt's plaster cast will probably come off this week—then crutches for a spell. Weather has been fine & hot for the past 2 days, so that all my writing has been done in the open. I found myself swamped with mail upon my return from Onset. Have just sent a bunch of oft-rejected tales to the new *Fantasy Fan*—no pay, but free copies—which are always welcome.[9] Hoping to see you ere long—In Eblis' name,

Notes

1. Alluding, apparently, to EHP's story "Shaykh Ahmad and the Pious Companions."

2. Hudson Motor Car Company had manufactured the inexpensive Essex from 1919 as a lower-priced vehicle line; the company merged Essex into itself in 1922. See EHP 54n1.

3. "My Country, 'Tis of Thee" (also known as "America") was written by Samuel Francis Smith (1808–1895), a Baptist minister, using the tune of the British national anthem. His daughter, Caroline Edwards Smith (b. 1843), was Morton's mother.

4. HPL refers to the ice cream parlor run by Charles R. Maxfield, Sr. (1879–1949), and his wife, Julia A. Maxfield, in Warren, RI.

5. An arsenal of the U.S. Army in Watervliet, NY, on the west bank of the Hudson River. It is the oldest continuously active arsenal in the country.

6. A character in EHP's story "The Fifty Grand Murder."

7. Edgar Wallace (1875–1932), British author and one of the most prolific writers of thrillers of the 20th century.

8. HPL had purchased "Robo: The Game that writes a Million Story Plots," devised by Wycliffe A. Hill (1883–1965), but ultimately found no use for it. EHP, however, found Hill's "Plot Genie" to be effective, probably using the detective fiction formula.

9. The fanzine published "Beyond the Wall of Sleep," "From Beyond," "The Other Gods," "Polaris," and four sonnets from *Fungi from Yuggoth*, and reprinted "Supernatural Horror in Literature" as a serial (incomplete).

[21]　[ALS, JHL]

Prospect Terrace
—Aug. 5, 1933

Dear Malik:—

Yours at hand, & the epistle to the fair satellite is duly in the mail. Congratulations on your faceless corpse novel[1]—which certainly combines clever more twists than any other yarn I've heard of lately! You're entirely welcome to use my anti-marine diet complex—& if you like, work my ailurophily into a later tale .... provided you don't express sentiments unfavourable to the felidae. The way you use the seafood point is infinitely ingenious—I don't wonder at your ready sales. Incidentally, I hope this tale goes over well. No hurry about Silver Key—it'll probably meet a turndown anyhow. Hope your Grey Sphinx will land.

As for Satrap Pharabozus–Pharnabozus's spacing of your tales in the publication schedule—I certainly give it up. That's exactly what he did with me in 1925, when I was flooding him with stuff. No matter how many he'd accept, he'd always let two or three months go by without any yarn by poor old Abdul—though in the interim Little Seabury was appearing right along & establishing the fame of the incomparable Jules. And I'll wager it would be just the same if I were to start in writing again now. The answer? Search me! But I wish you luck with your prodding. If in the end you can't make Pharny see the light, it would certainly be very logical to quit him cold & concentrate on the detective stuff that really pays.

Glad you're having at least a momentary rest, but sorry the prospects for a second Jugging hither aren't as bright as they were. However, we'll hope for the best. And if you can get to see Long & Morton, I'm sure you'll feel amply repaid. Too bad the mechanical work on Old Jug required costly professional intervention!

As for the hack-writing discussion with Long—I felt the same objection which you suggest; namely, that I could never put any real zest or personality into a job of plot-graph "revision." The whole field is so damnably repugnant to me! Long, however, has a chance. He has just sold a vile screed to the Macfadden bums for $100.00—a thing so bad he won't sign his name, although they make him give full personal data for their files.[2] He now lives in fear that some future literary historian will trace the thing to him . . . . all about how poor Sadie was ruined in the Great City. Who knows but that Little Belknap will become a successful confession specialist!

Just had a letter from the Knopf Co. asking to see some of my stuff with a view to possible book publication. After my experience with Putnam's & Viking I realise how little such gestures mean—but I've sent along 7 of my best junk for form's sake. They'll come back.[3]

Your 57th story! That's what I call quantity production! Congrats on the number in circulation.

Enclosed is some Gilbert Stuart stuff which may interest you, & which you needn't return if you have any permanent use for it. Today the Hannah Robinson play[4] is being held on the lawn of the plantation we visited—wish I had the cash to attend!

Morton & I had a great 3 days. Brobst was home in Allentown on his vacation, hence couldn't mix in. We took many rural hikes—on one occasion seeing an ancient well with wooden sweep, & ending up at the quaint village of Greenville, where the atmosphere of 1820 still lingers. We also went to Warren & Bristol—those colonial ports down the west shore where I wanted to take you—& ate a few of Maxfield's 28 varieties of ice cream. On another jaunt we took in old Pawtuxet, where I watched Morton eat a shore dinner of the traditional sort. Our final trip—Wednesday—was to Newport by boat. We had a fine day, & after exploring the ancient town spent the time lounging on the sea-cliffs where in 1730 Dean Berkeley sat & composed his "Alciphron; or, the Minute Philosopher". Morton has now gone on to Vermont & N.H. to climb mountains.

Good warm weather this week . . . 97°, 92°, 90° . . . though it's not so genial now. Am outdoors, though—seeing a great sunset. Hope you'll take a good rest before returning to the grindstone. ¶ Peace of the Prophets—

ꭦ Ƨ Ꙭ ꝯ

P.S. My aunt's cast came off Thursday, but the doctor is making her stay in bed for a week after the removal.

Notes

1. EHP called the story "The Corpse without a Face," but no such story was published with that title. Possibly published as "The Headless Corpse."
2. Bernarr Macfadden published various confessional magazines (*True Story, True Romance,* etc.), but since all stories were published anonymously, it is difficult to identify which might have been by Long.
3. "The Picture in the House," "The Music of Erich Zann," "The Rats in the Walls," "The Strange High House in the Mist," "Pickman's Model," "The Colour out of Space," and "The Dunwich Horror." A few days later he sent eighteen more stories. All were returned. See Schultz.
4. Unidentified.

[22]   [ANS, JHL]

[Postmarked Providence, R.I.,
11 August 1933]

Another victim for your boiling oil, O Peacock Lord! Just had word of the revival of *Astounding Stories* by Street & Smith (79–89 7ᵗʰ Ave., N.Y.C.) as a mainly *weird* magazine![1] If you want to give it a trial as a possible avenue of expression before applying the penalty, go to it! 1¢ per word ON ACCEPTANCE! Editor—Orlin Tremaine. Asst. Ed. Desmond Hall. Short sto 7500 nov. to 15,000 no serials ¶ Bought Nickel Detective yesterday, but Brobst begged to borrow it before I could digest the contents! Will report on contents when he brings it back.
Blessings of Nug & Yeb—

ꝑ ꙮꙅꙬ

Notes

1. The revived *Astounding Stories* published primarily science fiction.

[23]   [ALS, JHL]

The Wooded River-Bank
—whatever Wednesday is in
Arabic
[mid-August 1933][1]

Dear Malik:—

I have read with vast appreciation your note to Satrap Pharabo-zus (if you must have it that way!), & blush beneath the undeserved praise be-stowed upon my humble share in our joint effort. Let us hope that the Tyrant will be amenable to your persuasive eloquence—surely the tale must be pretty damn bad if that chrysostomic encomium won't put it over! And yet I enter-tain no false hopes. I am not at my best in collaboration—& the yarn is most distinctly not commercial . . . . & the caprices of Satrap Pharny are without number or assignable motivation!

By the way—here are two names to add to your bubbling dung & boiling lye list . . . . . new phantasy publishers as reported by the indefatigable Auguste-Guillaume, Comte d'Erlette. The names of their magazines are not yet known, but here is the dope transmitted by M. le Comte:

Rogers Terrill, Popular Publications, 205 E. 42nd St., New York City. Reli-able. Pays 1¢ per word promptly on publication.

Jay Publishing Co., 125 W. 45th St., New York City. Not so hot. Pays ½¢ per word tardily, after publication.[2]

Will you permit them to offer their wares before putting them out of the way? Incidentally, that non-paying *Fantasy Fan* (or did I tell you this before?) is go-ing weird altogether. The publisher—Charles D. Hornig—has been made managing editor of *Wonder*, & doesn't want to duplicate on scientifiction. As for Long—I wish him luck in the confession field. I'll tell him about Kline. He might be able to achieve your clever synthesis of commercial acceptability & personal expression, although I'm damned sure I never could.

Glad Two-Gun Bob liked my ghost-written attempt[3]—I'll lend you the magazine some time if you'd care to see it. I'm told the new W.T. is a pretty fair issue, tho' I've been too hellishly rushed to read a word of it. I shall try to get hold of the Nickel Detec on my first trip down town in business hours—surely this would seem to be a rare & notable issue! I note with pleasure the announcement of "Pale Hands" for the next *Magic Carpet*.

Sorry to hear of the coryzal affliction. I haven't had one since my memo-rable journey south prior to the 25½ hour call—but believe me, that speci-men was just as exaggerated in its way as the length of the ensuing social event! If I hadn't been virtually hypnotised with the beauty of the Shenando-ah, of Chattanooga, of the Cumberlands, of ancient Natchez, & of the Vieux

Carré, I'd have given myself up wholly to the enjoyment of my misery. I had to buy about 3 dozen handkerchiefs at various Woolworths along the route— N.Y., Chattanooga, Vicksburg—Canal St.—& was wheezing so persistently I could hardly ask directions to various archaic places! It took about 3 days of Nouvelle-Orleans to bake it out of me. Glad your malady was so short-lived—I'll have to try Turkish coffee the next time I'm stricken. Sorry you were forced to degrade your palate with Feringhi coffee[4]—better come to Prov. again & work your magic with my supply, which is smuggled across the void from the black fields of Yuggoth.

Glad you will maintain a proper respect for the felidae. You certainly can use a trait like ailurophily to immense advantage in a detective plot.

Glad the mill picture by your artistic relative appealed to you. This is quite an artistic season—only this morning a young fellow came to the door selling water-colours (black & white—very effective) of the ancient hill neighbourhood which he had painted; & my aunt couldn't resist buying one (for a dollar) of the college grounds looking downward over our street.

The 8-cylinder Jug sounds interesting, though you ought to think twice before going back on your present faithful steed. Welcome to Providence, whatever you come in!

Very decent weather today, though one needs a coat. I begin to feel the chill of the evenings, & have to head for my archaic hearthside sooner than in July. And now I must get to work on an unexpected job of verse revision.

Yog-Sothoth be with Thee!—

P.S. Epistle to Pharnabazus safely on file. Barlow ought to have a copy to add to his museum![5]

Notes

1. At JHL this letter (a reply to EHP of 8 August 1933) is accompanied by an envelope postmarked 31 October 1934, but this appears to be an error; the envelope presumably goes with letter 42.

2. Rogers Terrill of Popular Publications edited *Dime Mystery Magazine* (December 1932–September 1938), which began as a mystery magazine but switched focus to weird menace stories with the October 1933 issue. The magazine proposed by Jay Publishing Co. never appeared.

3. Probably "The Horror in the Museum," ghostwritten for Hazel Heald.

4. EHP to HPL, 8 August 1933 (TLS, JHL): "My supply of coffee is low—so I drank a pot of weak swill such as the Feringhi dogs drink up north, and claim it keeps them awake all night." *Feringhi* (more properly *ferengi*) is a term used by Arabs to denote foreign travelers coming to their country.

5. See Appendix.

[24]   [ALS, JHL]

Aug. 19[, 1933]
Eve of my 43d Birthday

Dear Malik:—

The enclosed sock on the jaw tells its own sad story.[1] Aië! Aië!
. . . or whatever is a good Arabic wail to echo about the time-weathered py-
lons of the Herati Gate. But it's no surprise. I see that Pharabozus is returning the MS. to me—but I'll pass it back to you, since the carbon (now with
Two-Gun Bob) is coming my way in the end. I'll leave it to your judgment
whether to attempt further peddling.

Hope you'll land something with the new *Astounding*. Wandrei has just
sold them a MS.[2] for 95 bucks—*on acceptance* [He has the cheque, has cashed
it, & the bank says it's all right!] Hope I can get a look at "The Hand of Hassan". Brobst returned *Nickel Detective*, & I enjoyed "When Winners Lose".
Very clever—I recall your outlining the plot some time ago. Haven't yet read
Burks & Mashburn items.[3]

Glad your current expenses haven't been as bad as feared—& hope you
get cheques enough to make a New England detour before heading south.
Actually, the climate up here isn't so bad in the first half of Septr., except that
the evenings get cold. I continue to do my writing outdoors whenever weather & programme permit. Aunt not yet doing much walking, but practices daily on crutches.

Regards & the Peace

Notes

1. See Appendix for Wright's letter to HPL of 17 August 1933 (ms., JHL).
2. Probably "A Race through Time" (October 1933).
3. *Nickel Detective* (August 1933): Arthur J. Burks, "Fangs of the Lily"; Kirk Mashburn,
"Minutes of Doom." The other story is by EHP.

[25]   [ALS, JHL]

Mosque of Shaitan
—Yaum el gumm'a[1]
[Postmarked 25 August 1933]

Dear Malik:—

Messages duly at hand. Your screed from Pharabozus seems to
be a duplicate of mine—but your answer is individual & splendidly effective.
I shall file these things along with your first letter to the Satrap. As for the tale
itself—I shall simply let it lie around for the present, until some really good
publication-prospect is sighted by either of the perpetrators. For the moment
it's lent to Brobst. But let me know whenever you want to see it. It is possi-

ble, as you suggest, that King Pharnaces may reconsider his rejection later on—I believe that is his tendency when he gives so tearful a turndown—but I shan't count extensively on anything of the sort. For the present the matter can rest so far as I'm concerned.

I shall get *All-Detective* the first time I pass an open news stand, & feel sure that "The Hand of Hassan" will form an interesting study. Yes—I'd be glad to see an analysis of that achievement, step by step, with the commercial reason for each particular twist explained. I have often wondered just what tricks differentiate the successful machine-made pulp tale from the unsuccessful. Not that I'll ever be likely to produce any myself—but simply from academic curiosity.

Good luck with the "Grey Sphinx" & other still unattached ventures. It would be splendid if you could make S & S—with their acceptance payment—a steady market. Good idea to recall stuff to[o] long buried in the catacombs under the Tigris! Glad the still further dismemberment of the Faceless Corpse had salutary results. Sabaean gold & the new venture sound promising, & I trust you can keep up the pace. The adventures of that cheque were picaresque indeed, & I certainly hope you can get cash out of it sooner or later!

News of Old Jug is always interesting—I await with bated breath the outcome of the gas test. Would that Frank Winfield might buy that novelette[2] & thereby turn your caravan to the East, where the unfinished bottle of curry powder still awaits the master hand! I envy you your winter in the south—to think I have not seen a bit of live-oak or a single strand of Spanish moss since I climbed the heights across the bay from Mobile over a year ago! But I don't envy you your tantalising dash past Fredericksburg, Richmond, *Charleston,* & Savannah without so much as a pause! Hope you'll get a good eyeful of St. Augustine—how I long to sit on the terreplein of Ft. San Marcos writing postcards & getting so brown that I patronise a Cuban eatery in Aviles St. in order to be inconspicuous! If you want a good Arabic vista, go south to the bottom of that long lagoon whose top begins in the old Spanish Quarter. Then looking back across the blue water, you will see in the distance the Moorish towers of the flamboyant Ponce de Leon hotel—softened by the intervening space, & ineffably glamourous against a gorgeous sunset. All the synthetic Victorianism goes out of the silhouette, & you have the magic of Bagdad, Damascus, Mecca, & Medina unalloyed. St. Augustine is probably the Florida town I'd most wish to live in—despite the greater climatic advantages of more southerly regions. No other place in the state is even half so interesting—& I'd rather partly hibernate there than live outdoors all the year in Miami, where everything is unpicturesquely new & where no live-oaks grow. Key West is another great spot—& the climate is even better than Miami's—but this town lacks good loafing places to read & write in. To enjoy K.W. one ought to be able to hire a cottage with a private garden. Whitehead's region on the west coast isn't bad—but it isn't old enough to have a permanent & pervasive charm. St. Augustine is my first choice, any day. However—in moving south one ought to consider *Natchez* before deciding. That place has scenery incomparably finer than even the best of Florida's, while its ancient charm leaves nothing to be desired. However—none of these places is in the running with *Charleston* as a town. I might choose that in spite of the reputedly cold Februarys. Charleston is a place of living tradition—a real home city in the sense that Providence is.

Rotten weather hereabouts, so I've been concentrating my activities indoors—trying to get my correspondence under control so I can do a little story-writing of my own. I must muster up some of your ruthlessness, cut out Boy Scout courtesy, & refuse to have ¾ of my time taken up by 20 to 40 page epistolary discussion without remuneration! Well—at last I managed to clean things up a bit, so have devoted the past three days to perpetrating a story. It is called "The Thing on the Doorstep", & runs to 37 pages of my average script, 8½ × 7 sheets. That will make over 40 double-spaced typed pages unless I cut drastically; & I shall not cut much more, since it would leave the climactic horrors insufficiently motivated. It is exceedingly gruesome at the end. I don't yet know whether it's any good, but shall keep it around & give it repeated perusals (& perhaps revisions) before exhibiting or offering it. It took me 3 days to write it, working every moment I could spare from sleep or nursing duty. The typing will be the hellish part . . . . . before I tackle that nightmare I may try some more stories—for in the old days they used to come in bunches. Alas—if everything one wrote would only sell!

Brobst was over last night & sent you his regards. Best wishes for all your ventures!

Salaam Aliekum[3]

Notes

1. Friday.
2. EHP submitted what he calls "Satan's Prayer Rug" to *Woolworth's Mystery Magazine*. (Note that EHP had sold a story called "Satan's Prayer Rug" [published as "Lord of the Fourth Axis"] to *WT*.) "Satan's Prayer Rug" was published in *Five Novels Magazine* as "Who Killed Gilbert Foster?" as by EHP and Ralph Milne Farley.
3. As-Salaam-Alaikum, the Arabic greeting meaning "Peace be unto you."

[26]   [ANS][1]

[Postmarked Providence, R.I.,
26 August 1933]

Congrats on "The Master of Assassins!" You certainly have all the popular ingredients present by droves & in triple strength!! ¶ Got Hand of Hassan last night & read with interest. It certainly is a tremendously clever & neatly dovetailed piece of work—with all the excitement & suspense one could well ask! I'll be interested to get an analysis of the various elements & their profession-al raisons d'etre. I recall one of the scenes—the escape—from our last year's conversations. Glad it found such an effective setting. ¶ Hope the new ven-ture goes over well—& luck with Grey Sphinx! ¶ Trust you'll have an inter-esting call on Long. I won't reveal any of your whereabouts from now on—so if he writes of your departure for Florida I'll merely express appropriate envy. By the way—if you could manage to call on Wandrei—84 Horatio St. (N.W. fringe of Greenwich Village)—I think you'd find him interesting. ¶ Regards & the Peace

Notes

1. *Front:* Brown University, Providence, R.I. The Carrie Tower, Hope, Manning and University Halls at left.

[27]   [ALS, JHL]

> Prospect Terrace, on the
> Ancient Hill. Sunset.
> Septr. 19, 1933

Dear Malik:—

Welcome home to the banquettes & galleries of ancient Cre-oledom! You are surely the antithesis of good old Morton with his minutely foreplanned schedules. Here I am fancying you headed for winter quarters in Southern Florida—when lo! the winds of Fate blow you back into the old pocket behind the levees of New-France's austral outpost! Ah, me—it makes me homesick for the Orleans, Gluck's, & my accustom'd benches in Jackson Square & City Park! Especially with chill autumn coming on.

I duly rejoiced when the card of the great convocation came, & have since been receiving enthusiastic panegyrics of you from the pens of Sonny Belknap & Mortonius the Great. I thought youse three guys would make a congenial team, & I see I was not mistaken. Glad you like the boys. Yes—you can see that old geezers like Morton & me still have a few interests left! James Ferdinand certainly is a philosopher of rare quality—& though his estimate of the cosmos differs almost diametrically from mine (he believes in some sort of deity, ethical values, & even immortality!), I cannot sufficiently praise the rational liberality of his perspective & methods. We can fight endlessly with-out becoming either angry on the one hand or bored on the other hand—& the same thing applies to Long.

But Belknap slipped up on one thing—for he was absolutely & unquali-fiedly wrong in believing that I have published non-weird fiction under a pseudonym. I not only have never done so, but have certainly never said anything from which such a mistaken inference could legitimately be made. That's the kid's one trouble—his imagination flies off on a tangent, & now & then goes beyond the plain facts. For example—when Putnam's asked to see some of my tales 3 years ago (they later turned 'em down), Belknap began telling the gang that they were going to publish a book of mine. And he really believed it, the young imp! In the present case I think Sonny got two separate things mixed up & exaggerated both. One element was probably that recent Cape Cod conversation I told you about—when we were discussing the *possibility* of my attempting general hack fiction with the aid of some device like a plot chart. But what I said I *might attempt* is a long way from anything I have ever *done!* The other element is the fact that I have ghost-written all sorts of junk for various clients. But here again—that's a long way from genuine & original pseudonymous writing. What's more—most of the tales I have ghost-written have been *weird*. And further—a lot of this ghost-written stuff has never sold, anyhow![1] So there is the end of a beautiful myth. May it rest peacefully in the bosom of Eblis beneath the crumbling pillars of Istakhar![2]

Your San Augustin card filled me with the greenest of envy, notwithstanding the sad news regarding the deleterious effects of Old Jug's recent diet.[3] Oh, to sit brooding in the old Slave Market, on the Bridge of Lions, or on the sun-baked terreplein of the ancient fort, or beneath the twisted, sinister live-oaks of the grove north of the town! And to think you voluntarily left it behind! Oh, well—you had New Orleans ahead! Some time you ought to run Old Jug up to Natchez if it holds together long enough. Did you see *Charleston?* And anything but the skeletonic outlines of Savannah? Your record of wakeful driving is certainly a distinguished one. Too bad you missed the heifer—which might have kept you in provisions all the rest of the way! I mourn at Juggernaut's indigestion, but am glad that some of the trouble dissolved on the post-Mobile run. Hope the rattle will mend in course of time, allowing you to take in such neighbouring spots as N. Michigan Ave., Auburn, Cal., & Cross Plains, Tex.

I shall be glad to peruse "Satan's Garden" when Satrap P. condescends to place it before the world. Hope you can find early placement for the Lilin with Hall. Wandrei & Long have called personally on the latter, & find him very affable & intelligent. He appears to be rather youngish—under thirty. Sorry some rejections have occurred—but you certainly have fewer of these than anyone else in the gang! You'll place Grey Sphinx (whose beginning, on the reverse side of your letter, sounds infinitely alluring) & Satan's Prayer-Rug yet! I'll be interested in your explanation of the fine points of "The Hand of Hassan" later on. Glad to hear of the Daigh acceptances.[4]

My aunt is much better now—all around the house on crutches or cane, though we have installed an electrical device for opening the front door from upstairs. The nurse went a fortnight ago, & my aunt has her principal meal sent in from the boarding-house across the back garden.[5] By the way—the nurse used quite a bit of our curry powder in preparing meals for my aunt during her regime!

Well—my trip was a magnificent surprise, & a splendidly successful jaunt from start to finish. I told you on the joint card with Cook of my unearthing of a 1637 house (with a secret room in the chimney) near Boston[6]—& on a later Quebec card I chronicled an ideal journey (no roystering beer-seekers on the train—hours spent in reading, drowsing, & [after dawn] landscape-viewing) & a delighted basking in the familiar antiquities of the Bayonne of the New World. Boy, what a town! Old grey walls, lofty citadel, dizzy cliffs, silver spires, ancient red roofs, mazes of winding ways, constant music of chimes & clopping hooves, throngs of cassocked, shovel-hatted[7] priests, robed nuns, & brown-cowled barefoot friars, vistas of huddled chimney-pots, blue river far below, vivid verdant countryside, & the dim, distant line of the purple Laurentians . . . . I also took some suburban trips—a walk to Sillery, up the river, & a trolley ride to the upper level of Montmorency Falls, where stands Kent House, the Georgian mansion inhabited by Queen Victoria's father in the 1790's. I loafed, read, & wrote in all the parks & on the citadel embankment which overlooks the whole city & surrounding terrain, & looked up the exact spot of Wolfe's ascent of the cliff—not an easy quest, since it is unmarked, & the local Gauls aren't a bit keen on pointing out the route of the guy who licked the pants off 'em! One of the things about Quebec that always strikes me forcibly is the *sky*—the odd cloud formations peculiar to northerly latitudes & virtually unknown in southern New England. Mist & vapour assume fantastic & portentous aspects, & at sunset on Labour Day I saw one of the most impressive phenomena imaginable from a vantage-point on the ancient citadel overlooking the river & the Levis cliffs beyond. The evening was predominantly clear; but some strange refractive quality gave the dying solar rays an abnormal redness, while from the zenith to the southeastern horizon stretched an almost black funnel of churning nimbus clouds—the small end meeting the earth at some inland point beyond Levis. From a place midway in this cloud-funnel, zigzag streaks of lightning would occasionally dart toward the ground, with faint rumbles of thunder following tardily after. Finally—while the blood-red sun still bathed the river & cliffs & housetops in a supernal light—a pallid arc of rainbow sprang into sight above the distant Isle d'Orleans; its upper end lost in the great funnel of cloud. I have never seen such a phenomenon before, & doubt if it could occur as far south as Providence. Another striking thing is the almost perpetual mist which hovers about the mountains & valleys near Lake Mauphramagog, at the Vermont–Quebec line. With such bizarre skies, I do not wonder that the northern races excel those of the south in fantastic imagination. On the inbound trip I paid Cook a second call—after a day spent in my beloved Salem & Marblehead (Arkham & Kingsport). Couldn't get to Newburyport (Innsmouth) this time. In Salem I came upon some interesting new sights.

For one thing, I succeeded in getting inside the old Richard Derby house (1762)[8] for the first time. This was the first brick house in Salem, & is finely panelled in a style which was somewhat old-fashioned even when the house was built. The Derbys were one of the foremost lines of Salem ship-owners & merchant princes—being virtually the originators of the East India trade. Another interesting object was the perfect reproduction of a gabled house of 1650 recently built on the grounds of the Pequot Mills. Every detail of 17th century work is duplicated with scholarly fidelity, & I could hardly believe it was a modern fac-simile. But the climax of all was another reproduction— that of the pioneer Salem settlement of 1626, carefully constructed & laid out in a park. This consists of a generous plot of ground at the harbour's edge, painstakingly landscaped & covered with absolutely perfect duplicates of the very earliest huts & houses—dwellings of a sort which have utterly vanished. All the early industries are also reproduced—these being such things as an ancient saw-pit, blacksmith shop, salt works, brick plant, fish-drying outfit, & so on. Nothing else that I have ever seen gives so good a picture of the rough pioneer life led during the first decade of New England colonisation. Marble-head possessed its accustomed charm—though my inspection of it was bro-ken by several showers. I finally got utterly drenched in Boston as I went to call on Cook. But all of my 4 days in Quebec were hot & fair.

On my return I struck a season of vile rainy weather, & nearly froze with the premature autumnal chill. Only my oil heater saved me. Yesterday & to-day, however, have been fair & warm; so that I've done quite a bit of writing outdoors. Indeed—I spent yesterday amidst rural scenes—in & around the Quinsnicket Woods 5 miles north of the city. ¶ Am getting my dinners at a new cheap eatery at the foot of the hill—Italian place called "Al's Lunch." Rock-bottom pre–N R A[9] prices! ¶ Blessings of the Djinns—Abdul

P.S. Klarkash-Ton tells me that one William Crawford of Everett, Pa. is about to start a new weird & scientifiction magazine (no pay) called *Unusual Stories*.

Notes

1. Such as "The Mound," ghostwritten for Zealia Bishop.

2. Istakhar or Istakhr was a city in ancient Persia, flourishing from the 3rd century B.C.E. to the 3rd century C.E.

3. EHP's attempt to seal a leak in the car's radiator with an additive resulted in the radiator needing to be replaced.

4. Ralph Daigh was the editor of *Strange Detective Stories* (formerly *Nickel Detective*). The accepted stories likely were "Spirit Madness" (also titled "The Dead Return") and "The Crooked Square."

5. The Arsdale, at 55 Waterman Street across the back garden from 66 College Street, where HPL often directed visitors from out of town to stay.

6. The Deane Winthrop house in Winthrop, Mass. The house was in fact built in 1675.
7. A hat, worn by some ecclesiastics, with a broad brim turned up at the sides and projecting with a shovel-like curve in front and behind.
8. At 168 Derby Street, Salem.
9. National Recovery Administration, a major New Deal program.

[28]   [ALS, Place of Hawks]

Irem—the City of Pillars.[1]

Sept[r]. 29, 1933

Dear Malik:—

Good luck with your twenty-emmer![2] By this time I presume the street fight has gone into literary history, with all hands safely killed or mangled. Hope the rumour about "The Dead Return" was correct—I must give the stands a looking-over. And so Pharabozus' immediate advice is "Lord of the 4th Axis". Well—I shall welcome it, & I hope the remuneration will not be too long deferred. Your future writing plans are as dizzying as novel, & make one envy the store of energy which enables you to make them—to say nothing of carrying them out!

I secured & perused the revived *Astounding*, & was vastly disappointed in the general contents. The opening tale[3] is the cheapest of claptrap, & in no case is there any escape from the hollow structure & thin, unsatisfying atmosphere of pulpdom. Not once can the reader catch any trifle of the momentary illusion which gives to weird fiction whatever it has of emotional value. Wandrei's opus was the best of anything in the book, but isn't even in the running with his best (& professionally rejected) material. I don't know whether Satrap P. ever had a look at this. It's a rather too bad you didn't get in touch with Wandrei in N. Y. But in general, I must say that Editor Hall's advance account of his literary ideals was hardly borne out by this opening performance. The thing does not excel the average W T quality, nor does any of the tales I read get as far from the sapless pulp convention as many of Frere Farnsworth's features. Likewise, I doubt very much if Hall would accept my material. Everything about the atmosphere & overtones of his venture seems remote indeed from what I write or try to write. I may have mentioned that he lately turned down a tale of Long's. He is, however, very much of a good fellow—about 27 years old, seemingly cultivated, & exceedingly genial. He has attended one of the informal meetings of our gang—at Wandrei's—& produced a very favourable impression. Unfortunately, being affable is an entirely different matter from accepting one's contributions! Eventually—with your adaptability & conscious workmanship—I feel sure that you can make *Astounding*, whose pay-on-acceptance policy certainly renders it a first-class market to cultivate.

Possibly the explanation of Belknap's overstatements about my fictional work is as you suggest. The kid has a dramatic fluency which makes it necessary to analyse his statements before acceptance. Incidentally—he turned 31 five months ago, the date of his advent to this planet being April 27, 1902.[4]

The Knopf bubble burst, as expected, a couple of days ago; when I received the usual polite letter heralding the return of the MSS. All very suave—the stories had full editorial approval, but commercial possibilities were few, &c. They did go to the length of asking Satrap Pharabozus if he could help in the marketing in event of publication but he was unable to offer them the requisite assurances. Well—nobody's surprised, & the only loss on my part is the postage one way. I hope they haven't soiled & rumpled the MSS. as badly as Putnam did.

So you never even went near Charleston! Well—that isn't as tantalysing as going through it & not stopping. As for the delights of thunderous, meteoric Juggernauting through mysterious & briefly glimpsed zones of strange light, shadow, mist, & contour—a process having a touch of the cosmic in its likeness to a comet's course through unforeseen, unplumbed spatial abysses—I can certainly understand your attitude to the limit, & share it under many circumstances. The difference is that I would want my cosmic burstings to involve some territory whose details did not fascinate me—some raw, modern, or untraditional region which I'd never care to linger over in detail. Otherwise a hasty passage would produce such bitter tantalisation that the enjoyment of the dash would be overbalanced. Another point where we differ is that of sightseeing. Unlike you, I am able to extract a great amount of satisfaction from a very brief glimpse of a quaint or beautiful place, provided I can include all the salient features. This is probably because the sensation of *time* is highly subjective with me—the ticking of the clock or turning of the calendar-leaves meaning relatively little to me as contrasted with the sheer, non-chronological flow of events. Many technically long periods seem negligibly brief to me if not filled with memorable landmarks; & conversely, I can extract a sense of ample time from my wide variety of vivid & pleasing impressions, no matter how technically swift (within certain limits, of course) their succession may be. I can see any *average* city quite adequately in a single day, although of course I *prefer* to have unlimited leisure. (This would not, of course, apply to places like Quebec, Charleston, or New Orleans, which contain too much vital detail for quite so brief an assimilation.) When I know I shall have very little time in a place, I always try to get as thorough as possible a book-&-map knowledge of it in advance. I then know about what I want to see & how to get to it, & can guess or deduce what sections are likely to be old & interesting. With this preparation, & with the aid of feet, street-cars, & (in certain cases) rubberneck-wagons, there are comparatively few towns which one cannot cover in a day, provided one eschews long visits to museums & long surveys of interiors. That single day will give all the salient & typical landscape & architectural vistas, will make one familiar with the principal buildings of interest, & will indicate the general atmosphere & colour of most of the important sections. Keeping one's attention alert, & not allowing impressions to overlap or coalesce, it is possible to make each momentary glimpse so keen & inclusive that the mind registers a picture conveying a sensation of substantial time. I can attest this from personal experience, for circumstances have forced me to begin acquaintance with many places—Portsmouth, N.H., Newburyport, Mass., Washington, D.C., Vicksburg, Miss., Mobile, Ala., Key West, Fla., Petersburg, Va., Montreal, &c—on a one-day basis. From each of these I carried away a sense of genuine familiarity, & when I was able to revisit certain ones I found that my brief first impression was perfectly valid. Revisiting a one-day-glimpsed city can be very much like a homecoming if the first glimpse be observant, inclusive, & emotionally well-assimilated. If the place is a large one, a preliminary orientation-tour on a sightseeing coach is the best general introduction. This translates the map into concrete terms, & gives the explorer a solid basis for special expeditions later in the day. Of course, there are many places of which it is impossible to get good guidebook-&-map material in advance. In such a case, the best way is to seek out the Chamber of Commerce at the earliest possible second & cram one's head & pockets with all the dope obtainable either there or at recommended bookstores. That's what I had to do at Vicksburg, & yet I retain to this moment a highly vivid picture of the mellow, shabby old town on its high river-bluff. That's also what I did at Montreal—aided by trips in sightseeing 'busses & trolleys. Naturally, all this postulates sufficient interest to make one unsparing of his feet. Nothing but brisk, tireless walking—even when supplemented by occasional transportation facilities—will enable one to pick up the right variety of impressions. Cruising around in a juggernaut won't do it—valuable though such a thing is for *non-urban* exploration. I was taken around Plymouth by car in 1926, & yet what I saw then was nothing as compared with what a pedestrian tour shewed me in 1931. Of course, one-day exploration is best in summer, when the available daylight period (especially in the north) has hours more than in winter. With 2, 2½, or 3 days a marvellously close acquaintance with a city can be obtained if the time be well-crowded. My first trip to Quebec[5] allowed only 2½ days, & yet I returned home with a virtually complete picture of the place—so that it was old familiar ground during my two subsequent visits. Adding all the days up, my three trips combined have given me little more than a week on Quebec soil, & yet I feel I know that city as well as Providence. I have traversed the full length of every notable street in the old section, have seen all the buildings of interest, have absorbed the landscape from every angle, & have recorded numberless little atmospheric details from the wooden suburban sidewalks, outside staircases, & NE STATIONNEZ PAS signs to the policemen's white helmets, prevailing cloud-formations, & constant music of chimes & clopping hooves. However—that's not saying that I wouldn't like to spend weeks in

Quebec, rolling around at leisure amidst the atmosphere & colour I have absorbed so swiftly & concentratedly. But if I *can't* get the big dose I'm willing to take a small one! Luckily, I did have liberal time-allowances in New Orleans, Charleston, & St. Augustine—though I'd like to spend months more in each. I surely hope you'll juggernaut around to Quebec some time. If you're then looking for a guide, you'll find my application high up on the waiting list!

I followed your analysis of "The Hand of Hassan" with the keenest interest, in many cases finding my own estimates of your purposes amply confirmed. The job is certainly one of the cleverest imaginable, & you manage very well to remove the plot from the realm of sheer abstraction. I can appreciate fully the extent to which an adroit & determined writer is able to circumvent the worst limitations of the pulp medium—although that does not alter the fact that this purely artificial burden (a burden not imposed by the legitimate demands of aesthetics, but by the ignorant, capricious, & irrelevant demands of those who have no interest in intrinsic merit & who, from their motives, have no right to make demands) represents a sheer waste of energy which any but a supercharged human dynamo would find disastrous. A writer with only the average store of energy has none to spare for things that are not essential. It may be that he could, through a dreary mental straining unrelieved by the zest which accompanies *artistically necessary* effort, succeed in the purely mechanical (but aesthetically meaningless & irrelevant) feat of producing a tale at once literarily respectable & acceptable to the low-grade tradesman of the editorial racket; yet when he has done this, he has *achieved nothing whatever* in the direction of anything he wishes or respects. The excess of exhausting labour he has spent in suiting the freaks of illiterates has not carried him a millimetre nearer to his one legitimate goal of emotional catharsis & harmonious expression, but has on the other hand lowered his vitality & creative energy, dampened the subconscious creative impulse which alone produces really powerful material, & confined him to a single set channel which—though he may have manipulated it till it does not flagrantly violate any aesthetic canon—is *certainly not better* than what he would have naturally used, & *probably much worse*. As an artist, he has flung away priceless strength to no purpose—wearing himself out in producing something *not as good* as he would otherwise have produced. No triumph is a real triumph unless it serves an end which the victor respects—& commercial advantage is an end which one can hardly respect unless one happens to be of a certain temperament. When so much ill-to-be-spared energy has to go into a field bringing no artistic return whatever, it is natural for the artist to prefer to *separate* his industrial from his personal life—using for honest, straightforward, non-pseudo-literary work of any sort the vast fund of energy which would have to be sunk futilely in his productions (& generally with a deleterious effect) in order to twist them into industrial material. All this, however, postulates the man of merely average or (like myself) sub-average energy—having no application to human dynamos like you & Derleth, who can pour out any amount of calculative cerebration independently of imaginative stimulus & without feeling the difference. Youse guys are damn lucky—but we plodders can't safely follow you any more than an average citizen can safely follow a tight-rope walker. What you are too lucky to be able to realise is that for a small-time writer *the whole bottom drops out of the creative process the moment it becomes consciously calculative.* Art is not the devising of artificial things to say, but the mere saying of something already formulated inside the artist's imagination & automatically clamouring to be said. That is the genesis of virtually every aesthetic product worth classifying as such. Art is potent only to the extent that it is unconscious. Of course, a great deal of careful conscious shaping is necessary, but this is always backed by a tense & effective emotional stimulus *as long as it is confined to the improvement & clarification of the original natural conception*—i.e., as long as it amplifies & promotes the basic subconscious desire which motivates & gives birth to the given aesthetic attempt. Even a comparatively sluggish & easily fatigued calculative intellect (like mine) can be spurred into fairly effective performances when the process promises to help in the fulfilment of the original subconscious expression-impulse. The hope of an adequate reward—a reward which seems adequate as measured by the then-ruling desire—is a stimulus of supreme potency. But set that same intellect to a calculative task *not* connected with the fulfilment of the dominant age—a task such as the laborious arrangement of expression to suit an artificial end *not connected* with the intrinsic perfection of the expression itself—& all emotional stimulus is lacking. The negative stimulus afforded by the fear of starving is not at all like the positive stimulus afforded by the desire for expression, dream-capture, or imaginative expansion. It produces—or tends to produce—a sort of paralysing desperation *hostile* to clear thinking rather than the expansive glow which strengthens, quickens, & fertilises thought. Thus the under-energised artist who finds no difficulty at all in arranging literary details *conducive to his own aesthetic ends,* encounters an unscalable barrier of exhausting & repulsive toil when confronted with the profitless & irrelevant task of artificially twisting his product—without hope of improvement & with vast likelihood of debasement—into some meaningless shape dictated by empty conventions which his whole nature execrates as disgustingly uncivilised & outside the normal field of consciousness of a gentleman. What happens when such an average-energied or under-energied artist attempts to link his personal expression with business depends altogether on the man himself, & on the attendant circumstances. In cases where the person has varied interests & holds on life—where his sense of integrity & existence is not bound up in the task of saying something which desperately clamours to be said—the solution is often a complete surrender of self-expression. Then, when the writer (no longer an artist) has ceased to have anything to say, there is no longer any emotional obstacle to the commercial juggling of rubber-stamp situations in accordance with the low-grade market's whims. While still lacking any *stimulus* for work, there is at least no *handicap*—& if ordinary cleverness be present, the writer can often succeed in gauging & pandering to the fickle boob-market—which he will do without any of the efforts at compromise made by the super-energied man, since his 'victory' in cheap fields will have crushed within him that sense of integrity which makes the super-energied hack still wish to retain something of artistic verity. True, he is not likely to produce any more art. That side of his life has been killed off. But if it was not his dominant & pivotal side, the loss is no greater than other curtailments of personality common in a barbarism where the profit-motive is forced on large numbers of cultivated persons. When, however, the capture of dreams & the utterance of dimly adumbrated conceptions *is* the primary & crucial element in a man's life—as it indubitably is in a substantial number of cases—then the attempt to suit artificial & contemptible tradesman's whims is foredoomed to failure except among the super-energied. Vast & insuperable emotional dykes are subconsciously reared against the diversion of intellection to base & ulterior objects, so that the listless & reluctant struggle toward industrialism can hardly be more than a dull tragedy consuming all & yielding nothing. It may kill the artist, but it will never make a business-man of the corpse. Nothing which is forced out of one at the price of his imaginative life is ever likely to have enough substance & skill to suit even the mind-struck three-penny cynics of the pulp. Compromise is impossible when the artist has not enough excess energy to make the irrelevant intellectual manipulations other than a prostrating & usually self-defeating drain. Remember that the slightest departure from the single aim of self-expression puts an instant damper on the very springs of creative zeal & creative intellect in the person of average or sluggish energy. The obstacles are too great to get around. Thus (in cases of average energy or less) when one bases one's life & self-respect on imaginative sincerity, it is really a bad business policy to try to tamper with self-expression or fuse one's dreams with the hard-boiled job of squeezing money out of indifferent & stereotyped tradesmen. It is bad business because it gets one nowhere. There isn't any money in it . . . . . an argument which even a tradesman can recognise as valid. When the only thing in life that one wants to do is to express himself aesthetically, it is foolish to embark on any course which will almost certainly defeat that end (though of course a good business-man doesn't even suspect what this is all about)—& *doubly* foolish when (here the business-man assents) that suicidal sacrifice will never lead to even the hollow compensation of material profit! The gist, of course, is simply this; that for certain types of persons the energy which would have to go into the artificial & repulsive task of hack-adapting would be largely wasted, & in any case grossly *disproportionate* as compared with the potentialities in other commercial fields where no disgust-barrier operates. If I reserve a certain quantity of mental energy from my personal & creative life to devote to the shelter-&-

nourishment-acquiring process, I want that energy to go as far as possible & to be wasted as little as possible . . . . & experiment seems to shew that it would go farther & bring better returns in some simple, honest, & non-charlatanic occupation like drug-clerking or bookkeeping or bricklaying—an occupation of a straightforward, need-filling sort without the servile taint of pandering & wheedling—than in any field which involved the element of mockery, of degrading parody, or of the diversion of exhausting intellection to an ulterior, irrelevant, & aesthetically wasteful aim. That is why I'd give a good deal for a real job, if I only knew how to go about looking for such a thing. My great mistake was in my younger days, when I thought that actual literary effort would surely manage to earn me a living somehow, some day. Had I known then what I know now, I would have hastened to fit myself for some steady routine work—of a sort mentally unexacting enough to leave my creative imagination free—as soon as my health became tolerable, & the ultimate exhaustion of drastically diminished resources apparent. But alas, these sensible perspectives generally come too late!

But remember that these observations do not apply to the super-energised, in whom the diversion of intellection to artistically irrelevant ends does *not* constitute a ruinous drain. Despite all that I have said, I appreciate none the less your own point of view—equally valid for the more fortunate type of person it concerns.

As for types of fiction—I hope you don't assume that I regard the weird tale as a superior form. Probably you don't, but one of your observations makes me anxious to rub the point in. My own devotion to this kind of thing is a sheer accident of personality, which only a psychiatrist, biologist, geneticist, or whatthehell could ever hope to trace to a source or sources—& I have never even dreamed of injecting such a personal bias into my general critical outlook. The proper function of a short story is to reflect powerfully a single mood, emotion, or authentic situation in life—& when you consider what a slight part the weird plays in our moods, feelings, & lives you can easily see how basically minor the weird tale must necessarily be. It *can* be art, since the sense of the uncanny is an authentic human emotion, but it is obviously a narrow & restricted form of art. I am sincerely sorry that my area of sensitiveness is so restricted as to make this the only province in which any urge for expression is really poignant and compelling. When I say that I can write nothing but weird fiction, I am not trying to exalt that medium, but am merely confessing my own weakness. The reason I can't write other kinds is not that I don't value & respect them, but merely that my slender set of endowments does not enable me to extract compellingly acute personal sense of interest & drama from the natural phenomena of life. I know that these natural phenomena are more important & significant than the special & tenuous moods which so absorb me, & that an art based on them is greater than any which fantasy could evoke—but I'm simply not big enough to react to them in the sensitive way necessary for artistic response & literary use. God in heaven! I'd certainly be glad enough to be a Shakespeare or Balzac or Turgeniev *if I could!* If I should try to write a story outside the weird area which engrosses my emotions & drama-sense, the result would be drearily *lifeless & artificial,* as all mainly objective work is. Not that any *repulsion* would be involved—the problem of course has no point of contact with the problem of insincere hack-writing previously discussed—but merely that a motive force & fine sense of zest & values would be lacking. I would heartily respect any medium, & would not regard as wasted any intellection spent on the solution of artistic problems of expression. I would, moreover, take a sincere satisfaction in any vivid capture of reality which I might be able to effect. So far, so good. But—unfortunately—there would always be the handicap *of having nothing to say.* I have no subconscious, ready-formed conceptions of a realistic sort. Whatever I treated of would have to be dragged in from outside, & would consequently have to be handled without the innate fire which animates any true work of art, however humble. I might, through study, produce something coldly correct & devoid of aesthetic gaucheries or untruths—but it would be a dead, mechanical thing unacceptable to others & unsatisfying to me because it would not involve the expression of a preëxisting urge. I respect realism more than any other form of art—but must reluctantly concede that, through my own limitations, it does not form a medium which I can adequately use. Even the faking of realistic fiction would be a thing of infinite difficulty for me, since my lack of vital interest in the details of daily life has caused me to remain blind to all those typical particulars about men & their customs & transactions which are so essential to the equipment of the realist. You know, by instinct & from observation, how different people react in different situations—while with me such knowledge is vague, generalised, remote, & second-hand. You have a thousand homely customs & processes at your finger-tips—whereas to me such things as stock exchanges, gasoline motors, police procedure, night clubs, & so on are so unknown or dimly reported as to be little better than half-fabulous. That is, my knowledge of the intimate details of the material background of all but a small segment of life, so unbelievably slight, that it would require years of special study to enable me to handle even the scenery of a varied body of contemporary realistic fiction. Now as to the *action or mystery story,* & whether I consider it "intrinsically base"—let me say that I do not consider any story base as long as it honestly & accurately reflects a human mood, feeling, or situation. There are no doubt many genuine moods, feelings, & situations involving violent overt events & sudden revelations; hence we may not justly object to any tale depicting them sincerely & in the proportions in which they normally occur in life. But this holds good only so far as a tale is a natural expression of a preëxisting feeling. Most certainly I cannot endorse as artistic a tale which crowds "action" to an extent unrepresentative of life, or which deliberately concocts mysteries & thrills to gratify an exaggerated & unrealistic taste. This is simply showmanship or catering—not the process of catharsis or expression which is art. The result is tinsel—it does not convince or satisfy the adult reader. When we see such a thing we do not thrill with the illusion of witnessing a fragment of life. We recognise the dreary stage-properties & notice the familiar wings & drop-curtains & masks before we realise that they are supposed to be arranged into a story. You say that all story tempo is essentially unnatural—which is certainly true as regards the conventional "plot" story. But I do not regard the conventional story as art at all—except now & then by accident. It is the free, looser-knit sort of tale which O'Brien's anthologies feature that raises short story writing to an art. *I'll* never get that far—but I appreciate the thing from the outside! And of course I realise that there are infinite gradations between the purely charlatanic concoction & the purely aesthetic tale. One must not expect perfection, but must merely do the best one can. ¶ Blessings of the Prophet [invented characters]

Notes

1. The word appears in EHP's draft, "The Lord of Illusion." The epithet "city of pillars" meant that Irem (or Iram, a lost city mentioned in the Qur'an) was actually a city of tent-poles. HPL probably imagined a city of impressive stone pillars. He mentioned Irem in "The Nameless City," "The Call of Cthulhu," "The Last Test," "History of the 'Necronomicon'" (1927), and "Through the Gates of the Silver Key" (1932–33), where he refers to "Shaddad [who] with his terrific genius built and concealed in the sands of Arabia Petraea the prodigious domes and uncounted minarets of thousand-pillared Irem" (*CF* 3.283). HPL had copied a passage from the *Encylopaedia Britannica* mentioning Irem into his commonplace book (entry 47).
2. I.e., a 20,000-word story.
3. Nat Schachner, "The Orange God" (*Astounding Stories*, October 1933). Wandrei's story was "A Race through Time."
4. Long actually was born in 1901.
5. In September 1930.

[29]   [ALS, JHL]

Mosque of Azathoth,
In Pillar'd Irem—
April 9, 1934

Dear Malik:—

Well, I'll be damn'd! Satrap Pharnabazus said something last week about your pulling up stakes, & now I learn that the rumour is all too true! I surely am sorry that your snug tepee among the aborigines couldn't prove permanent—for Oswald will miss you—but the argument of bad business is one which can't easily be disposed of. Anyhow, as you say, your sojourn in the hunting-grounds of Broken Axe[1] has been a distinctly profitable one—leaving you with a stout & rejuvenated Jug, & with a fund of technical experience not less valuable. And I certainly envy you the pilgrimage which lies ahead of you; with its face-to-face glimpses of the grim & sanguinary Conan amidst his heaps of skulls, & of daemon-haunted Klarkash-Ton as he feeds the blue-flamed lamps of orichalch in the subterrene fanes of Poseidonis. Hope you can see enough of ancient Mexico to give you a picturesque & lasting impression.

Meanwhile I trust the thrill-mill continues to prosper. The isolated bits of "The Hand of Wrath" sound highly fascinating to me, & I hope the capricious Satrap will think the same of the whole production. Congratulations on the detective short & the 23-cmnier—may both be founts of riches! "Satan's Garden"—part 1—makes a fine showing in the new W T. I wonder from whom Mrs. Brundage[2] stole the cover design? (You doubtless know of her habitual plagiarism from Derleth's friend Utpatel) By this time I suppose you've seen the magazine. You certainly get a well-deserved round of applause in the Eyrie. The E. Irvine Haines[3] who lauds "Tarbis" is an historian of note, whose articles frequently appear in the N.Y. Times. It is he who recently proved beyond a doubt the complicity of Benedict Arnold's wife in the plot of 1780. On the whole, the new W T is considerably above the average. The reprinted Burks story is one of the few unforgettable classics of the magazine, while "Black Thirst" is a marvel of original imagination & latent terror. Two-Gun's Conan tale is distinguished by an unforgettable suggestion of unholy antiquity—especially those pre-human words in the parrot's mouth, while Klarkash-Ton's opus falls into the superior class. His drawing is clever though slightly stiff.[4]

Glad the architectural jottings helped. The word "Empire" in an aesthetic sense, when it stands alone, generally refers by common usage to the First Empire. But as I said, I don't think it's ever used architecturally. "Vilest Victorian" is the best possible phrase for a typical 1880 product. Sorry, by the way, that you couldn't include a brooding Sleepy Hollow background.

Pharnabazus dropped me a line about the *unnenbaren–unaussprechlichen* controversy, revealing his usual concern for the minutiae of verbal propriety.[5] His office seems to be in quite a turmoil over the matter, & the Austrian assistant Richard has been urged to rack his ancestral memory for suitable criteria & precedents. In view of that very mouth-filling rhythm which I mentioned, he hates to let the good old Sauk City gargle of *unaussprechlichen* go if the slightest justification for its retention can be found. I am leaving the whole thing to him & his staff of scholars. Anything that sounds formidable & sinister is good enough for me!

Your chronicle of mechanical wizardry fills me with respectful admiration—& a new conception of the glamour & poetry that reside in subtle transformations of nature's blind forces. The Lord of the Juggernaut Stable

ought surely to thank you for the synthetic acetylene plant you are leaving behind you—& you, in turn, are doubtless blessing the Prophet for your chance
to rehabilitate Old Jug so soundly yet reasonably. Do you think you'll put in
that 90-per-hour attachment? With such a thing as that, "floorboarding" sure
would be floorboarding!! I knew you'd be glad to learn that Jug is a First Edition, but I didn't know of the actual material advantages possessed by the
Class of '28. Congratulations! I don't think you need to worry about all the
imperceptible subtleties of "idling". Anyhow, it looks as if you'd have a pretty
smooth & rapid run to Cimmeria & Hyperborea, if the roads will only do
their part. Yes—I see there must be a good deal of my old friend of '33 left. I
didn't know but it was like the ship Argo, which after Jason's return was set
up for worship in a grove on the Isthmus of Corinth. As the generations
passed, & rotting planks were renewed, it came about that no piece of the
original vessel remained; & philosophers were then called in to determine
whether or not the existing ship was in truth the old Argo. I believe their decision was affirmative, emphasising the principle that the essence of a thing is
the *arrangement* of its parts, rather than the material substance of the latter.
Thus no matter what happens, Old Jug will always be Old Jug!

I don't think your oil-field observations will be too superficial for Talman. Two-Gun Bob is no driller, but Talman used something of his none the
less.[6] One of the magazines—the *Texaco Star*—is for stockholders rather than
employees & technicians, & laymen prefer general colour to blue-print details
& esoteric trade jargon.

Yes—I think a really good interplanetary story would be unsalable. The
best stories of all kinds are. As to my stuff—the Mts. of Madness is a novelette representing my most serious endeavour—Antarctic archaeology & polar
mystery of a type that has haunted me since I was 11 years old. Its rejection
by Wright in 1931 was a psychological setback doing much to freeze me into
silence. I agree that my best medium is realism, though I am not certain whether the widespread advice to stick to New England backgrounds ought to be
followed too literally. There is a kind of *archaeological* horror dealing with lonely & remote places which I have to get out of my system every now & then.
"The Outsider" is a thing I wouldn't be apt to duplicate. But what I want to
do is to embody certain moods & pictures in tales whose central horror-
causes are not too *concrete* or essentially *trivial* (material monsters, conventional
wraiths, &c) to be adequate. There is some vague dream-world of macabre,
cosmic conceptions which I can sometimes glimpse & adumbrate, but can
never pin down.

Prospects look favourable for my southern trip—to visit Barlow & more
than incidentally see Charleston & St Augustine again—& your next word
from me may be a card from the road. I'll use the Pawhuska address till further notice.[7] Expect to stop a week at Long's en route.

Blessings, bismillah, & all that—

P.S. One of my friends—a corresponding member of the K.A.T. in a market next the Art Club—has just sustained woeful injuries to his neck & right fore paw. I don't know the source, but if it was a canine I shall endorse the curse of Islam on the doggish train. The injured John Quincy Adams, however, is just as playful & friendly as ever—& seems to be in no pain despite a pedal mangling which will probably leave him with a permanent limp.

Notes

1. A Native American acquaintance of EHP.

2. Margaret Brundage (1900–1976), *WT* cover artist, known for her scandalous nudes. Although she sometimes copied art by others, her cover for the April 1934 *WT* is yet another depiction of flagellation of a scantily clad woman.

3. E. Irvine Haines (1877–1959), editor, author, historian, and businessman. His story "The Hand of the Invisible" appeared in *WT* (May 1928), and he also had six letters published there. His letter regarding EHP's story was in *WT* 23, No. 4 (April 1934): 527–28.

4. *WT,* April 1934: Arthur J. Burks, "Bells of Oceana" (orig. December 1927); C. L. Moore, "Black Thirst"; Robert E. Howard, "Shadows in the Moonlight"; CAS, "The Death of Malygris." HPL's commonplace book contains an old entry (127) about a talking bird: "Ancient and unknown ruins—strange and immortal bird who SPEAKS in a language horrifying and revelatory to the explorers."

5. HPL to Robert E. Howard, 8 April 1934: "Quite an amusing debate is going on over the original German title of our old friend von Junzt's 'Nameless Cults'. You'll recall that I got the rendering *Unaussprechlichen Kulten* from young Derleth—who ought to know, being one of a compact German-American community. Price, however, was not satisfied with the translation, and finally decided that *Unnenbaren Kulten* was much more exact. Wright is now trying to decide what he'll do. *Unnenbaren* is probably more exact—but *Unaussprechlichen* has such a sinister, mouth-filling rhythm that it seems almost a pity to let it go if it can be found in any way usable" (*A Means to Freedom* 762). HPL to August Derleth, 29 March 1934: "Sultan Malik claims that *Unnennbaren* (= unmentionable) has some subtle preferability (in the way of unmistakable evil) over the earlier choice" (*ES* 628). The title as finally resolved upon is itself ungrammatical in German; it should either have been *Unaussprechliche Kulte* or *Von* or *Die unaussprechlichen Kulten.*

6. Wilfred Blanch Talman was editor of the *Texaco Star.* The magazine published Robert E. Howard's "The Ghost of Camp Colorado" (April 1931) and Paul J. Campbell's "The Joke Was on the White Man" (December 1931). The latter author was an amateur journalist and friend of HPL.

7. EHP had become a partner in a garage business in Pawhuska, OK.

[30]   [ANS][1]

[Postmarked De Land, Fla.,
5 May 1934]

Hail, Mighty Malik! Glad to see you pinned down to a reachable address! Meanwhile my own caravan ha[s been] on the move. Had a good week with Long & the gang in NY, then down to Charleston for a week, & now to De Land to visit young Barlow. You can reach me in his care for a fortnight or so. Very pleasant place—by a lake, out of the village. B. is an immensely bright & prepossessing kid. I'll be sending you the Charleston folder I couldn't previously send for lack of address. What a great old town! Also explored Savannah for 8½ hrs. Climate down here has livened me up tremendously! ¶ Vastly interested to hear of your Hegira & present surroundings. The new–old locale sounds delightfully snug & quaint to me. Good luck with the wealth of photographic materials—you may found a picture company & use the cinema camera in filming melodramas of Pierre d'Artois & the Assassins! ¶ Glad to learn of Mighty Juggernaut's choice diet & typical feats of valour. A tribute to the wonder workings of the lodge of Broken Axe. ¶ Trust you'll soon have a chance to see Klarkash-Ton. Bet you had an interesting time with Two-Gun Bob! ¶ Salaam Aliekum— 𐑿𐑣𐑮𐑪𐑻

Notes

1. *Front:* Independent Presbyterian Church, Savannah, Ga.

[31]   [ANS][1]

[Postmarked De Land, Fla.,
7? May 1934]

All hail, Lord Malik! Youthful host & aged guest salute thee in chorus! Would that thou mightest trundle Old Jug over here & participate in our sessions of lake-rowing, jungle-exploring, & delvings into the Vaults of Yoh-Vombis.[2] 86° today—& Old Abdul in his element. May all be well with thee in the City of the Himyarite Sultans!

In turn,

I trust my epistolary acedia will not entirely ban be [*sic*] from the Gates of Semaxxi. The distance you have covered in your Space-Eater is very imposing. //May I raise my hand for you-all's Ms. in case you h'aint forgot? I hope you will be able to see Klarkash-Ton in his bucolic dwelling.

By the Whiskers of Methuselah,
Ar-Ech-Bei

Notes

1. *Front:* Pine and Palm Forest in Dixieland. Card addressed by RHB.
2. I.e., the closet in which RHB stored his collection of books, magazines, and mss. Named after CAS's story.

[32]   [ALS, JHL]

℅ Barlow—Box 88,

De Land, Fla.,

May 30, 1934.

Dear Malik:—

Two cards duly recd.—& I enclose Providence & R.I. data requested. If this isn't sufficient, let me know, & I'll supply more. Also—I'll be glad to look over the rough draught of your story[1] when it's written, & correct any local allusions which may be erroneous. I'm surely eager to see what you make of the R.I. setting. Hope my memory of the Glebe is not all cockeyed—you'll recall that my own sight of it was just as brief as yours. I never beheld it before, & haven't seen it since! Meanwhile good luck with the Mexican border, Arabia, the Auburn mine, &c. &c. It probably is the best policy to vary environment, as you say. Congrats on Million Dollar Doom. That All Det. certainly is damn finical about its lengths![2] In general, your commercial record seems a very encouraging one; & I surely hope you can keep it up.

I continue to have a great time down here—the super-cordiality of my genial young host has kept deferring the date of my moving along. Hopes of Havana almost nil—but I shall certainly spend a week in ancient St. Augustine. Possibly Barlow will accompany me thither. Shall return home in slow stages—possibly visiting in Macon, Ga., & certainly pausing in Richmond & Washington. If not broke, I may visit Dwyer in West Shokan.

Shall be interested to hear more of your long odyssey, & of your encounters with Two-Gun Bob & Klarkash-Ton. Is Conan the Reaver as grim & sanguinary in person as on paper? Barlow has an idea of getting phonograph records made & sending oral greetings to C A S. No doubt you'll revisit Averoigne, since you're so relatively near there.

The genial climate here has taken 20 years from my shoulders—but day before yesterday there was a hell of a cold spell. In the house I wore a great quilt toga-wise over my suit, & outdoors I borrowed an overcoat. Cold is a devilish thing. There isn't any place on earth where I haven't shivered at one time or another!

Satrap Pharnabozus has been distributing the originals of the W T illustrations (as you doubtless know), but I've given all mine to my insatiable young host. The best of the lot was the "Strange High House" design by Doolin.[3] I hope our Silver Key next month gets a Rankin design. By the way, Pharnabozus intends to reprint my "Arthur Jermyn" before long.

Did I tell you what a sculptor Barlow is? He did a splendid bas-relief of Cthulhu, & has since finished a statuette of Ganesa, the Hindoo elephant god (a sort of prototype of Belknap's "Chaugnar"), for old William Lumley. If he only had better eyesight he could accomplish notable things in art.

About half the edition of my "Shunned House" has come from Cook, & Barlow intends to bind & issue it. Another scheme of Barlow's—which I hope vastly will succeed—is to issue 11 × 14 photographic reproductions (done by a professional) of Howard Wandrei's best fantastic drawings.[4] I guess I told you about these—later on I'll send some small photographs of them which Donald took.

This damn fountain pen is getting out of order—I'll have to see to it when I re-pass through N.Y. Fortunately I have another with me—though it is by no means as easy-writing as this.

Your recent Juggernauting exploits are surely impressive. Glad you now have the coöperation of a brother equally erudite in the lore of Juggernautive locomotion.

Peace be with you— 𝕾𝕳𝕷

[assorted enclosures: maps and sketches by HPL:]

On other side, rough map shewing relation of Glebe to Providence.

We left Prov. via Elmwood Ave. (The broad boulevard with car tracks on one side) & passed Roger Williams Park on our left. Then traversed Auburn, Norwood, Hillsgrove (seat of Prov. Airport), Greenwood, Apponaug* East Greenwich, (quaint old Village) & Wickford (*very* quaint old seaport where we saw Narragansett Church built in 1707 & moved to village in 1800).

Below Wickford is the Narragansett Country farmed in legend & song. Seat of prosperous culture before the Revolution—slaves & plantations like the South. Planters had their town houses in Newport across the bay. Narr. Ch. stood down here (a rural church in the woods like the old Virginia parish churches) till the prosperous rural life that nourished it declined. The Glebe (built circa 1730) was its parsonage. Here lived Dr. MacSparran (a fat, genial, cultivated cleric from N. Ireland) in the middle 18ᵗʰ century.

As for *mulberries*—I know nothing about 'em except that they're the kind of trees silkworms feed on. Their berries are rather like blackberries or raspberries (black), & they attract *birds* quite noticeably. They are originally Asiatic; & wherever found in America are usually reliques of attempts at silk culture. Specimens occur in Savannah (where Oglethorpe tried to found a silk industry) & in Williamsburg, Va. (where Gov. Francis Nicholson tried the same thing). I think MacSparran tried to found a silk industry in R.I.'s Narragansett Country. (or "South County") A mulberry tree exists in Providence close to

*APPONAUG, civic centre of Warwick

the house (598 Angell St) where I lived from 1904 to 1924.
Try the Britannica

Notes

1. It does not appear that a story set in Providence was ever completed.
2. It seems that EHP attempted to sell "Million Dollar Doom" to *All Detective Magazine*, but it apparently was rejected because of length, so he took it instead to *Super-Detective Stories*.
3. Joseph Patrick Doolin (1896–1967) was an artist for *WT* and numerous other pulp magazines.
4. Barlow bound only a few copies of *The Shunned House*. The photography plan also came to naught.

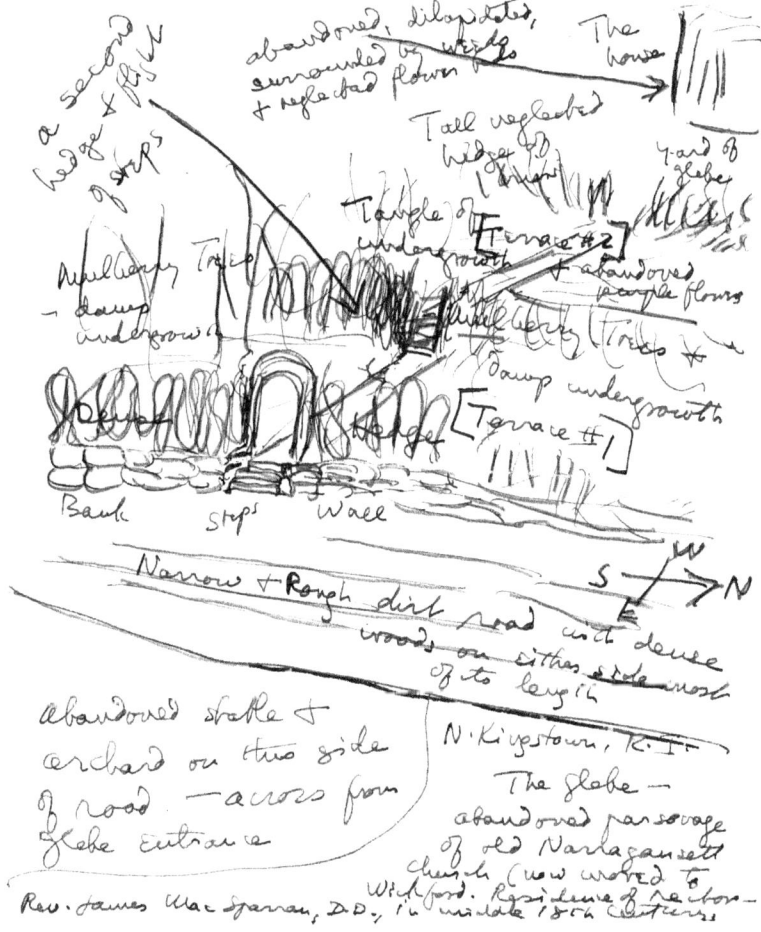

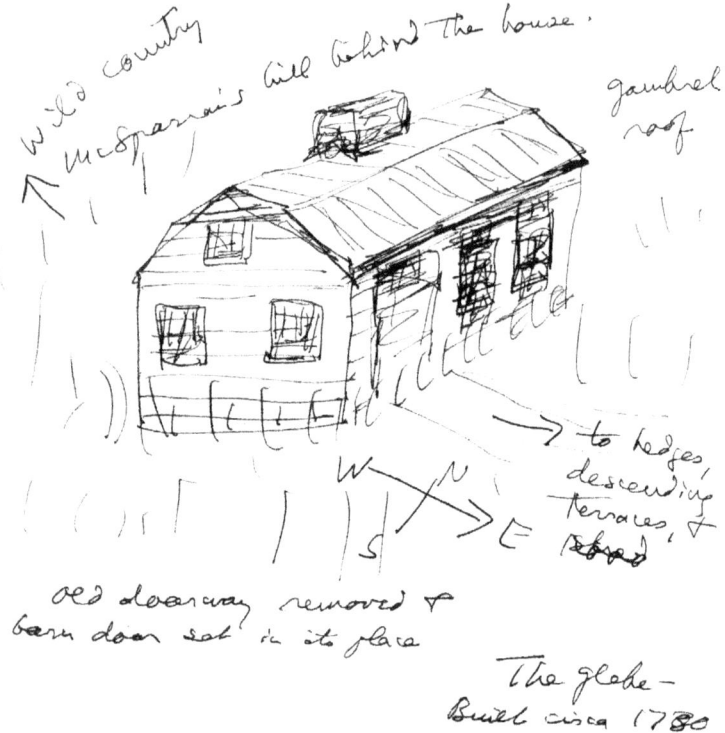

wild country
↑ McSpannan's hill behind the house.

gambrel roof

→ to hedges, descending terraces, & abroad

W N
S E

Old doorway removed & barn door set in its place

The glebe —
Built circa 1780

S←→N
E
Map of the glebe & its grounds

gradual ascent
woods + briars

wild terrain — going back to nature. McSpannan's hill rises behind house

house

abandoned flower gardens

neglected ┄┄┄┄ hedge ┄┄┄┄

upper terrace of tangled undergrowth + neglected purple flowers

steps deserted + sinister-looking
neglected ┄┄┄ hedge ┄┄┄

lower terrace or courtyard of neglected mulberry trees + damp weedy undergrowth. Very sinister aspect — always dark + shadowed

very high, dense hedge above low bank wall of stone.

steps + arch

very high, dense hedge above low bank wall of stone

Roadway — narrow, rutted, + primitive

☐ abandoned stable + orchard

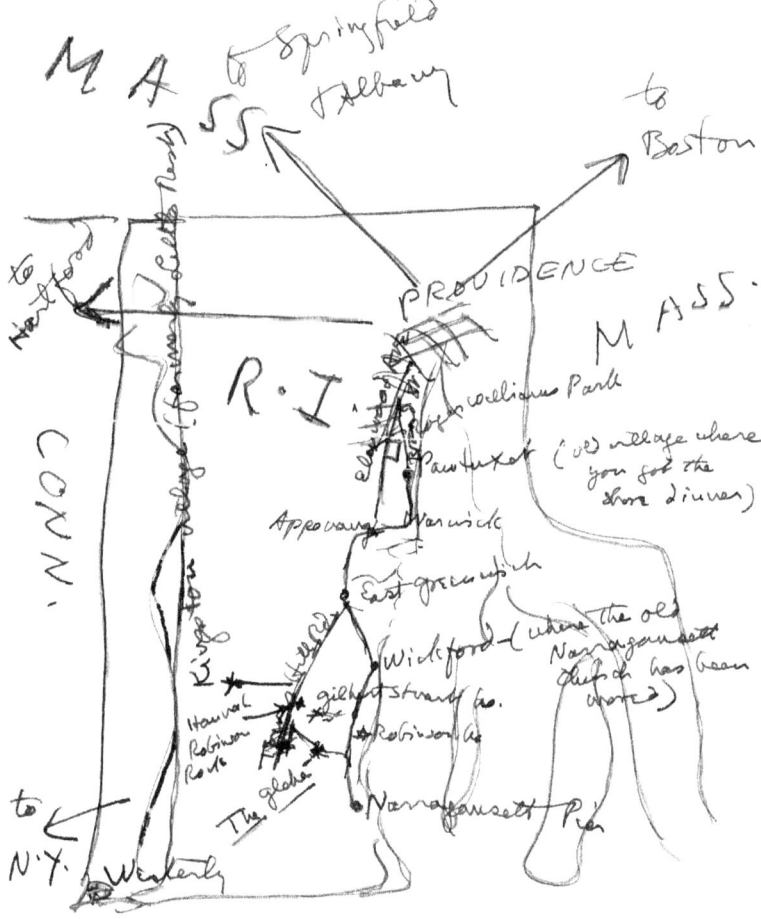

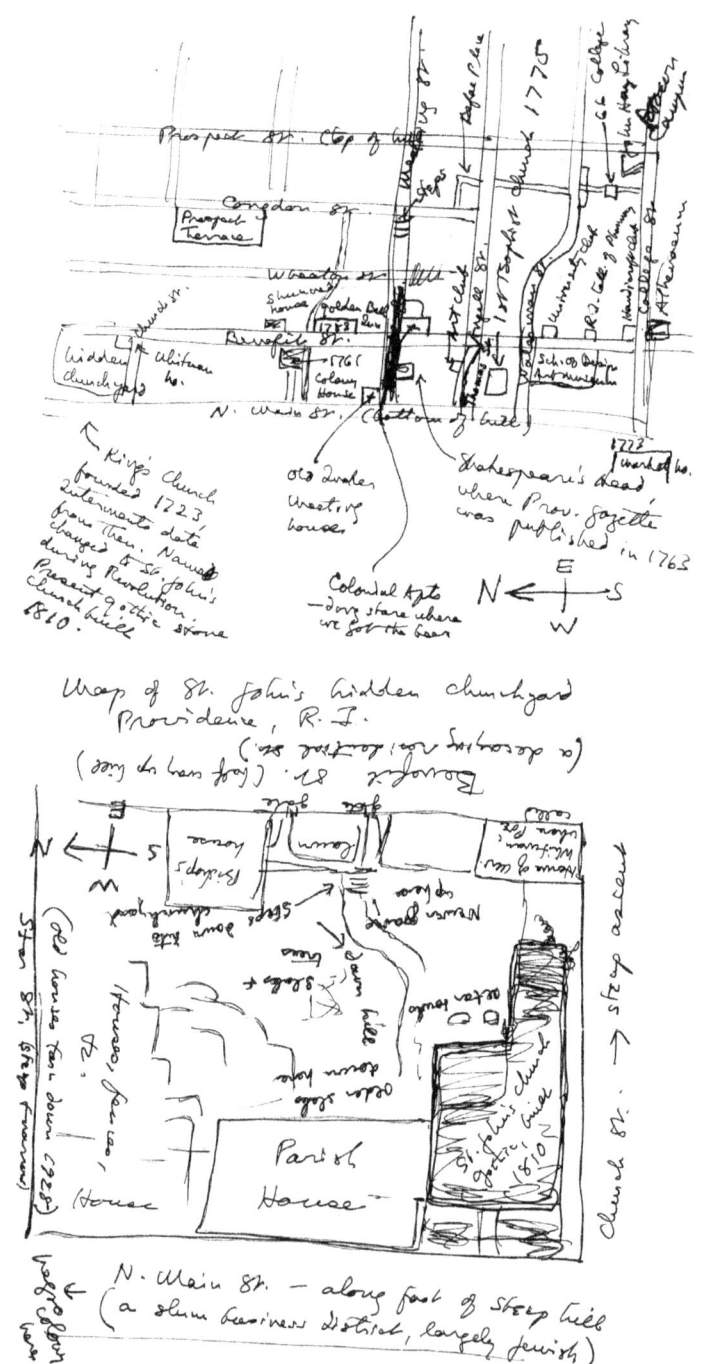

[33]   [ANS, JHL][1]

[Postmarked De Land, Fla.,
6 June 1934]

The house is undoubtedly Gothic—imitating the castle (with something of the manor-house also, perhaps), but Gothic none the less. The windows should be mullioned Gothic in type—such as were used in private houses. Diamond panes, of course. Here is a specimen. ————————>

Doorways—both exterior & interior—should have a flattened pointed arch, as in the second figure (which represents a heavy exterior door. Interior doors should be less massive. Heavy dark woodwork—panelled & perhaps carved. Windows can have two or three parts—the form shewn below is good for large ones. ¶ Porte cochere can be anywhere, but had better be at side door. Wings tend to be irregular—added quite unsymmetrically & at random . . . . houses tend to be rambling. In-

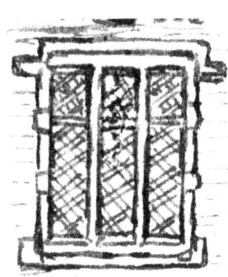

terior stairs tend to be in straight lines—right angle turns. Heavy carved balusters. There is sometimes an interior gallery extending along the 2nd story over the great hall. If the house is especially of the castellated type, there might be narrow, slit-like windows in the towers. Of course, this assumes fidelity to mediaeval Gothic types. In a Victorian house there would be all sorts of anachronisms & violations of type. ¶ Regards

P.S. R H B sends greetings, & wants to know whether you've received (& would part with) some of the originals of the drawings illustrating your tales.

Notes

1. *Front:* No picture.

[34]   [ANS, in private hands][1]

[Postmarked Ocean Grove, N.J.,
6 July 1934]

Greetings, O Right Hand of Suleiman ben Daoud![2] Glad to hear of your resent pilgrimages, but regret that sordid work closed the gates of the old mission to you. In the old days the friars were not so mercenary! Commiserations also on the new price of Juggernaut-fodder! Glad you had a good sight of San Francisco—which I suppose you know well. Yes—you'll have to train young Barlovius in the appreciation of velocity. He talks of dizzy speed at 35 mi. per hour! Congratulations on the sea-horse bargain—Belknap & I have paid 35¢ for such! Were the Chinese delicacies up to expectations? I've tried tamales, & liked them vastly—but fear they were not really representative ones. ¶ Congratulations on the cheque & the 20-emmer! ¶ Your plan for an M.A. or Ph.D. sounds magnificent—with such a distinction you can undoubtedly command a vastly increased range of opportunities—especially in the teaching line. And to a quick & thorough learner like yourself the work would really be inconsiderable. May Eblis & all the preadamite Sultans grant you the gold—& the ability to stay in one place long enough to finish your course! The Semitics course ought to be great for your Arabic soul! ¶ Trust you got my card from old St. Augustine. Took 2 days in Charleston, 1½ in Richmond, 1 afternoon in Fredericksburg, 2 d. in Washington, & 1 in Phila. Saw Poe's house in Phila., now open as museum. Nearly broke. I hit N.Y. Thursday night, & am now on a 3 d. trip to Asbury Pk. & Ocean Grove with our young friend Belknap. He will add his greetings to mine. Expect to be home before long now. ¶ Blessings— ⲟ ϳ˃ϳᲮ?·

Greetings and Salutations from the 'green and serpent haunted sea'[3] to Malik Taus. I have been meaning to write for Ages but the exigencies of pulp-hacking have virtually effaced me as a correspondent. I'll write soon, however. B.[4]

Notes

1. *Front:* Christ Church Where Washington Worshipped, Alexandria, Virginia.
2. I.e., King Solomon, who is a character in Rudyard Kipling's "The Butterfly That Stamped," in *Just So Stories*.
3. James Elroy Flecker, "The Gates of Damascus": "The dragon-green, the luminous, the dark, the serpent-haunted sea, / The snow-besprinkled wine of earth, the white-and-blue-flower foaming sea" (ll. 33–34).
4. Identified on the card with a pencil note as "probably [. . .] Barlow" but actually Frank Belknap Long.

[35] [ANS]¹

[Postmarked Providence, R.I.,
10 July 1934]

Home at last, & found your card of the 2nd awaiting me. I recalled from last year that the 3d is your anniversary—many happy returns! Trust the observance of the event was duly festive! Congratulations on the new work accomplished—& may the future outdo it! Yes—Satrap Pharnabazus did give us a great send off.[2] Hope he didn't overdo it, so that the readers will feel the story itself is a letdown! I shall probably send in the "Thing on the Doorstep" sooner or later.[3] ¶ Trust you got the joint card from Belknap & me. Upon reaching home I find myself utterly swamped by correspondence & other things to attend to. Have disposed of 5 letters & owe 17 more. And I have about 3 months of accumulated newspapers to skim over! ¶ Next convention of the National Amateur Press Association will be held in your town. ¶ Nearly froze on the bus coming home. ¶ Is "Ouroboros" safe?

Blessings— ✦ ⟿

[*On front:*] You ought to see the little coal-black kitten at the boarding-house across the back garden! Just a handful, & beginning to play.

Notes

1. *Front:* Old City Gates, St. Augustine, Fla.
2. On the table of contents, the story was hailed as "A brilliant story, cosmic in its scope, by two acknowledged masters of weird fiction."
3. In fact, HPL did not submit the story until the fall of 1936.

[36]   [ANS, in private hands][1]

[Postmarked Providence, R.I.,
c. 20 July 1934]

Hail, Lord Malik! Hope your pilgrimage to Averoigne proved pleasant, & that Old Jug managed to crawl along at least ¾ fast enough for you. After all, 70 an hour is some improvement on the average camel! ¶ Your recent composition record is enough to burn anybody out—I wonder you survive! Good luck with the 20-emmer, & congrats on the Million Dollar Doom cheque . . . . which I wish were as large as the sum mentioned! ¶ New Fantasy Fan & Marvel Tales just out—both above the average. ¶ Two-Gun Bob has visited the Carlsbad Caverns, & writes a veritable lyric masterpiece in his descriptive letter. ¶ Morton will be here Aug. 2–3–4, & I anticipate some great discussion. ¶ Trust you gave Klarkash-Ton my regards at Woods' Dry Diggings.[2] ¶ Still wrestling with the pile of accumulated stuff which I found awaiting me. The black kitten gets more fascinating every day—I must get a snap shot of him. ¶ Lately read "Peter Ashley", a novel of old Charleston.[3] Great real colour. ¶ Derleth's developing civic spirit. Has he told you of his campaign for better sidewalks in Sauk City? ¶ I continue to do most of my writing in the open, but today is so damn cold that I'll have to go in!

Blessings of Allah!

{invented characters}

Notes

1. *Front:* First Baptist Church, Providence, R.I.
2. The original name of Auburn, CA (where CAS lived), before it was renamed in the 1849 gold rush.
3. By Du Bose Heyward.

[37] [ALS, JHL]

Quinsnicket Woods–5 m. N.
of Providence. August 7, 1934

Hail, Malik!

The feline procession arranged to welcome me home was indeed impressive. Old black-&[-]white Pres. Randall of the Kappa Alpha Tau[1] was in the lead, followed by Count Magnus Osterberg (tiger) & other patriarchs of the clan. Then came the archers, & the kettle-drummers playing the Ulthar national hymn; followed by a festival chorus chanting the anthem of the fraternity.

Here we are,
The Kappa Alpha Tau boys;
We'll give a great meow, boys,
For Bast, & Sekhmet too.
Near & far,
We gather here as fellows,
And none may e'er excel
The Kappa Alpha Tau!

Here we shine,
The Kappa Alpha Tau boys;
Brave soldiers all allow, boys,
With many a victory.
Foes canine
In vain may seek to flout us,
For naught can ever rout
The Kappa Alpha Tau!

After that the mere rank & file—though a band so virile & formidable in aspect that no dog would venture near the place for a day. My new young friend Sam Perkins was too small to join these demonstrations, but he is now a little dynamo of kinetic sportiveness. I borrow him as often as possible, & the tiny black devil keeps my mind off my work . . . . . I play with him with a paper tied on a string when I ought to be writing!

But each afternoon I get out to the woods & fields where such temptations are absent. Today I have pulled the typically damn fool stunt of leaving my paper behind—hence this lousy ruled pad, the least evil purchasable at the one available roadside emporium. Programme still in a state of chaos, & have had to disappoint a revision client calling for copy on a stated date. Little though I do, I seem to be in as bad a rush as youse guys who really do something!

I presume you duly received the two joint cards from Morton & me. The Sage's visit was a highly delectable event, & we had three days of congenial debating & sightseeing. Newport was as welcome a sight as ever—though it was hellishly cold on the boat coming back. You must see this ancient town some day—as I told you, it was the urban focus of the Narragansett Country across the bay which we explored. It was in Newport that all the Narragansett planters—the Hazards, Robinsons, Updikes, Gardiners, Caseys, & so on— had their town houses. In view of our visit to the Robinson country house, I thought of you as Morton & I viewed the two Robinson town houses.

Your trip to Averoigne surely was an arduous struggle, & I regret all the various mishaps.[2] Glad to learn that Old Jug is as sound as ever after the necessary replacements. I think you'd better cling to the old boy even if he can't quite make the desiderate 90 an hour—for you & he have been through enough together to seal an inseparable friendship!

Regarding Ouroboros—tough luck, but don't worry about it.[3] Yuggoth knows I have enough to read as it is! I may find another copy some time, or you may. If you do, I'd of course be grateful for it—& if I do, I'll let you know so that you won't be on a needless quest. Meanwhile I can borrow Klarkash-Ton's copy for reading if I feel like an early perusal.

Your marketing exploits, as usual, command my congratulations & admiration. I'll bet Satrap Pharnabazus was an ass to reject Sekhmet[4]—but he'll probably take it later unless Lhen-Eighur or somebody else gets ahead of him. What you say of a new market sounds interesting, & I have half a mind to write Lhen-Eighur about it—although I hardly fancy anything of mine would be wanted. The pulp world is a cohesive unit, with laws & standards of its own, to which I have no relation whatsoever. I am not only not doing what they want, & not trying to do what they want, but actually trying my hardest to do something they don't want . . . i.e. to write sincere, disinterested phantasy.

Mortonius ought to be glad of those radio-active minerals—although you won't be able to hear from him on the subject till he returns from his present extensive wanderings. He's going to do some genealogical research in Boston, & will also visit his brother's summer camp in Frysburg, Maine. That lump of ore from Ashton-Smith Sr. must be quite a picturesque object, & I hope you'll never be reduced to the necessity of smelting it. Smith Sr. must be extremely interesting—C A S has spoken of his experiences in the tropics. It is perhaps from some of his tales of exotic scenery & strange happenings that Klarkash-Ton has derived a good share of his fantastic tastes.

Hope you'll be able to make that trip in 1935—I'm sure a week in Pawhuska will give Old Jug a second youth! Try to allot more time to ancient New England this trip—for as I assured you last year, you've merely scratched the surface so far. Think of Arkham & Kingsport—& all sorts of similar places—still unseen!

I've been invited to Boston Aug. 23d, & I think I'll go. Cook will be there—although he now has a plan of seeking professional affiliations in New York City. My host will be Edward H. Cole—one of the old amateur group. Naturally I shall also include some antiquarian sightseeing—& shall look in on our friend Brobst . . . who will be back in Providence in October.

The next really ambitious trip I shall take—although I doubt if it can be this year—is to the ancient island of *Nantucket;* which I have never seen, but where I am told an astonishing amount of colonial material survives. Morton was there 2 or 3 years ago, & says it is the most undilutedly early-American region—architecturally, socially, & otherwise—he has ever seen. I must explore it before it gets spoiled.

Enclosed is a F F of which I have a vast number of duplicates. I believe you don't see this humble struggler regularly, so fancied the issue might have at least a momentary interest. The story by me[5] is a relique of 1920—one of the few whose rejection by Wright I heartily endorse. Pardon the misprints—which I'd bitterly resent in a better story. If you look through the issue closely, you'll find your own name mentioned several times.

Just got the August W T, but have had no time to read it. I doubt if it's anything spectacular in merit. Did I mention the new magazine *Terror Tales*? According to the only one who has seen it (I haven't), it is pretty rotten—but markets are markets!

Am enclosing a cutting about Fez[6] which may please your Oriental soul. It is one of a regular travel series in the *Prov. Journal* by Marc T. Greene—a very brilliant local man whose aunt my family have always known very well.[7] He is a descendant of the famous Genl. Nathanael Greene of R.I.

Saw the second *Marvel Tales* some time ago—a vast improvement over #1. I think the story by Belknap is splendid,[8] though most dislike it. I've just sent Crawford an article on interplanetary fiction,[9] based on the synopsis I shewed you last year.

Recalling your occasional tutoring of boys for West Point, I've recently recommended you to a client in Kansas City who has a son with an eye on the academy. You may hear from her. If you render any service, be sure to ask for payment in advance or on a stated date, for this client (Mrs. Bishop) is rather slow pay, though reliable in the long run.

Well—it's getting too cold to write outdoors, so me for the homeward trail. I wish I were in Florida!

Blessings of the Preadamite Sultans

Notes

1. Because 66 College Street was on Brown University's fraternity row, HPL devised the Greek name K.A.T. (standing for *Kompsōn Ailurōn Taxis*, or "band of elegant [or well-dressed] cats") for the array of cats at the nearby boarding house. The names by which HPL referred to the cats are his own, not their real names.
2. Chronicled in EHP's "Clark Ashton Smith: A Memoir."
3. EHP lost HPL's copy of *The Worm Ouroboros*, which HPL had acquired in 1933 as a remainder for 79¢. He later offered to take $35 out of the $70 owed him for "Through the Gates of the Silver Key" from *WT* as reparation. See EHP 38.
4. I.e., "The Kiss of Sekhmet."
5. "From Beyond."
6. A city in northern inland Morocco.
7. Marc Tiffany Greene (1885–1966), reporter on Far East affairs.
8. Frank B. Long, Jr., "The Dark Beasts" (*Marvel Tales*, July/August 1934).
9. "Some Notes on Interplanetary Fiction." In the end, Crawford did not publish it.

[38]   [ALS, JHL]

Mosque on the Hill
[Postmarked 15 August 1934]

Hail, Malik!

Doubtless you received my card telling of the felicitous "Ouroboros" replacement.[1] All's well that ends well! Now I hope I get time to re-read the thing before long.

Interested to hear of your collaboration with Belknap, & am anxious to see the result. I don't think I ever saw the original MS.,[2] but I'll wager it's better for the expansion, motivation, & pepping up it has received. Now that you're worked into the technique of horror, you may try some blood-curdlers on your own hook! Hope you can land this composite with S & S on account of the quick pay & (I believe) higher rates. Belknap is becoming quite a devotee of your businesslike friend Kline, who seems to take a personal & helpful interest in his commercial strivings. By the way—I trust I mentioned the new *Terror Tales* (pub. by the *Dime Mystery* firm), which ought to prove a fair market for the products of adaptable pens. I've just read the first issue. Incredibly bad—but drawing contributions from chaps like Cave & Jacobi.[3]

Lenniger's "ultimate sales" theory is surely interesting, & seems to be founded on good sense. It does seem a waste to put time & effort into alterations when the same time & effort could go toward new work—while the unaltered old material would sell somewhere sooner or later. As you say, the application of this principle would markedly favour sincere as opposed to artificial & tailored-to-order composition—although of course it would scarcely mean that material utterly outside the pulp tradition would ever find a ready market. No modern catchpenny editor would ever accept a story like "The Willows" or "The Fall of the House of Usher" . . . . while a non-weird story of solid worth would have to remain homeless until it took the eye of a higher-grade sort of editor . . . . either a standard type, as of *Harper's* or *Scribner's*, or an aesthetic innovator like the publisher of *Story*.

Regarding my own stuff—it is a regrettable fact that I am never likely to produce anything of general acceptability. While having the highest respect for the authors of realistic fiction, & envying those who are able to accomplish the successful reflection of life in narrative form, I am sadly aware through actual experiment that this is a province definitely closed to me. The fact is, that I have absolutely nothing to say where actual, unvarnished life is concerned. The events of life are so profoundly & chronically uninteresting to me—& I know so little about them as a whole—that I can't scrape up anything in connexion with them which could possibly have the zest & tension & suspense needed to form a real story. That is, I am incurably blind to dramatic or fictional values except where violations of the natural order are concerned. Of course, I understand *objectively* what those values are, & can apply them with fair success to the criticism & revision of others' work; but they do not take hold of my imagination sufficiently to find creative expression. When I try to think up some vivid sequence of actual events I simply come to nothing. The spark of creation & instinctive dramatic arrangement simply isn't there. I'm not deeply interested, & I can't get deeply interested. What is more—I don't know enough about life to be an effective exponent of it. On account of my early ill-health & naturally retiring disposition my contacts with mankind—& with its varied aspects, folkways, idioms, attitudes, & standards—have been extremely limited; so that there are probably very few people outside the extreme rustic class who are more fundamentally unsophisticated than myself. I don't know what different kinds of people do & think & feel & say—their lives, languages, values, & technical processes are as remote from me as the manners & customs of the Cingalese. Now it is impossible to write about one's spatial neighbours as one would write about the Cingalese—as remotely & objectively, that is—so that the would-be realist who does not know life well is perforce compelled to resort to imitation—copying what he picks up from the doubtful & artificial media of books, plays, newspaper reports, & the like. That is what Long does—but I am too actual a realist in psychology to be able to do this. I know so damned well that the pictures one gets from books are unreal & distorted, that I *can't* sit down & transcribe those second-hand (& probably erroneous) impressions with all the assumed convincingness of one who really knows about them. I know that I *don't* know about the people I'd be writing about, hence I can't put up a jaunty bluff that their ways & speech & thoughts are familiar to me. Let us say that I'm called upon to portray the way one of your dashing young clubman-detectives responds to a given situation. Now I'm not a dashing young clubman-detective & never was one—nor have I ever been acquainted with any. Obviously, I don't know how the hell one of them (assuming that there *are* such persons) would react to any given situation. How, then, can I portray any of their deeds? If I copy from other writers I'll probably be copying artificial gestures remote from reality—& *knowing* this, I can't put any zest into copying. And this is true of so many different types of person—there are so *few* types that I really understand (& I'm not sure that I understand even them)—that I could never piece out the dramatis personae of any well-rounded work of fiction. My handicap is—all apart from the basic lack of interest—really twofold. First, my acquaintance with varied phases of life is too small for effective literary use. Second, I lack the natural faculty of imagination which gives the genuine innate author the instinctive power to understand & portray what different sorts of people would feel & think & say & do in various given situations. Long also lacks this faculty, but he won't admit. All his characters are little duplicate Belknaps in thought, manner, & speech. But I *realise* my lack & can't go ahead weaving vacuity when I *know* it's vacuity.

However—the crucial thing is my lack of interest in ordinary life. No one ever wrote a story yet without some real emotional drive behind it—& I have not that drive except where violations of the natural order . . . . defiances & evasions of time, space, & cosmic law . . . . are concerned. Just why this is so I haven't the slightest idea—it simply *is* so. I am interested only in broad pageants—historic streams—orders of biological, chemical, physical, & astronomical organisation–& the only conflict which has any deep emotional significance to me is that of the *principle of freedom or irregularity or adventurous opportunity against the eternal & maddening rigidity of cosmic law* . . . . especially the laws of *time*. Individuals & their fortunes within natural law move me very little. They are all momentary trifles bound from a common nothingness toward another common nothingness. Only the cosmic framework itself—or such individuals as symbolise principles (or defiances of principles) of the cosmic framework—can gain a deep grip on my imagination & set it to work creating. In other words, the only "heroes" I can write about are *phenomena*. The cosmos is such a closely-locked round of fatality—with everything prearranged—that nothing impresses me as *really dramatic* except some sudden & abnormal *violation of that relentless inevitability* . . . . something which cannot exist, but which can be imagined as existing. Hence the type of thing I try to write. Naturally, I am aware that this forms a very limited special field so far as mankind en masse is concerned; but I believe (as pointed out in that *Recluse* article) that the field is an authentic one despite its subordinate nature. This protest against natural law, & tendency to weave visions of escape from orderly nature, are characteristic & eternal factors in human psychology, even though very small ones. They exist as permanent realities, & have always expressed themselves in a typical form of art from the earliest fireside folk tales & ballads to the latest achievements of Blackwood or Machen or de la Mare or Dunsany. That art exists—whether the majority like it or not. It is small & limited, but real—& there is no reason why its practitioners should be ashamed of it. Naturally one would *rather* be a broad artist with power to evoke beauty from every phase of experience—but when one unmistakably *isn't* such an artist, there's no sense in bluffing & faking & pretending that one *is*. It being settled that I'm a little man instead of a big man, I'd a damn sight prefer to let it go frankly at that—& try to be a good little man in my narrow, limited, miniature fashion—than to cover up & pretend to be a bigger man than I am. Such a pretence can lead only to futile overreaching, pompous vacuity, & an ultimate loss of whatever little good I might have accomplished had I stuck to the one small province which was really mine. I am naturally a narrow specialist of very limited vision & power, & the only way I can ever create anything even half good is to stick to the area within which I have an actually genuine motivation—namely, the area of the cosmic & the weird. It I ever outgrow this area, it must be by very slow & gradual degrees; & only in the direction, & to the extent, that nature dictates. For example—it is barely conceivable that my longing for cosmic liberation might some time turn from the attempt to depict actual violations of nature to the realistic (but dream-overcast) portraiture of some fellow-dreamer with similar longings . . . . detailing dream-life *as* dream-life & constructing some half-mystical but non-supernatural narrative like Machen's "Hill of Dreams" or Dunsany's "Curse of the Wise Woman." But this must come only if it *wants* to come. Literature cannot be forced. Nothing really worth reading was ever deliberately or intentionally—or even wholly consciously—written. Art is not what one resolves to say, but what insists on saying itself through one. It has nothing to do with commerce, editorial demand, or popular approval. The only elements concerned are the artist & the emotions working within him. Of course, there is a business of magazine-purveying which is perfectly honest in itself, & a worthy field for those with a knack for it. I wish I had the knack. But this isn't the thing I'm interested in. If I had the knack, it would be something performed entirely apart from my serious work—just as my present revisory activities are. However, I haven't the knack, & the field is so repugnant to me that it's about the last way I'd ever choose to gain shelter & clothing & nourishment. Any other kind of a legitimate job would be preferable to my especial tastes. I dislike this trade because it bears a mocking external resemblance to the real literary composition which is the only thing (apart from sundry ancestral traditions) I take seriously in life.

Although greatly encouraged by the comments on "The Thing on the Doorstep", I do not think I had better attempt any more writing till my nerves are in better shape. I must finish an especially disagreeable revision job on which I am engaged, & must do more toward getting both the pulp models & my own previous attempts out of my head. Also, I must read more. Then, after a suitable fallow period, I *may* (though one can't tell) have another such creative burst as I had in 1920.[4] If not—that's simply that. It can't be helped. I may be as thoroughly played out as Blackwood now appears to be. I don't know—& there's nothing to do but experiment .... & keep as clear as possible of external criticisms & rebuffs. That's why I don't submit the "Doorstep" to Wright. For the present, then, I am a reader & appreciator rather than a writer. God knows I want a job—but I want it to be *anything*—elevator man, pickaxe artist, night-watchman, stevedore, what the hell—*except writing*. Anything except a parody on the only thing in life that means anything to me.

Speaking of reading—which I was a while back—I've just tackled some books by William Hope Hodgson lent me by H. C. Koenig. Having previously read & disliked a book of Hodgson's—"Carnacki, the Ghost[-]Finder"—I was totally unprepared for the excellence of this older work of the same author. "The Boats of the Glen Carrig" (1907), though a bit weak at the end, has much of the subtle, brooding power of "The Willows", & "The House on the Borderland" (which I'm half through) measures up well to it. One more awaits me—"The Ghost Pirates", with a frontispiece by Sime.[5]

Glad to hear of the marvels wrought upon Old Jug by your necromantically gifted brother. Iä! Shub-Niggurath! You & he will yet have the old boy doing the desiderate 90 per! Anyhow, I feel it would be a mistake to cast aside such an old friend—so I heartily endorse the idea of retaining him as a secondary chariot even if you feel forced to indulge in a newer & fleeter steed.

Well, well—you surely are becoming a prince of collaborators .... Long, Two-Gun, & now Kline again![6] Congrats on "Breath of Doom", & let us hope that its happy fate may be shared by the other allegedly "slow" pieces. The analysis of your sales certainly shows a gratifying emancipation from the clutches of Satrap Pharnabazus—& it can't be long before you achieve that significant 50th sale to which you look forward. I shall be listening for the camel-bells of Old Jug in the spring—& hope that eventually you may achieve that happy state of fictional "arrivedness" whereby a few lucky devils get such high prices for a moderate output that they can live in affluence without perpetual slaving. Indeed—I may say that I don't merely *hope* but positively *expect*—since your ability to analyse needs & adapt means to ends is too great to lead to anything but success in a chosen field.

Tried to introduce my little black friend Sam Perkins in the Kappa Alpha Tau last night, but he humiliated me by shewing hostility to old Pres. Randall—hissing, growling, & arching his little back. Only 2 months old, but an instinctive scrapper already! Pres. Randall, on his part, did no more than dignifiedly hiss & walk slowly away. Little Sam also tried to pick a fight with Vice-President Osterberg—a huge fighting tiger—but Mr. Osterberg likewise was too much of a gentleman to hit back at so small an opponent. These old K.A.T. boys always pick a fellow of their size when indulging in pugilism!

And so it goes. I shall be glad to see Cook next week—as well as my host Cole. Haven't seen the latter since 1931.

With all blessings of the Prophet— ꙭꚉꚉꙮ

Notes

1. RHB had just given HPL a copy of the book (see *O Fortunate Floridian* 162).
2. "Shape of Horror." It is unknown if the story was published, or if it appeared under only one byline (or pseudonym).
3. Hugh B. Cave's "Terror Island" appeared in the first issue (September 1934), Carl Jacobi's "Satan's Roadhouse" in the second (October 1934).
4. That year, HPL wrote thirteen stories (some in collaboration), most quite short.
5. HPL read Hodgson's *The Night Land* (1912) in November (see *ES* 666) but does not discuss it in letters to EHP.
6. EHP published three collaborations with Kline, including installments in the round-robin story "Cosmos.". EHP wrote no collaboration with Robert E. Howard. Clark Ashton Smith gave "The House of the Monoceros" to EHP, who (with Smith's permission) made a few revisions and published it under his own name. It was not a collaboration.

[39]   [ANS, JHL][1]

[Postmarked Salem, Mass.,
24 August 1934]

Hail, Malik! The old gang assembles once more, & wishes that you & old Jug were here to expedite transportation & feverish inspiration. Recd. your card just before hopping off. Good luck with the 20 emmer & other current produce. Hope Jug came out of its intestinal bath triumphantly. After all, every rival fades in comparison to the arch-Jug! ¶ Blessings

𝄞 ♒︎☞﹖⌒

This is not the Juggernaut but was a very jiggly trolley car in Charleston, man.
W. Paul Cook

Notes

1. *Front:* Bunker Hill Monument, Charlestown, Boston, Mass.

[40]   [ALS, JHL]

Ancient Nantucket
—Aug. 31, 1934

Dear Malik:—

Picked your card up as I passed through Prov. en route to the second stage of my present outing, & the subsequent welcome epistle has just been forwarded. As for "Ouroboros"—don't for gawd's sake bother about a trifle! Barlow's copy reached me long before either of us had any word from you, & my bookplate is irrevocably stuck in. If you ever want to make any ceremonious gesture of atonement, there are plenty of other books that would do just as well. For example—if you ever came across a copy of Blackwood's "Incredible Adventures" & shoved it my way, I'd effuse all over the place with fawning gratitude. Or M. P. Shiel's "The Pale Ape & Other Stories" [*sic*]. Or Gerald Biss's "The Door of the Unreal" . . . . or Lewis's "The Monk".[1] But don't pay a high price for any of these. It's a microscopic incident anyhow.

Well—by this time you've had some bulletins of my recent motions. The Boston sojourn was pleasant, & I got to ancient Marblehead (Kingsport) on Saturday. Cook, however, had one of his increasingly frequent nervous collapses & had to hasten back to Vermont. The Coles brought me home Sunday, but I did no more than stay over night before taking the New Bedford coach & Nantucket boat Monday.

And what a place is Nantucket! I *thought* I had seen something of colonial antiquity before—but just wait till I take you & Old Jug to this utterly unchanged fragment of early America! Ædepol! There is absolutely nothing else like it—& to think I never visited it before . . . . a place only 90 miles (6 hrs. by coach & ship) from my own door! Compared with this town Providence & St. Augustine & the Vieux Carré are positively modernistic! Whole networks of cobblestoned streets with nothing but colonial houses on either side—narrow, garden-bordered lanes—ancient belfries—picturesque waterfront—*everything* that the antiquarian would ask! I'm seeing the whole thing in a week's sojourn. Have a 3d story room at The Overlook (an ancient tavern with small-paned windows &c), with a splendid view of the town & harbour & sea. I've explored old houses, the 1746 windmill, the Hist. Soc. Museum, the whaling museum, &c.—& am doing every inch of the quaint streets & alleys on foot. Also took motor sightseeing tour around the entire island—viewing ancient Siasconset (a fishing village with tiny cottages & rambling lanes, now a summer resort) & other points. Yes—& just to echo faintly your Mt. Hamilton astronomical experience I had a fine view of Saturn through the 5″ refractor of the Maria Mitchell observatory. Yesterday I suffered greatly from the cold, but today it is warm again. One thing I'm strongly tempted to do is to follow the local fashion & hire a *bicycle* for a ramble around. I haven't been on a wheel in 20 years, & the idea has a subtly rejuvenating quality about it. In my youth I was a veritable bicycle centaur. Home on the evening of the 3d—& the next morning my aunt starts off for a fortnight in Ogunquit, Maine. I can't conceive of anybody going *north* at this time of year—but I suppose she knows what she wants!

So young Anger has already been to see you! Hope I didn't foist a nuisance on you by giving him your address. He seemed a very likely youth, amply deserving of encouragement. No doubt he can help to spread your fame. He has just written how grateful he is for suggestions that you gave him.

Congratulations, as usual, on your recent successes! The cesspool of the Dionaean Aphrodite is surely the one great meal-ticket in these neo-

Restoration days[2]—& I trust that the wallowings of Messrs. Farrell,[3] D'Artois, & Ismeddin may prove a dependable source of revenue! Good luck with the Kline & Long collaborations[4]—& may that 50th sale & 100th story be not long deferred!

I envy you the Mt. Hamilton trip, & am glad the soak was purged of his green snakes, pink elephants, & Brundage cover-designs in time to participate consciously.[5] Old Jug certainly help up his end of the expedition nobly! The largest telescope I've ever looked through is the 12″ of the Ladd Observatory in Providence. My own—on a none too firm altazimuth tripod—is a 3″. The 5″ of the Mitchell Observatory here in Nantucket is splendid for its size—an old-timer from the famous Alvan Clark works[6] which also produced the Lick.

As usual, I hear with the keenest interest of work on Mighty Juggernaut. Your brother is surely an invaluable fellow-wizard! It is rather dramatic to learn, at this late date, that the speedometer has been slandering Old Jug's potentialities in the velocity line—you'll have a keener respect for the old boy after this! After all, you may be able to get along without the 90-an-hour transit—especially since you see you can hit 60 now & then. I don't think you need to worry about that Hup-8[7] back in the land of John Broken Axe! What you say of that possible caravan of necromancers invading Mexico sounds alluring indeed, & I trust that events may eventually shape themselves in its favour. I'd surely enjoy such a jaunt to the limit—especially if it included a pause at the Carlsbad Caverns, which Two-Gun has so vividly described to me. Here's hoping I have the cash when you have the opportunity!

As for my inability to write realism or pseudo-realism—I gravely doubt whether I can ever shake it off; since my temperament is never likely to take me out into the world of varied experience very far, while my interest & imagination are curiously limited. Long may branch out in time—for he is relatively young, & is certainly interested in scores of worldly things which simply put me to sleep. But Grandpa isn't likely to diverge far at his age! Regarding mythical pseudo-realistic types like the "clubman-detective"—these are so unconvincing to me as characters that I could never make them convincing to anyone else. They don't represent anything I have either encountered or imagined—& when I depart from reality I have to turn to some form of unreality which is vivid & authentic to me. What I know of detailed human activities is very slight—& what I care about them is slighter still, except so far as the element of historic pageantry is concerned. Nothing but the element of *nature-defiance*—especially *time*-defiance—sets off the spring that starts my creative imagination running. Of the crimes & drunken hilarity & inane amusements of modern urban life nothing captivates my fancy. Set the calendar back a century & bring in some event involving old Nantucket or Providence or Charleston life, & my interest grows—since the drama of the time-stream will then figure—but even then my knowledge & technique are insufficient for the task of handling. If I *could* grind out unconvincing hokum to order I certainly *would*—but I know, after repeated experiments dating from 1921, that I can't. The element of *interest* plays a larger part in even the most mechanical hack writing than is commonly supposed. Take that out, & even the most industrious artisan is at least partly stalled. Also—the ambition to write seriously is a handicap to the hack. I think that, as a rule, the most successful hacks are those who stick to their trade with no thought of literary creation. Some can bridge the gulf, but the average plodder can be only one or the other—a pulp-producer or a serious writer. The writer must have no thought for either finances (in connexion with writing) or public demand. To him there are only two elements—what he has to say & how he wants to say it. His only concern is for *intrinsic excellence*—regardless of returns or popular taste. Literarily, the only thing for us to do just now is to keep quiet. I must try to get more leisure from correspondence & revision, & avoid the sort of nervous collapses that I used to have—& that Cook still has. First of all, to dispose of the loathsome prologue-writing & novel-revising job which stares me in the face when I get home. Then more reading & absorption—& then we shall see. I may eventually send Pharnabazus the "Doorstep", but I don't want the effect of a rejection just now. He is wholly commercial in his outlook—as witness his complaints against my "long" stories when he published gallons of utter drivel . . . . vast long serials . . . . by his trashy favourites. At a later period I may have more patience with that kind of thing—but just now my nerves are not in the right shape to confront it. This is the season for me to *absorb* impressions—not put them forth. I'm still revelling in the discovery of William Hope Hodgson—which, as I told you, I owe to the always-accomodating Koenig. Well—we shall see what we shall see. It's curious how the rejection of "At the Mountains of Madness" slowed up my whole writing career. I was the better for a pause between 1908[8] & 1917, & may be better for one between 1933 & gawd knows when! The more I stand off as a critical non-participant, the more avoidable faults I see in my stuff. I shall always make mistakes & perpetrate crudities, but certain specific types of error are not likely to reappear.

Sam Perkins is certainly a great boy—he'll doubtless be a full-fledged K.A.T. member by the time you & Jug get around—although he's got himself in bad with Pres. Randall & Vice-Pres. Osterberg by offering to fight them! I have apologised on his behalf to the old fellows, & they've promised not to blackball him when his name comes up. The brashness of youth must be excused! In Boston I encountered another likely sprig—at my host's home—who can give Sam a run for his money. This young gentleman is named Peter Ivan, & is a tiger angora of just about Sam's age. What a boy! He tears about continually, climbs up & down everybody, & then curls up to sleep in an ornamental basket which he chose & appropriated without asking anybody's permission. Like Sam, he shows fight toward his elders—the elders in question being my host's other two felidae—Napoleon & the Duke of Wellington. Peter was in my lap or around my feet during the bulk of my visit. Here in

Nantucket my greatest friends are three coal-black & precisely identical brothers at the restaurant where I eat. They were born last spring, & their perfect blackness & utter similarity caused them all to be retained. One is especially friendly—& jumps in my lap as I eat. He would like to ascend another stage & participate in the repast, but I discourage him from that procedure—preferring to treat him to select morsels where he is.

And so it goes. Yesterday I did a lot of historical & architectural research at the Athenaeum (1808—now a public library), but it was so damn cold that I could scarcely jot down notes. In the evening I draped a heavy blanket over my suit, but couldn't use my fingers very well. Today it is warmer, & I am out in the sun on Windmill Hill above the town. On my left is the ancient mill (1746) with its arms slowly turning—on my right the low rolling country that stretches 7 miles to the open sea. Good old Nantucket! Just as it has always been! And in fancy I can see the whalers of yesterday at the wharves, & the tarry sailors & beaver-hatted captains & merchants & drays & chaises & calashes in the cobblestoned streets. Here, indeed, is that *defiance of time* which stirs my imagination more strongly than anything else in the world! ¶ Peace of Allah upon thee— ✍

[Enclosures: 7 postcards][9]

Notes

1. HPL did acquire a copy of Lewis's *The Monk* in New York in December 1934.
2. HPL alludes to EHP's comment that *Spicy Detective* was popular among collegians, and that he could easily publish stories there.
3. Glenn Farrell, a character in EHP's "Silver Peacock." He appeared in ten stories by EHP.
4. "Volunteers from Venus" (with Otis Adelbert Kline). For the collaboration with Long see EHP 38n2.
5. EHP had written (21 August 1934): "I was subduing an old school mate with a mild case of delerium [*sic*] tremens. He stoutly alleged there were three more or less nude, lewd women pirouetting around my study, and asserted that I was a vile perjurer when I maintained that I could not find even one woman in the sacred preci[c]nts. However, I finally got the alcoholic to take a nap, and at 5 PM he was sufficiently recovered to join my party bound for Mt. Hamilton and a peep thru the 36″ refractor, (at the moon) and a look at Saturn" (TLS, JHL).
6. Alvan Clark (1804–1887), American astronomer and telescope maker. The firm Alvan Clark & Sons ground lenses for refracting telescopes.
7. Referring to a Hupmobile, an eight-cylinder automobile built by the Hupp Motor Car Company.
8. When HPL wrote "The Alchemist."
9. The Sounding Sea; Colonial Homes, Nantucket, Mass.; Sunset in the Harbor, Nantucket, Mass.; Harbor View, Nantucket, Mass.; The Chopping Bowl, Nantucket, Mass.; Colonial Mansions, Nantucket, Mass.; Moors End, Colonial Doorway, Nantucket, Mass.

[41]   [ALS, University of Minnesota]

Septʳ 7, 1934

Hail, Malik:—

Reached home Monday night & found your two cards awaiting me. Congratulations on the continued achievements! Hope you & W P C can get together on the private printing project. Cook, of course, has no press of his own; but is working in conjunction with Walter J. Coates of *Driftwind,* who not only has a press but makes a specialty of publishing books for authors. Any job thrown to Coates through Cook would probably redound to the latter's advantage.

Glad you enjoyed the Greene travel articles. This gifted author *has* written very vividly of Singapore in years past—when contributing to the *Sunday Journal*—although no articles on this region appeared in the recent *Daily Journal* series. I have no cuttings of his Singapore articles—& don't know whether or not the Journal Co. or the author himself could supply any. If you'd care to get in touch with the latter you could drop him a line—Marc T. Greene, % Prov. Journal Co., Providence, R. I. I don't know exactly where he is now—though I fancy it may be Boothbay, Ma., where his family own a cottage. As I said, I don't know him personally, though my aunts & late mother knew his aunt from girlhood. If you wanted to establish a quasi-personal touch in writing, you could say that his work had been brought to your attention by the son of an old friend of his aunt, Mrs. Nellie B. Pettis.[1] Actually, his travel material is about as interesting as any I've ever read—& I don't say that merely because he is a Rhode-Islander, either! On the chance that other specimens may be of interest to you, I am sending under separate cover all the rest of the recent series that I can find—& am enclosing one which treats of your own Golden Gate. Also—I'm sending an advertising booklet of a restaurant near Belknap's place whose Saracenic colour may appeal to you.

Your projected story[2] certainly sounds impressive, & I hope it may develop successfully,

And now to tackle the 16 letters I owe!

Blessings——— ℛ ℛℐℐℛℒ

P.S. In Nantucket I rode a bicycle for the first time in 20 years. It quite brought back my youth! ¶ Did I mention that H. Warner Munn's father has just been killed by a hit-&-run motorist? Damned shame!

Notes

1. Nellie Bissell Pettis (1859–1939) of Providence, RI.
2. "The Dragon's Shadow."

[42]   [ALS, JHL]

Septr 17, 1934

Hail, 𝓛𝓾𝓵𝓸!

All communications duly received—& you have no doubt meanwhile received my latest missive, plus the array of travel cuttings. I am certainly glad that you found the Nantucket material of interest, & can assure you that you will find the island no disappointment when you get there (may which time be not remote!). I'm enclosing herewith a booklet & folder which will add a few points concerning this unparallelled haven of the past.[1] If you'd like to read more on the subject, I'd be glad to lend you two smallish books—one on Nantucket history & the other on the folklore—which I acquired during my journey.[2]

My aunt will return from Ogunquit tomorrow, thus ending my solitary reign over these ancient precincts. At the present moment I am afflicted with dual pangs—an attack of indigestion which had me in bed two days, & grief at the death on Sept. 10 (apparently from natural causes) of my little black friend across the garden. Little Sam Perkins paid me an all-afternoon call as recently as the 7th—purring as he climbed all over me & played with the papers on my desk—but on the morning of the 10th he was found lifeless in the shrubbery he so loved to haunt. No sign of injury—& the cause still a mystery. He had a spell of illness early in August, but had fully recovered from that. Blessed little Piece of the Night! Born in June, gone in September. He never had to know what a savage winter is like!

> The ancient garden seems at night
> A deeper gloom to bear,
> As if some silent shadow's blight
> Were hov'ring in the air.
>
> With hidden griefs the grasses sway,
> Unable quite to word them—
> Remembering from yesterday
> The little paws that stirr'd them.[3]

Before his demise Little Sam had made his peace with the huge Toms on the shed roof, being duly initiated into the Kappa Alpha Tau. I saw him many times curled up within the sacred precincts. But now the elders drowse alone once more.

Congratulations on the cheque—& I hope the collaboration with Belknap will prove profitable. Belknap himself—largely with Kline's aid—has sold a surprising amount of work recently; having apparently gone into business with a complete relinquishment—or at least suspension—of his literary ambitions. Glad to hear that Pawang Ali[4] & Singapore are coming along well. Some day I hope you'll be able to travel in the Orient which, at a distance, you have visualised so vividly. And so the editorial diagram-merchants insist on a simplification & Occidentalisation of your style! Alas! It is certainly true that nothing can gain wide pulp consideration unless it becomes frankly juvenile! When I think of the harm done to literature by pulp influences—the number of writers withdrawn from or incapacitated for serious artistic creation through the pressure of this tawdry octopus—I do not wonder at my own venomous hatred of the whole "popular fiction" world!

I trust the massed efforts of the House of Price have by this time accomplished the needed miracles of surgery in connexion with good old Juggernaut. So faithful a steed surely deserves all the tender care that can be bestowed upon it! May it next year climb the ancient hill of Providence once more, cross the coastal plain to historic New Bedford (rich in whaling memories), find a comfortable stall between decks of one of the island packets, & eventually snort forth upon the ancient wharves & through the winding lanes of Nantucket!

Your remarks on Model T's & their economic possibilities are being filed for careful reference, & with appreciative gratitude. What a pity, these noble old standbys are manufactured no more! From my angle, the only reason why such a prehistoric Jug would not be an economy is that it would require storage expenses *all* the time, whereas my trips consume only a *small part* of the time. The element of *pure transportation* on all my trips this year—Florida, Boston, Nantucket—has not come up to fifty dollars combined. Could a T-Jug be maintained *& lodged* over an equal period for less than that? Garage board bills are the big problem. When one has a place to *store* a car, these T opportunities can mean a real saving. Otherwise, it seems to me that the economy is at least debatable. As to the mechanics—I am not, like Belknap, doubtful of my ability to *run* the thing. The point is that I could never locate & rectify ailments, & select & insert new parts myself, as you can. This would make my repair expenses considerable—having to call in a Jug-doctor when anything went wrong. How much I'd learn in time would remain to be seen. But alas—it may be that even the 'bus trips—& still more—will have to go soon. Outgo persists, income sinks to invisibility! Well—in the 13 or 14 years that my health has allowed me to get about, I've seen quite a bit of the elder world . . . . . enough to fit out a pretty fair set of images & recollections!

I envy you your recent glimpses through large telescopes. My sight of Saturn through the 5″ glass in Nantucket was just enough to be tantalising. The largest telescope I have ever looked through is the 12″ of the local Ladd Observatory.

Well—good luck with Pawang Ali, & may the dinars continue to pour in! Astaghifir, & all that![5]

Next Day—the 18th
. . . . Awaiting my Aunt's Return

Got yours of the 12th just as I was about to mail the preceding & enclosed parts of this communication. Note the typically Oriental thrift with which I have burglarised the envelope in an effort to make it do added duty! Glad to hear of Pawang Ali's doughty deeds—& interested to note, from your Greene letter, what minute points you are including. Surely this ought to be a triumph of verisimilitude, convincing every reader that you have lived in Singapore not less than a decade. I hope Greene will reply. Incidentally—his aunt's name is *PETTIS*, not *Paltis* . . . . but in view of my handwriting I don't wonder at the latter version. I must get the habit of printing out important proper names. As for Singapore—it keeps running in my head that the Natl. Am. Press Assn. used to have a member there—a native, but of English education. I'll try to see if I can find his name on some of the old lists.[6] He's no longer in the association—but might conceivably be reached through his old address. I never wrote or heard from him, but possibly mailed him amateur papers once or twice. He'd probably be glad to give any data he could. Another source of exotic data is the magazine *Adventure*—which had a question department & a staff of expert travellers. Also—an inveterate geographer & student of far-away life (also a story writer & critic—formerly connected with the Home Correspondence School) is Belknap's & my old friend Arthur Leeds, 2736 W. 16th St., Brooklyn, N.Y. ¶ After a search, I can't find that Singaporean's address. ¶

So the old Algiers' plain home cooking isn't exotic enough for you! Well—maybe they'd let you invade the kitchen in person & superintend the creation of something really bizarre! Right at this moment, though, I'd take the joint just as it is—or even milder! Gawd, how the old belly is backfiring! I've just graduated from crackers & Postum to Heinz's Scotch Broth (mutton & barley soup with vegetables)—which I seem to stand so far. But my favourite meat-balls & spaghetti will have to wait a while!

Glad to hear all the production dope—& I'm especially interested in the tale set in my beloved St. Augustine. I must get that when it appears. Too bad the old fort is in such respectable hands, so that you can't use its dungeons somehow. But how about unsuspected nether crypts—lying latent for a couple of centuries? Still, that might not accord with the particular plot in question. I didn't notice the Zorayda by name,[7] since modern real-estate Hispano-Moresque[8] is hardly what I was after—but I suppose I must have seen its facade. Ponce de Leon—Alcazar—Cordova—the whole neighbourhood is full of the stuff. To my mind, the synthetic arabesque towers of this region are best seen from afar—especially from the base of that long basin or lagoon which runs south from St. Francis St. to South St, & which was artificially formed from the upper end of the old Maria Sanchez Creek. Against a gorgeous sunset sky those old towers—plus the dome of the ornate Presbyterian church—do make just about as nifty & dream-waking a combination as can well be imagined!

Your recent dinner guest surely must have been a startling fount of provocative arcana. American civilisations contemporary with the European wars of Neanderthals & Cro-Magnons—canals & sea-walls of a lost continent atop the Andes—mesozoic mankind—Ædepol, I grow dizzy with such revelations! Of course, it may be that the bulk of cautious scientific opinion does not fully endorse some of these inferences . . . . . perhaps finding other explanations of the facts . . . . . but anyhow the challenge to speculation is stimulating!

Trust you can get some good Manila lore. Since you've been there in person, you have more to start with than Singapore offers.

Raining like hell—maybe my aunt won't come home today after all, since she was to motor with a friend. But I guess I'll keep the ice card up & get some butter just the same. I have private economies which my aunt can't parallel—I take no ice when alone, since there are things enough to eat which don't require it. Condensed milk—cheese—who the devil needs to bother with butter? This reminds me—I ought to look on the steps & see if the milk has come. It was to be resumed beginning today. Later I must don suitably disreputable attire & slosh down the hill for supplies. The damn grocery won't deliver orders under one dollar—or rather, it soaks you a dime extra for so doing. Same joint where we stopped to get the makings of that memorable curry feast last year. Which reminds me—Brobst ought to be back in town next month.

And so it goes. Wish little Sam Perkins were back to purr & curl up on my desk! ¶ Blessings & the Peace

Notes

1. *Whaling Museum of the Nantucket Historical Association in the Old Candle House at the Head of the Steamboat Wharf* ([Nantucket, MA]: [Nantucket Historical Association], [not before 1930]).

2. Probably William Francis Macy (1867–?), *The Story of Old Nantucket* (Nantucket: The Inquirer and Mirror, 1915; *LL* 630); William Francis Macy, ed., *The Nantucket Scrap Basket: Being a Collection of Characteristic Stories and Sayings of the People of the Town and Island of Nantucket, Massachusetts* (Nantucket: The Inquirer and Mirror, 1916; *LL* 631).

3. Now published as "Little Sam Perkins."

4. EHP wrote seven stories about the detective Pâwang Ali for *Clues*.

5. *Istighfar*, an essential part of worship in Islam, is the act of seeking forgiveness from Allah, generally done by repeating the Arabic words *astaghfirullah*, meaning "I seek forgiveness from Allah."

6. A search of available rosters did not find a member living in Singapore. HPL may have been thinking of James Guerrero Wingo of the Philippines, who tried to join NAPA in 1922, was a member in 1924–25 and then again in 1926–27.

7. Villa Zorayda (or the Zorayda Castle), the house in St. Augustine, FL, built in 1883 by eccentric Boston millionaire Franklin W. Smith as his winter home. It was inspired by the 12th-century Moorish Alhambra Palace in Granada, Spain, and named after a princess in Washington Irving's *Tales of the Alhambra*.

8. *Moresque,* an obsolete alternative to *Moorish.* By itself it pertains to stylized plant-based forms of tendrils and leaves in ornament and decoration in Renaissance Europe derived from the arabesque patterns of Islamic ornament.

[43]   [ALS, JHL]

Out on Prospect Terrace

Oct. 8, 1934

Dear Malik:—

Current bulletins at hand—& I must congratulate you on passing the 50 mark! Glad Pawang is safely on his way—& that Greene has furnished the desired Singapore data. You can use that in the sequel! I'll send along that Singapore amateur's address if I ever find it, but fear it's in one of the issues which I no longer have. Brobst isn't here yet—it's merely sometime this month that he's due back—but when he gets here I'll transmit your salaam & reading advice. Indeed, I'll pick those magazines up if I can find them on the stands.

You'll have to get to Nantucket some time! Yes—the old anti-motor law was repealed in 1918—largely to legalise the use of motor coaches to replace the narrow-gauge railway to Siasconset, which vanished in 1917. It was losing money, so they tore it up & sent the equipment to the U.S. Army in France . . . where rails & such-like were needed. Old Jug would find some excellent roads on Nantucket.

I must see that St. Augustine tale. And so it laps over on to Anastasia Island? The deserted beach just across the island from the bridge was a favourite haunt of mine—both by day & by full moonlight. I likewise visited the alligator farm, & the old Spanish well & chimney further south.

Your experiences with the batteries surely was both arduous & discouraging—but I trust you gained sufficient knowledge to repay you for the trouble, worry, & futile outcome. Your starting was a triumph of combined ingenuity & good fortune—& now I trust you will be exempt from electrical anxieties for some time to come. The new mat & window form still further steps toward the formation of a fresh vehicle—& I'm sure I'd hesitate vastly before casting the old boy aside in favour of some parvenu whose only added virtue is mere commonplace speed!

I note the remarks on T's & their approximate operative costs. Storage space surely is a great asset, even when it's in the open air—though a New England winter would probably knock hell out of even the hardiest Juggernaut left out in it. What you say of the advantages of Jug travel is certainly true, & if I were in better shape financially I'd attempt something of the sort. You have assuredly made the most of your faithful chariot!

Meanwhile your writing programme staggers me as usual. The new Farley collaboration[1] is likely to increase still further your always ample versatility—

for Chinese tongs must form quite a study in themselves!

It's certainly thoughtful of you to set Barlow after something to replace Ouroboros—but you really ought not to be so conscientious! As for a Washington street guide—I'd gladly have lent you mine . . . unless indeed you want one for your permanent archives.

Yes—I realise poignantly that you manage to get into every type of tale a certain nucleus of merit & good craftsmanship which other work in the same magazines is not likely to possess. Sometime I'll have to read a representative story of yours—selected as such by yourself—in each of the branches you have made your own. What a wide ground such an array would cover!

Wright's attitude toward "Sekhmet" is surely odd & exasperating enough—indeed, I have long maintained that it is impossible to find any guiding principle of consistency in his freakish verdicts. He pretends to be guided solely by reader reactions, yet repeatedly accepts stuff from unpraised & unmentioned nonentities (unless he suppresses most of his letters), while rejecting tales by those most repeatedly commended. And as for any standard of real *merit*—the idea is simply laughable! Some of the recent items—especially the tedious & annoying serials—are just about as flat & extravagant & poorly-written as stories could possibly be; so that the condemnation of "Sekhmet" as *banal* is simply absurd, whatever be the quality of the tale! I'll have to see it & judge for myself! Well—I'm glad "Cyclops of Xoatl" landed,[2] anyhow. All told, I fancy Satrap Pharnabazus values you as much as he values any of his contributors. You've fared well with cover designs, (I never had one), & your work is generally announced very glowingly—as mine never is. In the current issue your "Queen of the Lilin" gets a magnificent advance notice & quotation. By the way—this issue isn't quite as unrelievedly bad as the one preceding. "Black God's Kiss" & "7 Geases" good, & "Old Sledge" distinctly worth reading.[3]

Out on Prospect Terrace writing—for perhaps the last time this season. Gets beastly cold toward sunset. However, I hope to take several non-sedentary rural jaunts before the season is over. Feeling rather like hell—indigestion siege has left me weak, & a tendency toward insomnia doesn't help any. Must ease up my programme a bit—I have the most devilish & ill-paid novel-patching job saddled on me! Hence pardon any slips & incoherencies in this pallid epistle. Here's one more Greene article that I found. I'm sure fan letters to the Journal would be quite in order—& might induce them to start another series of his stuff. It really is great—both glamourous & intelligent.

This sunset promises to be a gorgeous one—but it's getting so damn cold that I fear I'll have to get into the house to enjoy it properly. We have steam daytime now, though I have to drag out the good old oil heater late at night. ¶ Salaams between shivers—

[P.S.] Failed to mail this till I got home—& now your triad of redwood cards is before me. Abundant thanks—& how I envy you the trip among these stupendous living messengers from prehistoric antiquity!

[P.P.S.] The cards go in my permanent files!

Notes

1. Unidentified.
2. It did not appear until December 1936.
3. *WT*, October 1934: C. L. Moore, "The Black God's Kiss"; CAS, "The Seven Geases"; Paul Ernst, "Old Sledge."

[44]   [ANS, in private hands][1]

[Postmarked Providence, R.I.,
19 October 1934]

Hail, Malik! Your message reaches me just as I'm about to hop off for Boston to pay Edward H. Cole—my host of last August—a week-end visit. Sunday he'll bring me back in his car, & if the day is any good we shall set out for the South County & cover as much of the old Malik–Abdul trail of July '33 as daylight will allow . . . Wickford, Stuart birthplace, Robinson house, Glebe, &c. &c. ¶ Glad to hear of current progress. Good luck with your Chink stuff! ¶ Yes, I'd surely appreciate a package of typical Malikese. ¶ Since you're doing so much collaborating, I may sic a new colleague on to you—old Adolphe de Castro (formerly known as G. A. Danziger), who collaborated with Ambrose Bierce in adapting "The Monk & the Hangman's Daughter" from the German. He's full of ideas, but can't do much with them. Just now he's in rotten bad shape—74, half blind, & with his wife wasting away with tuberculosis. Possibly none of his ideas will be of any use to you, but one never can tell. ¶ Greene will undoubtedly appreciate your writing The Journal. ¶ Well—more later. Now for the Boston stage-coach!
Blessings—

Notes

1. *Front:* First Baptist Church, Providence, R. I. / Founded by Roger Williams in 1638.

[45]   [ALS, JHL]

Eve of the Sabbat
[30 October 1934][1]

Dear Malik:—

Rec'd your second message just as I was about to reply to the first. Regarding old 'Dolph—I think he may have some usable ideas, though of course that's for you to judge. Naturally, you're not committing yourself to collaboration till you've seen the goods. I doubt if he'd be much good at plot construction—but that leaves you all the freer hand. The reason I sic'd him on to you was that you said you preferred collaboration to lone writing in the weird field. I thought some of his ideas might be just what you'd like to get going with. Of course, if you contributed most of the work you would naturally be entitled to the lion's share of the proceeds. You could make him understand that. I myself couldn't handle that kind of work at present—for collaboration is a tremendous handicap to me. I can do good work only when wholly independent—& working with my own ideas. I'm too near a nervous smashup to attempt anything with as much strain & forced labour as collaboration . . . that is, in the fictional field. If I ever expect to attempt anything of my own again, I must cut off all external influences fictionally. What I did tell the old boy I might do next summer is to help him with one of his historical or philosophical tomes—but I didn't really promise even that.

Old 'Dolph is a queer cuss. His original name is Gustav Adolf Danziger, & he was born somewhere along the Baltic (I don't know just where) in a German-speaking region belonging to Russia. He appears to be half Pole & half Jew in ancestry, & comes of a scholarly family. He graduated from the University of Bonn, in Germany, & became a scholar in all sorts of odd lines—languages, theology, folklore, philosophy, &c—but finally turned to dentistry as a profession. Coming to America in 1886, he went at once to San Francisco & set up as a dentist. There he made the acquaintance of Bierce, & helped him in the preparation of "The Monk & the Hangman's Daughter" from a German original by Richard Voss.[2] He was associated with Bierce for a number of years in various ventures, but they finally quarrelled (although he likes to minimise this latter fact). Meanwhile & later he wrote all sorts of books & articles—some published, some not—& did much reviewing for prominent papers. He no longer practices dentistry. Of his real scholarship there can be no doubt, but his very facility with different languages prevents him from expressing himself forcefully in any of them—hence his need of a collaborator. There is a touch of the poseur & charlatan about old 'Dolph, but I think he is always honest financially. He likes to strut, & probably mixes his reminiscences with myth—but there's no harm in him. Some years ago he went to Mexico & tried to get data on Bierce's disappearance, & in 1928 he wrote a life of Bierce which consists largely of subtle self-advertising. Long revised it & wrote the preface—after I had turned down the job. He undoubtedly capitalises his acquaintance with Bierce. He changed his name during the war, when everything with a Germanic suggestion was unpopular . . . de Castro being the name of a remote Spanish ancestor. He has dabbled in Republican politics for 40 years, & once drew as a reward the really important post of American consul at Madrid—under McKinley, I think. I've revised several tales for de Castro—you may recall "The Last Test" & "The Electric Executioner". Once in a while he has a really workable idea. Some of his un-published books really ought to see the light, although I doubt if they'd be sure enough of publication & circulation to make speculative collaboration profitable. And that's the only kind of collaboration old Dolph can offer, for there's no question at all about his down & outness. I haven't seen him in 6 years, but Belknap called on him a couple of months ago & was greatly moved by his predicament. His eyes are in dangerous shape, & his wife is an advanced tuberculosis patient. I wish I could help him, but I can't at just this juncture. There's something really likeable about the old cuss—a certain old-world charm mixed with cleverness & learning, which makes one wonder why he never quite succeeds in what he attempts. He is a very good poet, by the way—much better in verse than in prose. Belknap may be able to tell you more about him than I can—& his own letters may tell more than could ei-ther of us. He has ideas—& it may be that he'll have something just in your line. That's for you to see—now go to it! He can't be in any hurry—except that, naturally, he can very well use any spare cash whenever it may come in!

As for further news of Randolph Carter—I'm afraid that'll be darned hard to supply, unless you have special advices from Yaddith or Thok or any of the places where a bird in his odd position would be likely to hang out!³ If I ever use him again, I fear it'll have to be in my especial way—with the mys-tical & dream elements emphasised, & with no technical mathematical skele-ton to stick to. The idea you propose is infinitely clever, but it really ought to be developed by someone capable of appreciating the mathematical back-ground. That is the only way it can be really spontaneous. To me, mathemat-ics is a field too remote & abstract to form a basis for fictional imagination. Using it under external instructions, I find it a dead weight obstructing the free flow of fancy instead of a nucleus for the growth of fancy. It is a tool too large & complicated for me to work naturally with. Weird fiction, to have sig-nificance, must form an authentic symbol or picture of some genuine mood—& I can't interpret any mood mathematically. But there certainly is a great field for anyone who *can* translate those bold mathematical concepts in-to fiction without retaining the air of the classroom in the result. Why can't that pioneer be yourself? I don't believe I could tackle any collaboration at present—for I'm saving all possible energy for experiments in original ex-pression which will be miles away from anything externally determined. Col-laboration is the most exhausting of all work for me, since it entails the almost intolerable hardship of conforming my imagination to some prede-termined plan which chokes off all creative energy. The process is really wasteful—for with the same outlay of energy I could achieve infinitely better results if working alone & imaginatively unshackled. What I want to say is so infinitely different from anything that anybody else wants to say! That is why I absolutely could not collaborate with good old Whitehead on "Cassius".⁴

With me, collaboration tends to spoil both what I have to say & what the other fellow has to say! Clearly, it is something which can be truly successful only with writers much more objective than I. But, as I said before, that mathematical idea ought certainly to be used—& by someone to whom mathematics is a vivid emotional reality. Better tackle it independently unless you know of someone who is both a fluent fictioneer & a mathematician. If you don't want to try it as a Randolph Carter yarn you don't have to. It will be easy enough to get Randolph back to earth if he's needed—a bit of enlarging on the final phase of the Silver Key sequel would turn the trick. But I have my doubts about the real value of a repeated character. Such a being tends to grow deplorably hackneyed unless one has a clearly envisaged line of development to put him through—as in a novel—or unless one keeps him as a very subordinate element in the different episodes. The more I look over my old stuff the more disgusted I get with it—& with my efforts as a writer. Only once in a while do I approach what I am really trying to do. I need to make a clean break with whatever I have been doing, & start afresh after a rest—harking back to actual dreams & impressions as in 1917. My first attempts will probably have certain resemblances to my earlier stuff as distinguished from my later, although many typical crudities of the early period can be avoided. Adjectival extravagance will be restrained, but there will be an effort to present clouded pictorial effects rather than to indulge in prosaic pseudo-scientific explanation. Roughly speaking, I shall try to do with greater skill what I did crudely & half-accidentally around 1920 & 1921. My work of that period was—except for the Dunsanian pieces—especially my own, because I had no idea of publication. Once more I must forget that beings like Satrap Pharnabazus exist. Just as long as I think of anyone but myself, I shall never write. Any gains of mine since 1921 have been wholly *technical.* I can write better, but I have not so much to write. Therefore I am going to take my added technical knowledge & go back to 1921, emotionally speaking. It may be that I cannot regain the lost ground—that I am definitely written out—but the only way to find out is to try. I shall not exhibit to anyone the more unsuccessful attempts—of which I expect there will be a great number. But first I must arrange for leisure in which to make my attempts. I am accordingly being quite ruthless in pushing my way free of other obligations. It will, though, probably be quite a while before I can embark on any serious experimentation.

Well—the season of hibernation draws near. What was probably my last chain of outings occurred Oct. 19–21, when I again visited my host of last August in the Boston zone—Edward H. Cole. He has a modest young Juggernaut very useful in sightseeing, & two of our trips were especially notable. Oct. 20th we explored a section of N. Central Massachusetts which I had never before visited, & in which I saw some of the finest autumnal foliage & landscape vistas that I have ever beheld. The focus of the trip was West Townsend, where we lunched at a rambling, many-winged tavern built in 1774. We also patronised the quaintest general store that I've seen in 30 years. Nearby is the Willard Brook State Forest, where we revelled in wooded hills, rock waterfalls, & leafy gorges of indescribable picturesqueness. From nearly every point we had a splendid view of Mt. Wachusett's distant bulk, & of sundry steepled villages in peaceful valleys. Then—on the 21st—Cole & his wife brought me back to Providence in the car—picking up my aunt at #66 & setting out over the South County routes which you & I explored last year. We visited venerable Wickford with its drowsing wharves & elm-shaded main street, & later struck inland to the Gilbert Stuart birthplace. The landscape around the old snuff-mill—whose exquisite loveliness you will recall—is doubly beautiful in autumn; & Cole insisted on exploring the road beyond it (you & I turned back to the main road, as you'll recall)—so that we were quite lost & turned around for a while. Dusk came before we could see anything else—so that over half of the old Jug itinerary still awaits the Cole Chevrolet.

No very startling news around the circle—though two feline disappearances add their note of melancholy. Klarkash-Ton's Genl. Tabasco (whom you probably met) & Ar-E'ch-Bei's old white Doodlebug are both among the missing—hope being wholly relinquished in both cases. ¶ Did I tell you that Dwyer—despite his 38 years—has joined a CCC camp? He's just been made editor of the camp paper.[5] ¶ Here's a F F dedicated to the Old Gentleman—an undeserved compliment![6] Next issue dedicated to Klarkash-Ton. ¶ Heard a good lecture on the evolution of Am. music last week—by John Tasker Howard.[7] ¶ Exhibit of Thos. Holley Chivers material at the marble library next door.[8] ¶ Good luck with old Dolph if you take him up—& best wishes for the successful maturing of the mathematical plot.

> Bismillah, &c—

Notes

1. At JHL, the envelope accompanying this letter is postmarked 8 October 1934, but presumably goes with EHP 43. See also EHP 23n1.

2. It would be more accurate to say that Danziger approached Bierce for help polishing his translation of the German into better English. The two feuded later as to whose byline belonged on the story, even though the actual author was Voss.

3. EHP to HPL, 25 October 1934 (TNS, JHL): "I have detected, thru my espionage service, subterranean murmurings calling for further news as to Randolph Carter. Can you, in your odd moments, devise a way for him to return to earth? Carter, to me, has become so real—thru your sequence of stories—that I agree with those who deplore his present outrageous fate. In this connection, I have long been fascinated by the contemplation of a certain mathematical curve of infinite linear extent—but which despite its length, has the property of rotation about a vertical axis so as to generate a solid of finite volume. And there is the cardioid curve with a cusp: its properties are not particularly odd, but I have a hunch that some occult interpretation might be de-

vised for the inner solid generated by rotation of said cardioid about an axis. And perhaps we can devise spatial equations whereby Carter can be rescued from limbo; perhaps plot a curve whose equation necessitates a line passing thru 4th dimensional space. Although morally certain that not .1% of the fans can remotely grasp the mathematical implications, I feel that they would revel in the dramatization of a fictionized interpretation thereof. If in your leisure you can dig out an approach, I will uncork some calculus & other sinister mathematical engines to attempt the feat."

4. Whitehead based his story on an entry (133) in HPL's commonplace book.

5. Dwyer was the editor of *Blue Mountain Survey* of the Peekskill Civilian Conservation Corps camp. His story "The Old Dark House" appeared in it.

6. *FF* 2, No. 2 (October 1934), dedicated to HPL, contained "Beyond the Wall of Sleep," "The Favorite Weird Stories of H. P. Lovecraft" (compiled by H. C. Koenig), the first two sonnets of *Fungi from Yuggoth*, and an unusually long segment of "Supernatural Horror in Literature." As noted, *FF* 2, No. 3 (November 1934) was dedicated to CAS.

7. John Tasker Howard (1890–1964), music historian, composer, radio host, and writer. His *Our American Music* (1931) was an early history of music in the United States.

8. HPL to F. Lee Baldwin, 2 November 1934: "There has just been an interesting exhibit at the John Hay Library next door—books & papers & other reliques of Dr. Thomas Holley Chivers of Georgia, the contemporary of Poe who influenced & was influenced by the latter so considerably. [. . .] Prof. S. Foster Damon of Providence has written the only biography of him. The best existing collection of his works is that in the John Hay Library here—next door to 66 College St. Of these works one is the only existing copy. All Chivers students have to come to Providence for material." (*Letters to F. Lee Baldwin . . .* 108.)

[46]   [ALS, JHL]

Mosque of Eblis
—Novr. 18, 1934.

Dear Malik:—

That thin paper looks good to me—I've half a mind to see whether I can get some. I'd like to use it for first as well as second sheets, since the postage saving would be enormous.

Glad the F F proved interesting. With future dedications centreing in (a) Klarkash-Ton, (b) Edgar Allan Poe, & (c) the spirit of weird poetry,[1] I certainly have no reason, so far, to feel other than complimented by Editor Hornig's graceful tribute! What later dedications will be, Ye Ed has not yet mentioned.

Your remarks on phantasy in general, & on the quality of my attempts therein, proved most interesting & encouraging. Definitions of real weirdness or phantasy are almost impossible to establish. All one can say is that the weird tale or poem must form an authentic crystallisation or objectivisation of some deep & genuine human mood connected with the illusion of unseen worlds & the revolt of the emotions against the limitations of time, space, & natural law. The classification of weird tales which you present[2] is a very instructive one—& accurate, too, although I would not condemn all the members of Class B—the pure mood class. There are many authentic moods of the weird sort which are simply ruined by any attempt at excessive definiteness—for example, the items in Blackwood's "Incredible Adventures", or Klarkash-Ton's "A Night in Malneant." Then again, there are some moods capable of equally successful development in the short mood-sketch (more properly to be called a *prose-poem* than a *story*) & in the longer story of definite events.

I don't know just which type—B or C—is best adapted to me. So far as inclination goes, I seem to be drifting from B to C; but of the duration of this drift none may predict. I do not think that "The Thing on the Doorstep" represents a tendency which can be called permanent. Character-drawing will never be a major feature of my efforts, for the seat of my real interest is not in persons but in phenomena, conditions, & visual impressions. With me, realism can never be more than an accessory. What I am looking for is the best way to illustrate & embody the moods & visions which demand to be set down, & as yet I frankly don't know what that way is. All my knowledge is purely *negative*. I have learned a few things *not to do,* but which of the countless remaining courses is the best one to follow . . . . or whether *more than one* ought, on diverse occasions, to be followed . . . . . I really have not the slightest idea. All is experimental. I have a feeling that many typical features still persisting in my tales belong in the category of things not to be done, but so far I've not been able to discover what they are. When I do, I'll drop them overboard. One point concerns an occasional plethora of *visibly explanatory* matter. I feel sure that I ought to get rid of this—to substitute *brief implication or suggestion*—but at this stage I don't know how to make the substitution. Another point is the conveyance of shades of mood, & the presentation of events, in such a way as to give a full-bodied picture & *justify* the central weird assumption or climax . . . . that is, make this assumption or climax seem quasi-real or emotionally important rather than trivial, irrelevant, & unmotivated. At this stage I am unable to accomplish such a purpose without plenty of space for detail & 'building-up'. A better artist might do it through brief but potent symbolism or suggestion—but if I try that, the result is thin & hollow. Just now I am experimenting with an old plot idea of mine which I may have described to you—that of a man who, in excavating ruins palpably of incredible antiquity, comes upon (as an unmistakable part of them) *a specimen of his own handwriting in English.*[3] The explanation is that these ruins belong to a pre-human race of organic entities, infinitely above man in mental powers, who in their day ranged the whole gamut of time through mental transference. To learn of a future age, they would have one of their number project his mind ahead & displace the consciousness of somebody in the chosen period. Then the voyaging mind, in the body of its victim, would absorb all the information possible—& finally fly back through time to its original body, while the dis-

placed mind returned to the vacated future body. In the meantime the displaced mind had occupied the body of the pre-human voyager, hence had
had a brief life & consciousness in the immemorial past. And of course it
could then leave a *record* which, in its proper body millions of years later, it
could discover during the excavation of blasphemously ancient megalithic ruins. Well—I developed that story *mistily & allusively* in 16 pages, but it was no
go. Thin & unconvincing, with the climactic revelation wholly unjustified by
the hash of visions preceding it. So I've torn the whole damn thing up & am
re-writing it in my usual latter style—with gradual hints & slowly built-up
stages of unfolding. Am now on page 27, & fear it will run to 40 before I'm
through.[4] Naturally, I know what the majority will say—if I decide to type it &
show it around. "Verbose—long-winded—slow—nothing happens—novelette
length for short-story idea—&c. &c. &c." But the fact remains that it represents the best I can do with the given idea. The shorter treatment was wholly
inadequate—not even scratching the surface of the many bizarre implications
involved in the central assumption. And so it goes. Possibly I'll never succeed
in what I'm slowly fumbling for, but only experiment will decide.

No doubt you've heard more from old de Castro by this time. When I
mentioned a few of your many accomplishments to him, he seized delightedly
on your prowess as a maitre d'armes—for it seems that he is an old-time
swordsman who has given memorable exhibitions of skill & has even published
a small book entitled "The Art of Fencing."[5] Versatile cuss—I wouldn't be
surprised if he could discuss Persian rugs & epicycloids & acetylene burners
& Arabic roots with you . . . to say nothing of juggernauts! He has at last
wheedled me into letting him send me his latest philosophic tome, "The New
Way", for gradual perusal & still more gradual revision. Scholarship de luxe—
336 pages (condensed from *956*), & references to such authorities as

> SEYDEL, Das Evangelium von Jesus in seinem Verhaeltniss zur Buddah
> Sage und Buddah Lehre, Breslau, 1884
> LOISY, Essai Historique sur la Sacrifice, Paris, 1920. &c. &c. &c.

Here's a typical footnote:

> [1]Aristotle, De Divinat par somnum 1 & 2; compare also Talmud Babli
> Berachot 55a, & 56h & Hagigah 15.

Deep stuff . . . . I hope I'm not expected to pick errors in these learned citations . . . . . I always did get my Hagigahs mixed up with my Babli Berachots,
whatever they are![6]

I trust that Pawang Ali may eventually find a remunerative berth, & pray
likewise for the Cairo tale.[7] What you cite concerning the history of Cairo is
indeed interesting. I had commonly taken 938 as the date of origin. Fancy—
Cairo is only about as much older than St. Augustine, Fla., as St. Augustine is

older than ourselves! I did quite a bit of geographical research on modern Cairo in 1924, when preparing that ghost-written story "Imprisoned With the Pharaohs" for the late Houdini. You doubtless recall the item in the Great Anniversary Number. I believe that Satrap Pharnabazus ghost-wrote the other two Houdini stories in W.T., did he not?[8]

Glad you had a fruitful conversation with the super-editor in San Francisco, & wish you luck in meeting his schedule of quantity production. How you can keep up with the vortex of demands is beyond me! Only Comte d'Erlette & the late Edgar Wallace are in your class.

Hope you'll set Baedeker right on Bayonnais matters.[9] The central square of all French towns is usually called Place d'Armes—cf. New Orleans, Quebec, &c.—but where there is a specific other name, I fancy this title remains secondary. Therefore I guess you'd better stick to Place du Theatre for ancient Bayonne.

Regarding mathematics—I can fully realise the tremendous imaginative possibilities which lie in their more advanced concepts, but simply haven't the brains to take such things in. It requires a really profound assimilation of such abstruse complexities—something beyond even a cold working knowledge (which itself is more than I have!)—to transmute them into vital emotional forces; & no amount of study would ever get me that far. But there's a vast field for anybody who can at once feel this magic & embody it in symbols & images to which ordinary persons can respond. Possibly you'll be the one to turn the trick!

The K.A.T. is doing as well as can be expected in this cold weather. It is only frigidity which keeps Pres. Randall & Vice-Pres. Osterberg from their accustomed posts. I shall see Mr. Osterberg on warm days throughout the winter—though Mr. Randall will not again venture out till April. He & I have much in common! Met a very agreeable black gentleman with a white star on his chest yesterday—on the Waterman St. hill. Never saw him before, but he evidently belongs to the University Club in Benefit St. He accompanied me part of the way home, with plentiful purrings & ankle-rubbings. I shall propose him for membership in the K.A.T.

Was glad to see "Queen of the Lilin" occupying a place of honour in the current W.T. It surely is full of tense moments! But confound the Satrap for cutting out the vital quotation—& confound likewise the colour-blindness of the eminent artist who peroxided the *blue-black* locks of your she-ro in the cover design![10]

Hope all your plans for travel & transference develop well, & that old Jug may profit by a sojourn amidst the tepees of the Broken Axes. Providence would certainly hail your caravan with outflung banners—& New England holds in reserve other centuried, brooding arcana which you'd certainly find not less fascinating than the Glebe & Gilbert Stuart place. The narrow ways & crumbling houses of "Arkham" & "Kingsport" could not fail to stimulate your sense of the picturesque, & provide additional settings for fictional triumphs on your part. What an itinerary you could devise—New Bedford with its wealth of whaling traditions & reliques (including a genuine old whaler fully equipped); Nantucket & all that goes with it; Plymouth & the Mass. South Shore; Boston; Dedham & the oldest English house in America; Lexington & Concord; Salem & Marblehead; Newburyport & its deserted silences; Portsmouth, N.H. . . . . . . a whole surviving world of mystery & fascination!

By the way—here's a cutting from good old Nouvelle-Orleans which indicates that the stately Pontalba Bldgs. are getting a much-needed restoration. That's damned good news! The old Place d'Armes ought to be kept in the best possible condition, since it is obviously the focal point of the whole Vieux Carré. I wonder whether the threat of demolishing the old French market has yet been put into effect.

Another cutting ought to interest your Oriental soul—the Firdousi exhibition. I shall give this a look before the lapse of many days. I guess I mentioned seeing local exhibitions of Chivers reliques & of old Providence costumes. The other day I saw a splendid display of drawings of Providence scenes at the Art Club—pencil sketches which bring out all the quaintness in the crumbling byways & hoary vistas of the ancient hill.

Incidentally—speaking of old buildings—there has recently been an attack on the accepted belief that the St. Augustine post office is the original Governor's Mansion erected in 1597. According to the attackers, the old mansion was totally destroyed & replaced by a brand-new building instead of merely remodelled when the U.S. government located the Superior Court there in 1834. Extracts from the *Florida Herald* of June 5, 1834 seem to sustain this iconoclastic challenge to tradition. Thus vanish our cherished illusions, one by one! But if this is true, the U.S. certainly stuck to the old Spanish lines with uncanny fidelity . . . as I think you'll agree. Ah, me—I wish I were in ancient St. Augustine right now! ¶ Benedictions of the faithful—

P.S. Brobst is back—he was over the other night, & I gave him your regards. He sends you his, & says he greatly enjoyed "Queen of the Lilin." He appears to be hale, hearty, & flourishing. ¶ Am provisionally calling the new story "The Shadow out of Time." ﮮ ﯼﯼﮯﮯﮯﮯ

Notes

1. The December issue was dedicated to Poe. The January 1935 issue was a "special weird poetry number."
2. EHP to HPL, 5 November 1934, ms. JHL: "The weird story as she is published is
   A—An action story with sabre hacking dragged in by the heels to increase the one cent a word and to give it the 'speed' needed for a salable story. And a writer must eat, & buy gas.

B—A pitifully inadequate short story, wherein the 'mood' so dominates the writing and the structure that the result is so nebulous as to be utterly insipid. Damn it, I have moods aplenty, and the least of them are much more to my taste than the under-done quasi-presentations of the so called 'moods' of the Poe-esque dabbler who has not even his own word combinations and phrase building.

C—The occasional [*sic*] and all too rare story which really presents what 'B' foozles; and eliminating the extraneous 'action' of 'A', yet contains the fuller 'A' developement [*sic*] of the longer story. The full blown story with a thesis and developement that really leaves one thinking and feeling."

3. The idea dates to November 1930, if not earlier.

4. The ms. ultimately came to 65 pp.

5. No such work by Danziger/de Castro has been found.

6. Hagigah (or Chagigah; literally "Festival Offering") is one of the tractates comprising Moed, one of the six orders of the Mishnah—a collection of Jewish traditions included in the Talmud. Berakhot (literally "Blessings") is the first tractate of Seder Zeraim of the Mishnah and of the Talmud.

7. Either "Agents of the Iron Claw" or "The Sower of Swords."

8. Frank Parnell postulates in *Monthly Terrors* (Westport, CT: Greenwood Press, 1985) that C. M. Eddy or Walter Gibson was the author of "The Hoax of the Spirit Lover" (*WT*, April 1924) and "The Spirit of Hermannstadt" (*WT*, March–April 1924). Eddy seems an unlikely candidate, since HPL himself introduced him to Houdini in the autumn of 1924.

9. Probably referring to Karl Baedeker (firm), *South-Western France from the Loire and the Rhone to the Spanish Frontier: Handbook for Travellers* (Leipsic: Karl Baedeker, 1895).

10. EHP to HPL, 5 November 1934 (TLS, JHL): "Pharnabozus [. . .] excised from Queen of the Lilin its sole claim to authenticity: a rare & curious quotation from a rabbinical writer who is my authority for claiming that Lilith may properly be addressed or designated as 'Agrat bat Mahhat', or Daughter of the Dancer; that she was indeed commanded by Suleiman to dance before him—she, and a myriad of other female demons who walk by moonlight. Of course, this decapitation of the 'theme song' which followed the by-line does not affect the price of the story, but damn it, I did not as a childish whim include it in the text!" Margaret Brundage mistakenly made the queen a blonde.

[47]   [ALS, JHL]

Old 66—

Dec. 30, 1934

Dear Malik:—

Yours of the 15th, with subsequent bulletins, lies before me as I prepare to hop off on a midnight camel caravan for that neo-Bagdad wherein dwells the young sheik Abba 'l'nhap Longh & his brethren of the faithful. It will, according to all indications, be quite some event—for behold! In the metropolis there will be, besides myself, other devout pilgrims & Hajis from caliphates of the south & Emirates of the west . . . to wit, the youthful Ar-E'ch-

Bei of De Land & Washington, & the ever-restless Donald Wandrei, new-come by ship from your own Hesperian shores & from the sacred Tsathogguan groves of Averoigne. Of this convention you will hear more—but in the haste of imminent departure for it I fear I shall do your interesting & piquant communications but scant justice.

Imprimis—let me reiterate those congratulations on your proposed real-estate & housing scheme[1] which I extended not long ago by postcard. Verily, it sounds idyllic & marvellous—& withal eminently practical. With your artistic & mechanical skill you can certainly reduce building expenses to a minimum, & the location appears ideal. A Moorish abode of the sort you plan will be capable of infinite extension without any violation of architectonics, & I can picture the sort of interior you will devise with rugs & kindred accessories. The setting of the Arabian Nights—so dear to my youthful imagination—will rise anew in a western land! If you intend to keep up the present grind of production, you certainly need every favouring environmental influence you can get—& this arrangement would seem to promise just that. It suits all your diverse requirements better than anything else could even begin to do—& to cap the climax, is remarkably non-expensive. So once more I congratulate you on the prospect, & urge you by all means to go to it. And I'm glad Old Jug is not to be replaced. Young Anger has just written me of his delightful trip in it, & has expressed the hope that he can some day be conveyed by its magic to the Temple of Tsathoggua in fabulous Averoigne. Have you, by the way, seen Anger's writeup of you in the F F?[2] It is very pleasant & interesting, & if through any oversight you haven't a copy I'll be glad to send you one of my extras.

Your successes in the marketing of high-pressure, quantity-produced goods continue to leave me breathless. Verily, you literally exude auriferous words . . . . faster than you can write them down! For parallels one has to go back to the legend of Midas . . . or of the character in the fairy tale who spat a gold-piece upon each mouth-opening! I reel in admiring vertigo! . . . . . & the obtuse Satrap Pharnabazus may well reel in abasement & contrition. With such a greenback-factory founded on original manufactures, you certainly have no need to squander your time on arduous, thankless, & ill-paid criticism. Better tell the Dervish Eblis Adib al Klin to find another slave!

As for the Satrap's capricious rejection system—I have given up all efforts to fathom it. Thinking of that kind of thing simply prevents me from writing anything. Sometime I hope I can fix up a table of "fan reactions" to your tales from 1925 onward. It certainly ought to form an excellent selling argument! Often I wonder just how much Pharnabazus *is* guided by his floods of letters . . . or rather, I *used* to wonder. Nowadays I simply dismiss commercial editors from my mind as paralysing influences.

I'll probably submit the "Doorstep" when I finish the thing I'm now stalled on. A rejection at this juncture would still further aggravate the nervous disorganisation characteristic of recent months. This new thing—a second version—fails to satisfy me, & I don't know whether to finish it as it is or destroy once more & start afresh. Pressure of other duties has for the moment made any original writing impossible. The incomplete effusion is about ¾ done. It will probably mark my last attempt in the vein of recent years.

As for the S.K. proceeds-division—your idea is certainly fair & generous enough, & I shall either tell the Satrap (in case I have occasion to write him) to split the second cheque evenly, or effect such a cleavage myself upon receipt of the entire sum.[3] And meanwhile I'll notify Little Bobby to call off the book-quest on which you so ultra-conscientiously set him!

Congratulations on the dictaphone bargain! I really don't understand yet just how this will help your work—for the fact is, I don't think I know just what a dictaphone *does*. I've heard of office phonographs which take records of speech for later reproduction & copying by a stenographer—but these of course necessitate the employment of a stenographer . . . . & thorough revision would be hard to make. Is the dictaphone a step ahead of this process in any way? Regarding a letter on the dictaphone—I must warn you that I have no facilities for getting records reproduced if that is the form of epistle to be expected! Doubtless all these conjectures reveal a sad lack of knowledge of modern commercial devices—but I'm never one to conceal ignorance where it exists! I'm certainly curious to know just what a commercial dictaphone is, & what it does!

De rebus antiquis—how I envy you your actual sight of a Roman amphitheatre . . . aye, your actual entry into such! As you know, Roman antiquity is one of my hobbies—indeed, I finished an article on Roman architecture only a fortnight ago![4] Burdigala[5] was, as your guidebook has doubtless told you, a renowned centre of culture in the later days of the Empire. It is curious how the intellectual & aesthetic leadership of the Roman world shifted about after the Augustan age. In the 1st century A.D. all the best authors & deepest thinkers tended to be *Spaniards*, & after that the *North African* region centreing in Roman Carthage came to the fore. Then, in the last days of the Empire— the 4th & 5th centuries A.D.—the *Romanised Gauls* became almost the whole show, producing figures like Ausonius & Rutilius Namatianus. That was the heyday of old Burdigala—which had meanwhile become the capital of Aquitania Secunda. Its native son Ausonius (b. 310 A.D.) described it as a noble city "renowned for wines & streams & the manners & talents of its inhabitants"—& it was indeed the literary centre of Gaul if not of the whole dying empire. I understand that the amphitheatre is the only surviving relique of Roman Burdigala, & that it is (or was—it may have been restored in recent years) incorporated into some sort of mediaeval or modern edifice. Incidentally, something must be wrong with your guidebook account—for a structure erected in *A.D. 233* couldn't have had anything to do with the Emperor Gallienus. Gallienus was either a child or unborn in 233. His father Valerianus did not become Emperor till 253, & he himself reached the throne only in 260, when Valerianus was permanently captured & humiliated by the victorious Persian Sapor. I'd give anything to see genuine Roman remains—especially in Britain, where the stream of Roman civilisation meets my own blood ancestry. You may be aware that modern research—as ably summed up by the late Sir Arthur Weigall—has amply proved that the Romanised Britons are just as much our ancestors as the invading Saxons & Normans.[6] It is a complete error to fancy that all the Britons (Latin-speaking & Celtic-speaking) were killed off or driven out. On the other hand, they were enslaved, & ultimately merged into the conquering Teutonic population. The *language & culture* of Roman Britain perished, but not the *people*. In all probability half of our own ancestors once spoke Latin, wore togas, lived in Roman towns or villas, frequented baths, temples, & amphitheatres, & bore such names as Caius Julius Vitalis, Sextus Valerius Genialis, Titus Valerius Pudens, Lucius Martius Senacianus, &c. &c. &c. Not, however, that we have much real Roman *blood*. The legionaries who settled & intermarried among the Britons were in most cases Roman only in name & speech—Gauls & Germans largely predominating. Thus our Briton ancestry is about as Nordic as our Saxon & Norman ancestry.

Thanks for the tip on thin paper, which I'll follow up later. I had some good thin paper until lately, when the shop selling it went out of business. I used to be quite a Montgomery Ward catalogue patron 30 years or so ago, but gradually became more local—or more Woolworthian—in my shopping. Which reminds me—I've just found something very useful at Woolworth's—a set of 64-page booklets giving the history of Britain in pictures. Hundreds of line drawings—covering every phase of life from the ape-like dawn-men to George V & Sir Oswald Mosely.[7] Architecture, costume, utensils, typical scenes, historic events & personages—a veritable museum to consult in writing anything involving earlier ages. Diagrams of Roman villas, Saxon villages, Gothic castles & cathedrals &c—everything comprehensibly explained. The series is prepared by C. W. Airne of Cambridge, & ought to consist of 7 booklets—one giving the whole panorama of British history in rough outline, the next five treating periods (Prehistoric–Roman; Saxon–Norman; Mediaeval [Plantagenet]; Tudor & Stuart; Hanoverian & Modern) in detail, & the last covering the Empire. I have all but the last, which I can't find at the Providence Woolworth's, & which I shall seek in N.Y. Other recent Woolworth bargains of possible value to the writer are a series of miniature books with coloured plates which help one to identify birds, flowers, trees, & butterflies. These things will often help to make descriptions *concrete* & accurate. Really, Frank Winfield is getting to be quite a bookseller!

Continuing on the book theme—it is surely wise of you to accumulate a private library. It is almost suicidal for a writer to depend on public libraries—it causes delay & encourages vagueness & inaccuracy. I'm certain that many of the slips & anachronisms in Long's work come from his refusal to have a library of his own . . . & that doubtless applies to scores of others. I've heard of the David-Neel book—it ought to be a veritable mine of suggestions for you. Klarkash-Ton not so long ago gave me some highly interesting facts concerning the hideous Thibetan form of necromancy known as *rolang*.[8] An unabridged dictionary is a great asset—I use my father's two standbys . . . Stormonth's, & the Webster International of 1891. Up to a couple of years ago I used my grandfather's Unabridged of 1864, but that virtually fell to pieces . . . hence my coming forward one generation. I'll get around to the 1934 International about the year 2000! You ought to have a Roget's Thesaurus, of which there's an excellent dollar edition (Grosset & Dunlap) now out. Revised & amplified to date.

Your recent festivities must surely have been fascinating—especially the part including that teller of curious wonders, "Doc" Herrold.[9] I trust the good sage came across with many an inside story of strange carven marbles raised from the Pacific's depths, dark, non-human forms in iridescent armour found frozen in Greenland glaciers, & cyclopean sea-walls near the summit of Mt. Everest. Can't say I envy you the alcoholic & ichthyic delicacies—though your graceful descriptions give them an aura of charm at their proper distance.

I hope that nothing may intervene to curtail the aestival trip you outline. Cimmeria . . . Mexico . . . . . . Broken Axedom . . . . the Satrapy of Pharnabozus . . . the headquarters of the Interstellar Patrol . . . . Manhattan's zone of Chaos . . . . the ancient hill of Abdul Alhazred & the haunted woods around the Glebe . . . . brooding San Agustin . . . . the good old Vieux Carré . . . . . old Texas again . . . . & the old home—or the new Moorish palace at San Carlos. Some itinerary! And I urge you not to stint the Novanglian part of it, since you certainly ought to see Boston & "Arkham" & "Kingsport" & Nantucket (the latter sans Jug, since they'd probably soak you like blazes for the 54-mile ferriage from New Bedford) & all sorts of other colourful havens of the past.

I'll surely appreciate a glimpse of Pawang Ali, & so will Greene & Leeds. I saw Greene's aunt & cousin the other day, & spoke of your having been in touch with him. He is now in N.Y. I'm enclosing something about a new series of his which may interest you—& which will shew you what he looks like. Leeds spoke of hearing from you. I expect to see him quite often during the coming week.

Hope you & old de Castro can get together on something. Poor old duffer—his wife has now gone to the hospital (tuberculosis—she may never return), & he's in a pitifully distracted state. Belknap & I must call on him next week & see if we can't cheer him up. Now that I think of it, I haven't seen him in person since 1928!

Glad the Firdousi cutting was of some interest. I saw the exhibit in question. Since then there have been a phenomenal array of local art activities—part of Providence's "Art Week". One thing was vastly interesting—two prominent local artists, a landscapist & a portraitist,[10] painting in their respective veins in full view of the audience. Another event—a demonstration of that new aesthetic form, the correlation of shifting, projected colour with music—I had to pass up because of cold weather. More or less joined to this "art week" stuff was the first display of a choice array of the 717 Japanese prints just acquired by the local museum. This gave me quite a kick, since I am rather an enthusiast concerning Sino-Japanese art. The prints are of the finest quality, with plenty of Hokusais & Hiroshiges.[11] A couple of weeks ago an expert lectured on the making of Japanese prints, & exhibited some of the delicately carved blocks used in their preparation. Today there's a lecture on Mayan art—which I hope to take in before my journey. One must get a last taste of civilisation before embarking for the strident & decadent jungles of darkest Manhattan! Hades! I wish Belknap & the gang lived in some civilised town!

My aunt & I had quite a Christmas hereabouts—& I trust you had the same. Our downstairs neighbour[12] presented us with a *tree*—the first I've had in a quarter of a century or more—& it so tickled my fancy that I laid in quite a stock of decorations at Woolworth's .... tinsel star, baubles, tinsel rope, shredded tinsel (to hang like Spanish moss on the boughs), set of 8 lights, &c. &c. All my old ornaments were dispersed years ago. When the job was finished it certainly did look pretty neat—& it brought back my long-departed youth almost as vivibly as that Nantucket bicycle ride last summer. Around the base were piled our modest array of gifts .... my principal one, from my aunt, being a framed drawing of the ancient Stephen Hopkins house (which you saw) a block & a half from here down the hill. Christmas day opened most auspiciously with the great British Empire broadcast—which came at 8:54 a.m. here (1:54 p.m. Greenwich time), but which of course came to your part of the world at the godless hour of 5:54 a.m.! Conversations between London & all the Dominions—Australia, India, Canada, South Africa, &c— ending with messages from the Mother Land & a graceful address by the King! I don't know when I've ever had such an impressive phenomenon presented to me before. We had dinner at the boarding-house across the back garden, after which came sessions of gift-unveiling & conversation by candle light. The tree, with its illumination, certainly formed an entrancing & rejuvenating sight! On the previous night we listened to the carol-singing around the huge lighted tree in the courtyard of the ancient Beckwith house—home of the Handicraft Club.[13]

And so it goes. Tomorrow morning—unless headed off by a calamitous telegram—I shall be breakfasting at Belknap's & beholding Barlow. Later in the week there'll be a gang meeting with Morton, Leeds, Talman, Loveman, Koenig, & everybody. Hope the weather'll be decent—though the subway forms some protection in case of extreme cold. ¶ With all the Prophet's blessings
—Bismillah &c—

[P.S. on envelope:] Dear _____ [envelope torn] Am with _____ at 66——; just got back from a trip to the middle west. How are you faring? I think of you frequently. Regards.

H. Brobst

Behold the postscript of an honoured guest! Two letters for the price of one!

Notes

1. EHP was planning to buy a plot of land in Redwood City, CA, on which to build a house. He did, and lived there (2547 Woodland Place) until his death in 1988.

2. Fred Anger and Louis C. Smith, "An Interview with E. Hoffman [*sic*] Price," *FF* 2, No. 4 (December 1934): 60–61.

3. *WT* paid $140 for "Through the Gates of the Silver Key."

4. "A Living Heritage: Roman Architecture in Today's America." Published only in abridged form in HPL's lifetime.

5. The Latin name for the city of Bordeaux, in southwestern France.

6. HPL had derived this information from Arthur Weigall's *Wanderings in Roman Britain* (London: Butterworth, 1926; LL 1025), which he had read about a year earlier.

7. Sir Oswald Mosley (1896–1980), British politician who had served as an M.P. (1926–31) before establishing the British Union of Fascists in 1932.

8. The book is *Magic and Mystery in Tibet* by Alexandra David-Neél. HPL made the following entry (192) in his commonplace book: "Thibetan ROLANG—Sorcerer (or NGAGSPA) reanimates a corpse by holding it in a dark room—lying on it mouth to mouth & repeating a magic formula with all else banished from his mind. Corpse slowly comes to life & stands up. Tries to escape—leaps, bounds, & struggles—but sorcerer holds it. Continues with magic formula. Corpse sticks out tongue & sorcerer bites it off. Corpse then collapses. Tongue become a valuable talisman. If corpse escapes—hideous results & death to sorcerer."

9. Charles David "Doc" Herrold (1875–1948), American inventor and pioneer radio broadcaster. Beginning in 1912, he apparently became the first person to make regular entertainment broadcasts from his station in San Jose, CA.

10. Hezekiah Anthony Dyer (1872–1943) and John Robinson Frazier (1889–1966).

11. Katsushika Hokusai (1760–1849) and Utagawa Hiroshige (1797–1858), two of the leading Japanese artists of their era.

12. Alice Sheppard (1870–1961), HPL's downstairs neighbor at 66 College Street. She taught German at Classical High School.

13. The Truman Beckwith House (1826, John Holden Greene, architect; now the Providence Handicraft Club) at 42 College Street, only a few doors west of 66 College Street.

[48]   [ALS, JHL]

Garden of Hassan
—Jany 13, 1935.

Dear Malik:—

Yrs of Dec. 26 & subsequent bulletins duly at hand—& I am quite in suspense about your real estate decision. These bargains with house already built sound highly alluring—especially the hillside retreat with the near-colonial house & the sinister, twisted oak! The galleries of this edifice ought to remind you of the good old Rue Royale! But in my case I think the possession of a congenial & convenient headquarters is an exceedingly wise policy . . . . so here's hoping that you may soon be duly installed as the squire of San Carlos or feudal overlord of the Redwood region.

I appreciate the honour of receiving the first dictaphone letter from the Peacock Throne, & am glad you have found this means of facilitating your composition & correspondence. Even *with* such a device, I don't see how you can keep up such a schedule of quantity production as that which you have outlined. So Pawang is on the way toward becoming a standard figure of popular romance! Leeds spoke of hearing from you anent Singapore details— & by this time he has probably supplied you with such information as he can give. Incidentally—here's a fictional attempt by Marc T. Greene[1] which may interest you. It's the first story of his I ever saw. Perhaps he's written others in the past—or perhaps your example started him off!

Your Japanese Yuletide celebration must have been quite an experience—especially for a devotee of exotic nourishment. Sukiyaki, as you describe it, must be a distinctly toothsome dish; & I wouldn't mind trying it some time. Whether I could learn to manage chopsticks gracefully is another story!

The dictaphone certainly offers all sorts of possibilities, & I trust you'll get your full money's worth out of it. The sound effects—shots, battle-yells, &c.—would surely be worth trying if there were only a way of getting them across to the reader. As for studying Arabic—the phonograph is a well-known aid in linguistic instruction, & I have no doubt but that you could make great progress if the right kind of Arab were available. In the matter of speech correction—probably the ordinary daily use of the dictaphone will serve to point out to you any vocal tricks which you may wish to change. I once talked into a phonograph, & was horrified at realising—ruthlessly & objectively—the raucous squawk miscalled a "voice" which unkind nature fastened into my throat![2] Regarding the exchange of messages via dictaphone—that would surely have its advantages among a group of hurried persons uniformly equipped with phonographs. In time I suppose one could learn to get the maximum wordage on a cylinder, so that the latter would form the equivalent of about 3 double-spaced pages of ordinary typing. Just now, however, a correspondence in such a medium would be rather restricted for lack of widely diffused apparatus. Last spring in De Land Barlow wanted to get at a recording phonograph so that we could send our voices to Klarkash-Ton—who could get a record played somewhere in Averoigne. The plan fell through, however, since the machine he had in mind was out of order. Glad to hear that good old Jug seems assured of a permanent place in your stables. He certainly is hard to beat—& if you acquire a country estate you can provide a splendid refuge for his declining years. It would vastly add to the charm of that oak-studded hillside to have such a veteran steed put out to pasture—tied to one of the gnarled & half-sentient trees!

Meanwhile I trust that the production programme will spin merrily on. Hope you can get some fruitful ideas from old 'Dolph . . . . I see that he's been airing his opinions in the Eyrie.[3] Sorry I couldn't drop in on him during my recent Manhattan sojourn. *Spy Stories* ought to be quite a market for you—I hope you got that Jany. 5 item in on time. Hope to see the Egyptian magic story when it's done—also the other representative samples.

My last previous bulletin, I believe, was that mailed just before my departure for New York Dec. 30. The visit was extremely pleasant—expanding almost to the proportions of a convention through the presence of little Barlow (who stopped at the Hotel Clendening six blocks north of Belknap's) & both the Wandrei boys. Donald blew in from San Francisco the day before I arrived, & Howard came directly from St. Paul the day after. On Jany. 2 we had a gang meeting at Belknap's at which 15 were present—including Morton, Leeds, Kleiner, Loveman, the Wandreis, Barlow, Kirk, Talman, Koenig, &c. &c. &c.[4] This was Barlow's first N Y sojourn since infancy, & Belknap & I shewed him all the museums, galleries, bookstalls, &c. It was all we could do to keep the kid from spending his return fare once he got loose amidst the bibliophilic temptations of 4th Avenue. As it was, he picked up a bargain that turned me green with envy—George W. M. Reynolds' "Wagner the Wehr-Wolf" for 15¢! I, incidentally, landed a copy of Lewis's "Monk" for a dollar. One evening Loveman got out his full collection of Klarkash-Ton drawings—almost 400 of them—& nearly bowled the company over therewith. I had seen them in 1922—in Cleveland—but it gave me a great kick to see them again. Barlow, Long, & the Wandreis had never seen them before. From now on little Bobby will be pestering Loveman with requests for loans of drawings—so that he can photograph them.[5] The weather favoured the recent visit quite markedly, only 2 days being cold enough to give me grave inconvenience. I dropped in twice on the Wandrei's [*sic*]—who have taken an apartment together in Greenwich Village . . . at 155 W. 10th St., just above a rather noisy & well-known 'bohemian' restaurant named Julius's.[6] They are doing vast amounts of hack writing for Street & Smith—even though Donald's especial friend Desmond Hall has just severed his connexion with the firm. Tremaine is evidently just as well-disposed as his erstwhile subordinate.

The convention began its dispersal Jany. 7, when Barlow took the 11:30 a.m. coach for Washington. I left the following midnight—reaching home around 6:30 a.m. Tuesday. I drowsed most of the way, so that when the coach struck Providence I thought I was still in Danielson, Conn. Since my return I have been struggling desperately with an accumulation of tasks & correspondence, punctuated with a little museum attendance. One interesting exhibit is just next door at the John Hay Library—Sumerian & Babylonian clay tablets & cylinders as old as 3000 B.C., with cuneiform inscriptions. Another thing with an Oriental touch which might interest you is the exhibit of Cambodian stone sculpture & Javanese masks & puppets at Faunce House— on the Brown campus a block from here. I'll chuck in a catalogue which you needn't bother to return. This, of course, isn't in your Islamic line—but at least it has something to do with the general region represented by Pawang Ali. I don't care for Indo-Chinese, Malaysian, or Hindoo art, but the whole epic of the Khmers, with their brooding, deserted city of Angkor, has always fascinated me. It is curious to note the elongated ear-lobes of Cambodian statues—a link in common with the baffling colossi of Easter Island. I fancy a wave of Indo-Chinese culture spread all the way across the Pacific— entering Central America & giving many characteristic touches to Mayan & Aztec art. This would account for the puzzling resemblances to old-world forms noted in certain American antiquities. The idea of an "Atlantis" is really quite cockeyed, for all the evidence is against the existence of such a bridge to Europe during the age of man. Whatever European–Asian–African cultural influences reached America undoubtedly came by way of the Pacific—in which large land areas may or may not have subsided during the human period. A curious thing about these Cambodian statues is the archaic way of depicting hair—by thickly studded raised dots. This is characteristic of *archaic* Greek art, but disappeared in Greece by 500 B.C. In Asia, on the other hand, it kept right on through the centuries.

Well—I must lay off & get to work. Added to other tasks, I've got to write a critical report for the N.A.P.A.[7]—that society whose New York convention you & I & Jug *almost* attended in '33. By the way—the next convention . . . in July . . . . will be in *Oakland.* You ought to take it in!

Benedictions—

Notes

1. Greene had written "Heathen Chinee" (*Cornhill Magazine,* July 1935).

2. HPL to Moe, 15 May 1918: "Something over a decade ago I conceived the idea of displacing Sig. Caruso as the world's greatest lyric vocalist, and accordingly inflicted some weird and wondrous ululations upon a perfectly innocent Edison blank. My mother actually liked the results [. . .] but I saw to it that an accident soon removed the incriminating evidence" (*Letters to Maurice W. Moe and Others* 67).

3. De Castro had a letter in *WT* (January 1935) expressing admiration for EHP's "The Queen of Lilin."

4. Also present were Dean P. Phillips (a friend of Loveman) and his unnamed friend. The fifteenth person is unidentified.

5. Donald Wandrei to CAS, 11 January 1935 [erroneously dated 1934] (TLS, Minnesota Historical Society): "most of the evening we devoted to looking at Sam's immense collection of your drawings, water-colors, and grotesques. RHB was positively ill with envy, and made a pest of himself by trying to beg, borrow, or buy one or all of them until Loveman patiently but flatly stated, 'But Barlow, these are personal gifts from a very dear friend of mine.'"

6. In Greenwich Village. Now recognized as the oldest continuously operating gay bar in New York City.

7. "Report of the Bureau of Critics."

[49]   [ALS, JHL]

Jany. 29[, 1935]

Dear Malik:—

I feel honoured that I am the recipient not only of your first dictaphone letter, but the first message emanating from the new castle on the hill! Congratulations on your new setting—the bulletins of whose acquisition I have followed with the greatest interest. Judging from your description, your present locale is about as idyllic as one could well ask! The vistas from every part of your hilltop eyrie must be delectable in the extreme, while the whole countryside is well calculated to tempt you forth for excursions of every degree of length. With such a place to show off, you ought to kidnap Klarkash-Ton (who is really in desperate need of a vacation & relaxation from his eternal grind) & make him pay you a visit! Your desk surely has an interesting history—& must bring up many memories of its former owner. When you toil too hard over it, I presume you take one of his powders to ease your aching brow! I'd need a whole carton per day if I even began to attempt a programme like yours! The improvements scheduled for your estate all sound desirable. When you get those terraces all done, you'll have a layout something like that of the Glebe—save for the picturesque neglect of the latter. I'm not surprised that the place has an invigorating effect from the very start. It seems to me that it forms precisely what you need—& I'm certainly glad you chanced to discover it & to find it within your financial reach.

As to the production programme—Ædepol, but it makes one dizzy! To think of markets clamouring for material faster than one can dictate it at top speed! You will become a legend in future ages—Edgar Wallace & Augie Derleth are mere specks left behind in the dust from your juggernaut-wheels! But don't overdo—good health is worth more than pieces of gold! Glad Pawang made the deadline, & hope all the other ventures will fare equally well.

Was sorry to hear from old de Castro that his wife died Jan. 23 at St. Joseph's Hospital. I've sent him a line of sympathy, & imagine he'd appreciate one from you—if indeed you haven't sent one after a more direct notification. The whole ordeal of Mrs. De C's illness has had old 'Dolph pretty badly broken up—he spoke of a fortnight's nervous collapse some time ago.

Marc T. Greene seems to be following in your footsteps geographically as well as fictionally—note the two enclosed items from the old Nouvelle-Orleans stamping-ground! He ought to have mentioned the literary shrines in Rue Royale & Rue Josephine!

Well, I wish to gawd I were back at the good old Orleans in Rue St. Charles right now . . . for Providence is in the grip of a hellish visitation from the arctic! Zero temperatures day after day, & a 13-inch snowfall which has tied up every sort of traffic. I haven't been outdoors for a week—& no relief is yet in sight! Here's a picture to make you damn glad you're safely out of it on the crest of the terrible Kaf! You may recognise the scene, although you beheld it under vastly different conditions.

Speaking of furniture—as we were some distance back—I am impelled to mention a bargain I secured just before the cold drove me into retirement a week ago . . . . at a department-store fire sale. Two dark walnut chests of drawers at $4.44 each—which I have piled up vertically to form one capacious file. I've been looking for something of the kind for years—to take care of the papers, MSS., cuttings, &c. which are sprawled over everything. The drawers are large enough to take a newspaper folded twice. The style & colour look delightfully antique, so that the outfit blends finely with the archaic tone of my dump. I have located it without disturbing any previous piece of furniture—on the south wall beside the tall black-walnut bookcase, & encroaching only slightly on a window. On the other side is the low stand or bookcase near the corner morris-chair. Here's a rough idea of how it looks. Long had a similar thing (*one* chest) for Christmas, which made me quite envious—but now chance has enabled me to go him one better! His is painted a delicate light green—which wouldn't harmonise with my austere & archaic study—but my two are just the kind of dark wood I want. They really look enormously colonial.

Read the Jany. W T some time ago. Klarkash-Ton's "Dark Eidolon" is certainly magnificent! Have been going all over my new story again—providing a new beginning. Hope I can get the leisure to finish it before long!

Well—again let me congratulate you on your Djinn-builded palace on the peak of Mount Kaf! I'd like to see snap shots of it when you get around to taking some. Glad Jug will be well housed! Blessings— C⌐ʒ⸝⌐

[50]   [ALS, JHL]

Plateau of Leng
—Chinese New Year's
[Postmarked 4 February 1935]

Dear Malik:—

The enclosed, I take it, is quite self-explanatory. Now nobody owes anybody anything anent the "Gates". Am snatching moments & getting near the end of the "Shadow Out of Time", but doubt if that will ever draw down anything like the enclosed. Satrap Pharnabazus will undoubtedly pull that "too-long-&[-]slow-moving" gig when (or if ever) he sees it. I hope to continue my revolt against revision & extensive correspondence long enough to do something on another yarn (of possibly greater chances of favourable Pharnabazian consideration) which I have in mind—something with an Arkham scene. Oddly enough, both that & the present "Shadow" are basically non-supernatural—i.e., with science-fiction explanations of the marvels & horrors.

Regards to Hassan Asdeev[1] . . . . has he burst yet with milk & spaghetti? This morning I was delighted to see Vice-President Osterberg of the K.A.T. on his accustomed fence. He walked along to the clubhouse & tried to get on the roof—but the latter was a foot deep with snow! However, there was a melted margin close to the edge, so he finally leaped up & made the circuit. Not finding any good resting-place, he turned around & went home. He cast several enquiring glances at Pres. Randall's house, but old Peter is like me about winter weather, & won't be seen around the club till April.

The cold snap is broken, though. Over 40° yesterday, & I went with my aunt to a poetry reading at the college[2] & later took a walk through the snowy streets—getting some marvellous sunset effects on the edge of the hill, with colonial roofs, an 1816 steeple, & picturesque tree-branches against the flaming west. This afternoon is mild also—hence my ability to get down to the bank & post office & attend to the accompanying detail of vulgar commercialism. But hades! if the lax city fathers don't get some of the mountain-high snow carted off before the really serious melting begins, there'll be boating in the streets, & a greater Niagara down College Hill!

Got the new W T t'other day, but have had no time to read it. Nor have I had a chance to fill up my new cabinet outfit with properly classified material. Hope the settling is progressing auspiciously atop the daemon-haunted Kaf, & that the landscape vistas aren't beginning to bore you!

Blessings of the Elder Ones
⌐ ꞵ⌐ʒ⟩⟩⟳⌐⟩

Notes

1. Referring to EHP's cat, Nimrod. Asdeev (or Asdiv) is a giant white Persian dragon.
2. By Susanna Valentine Mitchell (1896–1979), author of the poetry volumes *Journey Taken by a Woman* (1935), *In the Bright April Weather* (1952), and *Make New Banners* (1954). Her *Collected Poems* appeared in 1966.

[51]   [ALS, JHL]

Kadath in the Cold Waste
[Postmarked 16 February 1935]

Dear Malik:—

Thanks immensely for the graphic chart displaying the new location of the Peacock Throne! I had located Redwood City on a smaller map—but now the whole thing, including the relation of Mt. Kaf & the Green Tarn to the bazaars & market-place, is straight in my mind. The walk to town must really be fascinating & invigorating—I had not realised that the hills had such a parallel-line arrangement. Most assuredly you are in the right place, & I have no doubt but that the stimulating environment will become manifest in your work. Hope you'll soon have all your belongings imported from 5314, & that you'll get the necessary cards, &c. at the Redwood City public library. How big a place is Redwood City?[1] I don't seem to find it in any of the census tables at my disposal. I notice a road to the S W of you which the map designates as leading to *Islam* Redwood Shrine. Decidedly appropriate for a Peacock Sultan! You can use it as a sort of Mecca—installing, if such is not already supplied, a suitable Kaaba Stone.

Of Nimrod[2] the Babylonish gourmand I learn with the acutest interest. Ay, he shall be overlord of all the mosques of the K.A.T. west of the Rockies! Even the equally snow-white Crom of Cimmeria—up in Asotin[3]—shall bend the furry knee to him! For verily, such prowess like his—both in the field & at the table—is such as makes men Sultans & Emirs! Only Conan the Reaver—or perchance King Kull of Valusia—could be mentioned in the same breath as a rival. Well—if you bring him east, I hope he won't challenge Vice President Osterberg (tiger) to single combat . . . . for Count Magnus is something of a warrior (always defensive, however—he is never an encroacher or aggressor!) himself, & if two such ever met in the field the result would (as in old Kilkenny) be likely to be merely a seething vacancy of dissociated electrons. The count had a fearsome set-to with a large dog last autumn, though his person no longer bears any evidence of it. Anyway—here's to good old Nimrod . . . & may the gopher-dog food–milk–cheese–oatmeal–spaghetti–fried egg supply never run low!

I likewise welcome news of good old Jug—who surely can cover the ground, whatever the technical minutiae may be! He flourishes as well on his petrol & ile as Nimrod does on his gophers & dog food—a sturdy, virile, pair! Next summer, I trust, one or both may come snorting into the marble-walled lane which leads to the Ancient Citadel of 66! Just now that lane is choked deep with an obstructive medium from which Nimrod could scarcely be chromatically distinguished.

And so Brother Dick[4] isn't as universally helpful as you anticipated? Well—he may come in handy now & then, & possibly you could pass him along to some other rapid-fire action-grinder! I noticed your description (& also your dual honours as a technical consulting expert) in a recent number of the Am. Fiction Guild's bulletin . . . which comes to me regularly (forwarded from the old Barnes St. address) despite my settled non-membership. Congratulations on becoming such a high light at the very outset!

As to "Wagner the Wehr-wolf"—it isn't such an indispensable item intrinsically, but is remarkable as one of the last examples of the thoroughly old-school Gothic tale. Reynolds also wrote another—"Faust & the Demon"—both of which I read in 1923. I think there were still others which I haven't seen. Although the importance of these items is probably more historical than literary in the strictest sense, they do have a very genuine interest & occasional dark potency if one has no prejudice against a leisurely, archaic style. They are damned hard to get—I know of no copies in any public library, the ones I read having been lent by a friend who in turn had borrowed them from a cousin in Madison, Wis. Barlow was a lucky little rascal to pick up "Wagner"—& for *15¢!* I'll bet he never gets "Faust & the Demon" so easily!

Glad to hear of all the progress on work, & will wager that Damascus stuff is potent & animated. Hope all the missing items turn up before any harm or inconvenience results from their absence. Thanks for the tip on Oriental ear-lobes. I'll bet a dime the thing indicates a connexion betwixt Easter Island & prehistoric Asia—especially since many find a close resemblance betwixt the hieroglyphs on a wooden club dug up on Easter Island, & those carved in the ruins of that prehistoric city—Mohenjo-Daro—discovered on the Indus River a few years ago.

About the Oakland convention—I doubt if any of our especial gang will be there, but the event will be festive for all that. The local leader is one Anthony F. Moitoret[5]—a newspaper reporter of some prominence. He used to be one of my chief enemies in amateurdom 20 years ago—battling for slap-dash, rough & ready papers while I fought for genuine literary standards. To-day he has probably forgotten my name & existence, except as reminded by current amateur papers. I'll enclose some Oakland amateur stuff—the products of Moitoret & his kid sons. ¶ Glad the cheque duly arrived & was useful . . . & trust the demands of Pawang & the dirt-pedlar won't drive you to distraction.

Peace upon thee—

[P.S.] Congrats on Old Jug's Chink New Year performance![6] That ought to reconcile you, at least in part, to the non-purchase of the decade-old chariot! The Chinatown glimpses surely sound fascinating. Congrats on that Singapore map! I wouldn't mind having similar charts of various exotic places. I have excellent London & Paris maps.[7] De Castro will surely appreciate your message.

[P.P.S. on envelope:] Loring & Mussey[8]—prompted by Derleth—just asked to see some of my junk. They—as you probably know—are the publishers of his books.

EXTRA

Just learned that there are 4 coal-black kittens at the boarding-house across the garden!

Notes

1. In 1930 the population was 8,962.
2. One of EHP's cats (the other was Battle Axe). According to the Book of Genesis and Books of Chronicles, Nimrod was the son of Cush, the great-grandson of Noah. He was "a mighty hunter before the Lord" (Gen. 10:9).
3. A cat belonging to Duane W. Rimel, who then resided in Asotin, WA.
4. I.e., EHP's dictaphone.
5. Anthony F. Moitoret (1892–1979), editor of the *Cleveland Sun, Seattle Sun,* and *San Francisco Sun.* His sons were Victor A. Moitoret (1919–2005) and Felix U. Moitoret (1923–2005).
6. In 1935, Chinese New Year was on 2 February.
7. J. Forest, *Plan de Paris* ([Paris:] A. Tirade, [1900]; *LL* 344). HPL's ownership of this item is conjectural. The London map is unidentified.
8. The publisher of Derleth's *Place of Hawks* and several of his detective novels.

[52] [ALS, JHL]

March 14, 1935

Hail, O Malik!

All bulletins & epistle duly at hand—& I have followed with the keenest interest the current adventures of yourself, Old Jug, & Nimrod the hunting leopard. What a trio! Congratulations on the dizzy Oakland drive, the 60,000th mile, the excursion to Half Moon Bay, & other achievements in higher juggernauting! Who wants a Rolls-Royce when an old friend is so faithful? Hope the dime remedy & diagnosis duly alleviated the worthy veteran's ailments! That expedition to the scenes of 1769 with its sunset ocean view & perilous mountain-trail-climbing by Jug (well—couldn't he climb trees back in '33?)[1] sounds impressive indeed, & I trust Nimrod enjoyed it if he was along. His exploits are surely of epic calibre—before long he'll have the whole neighbourhood purged of dogs . . . . unclean beasts in the sight of the Prophet.

Local felidae have shrunk to the extent of three exported kittens—but one of the four remains permanently. Coal-black little imp . . . whom I shall call John Perkins. Here's hoping he duplicates the multifarious & inimitable graces of his late brother Samuel (June–Sept. 1934)—though he'll have hard work doing that. In the course of time I trust he'll become a member of the Kappa Alpha Tau . . . . . little Sam had just joined when his untimely end overtook him.

Thanks abundantly for the cuttings. Chinatown must still be a fascinating & mysterious place, even though old-timers say it is merely a pallid echo of the original pre-1906 quarter. The only Chinatowns I've seen are those in Prov., Boston, & N.Y.—the latter the most picturesque of the three. Kirk, Leeds, & I once explored the N.Y. Chinatown during a tong war, when there were pairs of policemen stationed around at short intervals apart to prevent trouble—but we couldn't scare up a single flying bullet.

That account of Maine's Sahara certainly is fascinating in the extreme—it has the true quality of baffling *outsideness* which sends the imagination off on all sorts of flights . . . . & is the kind of thing which the late Charles Fort[2] would have avidly eaten up. I am enormously grateful for the account, & am filing it carefully in my "morgue" of weird ideas. Just *how* to use it is of course a question—although the basic idea would obviously be that of some inner-earth influence hostile to mankind. It ought to be handled in the subtle, restrained manner of Blackwood's "Willows"—with hints of possible horrors to come, & vague references to similar things in the past . . . . . the immemorially ancient past. It might be suggested that the Sahara Desert itself—once a fertile valley—became what it is through a similar process. But of course one ought to plan & ponder for ages before starting work on such a thing. Indian legends—the significance of the bull (vague allusions to Apis cult of Egypt & bull-worship of Crete)—hints of what lies underground—a possible journey of a human being through nighted labyrinths of inner earth—the notion (rather old, but still good for occasional use) of the earth as a single living organism—excavations of sand hills in various parts of the world shewing ruins of primal (sometimes pre-human) buildings, as if these had been engulfed by the vengeful & insatiable influence within—notion that the Gobi Desert—all deserts, in fact—thus arose . . . . any or all of these concepts might finally be used with a certain amount of effectiveness. I won't stake any claim around the idea. Let it remain common property, & good luck to the first one who utilises it adequately.

Glad the fiction-mill still pours forth its tireless stream, & shall appreciate the set of samples. Bless my soul! but do you mean to say that some fictioneers grind out still *more* than you do? Well—the pulps reveal that fact in a way . . . . since the overwhelming bulk of their contents seems to be simply slightly rearranged stock clichés & gory spatterings. I wouldn't envy such "masters" as Messrs. Brand & Bedford-Jones[3] too acutely! As for the young Comte d'Erlette—I really don't recall his latest figures, since such veritably astronomical magnitudes are too dizzying to hold in an old man's memory! But I dare say they form only a fraction of yours. I don't know the particulars of his work, but suppose his pulp junk is simply a rearrangement of the old "action" formulae—whether or not the details are previously decided on. This applies also to his detective books—of which he has fully completed three since the first one (one of these was published last autumn, another due this month, & another in September),⁴ virtually completed another, & planned still another. These detec items are rather above the average—with mechanically clever plot twists & surprises. I haven't asked him whether he still sticks to his 1-week schedule for deteckatiff novels.⁵ As for where his stuff appears—I suppose the books & a few pulps like W T account for the commercial junk. But it must be remembered that commercial stuff is not Derleth's real aim. It is merely a means of getting cash, & wholly disconnected with his serious work in the writing field—just like my revisory efforts, or the telegraph-operator's job held by R. E. Spencer, or the French instructor's job held by a friend of mine whose serious work is music.⁶ Probably the bulk of Derleth's real work—of which an increasing amount is poetry—occurs in the little high-grade magazines (*Midland, Pagany*, &c.) not on a commercial basis. He has also made *Scribners* & *Story*. One needn't think it is any *easier* to "make" these magazines than to make the commercial pulps—for as a matter of fact their standards of admission are *far more exacting* than those of any cheap trade proposition like W T or its congeners. While they don't of course demand the inartistic use of special formulae & "action" cliches as the pulps do, they have very rigid standards of *actual merit* which the pulps know nothing about. I doubt if I could ever write anything good enough for such non-trade magazines as *Pagany* or *Frontier*—indeed, I know of endless cases of their rejection of material which seemed to me quite excellent. Many—like young Bloch—who have made the pulps find it impossible to get anything into the small non-commercial quality magazines. With the latter there is no such thing as mastering a formula & indefinitely repeating. A story must have genuine aesthetic merit, or nothing doing. I have never had the audacity to send anything to magazines of such high quality. The fact that their acceptance is not "buying" means nothing at all. The profit motive is of no significance whatever in any work even remotely connected with the genuine arts. It is not likely that even a quarter of the work goes into one of Mr. H. Bedford-Jones's mechanical trade products, that goes into a really serious piece of writing of equal length (say by Machen or Blackwood) which may have escaped commercial publication . . . or may have never have been offered for publication. The idea of measuring the magnitude of a piece of work by its commercial reception or financial return is plainly a fallacy born of the transient conditions of our tottering bourgeois "civilisation"—especially that openly tradesmanlike phase of it which has flourished in the U.S. since the Civil War. Incidentally—Derleth's first serious novel, "Place of Hawks", will be published April 24.

This will form his fourth full-length book to appear in print. All are published by Loring & Mussey. And speaking of L & M—I'm expecting my own junk back any day now. After four previous fiascos in the book line, I am convinced that my products lack some essential quality of real merit—for these book propositions do not rest on the pulp formula basis. If an author can't get anything published by a quality (non-commercial) magazine or book-publisher, the fault would certainly seem to rest with him. By the way—I finished "The Shadow Out of Time" last week, but doubt whether it is good enough to type. Somehow or other, it does not seem to embody quite what I want to embody—& I may tear it up & start all over again. It came to 65 pages in all—but I don't see how it could be made any shorter without a loss of the essential effect. It is valueless to set down weird effects without adequate emotional preparation. As soon as I get a chance, I am going to experiment on other story ideas which repose in my note book.

Sorry local public library facilities are so poor—but the seeker after the unusual is always out of luck, even in the largest cities. It is surprising what books one *can't* find in the N.Y. & Boston libraries. After all, a private collection is the only dependable thing. However, for general small supplies Redwood City must be very convenient. Glad the environing country gentry use plenty of cat food . . . . though if Nimrod keeps up his present series of nocturnal forays he won't form a very steady customer of the urban emporia!

Harut & Marut[7] must make an interesting pair—though I should think their posture would interfere with their success as lecturers! I believe the mad author of the Necronomicon visited their hellish well near the site of Babel, though he is significantly reticent about its location in his abhorred & forbidden volume. I've never read Burton's[8] Arabian Nights—or any version except the small & ordinary popular ones. Probably it contains more than one valuable bit of weird source-material. It is, I believe, from the A. N. that most of our *ghoul* legendry is derived.[9]

Glad you're again finding the dictaphone of use—it would have been too bad to have purchased so elaborate a device in vain. Some day, perhaps, you can sell your used dictaphone records as valuable literary reliques instead of shaving & re-using them! What would we not give today for a wax cylinder holding the voice of Shakespeare or Milton or Keats!

Regarding the Oakland convention—thanks a million times for the proffered hospitality, though I hardly fancy I shall be able to make it. As a matter of fact, this especial convention isn't likely to draw enough of the old crowd I know to make it an overwhelming drawing card in itself. But I certainly do want to get out to California some time—to many-pillar'd Irem & vampire-haunted Averoigne—& when that time comes, your generous invitation will certainly be accepted with abundant appreciation! Probably the time I'll attempt the trip will be when you go east—so that I can avail myself of your generous suggestion & make either the outbound or inbound trip with you & Jug. If I ever go to the Pacific Coast, I'd like to have one trip by the northern route—taking in Wisconsin, where I have many friends,[10] & possibly including Asotin, Wash.—& the other through the southwest & south. But I wouldn't be any too particular if I could get across & back somehow! However—all that is for the remoter future. In any case, I hope you can get east again in course of time, & behold once more the huddled gambrel roofs of New-England's ancient seaports & the shadowy, brooding horrors of the secret-guarding glebe.

Had an interesting visitor March 2–3—the son of one of my old colleagues in amateur journalism who lives in Milwaukee. The youth—now 22, & 2 years out of the U. of Wis.—is an electrical engineer, & has recently been stationed by the Genl. Elec. Co. in Bridgeport, Conn. (130 m. from Prov. & 60 m. from N.Y.) He came in a juggernaut named "Skippy", of the same birth-date & parentage as your own immortal Arch-Jug—though it is only a runabout seating two instead of a capacious chariot. He is inclined to agree that the 1928's are about as solid & promising as any of Marse Henry's products.[11] Like you, he is skilled in mechanical mysteries, & has tinkered with brother Skippy's innards to a surprising & beneficial extent. On good roads he habitually makes 55 m. per hour when permitted by law or opportunity—though his ambitions have not soared into the 90 m. class as yet. By the way—this young man, whose name is Robert Ellis Moe, is a follower of weird & science fiction & a great admirer of "The Stranger from Kurdistan", "The Dreamer of Atlanaat", & other products of the Peacock Throne. Well—I showed him around the town, & lodged him on a camp cot in the living room . . . where I trust I may lodge you some time in the not too remote future. The next day we explored the countryside in Skippy—this forming my first real outing of the 1935 season. Most of the snow is gone, & the days are averaging between 40° & 50°. We went down the east shore of the bay to the ancient villages of Warren & Bristol, & later saw the west shore as far as East Greenwich. I left him there—giving him directions for reaching & seeing Wickford & Narragansett Pier on his homeward route. He expects to get up here several times more (& also to look up Long, Morton, & the gang in N Y)—& on some of those occasions I hope to shew him the Glebe & Gilbert Stuart's house & other notable scenes & objects which you will doubtless recall.

Good luck with your orchard—you surely will have a garden & estate worthy of any Sultan this side of Leng! Nimrod will guard the fruits of the sacred grove against all interlopers.

Regret to say that the *Fantasy Fan* has failed—which is unfortunate, since it really formed an invaluable forum for the exchange of discussion & information among devotees of the weird. Some of the material will be taken over by *Fantasy Magazine*—though it will of course be subordinated there, since Schwartz's specialty is science-fiction.

Heard some good recent lectures on Hokusai, contemporary Soviet art, & the mosaics of St. Sophia in Constantinople. Spring appears to be tardily creeping along, & I hope I can begin some real pedestrian outings within a month. Advices from Averoigne & Asotin indicate that your whole Pacific coast has been enjoying phenomenally vernal weather. Speaking of pedestrian trips, though—I did manage to work in a magnificent one March 6—when the mercury was up to 65° in the afternoon. I started out northward from the house, & eventually made a round trip of 12 miles—through five different cities & towns (Prov.–Pawtucket–Central Falls–Lincoln–N. Prov.), & including a plunge into my favourite Quinsnicket or Lincoln Woods countryside. Something of spring's intangible atmosphere was abroad—& at dusk an exquisitely slender crescent moon hung in the western sky not far from the blazing beacon of Venus. On the return trip—passing through the downtown section—I committed an extravagance which I'd been on the brink of committing for several days—bought the new 1935 edition of the 1-volume "Modern Encyclopaedia" . . . just brought out by Grosset & Dunlap for $1.95. I *almost* bought the original $3.50 edition back in 1933—& now I'm glad I didn't. A great book—I've long needed something with reasonably contemporary information, my newest other encyclopaedia being 1914. Contains all sorts of things which the older reference books don't have—not only recent events, but older things which weren't fully appreciated until comparatively recently. Thus an ordinary encyclopaedia of 20 or 25 years ago didn't have any of the French symbolist poets or any of the great Japanese printmakers—whereas this does. And as for recency—it mentions things as late as *last September!* But if you get one, be sure to get a *perfect copy.* Since it is a cheaply manufactured volume, some copies are likely to be slightly imperfect. I changed the first one I got—but even the new copy has a crease in one place . . . & a bit of glue from the binding in another place . . . &c. But for $1.95 it's a really record-breaking volume

Wish you could out-argue the commercial tyrant who wants you to twist Pawang out of character—damn these tradesmen & their doltish ideas! That was certainly a tragedy about the 5 wasted records—Yuggoth! but I hope you remembered the vital substance of what you had on them.[12]

Nimrod's appetite after his wounds certainly argues an exhaustless capacity. What a boy! Hope he fully avenged his injuries in the next foray. Yes—there's nothing quite up to the felidae . . . I've been devoted to them all my life. Some of the Kappa Alpha Tau are at the club today—I went out & had quite a conversation with the tiger vice-president a while ago. Pres. Randall has appeared on a few *very* warm days—but he's like me about weather!

The weird–science-fiction-fan population of Providence has just received an accretion of very energetic calibre, as I had impressed upon me last week. I was reading the paper in my study one evening when—after a ringing of the doorbell—my aunt entered to announce a caller . . . a "Mr. Sterling",[13] who had called to see the old gentleman. Close upon her heels the visitor appeared . . . in the person of a little Jewish boy about as high as my waist, with unchanged childish treble & swarthy face innocent of the Gillette's passage. He *did* have long trousers—which somehow seemed odd upon so small an infant. It appears that he is one of the innumerable kid fans clustering around *Fantasy Magazine,* the late F F, & the weird-science pulps in general, & that he had known my stuff & got my address from someone in the fantasy world. He is a New-Yorker, but his papa has just been made assistant manager or something at a local chain fur emporium of considerable N.E. fame, so he's a Providence citizen now—& in the Classical High School. And oy, vhat ah child! Vhat ah child! If they all come as precocious as this, I don't wonder the Nazis are afraid they'll juggle the shirts off the German people! Damme if the kid didn't talk like a man of 30—correcting all the mistakes in the current science yarns, reeling off facts & figures a mile a minute, & displaying the taste & judgment of a veteran. He has already sold stories to *Wonder* & other pulps, & is bubbling over with ideas. Others in his family, he said, have written book reviews for the N.Y. *Herald Tribune* & contributed to various "slicks". And now—being fully weaned from the bottle—he has put on long trousers & is prepared to conquer ancient Providence! He vants he should organise a branch of the Science Fiction League, &c. &c. &c. Well, well! I gave him some F Fs & other items—& he says he's going to call again. Hope he won't become a nuisance—I don't want to discourage him, for he really does seem like an astonishingly promising babe.

Had a good glimpse of the countryside March 9—some friends took my aunt & me on a motor ride through the region just east of here—the Massachusetts border. Fine old farmhouses & village vistas—& the magic of approaching spring more & more apparent.

Heard a fine lecture at the college—with slides & instruments—March 11, on the cosmic rays, by Prof. W. F. G. Swann of the Franklin Institute.[14] He made several things clear which I had not fully comprehended before. ¶ Congrats on sampling your old Va. friends! I used to see 'em advertised everywhere, though I don't recall Gen. McArthur.[15] ¶ Well—Blessings of all the Djinns & Afreets!

ꓛ ꙅꙅ ꙅꓯ

Notes

1. EHP did in fact write twice about using his car for tree-climbing.

2. Charles Fort (1874–1932), American writer and researcher specializing in anomalous phenomena. The Desert of Maine is not a true desert, since it receives abundant precipitation and surrounding vegetation encroaches on the barren dunes. The 40-acre tract of exposed glacial silt is surrounded by a pine forest near Freeport, ME. It originated when land clearance and overgrazing by sheep led to soil erosion, exposing a dune of sandlike glacial silt. It was turned into a tourist attraction in 1925.

3. Frederick Schiller Faust (1892–1944), American author known primarily for his

thoughtful and literary Westerns under the pen name Max Brand. He wrote more than 500 novels for magazines and almost as many shorter stories. Henry James O'Brien Bedford-Jones, or H. Bedford-Jones (1887–1949), was a Canadian historical, adventure fantasy, science fiction, crime, and Western writer who became a naturalized U.S. citizen in 1908. He wrote more than 100 novels, earning the sobriquet "King of the Pulps."

4. *The Man on All Fours* (1934), *Sign of Fear* (1935), and *Three Who Died* (1935). HPL owned all these books (presumably given to him by Derleth). Loring & Mussey went out of business, and so the works in progress, *Sentence Deferred* (1939) and *The Seven Who Waited* (1943), were not published for some time.

5. See August Derleth, "Novels at 10,000 Words a Day," *Writer's Review* 2, No. 4 (January 1934): 3–4.

6. Robin Edgerton Spencer (1896–1956) was later Assistant Chief of Office of Climatology, U.S. Weather Bureau, Washington, D.C. He wrote four novels, including the weird novel *The Lady Who Came to Stay* (1931), which HPL admired. HPL's friend was Alfred Galpin (1901–1983), French scholar, who composed a "Lament for H.P.L." following HPL's death.

7. Two angels mentioned in the second surah of the Qur'an who were present during the reign of Sulaymân and located at Bâbil.

8. Sir Richard Burton (1821–1890), British Orientalist who prepared an unexpurgated translation of the *Arabian Nights* (1885). HPL read an unidentified abridged translation in 1895, then was given a copy of Andrew Lang's selection (1898) as a Christmas present by his mother in 1898.

9. HPL derived his information on ghouls from Samuel Henley's notes to William Beckford's *Vathek* (1786).

10. In Wisconsin, HPL knew Maurice W. Moe and Robert Bloch in Milwaukee, Alfred Galpin in Appleton, George S. Schilling in Madison, and August Derleth in Sauk City. F. Lee Baldwin and Duane W. Rimel lived in Asotin, Washington.

11. I.e., Ford automobiles.

12. EHP had mistakenly "shaved" five recording discs before having their contents transcribed.

13. Kenneth J. Sterling (see Glossary). His father was Lee Welvan Sterling (1890–1980?).

14. William Francis Gray Swann (1884–1962), British physicist and director of the Franklin Institute (1927–59).

15. A brand of cigarette.

[53]   [ALS, JHL]

Ancient Kingsport—May 4[, 1935]

[Postmarked Providence, R.I., 7 May 1935]

Hail, O Malik!

Behold me in the centuried lanes of hoary Marblehead— prototype of Kingsport—in the course of a week-end outing & visit. Weather was rotten yesterday, but today is sunny . . . though not as warm as I'd like. In a borrowed topcoat, however, I'm all right—& I'm endeavouring to keep up with my neglected correspondence by writing (as I usually do) between sight-seeing glances. Am sitting just now in my worthy host's Juggernaut—but later paragraphs may be written in one or another of the harbour-overlooking parks of this fascinating & venerable town (which dates from about 1639). I suppose I've described Marblehead to you many times before, so that you are no stranger to its crooked alleys, precipitous hill streets, & 18th century gam-brel-roofed houses perched at irresponsible angles on rock cliffs & surprising slopes. There's no other place like it in creation—& I like it best at this time of year, before the self-conscious summer people & "art" colonists begin to clutter it up. Spring—of a sort—is here despite the chill of today. Trees & shrubs in feathery green, & forsythias a blaze of yellow. Here in Mass., though, the season is not as well advanced as in R.I. They have a hellish east wind here which we don't get. My host is the pleasant Edward H. Cole whom I've mentioned to you before—one of the old-time amateur crowd, though he won't be at the Oakland convention. Teacher of English & of Am. history in Chauncy Hall School, which prepares boys for M.I.T. I may have men-tioned his household of felidae—grave grey & white Napoleon, lean, tiger Wellington, & tiger-angora Peter Ivanovitch Romanoff . . . who has grown to huge size since last August, & whose battles with the Iron Duke are epical in their intensity. If these warriors ever united in a common cause, I'll wager they could give even Nimrod a tough tussle!

Well—I read your epistle & postcard bulletins with the keenest of pleas-ure, & sincerely envy you the Yosemite trip. Scenic *grandeur* is something with which I am almost unacquainted at first-hand—a glimpse of the White Mts. & ascent of Mt. Washington by cog-wheel railway in 1927 being my only ap-proximation of it. I have, of course seen pictures & read descriptions of the Yosemite—but such can hardly convey more than a faint shadow of the real thing. El Capitan—3604 feet above a 3090 feet floor—must be a tremendous sight. I once revised a poem describing—or purporting to describe—it.

Congrats on Old Jug's renovation! Hope the eastern trip will materialise in course of time. A tour with dictaphone & all the trimmings—combining work & pleasure—would surely be a great idea . . . . though it's a pity such a peregrination couldn't be accomplished in the faithful old Jug of yore!

Glad Pawang & his brethren are prospering, & hope their various con-spiracies & slaughterings may soon have that mortgage & all other obligations disposed of. As for Satrap Pharnabazus & his caprices—he has long been past my explaining. Your were-leopard tale[1] sounds to me like a tremendous improvement on the silver-bullet stuff—indeed, your explanation of the na-ture of the phenomenon is precisely like that offered back in the 15th century by Kramer & Sprenger (authors of the famous Malleus Maleficarum) in con-sidering some of the phenomena of witchcraft-metamorphosis. Why Wright did not appreciate the departure from the usual cliché is beyond me—though it is easy to see that he has a weakness for conventional tripe. As for a commercial policy to adopt toward him—I suppose the wise thing would be to cease "slanting" any commercial fiction in his direction. If a tale designed for another market happens to fall within the conceivable sphere of W T, you might send it in after rejections by higher-paying media—letting Pharnabazus being [*sic*] a sort of incidental, as it were. But commercial material designed to suit W T & no other possible market is obviously unprofitable. However— W T is always a *conceivable* market for certain types of serious weird fiction as distinguished from the profit-seeking product. One can never depend on Wright either for acceptance or rejection—but if a tale is short, & not extremely gruesome or strikingly original, it always has a *chance*. And the fact that Pharnabazus will (as many others will not) guarantee to print a story *exactly as written* is in his favour. I think he used to be even more liberal & open than he is now. His timidity about gruesomeness is increasing, & he is getting so soaked in the lifeless & mechanical formula & jack-in-the-box action clichés of commercial fiction that he appreciates a real story less & less. His recent attempt to compete with certain other magazines by encouraging science fiction & weird detective stuff is a loss to lovers of the weird.

Well—good luck to your production schedule! I've heard a good deal about these plot devices, & once thought they might be of help to me in concocting commercial junk. I argued that, except for the disgust & repulsion which keep one from devising *unguided* pulp puerilities, I could concoct independent synthetic crap as easily as I could tinker with the kindred crap of other would-be hacks. If, then, I had a conventional mechanical plot doped out by some external agency—which is as much & more than I have to go by in many revision jobs—why could I not do with *that* what I ordinarily do with the feeble conventionalities of others . . . . the only difference being that I could collect *all* the possible proceeds instead of merely a fee? The 'plot elements' arrived at through these gadgets would be equivalent to a bum story offered for revision by Mrs. Heald[2] or old 'Dolph de Castro or some other aspiring pulpist. Well—I got to the point of sending a dollar to one of those companies in Los Angeles (the same one, I think, which makes the Plot Genie) for something called the *Plot Robot*—a set of lists of stock characters, situations, climaxes, difficulties, &c. &c. &c. &c. to be chosen in juxtaposition by the twirling of a pointer on a dial. God, what cheap hokum! To make matters worse, they sent a set of lists pertaining to a branch of fiction utterly & especially antipathetic to me—romance-adventure, or something like that, with noble hero, beautiful she-ro, black vilyun, stirring deeds, & all the rest. It was simply too much for my stomach—& ingenuity. Other types of plot creator might not be so hopeless. I don't know. But that contemplated tripeworks of mine certainly never got to the stage of actual operation or even preliminary experimentation! However, I know that a cleverer person than I might well find some such apparatus prodigiously helpful. It might be possible to use only *part* of a formula arrangement—or to depart widely from the plot originally selected. There is certainly a place for such things among mechanical fiction-purveyors, & if I had the cash I'd probably sample all the various brands on the market. By the way—I can well imagine how valuable the Malay & Hindoo manuals are proving. Touches of authentic speech here & there must go far toward making an exotic locale convincing.

About old de Castro—I really feel guilty in having sic'd him on you, but when I did so I thought you were anxious for collaborative connexions & plots from outside sources . . . . human Plot Genie stuff, as it were. Indeed, I think you were at the time collaborating with Long. Too bad his ideas are so archaic & undeveloped—I can understand what a problem their proper formulation would be. That's about the way I feel concerning his philosophical book MS. "The New Way"—on which I rashly promised to help him. Like you, I hate to let the old chap down—especially in view of his present bereavement. He is really very generous & likeable—only the other day he sent me an edition of Baudelaire's letters. In your case I hardly know what to advise. You certainly ought not to assume any responsibility injurious to your own programme. Perhaps a few words of praise & constructive criticism—with a delay savouring more of postponement than of downright dismissal where actual revision or ghost-writing is concerned—might help to tide things over without giving the old boy either offence or discouragement. Incidentally—I don't think he'd mind having another's work passed off as his own. As I once told you, there is a persistent touch of the charlatan in his makeup. About Mortonius—I'll tell him those minerals are safe, & that he'll get his supply in due course of time. And so Miss Moore is considering the A.F.G.? Young Bobby Barlow is afraid she'll go commercial[3] & lose the potency & freshness which come of spontaneous, non-formula writing—which may be so, especially since she uses stock romantic characters & situations anyhow, as a result of a somewhat unclassical taste. Her work seems to be like that of Two-Gun Bob in spirit—accidentally suited to the herd's taste, yet motivated by a genuine self-expressive instinct. If she became a general fiction-factory she'd lose the distinctive merit she now has—though possibly turning out an acceptable grade of formula-junk. One can never tell in advance about any given case. As for the least absurd interplanetary stuff in the pulps—I think the rather light tales of one Stanley G. Weinbaum[4] in Wonder & Astounding (recently brought to my notice) almost merit that designation. They relate events not conspicuously removed from plausibility. Young Anger spoke of his enjoyable visit to many-pillared Irem, & of Nimrod's surprising friendliness toward him.

Home Again—May 7

Didn't have time to finish this while on the road. The visit as a whole was badly ruined by the cold weather, though of course congenial conversation made up for much that was missed.

Glad to hear news of the orchard, & trust it may flourish in spite of the gophers, afrites, & other evil influences. Your selection of trees is surely artistic & judicious . . . . & the name *Black Mission fig* suggests almost anything! Perchance it pertains to that Black Pilgrimage so potently alluded to in M. R. James's "Count Magnus."

The description of Nimrod & his current activities is as fascinating a piece of feline literature as I've read in recent years, & will gain a permanent place in the Kappa Alpha Tau's archives. What an engaging old reprobate Nim must be! I hope you'll let me see any snapshots of him which you may take. You would, I presume, choose some moment (if any) when his ears & countenance are reasonably intact. Good old rascal! May his be a peaceful & pious old age—& may many a dream of glamourous & victorious yesterdays come to hover round the red cushion in the throne room during the future years of repose. By the way—little John Perkins is here today, & sends his regards to Nimrod. Enclosed are snaps of both Perkinses—little Sam (June–Sept. 1934) & Johnny. I started a new role of film with Sam last August, & didn't finish using up the 8 pictures till this April—so that the departed & the living are preserved on one celluloid strip. I haven't yet been able to get a very good snap of John—but am still hoping. The present one is a crude silhouette made with a portrait lens. The little devils simply won't keep still! You might return these prints unless you have some permanent use for them—though there's no hurry about the date.

Some good lectures recently—one on Albrecht Dürer by Prof. Pauli,[5] director of the Hamburg Kunsthalle, & one on Italian baroque architecture by the great-great-grand-nephew of the bird who chose the Gibbs designs for our First Baptist Steeple in 1774.[6] The latter was especially interesting—I had not realised before how much freer from the extreme phases of baroque extravagance Northern Italy was, than Rome & the South. No wonder our own Georgian architecture is far purer & more classical than the Renaissance architecture of other nations—since it was from Palladio (of Venice & Vicenza) that Inigo Jones drew his primary inspiration.

As for travel notes—though cold weather played hell with the recent week-end, its predecessor was almost ideal. Blazing sun—& up to 82° in Providence. Fortunately I got in a lot of exploration & sightseeing through a visit from young Moe—the chap who was here early in March. The visitor blew in Saturday, Apr. 27, in his faithful Skippy—brother of Old Jug—& we put in a strenuous 2 days in that venerable vehicle. Saturday we visited old Newport—seeing 2 ancient windmills; a flock of sheep with sportive lambkins in the best pastoral tradition; "Whitehall", the 1729–32 home of Dean Berkeley; the Hanging Rocks where that good cleric composed his famous "Alciphron"; the lofty cliffs; the strange rock cleft called "Purgatory", where the ocean pounds thunderously in; the Overing farmhouse where a small rowboat party of rebels under Col. Wm. Barton captured Genl. Prescott of

His Majesty's Regulars in 1778; & the centuried town itself—with 1698 Quaker Meeting House, 1726 Anglican church, 1739 Colony House, 1749 library, 1760 market-house, 1763 Jews' synagogue, & private dwellings as old as 1675. Glorious hot day—up to 82° in Prov., though not quite so good in Newport. Took some pictures which I'll show you if they turn out well. Sunday the 28th we went to ancient New Bedford, the quondam whaling centre (after Nantucket's decline). The marine museum was closed—but after a tour of the picturesque waterfront we set off southward to sample something still better. This was the Round Hills estate of Col. E. H. R. Green (son of old Hetty the miser) in S. Dartmouth, where the old whaling barque *Charles W. Morgan* (built 1841) is preserved at a realistic-looking wharf—but solidly embedded in concrete as a permanent exhibit. We went all over the vessel—which is tremendously fascinating—& snapped some pictures of it. On the Green estate is also an ancient windmill moved from Rhode Island. We then explored a region—where southern Mass. adjoins southeastern R.I.—which I had never seen before in my life. Splendid unspoiled country with rambling stone walls & idyllic white-steepled villages of the old New England type. Of the latter the best 2 specimens—Adamsville & Little Compton Commons—are both in R.I. Adamsville contains the world's only known monument to a *hen*—perpetuating the fame of the Rhode Island Red, a breed evolved in that village from East Indian (page Pawang Ali!) & Chinese gallinaceous forbears. At Little Compton Commons can be found the home & grave of Elizabeth Alden Pabodie—daughter of the famed John Alden & Priscilla Mullins of Plymouth, & first white woman born in New England. This region was once the seat of the Sakonnet Indians—whose squaw-sachem Awashonks was persuaded by the noted old warrior Capt. Benjamin Church not to join King Philip's conspiracy in 1675. It was settled from Plymouth about 1673, & (like Barrington, Warren, & Bristol) came into Massachusetts in 1691 & into Rhode Island (when a boundary dispute was settled by George II) in 1747. Capt. Church lies buried not far from Little Compton Commons. Well—at last we turned north through Tiverton, where on our left we had some marvellous vistas of low-lying fields & blue water. Here we passed the home of the navigator Capt. Robert Grey, who in 1792 discovered the Columbia River on your own Pacific coast—naming it after his stout Rhode Island brig. Then back home via Fall River (an ugly mill city over the line in Mass.) & Warren . . . at which later place we paused at the famous Maxfield's (a rendezvous of Mortonius & myself, of which I think I've told you) for a dinner consisting entirely of ice cream—a pint & a half each. (6 varieties . . . I had chocolate, caramel, banana, coffee, lemon & strawberry; Moe had chocolate, caramel, banana, coffee, ginger, & pistachio) Finally back to #66—after which I regretfully guided the guest out of town & took a 4-mile rural walk before returning home. Quite a session—I wish to hades the later outing would have been equally favoured by circumstance!

Just got the May W T—which is reprinting my "Arthur Jermyn". Haven't had time to read it yet. Have you seen the March–April *Marvel Tales?* If not, I could send you a copy. And did you see the April *Fantasy Magazine* with my biography & portrait?[7]

Cook may be going to E. St. Louis, Ill. before long—if a certain possible business prospect materialises. If he doesn't, he may possibly go on a tour of Vermont in his sister's car—in which case I would probably accompany him. But I'd want any trip to *Vermont* to be considerably later in the season than this! ¶ Regards to you & Nimrod from all the K.A.T. ¶ Salaam aliekum—

[Enclosures: Postcard[8]] Probably Gov. Arnold's mill—built circa 1670.[9] [Clipping: "Indians on Relief Job Learn Thrift"] Broken Axe, him get busy!

Notes

1. "Naga's Kiss."
2. Hazel Heald (1896–1961), revision client of HPL.
3. So much so that he put HPL up to writing a letter to her (his first), attempting to dissuade her from doing so.
4. Weinbaum (1902–1935) died of throat cancer at the age of thirty-three. His writing career lasted a scant 18 months, but he is considered one of the greatest of science fiction writers for his realistic portrayal of alien creatures. Like Bloch, he was a member of the Milwaukee Fictioneers, which issued his book *The Black Flame* as a memorial.
5. Theodor Gustav Pauli (1866–1938), German art historian and museum director in Bremen and Hamburg.
6. Joseph Brown (1736–1803) selected the steeple designs.
7. By F. Lee Baldwin (biography) and Duane W. Rimel (linoleum cut).
8. *Front:* Ancient Viking Tower, The Old Stone Mill, Newport, R.I.
9. Governor Benedict Arnold (1615–1678) referred to the Newport Tower as his "stone built wind mill." HPL's notes for a possible story, "[The Round Tower]" (*CE* 5.253), seem to derive from this edifice.

[54]   [ALS, JHL]

May 29, 1935

Dear Malik:—

Aië! Aië! Aië! I mourn for Great Jogganath, Prince of Tree-Climbers & Leader of Caravans; mighty Jug, Great-grandfather of the Arrow & Brother of the Meteor![1] A star droppeth from out the sky; a mountain top-pleth into the plain; a titan redwood falleth from among its brethren. Aië! Aië! Great Juggernaut is no more! The lane outside the door weepeth for the wheels it will never again feel; up from the Glebe & the Stuart snuff-mill cometh a chorus of sighs. As sang Moschus of old in sun-blest Sicilia for the lost Bion:

'Plaintively groan at my bidding, ye woodland dells, & thou Dorian water, & weep, rivers, the mighty Juggernaut; now wail at my bidding, ye plants, & now, groves, utter a wail; now may ye flowers breathe forth your life in sad clusters; blush now sorrowfully, ye roses, now, thou anemone; now, hyacinth, speak thy letters, & with thy leaves lisp *aï! aï!* more than is thy wont: a noble chariot is dead.

'Begin, Sicilian Muses, begin the lament!'[2]

But let us bear up bravely. Le Roi est mort—Vive le Roi! May fortune & felicity attend Great Juggernaut II—which surely seems to take the throne under good auspices. The Essex is a worthy steed—& has been the official Long chariot since 1927. When Essex I became seedy, Doc Long could think of nothing better than an Essex II—the present family coach—as its successor. Your present buy seems to be a genuine bargain, & I think you were undoubtedly wise not to take the impressive & all-too-thirsty Pierce-Arrow. Hope all your expeditions will be realised, & that you'll shortly be beating every streamlined rocket in sight—soaring over the highways at a rate comparable to that of the Interstellar Patrol's space ships!

Thanks tremendously for the attractive snap of yourself & Great Nimrod at the Gates of Many-Pillar'd Irem. Nim surely is a valiant old boy, & a worthy member of the Pious Companions. I can picture him stalking nameless prey by night, & returning at dawn with the scars of cryptic & honourable combat variegating his snowy fur. Noble clawsman! May his red cushion ever be soft, & may the liver, cheese parings, milk, dog-food, beans, diced meat & spaghetti never run low! Let me add that I likewise rejoice at having a recent likeness of Nimrod's valiant comrade—& of the magic portal of Irem.

But tell Nimrod to be on his guard against evil spells . . . for lo! The *second* of his fleece-white brethren has now vanished into ethereal space! I sadly told you about the evaporation of the sturdy & alabaster Doodlebug at the Villa Barlovia last winter. Now the curse has crossed the continent & attacked the Kappa Alpha Tau's stronghold in Asotin, Wash! For alas, young Rimel's marble-hued Crom has floated out of this tri-dimensional world into some forbidden realm of the 4th Axis! What hidden enemy is at work against our clan? Perchance it is this continent-spanning Malevolence which Nimrod battles by night! Well—I trust the teeth & talons of this last & mightiest of the Sons of Snow may prove victorious! Death to all oppressors & enemies of the K.A.T.!

Congrats on the 2nd anniversary of the Irem Fiction Works! You certainly have developed production in a big way! I don't wonder you celebrated—but shame on you for not taking Nimrod along to share the festive gorge on marine obscenities! Well—see that he gets plenty of the Chorazin[3] Pilgrimage Figs when they're at the right stage of unholy ripeness!

And thanks most effusively for the vivid travelogue & map of the Monterey peninsula trip! Your notes make the reader visualise the voyage with remarkable clearness—the sinister shadows of La Honda, the melancholy &

desolation of the abandoned oil country, the bronze footprints of Don Gaspar de Portola,[4] & the lingering charm of leisurely old Monterey itself. I fancy I'd like Monterey about as well as any town on the Pacific coast—it certainly sounds like my kind of a place! The presence of an *American Consulate* adds an unique touch . . . . I wonder if they had one in San Augustin, Florida-Oriental, prior to 1819? Well—if I ever do get out to the Pacific, I certainly mustn't miss Monterey! But to think that this memorable jaunt formed Old Jug's last ride! Eheu, fugaces!

Speaking of trips—there is a possibility that I may see ancient San Augustin before long, for Barlow is urging me to visit him after he gets home from Washington. It will be a perilous financial squeak—but I may try it for all that . . . . cutting out all intermediate stops save Charleston & St. Aug. I certainly hope I can make it. This spring has been lousily chilly, so that I really need a genuinely warm place to thaw the traces of winter out of my aged bones!

Had a visit from young Hornig, late editor of *The Fantasy Fan*, last Saturday. He's a pleasant chap of 18 or 19—tall & lean, & resembling Donald Wandrei except for a vaguely Semitic cast of countenance. Capable & intelligent—as indeed he must be in order to edit *Wonder Stories*. He seemed to appreciate the antiquities of centuried Providence very keenly—I shewed him the high spots, including the hidden churchyard which you & Brobst & I saw by night.[5] Young Sterling (who returns to N.Y. shortly) was also on hand.

Speaking of antiquarian high-spots—aïë! aïë! aïë! Another row of ancient buildings in this vicinity is about to feel the vandal's hand! The scene of devastation is College St. itself—the doomed row being that huddle of quaint houses & archways reaching from Benefit St. (where that tailor said he couldn't have your suits cleaned by the following Monday)[6] downward to the foot of the hill—on the same (north) side as the court leading to #66, but beginning ¾ of a block lower down. Included in the cataclysm are the house of Brown's first president (1771), a fine 1750 specimen, & one of those rare old archways leading under parts of a building to inner courtyards[7] . . . . . of which the only perfect specimens left in America are those on Providence's ancient hill. (There is a bricked-up example in Richmond, & a boarded-up one in Philadelphia) On this site will ascend the new main building of the R.I. School of Design. Two palliating & consoling factors exist: (a) The preservation, restoration, & incorporation into the new building of the bottom (& only brick) house of the ancient row—the old Franklin Inn, with its quaint innyard archway. Thus the survival of *one* of the archways is assured. And (b) the choice of a splendid Providence-Georgian design for the new edifice. The structure's lower units will harmonise with the surviving Franklin Inn, while the upper units will blend with the residential buildings higher up on the hill. One part will even have a "monitor roof" like #66—
—a form especially typical of Providence in the 1790–1810 period. The architect is the same bird who did

the new Providence-Georgian court house across the street from the proposed structure (you saw this). The change is regrettable, yet it is fortunate that the character of the new building will be the same. Obviously, Providence is remaining dominantly true to its traditional Georgian heritage, & avoiding the 'modernistic' epidemic from which even old Boston is not quite immune.

Had my pictures of the April 27–8 outing developed at last, & they all came out fairly well. At the moment all the sets are lent, but when one comes back I'll let you have a look at it. The shot I like best is of the pastoral scene I told you about—the green slope with the ancient windmill, flock of sheep, stone wall, & venerable farm buildings. If that isn't a bit of the 18th century—or the old world—I'll eat the negative!

Mr. Perkins sends his regards to Nimrod. He's getting bigger & scrappier every day, & by the time he formally joins the Kappa Alpha Tau I'll bet he can lick any man in it! He's over here a good part of the time—chewing up papers & scattering their fragments all over the room. His purr gets louder & louder, though he can't rival E. H. Cole's Angora—Peter Ivanovitch Romanoff—for absolute quantitative resonance.

Your composite Plotto–Genie tale certainly sounds like a triumph for The Fiction Works & its latest installations![8] The current Spicy must be quite an Irem issue![9] Hope the rejection mania won't spread—but of course such temporary maladies develop now & then even in the most advanced manufacturing circles—the business cycle, & all that! Glad to hear that the cost of Jug #2 has almost been recouped.

Now about the book I spoke of—it was none other than the famous MALLEUS MALEFICARUM [Hammer of Witches] by Jacobus Sprenger & Henricus Institor [Heinrich Kramer]—published in Germany about 1485 as a guide to inquisitors in detecting, examining, & punishing witches. The authors were priests connected with the Inquisition, & the occasion for writing the book was the extraordinary outburst of witch-cult activities in the 15th century which led to Pope Innocent VIIIth's celebrated bull of 1484—an edict which produced the greatest period of witch-burning in all history. Only one part of the book deals with the transformation of humans into other animals—but in this section it is suggested that the change is only an apparent one, caused by a spell laid upon the eyes of all beholders. This suggestion is not dogmatic or all-inclusive, but is advanced as tentative & probable in a great many cases. The *Malleus* proved to be the first of many similar works on witch-finding, of which those of Delrio, Remigius, Guazzo, Glanvill, & Boguet[10] are the best known. I don't know how much real help a perusal of the book would give you. There is nothing very complex or new in it. Perhaps the greatest advantage apart from convincing Wright would be in being able to quote verbatim from some ancient & important-sounding source. The modern English edition of the book is that translated & edited by the Rev.

Montague Summers (a rare old nut who actually believes in witchcraft) & published by John Rodker (London) in 1928. This is so famous a book that there is no chance whatsoever of Wright's not having *heard* of it. It is, however, less certain that he has *read* it—for it is somewhat hard to get at nowadays. The copy I read was borrowed from *H. Koenig, 540 East 80th St., New York, N.Y.*—who would be exceedingly glad to lend it to you . . . or to Wright, as might be preferable. It is, incidentally, silly of Wright to let such a thing determine his policy of acceptance or rejection. A plausible idea is a plausible idea—& it doesn't make a damn's worth of difference whether or not it has ever formed part of an actual mythological fabric. The fact is, I rather prefer *purely original* weird concepts as opposed to those derived from genuine folklore. Authentic folk-beliefs are likely to be insipid, ill-proportioned, freakish, & in general far less aesthetically effective than concepts formed by an author with a specific artistic purpose in mind. Quinn makes me tired with his dragged-in encyclopaedia-scrapings.

Well—in any case, I hope the *Malleus* reference will still Satrap Pharnabazus' objections & sell the story. It ought to, if folklore justification is what the cuss is looking for! Happened to be writing this letter when your 2 cards arrived, hence am saving the reply card for some future occasion.

Also during the course of this epistle I've received back one of the loaned sets of travel pictures—hence I'm enclosing it herewith. I think you'll agree that our expedition traversed a pretty interesting terrain! Have you ever seen any of the ancient windmills which abound on the flatter parts of the New England coast . . . Cape Cod, Nantucket, Aquidneck, Conanicut, Long Island? Hope Jug II will get around to their habitat in the course of time! No haste about return of pictures so long as they're safe.

Another item in the day's mail is from Barlow. He hopes I can get down to De Land as soon as possible after his own return June 3. I may try it—but address the next communication to #66 unless you get a postcard of contrary advice. If I go, I'll have to shoot straight down—trusting to luck to manage St. Aug & Charleston on the return trip.

My sympathy to Nimrod anent his gnawed ear. Undoubtedly he is being hunted by the same Nameless Night-Entity which has kidnapped good old Doodlebug & Crom . . . . but his supernal prowess prevents the Entity from getting him. Some black midnight he may even get the Entity—how would you like to have him dragging a Loathsome Shape into the house some morning, as he has in the past dragged gophers? Curious how these Entities concentrate their attacks upon *white* Kappa Alpha Tau members! Thanks again, by the way, for that attractive photograph.

Well—again I shed tears for Old Jug. That last Oakland trip surely attests his gameness! And again I will express my gratitude for that interesting Monterey travelogue.

With every good wish, & hoping that Jug II may yield the most brilliant possible results, I am
Ever your most obt h^ble Servt   ⌒⌒⌣ ᗡ ᑎ⌒

Notes

1. The Duesenberg Model SJ, better known as the Mormon Meteor, was built in 1935. EHP had previously written HPL about recently going to San Francisco to purchase a 1932 Essex Terraplane. He mentioned seeing a 1931 Pierce Arrow, though demurred at buying it because of its gasoline consumption.

2. From "Idyll III: The Epitaph of Bion, a Loving Herdsman," in *The Idylls of Theocritus, Bion, and Moschus: and the War-Songs of Tyrtæus,* Literally Translated into English Prose, by the Rev. J. Banks, M.A. with Metrical Versions by J. M. Chapman, M.A. (London: George Bell and Sons, 1878), 188–89.

3. Khorazin (or Chorazin) is a village cursed by Jesus (Matthew 11:20–24; Luke 10:13–15) for rejecting his work. Early medieval writers believed the Antichrist would be born there. Chorazin is cited in M. R. James's "Count Magnus."

4. Gaspar de Portolá y Rovira (1723–1786), Spanish soldier and administrator in New Spain. His expedition was the first from Europe to see San Francisco Bay.

5. At St. John's Episcopal Church (1810) at 275 North Main Street.

6. Probably John A. Stone at 238 Benefit Street.

7. The "rare old archway" to which HPL refers was at 20 College Street.

8. "Death Rides an Elephant." EHP used Plotto to begin the story and Plot Genie to finish it—hence HPL's reference to the "composite Plotto–Genie tale."

9. EHP had two stories in the *Spicy Mystery Stories* for July 1935: "The Garden of Evil" and "Corpse Crypt" (as by Hamlin Daly), and also "Private Graveyard" in the July *Spicy Detective.*

10. Martin Antoine Del Rio, or Delrio (1551–1608), a Jesuit priest, was the author of *Disquisitionum Magicarum Libri Sex [Six Books of Disquisitions on Magic]* (1633). HPL cribbed the quotation from Delrio in "The Horror at Red Hook" from the "Magic" entry by Edward Burnett Tylor in the *Encyclopaedia Britannica.* Remigius is the Latinized form of the name Nicholas Remy (1525–1612). *Daemonolatreia* was published in Latin in 1595; there have been two translations, one in German in 1693 and one in English in 1930 (by Montague Summers; as *Demonolatry*). It is a sort of guidebook to witch-hunting for witchcraft judges. HPL mentioned it in "The Festival" (*CF* 1.410) and "The Dunwich Horror" (*CF* 2.452). Francesco Maria Guazzo (1570–1640), an Italian priest, published *Compendium Maleficarum,* a witch-hunter's manual published in Milan in 1608. *Saducismus Triumphatus* by Joseph Glanvill (1636–1680) condemned skepticism about the existence and supernatural powers of witchcraft and included seventeenth-century folklore about witches. The book is mentioned in "The Festival" (*CF* 1.410), Glanville in "The Transition of Juan Romero" (*CF* 1.100). *Discours des Sorciers (An Examen of Witches,* edited by Montague Summers) by Henri Boguet (d. 1619) is the work of a French judge who sat on numberless witchcraft cases in the 1590s.

[55]   [ALS, JHL][1]

Deserted Mosque of Yoth-Kadar
in the tropic jungle of Zhun
[Postmarked 19 June 1935]

Dear Malik:—

All bulletins—direct & forwarded—duly arrived, & I had an anxious & melancholy day betwixt the message telling of Nimrod's vanishment & that announcing his triumphant return. Good old Nim! Even the sinister powers of darkness which engulfed his snowy brethren Crom & Doodlebug were powerless to prevail against his intrepid might! A true warrior & slayer of foes, even as the immortal Conan! Long may he flourish, & many may be the bowls of beans & Cals laid before his red-cushioned daïs! Which reminds me that there are vague rumours down here of old Doodlebug's survival—rumours of a white, panther-like form seen darting by night through the jungle by the white moonlit road. Possibly the old boy has not met his match after all, but has merely gone native . . . . introducing a curious white strain amongst the autochthonous bobcat population. I surely hope so, for like his chalky brethren of Irem & Asotin, he was a noble old potentate!

Delighted to hear of Terraplane's[2] performances—& feel sure you can learn to bear the 75 mph limitation with a truly Islamic resignation. After all, one *can* crawl around quite effectively at such a rate if one allows time enough. Old Terry surely seems to be giving valiant service, & I trust he may long serve to bear your caravan across the burning deserts. Here's to the day when he'll nose into the alley beside the John Hay Library's marble wall![3]

Your travel notes are surely fascinating & tantalising. That account of the Yosemite ought to be published—indeed, my youthful host may ask your permission to use it some time in an amateur journal. What a place! I surely must see it some day . . . it would doubtless give me an entirely new set of impressions of grandeur.

Congratulations as usual on commercial successes. Regarding the Leopard Man—don't mean to tell me that Satrap Pharnabazus *still* insists on a puerile & hackneyed silver bullet after being told how well the Malleus Maleficarum verifies your original ending? Alas, alas! Well—good luck with the interplanetary effort.

I shed tears for the Nighted Fig-Tree of Chorazin & other victims of the nameless blight of Irem. Do you think the evil Burrowers are responsible? Or are there less nameable night-things which only Nimrod has seen?

Regarding Miss Moore—I doubt whether she will ever be a successful commercial fiction-producer. While her work shows a willingness to compromise & to adopt herd romantic devices, it does not indicate any especial skill in fields outside the weird. In the general plot-manufacturing field she would have no especial advantage over any other alert & intelligent apprentice. She might succeed—but so might any high-grade layman. On the other hand, she has notable & spontaneous gifts in the field of fantasy—a peculiar mysticism of vision & sense of unreality—which will carry her far in that department if she is not prematurely sidetracked either by her own popular romantic taste or by an abandonment of sincere authorship in favour of commercial manufacturing. I doubt whether she could both write powerful stories & produce marketable editorial pap as some of the more *widely* gifted & consciously clever craftsmen manage to do. If she has any way of keeping alive without the sacrifice of her talent, I would advise the averting of that sacrifice.

As soon as I get home—gawd knows when, since the hospitality of the Barlows is infinite & overflowing—I'll send you that *Marvel Tales* of which I have duplicates, & also the copy of F M containing my biography by F. Lee Baldwin. Glad you saw "Arthur Jermyn". It is amusing to note that Wright always chooses, for reprinting, those tales of mine which were published *before* I reserved all save 1st. rights. When the supply of these is exhausted, he'll either have to stop printing my stuff or cough up something financially for second publication. I thoroughly agree with your opinion concerning his policy, & hope that the dreamed-of raid on the citadels of publication may occur soon—with fire & sword out in full force!

I envy you your colloquies with the learned "Doc" Herrold, whose interpretations of Andean antiquities & theories of vanished civilisations are so fascinating. He must be a source of infinitely fruitful suggestions. Also, I note with interest your explorations in the works of Don Gaspar de Portola. I had scarcely heard of Don Gaspar before you mentioned him, despite his presence in my favourite 18th century. Now he seems like a familiar figure. I must, however, read more of his explorations. I don't envy him his enforced fish diet—indeed, I think I could starve more cheerfully than I could adopt such a repulsive fare. Congratulations on Terraplane's hill-climbing accomplishments—I note both your comment & the interesting newspaper cutting.

The San Francisco trip, with its picturesque Chinatown phases, must have been tremendously pleasant. You certainly succeed in discovering picturesque food under any conditions! Congratulations on the purchase of the glasses, which will undoubtedly help things out in the Throne Room. And thanks for the postcards—which certainly reflect a vast amount of colour & interest. Nimrod's *second* disappearance must have been disconcerting—though probably it didn't cause as much worry as the first. You know the old rascal's tricks now, & aren't alarmed by his various vanishments. Glad his ears are being fixed up—as I learn from your message to Barlow. Barlow, by the way, was considerably interested by that picture of you & old Nim. It made him think wistfully of the disappeared Doodlebug. Enclosed is a map & guide of Washington which my young host says he promised you long ago in response to some expressed wish. R H B is as prolific as ever in literature & art . . . . note the sinister (or at least portentous) linoleum-block devices which adorn or deface this stationery.

Well—the last previous bulletin from me was sent in Charleston. My trip from there was pleasant & uneventful, & it gratified me to be entering the actual subtropics. The days are very warm now, & I feel vigorous & well to an extent seldom possible in the north.

All is much the same at Villa Barlovia, save that the household is larger now through the presence at home of Bob's father (Lt. Col. E. D. Barlow, retired) & elder brother (Lt. Wayne Barlow of Ft. Sam Houston, Tex).[4] The latter is a delightful chap of about 27—versatile & well-informed—a 2nd Lt. stationed at San Antonio, Texas, but now on a furlough. Bob (with assistance) is building a cabin in an oak grove across the lake from the house, & in this he expects later on to install his printing equipment. It will make an admirable retreat. We do, in the main, about the same things which we did last year . . . boating, discussing, & setting up type. Monday we rowed for miles on Black Water Creek—a stream so tropical in appearance that it might well have been the Congo or the Amazon. It made me think of the river which flows from Silver Spring, Fla.—which I described to you last year. Palms, curious tree-roots, &c. &c. abound. We gathered some odd-shaped white flowers which nobody could identify, but which grew in the jungle on the water's edge. One of the party left on shore saw an alligator, but our boating contingent missed it—although we did see & hear a water-moccasin rustling his poisonous coils on the bank. It is hard to convey the massed effect of a scene like this—though of course you've seen more of 'em than I have, & need no descriptive text. The black, silent, glassy river with its cryptic bands—the monstrously tall cypresses with their festoons of moss—the twisted roots clawing at the water—the ghostly, leaning palms—the riot of underbrush, vines, & creepers—the black, dank earth—the grotesque sunken logs—the muted, sinister, scarcely identifiable sounds of forest & water—the evilly beckoning vistas & funereal arcades among the towering trees of the wood— the fungous, leprous flowers that have never felt full sunlight . . . . . everything to suggest some exotic world of fantasy in which one would not be surprised to see the crumbling, aeon-decayed, moss-grown masonry of one of Two-Gun Bob's forgotten jungle ruins. On the whole, I got a bigger kick out this trip than out of the one last year, since on that occasion the boat was a launch which moved too rapidly for the kind of appreciative absorption I like to exercise. This time we had a lowly & primitive rowboat, & I drank my fill of tropical colour without haste or harassing. The general scenery near the river was correspondingly glamourous—certain areas of tall palms being as exotic & impressive as anything I've ever seen. Louisiana, I dare say, has much the same kind of thing—even more, perhaps—if one knows where to look for it; but during my sojourn of 1932 I had not the time or transportation facilities to penetrate the swamps & bayous & other remote regions of which I have read so much. Hence to me Florida & the tropics are still instinctively synonymous terms.

The local chapter of the Kappa Alpha Tau is still a flourishing one despite the loss of Doodlebug. High has moved over to the cabin of Charles Johnston,[5] but is still to be seen now & then. Jack is the dean of the clan at the Villa—his neck just the least bit twisted from his snake experience of a year ago. Henry Clay & Alfred A. Knopf are new kittens—yellow & grey spotted, respectively. Then there are 2 fluffy yellow Persians just brought down from Washington by my young host . . . Cyrus & Darius. Cyrus is very friendly, but Darius is austere & aloof. C & D are house cats—the others belong to the Great Outdoors. ¶ Well—more bulletins later. Good luck with Terry—& may Nimrod's wanderings all be temporary! Peace ﺎﻋﺭ ٢.

Notes

1. Stamped with RHB's design, depicting a "Coffin of Lissa motif [per August Derleth's story] in the N.W. & S.E. corners. Others typify the Fungi from Yuggoth permeated by subtle colours out of space" (*ES* 698).
2. The Terraplane was an automobile built by the Hudson Motor Car Company between 1932 and 1938. In its first year, the car was branded the Essex-Terraplane but in 1934 became simply the Terraplane.
3. The house in which HPL lived was set back from the street, but could be approached by automobile along the driveway he refers to as an alley.
4. LTC Everett Darius Barlow (1881–1952) and Everett Wayne Barlow (1908–1992). It was probably at this time that HPL and R. H. Barlow helped draft Everett's "National Defence" essay, published in the *Californian* (Winter 1935); rpt. *Lovecraft Annual* No. 14 (2020): 3–13.
5. Charles Blackburn Johnston (1902–1984) was the Barlows' handyman.

[56]   [ALS, JHL]

By the Tarn in the Jungle
—July 9, 1935.

Dear Malik:—

Sundry bulletins have duly appeared. Glad to hear of Terry's encouraging performances, & hope he'll prove in every way worthy of his illustrious predecessor. In a recent letter Klarkash-Ton speaks of the somewhat improved condition of his parents, & his hope that you & Anger can get to see him soon. Here, then, is a trip worthy of Young Terry's 70 mph . . . . a bulletin whereof I hope I may receive in the not remote future. By the way— C A S is developing a new hobby (or has he told you of it?)—sculptural carving in talc, rhyolite, dinosaur bone, & other materials local to Auburn. Specimens sent to Ar-Ech-Bei & me seem marvellously impressive—& he speaks of more ambitious pieces adorning the altars of Tsathoggua's temple.

Glad to hear of Pawang Ali's new honours[1]—long may he flourish! That plot genie surely seems to be a noble device. Your accumulation of guides, maps, currency information, &c ought surely to lead to striking results. My Cairo touches in the Houdini ghosting job of 1924 were secured with the aid of the Britannica and an archaic Baedeker.[2] (Just saw cover of Pawang Ali. Good!)

I shall await with much eagerness your coming immortalisation by Baldwin & Rimel.[3] As perhaps you know, they've just finished with Two-Gun Bob for the same series.[4] Hope pictorial results will be successful!

Dietary & potational notes observed with interest—glad you survived the bolshevik vodka from the quondam W T meteor,[5] & the molluscan shipment from Maine's rock-bound coast!

The item anent the valiant rifleman Wong Chu is surely entertaining.[6] He must have startled all the gods in Pagoda Place!

Of Nimrod's adventures I always read with interest & sympathy. Hope he's properly de-tarred & deflated—& glad the mange cure is beginning to work. All the felidae here send him their regards.

Glad Ar-E'ch-Bei's cryptical block prints duly impressed you. Yes—I don't see why Arabic characters—or other elements of Saracenic design—couldn't be used to vast advantage in block printing. Why not discuss the matter with my young host? Given the right suggestions, he could do wonders with his keen decorative sense & clever craftsmanship.

Which reminds me—Ar-E'ch-Bei duly received your card, & will no doubt reply in proper season despite his constitutional shortcomings as a correspondent. He will likewise appreciate tremendously the 1919 fantasy item—which, as your *first specimen of bizarre writing* (antedating, I judge, even the first version of Tarbis), certainly forms a collector's prize of the first magnitude. I hope it will come whilst I'm still here—for I'd appreciate a glimpse of such a thing myself!

Well—this is certainly a great visit. My health continues to be so damn good that I scarcely know myself—& interesting events continually turn up. Bob's cabin across the lake is now finished, & heavy printing operations are going on therein. The other day I cut a roadway from the landing to the older road which leads around the lake to the cabin. Our group is now, alas, depleted by the loss of one member—Bob's brother Wayne, who has returned to Ft. Sam Houston (where is he is a 2nd Lt.) upon the expiration of his furlough. Last Friday all hands went to Daytona Beach to celebrate the 54th birthday of Barlovius Pater.

Did I tell you about our trip June 17th to the tropical windings of Black Water Creek? A veritable jungle setting for one of Two-Gun's African tales . . . . moss-draped cypresses with twisted roots writhing at the water's edge—leaning palms—lushly convoluted creepers & half-sentient, ropy vines—pallid flowers & leprous fungi against the black, dank earth of the bordering forest aisles—grotesque sunken logs—snakes & alligators—all the paraphernalia of tropical exoticism . . . such as you've probably encountered yourself in the bayou country of Louisiana. It was very much like the river at Silver Springs which I described last year—but I enjoyed it even more because of the more leisurely observing conditions. At S. S. I was whizzed along in a launch, but here we had a slow rowboat, & could absorb each new vista & impression amidst adequate leisure. I hope for more such trips—the duration of the visit being apparently of indefinite extent . . . perhaps several weeks more. ¶ Blessings & the peace—

P.S. Hope Nimrod's disappearance is not permanent—I'd be worried if I thought it were! ¶ I envy you your Mt. Hamilton trip—did you get a look through the Lick Telescope?—Just recd. reassuring bulletin! Glad C A S trip seems imminent.

Notes

1. "The Claw of Iblis" was featured on the cover of *Clues Detective Stories*.
2. Karl Baedeker, ed., *Egypt: Handbook for Travellers* (Leipzig: Baedeker, 1878). There were revised editions in 1885, 1895, 1898, and 1902.
3. The piece was not published. See EHP 64n7.
4. Unpublished.
5. I.e., Robert S. Carr.
6. A citizen had been firing a rifle trying to kill rats and almost injured innocent bystanders.

[57]   [ALS, JHL]

% Barlow, Box 88,
De Land, Florida
July 25, 1935.

Dear Malik:—

Thanks endlessly for the piquant travelogue & generous-scaled map—both of which will go into my most sacred archives when I get home. Your trip was certainly vivid & varied—& I appreciated it all the more because of having seen pictures of the Lassen region.[1] Last autumn some friends motored over a route much the same as yours, & sent alluring descriptions of the devastated regions, fumaroles, lake of swans, sunrise from the heights, & other characteristic features. Your account certainly brings the scene close—& makes me wish I could go over the ground in person. Terraplane has in this trip amply proved its worth—& earned a niche in history comparable to that occupied by Old Jug! At odd moments I have been going over the map & acquiring a clearer notion of many places described in passing by various California voyagers. Again, my sincerest thanks! The outfit arrived in excellent condition.

By the way—I was sorry to learn that the visit to Klarkash-Ton had to be annulled. Hope Smith Sr. will soon be again in as good shape as his age & chronic infirmities allow. C A S recently sent Ar-Ech-Bei & me some specimens of the sculptural carving he has taken up, & his results are really tremendously effective. It is marvellous that he can do such good work amidst his many practical handicaps.

Interested to hear of An-Ghah's ancient Juggernaut, & hope its favourable performances may be repeated. Who is his partner in ownership—Louis C. Smith? Young Louis—more or less in collaboration with An-Ghah—has some quite ambitious publishing plans . . . including the issuance of a complete index to W T & a booklet containing my "Fungi from Yuggoth" complete—both on a mimeograph.[2] Both boys, I am sure, amply deserve the dignified title of *penghulu!*[3]

Meanwhile young Ar-Ech-Bei continues to earn *penghulhuminous* honours on this side of the continent. His printing outfit is now fully in operation in the new oak-grove cabin across the lake, & the first-fruits thereof promise to be notable indeed.[4] Of these more anon. Before long he intends to install *binding* facilities. I have been helping a good bit in all the operations, & have acquired (or reacquired, since I dabbled in boyhood days) quite a facility for setting type. Another recent accomplishment of mine is road-making—if that term may be applied to a process including little more than the clearing-away of underbrush & scrub palmettos.

Ar-Ech-Bei will be exceedingly glad to receive that early MS. Regarding his preference for *early* work—he does not mean to imply that your powers of imaginative evocation are less, but simply that you have less chance to *use* them when working with the mechanised, characteristically glib, conventionally speeded-up, & plot-ridden formulae imposed by professional pulp editors. He is well aware that you could still, if free of professional duties, turn out the same kind of unhampered & glamourous material as of yore . . . . imaginative pictures developed in the ample, leisurely way which enables the reader to duplicate the mood of the writer & feel the potent, compelling magic of a realm beyond reality . . . . . Atlanaat . . . . Kurdistan . . . . But of course myriads of touches of the old magic enter into the later material despite the handicap of "action", "plot", & other machine-made demands. In collecting MSS., one naturally looks for those which have in them the most of the author's real personality . . . things written for the joy of writing, & not as a business. Hence the call for things of the Kurdistan period . . . or of some later period of composition under similar conditions.

Congratulations on recent successes! You & young Derleth surely do paralyse an inactive old man with your achievements! Loring & Mussey turned down my volume of tales, just as I knew they would. I shall submit no more stories to professional publishers.

My visit continues to be delightful—& such is the super-hospitality of my hosts that its termination still remains indefinite. I guess I told you about that trip to Black Water Creek with its tropical scenery. Just now I'm out in the landscape garden writing—with a congenial menagerie of cats & one dog grouped around me. Now & then a shower drives me in, but I return as soon as it's over. All the felidae (of whom Henry Clay & Alfred A. Knopf are at this moment on the bench beside me) send their warmest regards to Nimrod. Old Jack could stage quite a championship fight with Nim—though from what I hear of the latter I rather think the title would remain on the West Coast! Hope the good old ruffian's absences continue to be temporary, & that all his wounds & ailments may soon succumb to the remedies applied. At least, I hope the healing can keep pace with the scars of battle! ¶ Yrs for the Peace— Є⌇ ⁇

P.S. Ar-Ech-Bei & I tried to see the eclipse, but dense clouds covered everything. Ironically enough, it cleared up toward morning—affording floods of burning moonlight. But I should worry—I, who have seen 2 total solar eclipses in my long & eventful life!

[Postcard enclosure:][5] Just recd. card telling of new feline. She certainly sounds like a marvellous little atom! What are you going to call her? Fatima . . . Zuleika . . . Amina . . . Roxana . . . Statēra?[6] . . . well, I'll leave the nomenclature to you! Trust her diet may soon be adjusted, & that she may grow up to become the mother of a noted line of valiant warriors. Jack, Henry Clay, Mr. Knopf, Cyrus, & Darius send her their regards—as do the members of the K.A.T. in Providence. ¶ I regret Nimrod's absence, but feel less alarm than I ordinarily would—on account of his former jaunts into the unknown. ¶ In Providence little Johnny Perkins is getting to be a formidable fighting man—the other day he put the aged President of the K.A.T. to flight! He now has a tiny black-&-white half-brother (destined for presentation elsewhere as soon as he graduates from a maternal diet) with whom he battles playfully, & who (so far as relative size allows) gives him back as good as he sends.

Notes

1. Referring to the area around Mount Lassen, the southernmost active volcano in the Cascade Range of the Western United States.
2. Both projects came to naught.
3. A local chief or governor in parts of Malaysia and Indonesia.
4. RHB's first publications (1935) were the first issue of the *Dragon-Fly*, Frank Belknap Long's *The Goblin Tower*, and HPL's *The Cats of Ulthar*.
5. *Front:* A Florida Sunset.

6. Amina (d. 1610) was a Hausa warrior queen of Zazzau in the northwest region of Nigeria. Zuleika was the heroine of Lord Byron's *The Bride of Abydos* (1813). Roxana (340?–310? B.C.E.) was a Sogdian princess of Bactria whom Alexander the Great married. Stateira refers to one of several royal women of the Achaemenid period. Possibly Stateira I (died 332? B.C.E.), wife of Darius III of Persia, who accompanied him while he went to war.

[58]   [ALS, JHL]

℅ Barlow, Box 88,

De Land, Florida.

August 3, 1935.

Dear Malik:—

Epistle & card duly arrived—& as you are aware, I answered the latter at once on the medium attached for that purpose. Hope all in the bibliophilic line will be adjusted to your satisfaction.

Glad to hear all the news, & hope all the scheduled social events will come to pass. The Hamilton–Williamson outfit surely is seeing the world![1] Ralph Milne Farley seems to be quite a bird.[2] Young Bloch speaks of attending the meetings of some society in Milwaukee which he has organised.[3] With all these visiting dignitaries you surely ought to provide a suitably costumed welcoming staff. To supplement the Vizier An-Ghah, why not drag in his young side-pardner Lwi-Sees-Mith of O-Khlan? The two boys, clad in green robes & properly equipped with flagons, braziers, kettle-drums, censers, scimitars, ankhs, arquebuses, or whatever belongs in the picture, would surely make a colourful guard of honour to stand before Irem's chalcedony pillars as the camel-caravans of the various pious pilgrims draw nigh.

I envy you your trips to the Lick Observatory. The largest telescope I've ever looked through is that of the Ladd Observatory of Brown University in Providence—a 12″. This, in the ordinary air of a commonplace residential hilltop, would not be equal to a telescope of the same size on Mt. Hamilton. The power you used—270—is about as high as is customarily used for ordinary observations with a telescope of any size. The advantage of a large aperture is the extra light-gathering power, which makes the image of a given diameter brighter & clearer & therefore fuller of detail. High powers are used sparingly & for special purposes. I have a 3″ telescope, on which I use eye-pieces of 45 (terr.) & 100 (celes.) Last year I had a good look at Saturn through the 5½″ refractor of the small Maria Mitchell Observatory at Nantucket—with a power of 150 the ringed orb was impressive indeed. Down here I revel in the glittering sky—broad horizons & no electric lights—& wish vainly that I had a good telescope at my disposal. The best we have is Col. Barlow's 5½-power field glass . . . which is not sufficient to reveal (to my aged eyes, at least) Jupiter's satellites or Venus's now marked crescentic phase. Possibly I can make out the latter when the crescent gets thinner & its semidiameter increases. It was in gr. elong. E. June 30, & will be in inf. conjunction[4] some time in September. Some time when you're in the southern part of your state you ought to see the Mt. Wilson Observatory & its great reflectors. And if you ever cross Arizona don't miss Flagstaff with its famous Lowell Observatory (24″ refr.) where Pluto was discovered. I was introduced personally to the late Percival Lowell in 1907 (a decade before his death), when he lectured in Providence.[5]

I absorbed the Kappa Alpha Tau bulletins with the keenest of interest, & would give much to behold the intrepid yet amiable Zuleika–Fatima–Amina–Ayesha[6] . . . microscopic great-great-granddaughter of the Sphinx. Hope you'll get a snapshot of her while she is still fuzzy & infantine. As I write these lines I am in very congenial K.A.T. company myself—for small tiger Alfred A. Knopf is ensconced in the curve of my left arm as I sit on a bench in the landscape garden . . . occasionally chewing the edge of your letter, & occasionally reaching forth a sportive paw to pat the moving Parker which indites this document. A black dog is bustling around near by, but Mr. Knopf is the object of my especial interest. I agree thoroughly with your view as to the relative civilisedness of felidae & canidae.[7] During the whole of a long lifetime I have been an unswerving & almost fanatical khatist. Hope Nimrod & Ayesha will get along well. What a great old fellow Nim is! It relieved me vastly to hear of his latest return—for even after many repetitions these absences worry one. Your description of him—& of his atavistic moments—proved highly fascinating to me. He has certainly done well in the hunting line despite the handicap of his snowy coat!

That book on mummies[8] must be great stuff—I'd like to see it sometime, though at the moment my programme wouldn't let me do it justice. G. Elliot Smith[9] is one of the greatest living anthropologists—the man almost solely responsible for the now universally accepted belief that all civilisations have sprung from a single source instead of having developed independently & without external contacts. Hope you'll find the work a vast aid in your story.

Your battery work sounds impressive indeed—surely you are the supreme Doctor of Juggernauts!

The other day we all visited a very picturesque spot about 20 m. S.W. of here—Rock Springs—where, in a tropical valley rich with exotic growths, an idyllic forest-shaded river springs with cold & crystal clearness out of two black, yawning tunnels in the side of a tree-crowned vertical cliff of hard-packed clay. One of these tunnels is large enough for a man to crawl in—& 60 feet from the mouth is a vast subterrene chamber of eternal night . . . beyond which the river comes out of the *utterly* unknown abysses of inner earth. This chamber is said to have been used as an Indian hiding-place in the old days. Visitors were once permitted to crawl in—but are not at present. The whole region, however, is infinitely glamourous & well worth visiting. I hope to get there again—as I probably shall before turning northward. Date of my return keeps getting postponed—the Barlows urge an all-winter stay, but I hardly think that would be practicable—since I can't do any serious work without my library. Every good wish—Your obt Servt ℰ ⌐⌐⟍⟍

[Postcard enclosure: P.S.:][10] Just recd. the tremendously interesting China-town travelogue. Thanks immensely—I shall keep this (like all your other sets of travel notes) for my permanent files. Your jottings are always piquant & keenly interesting—indicating the greatest possible skill in the selection of significant detail. I don't believe I've ever seen an account of Chinatown even half as graphic & vivid. You surely make the place live—in its minor as well as major aspects. The account of the Chinese opera is surely a classic—I really had no connected idea before of what a Chinese theatrical performance is like. The programme is a gem—I shall retain it to illustrate the travelogue. ¶ Am sure Farley must have had a great time in S.F. under your expert guidance. Now it's Hamilton's turn, lucky devil! Hope I can get out there some day. Meanwhile I surely will be grateful for that Shell Oil Co. street guide you mention. It will coöperate with the map of California in giving your geographic observations an air of added concreteness.

Notes

1. HPL refers to science fiction writers Edmond Hamilton (1904–1977) and Jack Williamson (1908–2006). RHB had proposed meeting them when HPL visited him in Florida in 1934 (the writers were wintering in Key West and contemplated a stop in De Land on their journey northward), but the meeting never occurred.

2. Roger Sherman Hoar (1887–1963), Massachusetts politician who wrote science fiction under the pseudonym "Ralph Milne Farley."

3. Ralph Milne Farley organized the Milwaukee Fictioneers in 1931.

4. A planet's elongation is the angular separation between the sun and the planet, with Earth as the reference point. An inferior conjunction occurs when the two planets lie in a line on the same side of the Sun. In an inferior conjunction, the superior planet is in "opposition" to the Sun as seen from the inferior planet.

5. Percival Lowell (1855–1916), American mathematician and astronomer who established his observatory in Flagstaff in 1893–94. For more on HPL's encounter with Lowell in 1907, see *Letters to Rheinhart Kleiner and Others* 53.

6. Fatimah bint Muhammad was the youngest daughter of Muhammad the prophet. Ayesha derives from *Ayesha, the Return of She* (1905) by H. Rider Haggard.

7. See "Cats and Dogs."

8. See Bibliography under G. Elliot Smith and Warren R. Dawson.

9. Sir G[rafton] Elliot Smith (1871–1937), author of *The Evolution of Man* (1924) and *The Migrations of Early Culture* (1929). Smith was a vigorous proponent of the theory that Egypt was the source of European civilization. See *The Ancient Egyptians and Their Influence upon the Civilization of Europe* (1911).

10. *Front:* Royal Palm and Hibiscus in Florida.

[59]   [ALS, JHL]

Aug. 11, 1935
[Postmarked Cassia, Fla.,
12 August 1935]

Hail, O Malik!

Map & bulletins received—& extremely glad to have this vivid key to the intricacies of the San Francisco Bay region at my disposal. Naturally it can't be expected to shew all the twisting alleys of Chinatown—but for general purposes it could scarcely be improved upon. In reciprocation, permit me to enclose the best map of Florida which I have on hand. Not so bad—but if I can pick up a better one I'll send it along. That California map you sent certainly was a bird! Yes—it had insets shewing the layout of the larger towns.

Congratulations on old Terry's latest feat! Mountain-climbing in high gear is certainly an accomplishment which no ordinary Juggernaut could rival! Glad you left your pharmaceutical rival in the shade!

Ar-E'ch-Bei sends salutations, & says he will be extremely grateful for that 1919-er whenever you come across it. Yes—I recall "Queen of the Morning"—what a pity the failure of M C has left it stranded.[1] As for a collaborative transformation into a weird tale—thanks for the compliment of suggesting that I could do it![2] Actually, however, I fear I'd only mess it up. I have virtually forsworn all collaboration—turned down requests from old de Castro & Mrs. Heald not long ago. Unless a story is closely akin to one's own style, any attempt at adding to another's work is bound to be inept & lacking in homogeneity. This is especially true where two deeply ingrained & antipodally contrasting styles are concerned. When I get at writing, I want to experiment in certain new directions of my own—so that I doubt if I could do justice to any new collaborative project. Why not try Long—or either of the Wandrei boys?

Lukewarm reception of my latest effort by Derleth & Barlow leads me to question the result of my last year's experimentation. Must try a new direction.

Thanks for the touching obituary of "Steamboat."[3] An appealing old tough! Would that he might have survived another 12 years! Sad news from home—Vice-Pres. Osterberg of the K.A.T. is no more . . . an encounter with a huge dog proved too much for him. A knightly warrior—never aggressive, but always ready to repel aggression. Game to the last—requiescat in pace! Another old tiger—Stephen Randall, brother of black & white Pres. Peter Randall—succeeds to the vice-presidency.

Ar-Ech-Bei's trans-lacustrine cabin is now filling up with binders' paraphernalia. He's getting a formidable plant! Still having a great time down here, but must break away soon. Thanks again for the map.

Salaam—

Notes

1. The story was never published.
2. In an earlier letter, EHP refers to the story "One Arabian Night" as the "sexification of Queen of the Morning." This story is about Glenn Ferrell, Pierre d'Artois, and Ismeddin saving a girl from ritual sacrifice.
3. A neighbor's cat.

[60]   [ALS, JHL]

Ancient San Agustin—
August 21, 1935.

Hail, Mighty Malik:—

On my way at last! I accompanied the Barlovii to Daytona Beach & helped them settle in the flat which they are to occupy for a fortnight—then boarded the diligencia for ancient San Agustin! It surely is damn good to be seeing centuried gables & facades & balconies & garden walls—& to be hearing the sound of tinkling fountains at twilight, & of cathedral chimes cast in 1682—after 2 mo & 9 d of rustic modernity! Am revelling in the atmosphere of a 370-year-old city—a city founded when Shakespeare was a year old, & still containing houses which had 50 years behind them when the Pilgrims landed on Plymouth Rock. Am staying a week at my usual hostelry—the cheap but cleanly Rio Vista on the bay front—& have secured a marvellous bargain in housing . . . a sizeable basement (but above ground) room, with bathroom & kitchenette annexed, for only *$3.50!* Have cut my food bill down to 20 or 25¢ per day—using beans (large cans for *5¢* here!) as the heavy staple. My dissipation is sherbet (good old Arabic name!)[1] which at certain places here is obtainable for *10¢ a pint* in orange, lime, & pineapple flavours. As may be imagined, I spend most of my time absorbing ancient vistas & writing on the sun-baked terreplein of the venerable Fortaleza San Marcos. There is, by the way, a delightful grey kitten around the fort—who the other day sat alternately purring & drowsing in my lap for an hour whilst I wrote letters. He sent his regards to Nimrod & little Ayesha. Last night I saw a glorious sunset from the far end of that basin or lagoon in the southern part of the town which stretches from St. Francis to South St. The distant Moorish towers of the ornate Ponce de Leon hotel, & the dome of that garish Presbyterian church, were outlined in black against the most fantastic sea of seething orange & green & purple fire imaginable—giving rise to a dreamlike Oriental effect which Cairo or Bagdad could scarcely suppress. Today I have been wandering among the tombs of the ancient cemeteries—especially that surrounding the chapel of Nuestra Señora de la Leche,[2] where neglected gravestones are almost lost among the lush underbrush & moss-bearded live-oaks which have overgrown the spot. I am now writing in the grey twilight of a mighty grove of gnarled oaks whose titanic branches over-arch the roadway & touch the ground on the other side.

Well—I shall have to move on at 11:15 p.m. Aug. 25. Reach Savannah at 4:50 a.m. the 26th, & think I'll stay exploring till the 10:30 a.m. coach for my beloved CHARLESTON. Charleston at 2:15 p.m.—& there I shall stick at the Y as long as my cash holds out . . . which won't be very long, from the present looks of things. The reason I'm taking the full week in St. Aug. instead of Charleston is that living is infinitely more expensive in the latter. But I'll set a day or two there if it kills me! Probably no stops north of Charleston—except brief intervals between coaches. I shall have an evening in Washington & most of a day in Philadelphia—& shall doubtless call on Belknap in N.Y. An-yhow[?], it has been a great outing, all in all! Left home June 5, & probably shan't be back there till well into September. Shall have 3 months of old pa-pers to read up—though the N.Y. Sunday Times was forwarded to me.

Glad the Redwood City factory continues its successful operation, & that Farley will collaborate on the Queen. As for submitting "Doorstep"—I may when I get home,[3] but want to look it over first. Barlow has typed my latest thing—"The Shadow out of Time"—& it comes to 88 pages.

About your idea of collaboration with all proceeds to go into a California trip for Grandpa in case of sale—bless my soul, but I can't say how much I appreciate the generosity of the idea! You quite overwhelm an old man! Actu-ally, though, you ought not to put so much constructive labour into anything with so doubtful a return. In the first place, the synthetic product probably wouldn't sell—since anything that *I* could do to a story would merely *unfit* it for the commercial pulp market. And in the second place; if by any miracle it *did* sell, it would be a pity to have a mere visit from an uninteresting old crank take the place of the quarter or half share (depending on the amount of mate-rial put in) which ought to be yours. I have grave doubts of whether any foundation-plot or synopsis of the pulp order would increase the chances of commercial acceptance of anything I might write. Such a foundation would form a proper starting-point *only for a story written in the same spirit & technique.* A building-up of *my* sort would only clash with such a start. The start would be handicapped by the story, & the story would be handicapped by the start. You can't make a good alloy of concrete & iron . . . or hatch a hen from a duck's egg! Of course, exceptions occur now & then. If the idea were of a not too pulpish sort, & if I happened to tackle it in a particularly objective mood, the result might assume a salable form. But your own development of your idea, or a story of mine from an idea of my own, would probably be much more effective. *Your* story would, in addition, be more commercially salable. Whatever I touch, I make *less* pulpishly acceptable. Well—think over all the drawbacks before being too definite. I might be tempted to try the thing some time—but not unless you realise all the handicaps involved. It goes without saying that I'd give a lot to see the Californian domain so vividly brought to life by your travelogues & accompanying maps!

Nope—never heard of the "Hung Society".[4] What is it like? ¶ Regards to Nimrod, little Ayesha, An-Ghah, & any other pious worthies you may encounter. ¶ Guess I'll pack up the black bag & transfer activities to the deserted beach on Anastasia Island—across the bridge. Want to pick up some tan!

Yrs for the Litany of Eblis— ⌒ᶜ ⌣ᴢᴿ Ω

[Enclosures: Two picture postcards, no writing: Old Curiosity Shop, St. George Street, St. Augustine, Florida; Patio, showing wishing well, oldest house in the United States.]

Notes

1. *Sherbet* is derived from the Arabic verb *shariba* (to drink).
2. I.e., the Nursing Madonna.
3. HPL did not submit the story for another twelve months.
4. Tiandihui, the Society of the Heaven and the Earth (also called Hongmen), a Chinese fraternal organization and secretive folk religious sect.

[61]   [ALS, JHL]

Home—

Septr. 28[, 1935]

Dear Malik:—

Cards of 17th & 23d duly received. Hope to see some of those photographs of Nimrod & Battle Axe. What a valiant & distinctive pair! Rimel showed me your letter in accordance with instructions, & I was interested in the accounts of linguistic accomplishments among the Redwood City felidae. I shall indeed be eager to hear more of the fine shades of meaning conveyed by Nimrod & his youthful disciple!

Congratulations on the San Gregorio expedition—which was certainly an education in marine biology! Some of the things you describe remind me of what I saw from a glass-bottomed boat in Miami Harbour—over a coral reef. The green-fleshed fish sound engagingly sinister—although *any* fish would be enough to give *me* a case of shudders, gastronomically considered! I don't blame Don Gaspar's men for cursing if they had to eat fish!

Glad the new Pawang tale[1] has found a suitable market, & hope the sundry smuttinesses will be enough to make possible the Mexican jaunt. And so the famous Plot Genie brings results, eh? Belknap wanted me to ask you just *which* of several similar devices had served you best. He has long hesitated on the brink of such a purchase, but has been deterred by stiff prices & doubt of results.

Well—as I said, Rimel sent me your letter, & I perused its various points with keen interest. I tend to agree with you regarding the working out of the commonplace pulp weird field—although I doubt if such a limitation applies to serious weird writing. The sincere weird story depends very little on plot or incident, but is purely & simply *a picture of a certain characteristic human mood.* Atmosphere & suggestion are the big things—even a hackneyed set of incidents can be re-used if presented with the proper emotional shadings. I have always preferred to use established folklore legends as little as possible, & see no reason to change my opinion. The weird artist should invent his own fantastic violations of natural law. Of course the growing body of genuine weird writing—Poe, Dunsany, Blackwood, Shiel, de la Mare, Machen, M. R. James, Wakefield, Benson, Hodgson, Ewers, &c. &c.—does narrow the field in a subtle way; just as the growing body of general literature makes it harder & harder for the realist or non-weird romanticist to say anything new. That is one of the inevitable aesthetic hardships of an aging civilisation. But this slow, vague narrowing has nothing to do with the sharp, definite exhaustion of the pulp formula field which deals with standardised ghosts, werewolves, & vampires. There is always a chance for the serious artist in weird literature. So far Rimel has shown a tendency to steer clear of pulp formulae & attempt original themes. He may not get far in the cheap magazines, but will perhaps become a serious fantaisiste to be reckoned with. Has he showed you "The Disinterment"?[2] About my own stuff—I'd hardly say that my newer experiments show any *general* drift toward the delineation of weird humanity & character as typified by "The Thing on the Doorstep". That piece is only one of several attempts to capture certain moods in various ways, & I don't recall using that especial method in any other case. I don't know yet what constitutes the best way of saying what I'm trying to say. Possibly all ways will be equally awkward. But for the moment it may be said that I have no settled method whatever. I'm merely looking around for one!

I noted Rimel's linoleum print of your physiognomy with great interest, & believe he caught a good bit of your expression. His cut, however, conveys a misleadingly heavy-jowled effect—as if you had put on about 30 lbs. of superfluous suet! By the way—did you receive the *Fantasy Magazine* with my picture & biography? If not, I'll send you a copy. And how about *Marvel Tales?*

Doubtless you received my card from the Boston zone telling of Klarkash-Ton's bereavement.[3] I was surely sorry to hear of the event, though it was of course long-expected.

My Massachusetts week-end surely gave me a vivid & comprehensive reintroduction to New England scenery after my long absence! Friday Nahant & Marblehead. Saturday the brooding "Dunwich" region—the exquisite hills of the Connecticut Valley around Wilbraham. Sunday we visited Cape Cod, where an opposite type of landscape—gentle, level terrain with sea-blown willows—prevails. We lounged on the sands of Chatham with nothing but the blue Atlantic betwixt us & Spain. It is possible that I shall have one more outing before winter sets in—over the Mohawk Trail & into Vermont when the autumn foliage is at its height—but this remains highly tentative.

Meanwhile I've made scarcely any progress against the engulfing mounds of piled-up work around me. Correspondence all shot to hell, & scores of obligations still undischarged. Have all the N Y Sunday Times's since Aug. 4 to read, & Harpers Magazine beginning with July. I surely wish I had a bit of your energy!

¶ Social notes—both Howard Wandrei & young Brobst married this month.[4] Brobst is taking a special course at Brown in addition to his nursing work.

Peace of the Prophet upon you—

[P.S. on envelope:] Abundant thanks for that brochure about Lassen Volcanic Park, which I devoured with extreme interest.

Notes

1. "The Hand of Subramanya."
2. *WT,* January 1937. HPL revised the tale to some degree.
3. CAS's mother, Fanny (Gaylord) Smith (1850–1935), died on 9 September.
4. Wandrei married Connie Colstock; Brobst married Judith Sylvia Heideman (1906–1988).

[62]   [ALS, JHL]

Octr. 13, 1935

Hail, Malik!

Cards at hand—& bon voyage to Old Mexico! The absence of Mimi-Battle-Axe"[*sic*] had me gravely worried until I learned of her providential return. Glad that her absence gave you an introduction to a chap as interesting as the old German adventurer! Meanwhile I rejoice in the gradual mending of old Nimrod's ears.

Congratulations on all the new successes—expected & unexpected! The landing of that Farley collaboration[1] must form a particularly helpful surprise. I envy you—& those along your route—the coming trip, & know that Two-Gun will rejoice in your advent to Cross Plains. He has just sent me an amazingly vivid & masterfully panoramic "history" of the prehistoric world he writes about. Everything is coherent, natural, & self-consistent—& I only wish he would get a new nomenclature to replace his present system with its annoyingly misleading resemblances. The article is designed for *The Phantagraph*[2]—only existing attempt to carry on the F F tradition.

Your exotic library seems destined to become a singular & distinctive collection, leading you to new levels of accuracy & detail in the creation of Orientalia. Thanks profusely for remembering me in connexion with the Cairene cartography!

October W T considerably better than Sept. The Machen reprint is of course a very minor production of its author—& is wholly new to me. The Flanders story is really quite notable—with some actually convincing atmospheric touches. I've seen fairly good stuff of his before—especially a yarn called "The Graveyard Duchess." The Moore tale has some very effective passages & bits of suggestion.[3] Other stories are just routine items—some, perhaps, not without possible promise.

I guess I told you of the New Haven trip I was about to make with my aunt. Well, it occurred last Tuesday, & was in every way a brilliant success. I had 7½ hours for exploration while my aunt visited a friend. The day was ideally sunny (though I could have wished it warmer), & the ride through autumnal Connecticut scenery (100 m. = 2½ hrs) delightful. New Haven is not as rich in colonial antiquities as Providence, but has a peculiar charm of its own. Streets are broad & well-kept, & in the residential sections (some of which involve hills & fine views) there are endless stately mansions a century old, with generous grounds & gardens, & an almost continuous overarching canopy of great elms. I visited ancient Connecticut Hall (1752—the oldest Yale college building, where Nathan Hale of the Class of 1773 roomed), old Centre Church (1812, with an interesting crypt containing the grave of Benedict Arnold's first wife), the Pierpont house (1767—now Yale Faculty Club), the historical, art, & natural history museums, the Farnam & Marsh botanic gardens, & various other points of interest—crowding as much as possible into the limited time available. Most impressive of all the sights, perhaps, were the great *new* quadrangles of the university—each an absolutely faithful reproduction of old-time architecture & atmosphere, & forming a self-contained little world in itself. The Gothic courtyards transport one in fancy to mediaeval Oxford or Cambridge—spires, oriels, pointed arches, mullioned windows, arcades with groined roofs, climbing ivy, sundials, lawns, gardens, vine-clad walls, & flagstoned walks—everything to give the young occupants that massed impression of their accumulated cultural heritage which they might obtain in Old England itself. To stroll through these quadrangles in the golden afternoon sunlight; at dusk, when the lights in the diamond-paned casements flicker up one by one; or in the beams of a mellow Hunter's Moon; is to walk bodily into an enchanted region of dream. It is the past & the ancient mother land brought magically to the present time & place. The choicest of these Gothic quadrangles is Calhoun College—named for the great South Carolina statesman (whose grave in St. Philip's Churchyard, Charleston, I visited less than 2 months ago), who was a graduate of Yale. Nor are the Georgian quadrangles less glamourous—each being a magical summoning-up of the world of 2 centuries ago. Many distinct styles of Georgian architecture are represented, & the buildings & landscaping alike reflect the finest taste which European civilisation has yet evolved. Lucky is the boy whose formative years are spent amid such scenes! I wandered for hours through this limitless labyrinth of unexpected elder microcosms, & mourned the lack of further time. Certainly, I must visit New Haven again, since many of its treasures would require weeks for proper inspection & appreciation.

Well—I surely envy you your coming jaunt to more exotic realms! Knowing nothing of mail-forwarding arrangements, I may hold this missive till I hear of a definite temporary address—or on the other hand I may just send it along & let Nimrod attend to the forwarding. At this moment Mr. John Perkins has somnolently sprawled on a neighbouring rug—in an absolutely straight line, like a long ebony club. He's active when he's active, but he certainly knows how to take his leisure!

Hope you'll give my regards to Two-Gun when you hit Cross Plains. Benedictions— ᴄⁿ ᴦᴗ∕ ᴗ

[P.S.] Just recd. carbon of Pawang Ali opening from Kline. Delightful! Glad to make the belated acquaintance of your appealing & redoubtable hero!

Part II—
Octr. 19, 1935.

Salaam once more, O Protector of the Poor!

Just received your extremely interesting communication of the 11th, & will add this reply to the envelope-full of messages held for your return. Your preparations for the Mexican voyage have surely been extensive enough, & I trust the event itself may yield justifying dividends of pleasure & imaginative enrichment. Good old Terry must be pretty nearly a new car after all the overhaulings & replacements! Hope Battle Axe won't pine unduly in the absence of the Master. Are you taking good old Nimrod along? The itinerary you outline excites my deepest envy— & I'll wager the Aztec pyramids & temples will set you off on a new cycle of dreaming & composition! Hope you have interesting sessions with Two-Gun & Mashburn—& that New Orleans will have lost none of its charm in your eyes. It's really too bad that you haven't more time to spare, since most of the points along your route ought to be savoured at length, in the most leisurely possible way. However, you're damned lucky to be able to make the trip at all!

Those maps & books which you've ordered are surely an impressive lot! With detailed alley maps of Cairo at your disposal, you can handle the city like an old resident—while the other items will further increase your easy & intimate familiarity with sundry Orientalia. Before long you ought to be eligible for appointment as Egyptian minister, Calcutta consul, Burmese ambassador, or something of the sort! As I said before, I shall be grovellingly grateful for the Cairo chart you mention. It will form an admirable complement of that 15th century map which I owe to your generosity!

I'll tell Belknap that your useful auxiliary is the "Plot-Genie"—& later on he'll be glad to have any more detailed tips which you may transmit to him directly. I've always thought that such things must aid quantity-production immensely. I'll wager that you can beat the enterprising Mr. Bedford-Jones when you start operations in his province!

I'll look up "Siesta" as soon as I get a chance to go over my files thoroughly. Who is the author?[4] Yes—I agree with your remarks on "The Woman of the Wood."[5]

About young Bloch's naively overloaded style—I've constantly been at him to prune away some of the baroque excrescences. It will, however, take time to make him spontaneously understand & recognise the extent of his excessive colouring. That kind of writing is an almost inescapable attribute of youth—a phase through which nearly every incipient fantaisiste must go—& it can no more be avoided than the cracked voice of adolescence can be avoided. In certain ways, it is a promising rather than discouraging sign—that is, it indicates that the young aspirant is trying for the right kind of style & effect (a style & effect in which the vocabulary, syntax, cadences, & modulations all conduce toward the emotional impression sought) instead of for the cheap skeletonic style which merely sets down statements without realising their emotional possibilities or making them come alive. Ordinarily this juvenile lushness modifies itself as the perpetrator gains in reading & experience. In Bloch's case, however, there is the complicating factor of his *commercial* ambitions—which may yet ruin him as a creative artist. He probably has the idea that cheap editors *like* heavy overcolouring in certain classes of tales—hence continues to pile it on in the hope of sales even when he knows it is excessive. Just how much conscious imitation of Poe is involved in such writing, one cannot be sure. In some cases the resemblance is more to the general school of narration to which Poe belonged, than to E A P personally. Certain words & constructions have picked up certain vague but powerful associations & overtones in the course of their age-old use, & occasionally the experimenting novice is independen[t]ly led to some of them in just the same way that Poe before him was led. It is occasionally better to run the risk of a little accidental resemblance, than to discard the discriminating plastic use of words & phrases altogether as the "action" hacks do. Well, it all remains to be seen. There's a lot in Bloch—& possibilities will be realised. One fears that his attempts to please editors will retard if not defeat his progress toward intrinsic excellence. Too bad he entered the commercial arena before a sound & disinterested style of his own had an opportunity to crystallise. What is more—many of his energies are scattered in other projects such as writing & arranging comic sketches for amateur theatricals, &c. Such versatility sometimes makes for superficiality—but one never can tell.

Good luck with your sales programme. I surely think you are entitled to include collaborations & verses in your reckoning of successful accomplishments, so that an immediate "centenary" celebration ought to be in order. But why not have *two* celebrations? Your "centenary" now, & a "centennial" later when you've finished & sold the 9 additional solo stories? Thus the Providence

Journal had two centennials—one in 1920, commemorating the 100ᵗʰ year of *existence*, & another in 1929, at the 100ᵗʰ anniversary of existence *as a daily*. Have you seen Barlow's amateur paper, *The Dragon-Fly?* If not, you must. Just received copy of Derleth's new detective novel, "Sign of Fear". Must read & tell A W what I think of it.

Well—here's wishing you luck on the trip! Hope to receive some tantalising cards as you advance from wonder to wonder.

Benedictions—

[P.S.] Thanks tremendously for *Monterrey Greeter*.⁶ It makes me anxious to get down into Nuevo Leon!

[P.]P.S. Schwartz tells me he has succeeded in selling my "Mts. of Madness" to *Astounding*.

Notes

1. "Who Killed Gilbert Foster?"

2. "The Hyborian Age" (*Phantagraph*, February, August, and October–November 1936). Later published as a pamphlet.

3. *WT*, October 1934: Arthur Machen, "The Lost Club"; Jean Ray, "The Mystery of the Last Guest" (trans. of "Le Dernier Voyageur" [1932], as by John Flanders); C. L. Moore, "The Cold Gray God." The other John Flanders tale is "The Graveyard Duchess" (trans. of "Le Gardien du cimetière" [1919]) (*WT*, December 1934).

4. Alexander L. Kielland (1849–1906), Norwegian realist writer. Marie/Maria von Borch (1853–1895) translated the story from Norwegian to German. It was then translated by Charles Flint McClumpha into English and published in *Modern Ghosts*, ed. George William Curtis (New York: Harper & Brothers, 1890). It appeared in *WT*, November 1930.

5. EHP had written of A. Merritt's story, "[it] is so utterly 'personal', so utterly independent of a legend that it lives." (TLS, JHL; 11 October [1935]).

6. *The Monterrey Greeter* was a monthly publication edited by the local Asociación Mexicana Automovilística club, distributed freely in AMA-associated hotels. Apparently EHP sent a copy to HPL from his travels. Monterrey is the capital of the state of Nuevo León.

[63]   [ALS, JHL]
        [2 postcards included in envelope; postmarked Providence, R.I.,
        10 November 1935]

[postcard 1:][1]
P.S. Even the New Haven trip didn't quite end my 1935 travels. On Oct. 16 at 6 a.m. Samuel Loveman blew into town on the N.Y. boat, & after a session at 66 we both started out for Boston to absorb bookstalls, museums, & antiquities. Stayed 3 days—stopping at Technology Chambers in Irvington St. Took in quite a few things (including the cinema "Last Days of Pompeii"[2]— quite a spectacle, though infantile as a story), but had no time to look up Cole or anybody else in the group. Back to Providence Friday, & did all the local bookstalls. Discovered one so good that Loveman may be back in a month or so to patronise it. Had fine warm weather throughout trip. Loveman left for N.Y. on the boat Friday evening. He is moving his book shop to the cor. of 5th Ave. & 14th St—near Dauber & Pine's, where he used to work. I forget whether or not you met Loveman when you were in N. Y. ¶ In the Boston North End near the ancient North Church (1726) we found a delightful grey cat whose master (an ancient Italian) said he was 15 years old. No marks of decrepitude—purring, friendly, & in general a handsome old patriarch. He treats mice as his master's compatriots treat the Æthiopians!

[postcard 2:][3]
P. S. Got your tarjeta[4] from Ciudad Mexico—& do I envy you? Boy! Hope you can stay for the session with Pawang. ¶ Tragic news—Long's aunt was instantly killed in a motor accident near Miami Oct. 20.[5] ¶ Barlow has just bound & sent to Long the volume of the latter's poems which we printed last summer as a surprise for the bard. ¶ And Barlow is also trying to get hold of you to invite you to visit him during your trip—hope he does! ¶ More good news for the old man. Wandrei submitted my new "Shadow Out of Time" to *Astounding*, & they accepted it! Some streak of luck[6]—but it won't last. ¶ Nov. W T above average, with 3 good stories. Your "Hand of Wrath" is splendid—outstanding among your recent productions. Two-Gun is his usual spirited self in "Zamboula". And "The Way Home", by Paul Frederick Stern, is highly remarkable. Real mood & atmosphere. This chap is new to me, but he'll be worth watching![7] ¶ Just recd. card from Houston. Commiserations on the mishap, but congratulations on the intensive local colour. You certainly met the emergency cleverly enough! I envy you your antiquarian sightseeing, & wish I could pick up some good fake Aztec stuff for decoration! Good luck with Pawang! ¶ Have been attending a very interesting course of art lectures, with eminent speakers from various points of the compass. ¶ Am experimenting with a new tale, though I don't know how far it will get.[8] ¶ Guess I'll mail this at last, since you'll probably be home soon. Johnny Perkins is over this afternoon. He's been rolling in catnip, but now he has ambled over

near Grandpa & gone to sleep on the green cushion of the semicircular chair. You ought to see what a fine big boy he is! We salute Nimrod & Battle Axe! ¶ Blessings— ᴙ ⁊⁊ ˎ

Notes

1. *Front:* King's Chapel, Boston, Mass.

2. *The Last Days of Pompeii* (RKO Radio Pictures, 1935), directed by Ernest B. Schoedsack and Merian C. Cooper (uncredited); starring Preston Foster, Alan Hale, and Basil Rathbone.

3. *Front:* New Providence County Court House, Providence, R.I.

4. Postcard.

5. Cassie Doty Symmes (1872–1935), sister of Frank Belknap Long's mother. HPL had ghostwritten for Long a preface to Symmes's *Old World Footprints* (Athol, MA: W. Paul Cook/The Recluse Press, 1928; as by "Mrs. William B. Symmes"). See David Goudsward, "Cassie Symmes: Inadvertent Lovecraftian," *Lovecraft Annual* No. 9 (2015): 130–35.

6. *Astounding Stories* accepted *At the Mountains of Madness,* submitted by Julius Schwartz as HPL's agent, and quickly thereafter "The Shadow out of Time," submitted surreptitiously by Wandrei after he hijacked the story from its intended circulation list (and after *Argosy* rejected it first).

7. *WT,* November 1935: EHP, "The Hand of Wrath"; Robert E. Howard, "Shadows in Zamboula"; Paul Frederick Stern, "The Way Home." Stern is the pseudonym of Paul Ernst (who also had a story, "The Consuming Flame," in the issue).

8. "The Haunter of the Dark." HPL wrote it on 5–9 November.

[64]   [ALS, JHL]

Citadel of Leng—
Last of November
[30 November 1935]

Dear Malik:—

Aië! Aië! Mraow! Mraow! The Kappa Alpha Tau of Providence lifts its collective throat in lamentation for valiant Nimrod's vanishment, & in prayer for his safe & speedy return! To Azathoth, Yog-Sothoth, Tsathoggua, Bast, & Sekhmet ascend our yowls . . . & I'm sure Cyrus & Darius & all the rest in De Land echo our petitions. Likewise the youthful & night-black Sotho in Asotin—successor to the departed Crom. We all hold our breath & hope for the best. But thank Yuggoth Battle-Axe is still safe—may his sojourn on this planet & within these three dimensions be long & happy! Glad his status as a true he warrior is established!

Well—you surely had a trip! I've been studying the map (for which extreme thanks) with envious interest, & shall take delight in the promised travelogue. The excursion seems to have been without anticlimax—delightful to the last, even on the return trip. I felt a twinge of quasi-homesickness at the New Orleans view. Ah, me—when shall I again tread the ancient banquettes of Chartres & Royal Streets, write letters in Jackson Square, & wander amidst the grotesque tombs of ancient St. Louis Cemetery? The 'Cajin[1] country—which I never saw—must have been fascinating. Did you get to see Two-Gun in Cross Plains? And I'm glad that the picturesqueness kept up to the very last, & included the final miles in Alta California. It surely was a memorable expedition, & its echoes ought to colour your imagination for many a long day! Glad old Terry behaved so well despite the ripping he received down in Hidalgo.

Meanwhile let me congratulate you upon the acceptance of Pawang #6[2]—completed under such strenuous circumstances! And to think future adventures are not only mapped out but provisionally spoken for! Pawang in the Occident[3] ought to be quite a success. If he passes through Providence tell him to stop at 66! You needn't regret your maps of Penang & the like—for in time you'll undoubtedly be handling more material with an Oriental theme. Hope you'll master London in short order. Would the loan of an excellent map do you any good? I've tried to master the salient points of London at various times in the past. The map I have is quite new, although all my real guide-books are hilariously out of date. Let me know if any of the stuff would be of assistance. I have one sort of running commentary on London scenes which is fairly contemporary—by Sidney Dark, with illustration by the late Joseph Pennell . . . . also another thing by Dark; a sort of superficial guide book. All these put together might give you a vague notion of the place. Say the word & I'll send them along as a long-term loan.

I was surely glad to dispose of those two tales to *Astounding*,[4] though I doubt whether such a winning streak could continue long. The recent story which I wrote Nov. 5–9 is now circulating amongst the gang, & will reach you soon from Klarkash-Ton if it has not already done so. Not the least hurry about perusal—but when you're entirely through with it you might send it on to Two-Gun.

I presume your course in returning Old Dolph's story is the only feasible one. His yarns haven't even the start of anything truly weird. Which reminds me—did I tell you that I patched up a story of Old Bill Lumley's, & that Satrap Pharnabazus actually *accepted* it?[5] The good old boy was so pathetically anxious to get some sort of story in shape that I couldn't resist doing what I could. He really knows what *weird atmosphere* is—though he can't put anything in any sort of form. I'm letting old Bill keep all the cash he can get from the enterprise—he needs the encouragement. In appreciation of my help he gave me a very attractive copy of "The Book of the Dead"—translated by Sir E. Wallis Budge.

I feel sure Mortonius will be grateful for the fragment of Cuichilconian lava—as well as for the earlier set of specimens.[6] He was wondering last Sept. what had become of that latter array! And speaking of stone—you ought to see more of Klarkash-Ton's new carvings! He has presented me with a hellish thing entitled "The Outsider", & shewed me another monstrous specimen—destined ultimately from [*sic*] Ar-E'ch-Bei—entitled "The Hyperborean Snake-Eater".

Thanks vastly for the proffered loan of pictures & monograph covering the weird antiquities you have seen. The subject is indeed a fascinating one to me—as is anything connected with archaeology. While I don't claim to know Spanish, I have in the past puzzled out texts with the aid of a fair dictionary & 2 or 3 grammars which I possess—& with the spur of curiosity & historical interest I ought to be able to get the drift of the author's remarks.

Just recd. *Fantasy* with your biography,[7] & was interested in the various details—some of which were new to me. The picture (at least in my two copies) didn't come out very well—but then again, it wasn't any too faithful in the beginning, as a proof from Rimel shewed. R. gave you a sort of heavy jowl which you don't possess. ¶ Benedictions & Peace—

P.S. HURRAH! Your *latest* card has arrived!!! Good old Nimrod!!!! Can't keep the Kappa Alpha Tau down! Give him the Providence chapter's most resounding regards!! Prrrr . . prrrr . . . prrr . . . .

[P.P.S. on envelope:] C A S will soon forward you my new tale. Will you add to the circulation list the name of
William Crawford,
122 Water St.,
Everett, Penna.   ?

Thanks in advance!

Notes

1. HPL's mark of elision serves to indicate his recognition of *Cajun* as an elision or corruption of *Acadian*. The Acadians who migrated from Canada at the end of the French and Indian War (1763) settled in the area of the Gulf of Mexico.
2. "Each Slew a Slayer."
3. "The Pawang Moves."
4. There appear to be no extant letters in which HPL notes the sale of *At the Mountains of Madness* to *Astounding Stories* through his agent, Julius Schwartz, in early November, just before Wandrei sold "The Shadow out of Time."
5. "The Diary of Alonzo Typer."
6. Cuicuilco is an archaeological site on the southern shore of Lake Texcoco in the southeastern Valley of Mexico, in what is today the borough of Tlalpan in Mexico City. The settlement dates to 1400 B.C.E.
7. Alvin Earl Perry, "A Biographical Sketch of E. Hoffmann Price," *Fantasy Magazine* 5, No. 4 (September 1935): 236–38, with linoleum cut by Duane W. Rimel (see Appendix).

[65]   [ALS, JHL]

Dec. 15, 1935

Dear Malik:—

Mourn not at the unavoidable absence of the large-scale map—for verily, I am profoundly in your debt for having any at all! The existing chart is a mine of fascination—& its wider scope atones nobly for its smaller scale. I like these panoramic & inclusive layouts—indeed, my favourite maps of Providence, London, & Boston are those which include the suburbs & condense the city proper. Of course, if I were going to explore all the minute alleys of a town—or write a story demanding accurate knowledge of such—I would need a large-scale map or set of maps. But for a merely laymanlike survey, the broader plan certainly has its advantages. Possibly I told you that I once made quite a study of Cairo—in a superficial way—when ghost-writing that Egyptian thing of Houdini's for the 1924 giant anniversary number of W T. This admirable chart brings back my fading memory of that study—& well supplements the old-time map sent last September (for which renewed thanks!) in making me feel at home in the shadow of the Pyramids. My only regret is that my good fortune should be Kline's loss. A pleasant note from him accompanied the welcome device. Again, let me express my sincerest gratitude!

Glad the composite tales in F M proved of interest.[1] The weird one as a whole is better than I expected it would be, though nothing so heterogeneous & uncoördinated could have much intrinsic merit. My section isn't very impressive—having been written hastily & to order in Charleston during my recent travels. Also, certain bad misprints create an effect of nonsense in 2 or 3 places. The styles of the various writers clash less than might be expected—though each shews certain individual traits. The mild professor becomes a raging Conan in the sanguinary hands of Two-Gun, while Belknap airs his favourite romantic notion that all human beings are violent savages, restrained only through constant social pressure.

Yes—a de Castro job would certainly be as exacting & time-consuming a process as the composition of an original story—more so, in fact, since a certain limiting background is present. About those tales of mine which *Astounding* has taken—I don't know when "The Shadow out of Time" will appear, but "Mts. of Madness" is scheduled for 3-part publication in the Feb., Mar., & April issues. Of these two, the "Mts." is the only one rejected by Wright. The "Shadow" had never been submitted anywhere before.[2]

I doubt very much whether I could write non-weird stories of any sort, since experience has proved that all non-spontaneous material of mine is very bad. I have no impulse to write anything which does not deal with shadowy borderlands, & terrestrial crime simply bores me to death. So far as standard detective stuff is concerned, I lack almost every element needed for successful production. I have no interest in the theme, no knowledge of detailed contemporary life & customs, no knowledge of criminal or underworld folk-ways, & no knowledge of police judicial procedure. Added to which, of course, is the antipodal gulf between my style & the "action" jargon demand-ed by pulp editors. Even successful collaboration in this field seems doubt-ful—for I hardly see how I could do otherwise than *decrease* the professional chances of any detective MS. I might touch. Thanks for the suggestion, though. Some time later, when I am less oppressed with various tasks than at present, I may try my luck with some of those recalcitrant MSS. of yours.[3]

Hope "The Haunter of the Dark" won't bore you too badly. No—I wouldn't mind a critique of its salability aspects—in fact, such a thing would be very interesting as a study in contrasts. Thanks for the idea. But I couldn't guarantee to follow the directions, since my great aim is to break away from all cheap & conventional patterns & really express certain shadings of human mood as Blackwood & Poe & other sincere writers have done. I read as little pulp material as I can, & try to purge my style of its influence—for such things affect one insidiously, & hamper genuine utterance. The Putnam edi-tor, in rejecting a collection of my MSS. in 1931, pointed to the traceable in-fluence of the commercial pattern in my tales, & I have been trying to eradicate it ever since. If I can't get cash without twisting my writing, I'll will-ingly starve. Probably I shall fail in my attempt to create anything real—but I don't know of any reason for remaining alive except to try to do the only thing which to me seems worth doing.

Well—may the Prophet reward you!

ᘚᗩᘐ ᖇ

P.S. That Mexican coffee sounds highly fascinating—but I'm sure it owes much of its merit to the skilled preparation it receives at your hands!

Notes

1. *Fantasy Magazine* (September 1935) published two round-robin stories titled "The Challenge from Beyond," one (science fiction) by Stanley G. Weinbaum, Donald Wandrei, Edward E. Smith, Harl Vincent, and Murray Leinster, the other (horror) by C. L. Moore, A. Merritt, HPL, Robert E. Howard, and Frank Belknap Long.

2. Unknown to HPL, Donald Wandrei had submitted the story to *Argosy* before he submitted it to *Astounding*

3. EHP had written: "If I could tempt you to turn your revisory talent to one or more of my mystery novelettes which for some reason remain on the shelf, you might prove my contention" (4 December 1935; TNS, JHL).

[66]   [ALS, JHL]

[Postmarked 24 December 1935]

Dear Malik:—

Well, well, I surely have been granted a sight of an historic document! The beginnings of a titan! And how beautifully yellowed & mildewed & tattered the antique papyrus is! Were it not for the typed hieroglyphs, I would vow it came straight from some rock tomb in the Valley of Kings! And it is good stuff, too. Not as well-rounded as mature work, perhaps, but full of vivid atmosphere & eloquent with promise. It carries within it the seeds which flowered into "The Dreamer of Atlanaat" & "The Hand of Wrath". Slips are few—though had I been criticising the story at the time I'd have noted the missing A in *Paracelsus*, & the attribution of a long life to that gentleman, whereas he rounded out only a measly 48 years (1493–1541). I might have had a word to say about etymology, too—since I believe *alcohol* comes from *al kohol* (the latter meaning antimony powder—transferred through a curious associative process), whilst *al kali* (glasswort—source of soda) was the parent of nothing more formidable than *alkali*. I enjoyed the story's swat at the daemon rum, to which I am no friend! The MS. has already gone forward to Ar-E'ch-Bei with appropriate explanations.[1] He is at home in De Land—indeed, he hasn't been away since last spring. Just now he is printing my "Fungi From Yuggoth" preparatory to tackling Klarkash-Ton's "Incantations".[2] Needless to say, he'll be overwhelmed with joy at sight of this crumbling document, though it will sadden him to have the threat of possible recall hanging in the offing. Wish you could find some other treasure for the Hierophant An-ghah—for I don't believe anyone could give the MS. as tender & museum-like care as could Barlovius. He would place each sheet in an envelope of cellophane—probably framed in stiff cardboard. However, I realise that faithful & energetic service like An-ghah's deserves some notable reward! You can depend upon Ar-E'ch-Bei not to let the tale get into print—& to keep it in the pink of condition, whether his tenure is to be permanent or not.

Glad all is flourishing atop the haunted Kaf. Old Terry's new speeds must be highly encouraging to a Brother of the Lightning, & I trust you may have many opportunities for exercising your champing charger without disasters or legal intervention! Glad the revolutionists appreciated your courtesies. Nobody can beat the Latins in politeness!

Thanks for the opportunity of copying your necropolitan chart! My cartography is very crude & amateurish, but I fancy I could give enough of an idea of the place to guide my spirit in case of any subsequent ghoulish dreamwanderings.

Got something amusing the other day from Pharnabazus—copy of "Midsummer Night's Dream" in format of pulp magazine with illustrations, announced as the first of "Wright's Shakespearian Library." Bless me, but the old boy is going classic! 35¢ per copy. I'd invest if there weren't from 4 to 6 sets of the Bard in the house—counting attic miscellany. But I've thanked Farny for the sample.

Instalment I of the travelogue duly goes forward to C L M. I await the later sections with accounts of Aztec antiquities & exotic adventures. Glad the novel goes ahead well. I've always maintained that a long thing is easier to write than a short story—indeed, I've about come to the conclusion that I *can't* write short stories any more. Whatever I want to say spins itself out to at least "novelette" length. Congratulations on the Swedish sales! I'd like to see one of your stories in Swedish—or Basque, or Amharic. Not that I could read it, but that it would look impressive!

It is possible that I shall be in N.Y. from Dec. 30 to Jan. 6, visiting Belknap & incidentally seeing Morton, the Wandreis, & other metropolitan imams & dervishes. Brobst was over here yesterday, & sent you his most particular regards.

Johnny Perkins sends his best regards to Old Nim & little Battle-Axe. I'm getting John some catnip for Christmas, & hope he'll be over here at Yuletide. Have got a Christmas tree, & shall complete its decorations this afternoon. Trust your own holidays may be festive & memorable.

Peace & prayer— ϱ ⌒ 𝒴⌐⟩

Notes

1. RHB had sought to obtain one of EHP's early mss. for his collection. See EHP to HPL, 26 August 1935 (TNS, JHL): "A message for Barlonius: an intensive search to find my first piece of fantasy fiction, written in France, April 1919, has completely failed. Somehow, I feel that it was not destroyed, but I may finally have scrapped it. The only relic I find is a typed copy of THE FIRST STORY I EVER HAD IN PRINT—March 1924. However, it is not fantasy, and thus despite its 'historic' value, it would not suit the Barlonius archives." The story was "Triangle with Variations" in *Droll Stories*, though it was published in the June issue.

2. *Fungi from Yuggoth* was never completed and *Incantations* never begun.

[67] [ALS, JHL]

Cave of the Afreets
—Jany. 20, 1936

Dear Malik:—

Only the maddening pressure of countless exacting & unexpected tasks has prevented me from sooner acknowledging your sundry bulletins, & the tremendously interesting & brilliantly edited 𝄞 日 矢 圀 —whose style is remarkably vigorous despite the slightly Cantonese provincialism of one or two of the editorials.[1] A message from An-Ghah the Hierophant confirms your report of a pleasant evening among Cathayan influences,[2] & I note with interest the increasing appeal which Chinese music has for you. About a year ago a Dr. Koo lectured here on the Far Eastern situation, & at the conclusion of his remarks rendered three selections on the flute of his native land.[3] All of these pieces had a strong & haunting charm, but I imagined he had purposely chosen melodies which happened to resemble western music more than the average.

Glad you duly received Ar-E'ch-Bei's surprise edition of "Ulthar". I hadn't an inkling of what the little imp was preparing, & was certainly pleased by his thoughtfulness. He was, by the way, very sorry that your recent trip didn't take you as far east as Florida. One of his great ambitions is to have Al-Tarah-P'lan draw up before the rugged facade of the Villa Barlovia.

Interested to hear that you are getting Pawang around to good old Ba yonne. Hope he'll clean up all the daemons in the prehistoric & forgotten crypts! Or you might pit him against an emissary of the frightful Hung Society—that book about which would surely seem to be a treasure. No hurry about that necropolitan loan—though I'll be glad to copy the chart when a convenient opportunity arises. With these desolate, moon-washed realms of the dead in mind, it wouldn't be difficult to imagine a *necropolitan police force*— whose members would move somewhat stiffly, with the rust of some 3000 or 4000 years in their joints. And so the dictaphone is once more of use? Such dizzy mechanical devices are beyond me! Glad that the offering of alternative tributes to An-Ghah is likely to prolong Barlovius' tenure of the treasured Paracelsian MS. If ever you feel justified in issuing him a patent of perpetual possession in fee simple, you will probably be the recipient of a most ceremoniously grateful demonstration. No—Paracelsus rounded out only 48 years despite his delvings into the obscure. Maybe he didn't think a longer life worth bothering about!

Glad that Battle-Axe seems to have recovered from his indisposition . . . . & congratulations on his first & gloriously successful gopher-hunt! Apparently gopher-hunting is one of the crucial feats of feline prowess in the golden west—I notice that Klarkash-Ton mentions a slackening in this pursuit as one of the signs of venerable Simaetha's advancing years. As for B-A's voracity—it must be either the climate of Mt. Kaf, or the bad influence of all-consuming Nimrod. I recall that B-A is prone to imitate his senior in speech & otherwise. Well—here's hoping he doesn't stuff himself to death before he's old enough to take it! As for old Nim himself—he surely *will* need a cage or chain before long! Look out for your knuckles! Glad he turned up as usual after his fortnight's sojourn beyond the river Skai[4] . . . one may imagine what nourishment bred his unwonted indifference to his accustomed 5-lb snacks of raw meat!

As for the Providence chapter of the K.A.T.—I am in sighs & tears! Not a blow of the grim reaper, but a cuff from the daemon of separation. For alas—the venerable black-&-white president & his tiger brother have *moved away* with their human family. Eheu, eheu! I gaze in sadness upon the untenanted expanse of the clubhouse roof, looking vainly for the sprawling forms of my furry friends. Other members will come with the spring—but who could be like old Peter Randall, with the white spot on the tip of his tail? Grave, ancient Peter, who finally came to recall so much of his lost kittenhood that he would roll over playfully when Grandpa spoke to him? I must find out whither Peter's household has moved, & pay him a call in his new locale. Meanwhile Mr. John Perkins waxes immense, & is a frequent visitor at 66—while his small brother, Gilbert John Murray Kynymond Elliott, Earl of Minto,[5] still remains at the neighbouring boarding-house. I guess they mean to keep Lord Minto, though they had promised him to friends elsewhere. He is a lively little cuss!

Your letter to old Dolph is a masterpiece of tact & gracefulness, & ought to leave its recipient in a mood of friendly understanding. It is so good that I am tempted to plagiarise it in formulating future turndowns . . . . not, however, that I could use the Mexican parts, or those speaking of a demand for original work! I didn't know old Dolph was contemplating a return to San Francisco. It would probably be a good move—indeed, I don't see how anybody can live in New York voluntarily.

Thanks immensely for the Texas map, which gives an added vividness to Two-Gun's odysseys of local travel. I hope to see more of your own travelogue in course of time—& am glad that Yule brought you a pictorial echo of the gleaming deserts you so extensively traversed. My files are getting very rich in maps—though I doubt whether I shall ever be able to cover the represented territory in person!

I had a pleasant Christmas—with a tree, as last year—though my holiday *did* lack a session at the morgue![6] Hugh B. Cave ought to appreciate your researches at this cheerful social centre. Years ago Belknap & I half-decided to inspect a morgue, but we never got around to it. I fear I might not be wholly appreciative, despite the gruesomeness in some of my pseudo-literary attempts. Piecemeal & putrescent cadavers are all right on paper—but when it comes to personal inspection, some aged horror-weavers harbour a strange squeamishness! No—of San Francisco's varied diversions I guess I'll chose the Chinese theatre!

Yes—I hope that trip *can* be managed some day—although I sadly doubt my ability to improve, in the ways commercially demanded, any crime novelette from a master hand! But we'll see later on, when my programme is less feverishly crowded than at present. This month I'm absolutely cornered—& have had to evade many of my duties (such as preparing a critical report) in the N.A.P.A.

Around New Year's I visited Long a week, & in that brief time succeeded in seeing most of the gang—Morton, Loveman, Leeds, Talman, Kleiner, Kirk, the Wandrei boys, Kline's son,[7] &c. &c. Met Otto (of "Eando") Binder, Arthur J. Burks, & Donald Wollheim for the first time—& saw good old

Seabury Quinn for the first time since 1931. Some of these glimpses occurred at a dinner of the American Fiction Guild which I attended. Morton, Long, & others sent you their regards—the first-named delicately hinting that he'd still be extremely grateful for any California minerals which might find their way to his museum.[8] We had several gatherings, & on the final day Long & I went out to Paterson to see J F M. Saw Loveman's new bookshop, & was delighted to get a glimpse of his new book—of which an advance copy had just arrived. You may recall my mentioning that I read its proofs last September. It really makes a fine appearance. Here's a circular including a description of it.

On two occasions I visited the new Hayden Planetarium of the Am. Museum, & found it a highly impressive device. It consists of a round domed building of 2 storeys. On the lower floor is a circular hall whose ceiling is a gigantic orrery—showing the planets revolving around the sun at their proper relative speeds. Above it is another circular hall whose roof is the great dome, & whose edge is made to represent the horizon of N.Y. as seen from Central Park. In the middle of this upper hall is a curious projector (that looks like an Hamiltonian "space ship" or like one of the armoured Martians in "The War of the Worlds") which casts on the concave dome a perfect image of the sky—capable of duplicating the natural apparent motions of the celestial vault, & of depicting the heavens as seen at any hour, in any season, from any latitude, & at any period of history. Other parts of the projector can cast suitably moveable images of the sun, moon, & planets, & diagrammatic arrows & circles for explanatory purposes. The effect is infinitely lifelike—as if one were outdoors beneath the sky. Lectures—different each month (I heard both Dec. & Jan. ones)—were given in connexion with this apparatus. In the annular corridors on each floor are niches containing typical astronomical instruments of all ages—telescopes, transits, celestial globes, armillary spheres, &c.—& cases to display books, meteorites, & other miscellany. Astronomical pictures line the walls, & at the desk may be obtained useful pamphlets, books, planispheres, &c. The institution holds classes in elementary astronomy, & sponsors clubs of amateur observers. Altogether, it is the most complete & active popular astronomical centre imaginable. It seems to be crowded at all hours—attesting a public interest in astronomy which did not exist when I was young.

Klarkash-Ton writes that his new sculptural activities have become paramount with him. There now seems to be even a professional demand for his work, so that it might well replace writing in the end as a source of revenue.[9] I am eagerly awaiting the loan exhibit of his figurines which is to go the rounds of the gang by express.

A little farther up the coast, Rhi-Mhel has just made that long-awaited article out of your forceful letter anent the decline of weird fiction. He has shown surprising skill in preserving your anonymity, & I fancy you will approve the result when he sends it for your imprimatur. Incidentally—Rimel has almost succeeded in placing a story with Satrap Pharnabazus . . . through Kline. The younger generation is coming along!

Haven't yet had a chance to read the Jan. W T. Have seen the *Astounding* with Part I of my "Mts. of Madness", & admire the skill with which the illustrator grasped the nature of those palaeogean Things from a purely verbal description.[10] Hope the text isn't mangled—I haven't been able to look it over as yet.

Providence is under a heavy snow today—it fell yesterday, perhaps to commemorate the joint birthday of James Watt, Robert E. Lee, & Edgar Allan Poe. Hope the winter isn't going to end up severely—it has been phenomenally mild hereabouts so far.

With all the accustomed blessings—
Yrs by the Prophet

[Enclosures: newspaper clippings; flyer for Caxton Printers.]

Notes

1. EHP had sent HPL a Chinese newspaper.

2. EHP and Fred Anger attended a Chinese opera on 29 or 30 December.

3. Tse Zung Koo (Gu Ziren; 1887–1971) was a preeminent Chinese Christian leader, a graduate of St. John's University Shanghai (1908), in government railroad administrative service, and master of literature (1911). Author of *Songs of Cathay: An Anthology of Songs Current in Various Parts of China* and *Chinese Christianity Speaks to the West* (1950). He played a split bamboo flute.

4. Referring to his story "The Cats of Ulthar."

5. Named after Gilbert John Elliot-Murray-Kynynmound, 4th Earl of Minto (1845–1914), Governor-General of Canada (1898–1904) and Viceroy of India (1905–10).

6. EHP to HPL, 31 December 1935 (TLS, JHL): "I spent Xmas day at the San Francisco morgue, viewing the 22 corpses in the refrigerator, inspecting the laboratory, scrutinizing the photo album, showing pictures of several ladies whose violent & mysterious deaths hogged the headlines the past year."

7. Allen Kline (not to be confused with Otis's younger brother Allan S. Kline).

8. In July 1939, Morton (and R. H. Barlow) visited EHP, who took Morton to various sites to collect mineral samples.

9. Such was the case. Smith devoted a longer period of his life to this than he did to fiction writing, and even though his writing of poetry covered a longer period, he worked steadily at carving for about 30 years.

10. Howard V. Brown (1878–1945) illustrated both *At the Mountains of Madness* and "The Shadow out of Time."

[68]   [ALS, JHL]

Citadel of Irem
[Postmarked 12 February 1936]

Dear Malik:—

Your many favours duly received—& I have just finished copying that graphic & interesting necropolitan chart. By adopting an equal scale & duplicating the squares I believe I have the salient features in something like their correct positions. I have indicated cliffs & rising ground without copying all the contour lines—& believe I have all the roads & ancient buildings. Now I ought to be able to find my way around when I get to immemorial Thebes! Eventually I shall ink over the lines which I have drawn in pencil. I'll wager the Bangkok map is fascinating—though don't believe I'll tackle the copying just yet. Probably it wouldn't pay to have a photostatic copy unless one needed the chart for specific use. But thanks endlessly for the Theban affair—which I am returning herewith in what I hope will prove an undamaged state.

Glad you found the "Mts. of Madness" readable. That was my attempt to pin down the vague feelings regarding the lethal, desolate white south which have haunted me ever since I was ten years old. It was written in 1931—& its hostile reception by Wright & others to whom it was shown probably did more than anything else to end my effective fictional career. The feeling that I had failed to crystallise the mood I was trying to crystallise robbed me in some subtle fashion of the ability to approach this kind of problem in the same way—or with the same degree of confidence & fertility. But it is some consolation to have the damn thing printed at last—as a posthumous effort, if nothing more. There are several inexcusable errors in the text—such as "palaeocene" for *palaeogean*—but the illustrations are excellent. The artist visualised the archaean entities perfectly from the written description—proving that he really read the text, which is more than most of Satrap Pharnabazus' picture-bunglers do.

I am grieved to hear of Nimrod's increasing absences, & hope his seeming lack of domestic appreciativeness is a purely transient phenomenon. Was interested to hear of the martial gathering on Telegraph Hill. Battle-Axe is surely inheriting the best Kappa Alpha Tau traditions of prowess & gluttony—the latter of which I trust may be curbed to an extent compatible with his own good. I mourn the canine loss, & place a figurative wreath upon the hillside grave. The local K.A.T. now seems, alas, confined to the citizens of the neighbouring boarding-house. Mr. Perkins continues to be a frequent visitor—& his brother, Gilbert John Murray Kynymond Elliot, 4th Earl of Minto, is developing into a most pleasing youth. Lord Minto is black & white—the former on top, the latter in his southern hemisphere.

Glad that Pawang & his contemporaries continue to prosper. Interested to hear of the curious ancestry of Kwan Shi Yin[1]—& of her connexion with the hideous Hung Society. You might set the Necropolitan Police after the Hungs, & make them live up to their name! Don't hurry unduly about the Mexican notes—I guess your memory will still retain enough to make absorbing reading! Hope the new refrigerator works well. Morton has one of these electrical contraptions—of the Norge brand—& it makes delectable ice cream. I ate about a quart of its choice product on the evening of Jany. 6. Haven't heard from de Castro since his note at Christmas, but he'll surely let you know when he returns to the realm of the Golden Gate.

I read with great interest & appreciation your careful analysis of the recent alleged story, & must thank you for the time, energy, & attention given to what is essentially only a trifle. I realised from the outset that the thing is a failure—as everything since the "Mts of Madness" has been. I simply lack whatever it is that enables a real artist to convey his mood. The sole purpose of this attempt was to crystallise (a) the feeling of strangeness in a distant view, & (b) the feeling of latent horror in an old, deserted edifice. Evidently I did neither. I don't know why I kept the thing after destroying dozens of similar attempts without shewing them during the past few years—but now & then one has a streak of ego. However, I don't know that there's much use in further experimentation. I'm further from doing what I want to do than I was 20 years ago. The peculiar faculty which Blackwood & Dunsany possess simply isn't mine.

Your verbal points are very interesting. I have always been aware that my use of *cyclopean* is not technically correct in a purist's sense, but have questioned the advisability of a too rigid purism. Regarding *eldritch*—I deliberately repudiate the idea that popular over-use of a word can destroy its permanent value. What appears in the pulps today is forgotten tomorrow—& any tale which survives at all will live to see its words appraised at their original worth. Not that this tale will survive—but that I don't care how bad it is *unless* it has permanent qualities. That is, the standard of *contemporary* as distinguished from *permanent* value is meaningless to me. If the tale hasn't gone on to 2-Gun, you might send it back to me—for after all, I'm not sure that I wish to circulate it.

As for the old *unaussprechlichen–unenbarren* controversy . . . I stand a helpless & ignorant bystander among experts! Possibly you recall the later preceding phases. Graf August-Wilhelm von Derleth stuck by his *unaussprechlichen* on the ground of living German usage as perpetuated by the people of Sauk City— who were recruited from an above-average section of the German people. Then the ex-W T artist *C. C. Senf* [2]—born & educated in Germany—cast his vote on the same side. He called at Wright's office while the debate was still hot, & in response to the Satrap's query (with explanations) backed up the Count. I wish all you linguistic sharks could be corralled together for a verbal debate—drawing on precedents in speech, literature, &c. About the only thing a poor know-nothing can do is to call the hellish volume "The Black Book" & let it go at that! But your explanations do sound damned convincing! Haven't had a chance to read the last two W Ts—duties of every sort have crowded oppressively in & completely wrecked my programme, added to which I've had a touch of grippe which put me out of business for a week & has left me as weak & sleepy as a dishrag. Derleth has sent me his first *serious* book—"Place of Hawks"—plus a nightmare anthology including a sketch by Blackwood.[3] Hope your forswearing of fantasy isn't too final. I certainly wouldn't recall anything accepted! Crawford is going to print my "Innsmouth" as a book, & hopes to get illustrations from Utpatel. Rimel has had a story accepted by W T—through the mediation of Kline

Hellish-scelerous-infandous-weather hereabouts lately. Snow in profusion, & day after day not much above 20°. I haven't been out of the house since Jany. 13. Well—next month contains the Vernal Æquinox! Again let me thank you for the painstaking criticism—which will substantially aid in giving direction to any fresh experiments I may make. Regards to Nimrod & Battle-Axe. And thanks for the chart—whose crude counterpart is now in my permanent files. ¶ Peace & prayer—ﻕﻮﻗ I don't know what this means, but if it's unpronounceable it ought to be a good signature!

P.S. Young *Donald A. Wollheim, 801 West End Ave., N.Y. City,* the second issue of whose rather crudely printed *Phantagraph* has appeared, wants to know the addresses of Edmond Hamilton & W. Kirk Mashburn. Could you supply him?

Notes

1. Literally "he who perceives the world's lamentations." In theosophical literature, Kwan-Shi-Yin is the Logos, as the highest principle in the manifested cosmos. Kwan-Shi-Yin is identical with the Sanskrit *Avalokitéshvara,* and as such is an androgynous deity, like the Tetragrammaton and all the Logoi of antiquity. It is only by some sects in China that he is anthropomorphized and represented with female attributes, when, under his female aspect, he becomes Kwan-Yin, the goddess of mercy, called the "Divine Voice." EHP had written (1 February 1936; TNS, JHL): "Kwan Shi Yin, the Goddess of Mercy, is said to be akin to Avalokitesvara, 'The Looking Down God', perhaps derived from the Arabian Al Makah, THE GOD WHO HEARKENS. This shift from masc. to fem. deity being not uncommon."

2. C[urtis] C[harles] Senf (1873–1949) was an illustrator for *WT* from 1927 until 1932, when he was edged out because of complaints about his artwork.

3. See Bibliography under Cynthia Asquith. The book contained Blackwood's "The Blackmailers."

[69]   [ALS, JHL]

March 16, 1936

Dear Malik:—

When I reflect that the earliest of your welcome but hitherto unanswered bulletins bears the date of Feby. 12, I am impressed with the extent to which my correspondence has lapsed. But the reasons therefor are all too compelling—& I fancy the account of them will quickly gain me pardon. The maddening overflow of work & the grippe attack of which I spoke in my previous epistle were only the *beginning* of local worries. The worst was yet to come—& 1936 certainly goes down in my annals as a bad year! In brief—in mid-February my aunt came down with a grippe attack far worse than mine—& complications have made a serious illness of it.[1] For a month I have been busy as a combined nurse, butler, secretary, market-man & errand-boy—with no time for concentrated thought or continuous work of any kind. My aunt will now be in the hospital (another building of the extensive institution which we visited in '33) for about a fortnight, & in a nursing home perhaps a fortnight more. Amidst all this upheaval & anxiety the state of my own programme can be imagined. I am having to resign one of the revision jobs I spoke of in an unfinished state—& correspondence becomes merely a series of idle jottings in moments when I am too exhausted to do anything else.

Glad to hear all the news, & hope the book comes out well. Good luck to Pawang in his war on the Hung Society—& may your microscopic rug article save at least one novice from the cheater's toils. You are to rugs what Morton is to minerals! Hope the Mexican swindle articles can be made at least sinister enough to get by![2]

Glad the good impression of "Mts. of Madness" holds. I'll ask Wollheim not to quote you regarding the story's original rejection—but appreciate the opinion none the less! Yes—I'd be pleased to hear opinions on the trouble with my writing, although my own tripartite view seems to me pretty valid. That is (a) lack of general ability [my stuff *never was* much good—its appeal, such as it was, being largely meretricious][,] (b) too much reading of pulp fiction, whereby I acquired mental patterns fatal to genuine expression, & (c) the fact that *fiction* is *not* the medium for what I *really want to do*. [Just what the right medium would be, I don't know—perhaps the cheapened & hackneyed term "prose-poem" would hint in the general direction.] Minor added factors are lack of the freshness of novelty in my efforts, & the subconscious effect of criticism—with the inhibitions it imposes on the spontaneous creative process. Probably I need another 9-year vacation from this type of thing—like my silence of 1908–1917. It will be time to begin again when I have forgotten all about magazines—pulp & genuine—& reading publics, & have returned to the complete state of isolation & spontaneous self-suiting which I possessed in 1905 & 1917 . . . in each of which years I began a series of tales which virtually wrote themselves. All good work must come from the subconscious, & pay no attention to any external standard or demand—to nothing but the instincts & taste of the creator as imperceptibly moulded by the education & impressions he has received. However—I doubt if I have the native capacity to do any first-rate work even under favourable conditions. If I had such, I would never have read pulp fiction, nor unconsciously acquired the taint of its perspective & materials—nor would I have persisted in a medium unsuited to my major (albeit unconscious) objectives.

Speaking of decline & death—my tears flow at the thought that Nimrod will devour no more gophers & bowls of beans, accumulate & inflict no more tattered ears, & doze no more on his accustomed red cushion. Aië! Aië! The resident remainder of Kappa Alpha Tau's Providence chapter yowl in chorus with me! But is it not possible that our apprehensions are premature, & that he may yet return, dragging the carcass of a slain dog or hyena or rhinoceros in his reddened paws? O Nimrod, how mighty a destroyer wert thou! The vultures mourn at thy passing, Nimrod—thou, who didst daily enrich their feasting & thine own! I still refuse to believe the worst as a proved thing—but if Nimrod has gone down into the long night I'll wager he went fighting, & circled by a ring of his foemen's slain forms. Weep, O Mavors![3] Sigh, Bellona,[4] for a son worthy of thy rage! In the words of the blind Bard, as Mr. Pope translates him:

> "Not yet, my brave companions of the war,
> Release your smoking coursers from the car;
> But, with his chariot each in order led,
> Perform due honours to our NIMROD dead.
> Ere yet from rest or food we seek relief,
> Some rites remain, to glut our rage of grief."[5]

Well—whoever his slayers are, I hope his five small sons will grow up into stout warriors to avenge him! Too bad you couldn't secure one of them—but perhaps a wider search might reveal other snow-white scions of the mighty warrior!

But Battle-Axe, I trust, still remains to carry out revenges of his own—he, who learned the accents of martial speech from the lips of the Great One. I rejoice to hear of his prowess, & of the instances of his shrewd cerebration. Mr. Perkins & his little brother Lord Minto continue to dominate the situation here. They were both over here visiting yesterday, & formed highly congenial company. John is quite devoted to his brother & often protects him.

Congratulations on the headship of the Am. Fiction Guild in San Francisco—an honour, even if a burden. The N.Y. chapter—a dinner of which I attended with Belknap & Howard Wandrei last January—seems quite thriving.

Glad the orchard on Mt. Kaf is beginning to show vernal signs. Weather greatly moderated here—the cold winter having broken up around the middle of February. Around 60° yesterday—& 64° last Tuesday. But nothing in the way of blossoms or kindred phenomena.

And now let me congratulate you upon the new steed Hu'd-s'un—third in descent from good old Jug! It surely sounds marvellous enough—& who would care for 113 or 121 horsepower when one has the mystical Thibetan 108?[6] Glad you got such a good allowance on old Terry. As for boosting the power—I surely *wouldn't* do it if I were you, for the added speed would scarcely be worth the sacrificed symmetry. Glad to hear of the notable Himalayan performances—though sorry that Hu'd-s'un is so much thirstier than Terry & Jug. I don't wonder that the local tribesmen stare in amazement at so huge & snorting an elephant. And by the way—I shall read with great interest the second instalment of your Mexican travelogue.

Just heard from Klarkash-Ton—which reminds me that I owe the ancient witch Simaetha, head of the Averoigne K.A.T., an apology! In writing you last—after a *hasty* reading of another epistle from C A S—I stated that the almost-century-old grandam[7] shewed "a little less energy" in hunting gophers. Perish the slander! When I re-read the letter I saw that it said she shews "*little* (*not* "a" little) less energy" in her pursuit of the elusive burrowers! In other words, though she has been a familiar black shadow on Indian Hill for almost as long as Klarkash-Ton can remember, her uncanny strength & daemoniac endowments stand apart from the common encroachments of Time! Always the same—while dynasties fall & generations pass from cradle to grave! A true ally of dark powers beyond the Pillars of Yoth.

Glad you've heard from Ar-E'ch-Bei. Yes—he's determined to save C L M for literature if he can, though it's probably a losing game. Incidentally—she & her mother stopped to see the Young Acolyte of Krang last month while touring Florida. The trip was a rather melancholy one—to ease the shock of a major bereavement (C L M's fiancè [*sic*], a mighty hunter, was instantly killed on Feby. 13 while cleaning his gun—a truly tragic accident to a youth full of promise)—& Ar-E'ch-Bei hopes for an ampler visit under happier conditions in the future.

Since you don't do science fiction, I presume that the sale of *Wonder Stories* to the Margulies group[8] which Belknap likes so well will be of merely academic interest to you. For those who *do* write science fiction it will be a godsend—like the founding of a new magazine, since Hugo the Rat was never to be depended upon financially. Margulies has asked me for material, but I have nothing on hand suitable for such a periodical. By the way—I am told that *Astounding* will use my "Shadow out of Time" in the June issue.

Crawford intends to print my "Shadow Over Innsmouth" as a booklet with illustrations by Derleth's gifted friend Utpatel. It will be a crude job, I suppose—but anything to get the text into an easily circulatable form.

Under separate cover I send a copy of *Causerie*—connected with the National Amateur Press Assn.—in which a not wholly sympathetic review of Long's "Goblin Tower" is given.[9] The detailed criticisms are just enough, but

By the way—I duly received the second instalment of your fascinating travelogue. You surely make the Mexican invasion live again! Discovering that Arab at the caravanserai must have given you quite a kick! In piecing together sections 1 & 2 I noted with regret that *p. 5* of the El Paso section is missing. Did it get left out when you assembled the copy?

Thanks immensely for the loan of the cutting anent the Cuicuilco excavations. It gives an excellent idea of the scene, & will form a useful footnote to your travelogue. Scientifically, however, it is all haywire. It says, for example, that Neanderthal man (a sub-human branch not belonging to our species) 'came long after the Pleistocene [glacial] system had disappeared.' Now anybody knows that the Neanderthalers lived principally *right in the Pleistocene age* (say 75,000 to 25,000 B.C. The Pleistocene itself lasted from about 475,000 to 25,000 B.C.), & did not long survive it—being rapidly killed off as soon as they came in contact with true men in Europe. And as for Pekin & Piltdown[2] & Heidelberg man—they came long before that, at periods varying from 100,000 to 250,000 years ago—& perhaps more. America has no human or sub-human remains of an antiquity even comparable with these. Moreover—these primitive sub-men had no pottery, nor any artifacts except chipped flints. Another 'boner' in the article is that 8000 years is 'well back toward the Pleistocene'. No modern authority puts the end of the glacial age at less than 25,000 years ago—& many seek to push it back 25,000 years more. 8000 years ago—6000 B.C.—is no older than many ruins in the Tigris-Euphrates valley. However—it would be an important thing if American ruins could be assigned so early a date. Very few are willing to grant a very high antiquity to Mexican & Mayan ruins, believing that none antedate the 1st century A.D. A few push the date back to 2000 B.C.—& *one* recent German scholar has an attempted interpretation of the Mayan calendar which would justify a date of 8000 or more B.C. for Middle American cultures. Authorities differ widely on the age of sub-pedregal artifacts. Some Mexican scholars push the date back to 19,000 B.C.—but few in the outside world agree with them. This dating is a very delicate process of estimation, involving the interpretation of geological evidence. The other night I heard an excellent lecture on Mayan ruins, & learned a great deal about them that I never knew before. American archaeology surely has made strides of late!

Well—I hope soon to hear the tinkle of the camel bells on the neighbouring sands! Keep me posted. ¶ Blessings ⨀

Notes

1. Raoul Riganti (1893–1970), Argentine racecar driver.
2. Piltdown Man was a paleoanthropological fraud in which bone fragments were presented as the fossilized remains of a previously unknown early human. The falsity of the hoax was definitively demonstrated in 1953; amateur archaeologist Charles Daw-

son was deemed its likely perpetrator. HPL cites it in "Dagon" (1917) and "The Rats in the Walls" (1923) (*CF* 1.57, 393).

[71]   [ALS, JHL]

Lamasery of Leng—
May 19, 1936

Mighty Malik:—

Your chronicle of the 4th duly arrived, & I mourn that all hope of the eastward hegira seems to have faded. Brobst shares my tears—as does Long. But let us hope that the autumn will bring better luck!

Hope your new products are all taking shape satisfactorily. Wandrei seems to have broken into *The Argosy*, & if he can, you certainly can.[1] Sorry the advertisement of the travelogue is so unscholarly—but perhaps the reader will realise that you are not responsible for the boners. Anyhow, a guy who can graduate from West Point before attending high-school is obviously an important character no matter how he *seems* to spell! Hope the book can be profitably placed. If it has the same freshness & vitality that the carbon instalments have, it surely ought to be a success! Thanks, by the way, for the missing p. 5, which I have appreciatively read & put in place. Hope to see later instalments ere long. You can probably work in the Cuicuilco material effectively without including the journalistic blunders of that article. I didn't know the pedregal lava flow had been traced to any particular mountain. Your volume will probably include much which is wholly new to the reader, since it draws on official native sources.

Glad to hear latest revised bulletins of orchard & garden. You Californians seem to appreciate cacti more than the Floridans do. My sole experience with the genus consists in helping Pa Barlow root them out of the lawn at Moon Pool Manor in De Land! However, I did persuade the Barlovii to retain at least a few finely-branching specimens at strategic points. Hope the plums will prove edible despite dire contrary prophecies—& my blessings attend the peach & the orangelets!

Battle-Axe seems to be a very distinguished youth, & a not wholly unworthy successor to the Great Departed as president of The California Chapter of the Kappa Alpha Tau. Hope I can see a picture of him some time. I duly note the Malayan usage in his alternative name.[2] Eventually I trust that he & Popocatepetl may work out some reasonably pacific modus vivendi. The Prov. K.A.T. flourishes—both Mr. Perkins & his brother having spent all Saturday afternoon at 66. There is still much of the kitten in John, despite his 1 year, 3 months.

Hu'd-su'un surely is a mighty beast—& I'm sure that *I* would be quite satisfied with speeds of 78.5 or 82.5 miles per hour! Congratulations on your record run from the great city—may you do as well in burning up the miles to ancient Providence later on! Too bad you can't train the beast to be as economical of petrol as he is of oil!

Thanks for that Belmont cutting—which surely describes a town made to order for Brobst![3] The City of the Mad . . . . assuredly, there ought to be a story in that for somebody! I return the cutting as per request.

Well—I'll be a candidate for Belmont myself if I can't get my programme straightened out somehow! I guess I told you that my aunt is recovering nicely now—returned home April 21, & takes walks each sunny afternoon. On April 30 we were both treated to a delightful motor ride through the awakening countryside to Westport Point, Mass. I shall feel better when warm weather is here to stay. Not till April 28 was there any really good day—but since then I've been out on Prospect Terrace with my work several times, & yesterday I took a sizeable urban walk. The landscape is now a captivating spectacle with its new verdure & abundant blossoms, & I hope to find time for some rural walks ere long. Barlow has invited me down to De Land again, but I greatly doubt my ability to accept.

On May 4 the R.I. Tercentenary observances began with a costumed parade which started at the college gate—just a stone's throw from here. Later there was a mock-session of the rebel legislature of May 4, 1776—held in costume in the selfsame room of the ancient colony-house (1761) where the original session was held. In this, each old-time deputy was impersonated by a lineal descendant. The acting & pageantry were so excellent that one might easily have fancied the bygone period returned—with the intervening 160 years merely a bad dream. I was one of the relatively few spectators lucky enough to get into the colony-house & witness the proceedings. In the afternoon—in a ceremony at the State House which I did not attend—Gov. Curley of Mass. presented to Gov. Green R.I.[4] a copy of the recent resolution of the Mass. General Court—rescinding the banishment imposed by that august body on Roger Williams in Oct. 1635. After 300½ years Mr. Williams no doubt appreciates this delicate mark of consideration!

Stumbled on an interesting genealogical discovery recently—when I learned for the first time that I am a great-great-great-great-great-great-great-great-great-grandson of the Elizabethan astronomer who introduced the Copernican theory into England! For one who has always been a keen amateur astronomer, this was quite a find. Ordinarily I'm not much at genealogy, being (unlike our friend Mortonius) content to take what existing charts tell me & let it go at that. The other day I ran into a caller of my aunt's—an old lady related to us in the Field & Wilcox lines—& she mentioned how proud I ought to be of our common forbear, *the astronomer John Field or Felde*. That had me quite floored, since our charts carried the Field line back only to the original Providence settler John Field, who died in 1686, & I knew damn well *he* was no star-gazer! Well—it soon turned out that the ancestry of this settler has been known for ages among genealogists, though I had no inkling of it. The 16th

Cent. astronomer (whose 1557 Ephemeris contained the first English account of the Copernican system, & who has been called "The Proto-Copernican of England") was the Prov. colonist's *own grandfather*—hence *my* 9-times-great-grandfather. It surely gave me a kick to get a real *man of science* in my pedigree—which as a general thing is lousy with clergymen but short on straight thinkers. [But damme if this new discovery hasn't added *one more* divine to the bunch—for it seems that the Prov. colonist's maternal grandfather was the Rev. John Sotwell, Vicar of Peniston in Yorkshire!] Later I looked up the standard Field genealogy (by F. C. Pierce, 1901), & found out all about the line. It comes from Sir Hubertus de la Feld [of the family of the Counts de la Feld, seated near Colmar in Alsace], a follower of William the Conqueror who took lands in Lancashire, Sowerby, Ardsley, & Thurnscoe. I've copied a lot of notes & now have my Field lineage straight back—in exactly 20 generations—to Roger de la Feld of Sowerby, born in 1240. But it's the *astronomer* who interests me—& about whom I must learn more. I have a triple allotment of Field blood, being descended from no less than three of the Providence settler's grandchildren.

1936 seems to be a bad year for others as well as for me. Both of Long's parents have been down with grippe, & he is virtually reduced to exhaustion. Wandrei has suffered from colds, influenza, & dysentery. Barlow's throat has troubled him greatly—requiring $AgNO_3$ paintings daily.[5] And Klarkash-Ton, burdened with the care of his place & of his increasingly feeble father, is about driven to the wall. If misery loves company, the gang has plenty!

I hear that the Tercentenary Commission is coöperating with the state in getting out a fine new historical map of R.I. If I can get a supply I'll send you one . . . hoping you can eventually put it to use! Salaam—

Notes

1. Wandrei's "The Monster from Nowhere" appeared in *Argosy* (23 November 1935).
2. EHP to HPL, 4 May 1936 (TLS, JHL): "the repetition is the Malay usage [. . .] corresponding to our indefinite article."
3. In 1900, Dr. Alden Monroe Gardener established a private sanitarium in the William C. Ralston mansion in Belmont.
4. James Michael Curley (1874–1958), four-term mayor of Boston and one-term governor of Massachusetts (1935–37); Theodore Francis Green (1867–1966), governor of Rhode Island (1933–37) and U.S. senator (1937–61).
5. Silver nitrate, sometimes used as a disinfectant.

[72]   [ALS, JHL]

The Antient Hill
—June 12, 1936

Dear Malik:—

Recent bulletins from Mt. Kaf have been, as usual, extremely welcome. Belmont certainly sounds like an idyllic place, & I must investigate its possibilities as my present tangle of assorted tasks (aggravated by a file-cleaning & MS. correcting which took 4 solid days—with 2 nights' sleep cut out!) drives me closer & closer to the stage of Napoleonic (or G-man) impersonation. Maybe you'll yet see the Brobst–Abdul duo on the highways of Belmont—the former in a keeper's white uniform, & the Mad Arab in a straight-jacket . . . or a high-powered Juggernaut!

Enclosed is one of the results of the above-mentioned Augean Stable act . . . the long-lost cutting about that sensationally ancient Maya chronology which I was trying to tell you about. This remote dating would be prodigiously significant if true, but it is only fair to add that the bulk of solid authorities do not yet back Dr. Henseling[1] up. I think this cutting dates from 1934, but I have seen no reference to the theory since. Please return this item some time—though there is no hurry.

As for genealogy—it certainly brings quite a kick now & then, as in the case of my long-lost astronomer; yet it is after all a rather limited & secondary subject, & one upon which I would never expend the time & energy that Morton does. I'm glad of a new glimpse of my family past when somebody else digs it up—but for the most part I take what's on existing charts & probe the vanished aeons no further. Morton certainly has a prize lot of early ancestors—including Zeus, Odin, Adam, & other standbys. I could match some of these if I wanted to take the trouble, since many old lines lay claim to such fabulous lineage & record it on their charts in a spirit of loyal household mythology. I'd be interested to hear of the Arabic customs you mention. Very recently Barlow has started tracing his forbears, & will sooner or later find how closely he is related to me. We both have Rathbone lines, & every colonial Rathbone in America is descended from a certain Richard Rathbone who settled in Roxbury, Mass. around 1630. I know my lineage from old Dick, but Ar-Ech-Bei has traced his Rathbone strain only as far as the Rev. Valentine Rathbone, a Providence clergyman of the late 18th century. I'm going to help him find where this pious old geezer hitches on to the main line. On his mother's side Barlow is a collateral descendant of Pres. James Monroe. Morton & I have an ancestor in common—one John Perkins, Jun. (after whom my black friend of the K.A.T. is named), who died in Ipswich, Mass. in 1698. Morton is now doing genealogical work professionally for others—& I threw him a new client the other day in the person of a Cleveland chap named Pabody,[2] who wrote me after seeing the name "Pabodie" in my "Mts. of Madness" [which on examination I find hideously mangled in A.S.]. Pabody thought I might have some data on the family—though in truth I merely picked the name (a typical Rhode Island one) at random. I told him all I knew of R.I. Pabodies & referred him to J F M—& the latter has now dug him up a tremendous mass of accurate information. Without doubt, if you gave James Ferdinand all the clues you have regarding Adolph Wehner, he would know just where to look for records & links & would eventually dig up a lot concerning his antecedents both immediate & remote. Some day I hope you'll be able to spare enough cash to set him on the trail!

Speaking of ancestors—I recently learned that the still-surviving homestead of one of mine (Thomas Clemence, a friend of Roger Williams, from whom I am descended in the 8th generation) is now considered the oldest house in Rhode Island. It stands on the fringe of the city's western suburbs—in good condition, though with some ugly Victorian additions, & with its immense stone chimney still intact. In the grounds is one of the very few *well-sweeps* remaining in the state. Clemence built the house in 1654, having purchased 8 acres of land from an Indian named Wissawyamake. It is now inhabited by an aged gentlewoman in destitute circumstances—& some day I hope some historical organisation will take it over. Upon learning of its acclaim as Rhode Island's oldest, I paid it another visit last week—finding it unchanged since my last previous glimpse of it.

Sorry your Mexican book is sidetracked, & trust you can arrange to resume it soon. Too bad W T's financial policy has become so shaky. Congratulations on the sales—diminution of which will doubtless soon be overbalanced by the good effects of your technical researches. ¶ Rimel says you may be passing through the Asotin region in the course of time. He'll be glad to see you! ¶ Blessings— ♀ ⚭⚭⚭

P.S. Enjoyed your vivid racing description, forwarded by C L M. Was that to be returned to you? As regards attending races, I'm somewhat like that late Shah of Persia![3] ¶ I understand that young Hornig is coming to San Francisco—on a newspaper job secured for him by good old Abe Merritt.

[P.P.S. on envelope:] Evil news since the sealing of this epistle. My two best friends are no more! Yowl, O Battle-Axe, in sympathy! Let the curses of the Kappa Alpha Tau ascend to nighted & cryptical Bast! Both John Perkins & Lord Minto have succumbed to some malady which is afflicting all the felidae of the neighbourhood—a thing which may be an obscure epidemic, yet which may be the malign activities of come contemptible poisoner. The sad end of the brothers seemed connected with some digestive disorder, & recalled the equally sad fate of their bygone brother—little Sam Perkins—in 1934. Is this a blow from the same cosmic malignity which erased mighty Nimrod from the scene?

Notes

1. Robert Henseling (1883–1964), German astronomer who claimed there was a relationship between the Maya and Chinese systems of astronomy.

2. Frederic Jay Pabody (1910–1993), would-be author who corresponded briefly with HPL. For HPL's letters to him, see *Letters to C. L. Moore and Others*.

3. The cover of *Le Petit Journal* (21 September 1902) depicted Mozaffar ad-Din Shah Qajar (1853–1907) observing an auto race.

[73]   [ALS, JHL]

Finished July [sic] 20
[Postmarked 20 June 1936]

Dear Malik:—

Following your example, I'll just *start* this reply to your epistle which crossed my last . . . . adding notes from time to time & mailing when I get a fair quota of them set down. Mourning still thick & heavy for John Perkins & his brother. Latest theory is that a poison called "mouse seed", sprinkled for mice in the boarding-house, is responsible for the tragedy. This stuff is *supposed* to harm only rodents—but who can say what may have happened if my friends mistook it for catnip? Eheu! Eheu! Which latter, I might as well remark now as any time in response to your query, is simply the Latin interjection equivalent to *alas*. [*eheu fugaces* means "alas for fleeting things" or "alas for the fleeting nature of everything"][1] Incidentally, the other word—*evoë* or *euhoë* in Latin & εύοῖ in Greek—is a ritualistic shout or exclamation used in the worship of Bacchus or Dionysus, & ordinarily associated with a state of joyous emotional exaltation. It is not an ordinary greeting among persons, but rather a hail to the god of the vine—uttered by his priests & maenads, or by the throng joining with those priests & maenads in worship. In its broadest sense, it can be called a joyous hail—its associative or figurative use extending somewhat beyond the domain of Dionysiac rites. However—in view of the recent K.A.T. developments, *eheu* is a far more frequent cry than *evoë* around here! Once more, *eheu!*

Well—I'm glad to hear that Battle-Axe still prospers, & hope that he may continue his valiant slayings & feedings untouched by the doom which has descended upon Nimrod & his Providence kin! His possible heeding of the noon whistle is highly interesting to consider—& is by no means beyond possibility as a matter of reflex-conditioning. Work with cats in psychological laboratories has shown tremendous reservoirs of intelligence on their part. Did I tell you that the late Mr. Perkins' mother was given to the Brown U. psychological laboratory in May? She is now home again—upon the earnest solicitation of one of the boarders who is tremendously fond of her.

Well—I hope she'll eventually have another coal-black son, & that he'll be permitted to round out a longer life than those of his ill-starred brothers. I foresee such a son, since the late Johnny's inky sire is once more a consistent caller around the ancient garden.

Your data on Arabic genealogical customs proved of extreme interest—especially since Sana'a in Yemen is the birthplace of the Mad Arab Abdul Alhazred. Did you know this, or have I neglected to shew you the outline history of the Necronomicon which I prepared in 1929 or 1930? Yemen, I believe, was an abode of darker sorceries than those found in the rest of the Saracenic world. As for the profession of "greeter"—I fancy Morton could practice that a lot better than I! With my shifty memory, I fear I'd have to do a lot of sheep-slaying! By the way—is it in *all* lines, or only the *direct paternal* line, that the dowshan has to go back 5 generations? If the latter, it may not be so bad . . . . just remembering 5 first names in connexion with every guest. Or did the illustrious deeds (if any) of each of the 5 have to be cited? Anyhow, I think Mortonius could lick me badly at dowshaning!

Congratulations on the exotic blooms in the Gardens of Irem! Really, the place sounds quite like a tropical paradise! I don't know how spectacular the blooming of the cereus really is, but from all reports feel sure that the phenomenon is not wholly a folk-myth. Oddly enough in view of my Floridan sojourns, I have never seen a cactus in bloom. I always seem to be in their midst in the wrong season! Well—I'm glad an apple-tree is appearing, since a few old-fashioned, homelike things form an excellent foil for the dominant exoticism. I do not think that the apple is one of those plants which revert disastrously when raised from seeds—though it would take a better arboriculturist than I to be positive on the subject. Sorry the plums fail to prosper, but fancy the orange crop will be good when the trees become larger. You surely have an ideal climate—& one which I envy as I sit shivering by my desk, waiting for the oil heater to take effect on the circumambient air. Hope you'll get rid of poison & inflammable material.

As for the book bargain you passed up—I'd welcome a chance of reading it, since I was almost brought up on Combe's earlier "Dr. Syntax" rhymes . . . of which, unfortunately, I possess only the first volume. William Combe (1751–1823) was a versatile literary hack with more than a slight touch of talent. Most of his work was anonymous—& the best of it consisted of comic or satiric verse written to accompany the famous colour-plates of Rowlandson. The earlier Syntax poems centre around Rowlandson illustrations—to such an extent that nearly everyone associates the figure of Dr. Syntax with the artist more than with the rhymer. I must admit that I never heard of this "Life of Napoleon"—or knew that Combe had worked in conjunction with Cruikshank—until seeing the item quoted in your letter.[2] But having read all the earlier Syntax couplets, I wish I could read these! I don't agree with you that it would be dull. On the other hand—judging from other Syntactiana— I'll wager it is quite witty & epigrammatic. What is meant by *Hudibrastic* verse is light satirical material in the octosyllabic couplet, usually briskly colloquial in style, & abounding in clever & unusual double rhymes . . . some of the latter created from apparently incongruous elements. The term is derived from the famous anti-Puritan satire of old Samuel Butler (1600–1680), entitled "Hudibras" (= Hugh de Bras) & written in this characteristic style. This poem—modelled somewhat after "Don Quixote"—has been a classic ever since its first appearance (in 2 parts) in 1662 & 1664. It has furnished a model for thousands of later satirists both good & bad, & some of its couplets live as common quotations on every tongue. For example—

"And pulpit, drum ecclesiastick,
Was beat with fist instead of a stick."

"We grant, although he had much wit,
He was very shy of using it."

"Besides, 'tis known he could speak Greek
As naturally as pigs squeak;
That Latin was no more difficle
Than to a black bird 'tis to whistle."

"And prove their doctrine orthodox
By apostolick blows & knocks."

"Compound for sins they are inclin'd to
By damning those they have no mind to."

"For those that fly may fight again,
Which he can never do that's slain."

"He that complies against his will
Is of his own opinion still."

I have a fairly good edition of "Hudibras". One of the most famous satires written in imitation is the American revolutionary product of John Trumbull of Connecticut (1750–1831 . . . . a 2nd. cousin of the famous painter of like name) entitled "McFingal". This poem contains many widely-quoted couplets, such as:

"No man e'er felt the halter draw,
With good opinion of the law."

I have a modern reprint of Trumbull's complete verses.[3]

Your observations on duplicated names in Burma & Malaysia (& Polynesia also, I believe) are extremely interesting, & explain forms which would otherwise puzzle the non-linguist. The critical clergyman surely spoke too soon, & without a proper knowledge of the given field. Thus with many scoffers who wax mirthful over the folkways of groups which they have not studied.

Glad to hear that Pawang's successor is developing well, & hope both editors & public will take kindly to him. Hope the adventure of Bast brings in some likely members of the K.A.T.! I doubt whether old de Castro was really offended by your inability to collaborate. He has not written anyone of the gang lately. I shall be glad to see the Mexican work when it reaches me—is it a continuation of the travelogue whose opening I already have? Meanwhile I believe I mentioned receiving the racing material— surely spirited stuff! Glad

C L M was able to supply so much kindred material from Indianapolis. Yes—she mentioned her commercial experiments under Kline. Hope they won't completely destroy her natural gifts in the field of fantastic expression.

Congratulations on the somewhat moderating thirst of Great Hu'ds'un! Hope the mighty beast will eventually become abstemious enough to warrant transcontinental travel!

Example of commercial-writing nerve. A friend of mine in Wisconsin[4] (an instructor in French at Lawrence College) has just written a detective novel (his first piece of fiction, except for a weird short story in 1919)[5] & expects to market it advantageously at once!!! Luck to him!

Later

Just had a most depressing & staggering message—a card from C L M with the report (source not given) that good old Two-Gun Bob has committed suicide. It seems incredible—I had a long normal letter from him written May 13. He was worried about his mother's health, but otherwise seemed perfectly all right. If the news is indeed true, it forms weird fiction's worst blow since the passing of Whitehead in 1932. Nobody else in the gang had quite the driving zest & spontaneity of Brother Conan. I surely wish I could get a bulletin saying that the report is a mistake. 1936 certainly is a hellish year! This loss will probably seem a more acute bereavement to you than to the others, since you are the only one of the group to have seen R E H in person. But if you can feel worse than I do about it, you'll be going some. Damnation, what a loss! That bird had gifts of an order even higher than the readers of his published work could suspect, & in time would have made his mark in real literature with some folk-epic of his beloved southwest. He was a perennial fount of erudition & eloquence on this theme—& had the creative imagination to make old days live again. Mitra,[6] what a man! It is hard to describe precisely what made his stories stand out so—but the real secret is that *he was in every one of them*, whether they were ostensibly commercial or not. He was greater than any profit-seeking policy he could adopt—for even when he outwardly made concessions to the mammon-guided editors he had an internal force & sincerity which broke through the surface & put the imprint of his personality on everything he wrote. Seldom or never did he set down a lifeless stock character or situation & leave it as such. Before he got through with it, it always took on some tinge of vitality & reality in spite of editorial orders—always drew something from his own first-hand experience & knowledge of life instead of from the barbarism of dessicated [*sic*] pulpish standbys. He was almost alone in his ability to create real emotions of fear & of dread suspense. Contrast his "Black Canaan" with the pallid synthetic pap comprising the rest of the current issue of W T. Bloch & Derleth[7] are clever enough technically—but for stark, living fear . . . . the actual smell & feel & darkness & brooding horror & impending doom that inhere in that nighted, moss-hung jungle . . . . . what other writer is even in the running with R E H?

No author can excel unless he takes his work very seriously & puts himself whole-heartedly into it—& Two-Gun did just that, even when he claimed & consciously believed that he didn't. And this is the giant whom Fate had to snatch away whilst hundreds of insincere hacks continue to concoct phony ghosts & vampires & space-ships & occult detectives! I can't understand the tragedy—for although R E H had a moody side expressed in his resentment against civilisation (the basis of our perennial & voluminous epistolary controversy), I always thought that this was a more or less *impersonal* sentiment—like Belknap's rage against the injustices of a capitalistic social order. He himself seemed to me pretty well adjusted—in an environment he loved, with plenty of congenial souls (like the "Pink" Tyson & Tevis Clyde Smith[8] of whom he spoke so often . . . did you meet either of these when visiting Two-Gun?) to talk & travel with, & with parents whom he obviously idolised. His mother's pleural illness imposed a great strain upon both him & his father, yet I cannot think that this would be sufficient to drive his tough-fibred nervous system to self-destructive extremes. Nor was his financial state at all desperate so far as I know. I wonder if he was alive when my last letter arrived—that must have been a week ago. Probably he never saw its 32 pages, that ended with an enthusiastic tribute to his serial & to "Black Canaan", which I had just read. Hell! Well, anyhow, I think he realised how keenly his work was appreciated. I hope the two *Phantagraph* boys had told him about their plan to issue his "Hyborian Age" as a separate pamphlet.[9] That ought to prove popular among Conan's thousands of admirers. By the way—as the only one of us who ever talked with R E H in person, I think you ought to prepare a brief obituary & appreciation for W T, as I did of good old Canevin. Some such word is a necessity—& you are the logical author. // Salaam ⟡⟡⟡

Notes

1. The expression is a partial quotation from Horace's *Eheu fugaces, Postume, Postume, / labuntur anni* ("Alas, Postumus, Postumus, the fleeting years slip away": *Odes* 2.14.1–2).
2. *The Life of Napoleon: A Hudibrastic Poem in Fifteen Cantos* by "Doctor Syntax." A verse biography of Napoleon. Illustrated with thirty engravings by George Cruikshank (1792–1878) featuring abusive caricatures of Napoleon.
3. See Bibliography under *The Colonnade*.
4. Alfred Galpin.
5. The novel was *Murder in Montparnasse*, never published. The story of 1919 was "Marsh-Mad: A Nightmare," published in Galpin's amateur journal the *Philosopher* (December 1920).
6. A deity from the Hyborian Age setting created by Robert E. Howard for his Conan stories; a personification of good popular among the Hyborian peoples. Thus, not a reference to Mithras, the Indo-Iranian god of sun, friendship, and energy.
7. *WT,* June 1936: Robert E. Howard, "Black Canaan"; Robert Bloch, "The Grinning

Ghoul"; August W. Derleth, "The Telephone in the Library."

8. Lindsey ("Pink") Tyson (1907–1994), Robert E. Howard's best friend in Cross Plains, shared with REH an enjoyment of the outdoors and sports such as boxing and football but had no particular literary interests. Tevis Clyde Smith, Jr. (1908–1984). He and REH met when REH attended Brownwood High School to complete his final year of schooling (1922–23), and they remained close friends for more than ten years. They exchanged hundreds of letters.

9. After being serialized in the *Phantagraph* (February–November 1936), "The Hyborian Age" was issued as a pamphlet in 1938. As an introduction it contained an extract from a letter by HPL to Donald A. Wollheim (7 October 1935; *Letters to Robert Bloch and Others* 319) discussing REH's work.

[74]　[ALS, JHL]

The Ancient Hill—
July 5, 1936

Dear Malik:—

Alas—the tragic news is now all too well authenticated. A letter & local papers from Dr. Howard tell the whole sad story—which by this time you may have heard directly. If you have not received first-hand information from Cross Plains, I'll send you the material I received. Like you, I feel clubbed on the head—or as if the whole thing were a nightmare from which one might suddenly awake. In case duplicate data hasn't reached you, I'll say briefly that grief about R E H's mother *was* the cause. When he was told that she could not live more than 48 hours, he entered his car, closed the doors, & shot himself through the head—never regaining consciousness & dying 8 hours later. That was June 11. His mother died the next day without regaining consciousness or knowing of his act. The shock to Dr. Howard must be devastating—wife & splendid only child gone in one dread blow. I only hope he can weather it successfully. I've just written him a letter of sympathy. His letter showed tremendous bravery, & the paper spoke of his being about to visit relatives in Missouri. One can imagine his suffering—as well as the degree of grief which drove R E H to his own desperate act. R E H's library will go to his alma mater—Howard Payne College in Brownwood—as the nucleus of a Robert E. Howard Memorial Collection which will later include letters, MSS., &c.

Poor old Two-Gun! His sombre, moody side—or else his general sensitiveness—must have gone deeper than we ever realised. Heaven knows the loss of a cherished parent is bad enough, but most can accept it as part of the inevitable order of things. R E H's idolisation of both his parents was always manifest, but the present sad extreme was hardly to be looked for—although his father says he feared it for some time. I suppose that, in the last analysis, his desperate reaction to his grief came from the selfsame endowment of sensitiveness & imagination which made his stories stand out so. He saw everything in the heightened light of its dramatic relationships to things behind &

around it, & subjectively *felt* the events of history, & the spirit & overtones of scenes & personalities, as very few are able to see & feel. Turned on the sorrow in his immediate life, this faculty must have given things an intolerable aspect & precipitated the fatal act. One could wish that, for once, he had been less of a sensitive artist!

Your impromptu reminiscence or obituary sheds a marvellously vivid light on good old Two-Gun—forming at once a revelation, & a confirmation of the impression derived from letters. Certainly, no more vivid & likeable individual ever existed—& I can scarcely wonder that at the moment your sense of personal loss transcends that of literary loss. Even without having met R E H face to face, I feel an acute individual bereavement which only the loss of a close relative could exceed. He had the fundamental honesty, simplicity, sincerity, & directness—the preëminently Aryan qualities—which have become so distressingly rare in modern urban life. While I basically disagreed with him regarding the superiority of barbarism over civilisation—& argued endlessly with him on that point—I respected his personality to a tremendous extent, & placed it miles above the "sophisticated" type of character. Indeed, I used him as a sort of model & example in arguing with persons like Long & Wandrei, who uphold a more disillusioned & decadent tradition. I told him how often I held him & his position up to extremists on the other side, so that he undoubtedly realised the depth & sincerity of my respect, even when I tore most vigorously into his pro-barbarian arguments. Well—he had the last word in our six-year debate, since the date of the tragedy makes it certain that he never saw my final 32-page letter. I don't begrudge him that advantage—although I am damn sorry he couldn't have seen the two solid pages in praise of his recent work—especially "Black Canaan"—with which my bulky communication concluded. But even so, he knew what I thought of his work—for I always commented on his current products (that is, such of them as I saw). He occasionally sent me magazines containing his prize-fight, western, & Oriental stories, so that my knowledge of his work is not wholly limited to the weird side.

Now as for the formal obituary in W T (for although he wrote for many magazines, I think the principal notice ought to go in the one which first discovered & developed him—& which for the past 2 or 3 years, if not longer, he has definitely dominated)—I still think (all the more so after seeing your extemporaneous tribute) you are the logical person to write it. You alone met him face to face. You alone can give a balanced estimate of his entire personality. As for hints on the best form—all I can say is that a fusion of your recent spontaneous remarks with a brief estimate of his work—plus the necessary biographical facts & dates—would seem to me to be the thing. Would you like the relevant pages of your letter returned? I may lend them to one or two members of the gang, but I could get them back to you in fair season. Enclosed is a copy of a tentative obituary which I wrote, & which you might use as a sort of quarry for dates & general ideas. This is meant for *Fantasy Magazine,* so that when you're through with it I wish you'd send it to *Julius Schwartz, 255 East 188ᵗʰ St., New York, N.Y.* He may not use it—but I'm letting him have it (as in your case) as a quarry for data. I'm preparing a shorter & entirely different notice for *The Phantagraph*—which is carrying Two-Gun's vivid "Hyborian Age" as a serial. Try to persuade Wright not to abridge your remarks. He nearly ruined my Whitehead obituary.

But it is damn hard to realise that there's no longer any R E H at Lock Box 313! I first became conscious of him as a coming leader just a decade ago—when (on a bench in Prospect Park, Brooklyn) I read "Wolfshead". I had read his two previous short tales with pleasure,[1] but without especially noting their author. Now— in '26—I saw that W T had landed a new bigtimer of the C A S & E H P calibre. Nor was I ever disappointed in the zestful & vigorous newcomer. He made good—& how! Much as I admired him, I had no correspondence with him till 1930—for I was never a guy to butt in on people. In that year he read the reprint of my "Rats in the Walls" & instantly spotted the bit of harmless fakery whereby I had lifted a Celtic phrase (for use as an atavistic exclamation) from a footnote to an old classic ("The Sin-Eater", by Fiona McLeod [William Sharp]).[2] He didn't realise the source of the phrase, but his sharp eye for Celtic antiquities told him it didn't quite fit—being a *Gaelic* (not *Cymric*) expression assigned to a South British locale. I myself don't know a word of any Celtic tongue, & never fancied anybody could spot the incongruity. Too charitable to suspect me of ignorant appropriation, he came to the conclusion that I followed a now-discredited theory whereby the Gaels were supposed to have preceded the Cymri in England— & wrote Satrap Pharnabazus a long & scholarly letter on the subject. Farny passed this on to me—& I couldn't rest easy until I had set the author right. Hence I dropped R E H a line confessing my ignorance & telling him that I had merely picked a phrase with the right meaning from a note to a Scottish story while perfectly well aware that the language of Celtic South-Britain was really somewhat different. I could not resist adding some incidental praise of his work—echoing remarks previously made in the Eyrie. Well—he replied at length, & the result was a bulky correspondence which throve from that day to this. I value that correspondence as one of the most broadening & sharpening influences in my later years. We were constantly debating sundry historical & philosophical points, & through these arguments (as well as through many passages of sheer description) I gained a much clearer perspective on various phases of history than I would ever have had otherwise. He made the southwest & its traditions live before my eyes—supplementing his descriptions with generous batches of pictorial matter (all now in my files) whenever he made a trip to any place of historical or scenic interest. He also sent various pertinent odd & ends such as rattlesnake rattles—with one set of which he included a page of comment so vivid & so finely phrased that I'd like to

publish it some day as a prose-poem.[3] (Indeed, I'd like to publish all his letters with their descriptive & historical riches.) I was glad to be able to recip-
rocate in a small way by sending him material from various points of interest
which I visited. I owe to Two-Gun my pleasant sessions at 305 Rue Royale, &
indeed my general introduction to the Sultan of the Peacock Throne—since
as you'll recall, it was he who telegraphed you of my presence in ancient
Nouvelle-Orleans in 1932. I had hoped to get to Cross Plains some time—
but now I shall probably never see the village whose name I have so frequently written on envelopes & postcards.

As for his work—while the King Kull series probably forms a weird
peak, I do not think the *best* of the Conan tales involve any radical falling-off.
Some were pure adventure-yarns with the touch of weirdness rather extraneous, but that is not the case with "Hour of the Dragon".[4] His best work
would probably have been regional & historical, & I was greatly pleased by
his recent tendency to employ his own southwestern background in fiction.
As a poet, too, he was phenomenally gifted—so that I always hoped to see a
collection of his verse. His scholarship in certain lines was truly remarkable. I
always gasped at his profound knowledge of history—including some of its
more obscure corners—& admired still more his really astonishing *assimilation*
& *vitalisation* of it. He was almost unique in his ability to *understand* & *mentally
inhabit* past ages—including many without any resemblance to our own. He
had the imagination to go beyond mere names & dates & get at the *actual tex-
ture of life* in the bygone periods which he studied. He could visualise all the
details of every-day existence in these periods, & subjectively enter into the
feelings of their inhabitants. As a result, the past was as alive for him as the
present—while his grasp of *general* historical & anthropological principles en-
abled him to construct from pure imagination those prehistoric worlds of
mystery & adventure & necromancy whose lifelike convincingness & consistent substance won such universal praise. No matter how assiduously the
profit-motivated critics & editors tried to warp him, he was always a step
ahead of them—& a step ahead of himself when he seemed to listen to them.
He had something to say—& all the hackneyed patterns & conventional
technique in the world couldn't stop him from saying it. Nothing could
squeeze the life & zest out of his work.

> "He was a man—take him for all in all,
> I shall not look upon his like again."[5]

I trust the Mashburn visit proved uniformly pleasant, & hope you could
include all the items planned—including the Lick Observatory & Chinese
opera. Glad to hear all the Irem news—& I envy you your sunset view of Mt.
Diabolo.[6] Congratulations on orchard developments—& on the increasing
prowess of Nimrod's disciple & successor. The latter's liking for cheese (my

favourite form of nourishment) indicates to my mind a very sound taste! Sorry he has suffered wounds—but hope his foes are in still worse shape! Those race notes surely were vivid & interesting, & I shall be glad to see their successors when they get around this way. Glad the Mayan cutting proved interesting—no hurry about its return. Here is something on another of your hobbies—rugs—which you need not return.

About Roger Williams—alas! I cannot claim him as an ancestor! Although at least two of my direct forbears (John Perkins & John Field) came to New England in the same ship with him (the *Lion*—Dec–Feb 1630), while others (Capt. John Whipple Sr. & Thomas Clemence) were excellent friends of his, I have not yet been able to find any line of direct descent from him to myself. However, I don't count that against him, & have recently read two biographies of him![7]

Speaking of genealogy—Morton or other experts could do more on your lines than you think. Given the approximate age of the fastidious Herr Wehner, such searches would comb official records in Germany—& in view of the European thoroughness in record-keeping could probably turn up some excellent clues sooner or later. Of course it would take time & cash—but some pretty tough riddles have been solved in the end. Even the reprobate parson might not prove to be an insoluble enigma. It is surprising what a science genealogy has come to be—I say *come*, because it is only since the development of America that *searching* has been such a specialty. In Europe, nearly everyone who was at all solicitous about his past had existing records at his disposal. One of the major feats of the present century was the tracing of Pres. Lincoln's ancestry—of which he himself had no exact knowledge. Today he is assigned a neat position on a spreading family tree which includes the main Lincoln line in America—the line springing from Hingham, Massachusetts & including the Providence artist James S. Lincoln[8] who married the aunt of my elder aunt's husband & painted the oval portrait which you probably saw over the living-room mantel at 66. (Not that that brings me & Honest Abe very close! For that matter, I have a real ancestor in common with Genl. Washington—but so remote as to make the amount of shared blood utterly infinitesimal.) A fascinating subject, & once in a while useful in historic research; but too secondary & localised to be of supreme interest to me as it is to Morton. Incidentally, good old Two-Gun was quite a hand at genealogy, & had himself pretty well linked with ancestors settling in Georgia & North Carolina in the first half of the 18th century.

Departing from the purely genealogical but continuing on the antiquarian—enclosed is a leaflet which may be of some interest. The other day I visited two colonial mansions on the ancient hill (just south of here—you saw both of 'em in '33) which have lately been thrown open as public museums—the leaflet describing the finer of the two. After a close inspection, I can say that John Quincy Adams (vide leaflet) was right[9]—& this after having examined 18th century houses all the way from Quebec on the north to St. Augustine & the Vieux Carré on the south. The edifice has an admirably classic symmetry & arrangement, its only possible flaw being a subtle tendency toward rococo over-ornateness on the lower floor. Like most houses in America even as late as the 1800's, it is untouched by the superior classicism of the Adam influence, which became manifest in Great Britain as early as the 1750's or 1760's. John Brown, the builder of the house, was one of four quite celebrated brothers belonging to a local sea-trading family descended from the early settler, Rev. Chad Brown. His nephew Nicholas Jr. is the one whose donations changed the name of Rhode-Island College to Brown University in 1804. His younger brother Moses was a well-known Quaker & philanthropist, while his grand-nephew John Carter Brown founded the world-famous library of that name. John himself was merely a shrewd grasper dependent upon other people's taste. The really civilised member of the family was his elder brother Joseph, who in the 1750's, 1760's, & 1770's played a great part in bringing Providence up to the cultural level of Newport. Joseph was a scholar & man of taste, & the greatest architect in the town prior to the rise of John Holden Greene. With Stephen Hopkins he helped to found the Providence Library in 1758, & in 1769 he imported a telescope (now at the Ladd Observatory—I've seen it) to observe the transit of Venus in that year. He designed the John Brown house, as well as houses for himself [his is the one in S. Main St. with the curved pediment which I shew'd you] & brother Nicholas—& to him are likewise due the plan of the Market House (1773— you saw it) & the selection of the Gibbs design for the 1st Baptist steeple (1775). In later life he became Professor of Natural Philosophy at the college. The house so well depicted in the leaflet is perhaps his masterpiece. He died in 1787, before its completion, but its splendid outlines survive as a memorial to his taste. The numerous French busts stuck around at various places are none of his doing. There is a legend that those on the gateposts turn & bow to each other at midnight—a phenomenon I have not personally witnessed!

The other house—of which I could secure no descriptive nor pictorial matter—is the Edward Carrington mansion, erected in 1809, & the work of John Holden Greene. This lacks the classic interior symmetry of the Brown house, but is extremely pleasing & homelike. It was recently presented to the R.I. School of Design—with all its original furniture & decorations to be kept intact for ever—by the last of the family, who resides in another colonial mansion inherited through another line. With its stables, coach-houses, cobbled courtyard, & extensive grounds & gardens, the Carrington house forms one of the most satisfying domestic units of the early-republic period now on exhibition. In its interior architecture it embodies a rather amusing hybridism seemingly peculiar to late 18th & early 19th century Providence—the use of rococo middle-18th-century architecture on the ground floor, & of the newer Adam-period design throughout the upper storeys. Some of the delicate Adam mantels upstairs are among the most exquisite I have ever seen.

Well–I'll call a halt & get this in the mail. Hope you'll have no difficulty in your melancholy task—& kindly send the enclosed obituary to Schwartz when you're through with it. What a hellish year is 1936!

¶ Peace & prayer—

ℂ ⌐⌐⊐⊣ ⸱ ⸱

P.S. The deaths of Montague Rhodes James (at 73) & George Allan England (at 59) sustain 1936's reputation as a bad year![10]

Notes

1. "Spear and Fang" (*WT,* July 1925); "In the Forest of Villefère" (*WT,* August 1925); "Wolfshead" (*WT,* April 1926).
2. In *The Best Psychic Stories,* ed. Joseph Lewis French (New York: Boni & Liveright/ Modern Library, [1920]; *LL* 355).
3. "With a Set of Rattlesnake Rattles," *Leaves* (Summer 1937).
4. *WT,* December 1935–April 1936 (5-part serial).
5. *Hamlet* 1.2.186–87.
6. HPL means Mt. Diablo, in Contra Costa county east of San Francisco.
7. By Emily M. Easton and James Ernst.
8. James Sullivan Lincoln (1811–1888), the "father of art in Providence," was a noted portrait painter and first president of the Providence Art Club. He married Rosina Child (Chase) Lincoln (1823–1910), aunt of Franklin C. Clark (1847–1915), husband of HPL's aunt Lillian, a physician and writer on medicine and local and natural history. HPL owned a portrait of a family member by Lincoln.
9. The leaflet HPL refers to stated that John Quincy Adams noted in his diary following a trip to Providence in 1791 that he considered the John Brown House (52 Power Street; 1786, Joseph Brown, architect) "the most magnificent and elegant private mansion that I have ever seen on this continent." It is now the home of the Rhode Island Historical Society.
10. M. R. James died on 12 June, George Allan England on 26 June.

[75]   [ALS, JHL]

July 29[, 1936]

Dear Malik:—

Current bulletins received & greatly appreciated. I am mentioning the R E H Memorial Collection to correspondents, & suggesting to the fan magazines that they publish a note about it. Thanks vastly for sending Schwartz a legible copy of the obituary—which he says he will (much my surprise) use entire. Schwartz also says he would very much like to have your proposed informal reminiscences of Two-Gun Bob—to which he would allot far more than his customary space in *Fantasy Magazine.* The new fan publication (*Science-Fantasy Correspondent*—Willis Conover, Jr., 27 High St., Cambridge, Maryland) also makes a bid for these reminiscences, & says they could be used serially if conditions forbade complete publication in one issue. I'll leave the choice to you. On the one hand F M is a going proposition, while S F C will not start till September. On the other hand, S F C may be the better magazine (one can't tell) when it *does* get going. Perhaps it would be safer to favour F M—but you can choose for yourself. As for a W T obituary—I doubt if Wright would let his feeling about reprints count in the matter. It seems to me that a brief character-sketch drawn from first-hand contact, plus a brief list of facts & summary of R E H's unique literary merits, would be extremely welcome both to him & to the readers. Hope you'll send one in. As for my F M obituary—you can do as you like with the longhand original. I'm sure the Collection is welcome to it if it wouldn't seem too trivial. I have of course told all the fan editors to be sure to send Dr. Howard anything they publish about R E H. Wollheim, as you know, is serially using "The Hyborian Age" in *The Phantagraph*. Barlow's elegiac sonnet[1] is splendid, though line 3 (at least in the carbon sent me) lacked a foot. I provided a correction (sending it in duplicate to Ar-E'ch-Bei & Satrap Pharnabazus) which I hope will be incorporated in the printed text. This is Barlow's first professional acceptance—& it is unfortunate that the debut should have so tragic a background! I hope you will be able to accept Dr. Howard's offer to serve as Conan's literary executor, for I feel that no one could administer the matter as well as yourself. Kline is of course an alert & dependable agent, but a competent expert on the spot could clear things up much quicker than anyone at a distance. There would surely be something peculiarly appropriate about a Cross Plains velocity test for Hu'd-su'un—savouring as it would of the Homeric funeral games which R E H would so keenly appreciate. No—I had never heard of the Sam Walser tales till you mentioned them, though last winter Two-Gun spoke of a contemplated invasion of the bawdy field.[2] His best work, I believe, would have been of some sort involving his tremendous love & encyclopaedic knowledge of his native region. He was slowly working around to it—& indeed, his voluminous letters were always full of lyrical & epical prose on the subject.

Sorry to hear of Ki-Ki's Job-like affliction, & hope the pizen will soon be worked out of his system. At least, I trust the malady is not accounted a dangerous one. Glad Hu'd-Su'un's thirst & velocity are assuming satisfactory proportions. Those freak races must have been extremely interesting—especially the one involving ancient cars. That would have made me homesick for the days of my youth! Those Chinese drinks sound potent & exotic indeed—a spoonful ought to put anyone in a coma peopled with visions of bygone Oriental wars & migrations!

Sorry another market has closed, & hope you'll be able to salvage what is owed you.[3] I can fully sympathise regarding the monotonousness of *series*— but hope you'll be able to finish the current chain in a financially advantageous way. As for W T reprints—I can't, as I believe I said once before, quite bring myself to endorse your position. The primary purpose of any legitimate enterprise is to fill a need—& there is a need of making certain old-time weird material available for a new generation of readers who could not otherwise gain access to it. Anything which tends to defeat the supplying of that need is, as I view it, to be deplored. All *artificial restriction*—of any kind—grates on some facet of my personality . . . . indeed, the A.A.A.'s efforts toward crop control form the one thing about the New Deal whose basic principle I cannot endorse.[4] I believe that surplus crops should be purchased by the government for charitable distribution instead of merely not grown. There is something wrong in any economic order which encourages the act of *keeping things away from people* for reasons of profit. I believe in doing everything possible toward securing the widest possible circulation for everything which is worth circulating. If such a course makes it impossible for the creators of material to secure an adequate return, then the system needs repair or oversight of some sort. But the creation of an artificial scarcity is not the proper course. Of that, I am convinced. The longer I live, the more tolerant I tend to become toward Belknap's radical position. Not that I could swallow orthodox Marxism as he does, but that I do believe in the adoption of a more or less socialistic pattern in which individual survival can be assured with less sacrifice of the general welfare. Socially useless competition, & profit secured through depriving others of what they might readily have, represents a fundamental *waste* of something or other which alienates me. A better economist or sociologist could phrase my vague position better than I can—but perhaps the general drift is comprehensible. I believe in adequate payment for service performed—but service is not *restriction*. Anything which is good for the public ought to be made as widely available to the public as it reasonably can be. When restriction becomes necessary for anyone's survival, something is wrong somewhere. Getting back to the case of W T—of course Wright ought to pay for the reprints (as he once *did* pay Quinn), & the only reason for letting him make them free at the present juncture is the precarious fiscal state of the magazine. That aspect of the matter is frankly a *favour* extended as an extraordinary measure at a time of extraordinary emergency. But there cannot be any valid objection against *paid reprints* in reasonable proportion. Every decade or so a new crop of readers arises & becomes curious about the stories of the past. Among these stories are several which the newcomers (especially in view of the highly special nature of the field) really ought to see. If the material is easily available in book form, well & good. If not, it ought to be reprinted. Not to reprint it would be an injustice to the faithful circle of readers. That the demand is genuine is proved by the vast number of youngsters who have asked me to lend them my old MSS.—which I have always done at a terrific cost of wear & tear. Of course this does not apply to *some* of the reprinting which Wright has done—using up space on famous old classics which any public library could supply. But it *does* apply to certain obscure but desirable items which have anciently appeared in W T or elsewhere. It would have been simply barbarous to prevent the present generation from reading "The Canal", "The Night Wire", "Bells of Oceana", "The Floor Above", "Beyond the Door", &c.[5] If this is "poor business", then I say damn business! Academically, I can see your side of the matter—but the contrary view is rooted deep in my basic philosophy of life. I can never countenance commercialism as an ultimate object, nor feel any lasting or genuine sympathy with its methods. It is of course necessary that every individual be provided with food, clothing, & lodging, but I can never accustom myself to the idea of acquisition as a primary object. That is, I can never think of the expenditure of effort in direct terms of profit. With me, objects are (1) the creation of something of intrinsic excellence if possible, & (2) the supplying of genuine needs. If my own survival cannot be ensured as an incidental to the pursuit of these objects, then I feel that something is wrong. Just what to do about it I cannot tell—but the acknowledgment of the difficulty does not alter my basic instincts & emotions. My tentative idea of a solution is to *separate* the problem of food, clothing, & lodging from one's most serious effort—putting forth *secondary* efforts toward physical survival while keeping primary efforts dedicated to the original objects of intrinsic excellence & general contribution. The "business spirit" & I can never have any point of contact. Much as I have laughed at Belknap's avowed attitude, there is probably a less impassable gulf betwixt it & my own than betwixt the commercial attitude & my own. My aesthetic & scientific feelings are equally outraged at the *waste of human energy* involved in competitive, profit-seeking effort which neither creates anything of excellence nor concerns itself with the maximum service of existing needs. Of course cheap weird fiction is a pretty small field, & some might think it a bit absurd in me to link its peanut problems with any expansive philosophy of life. Be that as it may. Some have a tendency to appear comical by seeing the general in the particular & the minute. I can't help the way I'm made! I recognise the theoretical absurdity of acting in accordance with a standard not generally adopted or recognised—of being uncommercial while all who deal with me are commercial. Wright undoubtedly wants to reprint things for *commercial* reasons, & I shall let him for *uncommercial* reasons. Paradoxical? Undoubtedly! But the fact remains that I am always at a lethargic standstill except when acting from one or the other of the motives which seem valid & rational to me—the creation of something as good as I can make it, & the performance of a service which needs performing. That most others aren't similarly constructed is damn fortunate for them! I can objectively envisage the purely commercial attitude as regards the production & marketing of fiction, & could sympathise with it more if I were less interested in good writing & the circulation of sincerely written material as ends in themselves. (Belknap is less interested—hence his recent success as a sheer hack despite his theoretical espousal of a non-commercial communistic order with service & excellence paramount. He has a shrewd essential *duality* which I lack.) Even as it is, I can understand why those who *do* regard writing as a business are anxious that its marketing operations be conducted according to the ethics traditionally recognised in competitive commerce. I can sympathise with such anxiety as long as it does not adversely affect the things I regard as paramount—excellence & faithful recording of material, & maximum circulation of anything worth circulating. Thus, while holding the attitude I do, I have not the least quarrel or criticism to offer those who hold the opposite attitude. They are probably more sensible realists than I. Certainly, they will get farther in the world! But Yuggoth, what a lot of talk about imponderables!

The recent warm spell filled me with new vigour, & I cleaned up more work in a week than in all the month preceding. On July 11 I took a boat trip to ancient Newport, seeing the ancient town & doing come writing on the rocky oceanward cliffs. Here's a view of one of the surviving antiquities of this fascinating region. July 18–19th I had an enjoyable visit from my old friend M. W. Moe of Milwaukee (poet–teacher–associate in the N.A.P.A) & his gifted son Robert (electrical engineer now of Bridgeport, Conn.—the youth who was here with his car in the spring of '35). It was my first sight of the old boy in 13 years, & I fancy he saw more change in me than I in him. Young Bob brought him in the car, & we covered quite a bit of scenic & historic ground in the all-too-brief span of 2 days. Went to the quaint village of Pawtuxet (where you had the shore dinner in '33 en route back from the South County), saw the view from old Ft. Independence, drove through Roger Williams Park (which you may recall), traversed the deep woods & colonial farmlands north of the city, & as a climax repeated the Warren–Bristol drive which young Bob & I took in March of last year. This was much more enjoyable in July than in March, & the ancient seaport villages (on the bay's E. shore) displayed their colonial houses & giant elms to maximum advantage. We also took the seaside drive on Popasquash Neck—a sub-peninsula attached to the main Bristol peninsula. In Warren we had an all-ice-cream dinner at Maxfield's (that famous Mecca of Mortonius, Cook, myself, & others)—mine consisting of grape, pineapple, peach, raspberry, banana, & chocolate chip. Old Moe had to call a halt after 2½ pints, but his son downed 3 pints—with difficulty. I surrounded 3 pines with ease & avidity, & could have relished 3 more! The visit was very much favoured meteorologically, for warmth & sunshine prevailed throughout . . . whereas the next day was cold & rainy, forcing me to crouch shivering & heavily blanketed over the oil heater.

Had a good look at Peltier's Comet the other night through the 12″ telescope (refractor) of the Ladd Observatory—a branch of the college on high ground about a mile N.E. of #66. It was my second visit to the observatory since 1908—though in the old days I used to haunt it constantly, thanks to the indulgence of the long-dead-&-gone authorities of a bygone age. The comet showed a slight disc with a hazy, fan-like tail. I could have seen it through my own small (3″) glass were the northern sky less cut off from the neighbourhood of 66.

Yes—you *did* duly return that cutting about Mayan chronology. Many thanks for the vivid racing report, which I am appreciatively filing. Glad that some of the primitive motors of my day can still give a good account of themselves! I note the joker in the idea of a super-charger as an economical device. That's true of many a modern gadget! But of course this device justifies itself in other ways.

I mourn for the lost Popo.[6] Alas, what perils & pitfalls the age of speed & machinery has brought with it! The funeral was surely appropriate— though I regret that such a thing had to be.

Glad Kiki's boils are clearing up, & hope he gets his feathery mouthful sooner or later. I'd like to see a photograph of the increasingly handsome gentleman when you get one. I learn with great interest of his neighbouring younger brother—& of the latter's insatiable appetite. No—I never heard of the special gustatory prowess of yellow Toms, though evidence for such a theory seems to be piling up rapidly on the slopes of cryptical & mameluke-guarded Kaf.[7]

Your glimpse of that far white form fills me with the intensest interest. Is the Mighty One indeed still among the living, & will he some day return from his wanderings to doze on red cushions & shew (by contrast) what slight eaters yellow toms are after all? I live to hope—indeed, I have never been fully willing to admit that Great Nimrod walks among the shades! I'd like to have seen that slate-blue Maltese gentleman. The local K.A.T. is very slow in reorganising its forces, so that my principal visitor these days is old Mrs. Spotty, who now & then forgets her recent academic dignity sufficiently to gobble the catnip purchased for younger mouths.

I endorse all that you say of the superior intelligence of the felidae. Never have I been able to associate the docile servility & satellitism of the canidae with mental power. Zoölogists seem to consider the cerebration of cats & dogs about 50–50—but my respect always goes to the cool, sure, impersonal, delicately poised feline who minds his business & never slobbers—the aristocratic, Epicurean philosopher who knows what he wants & tells interlopers to go to hell. There is no credit in having a dog attached to one—for a dog can be conditioned to become anybody's slave & property. But a cat is nobody's slave. You do not *own* a cat. If one lives in your home, it is because he regards your way of life favourably, & accepts you as a friend as one gentleman accepts another. He takes no kicks or insolence from anyone. If you are not worthy to associate with him, he will depart to seek an environment more suited to a gentleman's taste. Therefore he who retains the respect & companionship of a feline has proved himself to be essentially a superior citizen. For a human being, membership in the Kappa Alpha Tau forms a badge of distinction. Many are the eminent names on that membership list—Mahomet himself, Richelieu, Poe, Baudelaire . . . one could catalogue them endlessly. Certainly, I ask no greater honour than to be accounted a citizen of Ulthar beyond the River Skai!

Had a record-breaking bibliothecal windfall the other day—when the old lady downstairs (now leaving for a 3-years' residence in Germany) discarded a vast lot of old books & dumped them down cellar. I salvaged a 10-volume Chambers' Encyclopaedia, a learned biblical commentary in 5 huge volumes,[8] any amount of histories, a *good* Greek–English lexicon to replace my tattered one, &c. &c. &c. Also a splendid 11″ × 9.5″ cast of that famous Greek bas-relief of Orpheus, Eurydice, & Mercury in the Naples Museum.[9] Who says one can't sometimes get something for nothing?

Well—Salaam aliekum!— 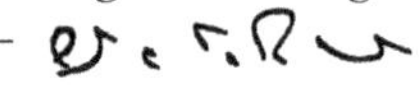

[P.S.] Latest! *Barlow* has just blown in for an indefinite stay. Has taken quarters across the garden from 66. Property adjustments at De Land made it a good time for a long visit. Ar-Ech-Bei is full of literary plans—& has grown a moustache & side whiskers!

Notes

1. RHB, "R. E. H." (*WT*, October 1936).

2. Howard published in *Spicy Adventure Tales* under the pen name Sam Walser.

3. In his letter of 15 July (TLS, JHL), EHP writes: "Another market shuts down: the bawdy books have bought (& PAID) for 20 stories since Jan. 1st, and have 15 still unpublished, and being similarly bought up on their other steady writers, they have declared a moratorium." In his letters, EHP tells of numerous "bawdy" stories he has written, but typically does not identify the publishers.

4. The Agricultural Adjustment Act was a federal law of the New Deal era designed to boost agricultural prices by reducing surpluses.

5. Everil Worrell, "The Canal" (December 1927; rpt. April 1935); H. F. Arnold, "The Night Wire" (September 1926; rpt. January 1933); Arthur J. Burks, "Bells of Oceana" (December 1927; rpt. April 1934); M. L. Humphries, "The Floor Above" (May 1923; rpt. June 1933); Paul Suter, "Beyond the Door" (April 1923; rpt. September 1930). HPL cites these stories, and also John Martin Leahy's "In Amundsen's Tent" (January 1928; rpt. August 1935), in a letter to Farnsworth Wright ([January? 1930]), not published in *WT*. See "Letters to Farnsworth Wright," *Lovecraft Annual* No. 8 (2014): 22.

6. Diminuitive of Popocatepetl, EHP's pet puppy.

7. *Mamluk* is an Arabic designation for slaves, most commonly used to refer to Muslim slave soldiers.

8. Probably William Jenks, *The Comprehensive Commentary on the Holy Bible*.

9. Roman copy of the Augustan age from a Greek original of the second half of 5th century B.C.E. by Alcamenes, a disciple of Phidias.

[76]   [ALS, JHL]

The Ancient Hill—
August 27, 1936.

Dear Malik:—

Yours of July 30 & of Aug. 7 found the Mad Arab doubly mad with a turmoil of conflicting social, epistolary, & near-literary duties. A certain revision job *must* be done by Sept. 1st[1]—letters *must* be answered—& guests *must* be kept entertained. Iä! Shub-Niggurath! The Goat with a Thousand Young! For be it known, the young sage Ar-Ech-Bei is not the only lettered visitor to brighten my ignoble threshold. On August 6 there loomed ponderously on the horizon the microscopic but venerable figure of our versatile old college chum *Adolphe de Castro*—whom I had not seen in person since 1928! He was returning from a melancholy pilgrimage to Boston to deposit his late wife's ashes in the sea in accordance with her ante-mortem request, & spent 5 days in Providentium's archaic atmosphere. One afternoon he, Barlow, & I sat on a tomb in the hidden churchyard & wrote rhymed acrostics on the name of *Edgar Allan Poe*[2]—who 90 years ago wandered among those selfsame slabs & mounds when visiting the town. Old 'Dolph spoke of you with great respect & admiration, & certainly harbours no grudge because of your inability to tinker with his stuff. He tried to unload a lot of aimless junk on me, but I managed to dodge it without offending him. He has not visibly changed in the last 8 years, & seems in pretty fair physical shape for a man of 77.

Both of your epistles interested me vastly, & only the prevailing congestion prevents my commenting more amply on their contents. I followed the varying fortunes of mighty Hu'd-Su'un with anxious absorption, & am relieved & delighted to learn that the intricate rites of the arch-imams & dervishes finally triumphed. Long life to the noble monster—may his strength & speed increase, & his appetite decrease! Here's hoping he'll be in good trim for an eastward hegira when the time comes!

Speaking of appetites—I extend obeisances to the Conquering Lion of Judah! He almost deserves to be renamed *Conan* in view of his ceaseless prowess! Sooner or later I hope to see a snapshot of the unconquerable warrior. I'm glad An-Ghah appreciates him, & wouldn't be surprised if there were something in his theory of the superior grimness & virility of California's feline mountaineers. Surely, it must be more than chance which brought *two* such indomitable men-at-arms to the colonnades of many-pillar'd Irem!

As usual, good luck to the gardens & orchards of ancient Kaf! Your descriptions sound alluring indeed despite the occasional reverses, & I can picture the endless bowers of peach-trees, hibisci, & other exotics from the cryptic conservatories of my old friend Frank Winfield Woolworth.[3] Good old Frank! How I've come to depend on him for things as varied as pads, lamp shades, socks, electric light bulbs, underwear, crockery, tooth paste, ink, postcards, Worcestershire sauce, mouse-traps, chocolate bars, gift pictures, cravats, elastic bands, & what the hell!

Your call on your valiant & eloquent uncle must have been a refreshing event—& I presume many reminiscences of your capacious ancestor Wehner were exchanged. A good concrete start toward genealogical research! Did I mention that Barlovius has been delving into his New England lines at the local libraries, & that he has discovered himself to be my *6th cousin?* Here is the way we descend from a common ancestor:

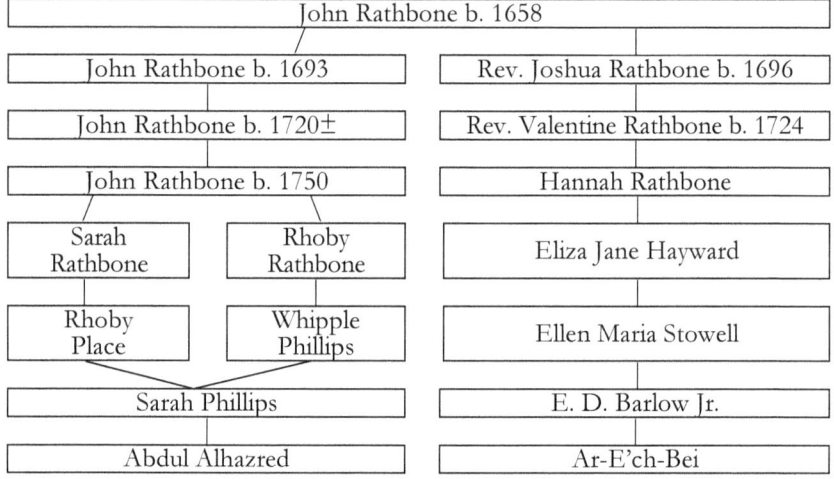

John Rathbone b. 1658	
John Rathbone b. 1693	Rev. Joshua Rathbone b. 1696
John Rathbone b. 1720±	Rev. Valentine Rathbone b. 1724
John Rathbone b. 1750	Hannah Rathbone
Sarah Rathbone / Rhoby Rathbone	Eliza Jane Hayward
Rhoby Place / Whipple Phillips	Ellen Maria Stowell
Sarah Phillips	E. D. Barlow Jr.
Abdul Alhazred	Ar-E'ch-Bei

It's an odd thing that Barlow & I represent the same number of generations from old John, although R H B is young enough to be my son.

I'm interested to hear of your new market, & to note your use of the Two-Gun locale & tradition in building up a living Western hero. Long life to Simon Bolivar Grimes!* From all you say of him, I'm sure Two-Gun would have hailed him with zest & fellowship.[4] The plot & sundry devices you cite seem to me inimitably clever, & I hope some day to read one of the epics of Simon's valiant deeds. I can see the vital relationship to R E H's spirit—having read at least one of the Breckenridge Elkins yarns, & having seen that final "Jeopard" story[5] reprinted in the Cross Plains paper. Good luck to the new line—may it bring you wealth & fame, & aid in keeping green the memory of one who might have been a flourishing contemporary in the same field! I'm sorry, by the way, that you couldn't get to Cross Plains to act as Two-Gun's literary executor.

I am indeed anxious (whetted by the spontaneous sample in your letter of some time ago) to see your R E H reminiscences, & agree that they ought

---

*can't you keep the greedy commercial editors from ruining him with cheap bawdry?

to be circulated as widely & freely as possible. Not a bad idea—sending the MS. to *all* the fan magazines! Hope it can be adequately arranged. When the time comes I'll give you a list of all I know. I'm sure W T will print a fuller obituary than the "stop press" note in the August issue. Another timely item is a detailed biographical & chronological sketch of *Conan* by P. Schuyler Miller—a list of all the Conan tales arranged according to their proper time-sequence, with a stream of running comment outlining the life & development of the hero from his first appearance at 15 to his days of kingship in Aquilonia around the age of 40. Miller showed this to Two-Gun last March, & received his enthusiastic approval. It is not yet published, but I hope it will be soon. As for the Conan tales themselves—I agree that they're not up to the King Kull standard. I wish Ar-E'ch-Bei *could* issue a best of Two-Gun's fiction*, but it isn't likely he could tackle any typographical job so ample. He does, however, want to publish Two-Gun's collected *verse*—if Dr. Howard will furnish the copy.[6] As soon as he gets re-settled & in contact with his printing-press he will write Dr. Howard. Incidentally, I shall soon be sending the Memorial Collection a bound copy of "The Shunned House".

Glad you received "The Goblin Tower" & *The Dragon Fly*. Edkins is indeed an acute commentator on verse, though perhaps you are excessively modest in believing that all your early attempts would fall under his ban. Just now Edkins is having a fearful time with his health—back in the Evanston Hospital for a second serious operation, with no prospect of being on his feet again until well into September.

Here's wishing you luck on the completion, coördination, & publication of your Mexican saga. If the notes sent to me form a fair sample, there is no question about the vitality & keen interest of the chronicle. It would be hard for any competing travelogue to parallel it in graphic choice of material, apt anecdotes, spirited style, racy, colloquial language, &c.—& it seems to me there ought to be some professional market for it. Speaking of professionalism & its problems—in particular as applied to W T & its reprints, pay rates, &c.—as I said before, I can understand very sympathetically the point of view you represent, & can admire the consistency with which you act upon it. If I differ, it is because I approach the field from the totally different angle of the *reader*—who very reasonably demands that reprints of substantial material be furnished, whatever commercial arrangements may be necessary to effect that end. That Wright is no philanthropist is self-evident, but reprinting prices are so slight in any case (tales used in "Not at Night" bring only $12.00, & so on) that it seems to me a bit hard to deny the readers what they ought to have in order to discipline the rascal! That of course is merely my own personal attitude—& I don't blame others for having other attitudes. Incidentally—I shall await with interest the appearance of "Cyclops of Xoatl" . . . hoping that

---

*Wilson Shepherd of The Phantagraph has an idea of such a volume

Kline's share is not sufficient to devitalise it to the usual pulp level.

Glad you had an enjoyable visit from An-Ghah—to whom I trust you will convey my regards. Rimel is just now in Shelby, Montana, in his capacity of pianist in a travelling orchestra. The life of a wandering minstrel! The ice-cream possibilities of your refrigerator sound masterful indeed—though they'd be taxed to capacity if ever Mortonius & I paid you a joint visit! By the way—I duly sent your note on to young Bloch, & am sure he will appreciate it. I also suggested Bloch as a possible fictional collaborator of old de Castro—since he has been doing quite a bit of collaboration of late . . . & with oafs as insubstantial as Forrest J. Ackerman![7]

Thanks vastly for the cutting giving Redwood City's historic background. I always like to have familiar places well oriented in the time-stream. Do you wish the item returned? It is safe & at your disposal. Otherwise it's something for the all-engulfing files.

Barlow & I had an enjoyable trip to Newport Aug. 15. On the 20th—my 46th birthday—we visited ancient Salem & Marblehead ("Arkham" & "Kingsport"), pausing in Lynn to pick up young Sterling. The latter is recovering finely from last spring's operation, & has passed his Harvard entrance examinations with highest honours. We went through the House of the Seven Gables & other centuried piles, & beheld a profusion of ghoulish churchyards with picturesquely crumbling slabs. Some day you surely must visit these venerable scenes! At the moment Barlow is visiting cousins in New Bedford. He'll be back Saturday morning, & that evening Brobst & his wife are coming over. On Sept. 1 Barlow leaves for Kansas City—stopping en route in New York, Washington, & Indianapolis. The week after that I expect Mortonius here. Too bad he & Barlow couldn't meet.[8] By the way—Wandrei is now back in St. Paul.

¶ Salaam—Ω ᘐᢞᡕ ᐧ

Notes

1. The job was *Well Bred Speech* (1936) by Anne Tillery Renshaw. Much of HPL's work, including "[Suggestions for a Reading Guide]" (in *CE* 2) and "Unpublished Parts of Well-Bred Speech . . ." (in *Letters to Elizabeth Toldridge and Anne Tillery Renshaw*), was excised from the final work.

2. Adolphe de Castro, "Edgar Allan Poe" (*WT*, May 1937); RHB, "St. John's Churchyard," and HPL, "In a Sequester'd Providence Churchyard Where Once Poe Walk'd" (*Science-Fantasy Correspondent*, March–April 1937). HPL's poem was reprinted in *WT* (May 1938) as "Where Poe Once Walked: An Acrostic Sonnet." Maurice W. Moe wrote a poem of his own and published it, along with HPL's, RHB's, and de Castro's, in a mimeographed pamphlet, *Four Acrostic Sonnets on Poe* (1936). Moe's poem was published in *Poetry out of Wisconsin*, ed. August Derleth and Raymond E. F. Larsson (New York: Henry Harrison, 1937). Kuttner's "Where He Walked" was not pub-

lished. The five acrostic poems are published in *Letters to Alfred Galpin and Others,* pp. 464–66.

3. Frank Winfield Woolworth (1852–1919), American entrepreneur, founder of F. W. Woolworth Company, and the operator of variety stores that featured a selection of low-priced merchandise.

4. Grimes is a western character in roughly twenty-seven stories, all in *Spicy Western Stories* except for one in *Fighting Western.*

5. "A Man-Eating Jeopard" first appeared in *Cowboy Stories* (June 1936).

6. RHB planned to issue Robert E. Howard's verse, *Echoes from an Iron Harp,* but the project came to naught. A book of that title was published in 1972.

7. Forrest J Ackerman (1916–2008), American science fiction fan, agent, author, and editor. HPL lampooned him in "The Battle That Ended the Century" and "In the Walls of Eryx."

8. RHB and James F. Morton met Price when they visited him in July 1939.

[77]   [ALS, JHL]

The Ancient Hill
—Finished
Octr. 13, 1936

Dear Malik:—

Effusive thanks for the portrait of you & the Conquering Lion! Not seeing any "please return" motto attached, I am adding this item most appreciatively to my gallery, & am abundantly glad to have both likenesses. Ki-Ki surely is a noble & patrician creature, & I only wish good old Nimrod could be around to behold the result of his patriarchal tutoring. The Conan-like jaws & Shah-Abbas[1] moustachios do not escape me, & I can trace the touch of wistfulness inspired by 7 months' refrigeratorial defeat. Looking, however, at the leonine air of determination, I would not be surprised if the valiant warrior were some day to turn that defeat into victory!

Congratulations on your Mexican volume's completion! With its piquant descriptions & apt photographs it ought to be a highly marketable item, & I surely hope you can ultimately place it to advantage. Glad you had the help of an expert in checking up on details. I shall certainly welcome any circulated copy that comes my way—& would be interested in seeing the original dicta-phoned text with its later refinements. Your postcard description of Mexico's prehistoric allurements is tantalising indeed, & I wish I might be able to join in some such expedition as you describe. Who knows what the future holds? Certainly, this continent holds no richer repository of the primal past's secrets!

Barlow started west Sept. 1, but did not see as many people en route as he had hoped to do.* His address in future will be % *H. M. LANGWORTHY,*[2]

---

*He saw Long, Sterling, Howard Wandrei, & Koenig in N.Y., & Miss Moore in Indi-anapolis.

810 W. 57ᵗʰ ST. TERRACE, KANSAS CITY, MO.

Had a very interesting letter the other day from Virgil Finlay the illustrator. He seems to be an extremely pleasant as well as brilliant chap. Glad you've heard from Bloch, who is steadily gaining in ability & will be quite a figure in the weird field before long.

As you now know from the tripartite postcard, Mortonius was here Sept. 11–12–13. We accomplished some prodigious feats in the ice-cream-eating line, & had a pleasant visit with Brobst on the evening of the 12ᵗʰ. As indicated on the card, Don Jaime Ferdinando would indeed appreciate the bit of pedregal—as well as that other lot of minerals promised him in '33. He'd also enjoy hearing from you—for his interest in many-pillar'd Irem & its resident Mullah³ is keen & cordial indeed. Incidentally, J F M brought me a gift of a new ancestor—a bird named Sylvester Eveleth, who was flitting around Boston (he was the first baker—whether of beans or not I don't know—in that historic town) in the year 1643. This gent turned up on the one line which Mortonius & I have in common. From here Mortonius returned to Boston, where he shone at the Harvard Tercentenary exercises. Possibly we mentioned on the postcard that J F M had just won the crossword puzzle championship (for which he'll get a silver loving-cup) at the Boston convention of the Puzzlers' League.

Wilson Shepherd (Oakman, Ala.) continues to be interested in the idea of a book of Two-Gun's best work, & wants your advice in the matter. He has, I think, already written Dr. Howard. If all developed well, he would probably wish you to act as editor—a task which I believe you would welcome even amidst your plethora of other activities. You would, of course, want to discuss the mechanical & financial side very thoroughly with Shepherd—taking care that the volume be accurate in text (I'd volunteer for the proofreading) & tasteful in format. If you don't hear from Shepherd, & are interested, you might write him—the address given above being sufficient.

Thanks in advance for any Mexican photographs which may come around this way—& equal thanks for the fascinating view of the pyramid-leading avenue of cacti. Is this latter to be returned? If so, let me know. Your descriptions of other views are very alluring—& I'm sure these pictures ought to aid in the marketing of the MS. Sorry so many mechanical obstacles appeared in the enlarging process—but I dare say the present experience will lead to greater success in the end. You'll be on guard concerning equipment from now on. A full set of your snaps would surely make a marvellous record—& even a few ought to whet anybody's appetite for the exotic marvels of ancie[nt] Tenochtitlan. Those primal pre-Aztec pyramids you speak of must be unutterably impressive, & I trust you were able to capture some of their brooding & immemorial mystery. You certainly caught the charm of those titanic cacti—specimens which tower considerably over those which I helped to root out of the Barlow lawn last year! Altogether, pictures & text ought to present an irresistible combination—making Mexico live in the reader's mind with a vividness not often achieved in travel books.

I learn of the new Kappa Alpha Tau member with utmost interest & envy, & hope in time to behold his portrait. From your account, he must be one of the most fascinating little devils alive, & I trust that before long the Conquering Lion of Judah will be able to regard him with true semi-fraternal cordiality. His name is surely picturesque & appropriate, & I hope he may never lack for pots to lick! Doubtless Ki-Ki will pass along to him the rudiments of that Great Tradition into which he himself was initiated by Mighty Nimrod—so that in time the furtive dwellers of the mountains will come to fear the Black Death that walks by night as they have feared the White Death & now fear the Striped Death! I'd like to see the two rascals at some of their bouts & lickings & cake-eatings. Perhaps the Conquering Lion *will* begin to roar in the course of time. Those rumblings may be preliminary practice work! I was greatly interested in hearing of the bleached-tiger President of the San José K.A.T. Chapter, & sorry that you had to frustrate his wishes for egress on the evening of your call. His thwarted ambitions for nocturnal slaying remind me of my friend Cole's senior companion Napoleon (now, alas, in the fields of eternal catnip) in Wollaston, whose howls at the front door after twilight were poignantly affecting.

I note the facts of authorship of "The Cyclops of Xoatl", & hope to peruse the tale itself ere long. I haven't had time to glance at W T for two months. Hope you get paid before long for "The Hand of Wrath". Glad to hear that your productivity is increasing, & trust all the new yarns will find a ready market.

Glad, too, to hear of the prosperity of the Gardens of Irem with their strangely hued blossoms & cryptical cacti. Mortonius—who has quite an eye for vegetation—would appreciate them. When we were in Warren on our ice-cream gorge he was prodigiously impressed by the strange, gigantic, & overnourished beech-trees in an undertaker's back yard . . . . . monstrous organisms upon whose source of nourishment one may only speculate vaguely.

Interested to hear that you've given young Conover an account of the genesis of the "Silver Key" sequel! That endless session in the Rue Royale, with its plenteous coffee & chili, ought to sound duly picturesque in print.[4] Incidentally, chili in cans (Rath's or Derby) is perhaps my favourite delicacy nowadays—shewing how much that session did to mould my permanent tastes. Wish I could get to ancient Nouvelle-Orleans again, but don't know when it will ever be financially practicable. Conover seems to be planning quite a magazine, though I haven't seen any actual issue of it as yet.

That genealogical research bureau surely is a helluva graft! Each MS. is doubtless a brief mimeographed script costing perhaps a nickel to produce, & containing highly generalised information about the early background of various families—which may or may not be those of the persons of identical name who send for them. To hitch one's *own* line on to any of these remote efflorescences is something else again! The stuff is doubtless merely copied out of standard books such as those Barlow & I studied during his visit. It would in some cases be interesting to have—when (by accident) the family treated under a certain name happened to be really one's own—since one may not have had a chance to consult the especial book which the "Bureau" got hold of. But the guy who sent in 20 or 25 bucks for complete histories of his various lines (15 of mine* are represented in the list of names, & of these only four—where the Am. branch of a family is absolutely known to come from one definite source—are certain to be the ones described . . . Hazard, Place, Rathbone, Whipple) would be a sucker. I notice both *Hoffmann* & *Price* in the catalogue—but advise you to spend your $3.75 (cost of 2 MSS.) on chili or petrol or something you're sure of!

Later

Just recd. the pictures, plus your late-Sept. notes. Overwhelming thanks! That Vale of Teotihuacan is surely a challenge to the imagination—& *what lies beneath that gaping aperture?* The enlargements seem to me really splendid—fully capturing the haunted atmosphere of the region. The classic symmetry & austere beauty of the temple of Quetzalcoatl impress one tremendously—& over all hangs the brooding mystery of the elder ruins . . . & the challenge of those enormous areas hitherto unexcavated, where centuried secrets brood & fester in eternal night. Your descriptions add enormously to the value of the pictures, & I shall preserve all most sedulously in my files—assuming that the pictures *are* gifts rather than loans. I also appreciated the landslide view with its distinguished component, & the two glimpses of Spanish Mexico—Market-Day & Cathedral. Most certainly, I hope that circumstances will eventually permit me to take advantage of your alluring tourist proposition—for to me Mexico would have a *double* charm—hitting two distinct sides of my interests. First, the primordial mystery of the great ruins—the spell of dead millennia & utter alienage—& second, the more recent historic antiquarianism of the European Colonial . . . . the kind of thing I seek in Quebec, Charleston, Nouvelle-Orleans, Natchez, & my own Providence. Well—we'll see what the gods dope out! Incidentally—I am reminded of a curious note I lately received from a bird in San Francisco, who claims to be a librarian who has travelled all over the world & examined strange & forbidden volumes in Budapest, Madras, & where the hell not. This guy—whose name is Stuart Morton Boland[5] (ever hear of him? Not that the S.F. zone is so small that you necessarily know all the villagers!)—addressed me through W T, & seemed tremendously interested in the Necronomicon & all that. He seems to be a sort of occultist, & sent me a fascinating Japanese postcard shewing the crew of a ship repelling the onslaught of a legion of sea-daemons & lemurs. Well—the connexion is that Boland says he visited Teotihuacan this summer, & that

*& about as many of Barlow's & Morton's

he is about to send me some "peculiar objects" which he secured there near the Pyramid of the Sun. Iä! Shub-Niggurath! What alien entities are about to enter the ancient portal of #66? Did they come up out of that gaping chasm amidst the palaeogean megalithic masonry? Are they shapes of a sort intelligible to mankind—or *something else?* My curiosity is piqued . . . . I am vaguely & subtly disquieted . . . . . Or are the "peculiar objects" mystical trinkets derived from the counters of Frank Winfield Woolworth or his equivalents & vended to a gullible touristry by an obliging peasantry? We shall see . . . . but it may be that an immemorially archaic curse is about to descend upon me! In view of this circumstance you can see how particularly & doubly grateful I am to have the landscape & structures of Teotihuacan made pictorially manifest to me. Again, my most profuse & effervescent thanks! Hope you'll have your $1650 Packard (145 HP) in time for the Great Expedition—although the $12.00 Flint would suit me just as well provided it got there & back somehow! 1925 . . . just the age of most of my suits!

Kappa Alpha Tau news is always welcome—& I feel sure that the Conquering Lion of Judah is the modestly anonymous hero of the Canine-routing episode. I hope he may eventually catch & unrecognisably mangle whatever enemy is responsible for the vanishment of Mighty Nimrod! I learn of Pot-Likher's cryptical & disquieting characteristics with the keenest interest, & hope he will aid in the avenging activities of the fraternity when he reaches military maturity. A good man to have on one's side, I judge, but a tough customer to have agin' one! No—I'm sure black cats do not form a separate *species*—for if they did they would not interbreed with others with full fertility. Most of them, I fancy, involve merely that minor racial variation which distinguishes white cats from tigers, grey cats from yellow, & so on. However— I wouldn't be surprised if *some* black cats involved the technically abnormal biological quality of *melanism* (excess of pigment—the opposite of albinism) which affects many organic species including the felidae. This is an hereditary tendency which crops out atavistically—& its extent varies in different individually [*sic*]. I believe some zoölogists believe that *all* black leopards & panthers are technically melanistic rather than belonging to normal variants—but the black felis domestica is so common & stable a type, & so often variegated with white areas (impossible in a case of melanism), that I don't think this theory could apply to him as a whole. However, there must of course be *some* melanistic common cats —& it would probably take a real zoölogist to decide whether or not any given K.A.T. blackamoor belongs to that cat-egory.

Glad to hear of Simon Bolivar Grimes's growing success,[6] & hope the novel & other material will prosper likewise. Congratulations on the bizarre & succulent fruits of the Gardens of Irem!

Activities hereabouts congested by hellish revision job—worked 60 hours last week without sleep to make a deadline. Autumn weather prevents working in open, but I get out for occasional rural walks. Lately I have taken to exploring a wooded hill—Neutaconkanut—on the western rim of the town, whence a series of marvellous views of outspread city & adjacent countryside may be obtained. I had often ascended it before, but have only recently examined & appreciated the exquisitely mystical sylvan scenery—curious mounds, flower-starred meadows, & hushed hidden valleys—beyond its crest. It shall henceforth be a favourite goal of mine. ¶ Salaam— ⳍ ⳃ Ⳍⳅ ⳡⳃ ⳍ

[P.S.] Last moment. Boland has just sent 14 fascinating small snaps of Aztec-Maya ruins, & promises to send more later. I'm getting a liberal education in American archaeology!

Notes

1. Shāh Abbās the Great or Shāh Abbās I of Persia (1571–1629), 5th Safavid Shah (king) of Iran.

2. Herman M. Langworthy (b. 1881), a lawyer, was married to RHB's mother Bernice Barlow's cousin Minnie Leach (b. 1879).

3. A Muslim learned in Islamic theology and sacred law.

4. Apparently EHP's memoir "The Sage of College Street," which concludes with a paragraph about HPL's visit with Price in New Orleans. It did not appear in Conover's *Science-Fantasy Correspondent* but in Corwin F. Stickney's *Amateur Correspondent*.

5. Boland (1909–1973), a librarian in San Francisco who corresponded with HPL in the 1930s, as recounted in his memoir, "Interlude with Lovecraft" (1945). HPL described him as "an occultly inclined nut in San Francisco who seems to be a sort of educated Bill Lumley" (*O Fortunate Floridian* 361).

6. EHP had sold "Grimes, Outlaw" to *Spicy Western Stories*.

[78]   [ALS, JHL]

The Ancient Hill
—All-Hallow's Eve
[31 October 1936]
Dear Malik:—

The recent bulletins from the garden'd slopes of Kaf were extremely welcome, & I rejoice to hear of the evidences of prosperity now hovering over many-pillar'd Irem. Here's wishing you luck with the Mexican epic—in Czechoslovakia & elsewhere—& many congratulations upon the increasing polyglotism of your various works! I envy you the photograph of Two-Gun. Hope something will come of Shepherd's plan for a volume of choice Hovardiana under your editorship. If it does, I'll be abundantly glad to coöperate in the choice of weird items.

I noted with interest your observations on sundry juggernauts & super-juggernauts, new & old. They surely do grow more impressive year by year—& yet I'm sure your present faithful Hu'd-Su'un ought to prove at least fairly adequate for a time. As for me—that 15-buck Model T would serve all my needs finely, & I'd be tempted to fall for such a bargain if my financial situation were less precariously acute! While I relish speed as an end in itself, I regard it as a sort of epicurean luxury wholly dissociated from the province of transportation & sightseeing. 30 miles per hour would do admirably in getting me over the country—indeed, I wouldn't wish to travel faster in regions where the scenery is good!

As usual, I relished the news of K'hi-K'hi & Photli-Khah, & am glad that they have learned to appreciate East Indian curry as prepared by their master's expert hand. With such a good beginning, let us hope that they will shortly see the light regarding chili con carne! Their military training—carrying on Mighty Nimrod's glorious tradition—is very gratifying to consider, & I can imagine the effectiveness of the Conquering Lion's tactical instructions if ever the fraternal pair set out together on a mission of joint slaying! Aye, I would give much to behold them as they stalk forth! *Melanism* is a curious thing, but as you say, it does not seem to characterise the ordinary Kappa Alpha Tau blackamoors whom we meet. I have noticed the half-buried spots on some black leopards in zoos—but of course, blends of heredity without melanism can produce analogous effects. My little late friend of 1934, Sam Perkins, had tiger markings clearly discernible beneath his black coat, yet had none of the general characteristics of melanism. His brother John, on the other hand, boasted an unbroken glossy blackness except for his diminutive white necktie. I'm interested to hear of the Conquering Lion's Afghan resemblance, & am sure Shir Ali would make an excellent alternative name for him.[1] His photograph clearly indicates the belligerent resolution & strength of character which are his!

I surely am grateful for the Mexican pictures—whose quality is amply good enough for me. The ones sent by Boland are small snaps—$2\frac{1}{4} \times 3\frac{1}{4}$—though they show up well under magnification. Did I add that Boland sent me a very lucid treatise on the Maya & Aztec civilisations—one of the handbooks of the Am. Museum?[2] Betwixt the two of you, I am surely doubling my knowledge of America's primal civilisations! If I ever attempt to utilise this scene & theme for a fantastic tale, I shall surely call upon you for the subtle & minute details which mean so much in the weaving of a background. Those subterrene gulfs & honeycombings deserve the most expert & authentic exploitation! Incidentally, I doubt whether I could beat or even equal you in visualising the majesty & the brooding mystery of the desert. You present so vivid & imagination-stirring a picture in even your impromptu paragraphs, that one is led to expect much of what you would write if seriously intent on putting over the palaeogean secrecy, weird beauty, & elusive glamour which you appreciate so keenly & sensitively. I surely hope that I may some time behold the Mojave in all its cryptic & varied grandeur. That I would be profoundly moved, it is impossible to doubt. Whether I could do it justice on paper is another matter. It is not likely that the region would hold for me that element of the *sinister* which the world of antarctic death holds, since in my mind only that which is *cold* is supremely associated with evil, horror, & death. I have vainly tried to lay weird tales in the south. No use! To me everything southern is friendly & benign—because *warm*. The north (or antarctic)—with its hideous torturing cold & long nights of stalking death—is in my consciousness the epitome of all that is hostile to mankind & to life. I am never far from the mood expressed in my old-time verses where I spoke of

"The mad time of unreason,
  The brain-numbing days
When winter, white-sheeted & ghastly, stalks onward to torture & craze."[3]

However—the sinister does not form the only effective element in fantasy, & I feel certain that the Mojave would start me off on some sort of imaginative spree—whether or not anything might ever come out of it! I've seen a number of crude postcards of the region—mostly sent by young Kuttner—& even these hold hints of the deep-seated impressiveness.

That quoted ritual of approach to the Rajah of Kandi surely does represent ceremony at its apex![4] The Orient knows how to stage such things with full strength & all the fixings! Well—I'm going through all the gestures, platter over head, in my approaches to Azathoth regarding the success of your transactions with the pious Miles W. Smith![5]

Mortonius will surely be glad to hear from you, & to see those deliberately labelled minerals when they arrive. I'll relay the latest from Belmont to Brobst. Evidently the Belmontani practice a policy which might well be expressed in a new parody of that line once so aptly parodied by Dr. Johnson— a parody reading

"Who rules o'er madmen should himself be mad"![6]

Hope the Yosemite, Death Valley, Mojave, & Baja California trips will duly materialise—& that some or all may be capable of lucrative exploitation in the manner of the Mexico City jaunt. That pearl fishery business sounds extremely picturesque. And here's hoping that some day Grandpa may get across the continent to all these scenes of glamour—in a 15-fish Model T or otherwise!

Speaking of scenic explorations—albeit on a more modest scale—I continued my outdoor rambles throughout October, & succeeded in unearthing still more territory close at hand which was absolutely new to me. Oct. 20 & 21 were phenomenally warm, & I went exploring on both days—finding a fascinating forest only 3 miles away which I had never seen before. This place—of which I had heard vaguely in the past, but which happens to be between my usual routes of travel—is called the "Squantum Woods", & lies down the east shore of the bay—in the town of East Providence. It is now a state reservation, & was made accessible by the cutting-through of the Barrington Parkway. Ædepol, but what I've missed for almost half a century! Still, I'm almost glad that some new discovery at my very doorstep was held in reserve for my declining years. It renews the illusion of youth & of adventurous expectancy to come upon something fresh & unexpected when one had thought all such things were past! Great oaks & birches—steep slopes & rock ledges—& on both occasions a magnificent sunset beyond the trees. Then glimpses of the crescent moon, Venus, & Jupiter—& the lights of far-off Providence from high places along the parkway. Another new goal for next year's rambles! On my expedition of the 20th a particularly congenial bodyguard or retinue attended me through the sunlit arcades of the grove—in the persons of *two infant members of the Kappa Alpha Tau,* one grey & one tortoise-shell, who appeared out of nowhere in the midst of the sylvan solitudes. Blithe spirits of the ancient wood—furry faunlets of the shadowy vale! I wonder where their mother was? Judging by their diminutiveness, they could not have been long graduated from her as a source of nourishment. Probably they belonged to an hospital whose grounds are contiguous with the mystical forest. Both were at first very timid, & reluctant to let Grandpa catch them; but eventually the little grey fellow became very purr-ful & amicable—climbing over the Old Gentleman, playing with twigs & with Grandpa's watch-charm, & eventually curling up & going to sleep in the grandpaternal lap. But little brother remained suspicious & aloof—clawing & spitting with surprising vehemence on the one occasion when Grandpa caught him. He hung around, however, because he didn't want to lose his brother! Not wishing to wake my new friend, I carried him about when I continued my ramble—little tortoise-shell brother tagging along reluctantly & dubiously at a discreet distance in the rear. When the grey faunlet awaked, he requested to be set down; but proceeded to trot companionably after Grandpa—sometimes getting under the Old Gentleman's feet & considerably retarding progress. Thus I roamed the venerable forest aisles for an hour & a half—till the ruddy disc of the sun vanished behind the farther hills & treetops. As I emerged from the wood, I feared that my faithful retinue might follow me on to the parkway & incur the perils of motor traffic—& was considering expedients for discouraging their further attendance—but discovered that they were not without native caution. Or perhaps they were wholly genii loci, without real existence apart from their dim nemorense habitat. At any rate, the little grey rascal paused at the edge of the grove with a mewed farewell—& naturally Young Tortoise-Shell had no great eagerness to follow. I bade them a regretful & ceremonious adieu—& on the next day looked for them in vain.

On Oct. 28 I opened up one more realm of fascinating terra incognita—the region west of the Neutaconkanut Hill which I described in a previous letter, & the western slopes of that eminence itself. At certain stages of this ramble I penetrated a terrain which took me half a mile from any spot I had ever trod before in the course of a long life. I followed a road which branches north & west from the Plainfield Pike, ascending a low rise which skirts Neutaconkanut's western foot & which commands an utterly idyllic vista of rolling meadows, ancient stone walls, hoary groves, & distant cottage roofs to the west & south. Only 2 or 3 miles from the city's heart, & yet in the primal rural New England of the first colonists! Just before sunset I ascended the hill by a precipitous cart-path skirting an ancient wood, & from the dizzy crest obtained an almost stupefying prospect of outspread countryside, gleaming rivulets, far-off forests, & mystical orange sky with the great solar disc sinking redly amidst bars of stratus clouds. Entering the woods, I saw the actual sunset through the trees, & then turned eastward to cross the hill to that more familiar cityward slope which I have always known. Never before had I realised the great extent of Neutaconkanut's surface. It is really a miniature plateau or table-land, with valleys, ridges, & summits of its own, rather than a simple hill. From some of its hidden interior meadows—remote from every sign of nearby human life—I secured truly marvellous glimpses of the remote urban skyline—a dream of enchanted pinnacles & domes half-floating in air, & with an obscure aura of mystery around them. The upper windows of some of the taller towers held the fire of the sun after I had lost it, affording a spectacle of cryptic & curious glamour. Then I saw the great round disc of the Hunter's Moon (2 days before full) floating above the belfries & minarets, while in the orange-glowing west Venus & Jupiter commenced to twinkle. My route across the plateau was varied—sometimes through the interior, but now & then getting toward the wood edges where dark valleys slope down to the plain below, & huge balanced boulders on rocky heights impart a spectral, druidic effect as they stand out against the twilight. I did not begin to cover the full extent of the plateau, & can see that I have a field for several future voyages of discovery. Finally I came to more familiar ground—where the grassy ridge of an old buried aqueduct gives the illusion of one of those vestigial Roman roads in Arthur Machen's Gwent country—& stood once more on the well-known eastward crest which I have gazed at since the age of three. The outspread city was rapidly lighting up, & lay like a constellation in the deepening dark. The moon poured down increasing floods of pale gold, & the glow of Venus & Jupiter in the fading west grew intense. Then down the steep hillside to the car line (too cold for enjoyable walking when there's no scenery to compensate for shivers!) & back to the prosaic haunts of man.

Later

Your second bulletin, with carbon of letter to Shepherd, duly received. I believe you are right in every phase of your advice to Shepherd—& am sure that neither I nor any of the others mentioned could possibly object to the reference to straitened circumstances. I couldn't cough up a ten-spot *now* to save my life—& Klarkash-Ton, Rimel, Bloch, & Belknap are undoubtedly in

H. P. Lovecraft ❋ 267

the same boat. When Shepherd spoke of subscriptions, I assumed he would approach only persons of known means, such as Koenig. Indeed, I'm sure I told him how absolutely broke I am. I also dwelt on the need of having the memorial to R E H an *adequate* one—a *good* collection, tastefully printed & well bound, or nothing. A smallish volume with *just the right stories* & with neat typography & format might not be so bad, but (as I tell Shepherd) the press-work would have to be a lot better than anything yet emanating from Oakman, Ala. So on the whole, I believe your advice is the best that could be given. A memorial collection is very much to be desired, but Shepherd is not the one to handle it *unless* (1) he can find a better list of potential subscribers, & unless (2) his mechanical skill greatly improves. Regarding point 2— he *is* learning printing at a very encouraging rate, despite his general illiteracy.

"Onery" is certainly a beast & a half! The pet leopards of Roman times had nothing on him! Too bad he can't sire a feline army of vengeance to extirpate the hostile influences which have worked havock with the Kappa Alpha Tau in Redwood City, Auburn, Asotin, De Land, Providence, & elsewhere! ¶ Congratulations on the sagacity of the Conquering Lion, as displayed in his disposal of the wire fence problem!

Congratulations on the Afghan story, & on the Aztec & Egyptian ideas! The El Kula pyramid item seems especially promising. Meanwhile let us hope that Rev. Miles & others will relish the Mexican travelogue.

Hope the Ensenada jaunt proves pleasant & fruitful. No—you hadn't mentioned those Mexico City traffic rules before. Thanks for the tip—I'll be on my guard if the 12-buck Flint or the 15-buck Model T goes wrong on the Paseo de la Reforma or Culla del Whatthehell! And the only corpse I'll haul will at least be alive from the neck down.

I'll hustle this off in order to endorse your Shepherd advice without delay. Am floundering in a sea of goddam proofs from two sources! Damn cold today— no more trips for Grandpa, I guess! ¶ Regards to the felidae—& numerous salaams. **ℰ ℵℐℱ**

Notes

1. Yet another name for Kiki. See 272n2.
2. Probably Herbert J. Spinden (1879–1967), *Ancient Civilizations of Mexico and Central America* (New York: American Museum of Natural History, 1917, 1922, or 1928; *LL* 901).
3. "The City" (1919), ll. 8–10.
4. EHP to HPL, 23 October 1936 (TLS, JHL): "An extract from acct. of an ambassador calling on the King of Kandi, 1762; or rather, the Raja of Kandi, Kirti Sri. 'He was admitted to the audience hall at midnight, and ordered to pull his shoes off & hold above his head the silver dish containing the letter for the Raja. Six seperate [*sic*] curtains, red & white, were withdrawn, and the king was then discovered seated on his throne. . .the envoy was forced upon his knees and had to make endless protstra-

tions [*sic*]. . .which ended at the foot of the throne, where he presented his creden-
tials. . .' Then the ambassador accounts, 'I should have been well enough pleased with
the appearance it made, had I been in a more agreeable situation. (he speaks here of
the monarch's costume). At the foot of the throne knelt one of the King's Prime Min-
isters, to whom he communicated what he had to say to me, who, after prostrating
himself on the ground, related it to one of the generals who sat by me; who, after having prostrated himself, explained it to a Malabar doctor, who told it in Malabar to my
dubash, and he to me. And this ceremony was repeated on asking every question. . .'"
5. EHP was trying to sell articles of his Mexico trip to Rev. Miles A. Smith, editor of
the American Baptist Publication Society. He did sell one article.
6. The line is a parody of "Who rules o'er freemen should himself be free!" from
Henry Brooke's tragedy *Gustavus Vasa* (1739). When this line was read in Samuel
Johnson's presence, he came up with the parody "Who drives fat oxen should himself
be fat." For Belmont see EHP 71. Dr. Gardener, founder of the sanitarium, himself
became a patient there.

[79]   [ALS, JHL]

The Ancient Hill
—Dec. 3, 1936.

Dear Malik:—

Your advice to Shepherd was undoubtedly sound—indeed, it
coincides to some extent with advice I had already given him. I had not dwelt
on the financing, but had insisted that any book serving as a memorial to
R E H ought to be one of reasonable size & really good appearance—not one
of those crude jobs such as Crawford, Shepherd, & other youthful aspirants
have hitherto turned out. I told him that he ought to consider such a venture
only after acquiring the skill & typographical equipment necessary for first-
rate workmanship. I'll let you know anything he writes regarding the matter—
but if he is at all sensible he ought to take your advice in good part.* He is a
somewhat illiterate "cracker", & was rather sharp & muddled in his dealings
four years ago, when he had quite a row with young Barlow;[1] but the passage
of time seems to have improved him vastly. He takes his enterprises with
commendable seriousness, & has really made remarkable progress in learning
how to print—as a comparison of his first *Phantagraph* (just a year ago) with
his latest products strikingly shows.

Young Conover is quite a different proposition—an educated & highly intelligent chap. His partner—Corwin Stickney Jr.[2]—who prints their joint paper
is an extremely brilliant kid of 14, who furnishes an excellent grade of press
work (beyond all comparison to Shepherd's & Crawford's) & shatters all records in his freedom from misprints. I hope you'll do everything in your power

---

*just heard from Shepherd. He is very grateful for your advice & will heed it. His *Fan-
ciful Tales* is out—the text of my "Nameless City" containing 59 misprints.

to encourage these boys, for they really appear to be the most promising publishing team of all the semi-pro juveniles. "The Sultan's Jest" will surely make a splendid feature in the S F C, & the publishers are accomplishing a real service in making it available to the present generation.[3] Your sketches of fantasy authors will greatly aid the popularity of the magazine, & I make a profound obeisance anent the undeserved honour of my choice for earliest dissection. I'll trust you not to be too libellous—anyhow, the 500-word limit will prevent you from revealing *quite* what a false alarm I am, even if you tried! That request for a sheet of autographs is a good measure of your growing fame. Bless me, but I wish I could make cash by just selling my signature—not on cheques! Hard to think of an easier day's work than just autographing:

H P Lovecraft	H P Lovecraft	H P Lovecraft
H P Lovecraft	H P Lovecraft	H P Lovecraft
H P Lovecraft	H P Lovecraft	H P Lovecraft

If every H P Lovecraft meant a dollar, I'd feel a damn sight freer of the poorhouse's shadow!

I trust you'll have an enjoyable session with the traveller from Pekin. You are surely able to offer your guests distinctive entertainment, thanks to the wizardry & exotic gardening on the slopes of Kaf. I was never previously aware of the technique required in serving cactus pears; but can, from your description, appreciate its necessity. Glad the local polo games are proving enjoyable, & that Mighty Hu'd-Su'un is displaying its manifold merits to advantage.

Kappa Alpha Tau news is always welcome, & I wish I might have seen the coal-black junior member who so nearly joined the caravan to manypillar'd Irem. The abstemious Maltese gentleman at the neighbouring winemerchant's is clearly a person of poise—but for diabolical picturesqueness I fancy the palm must go to the savage Onery! However, as a proved friend of the fraternity, you may yet have the old devil rubbing amicably around your ankles! My choicest regards to Khi-Khi & Potli-Khah—the latter of whom doubtless grows more formidable each day.

As for *cold* as an element of horror—to be sure, *I personally* would be past all conscious emotion, phobic or otherwise, at the temperatures of the antarctic continent. It is the *idea*, based on less extreme doses, which is hideous & sinister to me. And I assume, of course, that not everyone would be as thoroughly dead to the world as I amidst the frozen secrets of the white waste. Anyhow it seems a fact that frigidity & evil are inextricably intertwined in my emotional makeup. But that's not saying that I wouldn't find the Vale of Teotihuacan or the Mojave desert a source of inexhaustible fantastic impressions! I may yet call on you for colour & detail in connexion with some yarn based on those regions—& I thank you in advance for the idea. The southwest is probably richer in sinister possibilities than the south*east* which I know & love so well. I recall many awed reverences to its moonlit sands & half-amorphous ruins, its spectral colour-effects & its subtle suggestions of unholy antiquity— & only the other day someone was urging me to get in touch with an archaeologist who has monkeyed around a weird pueblo popularly called "The City of the Worm". Then there have been newspaper accounts of an incredible place in New Mexico—in the Navajo country—called "The Desert of the Black Blood."[4] This is a ghoulish & desolate area of broken lava which is rifted by great chasms & which has probably never been penetrated beyond a few miles by any white man—or any living Indian for that matter. Aëroplanes, flying over it, have spied what look like ruins at its very heart; & local legends tell of an ancient & mysterious city whose crumbling walls now harbour carnivorous dragons. Yea—the southwest is surely a place for the connoisseur in strange horror to visit—though one would need a guide to help one find the genuine high spots with a minimum of wasteful wandering.

Congratulations on recent work—Manchurian, Afghanese, Egyptian, Western, & what have you! That Cairene map makes your Sakhara locale much easier to comprehend . . . which reminds me that I once handled the Cairo-pyramid area (albeit rather superficially) in ghost-writing that yarn for Houdini—"Imprisoned With the Pharaohs"—in the anniversary W.T. back in '24. Your method of working sincere writing into pulp material, as practiced in the Manchurian yarn, certainly sounds promising—a variant of Derleth's ability to grind out pulp junk with his left hand while he slowly evolves authentic regional fiction with his right. I wish some of the other young pulpsters—Long, Wandrei, &c.—could be equally successful in keeping a firm grip on the literary standards with which they started out!

As to how I'd manage to refrain from lewd & obscene gestures in flivvering through Mexico City—that's a problem I'd have to study out with great care. Not knowing the region's code of symbolism, I might inadvertently pull the most outrageous faux pas's [*sic*] . . . when my real intent would be merely to point out some especially notable piece of architecture or wrought-iron work. It all depends on how vicious the imaginations of the gendarmes (or whatever they call 'em) are. There's no pleasing some people. Once in a while I'm both exasperated & amused by the cautionings of some over-sophisticated guy who urges me not to use this or that ordinary idiom or word on the ground that it has recently acquired some esoteric & repulsive meaning among the denizens of various sections of the underworld.

As for Henry Kuttner—he's a damn bright kid who resides at Beverly Hills, in your own state. He is securing an increasing foothold in the pulps, but nevertheless has a sound taste in weird fiction & can evoke powerful atmospheric effects when he tries. To shew how small the world is—when old de Castro was here last August I happened to mention Kuttner as a rising figure, & old 'Dolph was instantly all attention. He had known a Henry Kuttner years ago, & knew that he had a son of the same name—hence inferred that our energetic young colleague was that infant grown up. We at once dropped Kuttner a card—& it turned out that old Dolph's guess was right. Kuttner's late father—a bookseller—was indeed a pal of the venerable scholar's 20 years ago. Since the reëstablishment of the link Kuttner & de Castro have become regular & interested correspondents. Incidentally—the same town of Beverly Hills has lately yielded up another new correspondent (Holy Yuggoth, but how'll I ever handle my mounting list without a staff of secretaries!) who got hold of me through *Astounding Stories*, & who is probably the most brilliant & discerning student, analyst, & appreciator of the element of cosmic weirdness that I've ever encountered. His name is Fritz Leiber, Jr.,[5] & it doubled my interest to find that he is indeed the son & namesake of the (in those days) young Shakespearian actor whom I used to admire in parts like Faulconbridge, Edgar, Horatio, Macduff, &c. in Robert Mantell's classic repertory company a quarter of a century ago.[6] The kid certainly has papa's genius, & if it doesn't take him along in the thespian field (which he is entering) it surely will in the field of literature & criticism. He grasps the real *fundamentals* of the cosmic, & is able to distinguish the elusive essence of true weirdness from flashy imitations, better than anyone else I've lately come across. ¶ Regards & benedictions— ϙ𐤀 ϙ 𐤏 ϙ

[P.S.] Just had word "Pickman's Model" is to be reprinted in another British anthology.

[P.P.S.] Later—Behold! *I'm* a great man, too! Conover has just asked *me* for a batch of autographs!

Notes

1. The feud between Shepherd and RHB involved the trading of some pulp magazines in 1932, RHB offering to exchange eight bound volumes of *Amazing Stories* for a complete set of *WT* for 1923–25. HPL summarized the dispute in a half-flippant essay, "Correspondence between R. H. Barlow and Wilson Shepherd of Oakman, Alabama—Sept.–Nov. 1932" (*CE* 5.211–15).

2. Corwin F. Stickney (1921–1998), co-publisher with Willis Conover of *Science-Fantasy Correspondent* (1936–37), later titled *Amateur Correspondent* (1937f.), edited by Stickney alone. He issued the memorial volume of verse *HPL*, given free to subscribers to his magazine.

3. *WT*, September 1925. It was not reprinted.

4. HPL to Earl Peirce, 28 November 1936 (ms., Wisconsin Historical Society): "Then there have been newspaper accounts of an incredible place in New Mexico—in the Navajo country—called 'The Desert of the Black Blood.' This is a ghoulish & desolate area of broken lava which is rifted by great chasms & which has probably never been penetrated beyond a few miles by any white man—or any living Indian for that matter. Aëroplanes, flying over it, have spied what look like ruins at its very heart; & local legends tell of an ancient & mysterious city whose crumbling walls now harbour

carnivorous dragons. Yes—the southwest is surely a place for the connoisseur in strange horror to visit—though one would need a guide to help one find the genuine high spots with a minimum of wasteful wandering."

5. Fritz Leiber (1910–1992), a leading figures in science fiction and fantasy from the 1940s onward. He and his wife Jonquil (1907–1969) separately corresponded briefly with HPL.

6. Robert B. Mantell (1854–1928), a heralded Shakespearean stage actor who made several silent films.

[80]   [ANS, JHL][1]

[Postmarked Providence, R.I.,
11 December 1936]

KHI-KHI, CONQUERING LION OF JUDAH[2]

I wail! I yowl! I tear my fur & whiskers! The news casts a cloud of melancholy over all the Providence Chapter of the Kappa Alpha Tau! Khi-Khi, Great Battle-Axe of Eblis, Heir of the Preadamite Sultans, hath gone out into the night-hung Hills of Never to join Great Nimrod, the guider of his youth! Aië! Aië! M'row! M'raaow! M'raaaaaowwww!

I, too, am unable to do the calamity justice in a fitting dirge. Would that news of the hero's return might upset all our lamentation! May Potli-K'heh wax strong & vengeful, & rally around him all the savage warriors of the land for a mission of death in the purple hills! ¶ Congrats on your theological cheque[3] & other material acquisitions. Now to storm the gates of Popish, Mothereddy-ish,[4] Mormon, Jewish, Moslem, Buddhist, Shinto, & Confucian fanes! ¡Viva Mejico! Hope the other ideas for articles will come out well. ¶ Regards to Omar & Peter, & sorry they can't aid in the punitive expedition![5] Aië! Aië!

Notes

1. *Front:* Betsy Williams Cottage, Roger Williams Park, Providence, R. I.

2. Referring to EHP's cat Ki-Ki (also called Battle-Axe). The Lion of Judah is a Jewish cultural and national symbol of the Israelite tribe of Judah. According to the Torah, it consists of the descendants of Judah, fourth son of Jacob. The association between Judah and the lion can first be found in the blessing given by Jacob to Judah in Genesis. The Lion of Judah is also mentioned in the Book of Revelation, as a term representing Jesus, according to Christian theology. Cf. Rev. 5.5 (KJV): "And one of the elders saith unto me, Weep not: behold, the Lion of the tribe of Juda, the Root of David, hath prevailed to open the book, and to loose the seven seals thereof." The lion of Judah, a title of the Emperor Haile Selassie (1892–1975), was depicted on the flag of Ethiopia from 1897 to 1974.

3. EHP received a check for $27 for an article on Mexico for a Baptist Sunday school magazine.

4. Mary Baker Eddy (1821–1910), founder of Christian Science.

5. EHP described them as "two mighty K.A.T. potentates in Oakland. Alas, [who] can not leave their domains to avenge KiKi" (5 December 1936; TNS, JHL).

[81] [ALS, JHL]

The Hilltop Mosque
[Postmarked Providence, R.I.,
11 January 1937]

Dear Malik:—

Pleasure at your recent bulletins mitigates to some extent my lamentations at the vanishment of the Conquering Lion. But my heart is still heavy concerning this latest blow to the Kappa Alpha Tau. Aië! Aië! Miaow!

Glad the ghoulish-rakish yarn is at last out of the way. 181 tales! I reel in dizziness at the thought of so much industry! And yet if all this forms a school, as you suggest, in addition to providing liquid energy for Mighty Hu'd-Su'un, it is surely industry well rewarded. I can see how such apprenticeship might prove extremely valuable to persons of extra-acute mind, like you & Derleth, who are able to distinguish the valuable disciplinary elements from the elements of artificiality & charlatanry. Certainly, the basic problems of narration & incident-handling are the same in serious & in oversimplified popular fiction—& as you say, the qualities of clearness & simplicity are classic ones whose acquisition in any way is to be encouraged. I certainly hope that a good proportion of the readers understand & appreciate the amount of research you put into your tales. *Some* certainly do—& even if they form only a minority, they are surely worth playing up to. There is undoubtedly a great deal of general educational value in pulp material of the highest grade. Talbot Mundy makes the ancient world live again in authentic colours, while Harold Lamb vividly re-creates the Mongol empires of the Middle Ages.[1] You are assuredly in the same group—& observation will tell you that its members are pretty generally recognised as above the charlatanic level. It is a pity, though, that to the herd there is no difference between a careful researcher & a clever ignoramus who juggles glamourous names & throws an impressive bluff! That's life! Undoubtedly your serious work of the future will combine the re gional & the exotic—that is, it will pertain to strange & distant places, & embody the fascination they have for you, but will likewise be based on accurate geographical knowledge & familiarity with the historical & anthropological background. That Mexico will form at least one of the fields would seem to be a very strong probability—& I fancy the land of oil & Broken Axe, & the brooding ruins & mysterious deserts of the southwest, will not be unrepresented in your repertoire. Likewise, I'll wager that the good old Orient—historically & traditionally treated, will always be on the list of subjects!

Speaking of the southwest—I certainly shall call on you for background & colour if I ever do try to exploit its atmosphere myself. And this reminds me to enclose the only cutting which I possess concerning the "Desert of the Black Blood" in Nueva Mejico. When I read this, it *seemed* to tie up with other stuff I had read or heard of before; but when pinned down, I can't cite a single additional authority. It may have been merely conversational fragments . . . but in any case you have a fair account here. Further information might be forthcoming from the U.S. Biological Survey & Conservation Service—or from the author of the article, the well-known science columnist Thomas R. Henry of the *Washington Star*.[2] But wait a moment—I *do* recall one other lead. One of the innumerable Eyrie-followers who have fastened themselves on my correspondence list—a kid named Earl Peirce[3]—has been urging me to get in touch with a friend of his who has done archaeological work in the southwest & who has spoken of a curious Pueblo ruin known as "The City of the Worm". I haven't yet looked up the gent (who is also, I believe, a pulp fictionist), but his name is Bruce Bryan,[4] 1334 Columbia Road, N.W., Washington, D.C. You might drop him a line if you think he might have useful ideas or information. Incidentally—please return the Black Blood cutting some time, since it is one of a series on the Navajos & their country which I'm saving. No hurry, though. Conversely, if you'd like to borrow the rest of the series—anthropological rather than weird—it is completely at your disposal.

And now I must, with becoming obeisances, acknowledge the all-too-flattering sketch of Abdul the Damned[5] which you have so adroitly drawn up for the readers of the S F C. I recognise the plan & scope, hence am making no attempt to substitute Lucretius for chili con carne on the list of tastes. My only corrections are on minor matters of fact—for example, that my middle name is PHILLIPS (my mother's maiden name) & not "Philip", that my height in average shoes is 5 feet *11* & not 9 or 10, & that the thinning lint on top of my ugly bean is no longer dark but grey. (You'd be surprised as to 3½ yrs' possibilities of senescence!) I'm sure Conover will be very glad of the piece despite its lowly subject. He recently expressed his feeling of tremendous gratitude & indebtedness to you. I sent the sketch along as soon as it arrived.

Your advice on the Howard Memorial question seems very sound, & I think Shepherd accepts it completely. Assuredly, no tribute ought to be even partly a vehicle for the ego or interests of those who profess to pay it. Nothing is more repulsive than the spectacle of a herd of crawling parasites trying to cash in on the death of a titan. I can see your point about the preferability of a Cross Plains pilgrimage to a contribution to a Memorial Edition Fund. Undoubtedly—undervaluing his own achievements as he did—good old R E H would have considered such a pilgrimage the greater tribute. I can also see the point regarding the superior fitness of contributions to the Memorial Collection in Brownwood. I've already sent "The Shunned House" (bound by Barlow) & the little "Cats of Ulthar" pamphlet, & am now about to send the Crawford-published "Shadow Over Innsmouth." I hope Howard Payne College will take this collection with proper seriousness; keeping it catalogued, & calling adequate attention to it in the bulletins & other publications of the institution. I recall R E H's reminiscences of breaking into school libraries for out-of-season borrowings—& can attest that he certainly made good use of his temporary booty in building up an imagination-seasoned background of historical & mythological erudition! Apocryphal or not, the anecdote is typical & character-revealing. Good old Two-Gun! We shall not look upon his like again!

Many thanks for the scholarly exposition of the ancient gesture or manual symbol which Mexican officialdom recognises as 'lewd & obscene'. I am greatly relieved to learn that it is a highly specialised affair, & not one of those simple motions which might easily be duplicated—to the duplicator's detriment—in complete unconsciousness & ignorance! It is safe to say that I shall be able to traverse Mexico & China in a wholly off-guard & unconstrained way, without any danger of drawing crowds of frowning gendarmes or shady señoritas in the one country, or of assassins & torturers in the other! Your clever correlation of the Chinese sacred symbol with the Mexican profane one deserves recognition as a piece of serious research, & I trust it will be suitably acclaimed when your volume appears. The antiquity & universality of certain basic gestures are fascinating to contemplate, & arouse all sorts of speculations as to the early distribution of mankind, & the extent to which sheer biological or psychological makeup, responding to environment, can give rise to independent parallel phenomena in wholly separated human groups.

I read with great interest of the current performances of Potli-Khah, sole survivor of the Kappa Alpha Tau in many-pillar'd Irem. His emulation of canine ways reminds me of a K.A.T. member whom I met years ago in "Dunwich" (Wilbraham, Mass)—one of a flourishing chapter of seven at a farmhouse. This fat yellow rascal went over to the enemy to such an extent that he actually preferred the society of the two local canidae to that of his own fellow-felidae—I can see him now in his characteristic evening setting, curled up on the sofa beside his especial boon companion—an aged collie—while his fraternity brothers foregathered elsewhere around the fire. That was a great organisation—one of our soundest units! The dean & president—called "Printer"[6] [aff. dimin. of "Prince of Orange", in turn derived from the colour of his eyes]—was a sage tiger 17 years old, & the only member of the clan who remembered how to use the ancient "cat ladder" of projecting bricks in the huge chimney in getting from floor to floor when the doors to the stairs were closed. Printer—recognising a fellow-elder—took a liking to me, & spent nearly every evening of my visit in my lap, alternately dozing & wheezing . . . for he had asthma in his advanced years. Alas! Two years afterward I was called upon to write his elegy—which I did, in most sincerely mournful numbers.

Good old Printer! Another distinguished Dunwich member was the Prince of Wails (named for his vocal attainments), whose skill in threading his way damagelessly through labyrinths of antique glassware was well-nigh fabulous.

Hope your Yuletide was suitably cheerful & gift-bestrown. Ours here was commendably festive—including a turkey dinner at the boarding-house across the garden, with a congenial Kappa Alpha Tau dignitary meandering among the tables & finally jumping up on the window-seat for a nap. We had a tree in front of the hearth in my aunt's living-room—its verdant boughs thickly festooned with a tinsel imitation of Florida's & Louisiana's best Spanish moss, & its outlines emphasised by a not ungraceful lighting system. Around its base were ranged the Saturnalian gifts—which included (on my side) a hassock tall enough to let me reach the top shelves of my bookcases, & (on my aunt's side) a cabinet of drawers for odds & ends, not unlike my own filing cabinets, but of more ladylike arrangement & aspect. Of outside gifts the most distinctive was perhaps that which came quite unexpectedly from young Khono-Vhah, our amiable editorial friend of Cambridge, Md., daown awn de Eastern Sho'. For lo! when I had removed numberless layers of corrugated paper & excelsior, what should I find before me but the yellowed & crumbling fragments of *a long-interred human skull!* Verily, a fitting gift from a youthful ghoul to one of the hoary elders of the necropolitan clan! This sightlessly staring monument of mortality came from an Indian mound not far from the sender's home—a place distinguished by many archaeological exploits on the part of the enterprising editor & his young friends. Its condition is such as to make its reassembling a somewhat ticklish task—so that I may reserve it for the ministrations of some expert mender like Ar-E'ch-Bei upon the occasion of a future visit. Viewing this shattered yield of the ossuary, the reflective fancy strives to evoke the image of him to whom it once belonged. Was it some feathered chieftain who in his day oft ululated in triumph as he counted the tufted scalps sliced from coppery or colonist foes? Or some crafty shaman who with mask & drum called forth from the Great Abyss those shadowy Things which were better left uncalled? This we may never know—unless perchance some incantation droned out of the Necronomicon will have power to draw strange emanations from the lifeless & centuried clay, & raise up amidst the cobwebs of my ancient study a shimmering mist not without power to speak. In such a case, the revelation might be such that no man hearing it could any longer live save as one of those hapless entities 'who laugh, but smile no more'![7]

Speaking of bizarre & distinctive gifts—I surely envy you the hellish entity received from Klarkash-Ton! From your description, I judge that it is *not* one of those which went the rounds last summer—& it certainly sounds like one of C A S's typical intruders from Outside. I suppose the artist has told you of the coming exhibition of his work in Sacramento, & of his experiments in *cast*-making. I surely wish his products could attain a remunerative vogue—as indeed they well might if the winds of caprice happened to blow the right way. A genuine artist of rare quality is Klarkash-Ton—here is a tribute which sprang to my pen a couple of weeks ago as I considered some of his macabre accomplishments:

> *To Klarkash-Ton, Lord of Averoigne*
> A time-black tower against dim banks of cloud;
> Around its base the pathless, pressing wood.
> Shadow & silence, moss & mould, enshroud
> Grey, age-fell'd slabs that once as cromlechs stood.
> No fall of foot, no song of bird awakes
> The lethal aisles of sempiternal night,
> Tho' oft with stir of wings the dense air shakes,
> As in the tower there glows a pallid light.
>
> For here, apart, dwells one whose hands have wrought
> Strange eidola that chill the world with fear;
> Whose graven runes in tones of dread have taught
> What things beyond the star-gulfs lurk & leer.
> Dark Lord of Averoigne—whose windows stare
> On pits of dream no other gaze could bear!

———————

Your Mojave–Salton–Ensenada trip must surely have formed a most enviable phenomenon, & I hope to hear echoes of it in later communications. I note the remarks on Pierce Arrows & their alluring possibilities, but trust you won't supersede Mighty Hu'd-Su'un until it becomes really advisable to do so.

Thanks for the Yule-Card—whose pensive reflections anent the Conquering Lion I can poignantly appreciate! By the way—Ar-E'ch-Bei has just sent me a fascinating miniature statuette of a sleeping Kappa Alpha Tau member—coal-black, & evidently his own sculptural handiwork. It will win a place of honour on the display shelves of my museum. Other tributes of the season featured the K.A.T. motif—including the calendar above my desk, which depicts 3 black junior members of the order.

Later

Your bulletin of Dec. 30–31 is now at hand, & I mourn the injuries which have beset Mighty Hu'd-su'un! Surely a grievous & exasperating tragedy—redeemed only by the facts that the noble beast is not vitally nor mortally wounded, & that the financial burthen of restoration is very obviously not yours. Or perhaps a third redeeming feature lies in the new appreciation of your steed which you have gained from your current experience with the uncertain Oldsmobile! Well—I trust that surgery & convalescence may be speedy, & that you will soon have the roaring monster restored to the stables of many-pillar'd Irem & ready to bear you to as distant points as fortune permits you to visit!

Glad to hear recent news of Potli-Khah—whose recent affectionate nickname curiously resembles that of the matriarch across the garden (Spotty = "good ol' 'Patty-Kitty'" &c. &c.), albeit through a vastly differently etymology. I hope in course of time to behold a snapshot of your discriminating ornithologist (no taste for gophers yet?)—perhaps one which I can retain to add to a gallery already containing Mighty Nimrod & the Conquering Lion.

Felicitations on the Mt. Hamilton trip. I assume that the Mojave trip has been postponed to a more favourable time. Hope nothing will interfere with that '38 jaunt to the Atlantic Coast—an event which will be welcomed equally by the assembled Field-Marshals up the Hu'd-Su'un & by the lone elder of the Ancient Hill.

Meanwhile I learn with interest of your local Sinological researches, & wish that I might investigate some of these Celestial strongholds—in a visual & aural even if not dietary way. Just now, though, I could use a bit of *ng-ka-pay* if its medical reputation be justified, since my lower extremities are very much swollen—so much so that I have to wear an old stretched shoe on the left one. That is a frequent happening with me in winter, & occurs whenever I get exposed for any length of time to temperatures under 20° or thereabouts. Once I get it on me, nothing but a long spell of hot weather (*not* house heat, oddly enough!) seems able to work it out of my system. The swelling goes up & down, but I never get wholly rid of it till late spring. This is the most emphatic case of it that I've had since 1930. I don't know what the physiology of the damn thing is—probably quasi-dropsical & based on the bad effect of cold on my cardiac action. Just now my general misery is aggravated by a slight touch of the prevailing grippe. Well—*ng ka pay* might or might not cure the trouble; but after a complete round of the medicines you mention—*mui kwai lu, sam* (not stretched) *shu*, & all the rest[8]—I am sure I would be quite oblivious to all mortal ills . . . until deprived of the strange cargo by the instant emetic called seaweed soup! One or two things on the list sound not so bad—minced pork & beef & onions, &c.—& I fancy I could make friends with soy beans . . . . especially since the small type on the label of my favourite (Derby) sandwich spread informs me that in that palatable concoction the devilled ham is pieced out with some kind of soy bean paste. I am told that few products of the earth are as wholesome & nutritious as the soy bean.

Hope your Yule & New Year guests brought festivity enough to atone for their adverse effect on your production programme. Congratulations on the orders & accomplishments alike, & let us trust that returns will pick up as the '37 season advances.

Heard a damned interesting lecture on Peruvian antiquities last Sunday by the curator of the local art museum, who is just back from an expedition to that region. Lantern-slides & specimens of pottery, mummy-wrappings,

&c. added to its concrete interest. I never before realised how architecturally advanced the pre-Inca peoples of the coast were. Their ruins display an art comparable to that of the Mayas, though the perishable adobe medium has caused all exposed ones to deteriorate rapidly. Nowadays when a ruin is unearthed it is quickly provided with a wooden canopy or shelter to prevent weathering. It seems that two coastal cultures—Nazca & Chimu—had successively appeared, & that the mountain or Tiahuanaco culture had passed through two phases, before the warlike Inca or Quichua race conquered the region. Most of the typical culture-forms which we recognise as Peruvian—including the social system—are basically the product of these earlier races. ¶ Just recd. second S F C. The kids surely are keeping up the standard! ¶ Peace & prayer 𝔖𝔯𝔩𝔞𝔱𝔥

P.S. Cook's newspaper venture has exploded, but he has a new position. Present address: 1305 Missouri Ave., E. St. Louis, Ill.

P.P.S. That brandy-snifter is surely a curious & esoteric device—& you seem to have done it full justice in your conscientious ritual!

Notes

1. Talbot Mundy (1879–1940), American writer of historical and adventure fiction. Harold Lamb (1892–1962), American novelist and short story writer who published many stories in *Adventure* and went on to write many historical novels.
2. Thomas Robert Henry (1893–1968) covered science for the *Washington Star* and was a charter member of the National Association of Science Writers, founded in 1934.
3. Earl Peirce, Jr. (1917–1983), writer of weird fiction and friend of Robert Bloch.
4. Bruce Bryan (1906–2004) published a few stories in *WT* and *Oriental Stories*. He collaborated with Earl Peirce, Jr., on "The White Rat" (*WT*, September 1938).
5. "The Sage of College Street."
6. A cat belonging to Edith Miniter. HPL wrote elegiac lines on him in "Veteropinguis Redivivus" (poems 6 and 8).
7. Edgar Allan Poe, "The Haunted Palace," l. 48.
8. EHP to HPL, 30 December 1936 (TLS, JHL): "*ng ka pay*, a blasting and deadly orange hued drink of uncouth flavor; a Chinese patron told me his father, formerly a miner in Alaska, found it a sovreign [*sic*] remedy for swelling of the lower extremities (whether dropsy, scurvy, or what, I know not) but I would prefer most maladies to drinking *ng ka pay*. [. . .] Then I drank a draught of *mui kwai lu*, literally, 'dew of roses'. It tastes like roses and smells like them; it is clear, water white; the rose flavor is faintly mingled with the taste of old fashioned sewing machine oil. But withal, pleasant. Then I quaffed a goblet of *sam shu*, a rice wine vaguely reminiscent of port with bitters added, + a hint of strange & barbarous medicaments. [. . .] I can not recommend *ng ka pay*, *mui kwai lu*, or *sam shu* under any circumstances, particularly not when driving—unless one has a strong stomach and takes but tiny sips."

Letters to Richard F. Searight

[1]   [ALS]

[H. P. Lovecraft
66 College Street
Providence, R.I.]

August 25, 1933

Dear Mr. Searight:—

I was very glad to hear from you, having always remembered your vivid story "The Brain in the Jar", written in collaboration with a Mr. Hammerstrom [*sic*]. It is pleasing to know that you are about to resume writing, & I surely hope you will meet with notable success.

Regarding critical & revisory work—I have been trying to cut down my quota of late in order to get some time for original writing, but might be able to coöperate in your enterprises—especially since your products would not appear to be in need of the most arduous kind of reconstruction. I could tell better after seeing just what your stories need; hence if you will send along a few, I will be more definite about the matter.

My fees in such cases depend wholly upon the amount of work necessary, as reckoned in terms of time & labour. I have separate scales of prices for light revision, extensive revision, & actual reconstruction or "ghost-writing". I usually ask part in advance & the balance on delivery. What I cannot undertake—except in the very rarest cases—is *speculative* collaboration; that is, work done for a share of the proceeds in case of acceptance, & without a flat "win-or-lose" fee. My reason for this reluctance is that such an arrangement almost always results in loss rather than gain for the reviser—even when the story is accepted. Revision is really not only as hard as original writing, but (for me, at least) actually *harder*. It takes just as much (or more) of my time & energy to give a tale a thorough re-writing as to create one of my own—hence it would be absurd for me to do this, with only part of the proceeds as my greatest possible reward, when I could just as easily compose an original tale & have an equal chance of *all* the proceeds. My only object in accepting revision is to eliminate the element of chance—to accept lesser returns *because they are certain* instead of contingent upon acceptance. The sole exception to this rule is when a tale contains some absolutely sure-fire idea which makes sale almost certain—more nearly certain than with a thing of my own—but it is seldom that one finds an idea of which this can conclusively be said. Of course, even in those rare cases the speculative element is not absent, so that I have to ask a greater share of the proceeds than any flat fee, on a non-speculative basis, would amount to.

As I have said, I would be very interested to see some of your recent weird work—for "The Brain in the Jar" impressed me most favourably. Anything you send will be appreciatively read & carefully returned, whether or not any revisory arrangement proves feasible. Bizarre writing has always interested me vastly, & I am more than professionally eager to help the cause along whenever I can.

With best wishes, & trusting to see some of your work,

  I am

    Yrs most sincerely,

    H P Lovecraft

[2] [ALS]

      66 College St.,

       Providence, R.I.,

        Aug. 31, 1933

Dear Mr. Searight:—

    Your MSS. reached me this morning—on the verge of a week's vacation in ancient Quebec—& I will try to reply before my temporary flight from the affairs of the world.

I read both your MSS.[1] with much interest, but do not think it would be wise to try to rewrite them—since their occasional shortcomings are matters of subject-matter rather than of technique. In a word, they tend to be more or less echoes of familiar plots & types—requiring the injection of some wholly new, unique, & striking conception in order to stand out successfully. This is something which only the author can well remedy. You are aware, of course, of the enormous familiarity of the two ideas in question—the beneficent warning ghost & the malignant attacks of extra-terrestrial hordes. It is true that some of the established writers—like Quinn, Hamilton, Ward,[2] &c.—do manage to 'get away with' a vast amount of plot-repetition; but this seems largely owing to their reputations with the readers—aided, perhaps, by a certain smoothness of technique which lends a transient vividness even if the material is deplorably hackneyed. But in most cases something fresher is demanded—& even these old standbys may not be able to repeat their conventionalities indefinitely. Many readers are beginning to revolt against the endless, quasi-hectographic self-echoings of "Single-Plot Hamilton". If you will send me your "Cosmic Horror" I shall be very glad to read & comment on it—I don't see the science fiction magazines regularly. I must warn you, however, that "scientifiction" is not my best field, & that my criticisms touching it would not be nearly as acute as those of a real specialist. For a truly searching & intelligent analysis of a science fiction tale I would recommend that you write *Clark Ashton Smith, Box 385, Auburn, California*—whose work is doubtless well known to you. He would probably be willing to take on a certain amount of revision in that line if you desired the services of an expert. Now about these MSS.—which I return herewith—"The Formula" is hampered exceedingly by its usual & conventional theme. The beneficent warning ghost is such a stock fixture that only the most unusual kind of auxiliary plot & setting can make it usable today—& in this case I fear the needed uniqueness is absent. Secret formulae, laboratory operations, quests for atomic energy, &c. are appallingly overworked nowadays, & are hardly enough to keep even the best-intentioned spectre afloat. The modern writer must be constantly alert for totally new character types, new incidents, new settings, new situations, *new motives*, unforeseen consequences, & anything which can help him to escape from the hackneyed patterns. It takes a very fresh & distinctive element (like that of your "Brain in the Jar") to seize upon the jaded imagination of the contemporary public. Another thing—it is well to strive for greater vividness in language & phraseology. Your prose tends at times toward a kind of heaviness—with a good many 'rubber stamp' phrases like "lump rose in throat", "scientists' paradise", "announce to the world", "infectious grin", "devil's tattoo", &c. &c. Also—at the outset of "The Formula" the characters converse in too stilted language. Conversation ought to be absolutely natural & realistic—though very few 'pulp' writers seem to have learned this fact. However—in the present case something still more subtle is involved. The prose lacks *weirdness of atmosphere* as determined by vocabulary, rhythm, tone-colour, & sundry devices of syntax & rhetoric. It is too journalistically matter-of-fact—too brisk, normal, & cheerful. There is no tension of mood—no vague, gathering clouds of menace. On the whole I would say that you model too much after the colourless, thin-blooded material in the popular magazines—which is basically a mistake. Fully 9/10 of all this magazine truck is sheer crap—hopelessly dead, synthetic, mechanical tripe. The models for a weird writer to study day & night are Poe, Dunsany, ("Dreamer's Tales", "Sword of Welleran", "Book of Wonder") Algernon Blackwood, ("Incredible Adventures", "John Silence", "The Willows", "The Listener", "Julius le Vallon", "The Centaur") Arthur Machen, ("The Three Impostors", "The House of Souls", "The Terror", "The Shining Pyramid") Montague Rhodes James ("Ghost Stories of an Antiquary", "More Ghost Stories", "Thin Ghost", "Warning to the Curious"), Ambrose Bierce, ("In the Midst of Life", "Can Such Things Be?") E. F. Benson ("Visible & Invisible"), & others of the more or less "standard" class.

But to get back to "The Formula" in particular—the beginning is rather too slow for fullest effectiveness. The scene in the attorney's office might be cut out altogether, & even the trip to the laboratory might be boiled down a bit. As nearly as possible, a tale of this kind ought to commence with the beginning of the actual experiment, with antecedent explanations worked adroitly into the first few paragraphs as casual remarks & allusions. Another thing . . . . the conversation after the first ghostly appearance sounds distinctly flat—the talk of changing laboratory, & so on. The spectral phenomenon seems to be received in too matter-of-fact a way. Then again—the ghost, when it finally becomes manifest, is much too conventional. The same old spirals of whitish mist, &c. As for the motivation—there is hardly enough of the *unique & abnormal* to give the tale a first-rate shiver. The search for atomic energy, the wish 'to save the world', &c. are relatively well-worn & expected. If something more had been made of the *kind of harm* done by the release of atomic energy, there might be great possibilities for *original & unusual* development. How about it? What could you imagine as a sufficiently hellish consequence of the conquest of energy? The opening up of another dimension & the submergence of our familiar physical universe by some influence from "outside"? The explosion of all the matter in the immediate space-time continuum? The total or partial suspension of physico-chemical laws, or the disastrous ability of users to effect such a suspension locally or universally? Any of these lines—& many others—would be promising. But at any cost get away from the beaten track!

"Rays of Madness" is a decidedly better story, though I have my doubts about its professional usability unless revised so basically & extensively as to involve a prohibitive cost. It would pay better to start an entirely new story with some more original & striking "slant." As with the other tale, conventionality is the chief fault. It is a typical "cataclysmic" story of the Hamiltonian category. The style also needs close attention—polishing here & there in syntax & phraseology, & the removal of occasional slips like "dove", or *"refractory"* (for *refracting*) telescope. Stock phrases & occasional naive expressions like "learned doctors" need weeding out—especially the melodramatic "but us!" on p. 2. Also—ideas & characters tend to be artificial, mechanical, conventional, & oversimplified. The emotions of the characters are always inadequate in view of the various abnormal & unprecedented situations facing them . . . . & the figures themselves are wooden, cut-&-dried "scientist" types rather than normal & diversified human beings. The whole setting & range of incidents is likewise inclined to be conventional & undistinctive. Another point—is it not a trifle ingenuous to postulate successful automobile-aeroplanes & clear television as soon as six years ahead?

Taking points in order—the very beginning is especially trite & conventional . . . . utterly typical of the popular "cataclysmic" yarn. Look for some *new* angle or mode of approach. Around p. 8 you had better try to account for the presence of a "vibrometer" in an astronomical observatory. What in particular was Mitchell studying? Cosmic radiation? Solar, planetary, stellar, or nebular light or heat? Give at least some convincing-*sounding* hints. As for the telescope business—I think the normal course in trying to locate a new celestial object today would be to expose a photographic plate in the right sort of telescope-camera; but it is just possible that some observers would stick to the old visual method. On p. 9 what is the idea of using an eyepiece while "standing away from beneath the opening"? In a refracting telescope the eyepiece is at the lower end of the tube, so that only the greater circumference of the tube & its clusters of accessories (finder &c.) can intervene betwixt the observer & the slit of open sky at which he is looking. When you say "eyepiece" do you mean the sort of "diagonal eyepiece" in which a prism allows the observer to stand at right angles to the tube? Again. On p. 10, *how* does Mitchell estimate the distance of the newly observed object? Distance calculations involve several complex factors. What is more—how can he tell that the object is "immovable in space" without a long wait to ascertain its relative bearings? And, what is meant by "immovable" . . . . *absolute* fixity (so that it rises & sets, though the driving-clock keeps it constantly in the field), or *relative* fixity, so that it follows the earth's rotation & hangs over the same terrestrial spot (in which case the clock would cause the telescope to move away from it after finding)? How about *size* in relation to distance & visibility? All these points should be carefully thought out.

Another thing at this point in the story—the attitude of the observers shews much naivete. The emotions of normal human beings at sight of anything as incredible as a sign of intelligent extra-terrestrial intrusion would be totally different from the matter-of-fact attitude delineated. As for the invasion itself—I hardly need point out the essential triteness of the general idea of extra-terrestrial attacks & invasions. It never seems to occur to "interplanetary" writers that expeditions from "outside" might have objects other than capture or warfare.[3] You do not suggest enough about the invaders to make them convincing. Who are they? How did they learn about the earth & mankind? Why are they picking on us? How do they manage to communicate in terrestrial languages? What is the principle behind the operation of their "space ship"? Another thing—you have the language of these invaders unnecessarily formal & theatrically archaic. That is a dying tradition of popular fiction—why follow it?

On page 15 you have the transition from the continuous opening line of action to the condensed & speeded-up action of the Washington trip too abrupt. Such a radical change of perspective & tempo should be marked by a distinct pause or break—a rhetorical lull involving a sub-conclusion & new beginning. Transitions of this sort are among the greatest of problems for beginners—novices always have trouble with them. The convention of scientific men sounds a bit naive in spots. Agreement as to trouble seems to be reached too quickly in view of the complexity of the problem. It would be better to have a longer debate—though not transcribed in detail.

On page 26 it is too much of a *coincidence* to have the invaders' ship descend in the neighbourhood of the one who first analysed the rays. Such a coincidence sounds artificial & unconvincing. On p. 28 it is naive to be astonished at the *bodies* of the outsiders—as if implying that the human form is a norm of physical development. All bodies are accidental products of particular sorts of environment, so that the most highly evolved beings in the universe may be utterly dissimilar in every way to the upright-walking primate mammals of the animal kingdom who happen to embody the highest degree of evolution under the special conditions of *this* planet.

But on the other hand, you represent the outer beings as paradoxically stupid & barbaric in proportion to their technological attainment. True, you realise & remark this—but the circumstance remains unconvincing for all that. It is basically improbable that a race capable of solving the most intricate secrets of nature should remain so undeveloped in other ways. Not only do you represent them as *savage,* but you give them an actual *stupidity* (as evinced in their attack on the aeroplane) which conflicts with their ability to navigate space & learn about the earth without landing on it. Another thing—you make them (despite some gravity references) too much at ease under the utterly novel conditions of a strange planet. Our atmosphere does not seem to bother them a bit! Your ending is pretty dramatic—good stuff. But more ought to have been told about the invaders. Incidentally—I think Wells's "War of the Worlds" remains the best of all "outside invasion" stories to date.

Now I hope sincerely that nothing I have said will sound at all discouraging! I have assumed that you are looking for searching criticism—a ruthless probing into all possible flaws, as best I can detect them, for the purpose of getting hints for future action—hence I have tried to give just that. Actually, I can assure you that your tales are quite as good as the bulk of things published in popular magazines—the structure & writing being generally of a thoroughly professional grade. There is nothing of the tyro's faltering in your work—all it needs is a certain amount of care, polishing, & more unusual subject-matter & development. As you take these precautions—either independently or in collaboration—there seems to me to be little doubt of your success in the professional field.

I shall be glad to see other MSS. of yours. As for my revision rates—I'll copy off a table for your benefit, though in specific cases (especially with weird work) I might undercut these as circumstances dictate. The "reading fee" table can be ignored under all ordinary conditions. I like to help on the cause of the weird tale whenever I can—so that this letter & letters like it can be regarded as wholly non-professional matters involving no financial obligations.

You will find Smith's brochure highly interesting—the tales representing the highest level of his fictional art.[4] Possibly you know that he is a poet of some reputation—largely in the macabre field[5]—besides being one of the most original pictorial artists alive. His coloured drawings of "nameless Things" & morbid non-terrestrial vegetation are as close to sheer, living nightmare as anything I've yet seen. He is also a notable French scholar, & has done a translation of Baudelaire which to my mind surpasses any of the published ones.[6] He—together with Long, the late Dr. Whitehead, & the earlier (before he "went commercial") E. Hoffmann Price—forms one of the few 'pulp' fantaisistes whose work is really worth following as a model. Of course, though, a great deal of his casual "scientifiction" caters to popular demands & is quite uncharacteristic of his main line of endeavour.

The revival of *Astounding*[7] promises to be a great thing for weird writers—though of course its policy in practice may not be quite as ideal as it now sounds from the lips of its optimistic associate editor. I shall try to secure an entry as soon as I have anything fit to send—I am trying to get time now for some new tales; though I won't preserve or exhibit anything below a certain level, & I don't always hit that level when I try. Is this *Dime Mystery* the thing edited by Rogers Terrill, 205 E. 42nd St N Y C? I've never sent anything to it. And have you heard of a weird magazine published by the Jay Pub. Co., 125 E. 45th St N Y C? *The Fantasy Fan* ought to prove a rather encouraging influence. Since its publisher[8] is also managing editor of *Wonder Stories*, it would probably pay in the end to extend him all possible courtesies—he'd probably remember such in passing upon anything you might send to *Wonder!*

Well—I trust the foregoing analysis of your MSS. may be of at least some trifling help to you in your work. I certainly wish you all good luck—& feel sure that you will be getting steady acceptances before long . . . . though of course all writers must face a certain percentage of rejections. Let me know whenever I can be of service. ¶ And now for old Quebec! My almost sole interest apart from the literary & fantastic fields is antiquarian exploration—my one recreation being trips to ancient & historic places. Quebec & Charleston, S.C. are my favourite towns—the 18th century still lives in such places! ¶ Best wishes—

Yrs most cordially—

H P Lovecraft

[Enclosure]

H. P. Lovecraft—Prose Revision Rates
Reading Only—rough general remarks

1000 words or less _____	0.50
1000–2000 _____	0.65
2000–4000 _____	1.00
4000–5000 _____	1.25

20¢ for each 1000 wds over 5000

Criticism Only—analytical estimate in detail without revision

1000 words or less _____	1.50
1000–2000 _____	2.00
2000–4000 _____	3.00
4000–5000 _____	3.75

60¢ for each 1000 wds over 5000

Revision & Copying (Per page of 330 words)
(a) Copying on typewriter—double space, 1 carbon. No revision except
spelling, punctuation, & grammar _____ 0.25
(b) Light revision, no copying (prose improved locally—no new ideas)__ 0.25
(c) Light revision typed, double-space with 1 carbon _____ 0.50
(d) Extensive revision, no copying (thorough improvement, including struc-
tural change, transposition, addition, or excision—possible introduction
of new ideas or plot elements. Requires new text or separate MS.) In
rough draught longhand _____ 0.75
(e) Extensive revision as above, typed, double space, 1 carbon_____ 1.00
(f) Rewriting from old MS., synopsis, plot-notes, idea-germ, or mere suggestion—i.e., "ghost-writing". Text in full by reviser—both language & development. Rough draught longhand _____ 2.25
(g) Rewriting as above, typed, double space, 1 carbon _____ 2.50

Special flat rates quoted for special jobs, depending on estimated consumption of time & energy.

Notes

1. "The Formula" and "Rays of Madness," both unpublished.

2. Seabury Quinn (1889–1969), Edmond Hamilton (1904–1977), and Harold Ward (1879–1950).

3. See "Some Notes on Interplanetary Fiction" (July 1934) concerning realism in science fiction.

4. *The Double Shadow and Other Fantasies.* RFS's copy, requested in a letter dated 6 September 1933, is inscribed by CAS and dated 12 September 1933.

5. CAS was the author of *The Star-Treader and Other Poems* (1912), *Odes and Sonnets*
(1918), *Ebony and Crystal: Poems in Verse and Prose* (1922), and *Sandalwood* (1925).

6. CAS translated nearly the entirety of Baudelaire's *Les Fleurs du mal* (sometimes only
in prose), but few of his translations appeared in print; most of those were published
in his column in the *Auburn Journal* and in *Sandalwood*. Now gathered in CAS's *The
Complete Poetry and Translations, Volume 3: The Flowers of Evil and Others* (New York:
Hippocampus Press, 2007).

7. *Astounding Stories,* under the editorship of Harry Bates, ceased publication with the
March 1933 issue when the Clayton magazine chain went out of business. It resumed
with the October 1933 issue under the editorship first of Desmond Hall, then F. Orlin Tremaine, and was owned by Street & Smith.

8. Charles D. Hornig.

[3]   [ALS]

66 College St.,
Providence, R.I.,
Sept. 10, 1933.

Dear Mr. Searight:—

I am very glad to hear that you found my critical remarks acceptable & helpful, & hope that they may be able to furnish one or two suggestions of use in future compositions. Thanks for the postage—though there was really no need of enclosing it. I shall be very glad to see the new tale you mention, & trust that you may round it out to your own satisfaction. In commenting on it I shall strive to be as impersonally ruthless as I was before.

Yes—I believe the Terrill magazine is called *Dime Mystery*, though I have never seen a copy. I don't know just what sort of a market it would be for my stuff. The other company I mentioned (on a tip coming from August W. Derleth) is the *JAY* Pub. Co. (pardon the wretched script which conveyed a different impression!) It is, if Derleth reports aright, inclined to be less reliable than the Terrill outfit—with slow & lesser pay, though perhaps not as bad as Gernsback. I don't know what the name of the magazine will be—but I think A.W.D. said that it wishes *ghost* material primarily. I'll ask him further particulars.[1]

The name of the *Fantasy Fan* editor recently made Man. Ed. of *Wonder* is *Charles D. HORNIG*. He says that Gernsback pays him his salary, even though the contributors suffer—& adds that the company is really in difficulty. W.S. owes Clark Ashton Smith almost $900.00—indeed, he is considering legal steps for the recovery of what is due him. Courtesies shown Hornig in his capacity as F.F. publisher would surely be likely to influence him favourably as W.S. editor. I don't know, however, just how much influence he has with the Gernsback treasury department. The editorial & financial sides of a magazine are often kept utterly separate—as with W.T., where all cheques come from somebody named Sprenger[2] rather than from Wright.

Science fiction, as you suggest, is hardly a fruitful field unless one has a particular knack for it—as I have not. So much technical care is demanded, that one has virtually to pursue a special education in order to qualify—especially for *Amazing*. Most of the magazine output in this field is appallingly mediocre—indeed, Verne & Wells really worked the vein out, leaving little save colourless imitation for others. Almost all science-fiction yarns are absurdly motivated, & with ludicrously inadequate emotional values.

Although I have a keen interest in the sciences—& no belief at all in the supernatural—my one natural medium is the tale of utter weirdness & cosmic horror. Poe, Dunsany, Blackwood, Machen, & James are my natural congeners. I doubt if I could produce any even half-effective work in any other field. This is a bad thing financially—for it is the versatile scribbler who commands the best markets. E. Hoffmann Price, for example, is now doing more with detective stuff than with his beloved Orientales. Glad you liked "The Dreams in the Witch House." Of late I am becoming dissatisfied with my attempts, & am striving to find ways to improve them.

My recent trip was enjoyable in the extreme. Quebec's charm is undying— & I took side-trips on both outbound & inbound voyages. On the inbound run I revisited my favourite towns of Salem & Marblehead—the "Arkham" & "Kingsport" of my tales—& basked in their atmosphere of massed & living antiquity. Enclosed are some cards illustrating my wanderings.

With every good wish, & trusting to see your new tale when it is done, I remain

Yrs most cordially & sincerely,

H P Lovecraft

[Postcard enclosure:[3]]
This is the sort of place described in my "Dreams in the Witch House". In 1680 or 1690 all the New England coast towns were built up with architecture like this—the classic styles usually associated with the colonial period being subsequent to 1700. Many of these houses were altered to later styles after 1700, but quite a few survived in original form till 1800 & later. They are now very rare. Salem has more remaining specimens than any other place. Providence (whose oldest house is of 1735) has none at all. Boston has *one*.

Salem is the "Arkham" of my tales—with certain adaptations.

Notes

1. See HPL to August Derleth, September 1933: "The Terrill prospect sounds moderately good—but the adjective 'ghost' connected with the Jay arouses thoughts of conventional limitations" (*ES* 602).

2. William R. Sprenger (1902–1972), secretary-treasurer of *WT* (see photograph in *SL* 5.294f.).

3. [Picture side:] House of Seven Gables, built 169460 [changed by HPL], Salem, Mass. [Message side:]

HOUSE OF SEVEN GABLES.
BUILT 169460, SALEM, MASS.

This house is the object of greatest interest in Salem connected with Hawthorne's name and one of which inquiries are most frequently made. Built about 169460.

The house actually was built in 1668. The other enclosures have not been found.

[4]   [ALS]

66 College St.,
Providence, R.I.,
Septr. 25, 1933

Dear Mr. Searight:—

I have read "The Haunted Relay"[1] with much interest, & certainly think it has the touch of originality which fiction needs. The atmosphere of suspense & uncertainty is very well sustained, & the actual growth of madness is wholly a surprise despite the ample preparation. The explanation seems wholly adequate—indeed, the layman would hardly see any difficulty of the phenomenon in these days of radio, & of tales involving the action of sundry accidentally situated devices as involuntary radio receivers. The style is good, too. Delineating the thoughts of the central figure in his own kind of language is an admirable device—one I try to follow myself on many occasions. Whenever I indicate what a character is thinking I always adopt a manner & diction more or less suited to him—a procedure which once drew a bewildered protest from the puristically inclined Wright, who thought I was lapsing into illiteracy when I used the rural "healthy" instead of the academic "healthful" in describing the reflections of a Vermont rustic.[2] No—I don't think any formal separation of such reflective passages from the bulk of the text is desirable. Let the one merge into the other. It seems to me that this tale ought to have a good chance of marketability—not only in the weird field but in that of "scientifiction". After all, it has a scientific explanation & does not involve the supernatural. But don't clutter it up with technical nomenclature. As for the text—I can't think of any especial change to make. I've rectified one or two points of dubious orthography, & straightened out a bit of indifferent syntax—getting rid of the definitely awkward if not downright erroneous combination "different *than*". The best thing to follow "different" is *from*, although *to* is theoretically admissible.

As for transitions between differently timed or placed passages in a story— what I meant was *in essence* equivalent to the device termed "curtain", although it need not always be as sharp or well-defined. There are many different ways—of varying subtlety—to indicate a pause in the flow of narration, & it can often be done without any actual juggling of incidents or any interpolation of descriptions. Mere choice of words as related to moods is often sufficient. Whatever, by associative force, implies a pause or conclusion, is effective in ending the older flow of action; & the adoption of a different *mood*—a mood of brisk beginning not necessarily including any actual preamble—is often sufficient to establish the fresh line of action in a fluent & natural way. To do this unostentatiously undoubtedly requires considerable practice & familiarity with the best models, but in the end it tends to become second nature. Essentially, however, the general idea is certainly that of the "curtain" you mention.

Glad to hear you are brushing up on the weird classics. I'm doing an extensive re-reading of them at present, in order to get reoriented away from the vile pulp-magazine patterns.[3] Blackwood should be read for *substance* rather than style, since [he] tends to lapse regrettably into journalese. Machen, Dunsany, & M. R. James are the ones to study for *style*. Smith's best work, too, is a good model. Almost any tale in "The Double Shadow" is well worth emulating.

Hope the *Dime Mystery* reveals possibilities. By the way, I asked Derleth about the Jay Pub. Co., & he said he knew nothing more than what the writers' magazines have printed—that it is to handle ghost stories primarily. Perhaps it will be a successor to the trashy & unlamented (Macfadden–Hersey) *Ghost Stories*. Derleth says that *Strange Tales* may be reëstablished shortly under new owners. Glad you've subscribed for *The Fantasy Fan*—I'm sending it a copy of my old history of supernatural horror-fiction (revised to date) for use as a serial. By the way—Smith tells me of a new weird & scientifiction magazine (non-paying) about to be established—*Unusual Stories*, edited by one William Crawford of Everett, Pa.[4]

I had a glorious time in Quebec—4 days of hot, sunny weather. The glamour of antiquity was undimmed—old grey citadel, city walls, dizzying cliff, ancient byways, silver belfries, & marvellous vistas of town, river, countryside, & distant mountains. The sky effects—peculiar to northerly latitudes—fascinated me as usual. One sunset there was a distant thunderstorm across the river, with lightning darting from a vast black cloud-funnel to the ground—yet with the flame-golden light bathing everything, & with a pale arc of rainbow over the Isle d'Orleans. On my outbound trip I paused to look up a 1637 house in the Boston suburbs,[5] & inbound I digressed to my favourite Salem & Marblehead—the "Arkham" & "Kingsport" of my tales. I certainly hope you can get around to the boreal country again some summer. I'll enclose some views as a tantalisation—or spur. Best wishes—

  Yrs most cordially
  H P Lovecraft

Notes

1. Unpublished.

2. HPL uses this word or its variant twice in "The Whisperer in Darkness"—"unhealthy" at *CF* 2.472, "healthy" at *CF* 2.511—but in both instances it occurs in the narrative of Albert N. Wilmarth, who is not a native of Vermont. "Healthful" never occurs in the text.

3. This reading resulted in "Weird Story Plots," "A List of Certain Basic Underlying Horrors Effectively Used in Weird Fiction," "List of Primary Ideas Motivating Possible Weird Tales," and "Suggestions for Writing Story" (revised as "Notes on Writing Weird Fiction").

4. An "Advance Issue" of *Unusual Stories* was published in March 1934, followed by

two issues, May–June 1935 and Winter 1935. In an undated letter to RFS (probably early 1934), William L. Crawford accepted "The Haunted Relay" for *Unusual Stories,* but it never appeared there.
5. HPL speaks of "the ancient Deane Winthrop house (1637) in a Boston suburb. This is probably the 2nd oldest house of English origin in the U.S., & is tremendously interesting. There is a secret room in the enormous brick chimney" (HPL to August Derleth, [early September 1933]; *ES* 607).

[5]   [ALS]

66 College St.,

Providence, R.I.,

Octr. 15, 1933

Dear Mr. Searight:—
Sorry to hear that Wright rejected "The Haunted Relay", though rejections from him are so common that I am quite calloused to them. His explanations are not always clear—"overwritten" possibly signify-ing a larger amount of detail & psychological reflection than he likes in con-nexion with the narration of a single simple event. This is really largely a matter of personal taste. Incidentally, I didn't know that madman stories were barred by W.T. That would exclude my old "Rats in the Walls", which Wright professes to like so well! Well—I hope your tale has better luck with *Astound-ing,* whose editor (Desmond Hall) my friends Long & Wandrei have met in person & like very much.

I also have read the *Dime Mystery,* & agree that Cave's tale is the only real-ly effective one in the issue.[1] The rest is just synthetic hokum. Incidentally, the quality of *Astounding* is also a vast disappointment after the expectations aroused by Hall's letters. Your analysis of the policy of *Dime Mystery* interests me exceedingly, & I agree that some of my more gruesome stuff might have a chance there if it were on hand at the present moment. Unfortunately I have nothing immediately ready—but I shall keep the matter carefully in mind, hoping that I may have something before the editor's policy acquires the usu-al conventional arterio-sclerosis. Cave, by the way, lives in Pawtucket, R.I., just north of Providence, though I am not personally acquainted with him.[2]

Glad you found something of interest in "The Festival" after all these years. For one thing, the text is correctly printed this time. The story as a whole disappointed me as I went over it with a ten-year perspective, for I can see some sadly crude & overcoloured patches in it now. The fact is, all my stories are beginning to disgust me . . . . . even the recent specimens, for as I avoid certain old faults I stumble into new ones. Most certainly would I chal-lenge any belief that my stuff forms a model even remotely comparable to Ma-chen, Blackwood, James, or Poe. Mere date & locale mean nothing. A really good story is timeless & placeless. As for a collection of my tales—I'd cer-tainly like to see such a thing published, but nobody seems to want to attempt the project. Four times—by W.T., (1927) by Putnams', (1931) by the Vanguard, (1932) & by Knopf (1933)—I have been approached with requests for MSS. to consider in relation to collected book publication, but in each case the requester has politely backed out after deciding that the venture would not be commercially feasible. Apparently my tales fall into that uncomfortable middle division which is not trashy enough to please the herd, & yet not meritorious enough to gain consideration as literature. It is certain that my style & methods have been much injured through my too great familiarity with magazine trash. Pulp models leave a cheapening & insidious mark on one's utterance, which only conscious & determined effort can shake off.

Regarding rare & antique books—I am no collector or connoisseur at all, although many of my friends are. To me books are valuable primarily for what is in them, & the intangible quality of being a first edition—or any of the other things esteemed by bibliophiles—means nothing to my callous, middle-aged emotions. However, what I most decidedly *am* is a confirmed antiquarian of general nature, with a curious sense of personal membership in the 18th century—hence I do have a tremendous affection for old books (irrespective of rarity or bibliophilic esteem) along with old houses, old furniture, old customs & literary styles, & everything else old. Of the 2000-odd volumes on my shelves, about 200 are probably over a century old & perhaps 100 anterior to 1800—with the "long ſ", connected ᬭ, &c. My oldest book is a translation of Ovid's Heroides (in black letter) printed in 1567. I also have an Italian geography printed in 1605,[3] a curious astronomical work (Wittie's Ouranoscopia & Gout-Raptures) printed in 1681, & a pamphlet copy of Dryden's "Wild Gallant" printed in 1694. These are all the items I can think of antedating the 18th century—though of that period I have a good representation beginning with Cotton Mather's "Magnalia Christi Americana", printed in 1702. This Magnalia is the one *really* valuable book in my possession—an hereditary copy, as most of my really old books are. It must be remarked that age alone does not make a book valuable. Dozens of 18th century books with the long ſ can be picked up on the stands for a nickel, & I hardly know just what combination of qualities it is that gives "bibliophilic items" their varying degrees of arbitrary valuation. Concerning your three bibles[4]—I have no idea what the cash value of any would be, though you might ascertain from a friend of mine (Samuel Loveman, 17 Middagh St., Brooklyn, N.Y.) who is a rare book expert & cataloguer connected with the firm of Dauber & Pine in N.Y. The oldest bible I have is one printed in Edinburgh in 1795. As for judging age from text—a text like this,[5] with the long ſ used in conjunction with modern capitalisation and with proper names in ordinary Roman type, implies ſomething from about 1780 to 1800. If the capitaliſation be modern, but the proper names in *Italick* letters, a date (roughly) betwixt 1760 and 1780 is ſuggeſted. If, on the other Hand, the Nouns be all given Capitals in this Faſhion, whilſt the capital U is of the modern Sort, the Text probably dates from about 1710 to 1760. A capital U like this, with a lower right-hand Prong as in the lower-cafe U, indicates a date prior to 1710. This pre-1710 Type alfo tends to be taller and narrower than later Fonts. As for semi-old books— after 1800—ꜩ continued to be connected up to about 1810. Around 1816 or 1817 a typical heavy type-face appears, lasting through the 1830's. It is hard to date anything after 1840.

Your dead man's vengeance story sounds good to me.[6] While the basic idea of a spectrally harmful bequest is not new, I fancy you could give such a tale a powerfully original cast. It would be like the genii sealed in jars in the Arabian Nights. Hope the Asiatic menace story goes over well.[7] There's a new magazine (*Unusual Stories*, pub. by William Crawford, Everett, Pa.) about to appear, which seems very hospitable to experimental work. No pay as yet, but an accepted contribution brings a *10-year subscription*. In view of the mortality amongst such periodicals, the editor would seem to be an optimist!

¶ With abundant thanks for your tip anent *Dime Mystery*—
Yrs most cordially & sincerely, H P Lovecraft

P.S. Speaking of books & antiquities—here is my bookplate, drawn for me by a young artist friend whose stories you may recall in W.T.—Wilfred B. Talman. It represents a typical Georgian or Colonial doorway of the type common from 1730 to 1820—of which Providence has many examples. I now have the good fortune to live behind one of these doorways, in a house built about 1800. Visiting old towns & examining their colonial architecture is virtually my sole recreation. New England is of course full of such.

Notes

1. Hugh B. Cave, "The Graveless Dead" (*Dime Mystery*, October 1933).
2. HPL did not meet Cave (1910–2004), but he had exchanged a few letters with him on the subject of writing pulp fiction. See RFS 16.
3. Unidentified.
4. Probably an S. S. Teacher edition of 1889 or earlier and German and Latin editions of the 19th century. Only the first survives.
5. Here HPL begins to print the text in letters resembling the type styles he is describing.
6. Probably "The Sealed Casket."
7. "Lord of the Living Dead," of which a synopsis and several story starts survive.

[6]   [ALS]
66 College St.,
Providence, R.I.,
Jany. 15, 1934

Nt dear Mr. Searight:—
Yours of New-Year's arrived during my absence on a

visit to Frank Belknap Long, Jr. (whose tales you doubtless know) in New York, & my aunt—not recognising it as 1st class mail because of the large envelope—did not forward it. Hence my seemingly inexcusable delay. I'm glad you found the random observations on book dates interesting. Books really shew almost as many earmarks of their period as architecture, furniture, & costume.

I have read your new story[1] with the keenest & most genuine pleasure, & believe it is unqualifiedly the best thing you have done so far. It hangs together perfectly, & the ending is vivid & unexpected—yet well-motivated & inevitable in view of the antecedent elements. I don't think the possible objections you raise are at all grave. The explanatory reflection at the start seems to me thoroughly justified by the type & setting of the whole tale—& is well linked to the main action by the frequent allusions to the present scene. As for the adequacy of the concrete horror in embodying the "daemon Avaloth"—I really don't think any valid objection could be made. This material manifestation might easily be only one of an infinite number which Avaloth could make if It chose. Nor do I think the climax is overcoloured. On the other hand I think it is admirably handled—with just the right atmosphere, & with the crowning terror coming in a potently *gradual* way. The ending, too, is splendid. Post-climactic explanations are whittled down to a minimum, & the final touch is unforeseen & striking. I like the fragment from the Eltdown Shards, too.[2] These cryptic & terrible records of man's earliest struggles with the survivors of the pre-human world—related as they are to the abhorred paragraphs of the Book of Eibon & the later (& purely human) sections of the half-deciphered Pnakotic Manuscripts—have always fascinated me . . . . especially in view of those tantalising & subtly disquieting references in the dreaded *Necronomicon* of the mad Arab Abdul Alhazred, & the more obscure (& often disputed) single allusion in the monstrous *Unaussprechlichen Kulten* of the ill-fated Friedrich-Wilhelm von Junzt.[3] No—I don't think the "quotation" is too much of a give-away of the story's plot—particularly in a popular magazine. Indeed, the complaint of cheap editors is always that tales are too subtle & obscure—never that they are too obvious. The only change I have made in the quotation is the substitution of a dissyllable for a trisyllable in one place in the interest of good prose rhythm. As you know, these pseudo-archaic passages depend very largely on their rhythm for effectiveness. Well—as I've just said, this story appeals to me tremendously; & I think Wright will be an absolute ass if he doesn't take it. However, one never can tell about that bird! He is capricious, & often reverses his own earlier judgments . . . for example, he turned down a collaborated tale of mine & Price's last September, & then asked to see it again & accepted it a couple of months later.[4]

As to the status of matter sold to periodicals—if you sell (as is always advisable) "First North American Serial Rights Only" you have full power to sell all over again in any way you can—except that the reprints must give credit to the magazine of first publication. Prices for second & later publication are of course far below that of first publication. You don't have to ask *permission* of the first editor for reprinting—the rights are your own—but you have to give his magazine *credit*. The "first serial rights" mean merely the right to print *for the first time*. As to the reprinting of tales of which additional rights have been sold—I have found that most editors are very generous & reasonable about waiving their technical hold—especially if the proposed reprinting is in a book or something equally dissimilar to the original magazine in province. There are many stages in the sale of rights. Some periodicals insist on buying all *magazine* rights—which stops you from reprinting in magazines, but leaves you free to reprint in book form. And a few magazines seek to buy *all* rights of any kind whatsoever—thus wholly severing your commercial connexion with the story. They often arrange for reprints—but they get whatever proceeds there are. Never sell more than first N.A. serial rights unless an editor insists on it. It is now customary to put the words "First N.A. Serial Rights Only" in the upper right-hand corner of MSS. As for the semi-amateur sheets of *Fantasy Fan* calibre—I don't think that any legal distinction can be established between them & regular magazines. If anything is printed in one of them, it has had technical first publication. However—if you sell only first rights you'll have no trouble about reprinting. Sometimes re-sales mount up substantially . . . . . my most favourable case being "The Music of Erich Zann", which has had the following stages of publication: (1) W.T. (2) "Creeps by Night" anthology. (3) British reprint of same. (4) London Evening Standard. (5) [prospective] anthology to be published in London.[5]

As for the "important announcement" about my tales—that was where Brother Farnsworth jumped to conclusions too rapidly & gave a rather embarrassing false alarm! Last summer the Knopf firm asked to see some of my yarns with a view to book publication, but finally decided that there wasn't enough of an assured sale to warrant the step. During the course of the deciding they wrote Wright to ask what he could do about promoting a market in case of publication—& he let his imagination get ahead of the facts to the extent of publishing the forecast you saw.[6] Alas! I've been busy deflating the canard ever since it appeared.

The seven-weeks' stay of your MSS. with *Dime Mystery* looks to me like rather a good sign. When a story is rejected by the first bunch of office readers it generally comes back very shortly—for readers are numerous & seldom leave a contribution unread for any length of time. When something is detained over a period of weeks, it usually means that the first readers have thought it good enough to pass on to one of the actual editors for a second & more serious scrutiny. This takes time, for editors don't grow as thickly as readers—& in most magazines a single chief editor has to get a personal look at a tale before it is accepted. Delays of 3 months are not at all uncommon—

but they tend to form a distinctly favourable augury. You certainly have no cause for worry yet.

Glad you have something in the current *Wonder*[7]—& hope you get paid for it some day. As for the *ethics* of submitting further stuff to Gernsback—I certainly don't see anything to balk at. If you want to take a chance, it hurts nobody but yourself . . . . & it doesn't even hurt you if you know the uncertainty in advance. Getting into print at all—even without the expectation of remuneration, as in the F F & kindred things—is a valuable & encouraging thing for the aspirant; & Hugo the Rat at least treats one no worse than the editors who frankly don't pay at all! There is, besides, the amusing sporting chance that one *may* get paid. A woman lawyer in New York—a Miss Webber, whose address I've forgotten but who could be located through Clark Ashton Smith—makes a specialty of collecting bad debts from Gernsback, & actually did extort $35.00 from him on behalf of a revision client of mine.[8] I'd probably try something on the old reprobate just for the fun of it if I had any unsold MSS. of the right length & character!

Your proposed tale of a musician whose strange notes unlock forbidden dimensional gateways sounds extremely good to me. While of course many minor uses of sound in occult evocations have been depicted, I recall very few cases where the cosmic possibilities of tones are given a thorough exploitation by one really versed in music or acoustics. The nearest thing to it in W.T. was a yarn called "Satan's Fiddle"—by George Malcolm-Smith—in the Aug. 1927 issue.[9] This story was woven around a mad 'cellist who had discovered a close approach to that "cosmic chord" or combination of vibrations which, if amplified & repeated, would wreck the entire fabric of creation through the disintegration of the atom. It seems to me that you have the equipment & ability to produce something quite notable in this line, & my advice would be to 'go to it' by all means.

My recent visit was very interesting—bringing me into contact with several weird fictional personalities of whom you must have heard. Besides my host Long & my old friends Wandrei, Talman, &c. I met Wandrei's younger brother Howard, a magnificent weird artist of whom much will be heard in the course of time. Also Desmond Hall, editor of *Astounding Stories*, & T. Everett Harré, who compiled the anthology "Beware After Dark" (1929) containing my "Call of Cthulhu". But most interesting of all, perhaps, was the widely-known weird author *A. Merritt*, whose "Moon-Pool" & other tales you must have read & admired. He is associate editor of Hearst's flamboyant "American Weekly", but his chief interests are all in his original fiction. As you doubtless realise, he has certain absolutely unique powers in the field of atmospheric evocation, although he has allowed the popular magazine tradition to cheapen his handling of plot & character. He is now working on a sequel to "Burn, Witch, Burn"[10] (which I've never read, but a copy of which he has promised to send me)—with a setting laid in the fabulous city of Ys, supposed to have sunk off the cost of Brittany. Merritt is a stout, sandy, grey-eyed chap of about 45 or 50—very genial, intelligent, & well-read, & a fascinating arguer & conversationalist. I have admired him in the most whole-hearted way ever since reading "The Moon Pool" in the old *All-Story Weekly* for June 22, 1918. We had dinner at his club—The Players, which occupies the old home of Edwin Booth on the south side of Gramercy Park.

Yes—"Shambleau" was surely a most unusual tale . . . as was also "The House of the Worm" in the same issue.[11] The current number has a tale by the younger Wandrei—as well as Smith's first self-illustrated contribution.[12] Smith was a weird artist long before he ever tried fiction, & I've been urging W.T. for a decade to give his drawings a chance. This present specimen really doesn't do him justice—but I hope it will be received cordially enough to create a demand for more.

While in N.Y. I met the two youths who edit *Fantasy* (formerly *Science Fiction Digest*)—one of whom (Conrad Ruppert)[13] is also the printer of *The Fantasy Fan*. *Unusual Stories* has encountered obstacles, so that the first number will be delayed until March. I only hope the venture won't disintegrate entirely!

Well—let me congratulate you again on the excellence of your new story, & express the hope that it may achieve advantageous professional placement. You are certainly progressing finely in the fictional art, & I have the highest expectations for the coming musical tale—which I trust I may eventually see either in print or otherwise.

With every good wish for 1934, & thanking you for the attractive Yuletide card, I remain

Yrs most cordially & sincerely,
H. P. Lovecraft

Notes

1. "The Sealed Casket."

2. The fragment, serving as the epigraph to the tale, was omitted from the *WT* appearance. HPL reproduces it in a letter to CAS, [c. June 1935] (*DS* 606).

3. The Book of Eibon was invented by CAS, the Pnakotic Manuscripts and Alhazred's *Necronomicon* by HPL, and von Junzt's *Unaussprechlichen Kulten* by Robert E. Howard. But HPL devised von Junzt's first and middle names; Howard had failed to specify them.

4 HPL and EHP, "Through the Gates of the Silver Key."

5. The last item never appeared, but HPL nevertheless received payment of $32.50 (see HPL to August Derleth, 6 November 1934; *ES* 664).

6. "The Eyrie" for the December 1933 *WT* contained a letter from a fan inquiring about the possibility of collecting HPL's stories in book form, comparing him to Arthur Machen. The forecast to which HPL refers was the following brief note in response to the reader's query: "[We hope to have an important announcement to make

soon about Lovecraft's stories.—THE EDITORS.]" (p. 776).

7. RFS had only the one story, "The Cosmic Horror," in *Wonder Stories* (August 1933).

8. Ione Weber, whom CAS hired because *Wonder Stories* at one point owed him nearly $1000. The revision client is Hazel Heald, whose story "The Man of Stone" (ghost-written by HPL) appeared in *Wonder Stories* for October 1932. See RFS 13.

9. But recall HPL's "The Music of Erich Zann" (1921).

10. A[braham] Merritt (1884–1943), *Burn, Witch, Burn!*, serialized in *Argosy* from 22 October to 26 November 1932. The sequel was *Creep, Shadow!*, serialized in *Argosy* from 8 September to 20 October 1934.

11. C. L. Moore, "Shambleau" (*WT*, November 1933); Mearle Prout, "The House of the Worm" (*WT*, October 1933). See Will Murray, "Mearle Prout and 'The House of the Worm,'" *Crypt of Cthulhu* No. 18 (Yuletide 1983): 29–30, 39.

12. *WT*, January 1934: Howard Wandrei, "In the Triangle"; CAS, "The Weaver in the Vault" (illustrated by himself).

13. The other editor of *Fantasy Magazine* was Julius Schwartz, although others also held editorial positions.

[7]   [ALS]

66 College St.,
Providence, R.I.,
Feby. 3, 1934.

Dear Mr. Searight:—

I am sorry to hear that Wright returned "The Casket"— but that is quite typical of the essential capriciousness of his decisions. It discourages & bewilders one to see a tale like that turned down, & then to behold such unrelieved tripe as the current Dyalhis & Pope maunderings in print![1] But I'm glad one of the poems—even if the lesser one—landed.[2] Commercially, there is no question but that weird writing is a very unprofitable field. You are right regarding the recession of *Astounding* to the "scientific-tion" ranks. At present—*Dime Mystery* being apparently a sponsor of physically gruesome blood-&-thunder junk—good old W.T. would seem to be once more the only really fantastic magazine left in the field. The only reason anyone has for writing weird material is a genuine inward urge toward artistic expression in that direction. As a business, it doesn't pay.

What you say of adventure tales with an Icelandic setting[3] strikes me as eminently worthy of following up. I see no reason why such things should not be acceptable to the pulp magazines if the events & psychology are twisted & held down to the level demanded by their readers. Indeed, I fancy these readers would be glad of a repetition of the familiar "action" cliches against a novel & colourful background. What the herd want is a typical unreeling of certain crude & artificial stimuli which they have been taught to expect—& if an author is sure to include a preponderance of these old gags he is at liberty to place his action almost anywhere he wishes—from Chicago to Arcturus or the atom's inner core! It depends on his skill & temperament how much actual sincerity & literary merit he can manage to smuggle into a pulp tale without alienating the cheap editors & their microcephalic primer-public. Price is quite an expert in striking a compromise betwixt his own taste & the rabble's grotesque cravings—& Robert E. Howard is no slouch at the same game. I can't do it at all. The whole weary business of catering to the childish whines of an ignorant canaille is ineffably repulsive & infuriating to me, & I have found that the only attitude I can take toward popular taste is to ignore it altogether—writing sincerely with no one but myself in mind, having nothing but intrinsic excellence as a goal, & not expecting to sell anything except by accident. I have not even offered my latest story[4] to Wright or anybody else.

There is great possibility in Iceland as a story-background—& this refers to serious work as well as mob-tickling. Iceland has always fascinated me tremendously, so that I have read many volumes of various sorts pertaining to it.[5] Poised betwixt the old world & the new, bleak & sinister in its volcanic topography & sub-auroral setting, the home of a proud, pure race-stock & the lingering-place of ancient language-forms & traditions elsewhere vanished, this remote & mystical isle has much to hold the sensitive imagination. Its mediaeval literature is perhaps the latest-surviving example of that spontaneous singing of high deeds & marvels which lies at the base of Aryan epic poetry. For any born story-teller reasonably well-read regarding the place & period, mediaeval Iceland ought to constitute a rich fount of adventure-fiction. As for the best medium of narration—a pseudo-archaic style always seems to me slightly affected when another language is involved, & yet a racily modern idiom is even more out of place. To my mind the ideal course is to adhere to a style of great apparent plainness & simplicity—choosing the most *universal* words & *basic* constructions, & avoiding everything that is peculiar to any one period or typical of any one language. Robert E. Howard is unfortunate in his occasional use of jarringly modern phrases (mixed with archaic devices!), while Smith undeniably overdoes the archaic at times. In tales of epic atmosphere, it seems as if one's prose ought to be written with a sharp ear for harmony in accent & tone-colour—the most desirable effect being that of a subtle, imperceptible rhythm which rises at high moments to the fluency & poetic pulse of actual song. Wilde, Dunsany, & other titans in the field of prose-poetry are worth a close examination.

Regarding the advantages of amply-proportioned or "leisurely" fiction—they are so obvious . . . . so absolutely essential, indeed, to the adequate reflection of life & its shadings . . . . . that I do not think we can properly call such fiction obsolete. The "action" stuff of the moment simply *does not exist* as serious or permanent expression. It belongs to an underworld of writing in no way connected with literature, & can safely be ignored by the genuine student of the latter subject. You will find that the *real* works of literature of to-day—of which Proust is without dispute the leading example—are fully as ample & slow-moving as anything of the past. The difference is in tone & treatment & perspective. Today we know more about life & human motives than at any previous period, hence can detect elements of falsity, bombast, & irrelevance in much of the literature of the past. We know now how cheap & artificial the element of "plot" is—hence the diffusive, amorphous patterns of Proust & Joyce. As for the low level of popular & bourgeois taste—to begin with, taste of this sort *never was* other than cheap even in the old days. The long-winded tripe of cheap Victorian scribblers like Hall Caine & Mrs. E. D. E. N. Southworth was just as low-grade as the staccato, skeletonic action-junk of the modern herd. But there is no question of the effect of silly modern overspeeding, mechanisation, & cinema-addiction in transforming the plebe-ian-bourgeois demand for rambling romance to a craving for equally tawdry high-speed nursery pap. The only consolation is that people of real taste don't allow themselves to become spoiled. A good index of serious modern taste in the short story is afforded by O'Brien's annual anthologies & by the newly-founded magazine *Story*. There is a good deal of chaos & uncertainty—but it is all outside the domain of the ha'penny "action" yarn.

My recent visit surely was enjoyable. However—correspondence with other writers is really just about as good as personal contact. I very seldom meet any of the group face to face, & there are many—like Smith, Howard, & Derleth—whom I have never seen. I've never met Wright, but fancy he must be rather pleasant. ¶ With best wishes for your new line of endeavour—

Yrs most sincerely—H P Lovecraft

Notes

1. *WT,* February 1934: Nictzin Dyalhis, "The Sapphire Goddess"; William H. Pope, "The Virus of Hell."
2. "The New World."
3. RFS wrote two Icelandic tales centering on the figure of Arnor the Priest, "The Cavern of the Dragon" and "Guardian of the Cairn."
4. "The Thing on the Doorstep" (written 21–24 August 1933).
5. E.g., William Lord Watts (1850–1921), *Snoiland; or, Iceland, Its Jokulls and Fjalls* (London: Longmans, 1875; *LL* 1017).

[8]   [ALS]

66 College St.,
Providence, R.I.,
March 17, 1934.

Dear Mr. Searight:—

Congratulations on the acceptance of "The Casket"! I knew it was a good story, & am glad to hear that Il Duce Farnsworth has seen the light at last! I'm sorry he has seen fit to demand changes—but mangled publication is better than no publication when one is starting out. I liked that extract from the Eltdown Shards . . . . . some day I'm going to mention those hellish & mysterious fragments (which anticipate very ominously many of the Necronomicon's hinted horrors) in a tale of my own![1]

Surely there's no hurry about tackling the Icelandic series. As to the matter of varied writing—some can do it & some can't. I can't. Although I am interested in dozens of things besides the weird, the latter is undeniably the only thing which I have any impelling urge to capture & reproduce in fiction—& the only thing for which I have any natural aptitude. But each different person has to find out for himself whether he can work in many media or whether he is confined to one. To make writing pay—even enough to support one frugally—is virtually impossible unless one has a particular aptitude in some popularly acceptable direction. The latest person to learn this is E. Hoffmann Price, who recently took stock of his diminishing sales & very sensibly sought another source of income—accepting a partnership in a garage business in Pawhuska, Okla. From now on—now that he doesn't have to grind out an incessant stream of tailored-to-order pap to suit a dozen yokel-catering editors—we'll probably see better work from Price . . . . . a return to the mood of "The Stranger from Kurdistan" & "The Dreamer of Atlanaat." Of course Price was lucky to be able to command a lucrative post at this time—not everyone could make so rapid a transition.

I greatly enjoyed your verses in the recent *Fantasy Fan*,[2] & hope you will contribute more to that piquant though unpretentious sheet. It pleases me to hear that Hornig seems to be overcoming his worst financial obstacles, for the F F really fills (or is capable of filling) a very useful niche. Smith's article on M. R. James[3] is an especially notable item.

I read the March W T the other day, & thought it a rather average issue. But Smith's illustration[4] surely is a high spot! Though the human figure is a trifle stiff, the whole conception is tremendously impressive—subtly & curiously haunting. That cyclopean pillared hall, & the two nameless corpse-bearers, arouse a vague, pseudo-reminiscent sense of nightmare very hard to shake off. If you'd like to see more of Smith's drawings—his marvellous heads of nameless insecto-reptilian & hybrid proboscidian entities, & his studies in morbid, poisonous vegetation from other worlds & other galaxies—I'll be glad to lend you the specimens I possess. He encloses one in his letters every now & then, & during 12 years of frequent correspondence I've accumulated quite a batch. As for his fiction-writing—the present period of it scarcely goes behind 1930, though he has written isolated tales at rare intervals ever since 1910 or so. Back in that period—1911, I think—he had several items in *The Black Cat* & other magazines; this work being more realistic than his present material. The first glimmerings of his new period appeared in 1925, when he wrote two tales—"The Abominations of Yondo" & "Sadastor." They were not published,[5] but they foreshadowed the steady stream beginning 4 or 5 years later. Smith—now 40—was a boy prodigy, & had a book of poems published at 17.[6] I may have mentioned that he was a friend & protege of the late George Sterling. His drawings & paintings have been exhibited in San Francisco galleries, & have elicited some very favourable critical comment.

Thanks tremendously for the offer of a glimpse of "Historic Pilgrimages in New England"[7]—which I hereby accept with pleasure & appreciation. I trust I shall not detain it too long, & will take all possible pains to return it in the precise condition received. I possess another book by Bacon—on the historic towns of Narragansett Bay in my own state—& can imagine how interesting he would be in a larger field. No matter how many different books of this sort one reads, there is almost always something new in each one. Glad you have had a chance to get some sidelights on "Arkham" (Salem) & "Kingsport" (Marblehead). By the way—if you'd care to read more in this line, I'd be delighted to lend you any of the antiquarian books in my library—such as Samuel Adams Drake's "Nooks & Corners of the New England Coast", &c. I must have 50 to 100 volumes on early American places & customs (I haven't recently catalogued any but the weird part of my collection),[8] & will send you a list of the best items if you're interested. Since you've read one of Bacon's books, how about seeing the other?

My recent reading includes Dunsany's new book—"The Curse of the Wise Woman", & that 14-year-old item of A. Merritt's—"The Metal Monster".[9] The latter is absolutely tremendous . . . . . what an ass I was to pass it up when it first appeared! Never elsewhere have I seen *utter non-human alienage* so powerfully, opulently, & convincingly delineated. The human characters are wooden & commonplace—routine pulp stuff—but the background of "outside" scenes & phenomena is overwhelming. Now I understand why Merritt calls this his "best—& worst" story.[10] There is no question but that he can suggest sinister alienage in a scene or landscape better than anyone else dead or living. I wish he could shake wholly free of the cheap pulp influence?

Winter's grip seems to be breaking up at last. Feb. 26 & March 5 formed a contrast in Mondays . . . . on the former date the worst snowstorm of the season, & on the latter date—just a week later—a summerlike temperature of almost 70°, which sent me out to the woods & fields to slosh around in overshoes & rejoice in the annual awakening of Nature!

Every good wish—Yrs most cordially & sincerely,
H P Lovecraft

Notes

1. Cf. "The Shadow out of Time" (*CF* 3.407) and "The Challenge from Beyond" (*CF* 4.551f). See RFS 25.
2. "Winds."

3. "The Weird Works of M. R. James," *FF* 1, No. 6 (February 1934): 89–90.
4. CAS illustrated his story "The Charnel God."
5. In fact, "The Abominations of Yondo" appeared in the *Overland Monthly*, April 1926; "Sadastor" in *WT*, July 1930.
6. CAS was nineteen when *The Star-Treader* (1912; *LL* 884) was published.
7. By Edgar Mayhew Bacon.
8. "Weird Items in Library of H. P. Lovecraft," now printed as an appendix to *LL*.
9. Serialized in *Argosy All-Story Weekly* beginning with the issue of 7 August 1920.
10. As quoted in F. Lee Baldwin, "Within the Circle," *FF* 2, No. 1 (September 1934): 7.

[9]   [ALS]
66 College St.,
Providence, R.I.,
April 2, 1934.

Dear Mr. Searight:—
Let me thank you exceedingly for the loan of the piquant & alluring Bacon volume, which I shall digest with keen interest & return without undue delay. The limited geographical scope is no disappointment, for it embraces the most vital & picturesque antiquities on the whole. I can imagine how fascinating you will find this ancestral region when you visit it, & hope that your contemplated pilgrimage may occur without a hitch. I'd enjoy guiding you about old "Arkham" & "Kingsport", & I hope you will also be able to include Providence in your itinerary. I may have mentioned that this venerable town (whose tercentenary falls two years hence) is especially rich in scenic beauty & architectural antiquities. Meanwhile I have sent under separate cover the first of the New England books mentioned—Drake's "Nooks & Corners". This writer—though not wholly exempt from Victorian unctuousness & floridity—is really admirably interesting & accurate. Incidentally, it is he who finally discovered—in England—the manuscript of Bradford's history of the Plymouth colony—one of the most important of America's early records. Later on I'll send you other volumes on kindred themes.

I will also send Clark Ashton Smith's drawings as soon as I get them back from their present loanee (or better still, I'll ask him to send them along to you when he's through with them). You will certainly find them highly arresting & unusual. Possibly you would also like to see the even more mature work of Howard Wandrei, Donald's younger brother—of which I have some fairly good photographs. This latter youth is obviously destined for considerable heights in art.

Yes—I inferred that "Eltdown" had some subtle relationship to "Piltdown", even though the gentleman unearthed there was rather too primitive to record any secrets of the pre-human past that he may have overheard.[1] The suggestions evoked by the name "Eltdown Shards" are to me tremendous, & I shall undoubtedly use these hellish fragments in some future tale—perhaps one dealing with Roman Britain, & with horrors trickling down from forgotten millennia before it.

Let me express my sympathy concerning the threatened fate of your old home—a sympathy heightened by the circumstance that an ugly addition is now being tacked on to my birthplace (in recent years a doctors' building housing many offices) by its present owner, while the stable was demolished two years ago to make way for a pseudo-Tudor residence. Sic transit gloria mundi! Your house is evidently of the same period as my old home[2] . . . . the Victorian mid-century. Not my favourite period architecturally, but capable of a solid homelikeness to which years of habitancy in impressionable youth add a more precious charm. Thanks immensely for the views, which evoke a wistful nostalgia for other years. Here's a crude suggestion of the place when I first saw the light.

By the way—if those prints were meant to be returned, let me know. They're safe in my archives meanwhile. I envy you the furniture, since most of our really colonial pieces—including a clock of the same general type as yours—went to other branches of the family before my time. When the above-sketched house was built[3]—in the 1870's—my grandparents stocked up with new Victorian furniture, & looked down very scornfully upon the really infinitely better material of the past! And yet I am vastly attached to the furniture, paintings, & objets d'art amidst which my earliest years were spent, & could not possibly exist without the presence of these things around me. No matter to what small compass my household accomodations have been condensed, I always crowd in as much of the familiar material as I can. Naturally, much has had to be dispensed with; but my aunt & I still have enough to give our current abode a typical family atmosphere . . . & we have more stored in a neighbour's abandoned stable. We choose such of the old material as is least obtrusively Victorian, & make the most of the few really old pieces (a chair of about 1705, some tip-tables & wooden chairs, a cabinet or two, several candlesticks & vases, some paintings & a statuette, together with a desk, chair, & bookcases of the 1830 period) we have . . . . achieving a result which at once suggests the old house, yet carries a general Georgian rather than Victorian impression. I enclose a snapshot of the really colonial house in which we now reside—a house of my favourite type in general, though I wouldn't mind a slightly earlier specimen. The edifice, yellow & wooden, is on the crest of Providence's great hill in a quaint & grassy court just off College St.—behind & next to the marble John Hay Library of Brown University. The fine colonial doorway is typical of the 1800 period, when the house was built—with fan carving & side lights.[4] In the rear & on the western side are picturesque, village-like gardens—those behind being at a higher level than the front of the house. In front there [are] some flower-beds, a hedge, & a row of picturesque, old-fashioned posts to keep off vehicles. The upper flat we inhabit contains 5 rooms & accessories on the main (2nd) floor, plus 2 attic storerooms—one of which is so attractive that I wish I could have it for an extra den! My quarters—a large study & a small adjoining bedroom—are on the south side, with my working table under a west window affording a splendid view of the lower town's outspread roofs & of the mystical sunsets that flame behind them. In general, the interior is fully as fascinating as the exterior—with colonial fireplaces, mantels, & chimney-cupboards, curving Georgian staircase, wide floor-boards, old-fashioned latches, small-paned windows, six-panel doors, rear wing with floor at a different level (3 steps down), quaint attic stairs, &c.—just like the old houses open as museums. After admiring such all my life, I find something magical & dreamlike in the experience of actually *living in one* for the first time. The house is owned by Brown University—hot water & steam heat being piped in from the system centreing in the college engineering building on the campus far above. The enclosed view is taken from the courtyard of the adjacent library—which, incidentally, houses the Harris Collection of American Poetry, greatest of its kind in the world. Really, the ancient hill neighbourhood is vastly more fascinating than the sunny Victorian region of trim lawns & cast-iron deer where I grew up. It always seemed subtly magical to me.

Congratulations on the library you are inheriting![5] I fortunately fell heir to several small collections in various lines of my ancestry, so that—after a couple of reluctant eliminating campaigns, & plus my own personal additions—I now have perhaps 2500 volumes—mostly in my study, but some in the attic & others in storage. They are about the last possessions I would willingly resign.

Yes, I wish Smith would write up Blackwood, Machen, &c. as he did James . . . supplying biographical data. As for biographies in W.T.—I hardly think the grade of work in the pulp magazines really warrants the exploitation of its perpetrators. The only circle where such poor hacks can really bask in the sun of celebrity-ism is that of the semi-amateur sheets like F F & Fantasy Magazine. These modest journals occasionally give the petty godlets of the weird firmament a bit of descriptive space.

Regarding James's collected works—I feel sure that any metropolitan bookseller could order you a copy. I don't recall the exact title, but think it is simply "Collected Stories of M. R. James." I have the separate volumes, & would be glad to lend you any you haven't seen. James is utterly unique in many ways, & I really don't see how he 'gets away with' that brisk, cheerful style & those injections of sly humour as he does. I, myself, think the tales would be stronger without these things—but the fact remains that they do not spoil the effect as they invariably do with other writers. What James probably wants to achieve is a sensation of tremendous surprise & contrast— a wholesome, commonplace environment, & then the shock of something sudden, abnormal, & loathsome. Of all the weird masters, he is the least amenable to copying. Of all his imitators, only H. R. Wakefield is worthy of notice . . . . & Wakefield is at his best when least Jacobean. With me, James is more or less an acquired taste. Long was an enthusiast from the start, but it took a second reading after an interval to make me appreciate to the full the depths & nuances of the wraith-evoking antiquary. Doubtless you know that James, besides being Provost of Eton & a weird writer, is perhaps the greatest living authority on mediaeval Latin MSS. & Gothic cathedral architecture.

I thought our Rhode Island winter was about the worst yet, but we at least have had no snowfall for a fortnight! I'm glad you can get some fun out of such climatic inflictions—they are the one enemy I simply can't fight. Cold affects me very adversely—I can scarcely sign my name under 75°, & it's actually unsafe for me to be out in temperature under +20°[.] I've fallen unconscious at +14°. On the other hand, tropical heat braces me up & awakes unsuspected stores of energy in me. I literally don't know what the phrase "oppressive heat" means. At 97° I feel at my best. I ought to live in a warmer climate; but am so tremendously attached to the scenery, architecture, & general atmosphere of my native region that the transition will be very painful if it ever becomes necessary. I couldn't live in any place without visible antiquities. If I do migrate, it will probably be to ancient Charleston, S.C.—which retains even more of the 18th century than Providence does. Whole streets in Charleston are unchanged since the 1760 period—though the local architecture differs greatly from New England's. Charleston houses are tall, with stuccoed walls, pointed roofs, tiers of verandahs, & adjacent walled gardens.

They display considerable Huguenot & West Indian influence. I have a hope of seeing Charleston before long, since Barlow has invited me to Florida for a visit, & I can arrange to pass through there. If this trip materialises—it depends on my finances—I shall also see ancient St. Augustine again. I was last in Florida in 1931, when I visited our late fellow-weirdist Dr. Whitehead.

Oh—before I forget it, let me correct a maddening error in my letter in the March F F. For "*an* especial morbidity" read "NO especial morbidity". The reversal of meaning is obvious. With the text as misprinted, I wouldn't blame any reader for inferring that I am 'crazy or have a deceased mind'! Also—the word (if it is a word) "prospection" should read PERSPECTIVE. Careless work—though the type-face & impression are greatly improved in this issue [6]

I've just learned that Robert E. Howard sustained a severe motor accident this winter—involving frightful cuts & crushings. It would probably have killed any ordinary man, though the iron-physiqued Conan the Reaver is pulling through without disastrous consequences. He ran into a dark-grey flagpole set in the middle of a poorly lighted village square—an obvious menace to nocturnal traffic which ought to be abolished.

Good luck with your new weird tale. I'm writing nothing at present, though I have a rather ghoulish Arkham tale half planned in my head. Incidentally, I recently drew a map of "Arkham"[7] embodying such casual geographical allusions as I have made in my various yarns. As such stories multiply, it becomes necessary to get their background somewhat systematised to avoid confusion & contradiction. I'll have to tackle "Kingsport" before long!

Again thanking you for the book loan, & hoping that the Drake volume will not prove a disappointment, I remain

Most cordially & sincerely yrs—

H. P. Lovecraft

Notes

1. See EHP 70n2.

2. I.e., 454 (then 194) Angell St. See EHP 10n12.

3. Recent scholarship by Donovan K. Loucks indicates that HPL's grandfather Whipple Phillips did not build the house, as HPL contends, but merely purchased the house from its previous owner.

4. Actually, the house was built c. 1825.

5. This would be the library of Dr. Ellsworth Stiles Ellis of Manistee. The bulk of it went to RFS, thence to Franklyn Searight. The prize possession is a volume entitled *Voice of One Crying in a Wilderness*, published in 1746, a book of sermons from the library of Rev. Isaac Stiles, a lineal ancestor.

6. The passage as printed in *FF* 1, No. 7 (March 1934): 105 reads: "It can be said that anything which vividly embodies a basic human emotion or captures a definite and

typical human mood is genuine art. The subject matter is immaterial. It requires an [*sic*] especial morbidity to enjoy any authentic word-depiction, whether it is conventionally 'pleasant' or not. Indeed, it argues a somewhat immature and narrow prospection [*sic*] when our judgment is by the mere conventional appeal of its subject-matter or its supposed social effects. The question to ask is not whether it is 'healthy' or 'pleasant,' but whether it is *genuine* and *powerful*."

7. "Map of the Principal Parts of Arkham, Massachusetts," reproduced in *Acolyte* 1, No. 1 (Fall 1942): 26 (as "Map of Arkham"). Another map is reproduced in *Marginalia*, preceding p. 279, and HPL drew yet another map for Robert Bloch in 1936; see *Letters to Robert Bloch and Others* 169. Around this time, HPL also told Duane W. Rimel he was planning an Arkham story, which the following year he described as the "Arkham graveyard tale," but he never wrote such a story.

[10]   [ANS postcard][1]

[Postmarked Charleston, S.C.,

30 April 1934]

Greetings from my favourite town! Had a pleasant week in N Y with Long, the two Wandreis, & the rest of the gang—& hopped off for the South at midnight Apr. 22–3. Spent Mon. morning in Washington—exploring the ancient Georgetown section. Richmond in afternoon; Raleigh, N.C. in evening. Hit Charleston at dawn April 24. Stopping at Y & doing the old town as usual. Marvellous place—perfect 18th century survival. Full summer down here—with green vegetation, hot days, straw hats, & all. Merely springlike—with delicate young foliage—in Wash. & Richmond. And when I left N.Y. it was still wintry there—with chill winds & bare boughs. Great kick in passing from winter to summer in a few hours. On to Savannah tomorrow, & in De Land May 2 unless plans change. Temporary address for a fortnight or so—℅ R. H. BARLOW, BOX 88, DE LAND, FLA. But I hate to leave Charleston!

Regards—

H P L

Notes

1. *Front:* Old Post Office, Charleston, S.C.

[11]   [ALS]

℅ Barlow, Box 88,

De Land, Fla.,

May 15, 1934.

Dear Mr. Searight:—

Well, I am fully within the subtropics at last, & having a great time. Spent 8½ hrs. in Savannah en route, & explored that pleasant old town rather fully. De Land is a delightful village overarched with great moss-draped live-oaks, & the climate gives me a double quota of vigour. 85° & 86° day after day—I go hatless & coatless, & am accumulating a fine layer of tan. The Barlow place is 14 miles W. of town, & out of sight of any other habitation. Its grounds are attractively landscaped, & in the rear is a picturesque lake on which we row. Young Barlow is an ineffably bright & versatile kid— writer, painter, sculptor, pianist, landscape gardener, book-collector, & then some—but is handicapped by poor eyesight. This autumn he will go north for ocular treatment. I have been here a fortnight now, but my genial hosts still refuse to hear of my moving along. On the return trip I hope to stop a week in ancient St. Augustine, & I may possibly visit an old friend in Macon, Ga.[1] When I do travel, ah sho' does travel!

Glad the Drake book proved of interest. The author certainly was a great old oracle on Novangliana in his day! I also have his compilation of old N.E. legends—which is at your disposal as soon as I get home. Probably you are right about the wisdom of deferring regional study until the season of one's actual visit. I always want to brush up on local history just before I see a place, & this year carried my own old travelogue to Charleston as a guide.[2] The Bacon book was certainly splendid—giving me, as I said, several absolutely new sidelights on my own section!

I thought you'd enjoy Klarkash-Ton's pictures. His sources are various, & his technical training almost negligible—but the net result is surely impressive enough! He certainly did justice to hellish Tsathoggua—a deity of his own invention. The utter originality of the half-insect, half-vegetable monsters, & of the non-terrestrial fungi & flora, is phenomenal to the highest degree. Only the abysses of dream can produce entities like these! By the way—will you please send these monstrous things to me down here, in Barlow's care, instead of to my home? I want to show them to my host, who is an especial enthusiast anent weird art. I hope very shortly to get a batch of Howard (*not* Donald, but his younger brother) Wandrei's weird designs headed your way. Incidentally—my host has a plan for marketing one or two of this gifted artist's designs in the form of 11 × 14 photographic reproductions for sale at $2.00 each.

Glad the crude diagram of my birthplace didn't seem too ridiculous. You are at liberty to retain the snap of 66 College if it is of any permanent interest. Thanks for permission to keep the pictures of the old homestead at Menominee.[3] Old houses certainly have a subtle magic which nothing else can supply—but well-situated new houses are by no means without their points. Your present location sounds very attractive indeed. At this moment I am in a dwelling so new that its inner parts are scarcely finished, yet the place is ineffably congenial. Barlow's father is a lieutenant-colonel in the army, just retired to this idyllic spot because of failing health. The landscape abounds in tall Australian pines, which stand out against the horizon like the trees in a Japanese print.

Pleased to learn that M. R. James is available at your local library—all too often these weird items can't be furnished by public institutions. James ought to be just the author for you. It seems to me that the type of the 1-volume edition isn't unduly small, but that is a matter which current inspection will reveal better than memory.

You have certainly had some trying experiences with motors, & I don't wonder at your growing alienation from such contraptions! I've never driven a car, though I used to be quite a cyclist in the old days. What you say of the arrogant psychology of drivers is certainly true—showing how dependent on accident & environment all the phases of human character generally are!

Glad to hear that spring has reached the north at last! Indeed, correspondents as close to the pole as Vermont have reported unusual heat. You are lucky in being able to stand extremes at both ends of the scale . . . . only the tropical end is without terrors for me! As for the weight of summer clothing—I'm not sure that I quite agree with you, although there's undoubtedly a great deal of sense in your contention that garments exclude as well as retain heat. To my mind, all tight & heavy clothing is a painful incubus, so that one ought to welcome any chance to get down to Palm-Beach weight. I lose half my energy in a thick woollen suit with vest, & am no good at all in an overcoat. And in hot weather the effect of tight & abundant clothing in confining perspiration is uncomfortable in the extreme. I am all for tropical climates & two-piece duck suits—indeed, at present I go coatless for lack of an upper integument of suitable lightness.

Yes—I know that the Virgin Islands must form a fascinating retreat from arctic rigours. Whitehead used to tell me of their ideal climate & fascinating antiquities. In Frederiksted[4] the shop where Alexander Hamilton worked still stands—& is still kept by descendants of Hamilton's employers! Danish & English reliques blend curiously, & the vast black population is amusing or annoying, according to one's tastes. There are peculiar social customs, & the visitor is compelled to observe many little formalities in order to maintain the status of gentility. In the French & Dutch West Indies things are different— while Jamaica & Cuba furnish two more utterly alien worlds. One could spend years in the West Indies & never suffer from environmental monotony. I only wish I had the cash to pay them a visit!

About writing Klarkash-Ton—certainly mention his drawings! He delights in appreciation, & would probably be glad to lend you other specimens if you expressed genuine interest. By the way—Price has called on both Howard & Smith during his recent wanderings; in each case forming the only fellow-weirdist ever seen in person by his host. Price's quasi-permanent address is now 5314 East 12th St., Oakland, California . . . . . the old family abode.

Have you seen the new *Marvel Tales*—Crawford's belated & retitled venture? Not bad for a semi-amateur sheet . . . . hope it keeps up! Barlow has it, but I've had no time as yet to read it through. Haven't read the May W.T., either. Barlow's printing of the Whitehead letters is held up through his ocular trouble.[5] Unbound sheets of my "Shunned House" lately arrived from Cook, but we can't tell how soon it will be issued.

A few interesting old places down here despite the newness of De Land. At De Leon Springs there is a Spanish sugar mill built before 1763, & at New Smyrna on the coast there are the vine clad ruins of a great Franciscan monastery built in 1696. I'm enclosing a view of the former.

With every good wish, & regards from my brilliant & youthful host, I remain

      Yrs most cordially—

      H P L

Notes

1. Apparently the amateur journalist John Milton Samples, editor of the *Silver Clarion,* to which HPL contributed a few items around 1918.
2. "An Account of *Charleston,* in His Maj[ty's] Province of *South-Carolina*" (1930).
3. HPL's error for Manistee.
4. A town in St. Croix, U.S. Virgin Islands.
5. RHB printed a few pages of *Caneviniana* but never completed it.

[12]   [ANS postcard][1]

      [Postmarked De Land, Fla.,

      23 May 1934]

Yrs. just recd. It is *perfectly all right* about the C A S drawings. I *had* told you to send the drawings to Rimel or Baldwin, but you evidently didn't get the postcard on which I made the request. Then, when I saw by your letter that you hadn't received this request, I changed my mind & decided to have the stuff sent down here. I had forgotten all about Baldwin's knowing that the stuff was headed toward him—possibly I did tell him last month that it was in your possession or en route. Let me apologise sincerely both to you & to Baldwin for hashing it up up [*sic*] so & causing you anxiety. But it's all right. Asotin is the place where the drawings really ought to go anyway. Baldwin & Rimel can send the stuff down to Barlow at leisure. ¶ Still having a great time. Hopes for Havana very slim, but shall spend a week in ancient St. Augustine. This climate is making a new man of me! Barlow sends best regards.

Yr ob't Svt

      H P L

Notes

1. *Front:* A picturesque scene on a Florida river.

[13]   [ALS, JHL]

De Land—

June 8, 1934

Dear Mr. Searight:—

Yours of the 1st. found me still at the Villa Barlovia, detained far beyond my originally set time limits by the enthusiastic super-hospitality of my hosts. You would certainly enjoy this setting—although I doubt whether the lake has any fauna aside from an occasional turtle or alligator. Some of the lakes, however, have fish—& the broad St. John's River, half way betwixt here & De Land, is quite a haven for anglers. I myself do not care for fishing, & have not pursued a finny prey since I was 9 or 10. My one outdoor sport is simply the absorption of landscape values in scenic walks or rides. In hot weather I am never under a roof if I can help it, but take my current work, reading, or writing in a handbag & make a bee line for the nearest woodland retreat where I can sit undisturbed till dusk drives me home. Fortunately Providence's residence section is well within reach of such agrestic havens—it is only a short walk to the high wooded bluff of the Seekonk River—a favourite haunt of my youth which still (since it is part of the Metropolitan Park System) remains in its pristine unspoiled state.

Glad you've got in touch with C A S anent methods of salvaging debts from Hugo the Rat.[1] It would be unfortunate if everyone sustained losses as supinely as Frank B. Long. Did I mention that my revision client Mrs. Heald collected $35.00 from Gernsback through Miss Weber? I certainly wish you luck in your campaign to claim your own! Old Hugo seems to be getting more & more unscrupulous, though he always did lean heavily on the old standbys of bankruptcy, underpayment, deferred payment, & so on. Sooner or later he will no longer be able to get contributions from any responsible writer—so that his policy will become really self-defeating. Yes—the grade of W.S. certainly is declining. And incidentally, you are right in pointing out the instructive value of crude tales as horrible examples. They do reveal dozens of typical banalities & stock devices which better stories conceal, & which might therefore be copied unconsciously from the latter.

Your perusal of the classics will certainly prove of high value to you in your writing—not only directly, but indirectly through its inculcation of sound narrative, descriptive, & image-using principles. I always try to encourage writers to read widely—so many of them fancy that cheap weird fiction is all they need to assimilate!

"Celephaïs" is an old tale—written in 1920, & a sample of my period of Dunsanian imitation. I don't think much of it. The tale whose unbound sheets (not *proofs*) Cook has sent to Barlow is THE SHUNNED HOUSE—not a novel, but merely a short story printed separately as a little book or booklet. You may have seen it in MS. or proof form if I ever lent you any of my old stuff. It was written in 1924, printed in 1928, & thereafter shelved on account of

Cook's nervous & financial breakdown. Barlow will bind & issue it eventually.

Your coming vacation sounds delightful indeed, & I trust you'll have a pleasant call on Wright.[2] I don't think you need to feel embarrassed by Hornig's classification of you with established writers—you have already produced good stuff, & will undoubtedly produce much more!

My aunt spoke in a letter of the safe arrival of the Drake book at College St. Meanwhile my visit continues to be delightful. Barlow sends you his regards. My hopes of reaching Havana are about gone, but I shall spend a week in St. Augustine if it breaks me. Then a very gradual return to the north, with pauses in places of antiquarian interest. More bulletins later. There has been some cold weather down here, but warmer conditions are now restored though not anything as blazing as Wright reports in connexion with Chicago!

All good wishes—
Yours for the secret of the Eltdown Shards—
H P L

Notes

1. RFS wrote to CAS on 20 May 1934 asking about CAS's attorney for dealing with nonpayment from *Wonder Stories*. RFS was owed $40. CAS wrote to RFS (24 May 1934) telling of the services of Ione Weber in recouping debts from Gernsback and urging RFS to contact her.

2. RFS did in fact call on Wright, although it is not clear whether he did so at this particular time. He describes him as follows in the unpublished article "Looking Back" (1975): "Wright was a tall, gaunt man afflicted with the typical hand tremor and facial expression of Parkinson's disease. No doubt realizing that I had observed his condition, he explained that nothing more could be done to alleviate the symptoms and that he had come to content himself with a semi-annual check up. It was then I understood why he never signed his letters by hand.

"He was an affable, courteous gentleman and as is well known his literary standards were the highest. While his selections for the magazine seemed highly capricious at times, his choices may often have been a compromise between literary quality and what he judged to be reader acceptability. He was extremely meticulous and his constant exhortation was to be 'more convincing'."

[14]   [ALS]

Home again—
July 17, 1934

Dear Mr. Searight:—

Your letter of the 9th reached College St. almost simultaneously with myself. I spent a pleasant week amongst the antiquities of St. Augustine, & enjoyed two more days in old Charleston. In Richmond I visited the boyhood scenes of Poe—stopping at an hotel only two doors from the site of the Allan home where he grew up. Another afternoon was spent in

Fredericksburg—little changed since Genl. Washington knew it as a boy—& after that came 2 days in Washington, where I explored the capitol, ascended the monument, visited Rock Creek Park, & inspected the newly restored & furnished Arlington mansion on the heights across the river. In Philadelphia I threaded the ancient streets as of yore, visited old Germantown & the magnificent Wissahickon gorge, & paid a call at the Poe home (1842–44) in N. 7th St., now open as a public museum. This latter place is furnished exactly as in Poe's time, & contains a valuable collection of reliques. When I struck New York I found Long & his parents about to depart for a week-end at Asbury Park & Ocean Grove, N.J., & at their invitation went along with them. I had not cash enough to linger in Manhattan, so returned to Providence without looking up many of the local group. It was good to be home again—though the northern landscape & chilly nights still seem a bit strange after my saturation with the subtropics. As usual, I do as much work as possible in the open—being at this moment on my favourite wooded river-bank. The amount of piled-up material—letters, papers, & sundry tasks—awaiting me was appalling, & has so rushed me that my valise is still largely packed!

Your vacation sounds alluring indeed, & I am glad the old home still remains to make it complete.[1] You will surely get an ample quota of wildness & ruggedness—especially, I imagine, on Isle Royale—which sounds like an almost incredible survival from the primitive. That will take you farther north—48°—than I have ever been . . . . 47° (Isle d'Orleans near Quebec) being my limit. I surely hope you will write that monograph on Isle Royale,[2] since the place is really very little known to the outside world. Have you a camera along, so that you can supplement your account with illustrations? The bulletins you promise will be very welcome, & will undoubtedly go into my permanent geographical files. Is Houghton a pleasant town? I see by the map that it is just a trifle farther north than my own Ultima Thule. Probably I'd find the climate a bit less congenial than Florida's for vacational purposes.

I'm glad you enjoyed the "Silver Key" sequel—which somehow fails to satisfy me. Yes—this is the tale which Wright accepted after a previous rejection. As you doubtless know, it is a continuation of my old tale in the Jan. 1929 issue.[3] Price kept egging me on to write a sequel embodying a mathematical explanation of what became of Carter, but I didn't feel like doing it & told him to do it himself. He prepared a 6000-word sketch[4] which clashed badly with the original, so I took the central idea of that sketch—plus a few phrases—& wrote a new story around it. The result is what you see—the idea of the alien planet Yaddith & the voyage through space being wholly my own. I can't really like the thing, for it isn't what I would have written of my own accord. Regarding the expression *as though*—I don't see any reason why it should not be employed as freely as any other traditional expression. It occurs throughout standard literature—including the King James Bible—& is authorised by Webster & Stormonth & all the other lexicographers I know of. I have no use for the ultra-modern pedantry which brings up mechanical or technical objections to various accepted expressions. There is no law of grammar superior to standard usage—grammar is merely a codification & explanation of what is commonly used. Another piece of pedantry which makes me laugh is the silly objection to the possessive *whose* when applied to inanimate objects. As if what was good enough for Addison & Swift were not good enough for the Alexandrian dryasdusts of today!

I saw that mimeographed spoof at Barlow's, & found another copy when I got home. Whoever launched it was surely in close touch with the gang. Its main trouble is that very few persons know *all* the figures touched upon—so that a good deal of the text must sound like inane maundering to any *one* reader. One or two of the allusions go beyond me—but I fancy that "C. Half-Cent" must be *C. C. Senf,* the mediocre "artist" who used to draw for W.T.; while "W. Lablache Talcum" appears to be *Wilfred Blanch Talman,* whose stories appear now & then. Oddly, Kline is mentioned by his real name.[5]

Congratulations on the acceptance of "Wizard's Death"! Wright's finical pedantry is especially amusing in view of the lousy stuff he *does* print—only about a tenth of the prose or verse in W.T. being worth reading. As commercial truck it may be all right enough—but as art, it simply doesn't exist. The current issue is especially bad—though April & May were excellent. Yes—the serials seem to be the weakest point of all, & I can seldom wade through one. But serials are very hard to place—Wright turned down one of my best things[6] because of its length.

Well—I trust your outing is coming up to expectations. Mine certainly did! All good wishes—

Yrs most sincerely,
H P Lovecraft

Notes

1. The reference is to the old Carpenter (RFS's wife's maiden name) Homestead at 1217 Jasper Street in Houghton, MI. It was purchased in 1883 for $150.00 and accommodated RFS's wife's parents and their eight children. It was torn down in 1968 and a food market now occupies the site.

2. RFS actually wrote an historical novel, *Wild Empire,* in which Isle Royale is featured. It was published posthumously.

3. I.e., "The Silver Key."

4. "The Lord of Illusion" (1932), first published in *Crypt of Cthulhu* No. 10 (Yuletide 1982): 46–56.

5. RHB and HPL himself were co-authors of the "The Battle That Ended the Century." Elsewhere HPL suggested the name Oatmeal Addlepate Crime as a parodical name for Kline.

6. *At the Mountains of Madness.*

[15]   [ALS]

66 College St.,
Providence, R.I.,
August 11, 1934

Dear Mr. Searight:—

Having already thanked you for some alluring glimpses of the Michigan copper country, I must again express my gratitude for the second lot—including the delightful snapshots—contained in yours of the 4th. I have studied them—& the enlightening inscriptions attached to them—with the keenest of interest, till I feel that I have quite a second-hand acquaintance with this imposing & distinctive region. The snaps show up well under a magnifying-glass—a device I always use to get full value from sharp but small-scale photographs. With these vivid illustrations, the interesting descriptions in your letter take on a double significance. Houghton & its district must be extremely quaint & attractive—I always find something fascinating about a placid backwater from which the high tide of industrial prosperity has ebbed. This material & quantitative decline often gives rise to a genuine enrichment in the quality of life—real cultural values coming uppermost as false values of financial prosperity fade. Leisure is appreciated as it ought to be; & the futile, tail-chasing bustle of a commercial & industrial "civilisation" gives place to the mellow savouring of tradition & unhurried experience which really is civilisation. The east is full of these backwaters—Newport & the Narragansett country in Rhode Island, which the Revolution financially ruined; Salem & Marblehead & Newburyport in Massachusetts, which were commercially slain by the Embargo Act of 1808; Charleston & Natchez, whose prosperity fell in the War between the States—& so on. Every one of these places is a thousand times more attractive than any spot where the ugly processes & vulgar ideals of gain remain paramount. Houghton, apparently, is breaking into this class—& I can imagine its subtle charm even though its antiquities are Victorian rather than Georgian. A town which has shrunk from a larger population has a peculiarly interesting quality—Newburyport, once 25,000 & now 15,000, being a classic example. Houghton's situation also makes for picturesqueness—for towns on waterfront terraces are always quaint. Providence is such an one—the old hill section rising like a precipice above the head of the bay—though the covering over & filling in of most of the water has detracted from its original aspect. Still perfect specimens are Norwich, Conn., & Newburgh, N.Y., which rise in imposing tiers above the Thames & Hudson rivers, respectively. Marblehead's hills are more irregular, so that the symmetrical effect of terraces is lacking. But on the other hand, it is in Marblehead where one most often sees odd outcroppings of rock. Providence, of course, shares the architectural problems of all hill towns—having houses whose basements are high above ground on one side & deeply buried on the other. In the case of tall public buildings on the steepest parts of the hill the results are often amusing. Thus the Court House in South Main St. at the foot of the hill has its rear in Benefit St., which runs ledgewise along the hill half way up . . . . & the *ground floor* of the Benefit St. side is the *fifth floor* as reckoned from the S. Main St. front. Indolent persons often get a free ride half way up the hill by taking the court house elevator from S. Main St. to the 5th floor & then walking calmly out on Benefit St.! The School of Design Art Museum is similarly situated—but hasn't any elevator to tempt the ride-seeker. College St. runs straight up the hill—#66 being in the rear of a quaint grassy court near the top.

From my west windows I have a delectable view of the lower town & the sunset. I'd miss the hill if I lived in a level city like Charleston or Philadelphia.

The College of Mines must be a great institution despite its dwindling student body—& its geological museum sounds like a place which would captivate any devotee of the mineral world—like my friend James F. Morton (curator of the Paterson, N.J. municipal museum, & specialist in minerals), who has just been visiting me here. Sorry you had to omit Isle Royale, & hope you'll find access more practicable on your next trip. But even with all curtailments you would seem to have had a splendid vacation—amply justifying the graceful verses[1] on the subject which I have read with the utmost pleasure & appreciation.

Regarding grammatical minutiae & doubtful points—it is certainly next to impossible to draw any hard & fast line betwixt the admissible & the inadmissible. No two persons can agree, & most have their pet extremes in either direction. A few years ago it was the fashion to be precise & pedantic—in the manner of Woolley's handbook & Bierce's "Write it Right." Today there is a tendency to rush to the opposite extreme—a tendency which reached its apex of absurdity in 1932, when the judges in a survey of linguistic usage conducted by the National Council of English Teachers gave formal approval (at least for colloquial purposes) to such things as "It is *me*", "*Who* are you looking for", "we will try *and* get it", &c. All one can say is that both of these extremes are overdone. Language is neither a bundle of formal rules nor a free-&-easy matter of newsboy & stevedore patois. It is a fairly coherent but moderately flexible affair whose sole criterion is usage—but not the slovenly usage of the streets. There is no "law" about *general usage*—but what is meant by "usage" is the intelligent employment of speech by persons of cultivation who have something important to say & who consciously adapt the verbal medium at their disposal to the most effective saying of that something. In a word, the supreme authority is the habitual usage of authors whose general aesthetic position shows them to be employing words thoughtfully with a view to their best effect. This does not let in such eminent authors as possess known defects in linguistic skill—Dreiser, Sherwood Anderson, &c. It refers rather to men whose command of language is undisputed—Addison, Swift, Lamb, Pater, & all the fastidious writers down to the living Cabell, Robinson, Wharton, & so on. What artists of this calibre habitually use may be considered good enough for anyone—no matter what this or that textbook or schoolmarm may say. On the other hand, it would be silly to sanction such absolute illiteracies as the increasingly popular *like* for *as* or *as if*, or the form "I wonder will he go" for "I wonder if he will go". Wright, incidentally, is an extreme pedant of the old school—averse even to the use of colloquialisms *as colloquialisms*. It cost him many a pang to use Alvin F. Harlow's series title "Folks Used to Believe" a few years ago . . . . he thought it ought to be "*Folk* Used to Believe"![2] As for the cases you mention—I do not think that "due to" is admissible, at least as yet. Regarding "farther" & "further", & "on" & "upon"—it seems to me that these two pairs require separate consideration. In the case of "farther" & "further", there certainly ought to be a distinction—*farther* for literal distance & *further* for distance in the metaphorical sense. On the other hand, I believe that good usage grants to *on* & *upon* a greater interchangeability—with this exception: that *upon* cannot well serve for *on* in the sense of *direction forward*. *Upon* suggests *superposition*, either literal or figurative; whereas *on* suggests all of this *& more*. *On* is the wider word—as preposition & adverb—signifying both *upon* & *onward*. Apropos of the subject in general—I may say that I do *not* consider the indiscriminate use of *if* for *whether* as justified, nor do I see any reason for abolishing the distinction betwixt *shall* & *will*. I would also be very cautious about relegating the subjunctive mood to obsolescence—"if I *was* you", &c. It is well to be conservative, but not *mechanically* or *theoretically* so. The thing to be faithful to is the massed good usage of the last 300 years.

Regarding the original "Silver Key", which you missed—here is a copy which you can read at leisure & return. This is more my kind of thing than the sequel—& yet I wouldn't write a piece like that today. In retrospect it seems a bit mawkish & artificial—& anyhow, it is more of an essay than a story. I really wonder that Price liked it as he did. It was written in November 1926. When published, it got a single starring in O'Brien's year book—which is more than its sequel will ever get.

I haven't read the August W T yet, & don't know when I'll ever get the time to do so. Also unread is the new (& undoubtedly rotten) *Terror Tales* which I picked up the other day. I'll never get time to read all the stuff piling up on me—there are three borrowed books by William Hope Hodgson (weird writer of the pre-war period) which I ought to be returning to their owner right now![3]

Your plot of the released prehistoric monster[4] sounds admirable to me, & I hope you'll continue to experiment with it. The sheer horror style—presented through written reports—is by far the best. Or it could be written as simple narration—either 1st or 3d person—without resorting to the feeble action cliches of the Quinn tradition. A slow-moving style, full of macabre overtones, would be immensely effective in piling up atmosphere & preparing the reader for some hideous revelation.

The Poe house in Philadelphia surely was a fascinating place. But as to whether the bard's death at 40 deprived the world of any major literature, recent opinion is somewhat divided. A growing school, headed by Joseph Wood Krutch & Hervey Allen,[5] incline to the belief that Poe was pretty thoroughly played out by 1849, & that his genius would have lapsed into the status of a psychopathic case—without artistic productivity—had he lived longer. This seems to be borne out by the evidence of his letters & of the treatise "Eureka"[6] as viewed in the light of modern psychiatry. His case certainly forms one of the saddest on record, & probably had its roots in an early cardiac weakness which demanded the stimulation of alcohol or of some equivalent drug—all this, of course, joined to a basic temperament of the utmost neurotic sensitiveness. He was virtually foredoomed to a career of brief brilliancy—though modern medical science could probably have done much to assist him. Poverty, of course, was a severe aggravating factor. I've written a short account of Poe's different homes for an amateur paper, & will let you see it when it appears.[7]

As previously mentioned, I have been having a very interesting guest[8]— who was here August 2–3–4. We assimilated the leading local sights, & wound up with a boat trip to ancient Newport—30 m. S. of here, down Narragansett Bay. Newport has not changed much since the revolution, & the skyline of 17th & 18th century roofs is still crowned by old Trinity steeple, reared in 1726. Such public buildings as the Quaker Meeting house (1698), Trinity Church (1726), the Colony House (1739), the Redwood Library (1749), the Market House (1760), & the Jews' Synagogue (1763) still survive in excellent condition; & the narrow streets are solidly lined with fanlighted Georgian doorways. The wealthy parvenu estates are all south of the old town & do not interfere with it. On this occasion we saw the U.S. fleet at anchor in the harbour, explored the venerable streets, & walked & rested on the famous ocean cliffs.

On Aug. 23 I am invited to Boston for a few days, & shall doubtless make side trips to "Arkham" (Salem) & "Kingsport" (Marblehead)—as well as other places mentioned in that fascinating book which you so kindly lent me. Some time—perhaps not this year—I want to get to the island of Nantucket, where I am told the early American atmosphere survives more perfectly than anywhere else.

Well—again let me thank you for the pictures & descriptions, & for the vivid & pleasing poem in which your massed impressions are crystallised. With all good wishes—

Yrs most sincerely—H P L

Notes

1. Three unpublished poems by RFS on Copper County survive: "The Dream-House," "To an Isolated and Deserted House on the Shores of Lake Superior," and "Vacation's End."
2. Alvin F. Harlow (1875–1963), prolific writer for both the pulps and the slicks. Twenty-six of his articles appeared monthly in *WT* from September 1927 to October 1929.
3. HPL had borrowed *The Ghost Pirates, The House on the Borderland,* and *The Boats of the "Glen Carrig"* from H. C. Koenig.
4. Probably "The Cavern of the Dragon."
5. See Joseph Wood Krutch, *Edgar Allan Poe: A Study in Genius,* and Hervey Allen, *Israfel: The Life and Times of Edgar Allan Poe.*
6. *Eureka: A Prose Poem* (1848), a philosophical study of the mystical and material unity of the universe.
7. "Homes and Shrines of Poe."
8. James F. Morton.

[16]   [ALS]

66 College St.,
Providence, R.I.,
Septr. 8, 1934

Dear Mr. Searight:—

I am very glad you found "The Silver Key" of interest, since I have always had a sort of reminiscent affection for it despite its difference from anything I'd be likely to write today. There are spots which sound a bit mawkish & artificial to my maturer taste. However, it's a great deal more like *me* than is its sequel, in which I had to keep my collaborator constantly in mind. I'm through with collaboration—in fact, I'm turning down a suggestion of Long's that I do a story with him. Price, on the other hand, is planning two collaborations—one with Kline & one with Long.

As for the philosophy—if such it can be called—in "The Silver Key", I merely reflect casual observations. I am myself a recluse of recluses, & do not pretend to command any wide array of data. My remarks on agnostics & atheists—of which I am one—were not meant to apply to the quiet & disinterested thinker who repudiates the old myths without starting a circus about it, but had reference to the strident & assertive iconoclast who harbours the quaint delusion that a change of belief must necessarily involve an abrupt change of folkways. That is, I was taking a fling at the ostentatiously "emancipated" or "bohemian" type so pestiferously common amongst the small fry of writers & other artists. Such folk do not realise that the bulk of our social & ethical code comes from material historic evolution & not from religion at all—that it is a combination of the utilitarian & the aesthetic which religion *really* does no more than uphold & emphasise. Accordingly, the moment these birds throw off their primitive faith in a long-whiskered Jahweh they also proceed to throw off all the common decency & good taste they ever had— as if there were any relationship between the two! This *effect* of disbelief on a *certain type*—& not disbelief itself—is what I was hitting at. Actually, it is only a small proportion of mankind whom disbelief affects in just this way. Most educated adults under 50 have very little of the faith of their fathers left—yet the majority of them still plod along as ordinary citizens without turning into swine, drunkards, madmen, & criminals. Of course, their perspective is in many ways vastly altered—certain values shift in importance, & their sense of proportion suffers a substantial readjustment—but this does not mean any radical overturn of the foundations of taste & ethics. The latter have a far deeper basis—derived from fundamental & non-religious concepts of harmony, continuity, non-encroachment, & practical compromise—to be affected by any change in one's interpretation of the mechanism of the cosmos. As a matter of fact, we have seldom *really* believed all the myths to which we have outwardly subscribed—& during a large part of our cultural history we have followed religious & philosophic systems (Epicureanism, for example) which, if not denying the gods, have at least asserted that the gods have no direct oversight over—or interest in—mankind. Lucretius & the wide circle who believed with him held ideas of the cosmos not at all removed from what civilised & intelligent people accept today. And yet these older systems did not encourage the standardless "bohemianism" prevalent among our professional god-killers. The latter are, rather, cultural descendants of another school—the Cyrenaic school of Aristippus which went out after a positive orgiastic delight (ἡδονή) as distinguished from the tranquil & restrained well-being (ἀταραξία) which was the Epicurean's goal. The trouble with the disorganised bohemian is not that he does not believe in the gods or in the cosmic importance of mankind, but that he will not recognise the superior beauty, harmony, & practical effectiveness which reside in the codes, restraints, & compromises worked out by society. While faith has been used to uphold these things, they are certainly in no way dependent upon it. The unwisdom of a disregard for them is glaringly manifest in the wretchedness, disintegration, maladjustment, & general unrest of the drunken, loose-living, unscrupulous, & honour-less disciple of "emancipated bohemianism"—& in the misery he causes in those around him.

Now as to the effect of the church today on the mass of the population—I really don't know what to think. It is certainly a dead letter with all who have any coördinated knowledge or reflectiveness, but the masses are another problem altogether. It is really a more complex matter than we realise. Certainly, religion has been a very useful restraining influence in past periods—at least, certain religions such as Protestant Christianity have been—but can it continue to be such in the future, even if it survives as a genuine belief? Offhand, one would say that it might be—but here the complexity of human psychology comes in again. For there is no denying that the church is rapidly losing its hold over the *acts* & *feelings* of all classes—even the most gullible & thoughtless—even while it still commands the *conscious belief* of the ignorant. That is, the discrediting of religion among thoughtful people has been observed by the masses, so that they are subconsciously affected more than they understand. They know that the dominant classes are no longer ruled by religion; & since their acts are governed by imitation far more than by philosophy, they tend to become equally emancipated in an *objective* way, even while continuing to believe in the standard myths regarding the operation of the universe. This is the more easy because the masses never did associate religion very closely with conduct. Christianity makes demands which have habitually been ignored by all classes, & which to the lower classes seem almost non-existent. Catholicism has fostered this dualism by representing virtue as an all-but-unattainable ideal which ordinary men may only *approximate*—&, significantly enough, Catholicism is now dominant among the lower orders & is making inroads even among the higher. It is probably the only form of religion which will ultimately survive. Those who think will become agnostics—those who do not think will become Papists. And I doubt if it will be the credulous believers who will stand highest in the ethical scale. The fact is not so much that religion is dying—it isn't among the ignorant—as that it is losing its hold over the acts & motives of men of every class & race. As an influence it is petering out, belief or no belief. Therefore I do not feel as sure as I did in youth that faith is worth upholding among the masses. It is not the social & ethical weapon that it used to be—hence the wiser course is to leave it to its own devices & strive to encourage whatever will strengthen the popular morale.

But what, we may ask, *will* strengthen popular morale? Well—I'm hanged if I know yet, but I fancy that *the organised teaching of pure ethics* on a basis primarily utilitarian, but with sufficient emotional overtones to catch the enthusiasm of primitive minds, would form the foundation of any successful system. We must have an equivalent of what the churches used to be—& in the case of the Protestant churches, I don't see why the existing organisations couldn't keep on functioning usefully after the death of supernaturalism. The loyalty & interest of the herd must be caught by some movement which shall seem valid to them—as religion used to do, but as it can (so far as practical results are concerned) do no more. We can see something of the kind working more or less successfully in Soviet Russia & Nazi Germany, where the mystic ideal of a new society or of a racial state offers a tangible rallying-point for popular emotion & loyalty. We must give the masses something more than a myth to bite into if we expect them to be permanently influenced. They have seen the hypocrisy of a faith which promises everything to the humble & really gives him nothing. The herd—as well shown in Ortega y

Gasset's now classic volume[1]—has awakened to the raw deal it has always received from the shrewder, luckier, & more acquisitive classes; & will never subscribe spontaneously to any ideal which does not bring them some fresh hope of actual relief from their age-old burdens. There can be no widespread respect for any morality which impoverishes the many (especially amidst the present plenitude of resources) while it fabulously enriches the few. Thus a workable morality is bound up closely with the trying & complex economic issues of the day. A "New Deal" of some sort—of which Pres. Roosevelt's specimen forms an excellent beginning though it may not go far enough—is an absolute prerequisite to any profound moral equilibrium. It is only recently that I have come to realise this economic aspect in all its fulness, but the more I really reflect the more plainly do I recognise the inescapable facts. The old order is played out, & hope seems to lie only in some form of fascism which can recapture the loyalty of all classes through a more rational & humane distribution of resources. The alternative is a general loss of confidence in all laws & standards by the majority of people—a loss which will result either in anarchical chaos, or in some rigid & repellent form of communism sprung on the nation by those who are stealthily waiting for a chance to spring it. Most assuredly, the time has gone by when mere empty preaching of any sort can do any good.

I am glad you enjoyed the Nantucket folder, & am enclosing a card or two with other views of that delectable abode of yesterday. Positively, it surpassed all my expectations—& I really think it is in many respects the most fascinating place I have ever seen.[2] Nowhere else has the past survived so unchanged. The island was settled in 1660, & formed part of New York till 1692, since when it has been part of Massachusetts. In the 18th & early 19th centuries its whaling industries brought it vast prosperity, so that the town was built up solidly & tastefully. Then commerce declined—& everything was left as it was. Only the influx of summer vacationists has saved the island from dire poverty. The town still stands exactly as it was a century ago—cobblestoned streets lined with colonial houses, hitching-posts, horse-blocks, & silver doorplates, ancient windmill, picturesque alleys & waterfront, skyline of venerable spires & belfries . . . . . even Salem, Marblehead, Charleston & Quebec are scarcely in the running! It is odd that I never visited this wonderland before—only 90 miles from Providence . . . . a 6-hour coach & boat trip from my own doorstep! I lingered a week—in a 3d floor room with a splendid view of town, harbour, & sea. I explored all the ancient streets & lanes on foot, visited the historic houses & museums, examined the 1746 windmill, & saw Saturn through the 5″ telescope of the Maria Mitchell Observatory—which adjoins the birthplace of the celebrated female astronomer Maria Mitchell, professor at Vassar 1865–88. I also took a 'bus tour of the entire island, visiting among other points the quaint village of Siasconset with its tiny fishers' cottages & flower-bordered lawns. The country near the town I covered on a hired bicycle—the first time I had ridden in 20 years. The only flaw in the trip was the cold weather prevailing during the middle part. I really hated to come home when the time arrived! As for the narrowness of opinion prevailing in such idyllic backwaters—I know it exists, especially in the south; but I am too much of a hermit to let it bother me. I don't expect to find congenial people close at hand anywhere, but have always relied on long-distance acquaintances to keep interesting discussion going. However—I dare say I haven't encountered provincial bigotry at its worst, since I have never lived continuously in any of these towns that I so much love to visit. In De Land last spring I ran into a good many archaic views which amused me at the time, but which would doubtless have irritated me had I been confronted with them too long. Providence retains many village characteristics—such as the absurdly & even dangerously reactionary politics typical of a prosperous textile oligarchy—but is too large to let these assume a virulent form. Besides, it is a city of considerable cultivation, with the intellectual latitude which goes with enlightenment. In time it will lose its residual narrowness, as the immense bulk of its now inarticulate newer elements comes to influence the present reigning nucleus of old families.

I am interested to hear of Hugo the Rat's new ventures, & will warn Klarkash-Ton of the impending change. He has collected part of what is due him through that woman attorney I believe I spoke of—Miss Ione Weber of N.Y.—but I fancy the remaining debt is still considerable. Your idea of a joint suit sounds very sensible to me, & I trust others may coöperate in it. Somebody—or some group—ought to bring that unscrupulous rascal to an accounting sooner or later.

Terror Tales is pretty bad—it takes a rag like that to make me appreciate the merits of W.T. Cave is a perfect cynic regarding authorship. Though possessed of the highest talents, & of a genuine ability to create literature, he has no patience with any attitude save the commercial one. His object is to concoct what editors will pay the most for & purchase most widely—& he succeeds according to his own standards. I fear he didn't like what I wrote him about those standards, since he has never looked me up although he lives in the next town to Providence.[3] I hear rumours now & then of new weird magazines—an unnamed rival of W.T. to be launched soon, & a purchase of the defunct *Strange Tales* by Street & Smith, for high-grade editing by Desmond Hall (now asso. ed. of *Astounding*—a nice chap—I've met him briefly.)[4] All of these reports, however, must be accepted with a grain of salt till further evidence appears. Even if other weird magazines were founded, I doubt their ability to survive. There seems to be room for only one, & our old friend W.T. is safely in on the ground floor.

The case of your one-time collaborator Hammerstrom [*sic*] is certainly sad indeed—though I suppose his moments of realisation of his plight are relatively few.[5] It is tragic & ironic that, despite the advances of medicine in so many fields, the percentage of cures in diseases of the brain remains so low. However, I suppose it is only to be expected; since the brain is so much more delicate than any other part of the organism. To restore normality where such infinitesimal physical factors & such infinitely exact adjustments are concerned is certainly an Herculean task. And some progress has indeed been made—vast progress, if we compared modern results with the sordid & cruel "bedlams" of yesterday. A friend of mine[6]—a very brilliant young man—is a student nurse in one of the leading mental hospitals of the country; & he has made very clear the enormous variety of disorders—some of them miles apart in source & treatment—which are commonly grouped together because of their similar external manifestations. The line between sanity & insanity is really very thin, & millions of persons live all their lives in a borderland zone whence certain kinds of shocks might easily precipitate them into actual dementia. It would pay all nervously excitable persons—& persons subject to easy mental fatigue—to go easy & remember the need for rest. The cracking up of anyone as brilliant as Hammerstrom seems to have been is a genuine calamity.

Well—at last I am enclosing the elusive & long-promised photographs of Howard Wandrei's marvellous drawings. No hurry about their return so long as I get them back safely in the end. Naturally, the camera couldn't reproduce all the delicate colour values—but you can get a good idea of the artist's mastery of line. I'd recommend the use of a magnifying glass in studying these prints. I think you'll agree that H W is really an artist of astonishing power & imagination—far out of the amateur or semi-amateur class. I'm rather hoping for a visit from him—possibly with Donald along, too—later this month. Incidentally, if you'd like to have some really fine reproductions of these pictures, Barlow is issuing a few in conjunction with a professional photographer who uses colour-filters & similar devices.[7] He can supply 8 × 10 copies at $1.25, & 11 × 14's at $2.00. In case you're interested, you might write Barlow at 7019 Georgia Ave., N.W., Washington, D.C. He is in W. consulting oculists about his alarmingly bad eyesight.

All good wishes—

Yrs most sincerely—

H P L

Notes

1. José Ortega y Gasset (1883–1955), *The Revolt of the Masses* (1932), a translation of *La rebelión de las masas* (1929–30).

2. See "The Unknown City in the Ocean."

3. Cf. HPL to August Derleth, late August 1932: "I'm having quite a fight with Hugh B. Cave on the subject of literary motivation. When I mentioned Belknap's resentment at Bates's cuts in 'Space Monsters', he came back with a rather unsympathetic rejoinder, as if an author were an ass to mind the mutilation of his products—at least,

in the pulp field—& spoke of writing as a purely commercial game in which no one ought to pay too much attention to what he has written. All this, to me, was as a red rag to the proverbial bull—so I sailed into him & told him that not everybody could be satisfied to grind out colourless junk which could be slashed without harm & forgotten on the morrow. He replied with more hard-boiled arguments, & corroborated old Doc Johnson's Philistine dictum by averring that no one but a genius or an idiot writes from any but a mercenary motive. Naturally, this got Grandpa going again—& in a mild vein. I used you as the classic example of one with the rare gift of writing popular stuff with your left hand while your right turns out genuine literature. At present the combat is rather a draw—for Cave seems to differ less (except emotionally) from my position, at bottom, than either he or I though he did" (*ES* 498–99).

4. *Strange Tales* was never revived by Street & Smith.

5. Some time before 1930, Hamerstrom became a patient at the East Moline (IL) State Hospital for the mentally ill.

6. Harry K. Brobst, then an intern at Jane Brown Memorial Hospital (a branch of Rhode Island Hospital).

7. RHB's plan to sell photographs of Howard Wandrei's art came to naught.

[17]   [ALS]

66 College St.,
Providence, R.I.,
Octr. 13, 1934.

Dear Mr. Searight:—

I thought you'd find the Wandrei drawings of interest. Certainly, they belong to a school far different from Smith's—one stemming rather from Beardsley, Sime, & Harry Clarke. They display a strong *decorative* sense—an ability to balance masses & achieve a certain harmony betwixt the parts of a complex composition—which the hierophant of Tsathoggua has not yet achieved. Wandrei will be an interesting youth to watch—& I shall try to get as many as possible of the prints which Barlow is offering.

As to theism & its reverse—I would say that the existence of a guiding cosmic "consciousness" or "purpose" is *improbable* because (a) there is no evidence of it in nature, & (b) & because such examples of "consciousness" & "purpose" as we do know are strictly local & confined to one special type of material organisation. In other words, so far as we know, consciousness & purpose are very rare & specialised things—things linked with conditions apparently vastly different from any prevailing in the cosmos at large. To assume, gratuitously, that any such special arrangement (& one so rare amidst the infinity of other force-arrangements) exists on a magnified scale as the dominator of the entire cosmos—despite the lack of evidence that the entire fabric possesses any similarity to the local material nuclei which give rise to the only known cases of the given phenomena—seems to me a speculation so totally without basis as to be intrinsically absurd. And doubly so because we understand the psychological & anthropological forces which tend to create the illusion of a governing cosmic consciousness—through a well-known form of animism, or transference of human characteristics to inanimate objects & large natural forces. But—as I said before—I don't see why a realisation of the impersonality of the cosmos need make human beings disregard the rules whereby they can live collectively with a minimum of pain, waste, & disharmony. In other words, ethics ought to be able to stand independently—even if some organised emotional discipline (a successor to religion) is necessary to inculcate & enforce the right precepts among the less sensitive & analytical masses. As you say, a start has already been made in the evolution of the better Protestant churches toward a mainly ethical position. The N.Y. Riverside church under Dr. Fosdick[1] has progressed far in this direction.

I don't believe there'll be any rush for "The Shunned House"—if indeed Barlow ever gets around to binding it! There are 115 copies at his home, & W. Paul Cook probably has many more in storage somewhere.[2] I'll let you know when its appearance is likely—or if you wish, you can drop a card of enquiry to Barlow, whose present temporary address is 7019 Georgia Ave., N.W., Washington, D.C.

About bookplates—many firms offer standard designs on which one's name can be printed; but I prefer something more personal & individual— something expressive of my own especial nature & tastes. Thus the typical Providence colonial doorway & railing in my plate. The best way to get a plate is to discuss the matter with some suitable artist & agree on a design of maximum beauty & appropriateness. Then a large drawing can be made—& transformed to a cut by any commercial printer or photo-engraver. After that, editions can be struck off as needed. My plate was designed by my young friend *Wilfred B. Talman, Room 1830, 135 E. 42nd St., New York, N.Y.,* whose stories & verses you have probably seen from time to time in W.T. He is a very skilled amateur artist, & particularly good in anything approaching the *decorative*. My own plate was a gift—a recognition of gratuitous aid & coaching in the short story field—but Talman has made plates for others on a commercial basis, & to my mind furnishes the best work at the lowest prices of any artist obtainable. His rates go far below any others I ever heard of— indeed, I believe he is charging only $12.00 for drawing *& cut* in the case of a very fine & intricate plate he is making for a friend of mine—a highly individualised design minutely prescribed by the customer. If you consider my plate adequate in quality (& I am tremendously fond of it—we worked out the design through 2 years of discussion!), it would certainly pay you to write Talman & open up a discussion of suitable designs & prices. He is very conscientious, & would not be satisfied himself until you were. As for subjects— armorial bearings are not at all out of date. Talman uses his in his own plate, & I nearly had him use mine—although I finally decided that I preferred something more specifically expressive of my personal colonial antiquarianism. He is especially good at heraldic designs, & has done me a fine coat-of-arms on a large scale which I'd like to frame if that weren't a bit naive & ostentatious. But the whole matter is one which you ought to talk over with the artist—& I can't advise you too strongly to get in touch with Talman. I'd recommend that you choose a better paper stock than mine. My plates shew a tendency toward yellowing, & they look a bit cheap in books with especially fine end-papers & fly-leaves.

About that book you want—without question it is *The Frozen Pirate, by W. Clark Russell.* I have a wretched paper copy of it, & will gladly lend it to you if it is not available in your local public library.[3] Let me know. It is quite a famous tale in its way—or was, rather, in former generations. I read it in extreme youth—when 8 or 9—& was utterly fascinated by it . . . writing several yarns of my own under its influence. I don't believe I've read it since then, but every incident stands out freshly despite the years. I must skim through it again & see whether my infantile enthusiasm was warranted or otherwise! And don't fail to let me know if you wish the loan of my cheap & yellowed copy!

As for "Thrawn Janet"[4]—I thought I mentioned it in my history of the weird tale, but maybe I didn't (I haven't a copy of the *Recluse* at hand). At any rate, it ought to be mentioned. It is really a thing of vast & insidious power, & even the discouraging dialect can't quite kill it. "The Body-Snatchers" (which I read only once, perhaps 20 years ago) also seems to me to make the grade—at least, by a hair's breadth. Stevenson as a whole, though, has never been one of my favourites. He makes good light reading, beyond a doubt, but has a certain studied artificiality & unmotivated *jauntiness* which to me seem essentially hollow & at variance with artistic sincerity & real power. Both in fiction & verse he savours of the rather forced romanticism of the 19th century—thus being, in the last analysis, pleasant rather than vital.

Klarkash-Ton was highly grateful for your suggestions regarding Hugo the Rat; but doubts whether he could join in a collective lawsuit just now, in view of the *individual* suit which he already has under way through Miss Weber. He agrees that the joint plan would be ideal for smaller creditors if they could adjust the matter of initial expense. Curious that Miss W. does not reply to your letter. I haven't seen a copy of *Wonder Stories* for a year or two, but can imagine the nadir to which it must have sunk in view of the alienation of all its best authors. Sooner or later I fancy the Rat's tactics will prove self-defeating.

Have just read the new W.T. & think it is decidedly better than the previous issue. "The Black God's Kiss" leads by a wide margin, with "7 Geases" as an indubitable second. "Old Sledge" isn't bad.[5]

Autumn is now upon us, & I fear my outdoor reading & writing sessions are at an end. On my last trip of the kind I visited my favourite rural region north of Providence—writing first on a stone wall overlooking a magnificent sweep of verdant valley & distant steepled hillside, & later atop a rocky bluff by a small glassy tarn in the midst of deep woods. The leaves had begun to turn, but the bulk of the landscape was still aestival. During October I hope to have many rustic outings of a less sedentary character—& then the long hibernation!

With every good wish, & trusting that you'll let me know if you wish to see my copy of the "Frozen Pirate",

I remain

Yrs most sincerely,

H P L

Notes

1. Harry Emerson Fosdick (1878–1969), American clergyman and author who attempted to harmonize the findings of modern science with religious belief.

2. RHB bound only a few copies. The sheets RHB had were eventually bound and distributed by Arkham House in the 1960s. The sheets that remained in Cook's possession were rumored still to exist in the 1970s, but they have not yet come to light.

3. RFS did not obtain his own copy of *The Frozen Pirate* until 1964, when his son found a copy (Chicago: Donohue, Henneberry & Co., [1887?]) in a Detroit used bookstore and gave it to RFS as a Christmas present.

4. Robert Louis Stevenson (1850–1894), "Thrawn Janet," in *Dr. Jekyll and Mr. Hyde and The Merry Men and Other Tales* <1886, 1887> (London: J. M. Dent; New York: E. P. Dutton (Everyman's Library), [1914]–[1932]; *LL* 922). The story also appears in Joseph Lewis French, ed., *Masterpieces of Mystery* (Garden City, NY: Doubleday, Page & Co., 1920f; *LL* 356), 4 vols.; and Dorothy L. Sayers, ed., *The Omnibus of Crime* (1928; Garden City, NY: Garden City Publishing Co., 1931; *LL* 830). HPL mentions *Dr. Jekyll and Mr. Hyde* in "Supernatural Horror in Literature" but not "Thrawn Janet."

5. *WT,* October 1934: C. L. Moore, "The Black God's Kiss"; CAS, "The Seven Geases"; Paul Ernst, "Old Sledge."

[18] [ALS]

66 College St.,

Providence, R.I.,

Nov. 14, 1934.

Dear Mr. Searight:—

I surely hope you can find a copy of "The Frozen Pirate" for sale—it seems to me it ought to be in print somewhere, since Russell is one of the standard sea authors . . . . though perhaps his reputation has faded since I was young. Meanwhile my own copy is at your disposal for as long as you like whenever you wish to see it. I'll have to re-read it myself!

The W T story you are looking for is my own effusion—"The Whisperer in Darkness"—in the issue for August, 1931. If you'd care to re-read this I'd be glad to lend you the carbon of the MS. at any time. The scene is *Vermont*— & I tried to be rather realistic in describing the strange landscape of crowded green hills, deep woods, & the constant sound of trickling water. I visited Vermont for a fortnight in 1928, & the impression of that visit has never worn off.

Regarding the matter of cosmic organisation, & the question of a central consciousness or purpose, it would of course be departing from formal logic to speak of any such thing as technical *proof,* one way or the other. The bulk of the cosmos is entirely beyond perception or even imagination, & is likely to remain so permanently. All we can speak of are certain *probabilities,* as judged from phenomena within the small fraction of the cosmos which we do know. But probabilities can often be so strong as to suggest something practically equivalent to certainty. Thus, in the absence of any scintilla of evidence suggesting cosmic consciousness & purpose, & in the presence of strong evidence that all the consciousness & purpose we know are exclusive products of a certain form of complex material development utterly unlike anything conceivable as existing apart from compact organic matter, the chances for the existence of any universal mind or will become *practically* non-existent— though of course not *theoretically* so. And the final *practical* clincher is put on the argument when psychology & anthropology show us that the very *idea* of an universal mind & will is a common & inevitable type of illusion in the development of primitive man. That is, such an idea or belief is bound to exist at certain stages of racial growth—irrespective of what the realities may be . . . . the notion being due to the characteristic imaginative transference of human attributes to non-human objects, phenomena, & abstractions . . . the anthropological process called *animism.* Thus the existence of a system of belief in a cosmic mind ceases to be even a faint & presumptive indication of the real existence of such a mind. Nay, it only emphasises the utter improbability of the popular idea. We know (a) that the idea itself is a natural delusion common to mankind & wholly unrelated to any truth or evidence, & (b) that the real facts are totally & permanently inaccessible. Would it not, then, be an accident or coincidence *utterly beyond all probability* if the *real* nature of the unknowable cosmos were to be *precisely like the common delusion as to its nature* which known natural causes make it inevitable for us to harbour anyhow? All *likelihood* of the truth of the cosmic-consciousness concept is removed when we understand that this concept has a known & definite source in primitive illusion & personification. Returning to the *positive* improbability of a cosmic consciousness—of course, as you remark, some of the lower animals possess consciousness as well as man. But that means nothing, since man's distinction from other animals is very trivial & slight. The fact remains that *consciousness, so far as any trace of experience goes, is absolutely & inescapably a function of a certain complex type of organic material development AND NOTHING ELSE.* That is, there can be no consciousness without matter, protoplasm, & a long evolutionary process of the subdivision & building-up of complex forms of protoplasm. *To have anything like consciousness, purpose, mind, or will we must have a highly evolved physical brain.* No trace, indication, or tendency suggesting consciousness has ever been discovered except as an attribute of the highly evolved animal cerebrum. If there isn't a *physical brain* behind the universe, there isn't any will or consciousness there, either .... & who imagines that a governing physical brain of colossal magnitude exists somewhere in space? The idea of *consciousness* or *will* apart from the *complex physical tissue* which is, according to *all* our observation & experience, the *sole & essential basis* of such things, is really too childish for adult consideration, as Haeckel long ago pointed out. It is he who aptly called the mythical "god" a "gaseous vertebrate"—meaning a thing supposed to be as ethereal & pervasive as a gas, yet possessing qualities which only a vertebrate animal with a complex physical brain could possess.[1]

Here, then, is the list of conditions before us:

(1.)   There is no evidence of any "mind" or "will" in nature-at-large, & no trace of any reason why there should be such.

(2.)   There is, on the contrary, overwhelmingly powerful evidence that mind & will are local results of complex physical processes which could not exist in the fabric of the cosmos as a whole.

(3.)   Moreover, we now realise that the very *idea* of a cosmic mind & will is a fixed type of illusion, arising from natural & well-known psychological causes, inevitable to our species in its more primitive stages.

(4.)   In the face of all these indications, & in the absence of any hint impelling one toward a different assumption, it is certainly the height of absurdity & puerility to accept, FOR NO REASON AT ALL, the illusory myths of primitive man; myths whose natural origin & non-factual character have been so extensively demonstrated. What we *know* about the larger cosmos is absolutely nothing; & in the absence of knowledge we can only tentatively accept what seems to be the *least improbable* working hypothesis. Now *certainly* the old myths of a "cosmic mind" are not only *not the least improbable,* but are actually *the most wildly & absurdly improbable* of all possible theories of cosmic organisation & governance; *insomuch as they assume the diffusive presence, in the universe as a whole, of a type of definite force-pattern* [i.e., consciousness & will] *which* **all** *our experience indicates as confined to complex physical developments of matter incapable of a diffusive universal existence in the cosmos at large.* It is simple insanity—or would be if it were not merely the result of emotional inhibitions due to childhood training [a training which amounts to local mental crippling]—to prefer the wildly improbable mythical explanation of nature to some other explanation less violative of common reason. Indeed, it is almost equally insane to treat such myths as on any sort of plane of equality with really rational speculations. As to what the least improbable & irrational explanation of the cosmic mechanism is: we can only say that common sense bids us observe whatever fraction of the universal fabric we can; study the phenomena & underlying appearances of law in this fraction with the utmost care; note the dominant relationships of smaller units to larger units; & finally, through a process of frankly tentative extrapolation, make inferences regarding the *general state of things* of which our observable fragment is, so far as we can judge, a not untypical specimen. The net hypothesis which we thus derive is, of course, one of a cosmos of mutually interacting forces without beginning, ending, meaning, consciousness, or direction. Simply a *fixed condition* of infinite automatic mutations, of which such things as matter, stars, planets, living beings, & the like are only momentary & negligible byproducts. This, let us observe, is simply *the least improbable of all theories*. It accounts for what we know of the universe, & does so *without the direct contradictions of experience & common reason* which reside in any other conceivable theory. It is merely the thing which the evidence naturally suggests, in the absence of any evidence for any other theory, or of any reason for considering any other theory.

––––––––––

This, I guess, covers all your points. As you see, the reason for refusing to treat pro-cosmic-consciousness & anti-cosmic-consciousness theories as *equal* in the face of the absolutely unknowable rests primarily on what we know of the *nature of consciousness*. All our experience—& all the inferences suggested by our experience—point to *consciousness as an exclusive product of highly evolved solid physical matter*. Without a tangible physical brain, the phenomenon of consciousness is inconceivable. Is it not, then, folly to give serious consideration to myths which imply that consciousness exists as a spread-out abstraction in the diffused ether of the cosmos? Especially when we are able to *trace the origin of these myths & deduce the reasons for their persistence* through the sciences of anthropology & psychology? A good resume of the existing limitations of knowledge—involving an amusing exposé of the emotional factors causing elderly workers in single physical sciences (Millikan, Jeans, Eddington)[2] to cling pathetically to the shreds of their childhood theism—can be found in a back number of *Harpers* . . . . I forget the exact issue, but it was sometime last spring or late winter. You could easily find it in a file—its title is "Science Has Not Gone Mystical", by Henshaw Ward.[3] "The Modern Temper", by Joseph Wood Krutch, also sheds sensible light—as do sundry works by Santayana, John Dewey, Bertrand Russell, & others of foremost intellectual eminence. It is pretty safe to say that religion or anything like it is definitely out as an adult explanation of nature & the cosmos. True, all is unknown & unknowable—but we certainly have to make some pretty strong guesses when we look the evidence over!

I surely hope that you & Talman can make some satisfactory arrangement regarding bookplates. You don't need to send him a *pictorial* representation of your arms. Heraldry is a precisely conventionalised science, with every feature exactly indicated in words. Give Talman an accurate *verbal* description of your coat—a "blazoning" in the language of heraldry—& he can draw you a design as perfect as if he had seen it depicted.[4] You doubtless know how a "blazoning" runs—such being common in books of genealogy. For example, my own outfit reads thus: "Vert, a chevron, engrailed, or, between three foxes' heads, erased, or. Crest: on a wreath, a tower, or. Motto: *Quae amamus tuemur.*"[5] With that description alone, heraldic artists all over the world would be able to draw exactly the same thing—varying only in subtle & inconsequential shadings & decorative backgrounds determined by individual taste. In your case, Talman would of course show you samples of various sizes & techniques in advance, so that you'd know exactly what you were getting. I feel strongly that he will be able to furnish eminently gratifying results.

I haven't seen the latest W T, hence cannot as yet comment on its contents. What you say of Gurwit[6] is indeed interesting—I never heard of him before except as a name attached to certain distinctly mediocre tales. Hope the F F can carry on despite the financial straits emphasised in the new issue. "Beyond the Wall of Sleep" was written in 1919 & has many crudities—yet Wright has accepted worse in his day.[7] Hope the appearance of your tales in F F & W T won't be indefinitely delayed—though Wright is famous for his deferred publishing of stories. A client of mine has had a story awaiting publication for over a year & a half. One thing in the new F F which interests me is the allusion to a *high-grade* weird magazine (first of its kind in the world, I fancy) just established in England—*Tales of the Uncanny*. Tales by Blackwood, Wells, &c. are said to be featured—though I suspect they must be largely reprints. Anyhow, I'd like to get hold of its address & see what it's like. I was glad to see Klarkash-Ton's "The Primal City" printed at last.[8] Wright was an utter ass to reject that.

Alas—the chill of late autumn is indeed upon us . . . though in Providence the leaves are still putting up a brave fight. The period of my outdoor explorations is definitely over—though I am grateful for the 24-hour steam heat so faithfully provided in my present habitat. I surely echo your hope that last winter's rigours may not be repeated!

What was probably my farewell to 1934's outside world consisted of a very pleasant week-end visit to my host of last August in the Boston zone—Edward H. Cole—Oct. 19–21; a visit including several rural jaunts in Cole's well-heated Chevrolet. On Oct. 20th we explored a section of N. Central Mass. which I had never before visited, & in which I saw some of the finest autumnal foliage & landscape vistas that I have ever beheld. The focus of the trip was W. Townsend, where we lunched at a rambling old tavern built in 1774, & patronised the quaintest general store that I've seen in 30 years. Nearby is the Willard Brook State Forest, where we revelled in wooded hills, rock waterfalls, & leafy gorges of indescribable picturesqueness. From nearly every point the distant bulk of Mt. Wachusett loomed up, & once we had a splendid view of a steepled village in a peaceful valley. On the 21st Cole & his wife brought me back to Providence in the car—picking up my aunt at #66 & setting out for the historic Narragansett country which E. Hoffmann Price & I explored last year.[9] We visited venerable Wickford with its drowsing wharves & elm-shaded main street, & later struck inland to the gorgeously lovely spot where Gilbert Stuart's birthplace—a snuff mill built in 1750—broods beside the Narrow River. This ancient structure has been fully restored—wheel & all—so that it can grind snuff as well as it did when Stuart's father ran it 180 years ago. The surrounding countryside is doubly beautiful in autumn, & Cole insisted on some adventurous explorations which resulted in our getting partly lost.

Well—I trust you'll let me know if you'd like to see my paper-covered "Frozen Pirate" . . . . & the MS. of "The Whisperer in Darkness."

All good wishes—Yrs most cordially—

H P L

Notes

1. HPL refers to Ernst Haeckel (1834–1919), German biologist and philosopher whose treatise *Die Welträthsel* (1899; Eng. tr. as *The Riddle of the Universe*, 1900) parodied the idea of God as a "gaseous invertebrate." HPL read the work around 1919.

2. The American physicist Robert Andrews Millikan (1868–1953) and the British astronomers James Jeans (1877–1946) and Arthur S. Eddington (1882–1944) all attempted to reconcile the findings of science with religious belief.

3. The article is actually in the *Atlantic Monthly* 152, No. 2 (August 1933): 186–94.

4. It was not until 1953 that RFS, while visiting Carlisle, PA, on a genealogical trek, was directed to Headlies Book Exchange in Pittsburgh where he acquired *Record of the Searight Family (Also Written Seawright) Established in America* by William Searight (Uniontown, PA, 1893). Within it he found the heraldic information necessary to recreate his coat-of-arms.

5. "We defend the things we love." The coats of arms HPL drew in letters to Frank Belknap Long (24 September 1927) and James F. Morton ("Lud's Day" [1927]; both mss., JHL) resemble what HPL describes here.

6. S. Gordon Gurwit (1890–?), author of "The Pistol" (*WT*, October 1934) and "The Golden Glow" (*WT*, November 1934).

7. Wright published the story in *WT* following HPL's death.

8. *FF* 2, No. 3 (November 1934): 41–45.

9. See EHP, "The Man Who Was Lovecraft" 285–86.

[19]   [ALS]

66 College St.,

Providence, R.I.,

Dec. 22, 1934.

Dear Mr. Searight:—

I am herewith enclosing "The Whisperer in Darkness",

which I hope will not prove a disappointment on second reading. It was not one of the most popular of my efforts, but it does get in a lot of my impressions of Vermont. No hurry at all about its return. I wish I'd purchased more copies of the magazine in order to have a lighter lending copy. I *did* have one, but some infamous scion of Satan borrowed it & failed to return it!

Regarding typing—I can't afford to hire it, so reluctantly do it myself except when I can strike some sort of bargain deal with somebody having a typewriter. For example—little Bobby Barlow has an insane penchant for collecting the original MSS. of nonentities, hence will often agree to type a MS. free if he is allowed to keep the longhand rough draught. In other cases I've traded superfluous books & other odds & ends for typing work. But generally I have no such luck . . . . the enclosed "Whisperer" MS. is the product of my own weary hands & aching head, assisted by the rebuilt Remington which I purchased in 1906! Like you, I can't compose anything of importance on a machine—& I marvel unendingly at those who (like Long, Howard, & others of the younger generation) can & do. I revise on my original MS. by crossing things out & making interpolations in minute handwriting—sometimes inserting whole paragraphs in the marginal spaces & connecting them to their proper places with carets & long leading lines. As a result, my rough draughts are virtually unreadable save by myself—indeed, when others type them I have to go over the result most carefully. I revise a great deal—always transposing the parts of a sentence or paragraph if the first version does not suit my rhythmical ear or rhetorical taste. This is something the apostles of typing seldom do—& I think their style is the worse for it. Indeed, I believe that the use of the typewriter with its distracting noises, artificial rhythms, & mechanical revisory difficulties has had much to do with the unmistakable deterioration of style during the past two decades. I am all for the easy, flexible traditional methods which have served the race for 10,000 years or more. Mechanical aid is quite all right up to a certain point—for example, I gladly avail myself of the fountain pen—but *beyond* that certain point it seems to me that it involves something like the 'law of diminishing returns' . . . . . . disturbing accustomed conditions & creating more fresh difficulties than it overcomes. This applies to more things than writing, too. While the machine has an enormous function to fulfil in the production of real necessities & the elimination of real hardships, & while it may well become (after the inevitable period of readjustment & confusion) an unprecedented force for social & economic liberation, it seems certain to me that the extension of mechanisation to every department of life is essentially a mistake. Beyond certain limits, the machine tends indubitably to form an actual *obstacle* between the performer & the task to be performed . . . . especially if the task is a flexible one involving delicate touches of shading & remodelling. I shall never be convinced that anything can equal handwriting for the production of really good prose & verse. But I do have the most damnable difficulty in getting a fountain pen to suit me. I write rapidly & voluminously, & become quickly fatigued unless the pen will operate virtually without pressure—& this rapid rate also calls for a very copious feed. It takes a week of exchanging & adjusting to get a pen smooth & free-flowing enough for me—indeed, no ordinary store clerk seems able to meet my apparently finical requirements. I always wait till I can get to a Waterman central office in Boston or New York, where there is an unlimited supply of points, & an expert to attend to the details of feed adjustment. My rule for the feed is to have it just as copious as it can be without actually dripping. I try usually to have two pens on hand—so that I won't be stranded when one of them gives out. Just now I have a pen pretty close to my ideal—plus one that rates as 'pretty fair'.

Yes—it is undoubtedly the emotions which keep alive the vestiges of supernatural belief in those who know the facts of modern science. Many of these emotions, however, are basically artificial—the results of the childhood inculcation of certain conventional expectations & points of view—so that they may be expected to diminish as the generations advance. Some of the articles in the Catholic Encyclopaedia must make highly interesting reading, & I can well understand how certain controversial points can be treated from both angles without any radical discrepancy in the record of external facts. History is certainly a chaos of prejudiced statements—& the only way to judge of the absolute merits of any issue is to read the statements on both sides & draw a probable average. As you say, the minute examination of points inspired by partisanship makes the arguments of extremists often more valuable than the casual comments of a genuine neutral might be.

I wish you luck in your heraldic quest. What a pity that the crucial volume perished in the flames! Hope you can locate another copy—at least, get access to it even if it is not purchasable. But I think you might find the Searight or Seabright arms in some work of more general character. For example—at the Providence Public Library there used to be a book listing virtually every coat-of-arms ever granted by the Heralds' College; & in such a compilation you would undoubtedly find several Searight (or -bright) shields. Your only rub would then be to pick the especial one belonging to your branch. Unfortunately, this book has vanished in recent years from the local shelves, & I don't recall the name of it. But similar works must be in all the leading genealogical libraries—of which I presume Detroit has its share. Have you given the local public library a thorough examination? And do you think your *latent* memory of your arms would be sufficient to let you pick the right set from among several of more or less similar nature? The history of your line & of its divisions & mutations is indeed interesting. There is something heroic & poetic in the thought of Eric [or Olaf or Bjorne or Thorfinn or whatever-he-was] Sea-Bright standing, sword in hand, in the prow of his Viking galley, with flaxen hair & beard streaming in the wind! The line of Lovecraft appears to begin more prosaically—indeed, it does not authentically reach back to the Conquest. It is of Devonshire origin, & first figures in records early in the 15ᵗʰ century. Of its Saxon source there is no doubt—& the original form of the name is Lovecroft; implying a devotion to ancestral acres rather than to art or shrewdness. It was most numerous in the region near the river Teign. In the reign of Henry VII Thomas LovecrOft bore as arms a chevron, Or, between three towers, Or, on a field Vert; & around 1560 John LovecrAft of Minster Hall near Newton-Abbot bore similar arms, but with foxes' heads, erased, Or, replacing the towers, & with engrailing on the chevron. The connexion is unmistakable, though I do not know the precise relationship. It is interesting to note that, a century afterward, one of the LovecrAft line married a woman of the LovecrOft line; their children taking over the crest & motto which had in the meantime become attached to the LovecrOft arms. This family did not emigrate to the colonies in early times, but waited for misfortune to wreck it on its own soil. My great-great-grandfather Thomas Lovecraft (1745–1826) appears to have been a wild & reckless old boy in his day, & certainly left his finances & estates in a sad chaos. By 1823 he had circumvented whatever entail provisions remained at that time, & was totally cleaned out. Directly after his death my great-grandfather Joseph struck out for the U.S. with his wife & six children & settled in northern New York state, but the trip & the break were too much for him, & he died in 1828. Thus I am much closer to Old England than the average Yankee—my own grandfather, George Lovecraft, having been born in 1815 in Minster Hall on the old Devonshire soil. He grew to maturity in Rochester, N.Y., afterward moving to Mt. Vernon near N.Y. City. My father was born in Rochester. Contributory lines—Fulford, Morris, Musgrave, Chichester, Legge, Carew, Jenkins, Parry, &c—are more ancient than the Lovecraft line, & include both Norman conquerors & Welsh aborigines. On my mother's side—Phillips—I represent the colonial New England stock; her ancestors arriving in America between 1630 & 1658. It is curious to note that of all the persons I have met in later life through literary contacts only *two* have any known link of blood connexion with me. These are James F. Morton, who shares my Perkins line (as does also Franklin D. Roosevelt), & young Barlow, who has a strain from my Rathbone ancestors. I never took any active interest in genealogy till recent years, when young Talman stirred me up to an examination of boxes full of long-untouched & occasionally rather disordered material. I have not yet prepared the set of coherent & complete charts that I ought to prepare .... although it doesn't greatly matter, since I have no descendants. It is my opinion that I am the only Lovecraft in the U.S. With one exception, I know of the extinction of all the other male lines from Joseph Lovecraft—& that exception involves so complete a western disappearance & subsequent silence that I scarcely believe I have any unknown cousins today. Last spring I was quite excited over the appearance of a letter in the W.T. Eyrie signed "Edgar Lovecraft, Martinsburg, W. Va."[1]—& I wrote the gentleman a letter of enquiry about himself. My missive, however, was returned by the post-office; & I have since come to the conclusion that the name was a pseudonym—probably picked at random from the W.T. table of contents. Of course (since the stock still abounds in Devonshire) there may be American Lovecrafts today not descended from Joseph, but I do not know of any. There were none in America in colonial times, as records clearly show. So— as far as this side of the Atlantic is concerned—I tend to share with you a somewhat Usher-like distinctiveness. Which reminds me that there is an *Usher* line—of very ancient settlement—in Rhode Island . . . on the east shore of the bay (part of the old Plymouth colony & settled in 1677 after King Philip's War) which we took over from Massachusetts (after a boundary dispute finally settled by a royal decree of George II) in 1747.

Regarding Greek—alas, my present knowledge consists only of very meagre fragments surviving from a bygone knowledge (1 year in school—as far as the second book of the Anabasis[2]—plus more or less independent delving & browsing . . . all before 1909) which was never more than superficial. It is certainly true that with any foreign language, living or "dead" (to me the distinction between these two sorts never seemed important, since Greek & Roman literature lives for ever in the heritage of all Western Europe, while the literature of the different surviving languages influence one another much less), the literature can be better appreciated through really good translations (if we can find such) than through a laborious grammar-&-lexicon de-coding of the original texts. And unless one is a vastly more profound scholar than the average citizen is apt to be, any direct approach to the original text is likely to be only such a slow & painful de-coding. However, I believe that one's understanding of a foreign race & its mentality is enormously increased by a knowledge of that race's habit of expression as revealed in its idioms, so that at least a smattering of such knowledge is of great value. Even when one depends on translations for large-scale reading, those translations convey more if the reader also knows something of the elements & basic structure of the alien tongue. I wish I were a better linguist—as it is, I am a notoriously poor one. I am slow to acquire & quick to forget—except when the language possesses a particular hold on my imagination, as does Latin. For the Roman civilisation I have always had a singular feeling of affinity—as if it were my own. It is impossible for me to survey the ancient world except as a Roman; & I instinctively feel & use the term "we" or "us" in relation to the citizens or armies of the Respublica, just as I feel & use "they" or "them" in relation to the Greeks or Gauls or Parthians or Syrians or Egyptians or Carthaginians. Curiously, this feeling triumphs over blood itself—for while (aside from the Roman element in Britain, which the late Sir Arthur Weigall[3] showed to be not inconsiderably represented in modern English veins) it is the Teutonic & Celtic tribesmen of antiquity who are my own actual progenitors, these tribesmen always seem like "them" to me, whereas their Roman opponents seem like "us". In reflecting on Claudius' conquest of Britannia it is with the invading Roman rather than with the defeated Celt that I feel identified—& when I think of the tragedy in the Saltus Teutobergiensis I weep (like Augustus) for Quintilius Varus rather than exult with Arminius & his Germans. Why this is, I do not know—but the fact is that when I imagine myself anterior to the Dark Ages it is always as a Roman & not as a Northerner.* Remoter antiquity—the Egypto-Chaldaean age before the tribes of Italy had any coherent culture—arouses no subjective reaction whatsoever in me. All of which explains why I "took to" Latin as to no other foreign speech. Even now, French & Spanish & Italian seem to me only debased dialects. I agree with you that it would probably be better to teach languages with phrases & sentences than to follow the present mechanical procedure. Indeed, (as you point out regarding your H.S. German & regarding priesthood Latin students) attempts have been made to do so. One of the most useful of all introductions to French is (as I view it) a little volume popular a century & a quarter ago & now unfortunately obsolete & forgotten— Wanostrocht's "Recueil Choisi de Traits Historiques & Contes Moraux", of which I have the 1810 edition used by my great-grandfather Jeremiah Phillips in his boyhood. This consists of little historical anecdotes & fables in simple, idiomatic French—with no rules, declensions, or conjugations whatsoever, but with footnotes explaining every word not likely to be recognised through English resemblances. In the earlier tales words & idioms close to those of English are used as much as possible—the idea being to take the mother-tongue as a starting-point & work away from it gradually. To me—& a French instructor of long experience agrees with me—more can be obtained in a short time through these exercises than through any amount of drilling with precepts & tables. Here is a specimen of the early text—the part below the line being footnotes. Certain basic & oft-repeated pronouns, prepositions, &c. are given at the outset in a simple list.

> L'Empereur Aurelieu, étant arrivé devant la ville de Tyane, et en ayant trouvé les portes fermées, jura, dans sa colère, qu'il ne laisseroit pas seulement un chien en vie dans cette cité rebelle.
>
> Empereur, *emperor*; arrivé, *arrived*; ville, *city*; trouvé, found; portes, *gates*; fermées, shut; jura, swore; colère, anger; ne laisseroit pas, *would not leave*; seulement, *single*; chien, *dog*; en vie, *alive*; cité, *city*; rebelle, *rebellious*.

After a word has been defined in footnotes two or three times, the definition is not repeated; thus forcing the pupil to go "on his own". With a good teacher,

---

*This gets me into furious verbal clashes with Robert E. Howard, who is as fanatically anti-Roman as I am instinctively Roman. It is curious that he & I both feel antiquity very keenly as a living essence—albeit on bitterly opposed sides. He is always the primal Celt.

tremendous progress ought to be made—& indeed, the book was highly popular both in England & America from its first appearance in 1799 down to the 1830's or later. I have seen an edition as late as 1825. The author, I judge, was a Royalist refugee from the French revolution—his sentiments indicate such, & the volume was written in England. Some day I'm going to read the Recueil through again—heaven knows I need it, for Gallic speech has so slipped away from me that I wouldn't tackle anything harder than the "Ne stationnez pas" or "Traverse de Chemin de fer" signs of Quebec without a dictionary! German I never learned. I had a half-year of it in school, but it was absolutely repulsive to my Latin-biassed taste. The whole vocal timbre of it grated on me—it seemed as *hostile* as Ariovistus to Caesar or Arminius to Varus or the Marcomanni to Marcus Aurelius! So nowadays when I want to concoct a learned-sounding Germanic phrase to trick out a story, I have to call on an expert like E. Hoffmann Price or little Augie Derleth.[4] Did I, by the way, ever tell you about last year's heated controversy regarding a German equivalent for "Nameless Cults"? Robert E. Howard invented the mythical von Junzt opus, but did not give it a German name—since he is as ignorant as I of German. I thought it would be more convincing to have one, so passed the question to Derleth—who responded with *Unaussprechlichen Kulten.* Not long afterward Price, recalling his scraps of West Point German, began to question the correctness of this phrase for the exact shade of meaning intended, & offered *Unnenbarren*[5] as a substitute. Wright—who prides himself on a smattering of German—became convinced that Sultan Malik was right, & refused to use the Derleth version . . . . forgetting that Sauk City was settled by Germans of great cultivation, among whom the language was kept alive in its best form as a heritage, so that little Augie knows what he's talking about. Thus matters stood deadlocked until, one day, the ex-illustrator Senf happened in at 840 N. Michigan to talk over old times. He was born & educated in Germany, & obviously has the right dope. The subject was brought up, & C. C. unhesitatingly voted for Derleth . . . thus settling the matter, & atoning for all the third-rate "art" he perpetrated in the dear dead days gone by! So it is certain that the monstrous compilation of Herr von Junzt (with its cryptic borrowings from the Eltdown Shards) was issued in Düsseldorf under the title *Unaussprechlichen Kulten!*

Thanks extremely for the glimpse of the recent verses, which I greatly enjoyed. "The Road" is exquisite—conjuring up a vivid picture & evoking hints of alluring mysteries beyond the visible scene. I surely hope it may find appropriate publication in due season. The Yuletide piece is full of sprightliness & charm, & ought to delight the juvenile & parental public alike. As for a title—a poem with this theme & treatment, it seems to me, ought to make no attempt at the allusive, artificially brilliant, learned, or figurative type of nomenclature. I'd advise something absolutely simple & descriptive, such as "The Christmas Visitor."[6] Toward the end I see that you have rhymed a syllable *with itself* (star-*light*—de-*light*)—hence would suggest a rectification through the change of the first line involved to "Speeding off in the star-gleaming night".[7] Or perhaps you can think of apter equivalents. As per request, I am sending both poems on to Baldwin—who I am sure will like them. Incidentally, the time to submit Christmas poems to the larger magazines is, I believe, *June*— which allows for leisurely consideration & ample location-planning if accepted.

You have certainly had an early touch of winter—but so have we; although no snowfall of any magnitude or duration has accompanied it. The worst cold spell was that of Dec. 8–12 inclusive, when the mercury fell to 10° repeatedly, & attained a record (for the season) minimum of +8°. I, of course, was a prisoner indoors all this time; since I cannot safely expose myself to anything under +20°. But between cold spells I have managed to be reasonably active. I was in Boston late in November, & early this month I attended several lectures on aesthetic subjects—a series connected with the local observance of "Art Week." Some of these events were really very interesting— especially a demonstration of painting by two of Providence's leading artists, during which they finished a picture apiece in their respective media . . . landscape & portrait . . . in full view of their audience. Another event was the display of the choicest of the 717 Japanese prints just acquired by the local art museum. This is a really important accession—placing our museum in competition with Boston's . . . . which boasts of having the finest Japanese print collection outside Japan itself. The Providence collection is of the first quality, involving large numbers of items by Hokusai, Hiroshige, & kindred standbys. A later event of much interest was the demonstration of the new aesthetic form—the correlation of shifting colour with music. I had to pass this up, however, since it came after the beginning of the cold spell.

Just now I'm trying to decide whether I dare accept Long's invitation to visit him after Christmas. Possibly I will—for the subway system in N.Y. enables one to get about under cover & escape the worst rigours of whatever cold weather may ensue. Barlow has a notion of coming up from Washington if I go, & letting me introduce him to Long & the Manhattan group. I went last year & survived—so we shall see! But first I must get my programme of work at least moderately under control.

The Dec. W.T. strikes me as much superior to the Nov. issue. Klarkash-Ton's "Xeethra" easily leads the contents, with Miss Moore's "Black God's Shadow" a good second. Derleth, Flanders, & Byrne are not bad, & Morgan gives a pleasing embodiment of his single plot-idea. Two-Gun Bob's story is more an adventure yarn than a weird tale (for the monster toward the end is rather extraneously dragged in), but it is good of its kind.[8] I hear of new weird magazines appearing, but doubt if they would care for anything in my line. The report of a high-grade British weird magazine in the F F turned out to be a mistake—young Schwartz having confused an *anthology* with a magazine. *Marvel Tales* came some time ago, but the only first-rate thing in it is Keller's "Golden Bough".[9] I also received Crawford's brochure with C A S's "White

Sibyl" & Keller's "Men of Avalon"—but here Keller is hopelessly outclassed. New F F came the other day, & I was sorry to note the absence of a cover. But if Hornig can keep it going at all, he's doing well! When I get some more time I'm going to resume my weird background-reading—belatedly forming the acquaintance of the famous "Malleus Maleficarum", lent me by the always-accomodating Koenig. I'm also trying to write a new story,[10] though other demands have left me stalled about ¾ through it.

With all good wishes for the holidays, & again congratulating you on the excellence of your new verses, I remain

Most sincerely yours——H P L

P.S. Wandrei has been visiting Klarkash-Ton in Auburn. ¶ Don't fail to let me know if you'd like to see "The Frozen Pirate."

Notes

1. *WT* 23, No. 6 (June 1934): 783. Probably a hybrid pseudonym combining *Edgar* A. Poe and H. P. *Lovecraft*. "Edgar Lovecraft" had written: "[Margaret] Brundage is the greatest artist yet. His [*sic*] alien exotic use of rainbow tones is describable alone as breath-taking. As for the birth-nude female form, he depicts it in such a manner that it is not vulgar, but is simply beautiful. By all means keep Brundage. . . . The covers for June, July, September and January are the best yet. Black or jade backings instill a feeling of bizarreness and grotesqueness." Such sentiments were certainly antipodal to HPL's.

2. The *Anabasis* or "The March Up-Country" by the Greek historian Xenophon, still a standard text for beginning Greek.

3. Weigall died on 3 January 1934.

4. The only "learned-sounding Germanic phrase" in HPL's stories is in "The Horror at Red Hook" (1925), *"es lasst sich nicht lesen"* ("it does not permit itself to be read"), taken from Poe's "The Man of the Crowd."

5. I.e., *unmentionable*.

6. RFS in fact entitled the poem "The Christmas Visitor." It is unpublished.

7. RFS has written "Speeding off through the star-gleaming night" in the final draft of the poem.

8. August Derleth and Mark Schorer, "A Matter of Faith"; John Flanders, "The Graveyard Duchess"; Brooke Byrne, "The Werewolf's Howl"; Bassett Morgan, "The Vengeance of Ti Fong"; Robert E. Howard, "A Witch Shall Be Born."

9. David H. Keller, "The Golden Bough" (*Marvel Tales*, Winter 1934).

10. "The Shadow out of Time."

[20]   [ALS]

66 College St.,
Providence, R.I.,
Jany. 26, 1935.

Dear Mr. Searight:—

Immediately upon receipt of your letter I sent along my copy of "The Frozen Pirate"—which I trust has reached you safely. If the edges are crumbled away, I have only myself to blame—for I didn't stop to hunt up any protective cardboard. I surely hope you won't find it disappointing upon re-reading. There is no hurry whatever about its return—take all the time you wish for its leisurely savouring.

Glad the "Whisperer" didn't lose ground on a second perusal. One trouble with this yarn, perhaps, is the divided object with which it was written. For the most part the weird element is paramount—but now & then the desire to depict Vermont scenery & atmosphere got the upper hand. But at least it forms an attempt at sincere expression.

Regarding composition—yes, I suppose there are a few of us old longhanders left; though the younger generation seems curiously fond of its mechanical gimcracks! In the field of pens—I have indeed had the merits of the Shaeffer & the Wahl pointed out to me . . . . the latter as recently as last September, when I took this Parker into a local shop for treatment. If I were ever to get an absolutely new pen—independently of the replacement opportunities of the Waterman & Parker outfits—I think I would try a Sheaffer. Some of the new models seem to provide for just the sort of feather touch & Niagara-like flow I require. I never had a better fountain pen than my *first*—a Christmas present in 1903. Its flow & touch were fabulously perfect, yet if I recall aright it was rather inexpensive. Its name was *Remex*—long forgotten, no doubt, in the annals of merchandising. Another beloved standby was the Waterman I bought in 1906 & used continuously (with occasional replacements of point) for *seventeen years*. Both vanished tragically. I lost the Remex a year after its acquisition—from my pocket as I was shovelling snow. There were no clips in those days. When the snow melted I found it—with the barrel cracked! The 1906-er vanished amidst the sands of ancient Marblehead ("Kingsport") in 1923. It had a clip, but not a very good one—& I probably yanked it unknowingly out of my pocket when extracting some papers. Its successor was a Conklin—which I lent to a chap[1] for an afternoon . . . & which he at once proceeded to lose. That had a good point & feed, but didn't hold much ink. It was my first self-filler—& tanked up in a curious way, through twisting a ring around the barrel. From 1926 to 1933–4 I had execrable pen luck—but now (as I have mentioned) this gift Parker[2] & a Waterman which I've had adjusted endless times are in some kind of shape. I want two decent pens on hand in case one gives out—for replacement, as I have sadly learned, is no swift process! Sorry your Conklin has temperamental spells—possibly some specialist can eventually analyse & remedy the trouble.

Regarding genealogy—I have an Ellis ancestor, though unfortunately I don't know how she hooks on to any continuous Ellis line. Even the dates of her birth & death are absent from my charts—but her name was *Dorcas,* & she married my lineal ancestor Samuel Casey Sr. (1686–1752) of Newport (later Kingston) R.I. on Sept. 23, 1715. This bird Sam had a curious heritage. His paternal line was Irish, stretching back to one Cathasach of the Ui Nialls (O'Neills) of Tyrone, & claiming descent from Baudoin Ui Niall, 137th legendary king of Ireland. In 1641 the line was completely Protestantised & Anglicised through intermarriage, & dwelt amongst the Anglo-Irish—with a town house in Dublin. Then came the historic massacre by the Papists, & the grandparents of the above-mentioned Samuel were murdered in their own home in Dublin. Their small son Thomas, however, was saved by his nurse & taken to his mother's people in England—Gloucestershire. There he grew up, & thence at the age of 22—in 1658—he emigrated to Newport, R.I. From him stem all the colonial Protestant Caseys in New England . . . . or in the U.S. for that matter. Gen. Wanton Casey of the Revolution, Gen. Silas Casey (author of Casey's Military Tactics) who was killed in the Mexican War, the Casey who served as engineer in building the Washington Monument, & Edward Pearce Casey, architect of Washington's Congressional Library (for which gawd forgive him!), all trace their lineage back to little Tom from Dublin. So, too, does the famous silversmith & counterfeiter Samuel Casey Jr. . . . son of old Sam & Dorcas Ellis . . . . whose tankards & porringers are treasured in the Metropolitan, Boston, & other museums today, & who in 1770 was nearly hanged for coining Spanish milled dollars & Portugese moedores. He was freed through a general gaol-delivery at Kingston (by a band of men with blacked faces) on the night before his scheduled execution. Probably his neighbours were as deep in the coining plot (then rather lightly regarded in the colonies) as he was, & feared what he might reveal at the last moment. He vanished westward & was never heard of again, though rumour once hinted at his possible presence in Philadelphia.[3] A Vermont line of Caseys, whose progenitor came from Philadelphia in the late 18th century & vaguely spoke of descent from the Rhode Island stock, fondly believes that it forms the posterity of the fugitive . . . though no proof is possible. I am descended from the fugitive's more respectable but less artistic elder brother John (b. 1723), who married Mercy Dyer, a descendant of the famous Quaker martyr Mary Dyer (she, unlike Sam Casey Jr., *really* got hanged!). John's daughter Sarah married John Rathbone of Exeter R.I. in Oct. 1776, & *two* of their daughters—Sarah & Rhoby Rathbone—are my great-grandmothers. Sarah's daughter Rhoby Place (named for her aunt & mother-in-law) married Rhoby's son Whipple Phillips—& from that cousinly union sprang my mother Sarah Phillips. The Rathbone line extends to one Richard, born in 1574, who settled with his family in Roxbury, Mass. (now part of Boston—& adjacent to Dorchester) His son John (b. 1610 in England) had a son John (b. 1634 in Roxbury) who became one of the original purchasers of Block Island & later settled there. He was a representative in R.I.'s General Assembly in 1682, & in July 1689 (during King William's War) barely escaped the French privateers then pillaging Block Island. He had buried his money & silver plate, & was avidly sought by the enemy . . . . who indeed captured his son John (also my lineal ancestor—b. 1658 in Roxbury) & tortured him (though vainly) in an effort to make him reveal the hiding-place of the family possessions. This son John filled many public offices, & was a witness in an important pirate trial in 1712. He died in 1723. *His* son John (1693–1752) [there are *6 John* Rathbones in di rect succession in my ancestry—& certain distant cousins can reckon even a *7th!*] migrated to Escoheag on the R.I. mainland in 1744 & became my forbear. Other sons stayed on the island—& from one of those insular lines young Barlow is descended. His father still holds land there. I have the original will of the 6th John Rathbone (father of Sarah & Rhoby, my greatgrandmothers), who died in 1810 . . . . it is almost falling to pieces, & I must see about repairing it. The Place line into which Sarah Rathbone married stems from Dorchester, Mass.—one Enoch P. of that settlement coming to R.I. in the 1660's, when a number of Mass. colonists purchased land in the Narragansett Country on the west shore of Narragansett Bay. This Narragansett region developed a form of life utterly unlike anything else in New England, & closely parallelling the patriarchal plantation life of the South. Large landholding was common, & negro slaves were owned in large numbers. A typical plantation civilisation sprang up—with great estates, squirearchical institutions, & town life & town's houses in Newport across the bay. Stockraising & dairying were the leading economic reliances—& Narragansett pacers & Narragansett cheeses attained a fame which reached to Europe & Asia. From this rich & mellow existence sprang up a heritage & tradition & body of folklore not yet extinct. Ties with Virginia & the Carolinas were very close—so that many of the great families of those regions became intermarried with the Narragansett-country (or "South Country") stock. The Revolution destroyed this idyllic mode of life, though a few of the old families kept afloat by turning to manufacturing industries. Thus the still-opulent house of Hazard. I have two Hazard lines—but none of the surviving opulence! Robert Hazard, my great-great-great-great-great-grandfather (1635–1710), had 133 slaves, & a house so large that he was once jocosely asked whether he rode from front to back door on horseback. The houses of that region were of the common New England gambrel-roofed type, but constructed on a vast scale. I know of only 2 surviving specimens—one of which I explored with E. Hoffmann Price in 1933. Robert Hazard's wife Mary Brownell (1639–1739) is the only known *centenarian* in my ancestry. Their granddaughter Hannah Wilcox married Enoch Place's grandson—also named Enoch. (1701–

1789) Their son Stephen Place Sr. (1736–1817) built a homestead in Foster R.I. which still stands, & in which my grandmother & mother were both born. A picture of it (drawn by my mother from an original painting by a great-aunt) now hangs above my desk⁴—& I have several times visited it. It is out of the family now, but in fair condition. Beside it is the ancient Place burying-ground holding much of my ancestral dust. Stephen married Martha Perkins, descended from that John Perkins of Hillmorton, Warwickshire (1583–1654) who came to Boston (as a shipmate of Roger Williams) on the *Lion* & settled in Ipswich in 1633. From his son John Jr. (1609–1684) both I & my friend James F. Morton are descended. Morton & young Barlow are the only literary friends having a known blood link with me. It is through Morton (curator of the Paterson N.J. Museum, & in latter years a genealogist of sorts) that I have learned of the remoter ancestry of our common Perkins line (from which F. D. Roosevelt also descends). It appears that the visible start is with one Peter or Perkin (= Peterkin) Morely of Shropshire, a steward or bailiff to one Sir Hugh de Spencer in 1380. His grandson John Perkins, seneschal to Thomas de Spencer, received a grant of land & the arms & status of a gentleman in 1390. John's grandson, Thomas Perkins of Ufton Court, was a co-trustee with that Earl of Warwick called "The King Maker". The emigrant John Perkins was of the eleventh generation from Perkin Morley. I am of the twentieth—& Morton of the 19th. John's grandson Samuel fought in King Philip's War in 1676 & was subsequently given lands in Conn. His son Ebenezer crossed into Rhode Island, served in the Narragansett War of 1735, & became the founder of the main R.I. Perkins line. Ebenezer's granddaughter is the Martha who married Stephen Place & became my great-great-grandmother. So many scattered threads! I have not the patience to dig them out for myself, but they certainly are fascinating when one does get hold of them. Genealogy gives one a feeling of vital connexion with enormous reaches of time & space & history, & thereby acquires a certain dramatic or poetic value. Your lines are all immensely interesting. Though *Ellis* is the only name occurring in my own ancestry, I recognise several as belonging to my friend Morton's lineage. He, for example, descends from Roger Clap, & also has Clarke (Richard & Rowland), Ford, (Thomas) & Day (Robert). My late elder aunt's husband, Dr. Franklin Chase Clark, was descended from the Clarks of Plymouth Colony—& also from Gov. Winslow of that colony. R.I. has received much Plymouth-Pilgrim blood through her annexation in 1747 of a large region east of Narragansett Bay (Barrington, Warren, Bristol, Tiverton, Little Compton) settled by Plymouth stock. I, personally, have none of this blood—being without a single drop of the *Mayflower* strain. Regarding a possible link between you & Farnsworth Wright—you might or might not find such. *Wright*, of course, is a frequently duplicated surname. His *Farnsworths* came from New England—as I learned from some remarks of his last year. About Castle William in Boston, where Clap commanded—yes, it was on the island bearing what is now called Ft. Independence. I've been there many times. The fort is abandoned; & the island—connected with the mainland by a causeway—forms part of a marine park & is devoted to public enjoyment. Speaking of the execution of Maj. Andre—at which Eliakim Clapp was present—the tavern in which the hapless prisoner was confined was kept by a collateral ancestor of the weird tale writer Wilfred B. Talman, whom I recommended to you as a bookplate artist. It is maintained today as a public museum. Nearby is the house where Gen. Washington had his headquarters, & where Eliakim must have spent much time. This belonged to Talman's maternal line—& his mother was born there. The entire village of Tappan looks much as it did in that sad year of 1780 . . . . a fascinating place.

About the bookplate[5]—the specimen you enclose seems to me altogether delightful, with its classic framework & glamourous bit of garden vista. One could scarcely ask for a more pleasing or appropriate device! But I'm sorry the search for the coat-of-arms is proving so difficult. Have you tried looking it up in encyclopaedic works on heraldry, as I suggested? I wish that old book I spoke of were still in the library here—if it were, I'll bet I could find you the Seabright arms in two minutes! However—such a general work might possibly fail to give the exact modification used by your particular branch. Different branches often made minor variations in their arms, so that, even if all were given, considerable doubt might occur as to which of several closely similar versions is yours. I trust you can get to Carlisle in time—& meanwhile your present bookplate is surely attractive enough to satisfy any reasonable taste.

As I said, I liked your recent verses exceedingly; & don't see why you need to be seriously dissatisfied with either of the poems. Of course, we don't always hit the mark aimed at during the earlier stages of experimentation; but even among recognised bards there is always something of uncertainty & fortuitousness. Often a poem will be good, despite the fact that the author strove for something still better. The only sound policy is to keep on producing material, acquiring technical practice, & learning more & more about what one wants to say & how one can best utilise one's own particular gifts in saying it. These specimens are both excellent—& I fancy you'll find that Baldwin & others will confirm my opinion. Hope each will achieve suitable placement.

Regarding the sense of identification with other periods—I doubt if any such thing as hereditary memory (which really does not exist in any definite sense) can be held responsible for it. Chance events of association in infancy & early childhood—things too obscure, indirect, & complicated for conscious tracing—are almost certainly responsible for all phenomena of this sort. Pictures idly glimpsed, stories idly heard, chance phrases accidentally picked up . . . . any of these things, singly or in combination, may become unconsciously linked with sensations of pleasure, mystery, expectancy, advantage, identity, &c. at a time when analysis is impossible & new impressions are readily formed. In the case of Rome & myself, an elaborate set of converging influences might be cited—some of infinite complexity & indirectness, others involving sheer coincidence. A *general* love of the past—the fact that in Providence the visible reliques of the past are largely Georgian & classic, involving Graeco-Roman ornament—the fact that of all ancient alphabets, only the Roman is ours—a love of phantasy leading me to the Graeco-Roman myths through Hawthorne & Bulfinch—an early rebellion against the surrounding orthodox religion, & a consequent exaltation of the Romans who opposed that religion in early imperial times—the fact that an excellent art museum, with classical sculpture, opened in Providence in 1897—the fact that my favourite (for a largely separate set of reasons) 18ᵗʰ century literature is full of Roman classicism & includes many translations of Roman classics—Dryden's Virgil, Ovid by various hands, Rowe's Lucan, Lewis's Statius, Murphy's Tacitus, & Dryden's & Gifford's Juvenal, &c. &c.—the fact that Rome stood for the order & logic which naturally appeal to me—the fact that my uncle was a devoted classical student & had translated Virgil, Lucretius, & bits of other Latin poets—the fact that my grandfather had enjoyed Italy more than any other part of Europe, & had brought back many things from there, including Roman coins, booklets with pictures of Roman ruins, & a life-size copy of the famous Roman portrait bust commonly but erroneously called "Clytië" (all of which we still have)—the chance circumstance that a child's reader which I devoured at the age of 6 had a very alluring selection about Rome & Pompeii—the equally chance circumstance that at 3 or 4 I was impressed by the great railway viaduct at Canton, between Providence & Boston, which has great masonry arches like a Roman aqueduct . . . & that my mother, in connexion with it, told me that arches were first extensively used by the Romans, & described the great aqueducts . . . which latter I soon saw in pictures—& so on, & so on, & so on. The fact remains, that by 1896 I felt somehow that I—or whatever projection of myself could coexist with antiquity—was a Roman. From that period onward, any aspersion against Rome, or any expression of hostility toward the Roman imperium, seemed to me like a personal affront. I always hated the Middle Ages like poison, & despite my admiration for Greek culture, have had hard work to escape the Roman's feeling of slight patronage for it (as the culture of a *conquered* race) . . . . the sort of feeling summed up in the term *"Graeculus"*. To this day, the hard old faces of republican Romans, as presented by the photographically realistic portrait busts in museums, strike me as *familiar* in a deep, peculiar way—as if these were men, or the sort of men, whom I have known. Of all racial physiognomies differing from the English norm, the hawk-nosed, broad-templed Roman physiognomy is the only one which does not seem "foreign" to me. It is the only one I really like & admire—the only one I would be willing to have as my own.

Like you, I have delved very *unevenly* into the past, & probably have spots of ignorance far vaster & grosser than any of yours. For example—the Middle Ages, which I abominate, are known to me only fragmentarily. When I come to think of it, it is really only through England & France that I have kept any continuous track of events from the 6ᵗʰ century A.D. to modern times. What I know of Spanish or Italian or Eastern & Central European history in mediaeval times is merely a meagre skeleton with irregular patches of meat on it. Even our own history doesn't begin to interest me vitally till about the time of Chaucer—when the towns began to bristle with the gabled, half-timbered architecture familiar to us in pictures & through modern imitations. Then, in the 18ᵗʰ century, I strike another "home" period—with which I feel as utterly identified as with Rome. About 1820 things begin to seem remote & alien again—& the era of the 1870's & 1880's is as dim, fabulous, & repellent to me as the eleventh century. I was born in 1890, & my memories date from the summer of 1892—but the actual world of that period seemed somehow absurd & unreal to me. It was only later, amidst the growing rationality, rising taste, & increasing philosophic scepticism of the 20ᵗʰ century, that I felt any links at all with the present. As it is, I touch the age only at certain points. In many ways the 1930's shew a curious chaoticism & aesthetic decadence which does not attract me; whilst a good deal of contemporary philosophy is as hasty & immature in its way (overinfluenced by superficial interpretations of relativity & ill-digested theories of the utilitarian & functional bases of all human expression) as was that of the Victorian dark age. However, I don't feel *quite* as lost as I did in 1900. There is, despite a vast amount of decay, a real net gain since that period—mainly on the intellectual side, slightly on the aesthetic side. But I really don't *belong* to the present age any more than I did to the age of 1900. I merely observe it, just as through reading I observe the Tudor or Plantagenet ages. The only periods with which I have any *special* kinship are those of the later Roman republic & the English 18ᵗʰ century. I belong amidst arches & Corinthian colonnades, clean-shaven faces, ideals of logic & order, & a rational, materialistic explanation of the cosmos. The one incongruous note is my devotion to the spectral & fantastic—an undoubted heritage from the Gothic, mediaeval element (otherwise ignored) in the complex mixture of traditions extending behind us. Or perhaps one should add something which may or may not be separable from the foregoing—my tremendous absorption & fascination by the idea of *time* & its monstrous drama & pageantry. This *time-sense*, as Spengler points out,[6] certainly was not characteristic of classical civilisation. Hellenism—& to a lesser, imitative extent, Roman culture—lived for the moment.

But—also like you—I wish I had been more evenly educated. A state of almost semi-invalidism in youth made my school attendance very irregular, & deprived me altogether of college—I was in the midst of a nervous breakdown in 1908–12, when I expected to be in the university. I surely hope that the youthful heiress of the Sea-Brights[7] will be able to profit to the fullest extent by the reading-course which you are so carefully preparing. She will have reason to thank you for it twenty years hence!

And here I must present a blend of thanks & abject apologies in connexion with the winsome likeness enclosed in your letter & returned (vide enc.) in such a state of photochemical ruin. Vae mihi! Mea culpa! Peccavi![8] & more to that effect. I ought to have known that anything with that ruddy hue was a *proof* & therefore in need of guarding from the solar glare . . . . . but, unfortunately, no such consideration occurred to me! The picture was in fine shape when it came, & I admired most appreciatively the sprightly grace of the small subject—but now look at it! I can't yet fully account for the disaster. The print at no time lay in the sun, but of course it was more or less subject to diffused daylight as it reposed in the envelope chosen to bear it back to you. Common paper is undeniably translucent, & evil fate made the print happen to repose face upward. At any rate, the damage is done, & I am monstrously contrite about it. I wish there were some way I could rectify the harm! Anyhow, I hope most fervently that you still have the negative. Thanks again for this delightful glimpse of the rising generation. Some day—if you feel you can ever entrust a photographic specimen again to so lax a custodian—I wouldn't mind a glimpse of the features of Marjorie's gifted pater!

I saw a full-page rotogravure reproduction of some of the high spots of your local Hals exhibit in the N.Y. Times.[9] It must be a tremendously notable display—which I would keenly appreciate seeing, even though the artist is not among my favourites. I'll be interested to learn how it strikes you. Detroit is really getting to be a notable centre of all the arts—as I was recently reminded by a friend who has just been visiting there.[10] Incidentally, he & I had quite a debate about your Diego Rivera murals.[11] I dispute the aesthetic value of this intellectual, socially motivated art. Not that I can't appreciate the intellect behind it, & the intrinsic mastery of colour & design inherent in its pattern—but that I think the whole principle involves an essential disparity of elements. What Rivera wants to do is something that can't be done through painting. When anybody tries to do it through painting, the painting suffers.

Providence also is staging an exhibit of Persian art at the museum in commemoration of Firdousi[12]—indeed, the display has been on view in a special room for several weeks. Mostly paintings, illuminated MSS., & pottery. Regarding English translations of the Shah Namah—let me reveal the depth of my illiteracy by admitting that I don't know of a single one, either prose or verse![13] I never heard of any version in any European tongue except the French translation common a generation ago—but of course the past few years may have brought out all sorts of things. I don't keep track of new items as I did when I was young. E. Hoffmann Price, the arch-Orientalist, ought to be the boy to tip you off on all the latest Firdousi news. I was enormously fascinated by the Saracenic civilisation when I read the Arabian Nights at the age of 5, but did not keep up my interest as Sultan Malik did. Speaking of exhibits—I enclose a catalogue of a curious display of Cambodian & Javanese material at the college. Another interesting thing—at the library next door to #66—is an exhibit of Sumerian & Babylonian clay tablets & cylinders with cuneiform inscriptions—reaching back almost to 3000 B.C. Speaking of sundry Orientalia—last week I heard for the first time in my life some *actual* Chinese music. It was rendered on a native flute by the Chinese lecturer & diplomat T. Z. Koo,[14] who spoke at the university on the Manchurian question. There were four selections, & in general the departure from Occidental tonal qualities was far *less* than I had expected. It was distinctly *music*, even from the most purely European point of view—which is scarcely true of many exotic harmonic traditions.

My visit to Long did indeed materialise—& only 2 days were so cold as to give me serious trouble. A combination of circumstances made the occasion quite a convention—young Barlow was up from Washington, & both the Wandrei boys simultaneously blew in—Donald by boat from California, where he visited Clark Ashton Smith, & Howard directly from St. Paul. The brothers have taken a flat in Greenwich Village, & hope to hang on through hack writing for Street & Smith. Donald's especial friend Desmond Hall has just left the firm, but the remaining editor Orlin Tremaine is very favourable toward his stuff. This was Barlow's first Manhattan sojourn since infancy, so that Long & I were kept quite busy introducing him to the various museums, galleries, & bookstalls. He picked up some marvellous bargains—including a fine old copy of George W. M. Reynolds' "Wagner the Wehr-Wolf" for *15¢*. I secured a good modern edition of Lewis's famous "Monk" for a dollar. Our general gang meeting of Jany. 2 was one of the best in the history of the group—15 being assembled at Long's . . . . Morton, Barlow, Talman, Loveman, Kirk, the Wandreis, Koenig, Leeds, &c. &c. Two evenings later we assembled at Loveman's Brooklyn flat & were shown his collection of 300 or 400 Clark Ashton Smith drawings—only lately brought from his old home in Cleveland. Some of these were prodigiously impressive. I had seen them in Cleveland in 1922, but they were wholly new to Long, Barlow, & the Wandreis. On another occasion Koenig showed Long, Barlow, & me through the Electrical Testing Laboratories,[15] with which he is connected. A rather fascinating place full of weird-looking devices for measuring the safety & durability of every sort of electrical household appliance. Some of the bizarre modes of duplicating the precise conditions of ordinary wear & tear are picturesque indeed! I returned home Jany. 8, & have ever since been trying to catch up with accumulated work. The winter, on the whole, is not proving as severe as its predecessor—though two cold spells have made me a temporary prisoner within doors. Yes—I can readily appreciate the aesthetic & imaginative appeal of snow in connexion with the New England landscape . . . even though I prefer to read about it or see it in pictures rather than experience it! It is not only intrinsically beautiful, but as you say, is somehow associated with images of security, simplicity, & traditional living . . . . which one can appreciate keenly as long as the radiators hold their own. Poems like Whittier's "Snow

Bound" assist in promoting this appeal—& then again, it is the winter aspect of country life which is most purely historical & native . . . . least confused with the summer-vacation phase of rural existence. Still more—there is a definite psychology of protective *snugness* as typified by a *small* area tightly fortified against the encroaching cold. Well—the recent paralysing storm surely gave us all the snugness we could conveniently use!

No—I haven't had a moment to go on with the new story . . . . too swamped by other tasks. I have to have unhurried leisure for fictional composition. Your own new yarn sounds promising—that Warder of Knowledge must be quite a tough old customer, if I recall what was hinted on that 19th (& unaccountably cut off—*not* broken) table of the Eltdown Shards!

Derleth tells me of a new weird magazine—probably no good, but perhaps worth investigating. It is known as *Sensations,* & is issued by the Pierre Publications, 8th Floor, 120 W. 42nd St., New York City.[16]

Well—I certainly have rambled on to inexcusable lengths! For that—as well as for my possible carelessness with the photograph—I most humbly crave your pardon.

Yr obt hble Servt—H P L

P.S. I've just indulged in an extravagance—bought 2 dark walnut sets of drawers for filing purposes. My papers & cuttings were getting all out of control. Haven't yet worked out a permanent arrangement—I may superimpose one on the other & have a single tall cabinet. Long recently acquired something very similar. ¶ F F just came. Pleased to see your "Dead World".

Notes

1. Samuel Loveman.
2. From Ernest A. Edkins.
3. Note that a Casey disappears in "The Shadow over Innsmouth."
4. This painting was latterly in the possession of Ethel Phillips Morrish, HPL's second cousin; it was passed to her grandson Robert Harrall upon her death in 1987.
5. RFS did have a bookplate matching HPL's description made for himself, but it is not certain whether Wilfred B. Talman designed it.
6. HPL refers to Oswald Spengler's *The Decline of the West,* published in a two-volume English translation in 1922–26. HPL read only the first volume.
7. I.e., RFS's daughter Marjorie (Marge) Doris Searight, born 3 October 1930.
8. "Woe is me! My fault! I have erred!"
9. "Hals in Detroit," *New York Times* (30 December 1934): X9.
10. Harry K. Brobst.
11. Diego Rivera (1886–1957), one of modern Mexico's foremost painters, executed twenty-seven murals in the courtyard of the Detroit Institute of Arts.
12. See EHP 13n3.

13. There were three full or partial translations of the *Shah Namah* prior to 1935: *The Poems of Ferdosi,* translated by Joseph Champion (Calcutta: Printed for J. Hay, 1875; Vol. 1 only); *The Sháhnáma of Firdausí,* translated by Arthur George Warner and Edmund Warner (London: Kegan Paul, Trench, Trübner & Co., 1907–25; 9 vols.), and *The Shah-Namah of Fardusi,* translated by Alexander Rogers (London: Chapman & Hall, 1907). There were also several paraphrases or retellings of the poem.

14. See EHP 67n3.

15. At 2 East End Avenue at 79th Street.

16. No magazine of this title was published at this time.

[21] [ALS]

66 College St.,
Providence, R.I.,
March 5, 1935.

Dear Mr. Searight:—

I am surely glad to know that "The Frozen Pirate" formed a welcome echo from the past, & am looking forward to my own re-reading of it. Probably my impressions will closely duplicate your own. Certainly there must have been a rather potent evocation of the antarctic's horror & majesty in order to impress me so indelibly 35 years ago. Did I ever mention that the whole subject of the Great White South & its lurking, aeon-dead secrets has held a profound & particular fascination for me ever since I was ten years old? Something about its utter deadness & isolation—a remoteness making it more like another planet than like a part of earth—had an almost hypnotic effect on my childish imagination. It was the only *wholly unexplored continent* left on the globe. No mortal had ever penetrated its brooding mysteries or scaled its preternatural barrier of age-old ice . . . . indeed, no human foot had so much as touched its outermost fringe till a few years before, when (Jan. 23, 1895) the Norwegian C. E. Borchgrevingk had landed a party at Cape Adare. I think it was the newspaper accounts of Borchgrevingk's second expedition of 1900—when he made a new farthest south & wintered on the Antarctic Continent (among his party was the immortal Dr. Cook of subsequent dubious fame!)[1]—which first captured my attention & interest. I had been lamenting the tame *known-ness* of the world in general—that world which had been so fascinating & mysterious in the days of Columbus & the Cabots—& here was a modern world just as little known as the globe of the early 16th century . . . . a world whose map was as alluringly fragmentary as the map of America in Verrazano's & Jacques Cartier's age! By '02—when I was 12—I had read virtually everything in fact or fiction concerning the Antarctic, & was breathlessly awaiting news of the first Scott expedition. Those were great days—the beginning of a new wave of antarctic discovery after virtually half a century of neglect . . . for nothing of real moment occurred between the great work of D'Urville, Wilkes, & Ross (when the polar continent was first recognised) & the age of Borchgrevingk. Afterward, though, things speeded up & are still going on—Scott, Shackleton, Amundsen & the pole, Byrd, Mawson, Wilkins[2] . . . & their successors of the future. Such antarctic novels as I bought, I have still kept—& will be glad to lend, although they are more important for subject-matter than for merit. "Beyond the Great South Wall", by Frank Savile, "MS. Found in a Copper Cylinder" by James De Mille, & "Revi-Lona", by Frank Cowan. In recent years antarctic novels have been fairly frequent—if one counts the worthless serials of the science fiction pulps. I haven't even begun to keep track of these. I have always scribbled about the antarctic—beginning with my erudite "Antarctic Atlas", drawn by hand & published by myself in an edition of 1 copy in 1902. Did I send you my longest & most recent antarctic effort—"At the Mountains of Madness", written in 1931 & rejected by Wright? That opus catches just a bit of the mood I've tried to formulate & express for 35 years . . . . & Wright, damn him, *would* have to turn it down!

De re iconographica—there is really no excuse for my not recognising that proof as a proof. Its ruddy finish told the story—or should have to any alert eye, but for some reason or other I missed the idea entirely until *after* the blackening process began. Well—I'm glad no harm was done . . . & it certainly gave me an excellent idea of the comely & diminutive Sea-Bright heiress before the shadows began to gather. Thanks exceedingly for the current glimpses of the household—which I return herewith. With a strong magnifying glass (which I always use on snap shots) I believe I can get a very fair idea of the translator of the Eltdown Shards, & I must say that I think that eminent palaeographer has no reason at all to keep his picture out of the papers! And the rest of the family well maintain the decorative scheme—not excluding the aërially suspended Vito. That snap surely looks as if you were stringing the poor beast up by his teeth or tongue & gloating sadistically over your infandous deed—but I know how tricky the camera is! A decade ago I was snapped—apparently—in the act of wringing the neck of an exquisite grey kitten [I am a fanatical devotee of all felines], whereas in truth I was merely inducing the wriggly little devil to face the lens in the gentlest & most affectionate possible way![3] I shall be glad to see the more representative portrait you promise when the time comes. In return, I'm enclosing not merely a couple of shots of my own ugly mug, but some views of others in the "weird gang" which I think may interest you. Of these, the views of Smith & Wandrei are several years old—1927, I think—though all the others fall within the past 4 years. My own portrait—taken last June—represents young Barlow's first experiment with a new camera, & really looks very much like me. I also enclose a full-length view of Long & myself, taken by Talman[4] . . . . the young man I recommended as a bookplate designer. Of the subjects of these pictures I have met all in person except Baldwin, Bloch, Derleth, Howard, Rimel, & Smith—not much over half, though, at that! 'Two-Gun Bob' surely looks the part of his Conan! Of all the rest of the group he has personally met only Price, who visited Cross Plains last year. Smith has met only Price & Wandrei among his fellow-weirdists. And the Asotin boys have met none of their scattered colleagues. I shew the late Dr. Whitehead in his full ecclesiastical outfit—a rig he deeply appreciated as an aesthete, although he generally wore sport clothes & bright ties outside his 'working hours'. A great chap— probably the most broadly scholarly of us all. He was a Ph.D., & had studied under Santayana & Münsterberg. Derleth's picture looks a bit "arty" & affected—but since it was taken he appears to have 'snapped out of' the most virulent phases of his aesthetic self-consciousness. That kid is going far in serious general literature unless I'm much mistaken. As for the pictures—no hurry at all about their return, so long as they get back safely some time.

Just heard a rumour that the *Fantasy Fan* is about to fail—that the February issue will be the last. This is truly unfortunate, since the unpretentious little fellow really fulfilled a valuable function in encouraging the incipient weirdist & giving all the clan a convenient forum for the exchange of ideas. I suppose Schwartz's *Fantasy Magazine* will take over some of the material & departments, but its devotion to science fiction will make the straight weirdist get rather a poor break. Glad you like the Yuggothian Fungi in the Jan. issue. Yes—the Wooley & Howard material is really admirable.[5] Both writers are genuine poets, & really ought to be able to have verse in the remunerative magazines right along. Most of Two-Gun's verse has never been submitted for publication. Some of it [is] really marvellous in its savage, barbaric potency.

Incidentally—last week I had a letter from Loring & Mussey of N Y . . . young Derleth's publishers . . . asking to see some of my junk with a view to possible book publication. Since this is the 5th time I have received such a request (W T 1927, Putnam 1931, Vanguard '32, Knopf '33) without any tangible results so far, I'm not as naively excited about the matter as I might otherwise be. However—I'm shooting along a few tales just on the general principle of leaving no stone unturned. I'd hate to think, later on, that I *might* have had a book published *if* I'd responded to the request.

The piled-up chests of drawers certainly will form an admirable resolver of the prevailing chaos hereabouts—although, amusingly enough, I haven't yet had a moment in which to accomplish the necessary classification. Sorry you haven't space for a cabinet of the sort. Of course, I have to sacrifice perfect aestheticism in stuffing my quarters with such material. My study would be called grossly overcrowded by any smug interior decorator—but I can't help that! Glad you have a good new desk & bookcase. My desk is an old flat-topped affair—black walnut—in the family since about 1840, with a chair to match. As for bookcases—I have all sorts of odds & ends, mostly open shelves. Two huge glass-doored affairs house some of the choicer items—but the rest is rather haphazard. I have built up certain cases by finding others which fit accurately on top of them—thus reaching almost to the ceiling. I put less important volumes on the top shelves—reachable only by standing in a chair. One wall is solidly built up with shelves, & I have odd small cases tucked around everywhere—under windows, &c. I suppose I have about 2500 volumes in my study & bedroom together—with more in the attic & in storage. My last great weeding-out was in 1924,[6] but I shall have to attempt another some day. I hate depending on public libraries—it annoys me to be held up for lack of immediate volumes to consult—hence like to have most of the standard classics, reference works, & text books in my especial line on tap. Most of my books are getting in frightful condition—I wish I had cash enough for a general re-binding orgy. Some items are virtually falling to pieces—perhaps because of the dry heat which I have to maintain all winter. I can't stand cold.

Regarding genealogy—I've really done almost no research myself. I merely amuse myself with what others have dug up or preserved. The difference between *real* research (involving records, tombstones, libraries, &c. &c.) & just going up to the attic & dusting off pre-existing charts & notes is something I've come to appreciate poignantly since watching my *genuine* genealogist-friends Talman & Morton in full cry after some elusive progenitor. Those boys are out of my class! I'm just a surface-skimmer—enjoying a vague anecdotal knowledge of what some of my forbears were doing in my favourite 18th century, but being too lazy to clear up the various stub ends & blind spots in my lineage. It would indeed be interesting to learn something of my ancestress Dorcas Ellis—which reminds me that I am daily expecting a young visitor whose mother was an Ellis[7] of the Middle West, & who may very conceivably be a kinsman of yours. I shall ask him about his maternal ancestry, of which I know little, since it is his father who is my especial friend. He comes from Milwaukee, & bears the name of Robert Ellis Moe. Pater Moe is an English teacher at West Division High School, & author of a number of notable pedagogical devices such as the Moe Book Tests—extensively used in schools. Young Robert is an electrical engineer—just transferred to Bridgeport, Conn. (130 m. from Prov.) by the General Electric Co. Speaking of Connecticut—I regret to say that I have never been to Windsor; my acquaintance with the Hartford region being limited to a superficial knowledge of the city itself (which hasn't kept much of the quaint except the Bulfinch State House) & a more critical examination of its ancient & still-colonial suburbs Farmington & Wethersfield. As chance would have it, I've never explored Connecticut with the same thoroughness as Massachusetts, so that many striking historic & architectural vistas still await my discovery. *Hooker* is a great Connecticut line—the Rev. Thomas Hooker, whose grave in Centre churchyard I have seen, being the chief founder of Hartford. I was interested in the account of Wright's lineage. He had previously mentioned the Farnsworth line, but not the paternal one. Hope you'll be able to locate a good work on arms at the downtown library.

About the Narragansett Country—which is indeed the seat of a great deal of spectral & macabre legendry—I actually have thought of using it in a weird story some day. Currently, though I can't feel the same insidious sense of brooding, lurking *evil* in Rhode Island (or the South, either, for that matter) that I can in Massachusetts. We never had the grotesque abnormalities, blackly hideous legends, & actual witch-trials & executions which the Puritan colonies (Mass. & Conn.) had. At any rate, I seem to find northern & central Massachusetts (*not* the southeastern "Old Colony" section taken over from Plymouth in 1691 . . . New Bedford, Taunton, &c.) the most suggestive of horror of any regions I know. Almost *anything,* it has always seemed to me, might happen in one of those isolated hillside farmhouses on winding sideroads in Wilbraham [= Dunwich] or Monson or Hampden . . . . or in some of the half-abandoned, rotten-wharved seaports whose crumbling gambrel roofs huddle around sand-choked harbours on the coast north of Boston. The Narragansett County still harbours the same dreamlike beauty which it had in the 18th century. Apart from the main highways, the old rutted roads still wind between their ancient, briar-grown stone walls across the drowsy, rolling meadows, past willow-bordered curving streams, & up over shadowy wooded hills. The huge chimneys & cottage roofs of 200 & 250 years ago still pierce the foliage of great elms & oaks, & the same gnarled orchards still climb the hillsides behind them. Beside the reedy Pettaquamscutt the birthplace of Gilbert Stuart is still just as it was in 1755. Only the great plantation-houses have gone—save for one in perfect condition & one or two others more or less altered or in decay. The white church—which stood in the midst of the woods like old Virginia churches—was moved up to Wickford in 1800, & its abandoned churchyard is a spectral, shadowy place. Nearby the glebe house broods behind its overgrown terraces & courtyards—but I guess I told you about this (& how it fascinated E. Hoffmann Price in '33) before.[8] There certainly ought to be a story or two somewhere amidst all this! I really don't know the Narragansett Country as well as I ought, considering that more than a third of all my ancestral lines come from it. No lines of public transportation extend through its real & unspoiled heart (that's *why* it is unspoiled—& it has no attractions for the vulgar motorist . . . . whose cars its roads would tend to shake to pieces!); & since I have no means of private transportation, I have to do my exploring piecemeal as transient opportunities appear. From a certain high spot near the Tower Hill Road (which *is* a travelled highway) there can be obtained what I firmly believe is the finest landscape vista in America—nothing rugged or sensational, but a dream of quiet sloping meadows, forest-bordered stream, roofs & chimneys in distant valleys, a far-off white steeple, & in the remote background a misty blue glimmer of the ocean. It is such a landscape as our fathers knew in Old England—& while hereditary memory is no fact, we cannot but be doubly sensitive to something which 1500 years of cultural heritage has made a prominent & ineffaceable part of our racial tradition.

I envy you your early familiarity with the Shah-Namah—a thing which must make the current Firdousi celebration quite a personal event with you. I might have got to it if Graeco-Roman myth had not so suddenly & completely sidetracked my Oriental interests & Arabian Nights allegiance. It really is unfortunate that no complete English translation exists (that is, so far as I know), & I hope the condition may some time be remedied. Perhaps the anniversary will arouse enough interest to start somebody on the titanic job. The lecture by Dr. Aya must have been tremendously interesting—for Persia is really one of the most significant of all nations . . . . the first Aryan people to appear on the stage of the western world. While always the enemies of the especial culture streams from which we stem—Greece & Rome—the Persians nevertheless exercised a vast influence on the ancient world.

Speaking of lectures—I possibly mentioned the poetry reading by Archibald MacLeish which I attended Feby. 3. More recently I heard a fine discourse on Hokusai (an old favourite of mine) at the art museum in connexion with an exhibition of his prints. Sino-Japanese art has always fascinated me extremely, & I wish I could afford a Japanese print collection of my own. Still another lecture—Feby. 20—was on contemporary Russian soviet art. It appears that, in spite of the Marxian fallacy of a social motivation in art, the Russian painters are not as badly off as I had imagined. A good deal of sound traditional feeling from the old Byzantine stream still persists, & may revive & flourish as the political novelty of the existing regime wears off. Paradoxically enough, modern Russian work is not nearly as freakish as the decadent aesthetic abstractions of the current western artists. Rivera, I judge, is strongly influenced by soviet art—though he tends to go beyond it. My principal objection to him is not so much his subject-matter (for all things are equally fitted for artistic treatment, provided each is dealt with in the manner appropriate to it) as the manner in which he presents it. He is working *through intellectual perception instead of through symbolism.* The spirit of machinery could be symbolised in some fashion other than the sort of diagrammatic depiction which Rivera employs. However—my whole attitude toward the murals (& toward similar things elsewhere) goes rather farther than this. I question not only the manner of depicting the spirit of machinery, but the *choice* of this spirit as symbolic of Detroit. This does not contradict my just-expressed belief that such a spirit is capable of aesthetic treatment. It merely questions the appropriateness of the spirit *as the main symbol of a city*. I challenge the popular belief that the most important thing in life is amassing material resources, & that the most typical thing about a man—or a city—is the particular way he—or it—gains a material livelihood. To my mind, *living* is a process of emotional & intellectual experience—a matter of appreciating, understanding, & enjoying the external world. That is the *reason* for being alive—& the typical thing about a person or a place is his or its characteristic set of aesthetic & intellectual interests & folkways. The especial way in which the person or place makes a living is not primary but secondary; not an end, but a means to an end. It is important, but so only in the sense of a contributing mechanism. It is like the organs & entrails which contribute to the life of the brain, or the wheels & springs in the phonograph which plays a lovely & immortal melody. Therefore I disavow all use of an occupational or commercial symbolism in depicting the spirit of a city. Naturally, the daily life & habits of a population must not be left unrepresented. The industrial habits of a city deserve just as careful chronicling & representation as any other habits. Let us shew them in their true proportion, side by side with the rest . . . . . but let us beware of talk ing them as the city's supreme symbol. The exact amount of representation appropriate to industry depends of course on all sorts of individual considerations. When a particular industry has wholly created a city—as the fishing trade created Marblehead & the river trade plus cotton created Natchez & the falls of the Blackstone with their mills created Pawtucket, then it has to figure more prominently than otherwise in its traditions. Thus the gilded codfish— symbolic of Massachusetts fisheries—which has hung since colonial times in the Boston state house. (But observe that a golden cod is far better art than a Rivera-like blue-print diagram of a steam trawler!) Also, when a certain industry has a distinct *beauty* of its own—traditional or intrinsic—common sense assigns it a larger place in the general civic consciousness of a region. Thus a town with a picturesque sea-trade, or ancient agricultural supremacy, or educational & publishing activity, or artistic pottery or textile or other manufacturers, can well make more of its industries than a beer-brewing or fertilizer-making centre. But of course many of the ugly industries can be symbolised in a truly aesthetic way if the artist will only remain faithful to the principles of art. Thus a steel-working or mining centre can have its industry represented through images relating to the basic, historic, traditional, & on the whole beautiful early aspects of the craft—Tubal-Cain, & the picturesque pioneers of the Iron Age. Or else the *massed rhythms* of modern industry can be suggested in a broad way eliminating inharmonious detail.

It is very hard to formulate any central principle which governs the various manifestations of art—indeed, I rather doubt if there can be any. For no matter what the "abstract" moderns may say, there is no such thing as *effective* pure art. This is not to say that a separate & distinct aesthetic principle, based on harmony & proportion, does not exist. Almost undoubtedly, it does exist. But I doubt whether it can ever produce any major emotional effect *by itself*. We always have to receive it *in combination with something else*—personal or historic association, personal or group pride, physical comfort or pleasure, intellectual satisfaction, &c. &c. &c. No two arts are exactly the same in essence. A common strain of the purely aesthetic principle runs through them all, but each depends so much on a typical set of added factors that in many cases comparison is virtually impossible. Both the Parthenon & Dreiser's "American Tragedy" are major works of art—yet the amount of *material in common* forms only a fraction of each.

Certainly art has to be *selective*—picking out of its subject-matter that which has the greatest symbolic significance—but I have a hesitancy in applying the word *idealistic* to good art. I do not think that art can legitimately depict anything as other than it is. Of course *weird & fantastic* art would *seem* to form a glaring exception; yet even in this special instance I think the essential principle is maintained. For that which fantastic art portrays is *not the objective array of things & events described*, but simply *the human mood which perpetually reacts against reality in certain characteristic patterns*. A weird tale is *not* a description of certain things & persons & events, but a *picture of a typical human mood*. But this mood-picturing principle cannot be carried too far. It will work when concerned with *violent departures from nature*, but encounters powerful psychological obstacles when attempting to reproduce moods dependent on feeble aspirations regarding reality. We cannot write a novel in the Victorian manner—misrepresenting human acts & motives to conform to namby-pamby conventions of the moment—& expect it to be received as a really artistic picture of a basic human wish. The element of *mockery* is too great to float the wish-picture. The erroneous picture of life is not boldly fantastic enough in its unreality to rise to the level of a wish-symbol. It has so much *superficial resemblance* to reality that the only emotional effect is one of mockery, silliness, & feebleness. That is why most middle & late 19th & early 20th century Anglo-American fiction is almost devoid of any real value. For after all, the element of *truth* can't be taken too completely out of art. When a picture misrepresents any fact in nature without affirming some deeper truth in the apparent act, it simply falls flat. That is the reason I rate *romanticism* very low in the aesthetic-intellectual scale. Aside from sheer fantasy, I think that realistic fiction is the only sort worthy of the name. That is not to say that mere photographic reproduction is the ideal. Rather must the authentic subject-matter be given a thoroughly selective & symbolic treatment according to the temperament & object of the artist. No two artists can see or treat the same thing in the same way. *But the process of selection & symbolism must not involve misrepresentation.* You can easily see the difference between selecting significant details from a true-to-life series of events, & setting down a series of events which are not true to life. The latter process (with the sole exception of fantasy) can have no possible excuse. Regarding 'ugliness' in music, painting, sculpture, architecture, & decoration, a great deal depends on the observer & the set of traditions & associations behind him. I am rather a traditionalist (an extreme one in architecture & decoration, where the *associative* element is paramount) in this field, & do not think anything is gained by opposing too violently the habits of the long culture-stream behind a given aesthetic manifestation. And yet individual latitude within a single tradition is considerable. What is ugly to one is beautiful to another—& certain forms of physical or psychological ugliness possess a perverse & macabre impressiveness which is in itself a shadowy form of beauty. Hence the art of the horror-tale or nightmare painting. Emphatically, I can't endorse the Victorian cult of mere *prettiness*. The ugliness as well as the suave glitter of life demands suitable aesthetic representation. Of course—there is a strong code of *appropriateness in the use & location of various forms of art*. The pictorial nightmares of Doré & Hieronymus Bosch are splendid art, but would not form ideal frescoes for a child's nursery or ideal pictures for a general living-room. The novels of Zola take a high place in literature, but they are out of place as third readers or after-dinner brain-relaxers. It seems to me that much of the opposition to grim, terrifying, & sordidness-portraying art arises not so much from the existence of such art as from the obtrusion of it in places where it does not belong. The sound aesthete puts every manifestation in its place. I enjoy weird literature & art as a specific activity—but the scenes & decorations I like to have habitually around me are of the classic & quietly pastoral type. My *actually favourite* artists are not horror-mongers at all, but glamourous landscapists like Ruysdael, Hobbema, Claude Lorrain, & Constable. And the bulk of my favourite reading is history, antiquarianism, & 18ᵗʰ century & Graeco-Roman poetry with emphasis on the pastoral. Even in scenery I prefer the quiet loveliness of an England-like countryside to any amount of macabre mountain grandeur.

No—I missed the Poe's birthday exercises this year, although I got them last year . . . . when the brick cottage in Philadelphia was dedicated. I'm glad the performers didn't murder "Usher". Usually the "horror" attempted by radio artists becomes a species of low comedy! I miss many things which I'd probably enjoy through my utter inattentiveness to both radio programmes & cinema advertisements.

I was greatly interested in the notes on your early life & career. My own nervous state in childhood once produced a tendency inclining toward chorea, although not quite attaining that level. My face was full of unconscious & involuntary motions now & then—& the more I was urged to stop them, the more frequent they became.[9] But in time the tendency died down, & in later life I was not given to any extremes of expression. I was also hyper-sensitive & unadapted to discipline—with a very violent temper which has now wholly vanished. At about eleven—as a protective colouration & foil to ridicule-exciting bookishness—I cultivated the 'rough guy' attitude among my contemporaries, so that during one of my brief school periods I shared with one rival the distinction of being the worst boy in my room.[10] In high-school, however, the more mature & scholastically interesting environment caused me to reform. Dignity belonged with long trousers, anyhow. I then adopted a new attitude of elderly austerity, & earned the nickname of "Professor." But I was always on the edge of a nervous breakdown, & had to drop out a while in the middle of the course. By the time I was through—in 1908—I was pretty well all in—& college was not to be thought of. My seclusion became very complete—but I was always reading or writing or investigating something or other (chemistry & astronomy were my great interests at that period—I had a well-equipped laboratory & a 3″ telescope on a tripod . . . which latter I still possess), so that in the end I probably picked up a few of the things I didn't get at the university. I began contributing to the press in 1906—while in high school—writing a series of monthly astronomical articles for a local daily, & dumping other pedantic concoctions on a rural paper in my ancestral region of western R.I.[11] For commercial pursuits I never had the slightest aptitude— indeed, my lack of any skill in this direction amounts to a positive cerebral blank. I simply *cannot* think or calculate in terms of gain . . . . . a weakness which will prove my destruction in the end. I certainly envy you the enter- prise & stamina which have given you a firm foothold & a future! Incidental- ly, I imagine that your telegraphic work must have certain points of interest in addition to its economic value. I never realised before that the Morse code is extinct—but suppose it is only natural that telegraphic typing should replace it. Regarding music—did I mention that I studied violin between the ages of 7 & 9, then experiencing a violent reaction against all good music? To this day, music is my principal aesthetic blind spot.

Regarding a juvenile reading course—I am very hesitant about sugges- tions, since my acquaintance with such literature is so remote . . . . & anyhow, my early reading was lopsided, & coloured by my fantastic & archaic tastes. I guess I mentioned my browsings amongst the 18th century books in the black trunk-room upstairs. And yet I think that a good many of my early favourites would do for any child. So far as verse is concerned, I think that a few items like Stevenson's "Child's Garden of Verse" make a good preparation for some regular anthology like the "Golden Treasury".[12] And of course integral parts of racial folklore like "Mother Goose" cannot be omitted. Grimm's Fairy Tales are indispensable—& Andersen's are also splendid, although I didn't care so much for them. Lang's various fairy books—the Green, Blue, Red, &c.—are excellent, & his version of the Arabian Nights cannot be omit- ted. Hawthorne's "Wonder Book" & "Tanglewood Tales" are important (as is his "Grandfather's Chair" for New England history),[13] & for a child of 7 or more Bulfinch's Age of Fable (& his other legendary compendia—now in the Modern Lib.) is a delight. For classic background nothing is so good as Church's "Stories from Homer", "Stories from Livy", & "Stories from the Greek Tragedians". These have Hellenic-spirited illustrations in the Flaxman manner. [marginal note: Kingsley's "Greek Heroes" is fine.] Regarding Shake- speare—I am dogmatic enough to say that there is only one possible intro- duction . . . the long-familiar "Tales from Shakespeare", by Charles & Mary Lamb. Gradual reading of the actual plays can come after the stories have be- come familiar. Yes—Eugene Field & Longfellow are both good starters. Whittier also fits young minds—his "Snow Bound" cannot be omitted. Milton's lighter stuff—L'Allegro, Il Penseroso, Comus—are better as a starter than his epics. Coleridge's Ancient Mariner is a delight—how I ate it up, Doré plates & all—at the age of 6! Translations of the classics* will form a natural sequel to Bulfinch . . . . which is full of delectable verse extracts. In history & science there are many excellent juvenile things. Van Loon's "Story of Mankind" & "Story of the Bible" are very good. Later Wells's "Shorter History of the World"—an abridgment of the ["]Outline of History"—is useful. I'm not posted on the recent science books—but there are some fine old ones which are still authentic so far as the rough outlines of the various sciences are concerned. I don't know what I'd ever have done without the famous Science (& History & Literature) Primer Series, & Steele's various "Fourteen Weeks" manuals.[14] But to get back to the *small* child—there's really no one thing even half as good as the much-advertised "Book of Knowledge". That thing really is not overrated. It has a little of everything that the expanding mind wants & needs—verse, facts, science, history, legends, pictures, &c. Which reminds me that all children ought to know the great pictures through reproductions. *Reference* books ought to be immediately at hand, so that the child's curiosity can be satisfied *at once,* while it is still keen. That child's Encyclopaedia Britannica[15] recently advertised ought to be splendid—I've never seen a copy but it sounds great. And Webster's International, a good *Atlas,* Brewer's Dic. of Phrase & Fable, & Harpers Dictionary of Classical Literature[16] & Antiquities ought to be on every parental shelf. Good juvenile *geographies* & travel books are valuable. Also—the early volumes of many series of school readers are veritable treasure-houses. A good juvenile *magazine* is essential. Hasn't *St. Nicholas*[17] been revived? But as you say, all children are different, & each one ought to be encouraged to steer his own course to a very great extent. Open up all the avenues—but let the youngster chose among them.

Yes—the meetings of last January surely formed a festive season. It certainly is hard for anyone to find a circle of kindred minds unless one has an enormously large field to pick from. I've lived in Providence virtually all my 44 years, & have never come across anyone with any amount of permanent congeniality. This may be mere chance, & it may be owing to some philosophic or aesthetic perspective of mine which clashes with the orthodox New England temperament. For example—I have no use for religion, & consider the insidiously utilitarian & semi-moralistic attitude in art unqualifiedly ridiculous. Then again, though preëminently a traditionalist & antiquarian, I have no patience with the excessive & disproportionate idolatry of *forms & customs* so characteristic of this region. I consider folkways highly interesting as a subject of research, but refuse to attach importance to hours of rising, choice of

*For Homer, the prose version superintended by Lang is unquestionably the best. It's now in the Modern Library—& I mean to get both Iliad & Odyssey

breakfast, manner of having the window shades, & all that. Convention—
unmotivated custom—regularity—primness—all these are anathema to me.
Furthermore—I cannot attempt to suppress my utter amusement at the local
scale of values as attached to persons & families. I refuse to consider financial
solidity an especial merit, or to value mere *industriousness* when it is not necessary. I consider aesthetic & intellectual activity of more importance than
wealth or commercial & political activity. I am likewise unimpressed by certain of the imponderables which figure largely in Providence. While I am
vastly appreciative of the poetic beauty of long association with the same soil,
& think that nothing is more fortunate than a family's ability to stay rooted to
the same spot for endless generations, I cannot conceal a trace of scepticism
when membership in certain ancient & particular local clans is naively cited as
a badge of merit transcending all personal—or non-local hereditary—points
of excellence. Why a commonplace local Brown is necessarily more important than a highly intelligent & deeply cultivated Smith from New Hampshire or Pennsylvania, is a mystery I have never taken seriously enough to try
to solve. In short, I have been forced by observation to come to the conclusion that much in the ideology of local "nice people" is ludicrously—even
tragically—hollow & decadent. Dominant principles of appraisal are founded
on childishly trivial or completely irrelevant superficialities, & the whole basis
of opinion & motivation is tangled up with traditional false beliefs respecting
the nature of the universe & of mankind. Side by side with the surface-
qualities of prim cultivation there exists an ignorance & bigotry of almost
breath-taking depth—as evidenced by the incredible social-political naivete
which keeps the fashionable community solidly Republican & conservative in
the face of their system's complete & inevitable breakdown. These people
read all the facts in magazines like *Harpers,* & then proceed to ignore them
with smug & superior smiles . . . . as a child who has never seen winter might
arrogantly smile at the notion that there can be any season except summer.
The hypocrisy whereby they can profess the Christian religion, & at the same
time uphold a social & political system which must inevitably reduce millions
to suffering & starvation for no adequate reason, is something whose explanation I am forced to leave to the professional psychologist. But of course,
certain *individuals* are breaking away from the pattern—like our admirably intelligent Governor Green,[18] who is likewise the city's leading art connoisseur.
On the whole, it is not remarkable that I do not fit into my native milieu! And
yet my views are not always the precise *opposite* of its views. I certainly advocate no ideology favouring anything less than intrinsic excellence . . . but
would have *excellence* more justly & realistically defined. I have no excessive
fondness for the unwashed masses—although I *do* insist that no government
is worth maintaining unless it both feeds those masses, & gives them ample
chances to prepare their members for an ascent in the social scale. Personal
excellence must be substituted for the accident of property-possession as a

credential for power-wielding. The great problem of the future is to combine two outwardly conflicting elements—the guaranteeing of security to all, & the confining of executive power to the trained & competent few capable of wielding it intelligently. ¶ But I must cease this tedious rambling. ¶ Finished "The Shadow Out of Time", but am so uncertain about it that I may tear it up. ¶ All good wishes—Yrs most cordially—H P L

P.S. I must get the latest W.T. & see your "Sealed Casket" in print. Hope the text isn't too badly mangled. I think you said Wright had cut out the fascinating motto from the Eltdown Shards.

Notes

1. In 1909 Dr. Frederick Cook "falsely claimed to have reached the North Pole, was exposed as a liar, and later went to prison for a different fraud." Walker Chapman, *The Loneliest Continent: The Story of Antarctic Discovery* (Greenwich, CT: New York Graphic Society, 1964), 108.

2. HPL refers to the Antarctic explorers Jules Dumont d'Urville (French; 1790–1842), Charles Wilkes (American; 1798–1877), James Clark Ross (British; 1800–1862), Robert Falcon Scott (British; 1868–1912), Carsten Egeberg Borchgrevink (Norwegian; 1864–1934), Roald Amundsen (Norwegian; 1872–1928), Richard E. Byrd (American; 1888–1957), Sir Douglas Mawson (Australian; 1882–1958), and Hubert Wilkins (Australian; 1888–1958).

3. This refers to a photograph of RFS and his dog Vito, who is leaping up to catch in his mouth a stick held by RFS (see back cover of *Letters to Richard F. Searight* (Necronomicon Press). RFS has written on the back of the photograph: "This was taken some 3 years ago by a friend of mine who has a press camera. While it appears as if my dog were hanging from the stick, the camera actually caught the canine at the peak of his leap into the air to seize the stick. It's a better picture of Vito than of myself, I'm afraid." The picture of HPL and the kitten appears *Miscellaneous Writings* (1995).

4. 11 July 1931; see *SL* 3, frontispiece.

5. A reference to two poems in the January 1935 issue of *FF*, "The Alien" by Natalie H. Wooley (p. 74) and "Voices of the Night: 2. Babel" by Robert E. Howard (pp. 74–75).

6. Presumably upon HPL's moving from Providence to New York when he married Sonia H. Greene.

7. Laura Ellis Moe (1888?–?), wife of HPL's friend Maurice Winter Moe.

8. See RFS 18.

9. HPL alludes to these facial tics in "The Shadow out of Time" (1934–35), when Peaslee's body is host to the alien from the Great Race.

10. "Those were the days when a friend named Chester Pierce Munroe & I claimed the proud joint distinction of being the worst boys in Slater Ave. School." HPL to Helen V. Sully, 4 December 1935; *Letters to Wilfred B. Talman and Helen V. and Genevieve Sully* 453.

11. HPL wrote astronomy columns for the *Pawtuxet Valley Gleaner* (Phenix, RI, 1906) and the *Morning Tribune*, the *Evening Tribune*, and the *Sunday Tribune* (Providence, 1906–08).

12. Edited by Francis T. Palgrave.

13. RFS gave to his daughter Marjorie a copy of Hawthorne's *A Wonder Book* (Chicago: Rand-McNally, 1913) as a Christmas present in 1941.

14. HPL owned at least six of Joel Dorman Steele's fourteen-weeks titles.

15. Probably *Britannica Junior,* first published in 1934 in 12 volumes.

16. Edited by Harry Thurston Peck.

17. *St. Nicholas: An Illustrated Magazine for Young Folks* was a popular monthly American children's magazine. It was continuously published from 1873 to 1940 (there was a brief revival in 1943); but it did change publishers in 1935, from the American Education Press to the Educational Publishing Corp.

18. Theodore Francis Green (1867–1966), governor of Rhode Island from 1933 to 1937. He also served as U.S. senator from 1937 to 1961.

[22]　[ALS]

66 College St.,
Providence, R.I.,
April 16, 1935.

Dear R F S:—

Glad the snap shots proved interesting—& thanks exceedingly for the additional glimpse of yourself. Is this by any chance a permanent contribution to my Hall of Fame? If not, just say the word & it will return in the best of condition! Yes—a combat betwixt Two-Gun Bob & little Bobby Bloch would be quite a study in one-sided slaughter![1] That snap of Bloch was taken when he was 15 or 16—he must be close to 18 now. I don't imagine he is quite as fragile a creature as the picture would indicate. Two-Gun, on the other hand, is all that he looks & more. He wears a $^{#}$17 collar, & has such arms & chest muscles that he can't buy a ready-made coat! Whitehead was a great chap—as high-grade a person as ever contributed to W.T. His talents & energy were tremendous—& it is noteworthy to reflect that much of his work was carried on while he was almost incapacitated by his long gastric illness. Yes—I know what an exception *Adventure* made in the case of "The Black Beast" (whose proofs I read while in Dunedin in 1931) & other weird items.[2] I couldn't even begin to keep track of his minor items—& besides the magazine stories he had several ecclesiastical works & one juvenile novel[3] to his credit. Musician, artist, athlete, traveller, cleric, liturgiologist, author, boys' camp leader, psychologist, civic leader, anthropologist—no more versatile person ever lived, & his death in 1932 at the age of 49 was a calamity of the first water. Of other Whitehead pictures I can find only two in my files at the moment—one snap of himself & his (still living) father in early 1930, before illness had given him the extreme thinness manifest in later views, & one studio picture taken late in 1931. This latter—a reproduction designed for Barlow's contemplated edition of Whitehead's letters—you may keep permanently if it would form an acceptable memento of a remarkable writer, since I have not only another copy but the original photograph from which the reproduction was made. Please return the father-&-son view some time, though there is no hurry.

I still mourn the passing of the F F. Possibly Schwartz will use your vivid story, since he may try to bend F M weirdward just enough to hold some of Hornig's late clientele. I hope so, anyway. Crawford's "Marvel Tales" is another possible haven. The recent issue[4] of that shows a marked improvement in format, though the contents is nothing to become excited over. As to telegraph stories in general—it is unfortunate that the technical character of their background makes them hard to put across in ordinary magazines. I must have read some of the Lovett[5] tales in the old *Railroad Man's Magazine,* since I followed that fascinating, red-covered periodical from its start to its finish. Something about railways always strongly fascinated me. I haven't seen the revived magazine, but am told it does not follow its earlier avatar very closely. How to present plots connected with highly technical principles is really a vast problem—though I'd hesitate to call it beyond solution.

No news from Loring & Mussey about my MSS.—but I doubt if anything will develop. Something about my stuff seems to deter all publishers! I don't believe a sale of 3000 could be guaranteed. In 1933 Knopf was ready to publish if Wright (who was consulted) would give assurance that a certain number of copies could be sold—but no such assurance was forthcoming. Therefore my mood is far from optimistic.

Yes—I do like my study pretty well, crowding & all. Never before moving to this house (May '33) was I able to have a study separate from sleeping quarters—but I had a folding bed & dispensed with dresser &c . . . so that it may be said that I slept in my library rather than that I had my books & desk in my bedroom. Just now I have increased the crowding of my study still further by the addition of *more* filing cabinets—this time little fellows only 22 × 13 × 9½″ in total dimensions, so that they can be tucked in odd corners & under tables. They are a new invention—papier-maché with wood frame & imitation grained wood finish—& I got *6* of them at a bargain sale at a dollar each. I spent 2 days transferring material to them & to the 2 wooden cabinets purchased in January—& the result is almost miraculous! Scattered pamphlets & disintegrating boxes of papers are neatly assembled, well-protected, & coherently accessible for the first time in years—even though a good many stacks of magazines & boxes of cuttings still have to remain on the open shelves. Sorry you can't get all your bibliothecal & auctorial possessions into one definite room—but ideal housing arrangements are hard to light upon. One of my most learned friends today has no study—& young Long had to work in the family dining-living room & sleep on a couch in the parlour till he was 25 years old! Sorry rents are rising in Detroit. If that happens here, I see myself headed for the slums! I share your preferences for a non-urban environment—indeed, what makes me so fond of Providence is its persistently village-like aspect. The ancient hill still retains the quaint, quiet streets & garden oases which one would not expect to find in a city so large. And yet I'd prefer an even smaller town such as Newport or Annapolis or Fredericksburg or Natchez. The one thing I won't endure is a metropolis. My two years in Brooklyn—1924–6—drove me nearly to exasperation!

I had a delightful 2-day visit from Robert Ellis Moe, but he did not have enough genealogical information at his tongue's tip to establish himself as a definite relative of yours. Many names, of course, involve no family homogeneity. There are several utterly unrelated Phillips, Perkins, &c. lines in New England alone. You will undoubtedly find the Hooker volume a mine of interesting data.[6]

Haven't got around to "The Frozen Pirate" yet—so inundated have I been with loan-volumes demanding early attention & return or passing along. Last week I read Gustav Meyrink's "The Golem", lent by young Barlow. This is really the most magnificent thing I've come across in ages. The cinema of the same title in 1921[7] was a mere substitute using the name—with nothing of the novel in it. What a study in subtle fear, brooding hints of magic, & driftings to & fro across the borderline betwixt dream & waking, madness & sanity! There are no *overt* monsters or miracles—just symbols & suggestions. As a study in lurking, insidious *regional* horror it has scarcely a peer—doing for the ancient, crumbling Prague ghetto what I unsuccessfully tried to do for rotting Newburyport in "The Shadow Over Innsmouth". I had never seen the novel before, but mentioned it in my article as a result of having seen the cinema. Now I realise that I ought to have given it an even higher rating. Have you read it? If not, you ought to get on Barlow's mailing list!

Thanks for the cutting about "That Bennington Mob"[8]—which I hope I can get hold of eventually. Possibly the author's ancestry represents a branch of my own *Sufford* line. I have a well-known earlier novel on the same theme—Judge D. P. Thompson's "Green Mountain Boys", written in 1839. This is quite a storehouse of obscure Americana, though as a novel it suffers from the ponderousness of the Cooper period.

Hope my "Mts. of Madness" won't disappoint you. The sole coherent copy is now lent to young Emil Petaja, whose letters & verses you may have noticed in the F F. I have asked him to forward it to you as soon as he is through with it—so that it may be coming along any time, if indeed it has not already reached you. No hurry at all about returning it to me so long as it gets back safely in the end.

So you succeeded in being the absolutely worst—not merely one of the two worst—boy in your room in grammar-school days! I bow in acknowledged defeat! The parallelism of the laboratory, the "professor" nickname, & the telescope really is interesting! By the way—my first telescope (Feby. 1903) was a 99¢ mail-order-house specimen . . . a non-achromatic affair of vast size with papier-maché tubes obtained from Kirtland Bros. & Co., 90 Chambers St., N.Y. City . . . a firm still in existence. It wasn't bad for the price, though its illuminating powers were dubious. I still see telescopes of this sort advertised in the cheap magazines at $1.50 or $2.00. In July of the same year I got a really good 2¼″ telescope with two eyepieces (50 & 100 power) from the same firm for $16.50, & had a tripod mounting made by a local craftsman for $8.00. This served me 3 years—but in the summer of '06 I obtained my present Bardou 3″ from Montgomery Ward & Co.—for $50.00. It came on a pillar-&-claw table stand, but I shifted it to the old tripod, which I still use—keeping the other in reserve. After nearly 30 years the old fellow is rather battered & corroded, but it will still show the lunar peaks, Saturnian rings, & kindred celestial sights. A telescope is really imperishable—indeed, at the Ladd Observatory here there is still preserved the small reflecting telescope ordered from London by Joseph Brown of Providence in 1768 for the purpose of observing the Transit of Venus in 1769. The first astronomical telescope in Providence was owned by John Merritt in 1750.

Glad the juvenile suggestions seem useful. I wouldn't be in the least surprised if the Church books were the ones you read in childhood. They were very popular in my day, & I don't see why they shouldn't have survived. As for the Book of Knowledge—there was no such thing when I was young, & I wouldn't know much about it if my late uncle hadn't chanced to be connected with the company issuing it. As it was, he had a set which I looked through from sheer curiosity in adulthood—& which I now possess.[9] I soon saw that it really was a remarkable compendium of all the scraps of lore & knowledge bequeathed by the past to each rising generation—& unfolded in just the order & proportion best suited to the youthful mind. It is, I believe, kept abreast of the times through successive editions. The copy I have is of 1913 or 1914—& I can well imagine how the mechanical & scientific articles must have changed! By the way—since my previous letter, I've seen advertised a *child's dictionary*, which ought to be a very useful device in its way. It is said to define words in a simpler & more direct fashion than the customary Websters. I meant to sent you the advertisement (in the N.Y. Times Book Section, if I mistake not), but lost it before I had a chance. I'll probably come across it again, though. Glad the younger generation responds enthusiastically to poetry. Rhythm is a strong & spontaneous instinct in childhood—witness the universal appeal of Mother Goose, & the *unconscious* rhythm manifested in any repetitive childish cry or taunt—such as "John-ny / dass-nt / climb it / ; John-ny / dass-nt / climb it /" [two trochees & a spondee] &c. I was an avid Mother-Gooseist at 2½, & began devising rhymes of my own at 6.

The geographical & social distribution of conventional false values in society & economics would certainly make an interesting study. Within the United States it is just possible that the older sections tend to average more traditional prejudices in various fields than the newer—though there are some very conspicuous exceptions. For example—while the east may harbour more *political* & *social* blindness than any other region, the inner south (Ga. Tenn. Ala. Miss.) & middle west are infinitely more backward in their attitude toward science & the religious illusion. Those are the places at which Huey Long aims with his ex cathedra citations from 'de Bahble'. In many ways, it is paradoxically true that the regions with the greatest average of intellectual & aesthetic progress are most backward in social & political vision. The worst regions are those with a largely *commercial & industrial* tradition, & a ruling oligarchy of merchant-princes. This sort of plutocracy is less rational & malleable in every way than the genuine aristocracy of agrarian origin in which values other than financial & commercial are recognised. Both forms of oligarchy have their tendencies toward irrational clannishness & social myopia, but a true aristocracy is infinitely more fruitful in real thought & occasional concessions to actual needs & conditions than is an industrial plutocracy. Leaders of the people in the struggle for human rights come from the gentry much more frequently than from the upper bourgeoisie—witness Cleisthenes, the Gracchi, Caesar, Jefferson, both Roosevelts, John Strachey, &c—& such local examples as Thomas Wilson Dorr & Theodore Francis Green (now Governor) of Rhode Island.

Regarding Señor Rivera—of course he was not the sole or perhaps even the principal determinant of the subject-matter of his murals. Naturally he was told the kind of a job wanted. In some respects he may even have been hostile to the spirit given him to depict—certainly he must be hostile to the element of human exploitation & excessive private acquisition involved, since he is himself a Marxist. On the other hand, Marxists worship *the machine* as the basic source of the abundance which will one day make possible a wider distribution of resources—hence he may have been as sympathetic from his angle toward the mechanical basis of quantity-production, as are the plutocrats from their angle. That the machine does indeed have a high symbolic value in modern sociology no one can deny. The question is, whether the given *method* of symbolisation is a truly artistic one—& whether any purely economic factor ought to figure *so largely* in a representation of the *whole life* of a region or city. I am inclined to agree with you that a considerable amount of humour & satire enters into Rivera's compositions—as into the work of certain Gothic & Renaissance craftsmen. He has a certain impish independence—as his experience at Rockefeller Centre in N.Y. attests. I don't care much for his technique—but he certainly cannot be ignored or minimised. Incidentally—I'm no initiated expert in the matter of pictorial art. All my knowledge of painting & painters is of the most superficial, casually-picked-up sort—& some of my instinctive criteria of judgment are undoubtedly historical or traditional rather than purely aesthetic. Art critics would hoot at my taste. I don't care for representations of figures, but like landscapes & architectural views. I think my favourites are the Dutch landscapists of the 17th century—Ruysdael, Hobbema, Cuyp, &c—& also Claude Lorrain & Constable.

Regarding the delineation—in any of the arts—of what our especial age & culture-group considers distasteful or 'repulsive', I do not see where any definite line can be drawn. You raise a question as to the *purpose* of delineating objects considered 'mean', 'sordid['], or 'harrowing'—in reply to which I would say that no art can have any 'purpose' apart from the aesthetic satisfaction of the artist. To ask for any such added purpose is, it seems to me, to mistake the nature & function of art. That was the mistake of the old-time moralists—& is the mistake of the modern Marxists. As to the reason why the delineation of the "sordid" can satisfy an artist—I would say that there is a very profound & genuine satisfaction in any successful symbolisation of any essential phase of truth. Many are "repulsive" or "horrible" or both—& it would be absurd to think that anything so important . . . & therefore so potentially the material of the aesthetic symbolist . . . . could be overlooked. The joy & beauty are in *the process of successful creation.* Now although *intellection* really has no place in prose art, it is likewise a fact that many sombre or "sordid" art products do indeed exert a marked intellectual stimulation on the beholder. Intellectual satisfaction hinges on *the perception of new, complex, or obscure truth—* & this of course has nothing to do with any classification into "pleasant" or "repulsive" truth. There can be the highest satisfaction, both artistic & intellectual, in some great work of literature which reveals the repulsive facts behind some fair exterior. There may indeed be accompanying emotions of pain or distaste from sources other than artistic & intellectual—but these may justly be held irrelevant to the issue. In the end, the repulsive conditions depicted may be abolished all the quicker because of their powerful emphasis through art. Another thing, too—a highly horrible work of art may represent an emotional catharsis of the most useful sort . . . releasing gnawing & debilitating emotions connected with the general hideousness of life & its endless cruelties & frustrations. A concentrated picture of pure horror may well prepare the creator or beholder to bear all the better the long-drawn horror which is conscious existence. Of course, art which lays a markedly disproportionate stress on isolated & not especially significant details of horror is generally inferior. But any system of criteria which would bar out Zola & Poe & Baudelaire & Bosch & Goya is obviously unsound.[10] So far as Dickens goes— though I have no aesthetic objection to raise against the use of squalor in its place, I am infinitely wearied by his novels because they do *not* contain good character-drawing. Dickens never drew a real human being in all his career— just a pageant of abstractions, exaggerations, & general caricatures. Each "character" is merely an abstraction of a single human instinct. Of balanced psychology & lifelike roundedness there is nothing. Character—motivation— values—all false, artificial, & conventional. What gets Dickens by is a certain emotional drive—a reflection of his own creative impulse—plus the mechanical skill of his plot-patterns, whereby such varied scenes & pseudo-characters are brought to a neat focus. But all that kind of thing seems jejune & 19th century today—& I simply can't keep awake over it!

I certainly welcome the spring—whose degree of progress is probably about the same in Michigan & R.I. My hibernation is gradually breaking up—there have been days as warm as 65° & 71°, & on several occasions I have had outings in the countryside—once taking a 12-mile walk. But I don't get any really congenial weather up here till late May or June—hence I wish I could manage to amble down to Charleston!

Picked up a useful book the other day—the new 1-volume Modern Encyclopaedia, now issued at only $1.95 by Grosset & Dunlap. I've needed something of the sort—my latest other encyclopaedia being of 1914.[11] It seems curious to have a general encyclopaedia with events as late as *last November* mentioned. ¶ Read Derleth's new detective novel—"Three Who Died"—& guessed the outcome in full on p. 145 (out of 252).[12] Distinctly clever—an improvement on its predecessor.

All good wishes—Yrs most cordially—H P L

P.S. Glad to see your vivid verses in the April W T.[13] Haven't had time to read anything else in the issue as yet.

Notes

1. Apparently a reference to Bloch's letter in *WT*, November 1934, in which he attacked the fiction of Robert E. Howard, referring to Howard's popular hero as "Conan the Cluck." Bloch was only seventeen when he made his first appearance in *WT* with the well-received "The Feast in the Abbey" (January 1935).

2. "The Black Beast" appeared in *Adventure* for 15 July 1931. Whitehead had many stories in *Adventure*.

3. *Pinkie at Camp Cherokee* (New York: G. P. Putnam's Sons, 1931).

4. Presumably the issue for March–April 1935.

5. Possibly Robert Scott Lovett (1860–1932), author of several nonfiction works on railroads. *Railroad Man's Magazine* ran from 1906 to 1919, when it merged with *Argosy All-Story Weekly*.

6. *The Descendants of Rev. Thomas Hooker: Hartford, Connecticut: 1586–1908*. The volume contains references to Ruth Stiles, RFS's great-grandmother, and to Ebenezer Stiles, RFS's grandfather.

7. *The Golem* (UFA [Germany], 1920, silent), directed by Paul Wegener and Carl Boese; starring Paul Wegener, Albert Steinrück, and Lyda Salmonova.

8. By Henry Barnard Safford. This is an historical novel about the Green Mountain Boys, a militia organization formed in the 1760s to resist the province of New York's attempted annexation of the so-called New Hampshire Grants (later the state of Vermont).

9. Perhaps the *People's Cyclopedia*.

10. The "system" HPL postulates is the subject of Ray Bradbury's "Pillar of Fire" and "The Exiles," stories about future societies in which the writings of HPL, Poe, and other horror writers are banned.
11. See *People's Cyclopedia* in the Bibliography.
12. Derleth's previous novel was *The Man on All Fours*.
13. "The New World."

[23]   [ALS]

66 College St.,
Providence, R.I.,
May 31, 1935.

Dear R F S:—

Let me hasten to express my sympathy concerning your recent illness, & my hope that you may very soon be wholly restored to accustomed vigour. Digestive maladies of any sort are distressing—as I am reminded by my own rotten upset condition at this very moment. However, yours was a definitely isolated phenomenon, from which no further results need be apprehended. You are, indeed, to be envied your general high average of health.

I am surely glad that you found something to like in "At the Mountains of Madness". Most certainly, I don't regret having written it—whether or not it ever sees the light of print. It was in my system & had to come out. Whether anything will come of Crawford's booklet plan I can't say. Even if he prints the text there will probably be no very good way of circulating it—the story of Klarkash-Ton's "Double Shadow" brochure all over again. However—a good array of extra copies for lending & presentation would be a sufficient repayment for the labours of proofreading. If Crawford doesn't take it, I may possibly submit it to *Amazing Stories Quarterly*—a market, recently suggested to me, which I had previously overlooked. Regarding the linkage to "Arthur Gordon Pym"—some have criticised this, since so much of Poe's narrative is definitely contradicted by modern exploration, but I could not resist the temptation. "Pym" impressed me profoundly in youth—so profoundly that I can scarcely think of the antarctic apart from it. When I visited Nantucket last summer one of the first things that came to my mind was the hero's origin in that ancient island port . . where his father was "a respectable trader in sea-stores". Yes—I did notice the recent press mention of old Tristan d'Acunha, & was very much interested both because of the Pym connexion & because of my perennial fascination with all lonely & remote isles.[1] These solitary outposts feel change less than other parts of the world . . . to such an extent that I'd like to live on a good tropical specimen with plenty of architectural reminders of the past!

Yes—"Out of the Æons"[2] was a ghost-written product of my own pen—the alleged author's part consisting solely of the vague idea of an ancient mummy being found to have a still-living brain. It is not, I fear, as carefully written as a signed story of mine would have been. "The Canal"—one of the high spots of W T history[3]—well deserved reprinting. I haven't had time to read the May W T yet, but have no very high expectations of it. Little Bloch's story is an earlier effort than the one previously printed.[4] He is struggling hard with his juvenile tendency toward more gruesomeness & overcolouring, & the next few years will reveal how much genuine literary ability he has. Two-Gun Bob is a definite recruit for adventure fiction.[5] He keeps up a thin allegiance to weirdness, but it is in the slashing & mangling & escaping that his real zest lies. At that, he is miles ahead of all the hack pulpists— Kline, Quinn & (alas, alas!) the post-1932 Price—since he obviously enters enthusiastically into all his sanguinary upheavals. His own personality & ideas stick out all over his stories.

Thanks for permission to retain the snap . . . & I'll be glad to see the future one promised. Whether good old Canevin's death was hastened by his extremely active life is one of those obscure physiological problems which can never be fully decided. It is possible that sheer accident entered into the matter—for the gastric trouble was distinctly improving when the collapse occurred. Physicians never agreed whether the final sinking was a direct sequel to the dizzy seizure preceding it, or a tragic result of a fall sustained in the night when the patient attempted to rise. The gastric trouble probably was indeed a result of habitual overstrain—plus rather sumptuous eating & a kind of tropical dysentery once experienced in the West Indies. Whether H S W could have extracted more from life by living less intensely & longer is something no one but himself could say. I myself am in the opposite or energy-saving class—indeed, I have to be . . . although I don't carry the incubator idea to the extent that Long & some others do. Whereas I am inactive as judged by the Whitehead or Bob Howard standard, I am activity itself as compared with Long . . . who thinks my long walks & kindred exertions are positively barbaric in their arduousness!

"The Golem" is great stuff. If you'd like to read it, drop a card to Barlow (1218—16th St., N.W., Washn. D.C.) & he'll see that it comes your way. It is going on a borrower's circuit whose present final link is young Rimel of Asotin. This edition is as recent as 1928—but it's very hard to get. None of the present borrowers have ever come across a copy before. Thanks vastly for mentioning the weird work of Morgan Robertson.[6] I used to read some of his sea-tales—in the old *Popular Magazine,* I believe—but never realised that he had dabbled in the macabre. I would indeed be most grateful for the loan of the volume you mention, & will promise its safe return. No hurry, though, about the matter.

I surely hope "The Haunted Relay" will appear—though F M has rejected my "Nameless City", passed on by the late F F. Wright's humorous lines in the recent issue[7] are distinctly entertaining—& confirm my belief that ol' Satrap Pharnabazus must really be exceedingly clever & likeable despite some of his capricious decisions & shrewdly commercial standards. The Baldwin biography of me[8] was the result of a questionnaire joined to Eph-Li's general correspondence knowledge of the subject. Rimel's linoleum block is excellent considering its medium—though it gives an amusingly rejuvenated effect.

That new encyclopaedia surely is a good buy. I've had occasion to consult it repeatedly. And so you've come up against my own experience in obtaining Dryden's Virgil? Well—it's nothing new, for my replacement dates back to 1906, when a family copy virtually fell to pieces. Then as now the only obtainable edition was the Oxford one—in a very attractive series called "The World's Classics." But I don't [think] the trouble lies in a decreased love of Virgil . . . rather is it a lack of appreciation of *Dryden*. You'll find that *Coningtan's* Æneid[9] is abundantly easy to get—at least, it was the last I knew, being one of the titles in Burt's Home Library. I never cared for it, though—since its metre (the irregular octosyllabic couplet of Scott's longer poems) is very ill-suited to the stately Virgilian spirit. Conington also published a *prose* translation of all of Virgil—of which I have seen only portions.[10] I have Davidson's prose Virgil in Harper's Classical Library (1855). My late uncle Dr. Clark made a pentameter blank verse translation of the Æneid & Georgics, but died before getting at the Eclogues. It has never been published, but I have the typed MS. Wish I could publish it some day—finishing the Eclogues myself. Pope's Iliad & Odyssey are fortunately very much alive. I bought the former when my old copy fell to pieces. I still have the old family Odyssey. But the really best Homer in English (that is, the really closest duplication of the Homeric spirit) is the prose version of Andrew Lang & his colleagues. I don't own it, but mean to get it now that it's in the Modern Library complete for a dollar.

As for the macabre & the terrible in fiction—I certainly agree that the *overemphasised & unmotivated* use of harrowing or repulsive themes (done merely as a bid for attention) is as cheap & ignominious as any other literary practice involving disproportion, ulterior motives, & an absence of purely artistic intent. One cannot judge a work of art by its subject-matter—but one can analyse the *motive & method*, & form judgments accordingly. If a hideous or disgusting picture is an *authentic* attribute of some sincere transcript of human life or mood, it is as sound a piece of writing as any other . . . no matter whether its emotional (apart from aesthetic) effect upon immature people may be depressing. One cannot gauge general literature by the tastes or needs of a class who have no real occasion to read it. On the other hand, if the gruesome or repellent material is obviously dragged in merely for the sake of shocking—without natural justification in the subject-matter, & with a cheap gloating on the horror or filth for its own sake—then we may unhesitatingly condemn the product as tawdry & inartistic. In this class of tawdry & inferior writing I would place most popular obscenity & a good deal of the physically gruesome or sadistic material of the *conte cruel* type . . . like some of Capt. G. F. Eliot's yarns in W T.[11] In stuff like this there is not even a pretence of artistic intent—poor Price, who nowadays reels off endless tripe for the "spicy" magazines (among others) tells dolefully & cynically how editors send back his yarns with instructions to "sex 'em up" or "get 'em hotter". One does not have to be an Anthony Comstock or John S. Sumner[12] in order to feel a limitless contempt & nausea at tactics of this sort! It is fortunate for Price's pocketbook that he has a strong stomach & a limitless objectivity in concocting synthetic crap. Regarding Dickens—heretical as it may sound, I don't think you've missed much. Some tell me I read the stuff too young to appreciate it, but from all I recall—& from all the allusions I hear—I don't think I'd react much differently today. The grotesque puppets & one-sided abstractions in those novels never came to life so far as I was concerned, while the mawkish sentimentality drew from me only a laugh. Indeed, the Victorian age never "took" with me. I was born & grew up in it, but was just as alien to it as any modern. Since there was then no modern age to look ahead to, I looked backward & became a psychological part of the 18th century. Those around me gushed over Dickens & Browning & Tennyson—but I went up to the exiled leather-bound reliques in the attic & became one with Addison & Johnson & Pope.

No—I haven't done anything to "The Shadow Out of Time" yet . . . since the young Comte d'Erlette has made no report on the rough scrawl now in his hands. After hearing what he thinks of it I can judge better whether it's worth typing. Glad to hear that "The Warder of Knowledge" is coming along. Certainly—Klarkash-Ton & Two-Gun & I are delighted to have our imaginary horror-volumes mentioned. It creates a convincing background when a wide range of writers darkly allude to the same ominous legacies from shadowy pasts. Possibly you know that Robert W. Chambers thus used a great many of the black hints (Carcosa, Hastur, Lake of Hali) of Ambrose Bierce. I've mentioned the Eltdown Shards in the "Shadow".[13] Some other hellish possibilities are Ludvig Prinn's *De Vermis Mysteriis* (Bloch), & the "Sigsand Manuscripts" mentioned repeatedly in the work of William Hope Hodgson.[14] Concerning the *date* of the Eltdown Shards—I'd put them back in the Miocene or even Eocene if I were you. They ought to be definitely *pre-human*, & new discoveries are tending to show that modern man in all his full development may have existed as far back as the Pliocene. The inscriptions, beyond a doubt, bespeak a very perfect & very ancient civilisation—such as must have flourished for millions of years on this planet (how long on any other, only Azathoth can say!) before the rise of the mammalia. I think the symbols were of those ancient roots which you cite.

Klarkash-Ton thought your tale the best in the March W T, & I agreed with him after analysing the elements of repetition & conventionality in "Julhi",[15] its only possible rival. I was very glad to have another glimpse of the unwisely deleted motto, & will forward the text to Klarkash-Ton after making a copy to insert in my own W T file. I cannot understand Wright's unjustified elimination of this necessary atmospheric & explanatory touch.

Your new MS. box ought to be a great help in keeping things straight around your working quarters. My new files are a godsend—indeed, I can't see how I ever got along without them. I keep my own MSS. in two large tin boxes of the old-fashioned sort traditionally used for legal papers & the like.

Yes—a telescope is a pleasant thing to have around . . . indeed, I think every household ought to have a good specimen . . . as well as a microscope, a globe, & other common scientific devices. Such an equipment was thought almost necessary in the 18th century. We used to have both terrestrial & celestial globes—& I'm sorry now that I let the celestial one go during a household upheaval of 1924.

The "early spring" I spoke of surely turned out to be a mocking false alarm! I have, though, managed to squeeze in a few congenial outings. The best of these was April 27–8, when—through some benign dispensation of Yog-Sothoth—a spell of fine hot weather coincided with a visit from my young friend Robert Ellis Moe (who says, by the way, that he may get in touch with you soon on the subject of Ellis genealogy). The visitor arrived on the morning of Saturday the 27th in his faithful 1928 Ford—& we put in a strenuous 2 days in that venerable vehicle. Saturday we explored old Newport—seeing 2 ancient windmills; a flock of sheep with sportive lambs in the best pastoral tradition; "Whitehall", the 1729–32 home of Dean (later Bishop) Berkeley; the Hanging Rocks where that good cleric composed his famous ALCIPHRON, OR, THE MINUTE PHILOſOPHER; the lofty cliffs; the strange rock cleft called "Purgatory", where the sea pounds thunderously in; the Overing farmhouse where a small band of rebels under Col. Wm. Barton captured Genl. Prescott of the regulars in 1777; & the venerable town itself—with 1698 Quaker Meeting House, 1726 Anglican church, 1732 colony house, 1749 library, 1760 market-house, 1763 Jews' Synagogue, & private dwellings as old as 1675. It was a glorious hot day—up to 82° in Providence, though not quite so good in Newport. Sunday the 28th we went to ancient New Bedford—Nantucket's successor as the world's great whaling centre—whose last lone exemplar of the industry put to sea only 11 or 12 years ago. The marine museum was closed—but after a tour of the centuried waterfront we set off southward to sample something still better. This was the Round Hills estate of Col. E.H.R. Green (old Hetty's son) in S. Dartmouth, where the old whaling barque *Charles W. Morgan* (built 1841) is preserved at a realistic-looking wharf—but solidly embedded in concrete as a permanent exhibit. We went all over the vessel—which is tremendously fascinating. On the Green estate is also an ancient windmill moved from Rhode Island. We then explored a region—where Southern Mass. adjoins southeastern R.I.—which I had never seen before in my life. Splendid unspoiled countryside with rambling stone walls & idyllic white-steepled villages of the old New England type. Of the latter the two best specimens—Adamsville & Little Compton Commons—are both in Rhode Island. Adamsville contains the world's only known monument to a *hen*—perpetuating the fame of the Rhode Island Red—a breed evolved in that village from East Indian & Chinese gallinaceous forbears. At Little Compton Commons can be found the home & grave of Elizabeth Alden Pabodie—daughter of the famed John Alden & Priscilla Mullins of Plymouth, & first white woman born in New England. This region was once the seat of the Sakonnet Indians—whose squaw-sachem Awashonks was persuaded by the noted old warrior Capt. Benjamin Church not to join King Philip's conspiracy in 1675. It was settled from Plymouth about 1673, & (like Barrington, Warren, & Bristol) came into the Massachusetts-Bay in 1691 & into Rhode-Island (when a boundary dispute was settled by George II) in 1747. Capt. Church lies buried not far from Little Compton Commons. Well—at last we turned north through Tiverton, where on our left we had some marvellous vistas of low-lying fields & blue water. Here we passed the home of the navigator Capt. Robert Gray, who in 1792 discovered the Columbia River in the far-off Oregon country—naming it after his stout Rhode Island brig. Then back home via Fall River (an ugly mill city over the line in Mass.) & ancient Warren. Finally I regretfully guided the guest out of town—on the Hartford Pike en route for Bridgeport—& took a 4-mile rural & suburban walk before returning home. Quite a session, all in all!

The next week-end—May 3–4–5—I visited my old friend Cole in the Boston zone (Wollaston, in N. Quincy, just south of Boston proper), but cold weather seriously hampered our sightseeing. We explored ancient Marblehead, however—which is attractive under any conceivable conditions.

Future events undecided—though there is a distinct possibility that I shall visit Barlow in De Land again after he returns thither in June. Going to Florida for the *summer* sounds odd—but there's no time of year that I don't prefer a subtropical to a northern climate. Naturally, I shall welcome the sight of Richmond, Charleston, Savannah, & St. Augustine en route if the event develops. I can't yet be sure. Financial conditions will determine.

On May 25 I had an interesting visit from young Charles D. Hornig, erstwhile editor of the late F F, & present editor of *Wonder Stories*. He is a very pleasant & intelligent youth—reminding one slightly of Donald Wandrei, though with a vaguely quasi-Semitic cast of features. He seemed to appreciate quite keenly the archaic charm of venerable Providence—which is in some respects not unlike his own town of Elizabeth, N.J. I showed him most of the historic high spots, including the hidden churchyard on the ancient hill[16] which I have probably described to you at one time or another. Young Sterling (a science fiction devotee temporarily in Providence) was also on hand most of the time, making rather a convention of the event. The weather was providentially warm & sunny.

Melancholy note—a solid colonial block on the lower slope of College St. is about to be replaced by the new building of the R.I. School of Design. Palliating features are (a) the preservation of the lowest ancient building [an

old inn with archway & courtyard—to be incorporated into the new struc-ture], & (b) the fact that the future edifice is to be of a pure type of traditional Providence-Georgian architecture.[17]
All good wishes——Yrs most cordially—
E'ch-Pi-El

Notes

1. Tristan D'Acunha (now rendered Tristan da Cunha), a group of volcanic islands in the South Atlantic, inhabited at the time by only 172 people. The *New York Times* (24 March 1935): Sec. 8, p. 15, reports that the King and Queen of England were sending gifts to the island. Cf. *Commonplace Book* (entry 209), referring to another item from the *Times* of three weeks earlier concerning "lonely and remote isles":

> Special Correspondence of NY Times—March 3, 1935
> "Halifax, N.S.—Etched deeply into the face of an island which rises from the Atlantic surges off the S. coast of Nova Scotia 20 m. from Halifax is the strangest rock phenomenon which Canada boasts. Storm, sea, & frost have graven into the solid cliff of what has come to be known as Virgin's Island an almost perfect outline of the Madonna with the Christ Child in her arms.
> The island has sheer & wave-bound sides, is a danger to ships, & is abso-lutely uninhabited. *So far as is known, no human being has ever set foot on its shores.*"

2. By Hazel Heald.

3. Everil Worrell, "The Canal" (*WT*, December 1927; rpt. April 1935).

4. Robert Bloch, "The Secret of the Tomb" (*WT*, May 1935).

5. Robert E. Howard's "Beyond the Black River" was a two-part serial in *WT*, May and June 1935.

6. Morgan Robertson (1861–1915), author of many novels and tales of the sea. The weird volume mentioned by RFS is *Over the Border* (New York: McClure's Magazine, [1919?]), a collection of tales. See RFS 26.

7. Wright published a poem, "Self-Portrait," in *Fantasy Magazine* 4, No. 5 (April 1935): 112; rpt. *Etchings and Odysseys* No. 3 (1981): 61.

8. F. Lee Baldwin, "H. P. Lovecraft: A Biographical Sketch," *Fantasy Magazine* 4, No. 5 (April 1935): 108–10, 132.

9. Cf. "Metrical Regularity" (1915): "We feel even unconsciously the fitness of certain types of metre for certain types of thought, and in perusing a crude or irregular poem are often abruptly repelled by the unwarranted variations made by the bard, either through his ignorance or his perverted taste. We are naturally shocked at the clothing of a grave subject in anapaestic metre, or the treatment of a long and lofty theme in short, choppy lines. This latter defect is what repels us so much from Conington's really scholarly translation of the Aeneid" (*CE* 2.11–12).

10. Conington's prose translation of Virgil appears in *Miscellaneous Writings of John Co-nington* (London: Longmans, Green, 1872), Vol. 2.

11. E.g., "The Copper Bowl" (*WT*, December 1928).

12. Anthony Comstock (1844–1915), secretary of the New York Society for the Suppression of Vice and a virulent opponent of birth control who spearheaded the passage of the Comstock laws in the late 19th century that banned most writings on contraception. John S. Sumner (1876–1971) was Comstock's successor and sought unsuccessfully to ban many contemporary novels for obscenity.

13. *CF* 3.407.

14. Cf. "The Gateway of the Monster": "I got the idea from the Sigsand MS., written, so far as I can make out, in the fourteenth century." *Carnacki, the Ghost-Finder* (1913; London: Sphere, 1981), 50. The Sigsand MS. is also mentioned in "The Hog," published after HPL's death in *WT* (January 1947).

15. By C. L. Moore (*WT*, March 1935).

16. St. John's Churchyard.

17. College Building, Rhode Island School of Design (1822, 1936), 2 College Street. The building, of the late Federal/Georgian Revival, ascends the steep hillside between South Main and Benefit Streets. At the western end on South Main Street, it incorporates the facade of the Franklin House Hotel (1823), designed by John Holden Green (1777–1850). It also has a large archway, suggesting a carriageway that had existed between the buildings that formerly occupied the site.

[24]   [ALS]

% R. H. Barlow,
Box 88, De Land, Fla.,
August 4, 1935.

Dear Ar-Eph-Es:—

Well—as you see, the southern trip did most emphatically materialise! I left home June 5th & shot straight down to ancient Fredericksburg—home town of Genl. Washington. Then down to my beloved *Charleston.* Reached De Land June 9th, & have been here ever since. My super-hospitable hosts won't allow me to break away—so that I may linger on till August. This is a marvellous climate. I was all dragged out in the north, but began to brace up as soon as I struck the general warmth of the Carolina low country. Now I feel so active & vigorous that my northern acquaintances would scarcely recognise me. I shall certainly have to live down here eventually.

The present visit is much like that of last year except that Barlow's father—a retired army colonel—is now at home. Bob's brother Wayne—a fine young chap, a 2nd. Lt. at Ft. Sam Houston, Texas—has been here on a furlough & has proved a delightful companion, but the expiration of his leave has now sent him west again. Our activities are varied—& include the building of a cabin in an oak grove across the lake to house Bob's [illegible] (& now largely typographical) pursuits. The edifice is now quite complete, & not long ago I cleared a road to it through the scrub palmetto growths. I am helping a good deal with the printing—some results whereof you will see in course of time. Local felidae show a lineup slightly different from last year's.

Old white Doodlebug has vanished—probably run wild in the jungle. High has seceded to the phantom cabin down the road. Low has been given to a grocery store in Eustis. Jack remains in full dignity as a first-class fighting man despite a neck slightly awry from last year's snake poisoning. His nephews—Low's sons—Henry Clay (yellow) & Alfred A. Knopf[1] (tiger) now form part of the ensemble. And within the house are two pampered yellow Persians—Cyrus & Darius—brought down from Washington by my youthful host.

Occasional explorations diversify the programme. On June 17 we visited a fascinating place—Black Water Creek, a tropical river whose lush scenery suggests the Congo, Amazon, & other exotic streams found in history & legend. It winds through a steaming jungle of tall, moss-draped cypresses, whose grotesque, twisted roots writhe curiously at the water's edge. Palms lean precariously over the brink, & vines & creepers strow the black, dank earth of the bordering forest aisles. Sinister sunken logs loom up at various points, & pallid flowers & leprous fungi gleam whitely through the forest's perpetual twilight. It is much like the river at Silver Springs of which I think I wrote you last year—though I enjoyed it even more because of the more leisurely observing conditions. At Silver Springs I was whizzed ahead in a launch; this time we (R H B, Wayne, & I) went along slowly in a row boat. Each bend of the stream brought to light some unexpected vista of tropical luxuriance, & we absorbed the spectacle to the full. Serpents & alligators were somewhat in evidence—though none came near our boat. I hope for more trips of this kind, since I find myself especially sensitive to the beauty of subtropical scenery.

Turning to your epistle—I hope you are in no hurry about "Over the Border", since I may not get at it till my return home. If there *is* any haste, let me know, & I'll have my aunt forward the package down. At present I am having only first-class mail forwarded. I'm sure I shall find the tales enjoyable. As for "The Golem"—Barlow *did* receive your card & has been meaning for a long time to answer it. He will be delighted to include you on the mailing-list of "The Golem"—in fact, has already placed your name thereon. The volume will probably come from Rimel or Petaja. You might drop a postcard to one or the other of them, reminding them of your inclusion. It certainly is a great novel—with a subtlety & atmospheric depth not commonly found in weird literature. Oddly enough, other things of Meyrink's do not seem to equal "The Golem" in power. The tale in the current W T,[2] for example, is only fair. The Prague Ghetto must have been a marvellously impressive place in its heyday. I've never read Crawford's "Witch of Prague", but Meyrink's descriptions are enough to suggest the general fascination & sinister grotesqueness of the place. From passages in "The Golem" I judge that it no longer exists—that the old houses & courts & archways were torn down some 40 or 50 years ago—new wide streets being cut through. Alas! Such vandalism is all too common in quaint districts. . . . Similar destruction took place in London (between Holborn & the Strand near Drury Lane, Holywell

St., &c.) in the early 1900's, & in 1927 Boston cleared out the tangled North End alleys which I described in "Pickman's Model". Providence has had similar upheavals—which reminds me that the lower half of *College St.* is about to lose its colonial houses & archways in favour of a new building for the R.I. School of Design. *One* of the ancient buildings, however, is to be preserved & incorporated into the new structure . . . which will be of colonial design.

I'm interested to hear of the 1-volume Hawthorne. My Hawthorne items are in a variety of editions—only a few being uniform. Barlow has 2 copies of the *1st edition* of "The House of Seven Gables". This latter, by the way, seems to me the finest weird *novel* ever written in America. Hope the Shakespearian programme will advance slowly & surely. As for Crawford—I really don't know him as well as I'd like to. He belongs largely to his period, but occasionally transcends it. I surely must read "The Witch of Prague".

Sorry to hear of the dismantling of the old home—a blow very much like that which befell me in 1904, when my birthplace left the family. Really, though, the present case is worse, since your home is to be demolished & replaced by such an unworthy successor. My house is still standing (though the stable perished 2 or 3 years ago) & in use as a physicians' building. Hope you can salvage as much as possible of the library & other moveable material. So far I've kept a goodly number of old family items around me—but when my final financial collapse occurs, there's no telling what will happen. I certainly don't wish to survive the environment created by the familiar books, paintings, furniture, vases, statuary, &c. which I have had around me all my life. Your mother's eastern trip must have been full of interest, & I am glad she was able to bring some reliques & souvenirs of interest. Her itinerary certainly included some marvellous havens of the past. Hope you can arrange an historical trip of your own before very long.

Congratulations on your cheque from Hugo the Rat! It's hard telling just what treatment you would have received but for Miss Webber. Hornig (whose visit to me May 25 I doubtless mentioned) says that the people generally paid are (a) those living in N.Y., & (b) those who storm the office in person at certain lucky times when funds happen to be on hand. The classic exception to (a) is the case of Long—still unpaid for his tale in the *Spring 1930* W. S. Quarterly. A systematic exposé of the Gernsback financial policy was recently undertaken by a bright young chap named *Donald Wollheim, 801 West End Ave., N. Y. City*. He has issued a mimeographed leaflet summarising his results, & it certainly presents a damning case![3] Glad the Rat coughed up interest as well as principal in reimbursing you!

Hope "The Haunted Relay" will appear soon. Just recd. M.T., & am not vastly impressed by the present issue.[4] Ambitious in size, but naive in editing & heterogeneous in contents. Hill-Billy Crawford has no more taste or discrimination than a stevedore or share-cropper—though I do admire the cuss's persistence in trying to publish a paper (or a paper & a half—or two papers—counting *Unusual Stories*) in the face of all the existing obstacles! By the way—a possible new avenue for weird material is afforded by *The Phantagraph*, official organ of the Terrestrial Fantascience League, now published by the young Wollheim person mentioned in the preceding paragraph. This incipient sheet has a sort of vague wish to emulate the late F F—though I have my doubts as to its success. Anyhow, it deserves the encouragement of all those who wish to expand the opportunities of weird fictioneers.

Yes—it certainly was hell typing the ["]Mts. of Madness" . . . but if I hadn't, nobody but myself would ever have read it! I certainly hope Hill-Billy Crawford intends to carry out his vague plan of publishing this—& "Innsmouth". Meanwhile I hope to see your "Warder of Knowledge" in course of time. I feel sure that your account of the Old One will not conflict with any of the various hints I have advanced regarding those ominous beings. Anyhow—it can't conflict any more than the hints already do among themselves! I trust the story will meet with professional acceptance in W T or elsewhere.

Thanks exceedingly for the new snap shot—in which I really can't see any trace of the quasi-simian effect you mention! It strikes me, on the contrary, as highly attractive & prepossessing. However—the idea you derive—however fancifully—from it; about the normal-looking man whose features present a vaguely pre-human suggestion in photographs; is really full of fictional potentialities. I hope you'll employ it in a story sooner or later.[5] Speaking of simian mugs—I'll let you have a print of that shot of me which was in the envelope I lent you. Since it was taken down here by Barlow last year, I'm in just the right place to get it. I feel sure he still has the negative. It really looks very much like me—& I don't suppose a year has aged me unrecognisably.[6]

I fancy your Dryden's Virgil is printed from the same plates as mine—though mine has a green binding with gold lettering & decorations. As for my uncle's translation—it is closer to Virgil than Dryden, but not so vigorous as English poetry. The Eclogues were not translated when F C C died. If I ever had an opportunity for getting it published, I'd take it—perhaps trying to fix up a version of the Eclogues in similar style myself.

As regards energy-saving versus energy-spending—time will tell which school is more nearly correct. Moderation is undoubtedly the best watchword. I have noticed that in many cases invalids & persons of frail constitution—who are prevented from using vast stores of energy—live longer & have a later senescence than the energetic souls who burn the candle under forced draught. My family tend to die relatively young—but an invalid great-aunt (whose sisters & brother died around 70) lived to be 91.[7] I have only one known centenarian ancestor (1636–1736).[8] Regarding health fads—it surely is amusing to see them come & go. It would be better if more people forgot all about health. A tremendous number of diseases or apparent diseases have a purely nervous origin. As to the value of traditional folklore regarding health—I am naturally a sceptic in view of the large admixture of the capricious & magical in such precepts, yet

I would be the last to deny some germ of empirical common sense in many of the popular notions. After all, certain scraps of genuine experience are mixed with the allegorical, erroneous, & distorted concepts forming the bulk of folk tradition. The extreme *adaptability* of mankind is certainly impressive enough. Esquimaux in Greenland—niggers in Africa; desert-dwellers in Arabia, swamp-waders in Louisiana; plainsmen in Kansas, urbanites in New York . . . . . & they all manage to keep alive for a while! When the cry of "back to Nature" is raised, one is tempted to enquire "what kind of Nature"? However, it is easy to pick out many specific customs of modern urban life which do definitely transcend the range of environmental conditions—wide though the latter be—to which homo sapiens can advantageously adapt himself.

Klarkash-Ton was greatly pleased at receiving the motto designed for "The Sealed Casket", & hopes to see other extracts from the monstrous & pre-human Eltdown Shards. He, by the way, has taken up a new aesthetic hobby—sculptural carving in talc, rhyolite, *dinosaur bone* (of which a considerable deposit exists near Auburn), & other suitable materials. Specimens sent to Ar-Ech-Bei & myself are really impressive. This art of *carving* is of course entirely different in technique from the clay *modelling* in which Ar-Ech-Bei excels. I believe I sent you pictures of some of the latter's work last year.

Something very convenient for W T fans will appear in about a month—a complete index of the magazine's contents from its inception to the present time, published on a mimeograph by Louis C. Smith, 1908—98th St., Oakland, Calif. I don't know what the price will be, but I mean to get one. Smith may later publish my "Fungi from Yuggoth" as a mimeographed booklet.[9]

Glad you've had some good weather. It has been ideal down here—between 80° & 88°—& most of the days are sunny despite the brief showers which mark this as the "rainy season". Don't know when I'll get on the northward road—I certainly dread returning to a region of chilly nights & early autumn. Hope to stop a week in St. Augustine & Charleston, briefly in Washington, & possibly in N.Y. I shall spend a day, also, in Philadelphia.

Read the July W T lately—an average & undistinguished issue. Hectograph Eddie is trying a new plot—good luck to him! The Moore story is so-so—& many will welcome the O'Brien reprint.[10]

Thanks for the warnings against allegedly weird cinemas. Someone has just recommended "The Werewolf of London"[11] to me—but I have my doubts.

With every good wish, & hoping to see "The Warder of Knowledge" either in print or otherwise, I remain—

Yrs by the Purple Cloud—E'ch-Pi-El.

P.S. Robert Nelson—author of verses in W T & of "Lost Excerpts" in the F F—died July 23 at the age of 22 or 23. Too bad. He was crude but promising. Barlow has specimens of his posthumous work.[12]

Notes

1. HPL named this cat.

2. "The Violet Death" (*WT*, July 1935).

3. Donald A. Wollheim's exposé of Gernsback's failure to pay authors for work published in *Wonder Stories* was "My Experiences with *Wonder Stories*" in the *Bulletin* (April 1935) of the Terrestrial Fantascience Guild, a science fiction fan club.

4. Presumably the issue for Summer 1935, the last issue published.

5. There survives a three-page start of a story by RFS about a man who begins to take on a simian appearance.

6. [On verso of photo:]

H. P. Lovecraft

————————

De Land, Florida,
June 16, 1934.

Photograph by R. H. Barlow

A ruthlessly good
likeness. The intervening
1¼ years has added grey to
my locks, but not enough
new wrinkles to make the
picture misleading.

7. HPL probably refers to his great-aunt Sarah Algood, younger sister of his paternal great-grandmother Helen (Allgood) Lovecraft, who sent him information regarding his Allgood ancestry in 1905. See also HPL to Frank Belknap Long, November 1927 (*SL* 2.179–181).

8. HPL identifies this centenarian ancestress as Mary Brownell, wife of Robert Hazard (1635–1710) in his letter to Maurice W. Moe of 5 April 1931 (*Letters to Maurice W. Moe . . .* 299). Her dates, given correctly in neither the 1931 letter to Moe nor here to RFS, were 1639–1739 (see Caroline E. Robinson, *The Hazard Family of Rhode Island 1635–1894* [1895], 3–5). HPL's great-great-grandfather Stephen Place (1736–1817) was the great-grandson of Robert Hazard and Mary (Brownell) Hazard. (We are indebted to Kenneth W. Faig, Jr., for the genealogical information in these two notes.)

9. Smith never published either.

10. Edmond Hamilton, "The Avenger from Atlantis"; C. L. Moore, "Jirel Meets Magic"; Fitz-James O'Brien, "The Wondersmith."

11. *Werewolf of London* (Universal, 1935), directed by Stuart Walker; starring Henry Hull, Warner Oland, and Valerie Hobson.

12. Robert Nelson (1912–1935) wrote a few poems and stories before dying one day before his twenty-third birthday. For HPL's letters to him, see *Letters to Robert Bloch and Others* (2015). His collected writings have been published as *Sable Revery: Poems, Sketches, Letters*, ed. Douglas A. Anderson (Marcellus, MI: Nodens Books, 2012).

[25]   [ALS]

Home at Last

—Sept. 26, 1935

Dear Ar-Eph-Es:—

Through a curious coincidence—involving the delayed forwarding of the last few days' De Land mail—I have just received simultaneously your letter of Aug. 25 & card of Sept. 21st. Congratulations on the advent of Ellsworth Franklin Searight—who I trust is continuing to prosper in health & gain in size & weight, & whose mother is by now, one hopes, again enjoying full strength. I am glad that Ellsworth's big sister takes kindly to his presence. It certainly shews much graciousness & unselfishness on her part to welcome & be proud of the one who has displaced her from her hitherto undisputed eminence as sole scion of the household! One can imagine the general upheaval caused by the new arrival, but by this time things have doubtless settled down to a steadier tempo. Glad you had at least a fragmentary vacation, & imagine the visit to Wright must have been interesting. I envy you the warmth you report—though New England has had its quota of genial September days. Thanks, by the way, for the pleasing portrait, which I'm adding with pleasure to my gallery. I can well imagine that it excels the other two in faithfulness. The background of greenery is surely attractive—& I rejoice that 19946 can boast such an asset.[1] Marjorie & Ellsworth are lucky in having such a setting for their formative years. I always pity children brought up in urban apartments, who know nothing of verdure & natural beauty save what they glimpse fragmentarily in formal, artificial parks. Enclosed is that view of me which Barlow took last year—for permanent retention.

I certainly had a great time in De Land. As you know from my card,[2] I paused briefly in St. Augustine & my favourite Charleston. Then came Richmond, Washington, & Philadelphia—& finally a fortnight in New York as guest of Donald Wandrei. I saw most of the N Y local group—Long, Koenig, Hornig, &c. &c.—as well as the son of Otis Adelbert Kline,[3] who is acting as his father's N.Y. agent. Reached home Sept. 14, & found myself confronted by a terrifying mountain of work—a hopeless accumulation, which will keep my programme disrupted for weeks. And yet, recklessly enough, I permitted myself one more brief outing—visiting a friend in the Boston zone & accompanying him on various scenic pilgrimages including Nahant & Marblehead, ancient Wilbraham (the "Dunwich" country, which I had not seen since 1928), & Cape Cod. This representative panorama of varied New England scenery was highly welcome after my long absence in subtropical landscapes. In Wilbraham—up in the central Massachusetts hill country—we found considerable autumnal foliage, although the greenery is scarcely touched in R.I. & on Cape Cod. It is possible that I shall have at least one more outing before winter closes in—accompanying the same friend over the Mohawk Trail & perhaps into Vermont when the autumn foliage is at its height of splendour.

But this is merely tentative. I have hard work getting used to the chill of the north, & need my oil heater whenever the steam isn't on!

Abundant thanks for the loan of the Morgan Robertson book—which I duly found awaiting me in company with similar loans from varied sources. So far I have had no chance for any reading save of old papers—but very soon I hope to peruse the tales. I look forward to the reading with usual interest. Possibly I shall recognise some that I once read in the *Popular Magazine* 25 or 30 years ago. Later on I shall be extremely glad to see "The Witch of Prague". Hope you've received "The Golem" by this time. I think you'll agree with me concerning its peculiar haunting power. As I said, there is nothing about it to suggest the cinema of similar title popular around 1921. Speaking of circulated items—you're on the list for my latest story (now typed by Barlow), "The Shadow out of Time", though it may be quite a while before it gets around.

I'm sorry indeed to hear of the irrevocable passing of the old homestead—but am glad that the cream of the contents has been salvaged. My own experience of 1904 makes me groan in sympathy. That ancient dresser is surely a prize, & I'm glad it has reached proper & appreciative hands. You're lucky in having a posterity to hand it down to! I'm sure that judicious refinishing won't detract from its charm. Congratulations on the spoon & lamp— & I hope you get the sleigh-bed!

Hope the "Warder" landed—or hasn't Wright come to a decision yet? I'm anxious to see this—as well as the contemplated one about the latently simian face. I guess I told you that I've used the Eltdown Shards quite prominently in a new fragment—my instalment of the composite story which Schwartz is assembling for *Fantasy Magazine*. (Other instalments by C. L. Moore, A. Merritt, R. E. Howard, & F. B. Long)

Klarkash-Ton's carven teraphim[4] certainly display marvellous cleverness, & I am anxious to see photographs of the best specimens. You'll be sorry to hear that C A S's mother died on Sept. 9—an event long expected, but no less a blow on that account. His father is likewise in feeble health & of advanced years, so that ere long the arch-fantaisiste will probably be alone in the world.

Your nephew's conical clock-case sounds to me like a veritable triumph in cabinet-making, & I surely envy you your possession of it. Its harmony with the decorative scheme, & its function in accomodating the grandpaternal chronometer, make it a double asset, & attest to the cleverness of your youthful kinsman. You are lucky, by the way, to have this watch—along with the other reliques which have come your way.

Commiserations on the fountain pen debacle—& I hope repairs were speedy & adequate. My battery of two—Parker & Waterman—continues to work after a fashion, though the point of the Parker could well bear a little attention. I think I'd try a Sheaffer if I were branching out & getting an altogether new instrument.

So your local feline population is shy & reticent! My furry friends have cordially welcomed me back—the aged president of the Kappa Alpha Tau[5] rolling over quite kittenishly in his hospitable recognition. Little Johnny Perkins is now a huge & impressive black warrior—but still remains a constant visitor at 66. He has spent most of his time over here since my return—purring & drowsing & rolling in catnip.

Well—I'll add more when I've read the Robertson book. Yuggoth, what a reading programme I have! Among the other loans is the Wells–Huxley "Science of Life"—which I've been wanting to see for a long while. Sept. W T rather a poor issue—I couldn't finish many of the yarns. One of them speaks of New Orleans as a full-fledged city in 1720, when the site was scarcely cleared in that year![6]

Best wishes—& renewed congratulations on Ellsworth Franklin.

Yrs most cordially—Ech-Pi-El

Notes

1. RFS's address in Detroit was 19946 Derby Avenue.

2. Nonextant.

3. Allen Sides Kline (1893–1971) was Otis's brother.

4. In classical rabbinical literature, *teraphim* means "disgraceful things" (dismissed by modern etymologists). Many English translations of the Bible translated it as "idols, or household gods."

5. HPL did not explain to RFS previously that Kappa Alpha Tau referred to a "fraternity" of cats: *Kompsōn Ailourōn Taxis* (i.e., band of elegant [or well-dressed] cats), but it appears that RFS understood the significance of Kappa Alpha Tau.

6. "One Chance" by Ethel Helene Cohen.

[26]   [ANS postcard][1]

[Postmarked Providence, R.I.,

15 October 1935]

Have at last, with abundant thanks & appreciation, read "Over the Border", & am herewith returning it under separate cover. The tales take me back very vividly to my earlier years, when I used to read Robertson's work in the *Popular Magazine*. They have a certain flavour of naivete & quaintness now—so completely has the mental world of 20 years ago passed away. In many of these, though, the intimations of unreality are extremely clever. I am extremely glad of the opportunity to see these old-timers—all of them are new to me. ¶ Had an interesting trip to New Haven a week ago. Fascinating old town, though not as rich as Providence in colonial antiquities. Fine ride through autumnal Connecticut scenery, too. Saw most of the ancient buildings & museums, & was especially delighted by the new quadrangles of Yale University— perfect reproductions of the best Gothic & Georgian architecture which form

veritable fragments of the past—complete little elder worlds in themselves. A stroll through them is like walking bodily into a dream! ¶ I told you, I guess, of my trips of last month—to Marblehead, "Dunwich", & Cape Cod. ¶ Again thanks for the loan. Best wishes—
E'ch-Pi-El

Notes

1. *Front:* The Main New York Post Office at Eighth Avenue and 31st Street, New York City.

[27]   [ALS]

Old 66—
Nov. 4, 1935

Dear Ar-Eph-Es:—

I read yours of 27ᵗʰ ult. with keen interest, & was delighted with "The Warder of Knowledge" & the unnamed sonnet. Both create a very effective atmosphere, & I trust that each may ultimately appear in print. For the sonnet I might tentatively suggest the title "Shadows"—though possibly you will think of something much more distinctive yourself.[1]

I like the story exceedingly, & hope you will not let Wright's rejection discourage you. The style does not seem to me at all unduly verbose—indeed, I prefer such a full style infinitely to the lifeless, atmosphereless, skeletonic jargon affected by the bulk of the cheap pulp writers—to which, of course, Wright has become used. As for the charge that the climactic events 'do not follow logically from the previous pages'—my only reply is the inelegant but expressive 'horsefeathers'! It is true that the *specific* occurrences in the 'dream' have no definite foreshadowings—but what of it? The *general* character of the dream—that is, the coming of the Warder from his primal lair, the landscape suggesting the original period of the Shards, & the unfolding of all terrestrial knowledge—follows very logically indeed from the original premises. Regarding the alleged resemblance of the prose to my own—I can't see this to any marked degree. Rather would I say that you have simply chosen the same general cast of language which I prefer—but which hundreds of others, long before I was born, have preferred. Many think I have derived this style exclusively from Poe—which (despite the strong influence of Poe on me) is another typical mistake of uninformed modernism. This style is no especial attribute of Poe, but is simply *the major traditional way of handling English narrative prose.* If I picked it up through any especial influence, that influence is probably the practice of the 18th century rather than Poe; since I always doted on the earlier authors. Despite changes of fashion, I still think that this full style, whose system follows the classic universal rules prevailing in all Aryan languages ancient & modern, is more effective in conveying exact meanings &

delicate shadings of mood, than are any of the choppy, half-baked types of prose now temporarily in fashion.

Now as to any criticisms of my own—they would be very few & general. Some might bring up the old point that (in the dream) you narrate events which had no means of becoming known to anyone but the dead Whitney—but I am not a stickler about that detail. Anyhow, you provide for it in a way by speaking of 'psychic impressions' received by Prof. Tarkoff. A subtler point would have to do with *the nature of the universal knowledge involved.* As delineated, this knowledge seems to involve only *the earth & its immediate solar heritage*—whereas of course all this is the merest drop in the ocean of *universal* knowledge. Also, the terrestrial knowledge imparted seems to tally too well with the high spots of history as commonly known & taught today; whereas in truth, an absolute grasp of the earth's annals would stress hundreds of events & characters & civilisations unknown to us, while reducing in relative importance many which bulk large in our conventional records. And more—would an unfolding of *all* knowledge be confined to what we recognise as *events*? How *would* such a thing begin? Would it not deal with wholly unfamiliar foundations such as eternal currents & vortices of force—their passing to the various interactions of such currents & vortices, & the laws behind such interactions, until (long before the trivial incident involving matter, the present cosmos, the visible universe, &c. had a chance to come up) the finite mind (even with its medical preparation) grew dizzy & unconscious with the sheer pressure of detail & the sheer strain of infinitely complex correlation? The idea of *universal knowledge* is truly a fascinating one, with all sorts of unexpected ramifications. But don't take these minor observations (which have nothing to do with the story's effectiveness as a story) too seriously. All fiction usually reserves the right of limiting the field of vision for dramatic reasons, & some of the most powerful classics might be subject to the same kind of analysis. I like the tale tremendously, & surely hope it will achieve publication in the course of time. The references to the Eltdown Shards are fascinating—but woe is me! I've given a lot of dope in that composite story which conflicts directly with the true facts as here revealed! I can't recall all I wrote (for I kept no copy), but I remember having a translation prepared & published by some scholarly enthusiast corresponding to the Rev. Montague Summers of real life. I also fear that I described the shards in a conflicting way. Oh, well—in sober truth relatively few people will ever see the composite yarn anyhow. The circulation of the "fan" magazines is really quite negligible—& the merits of a quasi-impromptu mosaic story are of course close to zero. By the way—*Fantasy* is badly delayed this autumn, owing to young Ruppert's inability to attend to the printing end. The Sept. issue has yet to appear—& I don't know what plans are made for the future. Returning to the "Warder"—I've pencilled a few suggested changes in single words—any of which I'll be glad to explain if the reason is not self-evident. The point concerning the hellish & unmentionable *Necronomicon* will be elucidated by the enclosed "history" of the frightful volume . . . which I drew up some years ago to save myself from inconsistent allusions.[2] (Please return—though no hurry) This "history" must be modified in one respect—since Klarkash-Ton's "Return of the Sorcerer" (pub. in *Strange Tales* 3 yrs. ago) tells of the survival of an *Arabic* text until modern times.[3]

Glad your Chicago visit was pleasant. I have no doubt but that Wright is a delightful & congenial chap, though his capricious editorial policy does give me a large-sized cervical pain! He has consistently turned down my best work (though I no longer send to him) on the ground of *length,* while at the same time taking *far longer* things (for the most part utter tripe) from others. It is clear to me that he does not like my work, no matter what he says to the contrary.[4] He might be willing to condescend to take *short* pieces, but (though accepting such from Kline, Bernal,[5] & everybody else) draws the line at *long* pieces. Well—he can go to hell for all of me—though I suppose I may some day shoot him some odds & ends if I ever get writing in quantity again & have a plenitude of left-overs. His financial policy, too, is not very encouraging. Wandrei thinks the magazine is hard hit—so I wouldn't criticise Wright if he shared the losses (as respects his salary) with those whose work makes the magazine possible. But they tell me he still draws his full salary on time! Glad to hear you've received a cheque for April contributions. That means, I trust, that my client Mrs. Heald will get paid for the "Out of the Æons" which I ghost-wrote—& she promised to pay for that job as soon as Wright paid her. I could use that cash right now to splendid advantage!

However—I've had one piece of unexpected good luck, for young Schwartz—to whose literary agency I gave the "Mts. of Madness" MS. last September at his insistent solicitation—has actually sold the damn'd thing to *Astounding Stories!* My astonishment is unbounded—you could knock me over with a feather—but I have a $315 cheque ($350 less Schwartz's 10% commission) to prove the seriousness of the transaction. The story is absolutely opposed to the formula-type favoured by *Astounding,* & I could have sworn that it had no more chance with Tremaine than a snowball in De Land, Fla. . . . . . indeed, I warned Schwartz that he was merely wasting his time handling it. But the little imp surely is some agent! In a way, this is a good one on Wright, who turned the story down in 1931 with such bland confidence in its professional uselessness! I had—as you know—decided to let Hill-Billy Crawford tinker with it as a booklet when Leedle Shoolie stepped in & vanted an agent I shood led him be a'ready! I may let Schwartz (& his partner Weisinger)[6] peddle other things of mine. At any rate, this incident is distinctly encouraging, & strengthens my resolution to fight for enough free time to get some more stories written.

You have my profoundest sympathy concerning the passing of Vito. I have always dreaded similar tragedies, & have often refused to own a cat (my favourite, by a wide margin, among all animals from homo sapiens down) for fear I could not guarantee him a full-length life & placid old age. I suppose the further tenure of your furry friend was actually impossible (as my own tenure of a cat at various stages of my existence would have been), but that does not make the melancholy any less. So again I extend my sincerest condolences. By the way—is the passing of Vito behind your recent sonnet? A certain possible connexion seems traceable.

Congratulations on the waxing of young Ellsworth! He'll be racing around the house & talking before you realise it. I feel my own years when I see how fast the coming infants of yesteryear are growing up. Only the other day, it seems to me, I used to hear from a certain old friend about his toddling young hopeful—& bless my old bones! last spring that young hopeful (a budding electrical engineer of 22 who graduated from college at 20) was around here in his car taking the old gentleman for a ride![7] Glad the young lady is joining the ranks of the literate—& fancy her progress will get more & more rapid as her interest grows. It won't be long before she appreciates the limitless avenues opened up—with *all* books just as accessible as *picture-books* have hitherto been.

"The Golem" seems to be slow in making the rounds—but that's always the way, it would appear, with widely-circulated matter. There are always one or two tardy ones in a long chain—like Derleth & Dwyer with the Hodgson books. Thanks exceedingly for the offer of "The Witch of Prague"—which I'd welcome at any time now, unless an especially speedy return is necessary. My programme is much less congested now than it was last month. The Robertson volume surely was enjoyable, & I am very grateful for the opportunity of seeing it.

Congratulations on the new Sheaffer! Judging from your writing, I'd scarcely call the point too coarse—but it's very hard to get a fine point which writes with perfect ease. I've virtually given up—although both of my pens are obviously too coarse for an handwriting as small-sized as mine. Every time I've tried a fine pen it has scratched intolerably. Recently—because of the comparatively high cost of Sheaffer's Skrip—I've been experimenting in cheap inks, especially for rough MSS. They wouldn't work in *this* pen, (the Parker) but I've had the feed of my Waterman increased so radically that it would almost accomodate molasses or axle-grease! Behold the result! Woolworth's nickel-a-bottle concoction functioning just as smoothly as you please. And it will work on cheap paper even *better* than Skrip, because its greater thickness makes it less easily absorbed. Haven't had such good luck with cheap *black* ink. Black has to be good (Skrip or Quink), else it is very bad indeed. During recent weeks I've been writing all my rough MSS. with this outfit instead of with a pencil. Pencil rubs out & blurs so readily that—with my small writing—it's hardly safe to use it for anything of importance. But this Parker (which demands Skrip) is the most *comfortable* of all pens. It seems to fit my hand better than the Waterman. Eventually—if muscular weakening makes my handwriting any worse—I may have to use the hated typewriter in order to be understood by my correspondents. Even now many have great trouble deciphering my feeble & chaotic hieroglyphs. If I were more affluent I'd experiment with different fountain pens.

That Schick electric razor sounds impressive indeed . . . bless me, but what new-fangled methods the Machine-Age has thought up! I've seen these devices advertised, but never before had a first-hand report on their operation. Do you mean to say there are no changes or sharpenings of blades? I use a Gillette, but haven't bought a blade in years—because of a peculiar combination of thrift & opportunity. When I began shaving in '08 I always saved my blades in the hope that some effective sharpening device would be available later. Around the 1912–15 period such a device *was* available in Providence, & I had all my stacks of saved-up blades—the accumulation of years—put in as good a shape as new. The Liggett drug stores were the best place to get this sharpening done. Well—about the time of the war this service began to disappear—undoubtedly under the greedy pressure of the rapacious Gillette firm, which naturally wants to coerce the public into buying as many blades as possible. *But*—having so huge a stock already sharp, I'm still going on the original accumulation . . . . being probably the last surviving user of the *old* shape ⊙ ●● ! And I *still* save the second-time-dulled blades in the hope of further adequate sharpening opportunities (I believe the hand stroppers are rather ineffective). Hoot, mon! Ah may be English in ancestry, but uh'm a guid Scutchman at harrrt!

Klarkash-Ton is just pulling himself together after the shock of his bereavement—not writing much, but devoting himself to the sculpture which he took up last spring. His father is bearing up rather better than was expected—& I hope he'll survive for quite a spell, though he's in the 80's & badly arthritic. C A S has a maternal uncle, but he'll be pretty well alone when his father goes. He is almost a hermit—having nothing in common with the bulk of Auburnites, & indeed knowing only one family at all well.[8] Whether he will in after years drift east where the bulk of his friends—all epistolary friends—are, remains to be seen. His present abode is a small cottage—with no modern conveniences—on a hillside some distance outside the village. I believe he was born there & has never lived anywhere else. His acquisition of a deep scholarship, wide & thorough cultivation, artistic skill, & literary mastery in two languages (the editor of a Paris review, in accepting one of his French sonnets in the style of Baudelaire, once told him it was almost impossible to believe he was not a Frenchman) under such narrow environmental circumstances, is one of the most remarkable proofs of innate superiority & cultural capacity that I've ever seen. His father, though—a roving Englishman of cultivated background who finally settled down in California in middle life after extensive travels & tropical explorations—probably inculcated him with a good many mature standards which an average Auburn villager wouldn't be likely to acquire. In adolescence & young manhood he knew the late poet George Sterling quite well, & visited him at length in Carmel & San Francisco—thereby receiving much encouragement in his literary pursuits. It is fortunate that his taste & writing habits became fixed before he began writing for the pulp magazines—else his work might have suffered like the work of most of the once-promising writers (such as Long & Wandrei) who are caught too young by the cheapening commercial octopus. As it happened, he was 35 before he began writing for W T, *Wonder Stories,* & such media—hence he holds out against their insidious influence as almost none of the others (except the remarkable & exceptional Derleth) do. Sometimes he puts forth an inferior tale or two—but he always snaps back into his old form again. His classical literary training is too strong for any new influence of middle life. There is no question but that he is the greatest figure in the weird magazine field today. Derleth may have a greater future, but it won't be in the domain of fantasy. And although others may occasionally outdo C A S in single weird tales, there's nobody in sight who can challenge his high level of continuous production.

I can share your enthusiasm for "My Study Windows"[9]—a book I inherited & perused early in life. The essay on Pope delighted my 18th century soul, while that on Chaucer made me a lasting devotee of the "well of English undefiled"[10] despite my dominant prejudice against the mediaeval. Another of the essays—on the redeeming features of winter—helped to make mentally bearable a season which was physically a torment. I have always had a great respect for Lowell, both as an essayist & as a versifier. His Bigelow Papers[11] are genuine folk documents, & preserve for posterity a dialect now spoken by no living person. I've often seen his Cambridge home—Elmwood—which may some day become a public museum. It is a fine Georgian house of the 1760 period—once a country-seat, but now overtaken by the spreading town. Lowell belonged to the main classic tradition, & shews it by a style which stands head & shoulders above the crude, amorphous slop of the young moderns today. Of his charm & urbanity in his day there can be no doubt—indeed, he belonged to a generation when authors were gentlemen instead of 'bohemians' or semi-hobos. That Boston–Cambridge–Concord circle may have had its naive & absurd side, but I'd give more for such a circle than for the gin-soaked Greenwich-Village cliques of the present. It is amusing to note how closely I approached its periphery at one point—at the age of 2½. My mother knew the poetess Louise Imogen Guiney, & in the winter of 1892–3 my parents & I stayed with the Guineys while preparing to settle (as my father's business demanded) in the Boston zone. This was in the suburb of Auburndale, & I can still recall the Guiney home on Vista Ave. with great St. Bernard dogs. Miss Guiney knew several of the Boston group, especially Oliver Wendell Holmes, & the latter now & then called on her, as did many lesser lights of the day. I have been in the same room with Dr. Holmes (in the last year of the latter's long life) though unfortunately I have not the least recollection of the occurrence. Indeed, the only literary caller I can recall is a youngish man with rather long hair (I don't know who he was) who had a peculiarly vigorous mode of expression. But I remember Miss Guiney & her family well.[12] Long before that, my uncle had had Dr. Holmes as a teacher in the Harvard Medical School, & I still have a letter which Holmes later wrote him—congratulating him on an article in a medical journal. Very few people seem to realise that Holmes was a really eminent physiologist as well as literary man. I am inclined to like him best of all the Boston gang (Hawthorne, the greatest of all New England authors, was never really a part of it)—not because he's the only one I ever saw, but because he had a certain 18th century touch of disillusioned reality which his cloud-dwelling contemporaries sometimes escaped. Also, he stuck to ancient verse-forms (which I like), while his fellows dabbled in the modes of the day. Longfellow must have been tremendously pleasant, though most of his mild, cultivated, & platitudinous doggerel makes my jaws ache with yawning. And, paradoxically, I can't bear the involved & mystical verse of Miss Guiney—the only one we really knew personally! Our sojourn in Auburndale was cut short by the fatal illness of my father, which cancelled all plans of Boston settlement & brought my mother & me back to the grandpaternal roof in Providence.

Rhode-Island has shared your mild & genial autumn—so that my hibernation suffered an unwonted postponement. I probably mentioned my New Haven trip of Oct. 8, when I was so greatly fascinated by the new pseudo-archaic quadrangles at Yale. Oct. 16–18 I was in Boston, doing the bookstalls, museums, & antiquarian high spots with the poet Samuel Loveman, who came on from N.Y. And any number of afternoons I took my reading & writing out to the neighbouring woods & fields. This season was really a vast boon—giving me an outdoor period in my own environment despite my spending of the whole summer in another environment!

Barlow has just sent Long the surprise volume of the latter's recent verse which we printed last summer.[13] But tragically enough, Belknap's aunt was instantly killed Oct. 20 in a motor accident near Miami.[14]

Best wishes, & renewed thanks for the glimpse of your recent work.

Yrs by the Elder Sign—Ech-Pi-El

P.S. Last moment. Holy Yuggoth! *Astounding* has just accepted "The Shadow out of Time", so that you'll see it in print instead of in MS. This pulls down $280.00

[P.P.S.] Nov. W T a little above average. Stern tale extremely good, & Two Gun & Sultan Malik also in a happy vein.[15]

Notes

1. The sonnet was in fact entitled "Shadows" at HPL's suggestion, although two other variant titles—"The House of Memories" and "The Stairway and the Room"—exist on the T.Ms. First published in *Crypt of Cthulhu* No. 80 (Eastertide 1992): 32.
2. "History of the 'Necronomicon'" (1927).
3. *Strange Tales,* September 1931. Cf. HPL's A.Ms., which reads "Arabic text now lost" (*Lovecraft at Last* [Arlington, VA: Carrollton-Clark, 1975], 105).
4. In chiding August Derleth for "aping" HPL, Farnsworth Wright told Derleth that "My admiration for Lovecraft's writing amounts almost to idolatry" (Wright to Derleth, 13 July 1931; ms., Wisconsin Historical Society). Derleth passed this information on to HPL.
5. A[rthur] W[illiam] Bernal (1913–1991), American writer who published 5 stories in *WT* (1932–37) and also published in the science fiction pulps.
6. Mort Weisinger (1915–1978), who teamed up with Schwartz in high school to edit various science fiction fan magazines and later became an agent.
7. Robert Ellis Moe.
8. Presumably a reference to the Sully family, especially Genevieve and Helen Sully.
9. By James Russell Lowell. RFS had a first edition.
10. Edmund Spenser, *The Faerie Queene,* Book IV, Canto 2, Stanza 32.
11. Actually *The Biglow Papers.* For the possible influence of this series of poems on HPL's use of New England dialect, see Jason C. Eckhardt, "The Cosmic Yankee," in *An Epicure in the Terrible: A Centennial Anthology of Essays in Honor of H. P. Lovecraft,* ed. David E. Schultz and S. T. Joshi (1991; New York: Hippocampus Press, 2011), 77–100.
12. Louise Imogen Guiney (1861–1920), essayist and poet. HPL's account of spending the winter of 1892–93 in Guiney's home in Auburndale has not been verified, but in the absence of contrary evidence it can be provisionally accepted.
13. *The Goblin Tower* (Cassia, FL: Dragon-Fly Press, 1935) was a small collection of poetry written by Frank Belknap Long, published by HPL and RHB as a surprise gift to the poet. HPL helped set the type when he visited RHB in the summer of 1935.
14. Cassie (Doty) Symmes (1872–1935), whose book, *Old World Footprints* (Athol, MA: W. Paul Cook [The Recluse Press], 1928), contains a preface ghostwritten for Long by HPL.
15. Paul Frederick Stern, "The Way Home"; Robert E. Howard, "Shadows in Zamboula"; EHP, "The Hand of Wrath" (see 63n7).

[28]　[ANS postcard][1]

[Postmarked Providence, R.I.,
26 November 1935]

Thanks for "Witch of Prague" just recd. I shall read it with the keenest interest, though I may be some time in getting around to it. Trust there's no especial hurry about its return. Would you care to borrow the weird books of William Hope Hodgson (extremely distinctive—a real discovery) which

Koenig is circulating among the gang? If so, he authorises me to place your name on the circulation list. ¶ Did I mention the new story which I finished Nov. 10?[2] You are on the circulation list of that. Hope it won't disappoint you. ¶ Had quite a fall of snow last Saturday—the *earliest* in the history of the local weather bureau. Outdoor season obviously ended, but interesting lectures continue. ¶ Some of the pictures in the "Witch" look distinctly promising—especially the study of one Mr. Keyork Arabian. ¶ Price is home at last, & promises a travelogue of his Mexican journey. ¶ Again thanks & best wishes—E'ch-Pi-El

Notes

1. *Front:* New Providence County Court House, Providence, R. I.
2. "The Haunter of the Dark." In fact it was finished on 9 November.

[29] [ALS]

Dec. 24, 1935

Dear Ar-Eph-Es:—

No doubt "The Witch of Prague" safely reached you. Thanks again for the loan. It surely did have some delightful atmospheric touches despite the amusing 1880-ish sentimentalities & juvenile emotional concepts, & it leaves an unforgettable picture of old Prague. I can still see in fancy that ancient city of eternal twilight & shadow—of misty greyness & pallid sunbeams; age-blackened masonry & winding ways; mysterious arches & aeon-old bridges; the unfathomable ghetto with crazily-leaning gables, the chilly, rushing Moldau, & the grim overshadowing heights of the Hradschin. The Crawford & Meyrink works, taken together, surely succeed in immortalising the old Bohemian capital in the world of dream & semi-fantasy!

Congratulations on the reprinting of "The Brain in the Jar"![1] That certainly is a W T classic—I recall how enthusiastic Get-Rich-Quick-Henneberger was when he described it to me back in '24. I feel sure that the present generation will appreciate it as keenly as did their elders—& hope you'll lay in a good supply of lending copies. Sooner or later I hope the "Warder" will reach the printed stage—as well it may, even in W T, since Wright is capricious in the extreme, & often reverses his decisions. Glad my comments seemed helpful

I feel flattered that you deemed my note on the Necronomicon worth copying. Really, all the hellish elder tomes of the W T world ought to be similarly described by their imaginers—& the whole published in F M or *The Phantagraph* or some similar "fan" sheet—just as Two-Gun Bob is about to publish a "history" of Conan's prehistoric world in *The Phantagraph*.[2] The Book of Eibon, von Junzt's *Unaussprechlichen Kulten,* The Eltdown Shards, Lumley's Book of Hidden Things, Ludvig Prinn's *De Vermis Mysteriis,* Comte d'Erlette's *Cultes des Goules*—all these monstrous & blasphemous horrors await the attention of the historical & bibliographical scholar. Which reminds me that Barlow has concocted an amusing fake bibliography of the von Junzt opus[3]—a copy of which I'll enclose (please return) if I can find it. Unfortunately he does not touch upon the original German edition published at Düsseldorf in 1839— just before the Doom overtook the hapless author. Of this edition only 6 copies (4 intact) are now known to exist. Yes—one might weave many a tale in connexion with Abdul Alhazred—as with von Junzt, whose hideous end (as well as the mysterious suicide of his literary executor) is hinted at by Two-Gun. By this time you've probably seen the composite story in F M with the erroneous history of the Eltdown Shards.[4] It would be amusing if you'd write the editor a letter of correction! I don't know what the circulation of F M is— the old F F had only *60* paid subscribers! F M is in difficulties—Ruppert being unable to handle the printing any longer, & other arrangements being still uncertain. The stories themselves are about as bad as one would expect. It is amusing to see how promptly Two-Gun made a rip-roaring, sanguinary Co-nan out of the mild & scholarly professor George Campbell! Glad the "Haunter" didn't bore you too badly. It fails to satisfy me—I certainly can't write anything well when I haven't novelette length to spread to. Just as an exercise or experiment I limited myself to short story size in this instance. The home of "Blake" as depicted is nothing more or less than good old 66— the view being quite literally what I am looking at this instant. The huge church, however, is idealised . . . the real one (St. John's Catholic) being a red brick edifice of the 1870's.[5] From my window the distant church has a very spectral cast—& up to last summer really possessed a mystical spire. Last June, however, the steeple was demolished by lightning; & the parish (Irish, though the Italian colony now spreads nearly a mile on every side) decided not to restore it. Instead, they put a conical cap—surmounted by a gilded cross— on the brick tower, & let it go at that. I was greatly disappointed when I got home & found it in this bobtailed form, but at last I'm getting used to it. The sombre edifice still looms up mysteriously against the west, & the squat tower has a quaintness all its own.

Concerning the Vitonian tragedy—a threat of the same thing hangs over the local Kappa Alpha Tau fraternity, since the owners of my friend John Perkins find certain faults in his demeanour & threaten to send him to the An-imal Rescue League if he does not amend in certain respects. I shall mourn any-thing of the sort most profoundly if it has to be—especially since Johnny has always been a perfect gentleman when over here. Hope has not yet departed.

Regarding *ink*—I am just now using up the last of my first Woolworth bottle. As the fluid waned low in the bottle it became too thick even for the Waterman pen—hence I'm now dipping in the ancient manner. Before long I shall start a new bottle. I have heard that adverse opinion anent black ink, & fancy there is truth at the bottom of it. Still, I've had pretty good luck with Sheaffer's. I mean to experiment with different brands—even trying Carter's Congo Black again in the Waterman. I shall also try the ammonia method of cleaning. But incidentally, I can assure you that "Quink" really *does* clean! My aunt now uses it (too expensive for me!), & I have twice cleaned a pen very adequately by borrowing an occasional filling of it. *Black* Quink, at that. Its chemical principle seems to differ greatly from that of Sheaffer's & other inks—for one thing, it is not so readily amenable to the usual eradicating fluids. . . . . This using up of dregs is getting to be a sort of *game*—I'm laying wagers with myself whether there's enough blue-blackish moisture at the bottom of this bottle to complete the present page!

That Schick razor certainly sounds like a marvel, & I fancy I'd try it some time if I were more affluent. Modern technology has surely produced the most incredible conveniences! That lamp also sounds highly idyllic. I need a *strong* light, & never use less than a 75-watt bulb. Actually, I prefer a *diffused* to a *local* light, & would rather have about 135 watts going in the chandelier than use a desk light at all—but economy forbids this lavishness. 135 watts is what I call an adequate lighting for the whole study—a 75 & a 60 both going. Others find this excessive—but I could use still more & like it even better. The shaded dimness which so many regard as an ideal lighting scheme leaves me cold—as well as dark. All of which reminds me that I must get a new *shade* for my desk light—the present one being reduced to just about the final stage of decrepitude! ¶ Yes—I *am* finishing the page with this ink—although the frequency & needed exactitude of dipping form considerably less than the apex of convenience!

Well—here we are, all filled up from the new bottle, with ol' Louie Waterman functioning under his own power! Not as free as he might be—yet, at any rate. Probably the thick ink of the old bottle has caused some clogging. We shall see.

Yes—"My Study Windows" certainly contains a vast store of fascinating material. It has the faults of its time—the smug artificial values of the 19th century, the rambling tone then thought proper for the genteel essay, & the almost naive display of bookish scholarship for its own sake—but despite all this its vigour of thought, keenness of observation & analysis, wealth of information, grace of style, & occasional soundness of aesthetic appraisal make it a delight to read & recall. That "Library of Old Authors" essay surely is a monument of erudition, scholastic ingenuity, & general judgment. I always liked the early part where mere mechanical bibliophily—edition-collecting—is reduced to its proper place & contrasted with true literary appreciation. That section ought to be compulsory reading for Tom-Folios like Koenig & Bobby Barlow! Another essay which I used to read with wry but appreciative face is "A Good Word for Winter." I have few such words—but I was nevertheless

amused by the glamour which the winter scene can be made to possess . . . when one is comfortably close to a good fire. Without doubt, Lowell was a great figure in his day—& a few of the solid qualities of that day (as distinguished from now-absurd attitudes arising from genuine misconceptions in philosophy, human psychology, politico-economics, & the physical sciences) would do no harm to the present literary generation. Those old fellows at least realised that they were the inheritors of a long, rich stream of continuous literary tradition, & they used their native language with unconscious grace & accuracy according to its own natural rules. They thought as clearly & consistently as the practice of their age permitted, & addressed a reasonably literate public instead of catering to the ignorance & tastelessness of a promiscuous herd. Of course their problems were easier than those of the modern, since they lived in a world which possessed a reasonable degree of unanimity concerning the nature & operation of the
[concluding pages missing]

P.S. "Mts. of Madness" in Feb. Mar. & April *Astounding*. Don't know when "Shadow" will appear. ¶ Just got something curious from Wright—copy of "Midsummer Night's Dream" in format of pulp magazine with illustrations, announced as first of "Wright's Shakespeare Library". I'd get a set if there weren't 4 or 5 or 6 sets of the Bard in the house, counting attic miscellany! ¶ Rec'd your card—thanks! I may be in N.Y. visiting Long from Dec. 30 to Jany 8.

[Enclosure:][6]
[With every good wish for a Merry Christmas and happiness in the New Year]
E'ch-Pi-El
—1935

Notes

1. The story was not reprinted until the June 1936 issue, so RFS must have simply received a notice from Farnsworth Wright of its impending reprinting.
2. "The Hyborian Age," published in three parts in the *Phantagraph* (February, August, and November–December 1936), and later as a separate pamphlet.
3. The existence or whereabouts of this item is unknown.
4. "The Challenge from Beyond" by HPL and others.
5. St. John's Roman Catholic Church (1871), 352 Atwells Avenue. The steeple of the church was removed in 1935 after damage by lightning, as suggested in "The Haunter of the Dark." The church was demolished in 1992.
6. Printed Christmas card, with illustration of the Old North Church.

[30] [ALS]

> 66 College St.,
> Providence, R.I.,
> Feby. 13, 1936

Dear Ar-Eph-Es:—

Yours of Jany. 24 found me in the midst of a chaos composed jointly of an overcrowded programme & a touch of grippe. The latter has largely vanished—save for a little deficiency of energy & a tendency toward easy ocular fatigue—but the former persists in full force. Hence any unusual incoherence in the ensuing lines.

I've had no reports on the commercial fortunes of Wright's Shakespeare Library, but see that it is advertised eloquently in the last two W T's. Possibly it will join "The Moon Terror" as a perennial drug on the market.[1] So far the library seems confined to Volume I—which bespeaks a commendable caution. If Satrap Pharnabazus *does* succeed in re-popularising Avon's Sweet Swan, he will indeed deserve well of civilisation!

Hope the "Warder" will eventually land in W T without too much concession to Wright's mania for full explanatory diagrams. Just what policy—if any—the magazine will turn to next, remains to be seen. Plenty of readers appear to be asking for a movement back to weird fiction—indeed, I see that F W has quoted in the Eyrie a passage of my own to that effect[2]—quoted from my acknowledgment of the Shakespearian opus. The last two issues are not among the worst. Each has a good Moore story, & "Norn" (in the Feb. issue—possibly by the old & excellent standby Everil Worrell, since "Lireve" is Everil spelled backward) is an admirable study in gathering menace. Also, Derleth's "Satin Mask" & Loretta Burrough's "Visitor from Far Away" aren't bad. I see that I am twice represented by reprints—I hadn't read "The Temple" in over a decade, & it sounds rather quaint now. It was written in 1920.[3]

Exact data regarding the Pnakotic MSS. are lacking. They were brought down from Hyperborea by a secret cult (allied to that which preserved the Book of Eibon), & are in the secret Hyperborean language, but there is a rumour that they are a translation of something hellishly older—brought from the land of Lomar & of fabulous antiquity even there. That they antedate the human race is freely whispered. Curious parallelisms betwixt them & the Eltdown Shards have been pointed out—as if both were remote derivatives of some immeasurably anterior source, on this or some other planet. They are perhaps too far back in the abyss of time to cover such secrets as that involved in "The Coming of Ourai-Adun"[4] (whose appearance I eagerly await), since this latter incident is a relatively recent episode of the age of mammals.

You have by this time, no doubt, seen both the Crawford-printed issue of F M, & the Shepherd-printed issue of *The Phantagraph*—a study in descending typographical values. Crawford is worse than Ruppert (old F M & F F printer), & Shepherd is infinitely worse than Crawford! Neither paper is very ambitious, though both mean well. I wish them well in their struggle against adversity, & hope their respective printers will improve. It would be really unfortunate to be without any "fan magazines" at all. Crawford, by the way, is planning to issue my "Innsmouth" as a book or booklet, & wants to get illustrations from Derleth's friend Utpatel. Hope he succeeds. He also intends to use the text in *Marvel Tales*.

That new & magical lamp surely sounds impressive—& ought to be, with 150 watts behind it! Hope I can afford one some day, for the *diffused* nature of the light is just what I dote on.

Yes—I guess a good deal of the more casual externals of "bohemianism" can be traced to sheer pose & jauntiness, supported by those 19th & early-20th-century tales which gild & glorify the squalor of the Parisian garret. When one is not too analytical, it is easy to confuse genius with whatever conventional symbol—long hair, flowing tie, iconoclastic epigrams—happens to be associated with it in the superficial best-sellers of the day. Being "an author" (or "an artist", "a musician" &c.) is a specific & serious business with these callow attitudinisers . . . . . & they endeavour to perfect themselves in the role before bothering to do any extensive work in such purely incidental fields as real literature, art, or music!

Glad you've seen the printed "Mts. of Madness". There are some bad misprints—such as "palaeocene" for *palaeogean*—but in general, the text is fairly decipherable. The illustrations are good—the artist[5] must have really read the text, since he has *almost perfectly* reconstructed the Old Ones from a purely verbal description. Long's story in the same issue[6] has some excellent touches of other-worldliness—& would have been excellent but for the alloy of cheap stock romance & melodrama.

It is certainly wise to find out all about tonsil matters from the best authorities before taking any decisive step. You are fortunate to have a specialist of the right species in the family! Nowadays, when commercialism & charlatanry are so often mixed into professional practice, it is a relief to have an absolutely dependable person to turn to. However, even under the best auspices, the prospect of tonsil operations is not an enviable one. Obviously a duty rather than a pleasure!

About the advisability of enclosing a note with MSS. designed for strange markets—I think opinion is divided. Certainly no long letter should be sent—but whether a brief note stating 'that such-&-such is submitted for consideration at usual rates' is desirable or not seems to be rather a moot point. I have usually sent such a note—but others point out that the very sending of the MS. forms a sufficient notification of the purpose of sending. I don't believe it matters much one way or the other. If the MS. gets past the readers to a real editor, nobody will care whether there's any accompanying note or not.

I certainly would try various unplaced verses on *Wings*—which has a very good reputation among the small poetry magazines. I have seen many newspaper articles & book reviews by Coblentz in addition to his verses, but never read one of his science-fiction products.[7] Others tell me that these things seem to form very subtle parodies on the common clichès of pulp "scientific-tion"—things written with tongue in cheek, though accepted at face value by the naive generality of fans. Whether or not Coblentz descends from Israel's ancient line I don't know, though city-surnames—especially Germanic ones—tend to point that way. But in any case he seems pretty well assimilat-ed to the Anglo-Saxon tradition.

Turning to your mention of Chaucer's unfinished narratives—I must admit that you have me floored in one case. My Chaucerian knowledge is nei-ther wide nor systematic, & comes from a very limited range of editions. And I must admit that I have *never heard* of any "Cook's Tale"![8] My edition has 24—Prologue, Knight, Miller, Reeve, Man of Law, Shipman, Prioress, Sir Thopas, Melibeus, Monk, Nun's Priest, Doctor of Physic, Pardoner, Wife of Bath, Friar, Summoner, Clerk, Merchant, Squire, Franklin, Second Nun, Can-on's Yeoman, Maniciple, & Parson—& I can't recall any others from any oth-er edition. Where—amidst this list—does the Cook's Tale come in in the edition you have? So far as I can recall, the only mention of the Cook except where he is catalogued in the Prologue is at the beginning of the Maniciple's Tale—the preliminary matter before the maniciple gets down to relating his narrative. Chaucer here as elsewhere reverts to the general affairs of the cav-alcade, & speaks of the cook as nodding drunkenly on his horse.

> "See how he nappeth. See for Goddes bones
> As he will falle from his hors at once.
> Is that a cook of London, with mischance?
> Let him come forth, he knoweth his penance,
> For he shall tell a tale by my fey
> Although it be not worth a bottle (= *bundle*) of hay.
> Awake, thou cook—&c."[9]

But the cook is too well soused to do anything except fall off his horse, & the host decides that he had better not attempt any story-telling. What he could tell in his condition wouldn't be worth much. So the maniciple gives him *an-other* swig of wine & calms the wrath which he had begun to display—reconciling him to drowsy silence. After which the maniciple embarks on his own tale. Thus so far as any knowledge of mine goes, the Cook's Tale is *never* told. I am certainly curious to know more about the passage you cite. From a reference of yours, I judge that the tale comes somewhat *before* the squire's. The only *unfinished* Canterbury Tale I know of beside the Squire's is that of Sir Thopas—supposed to be narrated by Chaucer himself. The host cuts him off on the ground that his rhyming is becoming mere frivolous doggerel, & switches him on to the serious prose tale of Melibeus. Your allusion to this other tale whereof "maketh Chaucer na more" surely fascinates & tantalises me. My ignorance is surely limitless! Yes—all texts are alike in having Sir Thopas & the Squire's tale incomplete. Thopas is *intentionally* so as part of the larger fictional framework of the Canterbury Tales. I really know nothing of the reason for the incompleteness of the Squire's Tale—but *certainly* it was not *meant* to be left as it is. I have seen one or two speculations as to the way Chaucer may have meant to finish it. Brewer[10] thinks he would have had Canace wed some knight able to overthrow her two brothers in the tournament. Milton alludes to the unfinished nature of this tale in "Il Penseroso", where he speaks of Chaucer as

".... Him that left half told
The story of Cambuscan bold."[11]

[Milton here gives a wrong accent to a name which *should* be pronounced *Cam'-bus-can".*]

I am pleased to say that my black friend Mr. Perkins seems to have weathered all the storms of domestic disapproval—so that he will unmenacedly celebrate his first birthday tomorrow. If he comes to see me on that occasion, I shall give him an extra-large portion of catnip! Incidentally, the household at the neighbouring hostelry seems inclined to keep Mr. Perkins's little brother as well as himself. This younger gentleman—known as Gilbert John Murray Kynymond Elliot, 4th Earl of Minto—is black & white & playful, & will make a delightful addition to the local Kappa Alpha Tau chapter. However—the chapter has sustained a grave loss, which no possible accession can repair. Not through death—but through the removal of both President & Vice President to another neighbourhood together with their human family. The ancient garden & clubhouse roof will not look the same without old Peter Randall & his tiger brother .... I must find out their new residence & pay them a call!

New England has certainly shared with Michigan the severe weather of later winter—though Providence's lowest temperature has so far been +4.8°. Except last night, when I attended a lecture at the college half a block away, I have not been out of the house since Jany. 13. Snow is deep, & temperatures stick close to +20°. Southern New England, because of the equalising influence of the sea, never has quite the extremes of the Middle West. Anything below zero in Providence is very rare—something occurring only about once in five years. Only twice in the history of the local weather bureau (estab. 1904) has the temperature been below -10° .... These exceptions being -12° on Dec. 30, 1917, & -17° on Feby. 9, 1934. Fortunately this house heats miraculously well 24 hours a day—with steam piped in from the central college heating plant.

We had a pleasant Christmas—with tree & accessories. Around New Year's I visited Long in N.Y. & saw most of the old group there—together with some new figures. Among those I met for the first time were Arthur J.

Burks, Donald Wollheim, & Otto Binder of the well-known "Eando" team. I saw good old Seabury Quinn for the first time since 1931. Of the older group I had a glimpse of everyone save Koenig & Hornig—the latter being on a trip to New Orleans. Koenig has since visited Florida & old Charleston—exploring the latter with aid of an itinerary furnished by me.[12] Lucky devils! We had several gatherings—attended (or held) by such persons as Long, Loveman, Morton, the Wandrei boys, Talman, Sterling, young Kline, Leeds, Kleiner, Kirk, &c. &c.—& on one occasion I attended a dinner of the Am. Fiction Guild with Belknap & Howard Wandrei. Loveman shewed me a copy of his new book—a circular of which I am enclosing.[13] The text ought to be fairly accurate, since I read the proofs five times last September. I'm distrib uting these circulars to all my correspondents—75 or more—as an effort to boost the volume! On two occasions I visited the new Hayden Planetarium of the Am. Museum of Nat. History, & found it a highly impressive device. It consists of a round, domed building of 2 storeys, joined at one point to the museum edifice. On the lower floor is a circular hall whose ceiling is a gigantic orrery—shewing the planets revolving around the sun at their proper relative speeds. Above it is another circular hall whose roof is the great dome, & whose edge is made to represent the horizon of N.Y. as seen from Central Park. In the middle of this upper hall is a projector (that looks like a fictional "space-ship" or like one of the armoured Martians in "The War of the Worlds") which casts on the whitened concave surface of the dome a perfect image of the sky—capable of duplicating the natural apparent motions of the celestial vault, & of depicting the heavens as seen at any hour, in any season, from any latitude, & at any period of history. Other parts of the projector can cast suitably movable images of the sun, moon, & planets, & diagrammatic arrows & circles for explanatory purposes. (Wright would no doubt enjoy these latter!) The effect is infinitely lifelike—as if one were outdoors beneath the sky. Lectures—different each month (I heard both Dec. & Jan. ones)—are given in connexion with this apparatus. In the annular corridors on each floor are niches containing typical astronomical instruments of all ages—telescopes, transits, celestial globes, armillary spheres, &c.—& cases to display books, meteorites, & other miscellany. Astronomical pictures line the walls, & at the desk may be obtained useful pamphlets, books, planispheres, &c. Very good planispheres are sold for only a quarter—the cheapest I ever saw. I got one apiece for Belknap & Donald Wandrei in the hope that these careless young scribblers will make fewer mistakes about the constellations than they've done in past stories! The institution holds classes in elementary astronomy, & sponsors clubs of amateur observers. Altogether, it forms the most complete & active popular astronomical centre imaginable. It seems to be crowded at all hours—attesting a public interest in astronomy which did not exist when I was young. Home again on Jany. 7—but at once plunged into a vortex of bad health & more tasks than I could perform. One of these multifarious demands is a request for an article on horror fiction from one B. C. Black, Box 53, Upland, Indiana. He is editing a new magazine called *Nuggets*, & appears to be on the lookout for MSS. No pay except subscription to the magazine—but this might be as good an outlet for rejected tales as Crawford's or Schwartz's or Wollheim's fan magazines. The thing is expected to start March 15.[14] I don't know yet whether I can summon up the time & energy to prepare the desired article.

With every good wish—

Yrs by the Thirteenth Shard——

E'ch-Pi-El

Notes

1. By A. G. Birch et al. The book sold very slowly. Both HPL and RFS had copies.

2. "*The Way Home* is one of the most atmospherically satisfying things I have seen lately, and I was interested to note that the author is Paul Ernst under an anagrammatic alias. I live in hope that the purely weird element may regain its ascendancy, as tales like that would imply. . . . Other good yarns in recent issues of WT are *The Cold Grey God, The Mystery of the Last Guest, Shadows in Zamboula, The Hand of Wrath,* and *The Chain of Aforgomon.*" *WT* 27, No. 2 (February 1936): 250. The stories cited in the last sentence are by C. L. Moore (October 1935), John Flanders (October 1935), Robert E. Howard (November 1935), E. Hoffmann Price (November 1935), and CAS (December 1935).

3. *WT*, January 1936: C. L. Moore, "The Dark Land"; August Derleth, "The Satin Mask"; HPL, "Dagon" (rpt. from October 1923). *WT*, February 1936: C. L. Moore, "Yvala"; Lireve Monet (pseud. of Everil Worrell), "Norn"; Loretta Burrough, "A Visitor from Far Away"; HPL, "The Temple" (rpt. from September 1925).

4. A story RFS did not complete.

5. Howard Brown, who also did the cover art based on HPL's story.

6. Frank Belknap Long, "Cones" (*Astounding Stories*, February 1936). This issue contained the first installment of HPL's novel.

7. Stanton A. Coblentz (1896–1982) wrote *The Sunken World* (1928) and other science fiction novels. He was a participant with HPL on "Cigarette Characterizations" (*Fantasy Magazine* 3, No. 4 [June 1934]) and editor of the poetry magazine *Wings*. Coblentz used two sonnets of HPL's *Fungi from Yuggoth* in his anthology *Unseen Wings* (1949).

8. "The Cook's Tale" is a 58-line fragment first published in a 1741 edition of *The Canterbury Tales*.

9. From "The Manciple's Prologue," ll. 9–15. "cockes bones" for "Goddes bones."

10. Probably E. Cobham Brewer (1810–1897), compiler of *The Reader's Handbook of Allusions, References, Plots and Stories* (1880). Brewer also compiled the celebrated *Dictionary of Phrase and Fable* (1870).

11. ll. 109–10.

12. Koenig mimeographed HPL's Charleston travelogue as *Charleston* (1936).

13. *The Hermaphrodite and Other Poems*.

14. No such magazine was ever published.

[31]   [ALS]

66 College St.,
Providence, R.I.,
April 15, 1936

Dear Ar-Eph-Es:—

Yes—the grippe left me at last—but what a minor introduction to subsequent troubles it proved! 1936 seems scheduled to go down
in history as my bad year—

"With ruin upon ruin, rout on rout,
Confusion worse confounded."[1]

I am absolutely sunk—letters since February unanswered, amateur journalistic
duties transferred to other shoulders, revision jobs returned unperformed,
borrowed books piled up unread, no writing done—& what the hell! Hence
the probable sketchy inadequacy of the present communication. The trouble?
Well—no sooner was I half-clear of *my* grippe, than my aunt came down with
an infinitely severer version of the selfsame malady[2]—tying me up at once as
a sort of combined nurse, butler, market-man, secretary, & errand-boy. All
my own activities went to hades. Complications having developed, my aunt
was forced to go to the hospital in mid-March—a step which somewhat
changed without materially lightening my duties. She is now recovering finely—transferred to a convalescents' home a week ago, & due back here in a
few days. But I see no hope of pulling out of my own morass of congested &
unperformable labours (even though I've desperately hung on to one revision
job, where an almost indefinite [i.e. September] time-limit extension was obtainable)[3]—& fear that if my programme is ever cleaned up it will be through
neglect & repudiation rather than performance. I can understand how the allied powers feel about those international debts! The trouble is of course aggravated by the weakness & nervous strain incident to the excess of labours—&
the indoor weather. I have to rest inordinately in order to do anything, & my
eyes are bothering me like the devil. However, I'm not forgetting that the whole
business is a damned sight harder on my aunt than it is on me!

Sorry to hear of your own colds & touch of grippe—but this winter has
spared few! We had a touch of mildness in March which brought the buds
out prematurely, but April has been cursedly cold except for yesterday &
today. I hope something approximating spring is here at last. Providence
wasn't harmed by the recent unprecedented floods, although streets were under water four miles from here—while Hartford, some 60-odd miles west—
suffered a major calamity.

Hope your *Adventure* story lands—although I believe they favour things
with an actually existing & definitely described setting. It sounds like highly
interesting material—& the Nibelung atmosphere ought to enhance its ap-

peal. I'm sure a series founded on the great sword has immense possibilities![4] No—the Pnakotic MSS. are translations, since the originals would be meaningless to any human beings of today. The Hyperboreans, though human, knew infinitely more of the elder world than we. Ask Klarkash-Ton!

Chaucer's "Cook's Tale"—of which I never even heard till you mentioned it—certainly captures my imagination! I hate to ask you to copy it for me, since I could probably get hold of the M. L. edition sometime, but if you ever do any typing purely for practice, & *happen* to choose this text as your theme, I'd surely appreciate having the result for preservation! Thanks in advance—& I wonder why this fragment does not occur in ordinary editions. Could it be recently discovered—or considered apocryphal until recent times?

Sorry the verses didn't land with Coblentz[5]—but it's a literal fact that all the "little magazines" are overstocked with verse—& in most cases *good* verse. So many persons can write really excellent verse nowadays that the market is veritably glutted. Old-timers find it much harder to place anything now—despite the plenitude of small magazines—than in their youth, when the Poets' Corner of the better newspapers found it hard to get sufficient material above the doggerel grade.

Glad you've seen the recent *Astoundings*. Yes—Long is learning all the tricks of the trade, getting an immense amount of scientific veneer from the popular science magazines. I wish, though, he wouldn't make so many concessions to the pulp style of writing. I think he could get by without it. I thought I had lent you my "Mts. of Madness" in the past, when we were discussing "The Frozen Pirate"—but I guess my aged memory is at fault. The antarctic has fascinated me ever since I was ten years old. Like you, I always save serials till they are complete before reading them.

Your Detroit winter temperatures make Providence's sound almost subtropical—though either one is bad enough! I could never live in the Middle West—or in central or northern New England. It is the relatively stabilising ocean frontage of southern New England which saves the situation for me.

That "Dictionary Companion"[6] interests me very much, though I never heard of it before. I've always spelled merely by instinct—though a smattering of Latin (& a lesser one of Greek) helps me to avoid mistakes w[h]ere classic roots are concerned. However—some of the typical errors of English spelling do not involve classic roots. The revision job I ought to be doing now—the one on which I obtained the time-extension—is a manual of English usage, & involves some interesting cataloguing of typical mistakes . . . not of spelling, but of syntax, pronunciation, & rhetoric. Part of the job was to double a list of 50 words commonly mispronounced—& when I came to consider it I was astonished at the number of *habitual* mispronunciations I could recall hearing. I've already gone 3 or 4 times over the 50-mark—since my list must include from 150 to 200 words. I keep adding to it. Only the other night at a philosophy lecture I heard a man behind me say *sŏn´-ō-rous* for *sō-nō´-rous*—& suddenly recalled that I had heard that selfsame boner from *other* persons of reasonable cultivation. Far more people mispronounce than mis-spell. I probably do myself even now, though I've caught a good many early slips (like *ver´-zhun* for *ver´-sion, pri-mar´-i-ly* for *pri´-ma-ri-ly*, &c) of mine. This book is rather an interesting job as a whole, & I hope I can arrange my programme in such a way as to let me go ahead with it. Another task is to fix up a list of 50 common *stock phrases* to be avoided.[7]

Loveman's book is a collection—one long narrative poem (the title poem), & a variety of short lyrics dating all the way from about 1912 to the present. No—the main poem has nothing to do with human abnormality, & will doubtless disappoint many smut-hounds who buy the book. It deals with a mythological being typifying pure beauty—the beauty that is *beyond sex*. It re-creates the atmosphere & colour of the Hellenistic world—the Graeco-Oriental era following Alexander the Great, when Alexandria, Antioch, & Pergamum were the prevailing centres of culture—as well as any poem I can think of.

Thanks immensely for the view of the young Sea-brights—which shows up well under a magnifying glass. The Crown Prince looks like a very promising & prepossessing young man, well worthy to carry on the traditions of his ancient line! And so he has three teeth? Bless my soul, but how the young do grow! Before I realise it he'll be writing fiction[8]—or at least listening to stories told by his sire & probably inventing imaginative variants of his own.

Hope you've seen *The Phantagraph* by this time—though it's a rotten enough sheet in mechanical aspect. No—I don't believe Hill-Billy Crawford has forgotten you. He hasn't published any paper in months, though plans for a new, bigger, & better *Marvel* are well along. He is also publishing my "Shadow over Innsmouth" as a cloth-bound book—with 4 fantastic illustrations by Derleth's gifted friend Utpatel. At least, I hope he's publishing it—I've seen only half of it in proofs as yet. W T seems to be picking up lately—both March & April issues being very fair. In March C A S, the Binders, Hamilton (incredibile dictu!), & the new writer Kuttner do very well. In April Jacobi, Derleth, & Bloch are likewise worth reading.[9]

Little Kenneth Sterling—the science fiction fan—has been desperately ill at the Mt. Sinai Hospital in N.Y.—operation for colonic abscess, blood-transfusion, intra-venous nourishment, &c.—but is now pulling around all right. He still dictates his letters, though. ¶ Price may get east next month—if so I hope to see him. ¶ *Wonder Stories* has been sold by "Hugo the Rat" to the Margulies group—which is very reliable financially. What will happen to its literary policy remains to be seen. Margulies invited me to submit a story, but I've nothing on hand & have no time to write one. ¶ Best wishes—

Yrs by the Eltdown Cromlech—
Ech-Pi-El

Notes

1. John Milton, *Paradise Lost* 2.995–96.
2. Annie Gamwell did not have "grippe" (an informal term for the flu), but had to have a mastectomy for breast cancer.
3. The job was *Well Bred Speech* (1936) by Anne Tillery Renshaw.
4. The reference could be to the sword Blueflame carried by Arnor the Priest, who is featured in RFS's unpublished stories "The Cavern of the Dragon" and "The Guardian of the Cairn."
5. Coblentz rejected some verse by RFS for *Wings* in a letter dated 21 February 1936.
6. By Christopher Orlando Sylvester Mawson.
7. This was a chapter entitled "Bromides Must Go" for Renshaw's *Well Bred Speech* but not published there.
8. Franklyn Searight in fact went on to write horror fiction, including "The Shadow of Thal-Omis" (*Weirdbook* No. 6 [1973]), "The Innsmouth Head" (*Dark Messenger Reader* No. 1 [1975]), and *Lair of the Dreamer: A Cthulhu Mythos Omnibus* (Hippocampus Press, 2007).
9. *WT*, March 1936: CAS, "The Black Abbot of Puthuum"; Eando Binder, "The Crystal Curse"; Edmond Hamilton, "In the World's Dusk"; Henry Kuttner, "The Graveyard Rats." *WT*, April 1936: Carl Jacobi, "The Face in the Wind"; August Derleth and Mark Schorer," "They Shall Rise"; Robert Bloch, "The Druidic Doom."

[32] [ALS]

The Ancient Hill
—June 12, 1936

Dear Ar-Eph-Es:—

Yours of May 14th found things a bit amended hereabouts, though my programme of work is still hopelessly congested & disordered. Eyes are rather better as summer approaches—for as I knew, much of their late trouble was generally physiological. I've had such trouble before—& have thrown it off by getting to Charleston or Florida. I've worn glasses off & on ever since I was 6 years old—my vision seeming to have ups & downs. In 1916 I had a bad spell of swimming vision, & for some time after that wore 'specs' constantly despite my detestation of them (they irritate my nose & ears). Just a decade ago I discovered I could leave them off for general walking around (I *never* needed them for reading—my trouble being near-sightedness plus a muscular defect in the left eye which retards quick focussing), hence have not worn them since 1926 except for continuous middle-distance vision—as at the theatre, lectures, cinema, &c.—when I feel a strain without them. This involves a lack of distinctness—but I'll put up with that for the sake of the freedom. I suppose I ought to have new glasses—or at least be examined again—but I hate to think of continuous wearing once more.

Well—as I said—things are slowly on the mend here. My aunt came home April 21, & is now actively up & about—taking longer & longer walks each sunny afternoon—though requiring considerable coöperation in household tasks. My own schedule is still badly awry because of my lack of energy—it takes me about an hour to do anything which I could ordinarily do in five minutes! But warmer weather & outdoor activities will be giving me a little more strength later on.

The weather in itself was enough to leave me limp. After a little deceptive warmth in March—followed by the memorable floods—there came a chilly April which about wore me out. Not till the 28th was there a really decent day. Since then I have been able to take my work out to Prospect Terrace several times, & on April 30 my aunt & I were treated to a delightful motor ride through the awakening countryside to Westport Point, Mass. The landscape is now a captivating spectacle with its fresh verdure & abundant blossoms, & I hope to find time for some rural walks ere long. Barlow has invited me down to De Land again, but I greatly doubt my ability to accept. This, I fear, is no travel year for me!

I've heard some pretty good lectures during recent months—at the college a block over the hill & at the School of Design a block down the hill. Subjects pleasantly varied—Plato's "Republic", modern painting, Chinese contributions to western culture, Gilbert Stuart, R.I. Silversmiths, archaic Greek art influences, early classical sculpture, philosophy & poetry, Mayan ruins, & the Michelson-Morley experiment. Never too old to learn in this informative neighbourhood!

On May 4 the R.I. Tercentenary observances began with a costumed parade which started at the college gate—just a stone's throw from here. Later there was a mock-session of the rebel legislature of May 4, 1776—held in costume in the selfsame room of the ancient colony-house (1761) where the original session was held. In this, each old-time deputy was impersonated by a lineal descendant—Gov. Green representing his ancestor Col. Arnold, who offered the original set of treasonable resolutions severing Rhode Island from the lawful authority of the Crown. The acting & pageantry were so excellent that one might easily have fancied the bygone period returned—with the intervening 160 years merely a bad dream. I was one of the relatively few spectators lucky enough to get into the colony-house & witness the proceedings. In the afternoon—in a ceremony at the State House which I did not attend—Gov. Curley of Mass. presented to Gov. Green a copy of the recent resolutions of the Mass. General Court, rescinding the banishment imposed by that august body upon Roger Williams in Oct. 1635. After 300½ years, Mr. Williams no doubt highly appreciates this delicate mark of consideration!

Apropos of the historic atmosphere—I stumbled on an interesting *genealogical* discovery recently, when I learned for the first time that I am a great-great-great-great-great-great-great-great-great-grandson of the Elizabethan astronomer who introduced the Copernican theory into England! For one who has always been a keen amateur devotee of celestial science, this was indeed a gratifying find! Ordinarily I am a very sluggish genealogist, being content to take what existing charts tell me & let it go at that. The other day I ran into a caller of my aunt's—an old lady related to us in the Field & Wilcox lines-& she mentioned how proud I ought to be of our common forbear, *the astronomer John Field or Felde.* That rather floored me, since our charts carried the Field line back only to the original Providence settler John Field, who died in 1686, & I knew *he* was no moon-starer! Well—it soon turned out that the ancestry of this settler has been known for ages among genealogists, though I had no inkling of it. The 16ᵗʰ century astronomer (whose 1557 Ephemeris contained the first English account of the Copernican system, & who has been called "The Proto-Copernican of England") was the Providence colonist's *own grandfather*—hence *my* nine-times-great-grandfather. It certainly gave me a kick to get a real man of science in my pedigree—which as a general thing is lousy with clergymen but short on straight thinkers. [But I'll be hanged if this new discovery hasn't added *one more* damn divine to the bunch—for it seems that the Prov. colonist's maternal grandfather was the Rev. John Sotwell, Vicar of Peniston in Yorkshire!] Later I looked up the standard Field genealogy (by F. C. Pierce, 1901) & found out all about the line. It comes from Sir Hubertus de la Feld [of the family of Counts de la Feld, seated near Colmar in Alsace], a follower of William the Conqueror who took lands in Lancashire in 1069; the Providence stock springing from the Yorkshire branch centreing around Sowerby, Ardsley, & Thurnscoe. I have copied an abundance of notes & now have my Field lineage straight back—in exactly 20 generations—to Roger de la Feld of Sowerby, born in 1240. But it's the *astronomer* who chiefly interests me, & about whom I am anxious to learn more. I have a triple allotment of Field blood, being descended from no less than three of the Providence settler's grandchildren [Ruth, James Jr., & John Mathewson, children of John Field's daughter Hannah who died in 1703.]

And while still on the old times—let me thank you most sincerely for your generous transcript of the Chaucerian "Coke's [*sic*] Tale"! I read it with great interest, & have since been trying to figure out whether the style *is* perfectly homogeneous with the rest of the Canterbury Tales, or whether it has certain subtle differences. I've seen imitations of Chaucer (especially one by my friend Loveman of the Herm) which have fooled me, & would fool anybody but a specialist in Middle English. I shall pass this MS. around & see what some of my better-informed friends have to say of it—whether they ever heard of the Coke's Tale before. Whatever I learn I'll duly relay to you. If I get any spare time I'll go over the various Chaucers at the library & see whether I can find the mysterious text in any but the Mod. Lib. edition. The whole matter certainly piques one's curiosity!

Sorry "The Cavern of the Dragon" hasn't landed yet—but my "Innsmouth", "Nameless City", &c. &c. &c. put me in the same boat! Kline might very conceivably help you place the tale—as he helped Long & Price & others—though all his advice will be in a commercial direction & sometimes directly contrary to the principles of serious writing. Bloch is certainly coming along. I enjoyed "The Druidic Doom" (which I never saw till it was in print), but have not yet had a chance to read "The Faceless God".[1] If this youth will steer clear of commercial models he will be heard from some day. Yes—Hamilton is shewing that he *can* break through his formula when he chooses. I hope to read his May story[2] before long. Haven't read the Quinn opus as yet—but good ol' Seabury is simply a business man following the market. If the new thing is repulsive, it's no doubt because Wright has sent out a call for "spicy" material.[3]

Glad the "Mts. of Madness"—with its atrociously mangled text—stands up under a second reading. "The Shadow Out of Time" appears complete in the June issue of *Astounding*—& will not, I hope, prove too great a disappointment.

That list of mispronounced words is beginning to look like a young dictionary! I think of new boners, & others offer suggestions—till the interpolations come close to exceeding the original specimens. There is something a bit humorous in the *revision* of a text-book on English usage, though it represents a far from uncommon situation. A teacher may know the elements of correct speech, yet lack altogether the ability to *formulate* the material in a neat & effective fashion. Using good phraseology & *organising a treatise* are two different matters. In this case the author's lack of time is the main factor. I expand or contract topics, hunt up new examples of this or that linguistic principle, & correct the historical, mythological, & literary errors (errors involving *general* rather than *linguistic* knowledge) in the chapters touching on familiar phrases & allusions. I also compile reading courses. Well—I hope I can make a decent job of it & get it out of the way before the new time limit (September)!

No—Loveman's "Hermaphrodite" is not *realistic* in any sense. It is the *spirit* of the Hellenistic world—the atmosphere & mood—rather than the actual scenes & manners, which the poem catches. I wish I could think of a novel or poem presenting the warlike Achaian (Homeric) period realistically, but can't seem to do so at the moment. This provokes me, because I seem to recall some such thing—centreing around Ulysses—in the chaotic welter of my early reading. I'll tell you of anything I discover or recall.

About "Innsmouth"—I haven't the least idea of when Hill-Billy Crawford will have it ready. His capacities for delay are infinite. I doubt if more than a quarter of the text is in print —though the vivid Utpatel cuts are made. The existing part contains bad typographical errors demanding a printed list of errata.

Your description of the opera "The Dybbuk"[4] is extremely fascinating to me, especially since I had the good luck to see the original play in 1925—when a translation was presented in New York. The mere play (which was very well staged & acted) was impressive enough, & I can well imagine the additional power derived from an appropriate musical score. From your account, I judge that the opera follows the order & events of the drama quite closely. Mention of a dance of beggars vaguely reminds me of something in the play—connected with a garden scene. The exorcism was very powerful, even without music. I surely hope I can encounter the opera sooner or later—though I don't know when I shall next visit New York. The play produced a very potent impression on me, & I had a vague idea of trying to base a story on the dybbuk idea. I saved my programme—which had copious notes on the particular sect of Jews most addicted to cabalistic research (I think they were called the Chassidim)—but that young rascal Long lost it when I lent it to him! Without this ready-made data, I let the story-idea languish—though I suppose I could find out about dybbuks, & about the Chassidim, in the great Jewish Encyclopaedia which is available at most large libraries. Price got a lot of stuff about *Lilith* from this source. What is more—this work might shed a picturesque light on the *Golem* belief. This reminds me, by the way, that the long-delayed Meyrink novel "The Golem" will reach you before long from young Petaja. Keep it as long as you like—& eventually return it to Barlow, its owner.

"Prince Igor"[5] must have been quite a spectacle. I believe this opera was left unfinished by its composer—though no doubt judicious editing has rounded it out into presentable form.

The Phantagraph does indeed seem a rather pitiful substitute for the late lamented F F, but some of its worst crudities may drop off as Shepherd gains skill in typography. #2 certainly shows a great improvement over #1. Suggestions—such as that of an open forum for discussion—would be heartily welcomed by the youthful publishers. The other day I had a request for a contribution from a couple of New Jersey boys who publish a sheet of the "fan" order called *The Planeteer*. I haven't seen it yet, but imagine it is mimeographed—& largely devoted to science fiction. I sent in a couple of decade-old specimens of weird verse, which were gratefully accepted & rewarded by a life (mine or the magazine's) subscription.[6] You may get a request from the kids for an Eltdown Shard or two. They were almost on the point of falling for that spoofing item in *The Phantagraph* & sending $1.49 for a copy of the Necronomicon![7]

This seems, in general, to be rather a bad year for the gang. Both of Long's parents have been down with grippe, & he is quite nervously worn out himself. Wandrei has suffered from colds, influenza, & dysentery, while Barlow's bronchial trouble has been very acute. Robert E. Howard is greatly worried over his mother's health, while Klarkash-Ton is having a frightful struggle keeping the place going & caring for his increasingly feeble father.

Young Sterling is recovering well from his operation, & is now tutoring like the very devil to see if he can make Harvard in the autumn after all—despite the 2-month interruption in his studies.

In the February issue of *Story* there is a very clever bit by Dunsany—"Two Bottles of Relish"[8]—which shows how the better magazines waive some of the taboos which bother Wright so much. If you can't find this issue at the library I'll lend you the copy I have. The tale—a *conte cruel*—is not at all in Dunsany's old-time vein, & does not contain any of his characteristic charm.

Best wishes—Yrs by the Eyeless Mumbler
—E'ch-Pi-El

[P.S.] Glad to see the reprint of "The Brain in the Jar"—an old favourite of mine. ¶ Hornig of the late F F has gone to San Francisco on a newspaper job secured for him by A. Merritt. He stopped in Indianapolis to see the author of "Shambleau" on his way out to the coast.

Notes

1. *WT,* May 1936.
2. "Child of the Winds."
3. "Strange Interval" (*WT,* May 1936). The story describes the capture and flogging of Colonel Willoughby Moncure Munro by pirates. When a beautiful woman captive of the pirates refuses the advances of the skipper and shows favor to Willoughby, the pirates stage a mock wedding, castrate Willoughby (whose voice laughably becomes high and feminine), cut his beard, pierce his ears for women's earrings, comb his hair in women's fashion, dress him in women's attire, and force him to watch the rape of the woman, Carmelita. Willoughby assumes a new life as "Joaquina" having become nearly thoroughly "feminized," and his relationship with Carmelita takes on a lesbian-like turn. See also letter 33.
4. Lodovico Rocca (1895–1986), *Il Dibuk* (Milan: Ricordi, 1934), libretto by Renato Simoni. Based on the play *The Dybbuk; or, Between Two Worlds* by S. Ansky.
5. Aleksandr Porfirévich Borodin (1833–1887), *Prince Igor,* completed by Nikolai Rimskii-Korsakov (1844–1908) and Aleksandr Konstantinovich Glazunov (1865–1936) (Leipzig: M. P. Belaieff, 1889).
6. *The Planeteer* was edited by James Blish and William Miller, Jr. HPL's poem "The Wood" was to have appeared in the September 1936 issue and the sheets containing it were prepared, but the magazine was never published.
7. "About the *Necronomicon*—bless my soul, but I thought you knew that was a strictly imaginary institution! The paragraph about its being for sale at $1.49 was a joke—I don't know who wrote it, but suspect young Bloch." HPL to James Blish and William Miller, Jr., 19 May 1936; *Uncollected Letters* (West Warwick, RI: Necronomicon Press, 1986), 37.
8. The actual title is "The Two Bottles of Relish," first published in *Time and Tide* for 12 and 19 November 1932. It is a sardonic detective tale involving cannibalism and one of the most frequently anthologized tales in modern literature.

[33]   [ALS, JHL]

66 College St.,
Providence, R.I.,
August 27, 1936.

Dear Ar-Eph-Es:—

Yes—Rhode Island had the warm spell, & I really think it saved me from a sort of general breakdown. My nerves were on edge with the cold weather, mental & physical exhaustion dogged me, & my digestion had begun to go to pieces. Then—on the 8th of July—the blessed heat came (though it did not exceed 92°) . . . . & in two days I was on top of the world! Exhaustion vanished, nerves relaxed, & digestion rapidly cleared up. In the 6 days of really hot weather I accomplished more than in all the six *weeks* preceding. When the heat waned, my extra vigour & alertness declined—but I have not fallen back into quite the morass I was in before. I am certainly an ass to continue living in this damned subarctic climate—but that's what attachment to childhood & ancestral scenes will do! Glad the warmth (more pronounced in Detroit than here) didn't wilt you. Certainly, light-weight clothing is the only sensible thing for weather over 85° or 90°. I have an old palm beach suit which I drag forth for the few really hot days hereabouts—though I seldom get a chance to wear it! Of course, I always wear a much lighter-weight suit in summer than in winter—but I need more than a palm beach or tropical worsted for temperatures under 85°.

Good weather was the inspirer of considerable outdoor activity & exploration on my part, so that I covered a number of sights in a very short time. I may have mentioned my trip in May to see the ancient Clemence house (1654), now recognised as the oldest edifice in Rhode Island. Since its builder— Thomas Clemence, a friend of Roger Williams—is a lineal ancestor of mine in the 8th generation, I have more than a superficial interest in it. It lies just beyond the village of Manton, on the western fringe of Providence's suburbs. Clemence purchased the land—8 acres—from an Indian named Wissawyamake, & proceeded to construct a typical stone-chimneyed dwelling of the period. It is much changed today—but the accompanying rough sketch shows it as it originally was. The changes are all *excrescences*—dormers, lean-to, porch, &c.—so that it could easily be restored if purchased by an historical society as I hope it may be some day. The present occupant & owner is an ancient gentlewoman in destitute circumstances. In the yard the old well-sweep still remains—one of the relatively few left in Rhode Island. Thomas Clemence's daughter Elizabeth married the grandson of the Providence colonist John

Field—thus joining the two lines of my ancestry. I was certainly glad to discover this latter John's lineage last May, & thus be able to list a man of science among my progenitors! Incidentally—speaking of forbears & old houses—a piece of very good news reached me last week. It seems that my favourite surviving ancestral homestead—the Place house in Foster R.I.—has just been bought by an interior decorator for thorough restoration in the original style. It has been out of the family since 1870, & had begun to show decided signs of wear. I have its picture (a childhood crayon drawing of my mother's, after a painting by a great-aunt) over my desk, & it is cheering to know that the original will be in good condition for an indefinite period.

But my recent old-house explorations have not been confined to person ally ancestral places. Last month two of the ancient mansions on the hill just south of here were thrown open as museums, & among my heat-induced activities of the season was a thorough exploration of both of them. The enclosed leaflet describes the finer of the two. After a close inspection I can say that John Quincy Adams (vide leaflet) was right[1]—& this after having examined 18th century houses all the way from Quebec on the north to St. Augustine (Key West hasn't any!) & New Orleans on the south. The edifice has an admirably classic symmetry & arrangement, its only possible flaw being a subtle tendency toward rococo over-ornateness on the lower floor. Like most houses in America even as late as the early 1800's, it is untouched by the superior classicism of the Adam influence, which became manifest in Great Britain as early as the 1750's or 1760's. John Brown, the builder of the house, was one of four quite celebrated brothers belonging to a local sea-trading family descended from the early settler Rev. Chad Brown. His nephew Nicholas Jr. is the one whose donations changed the name of Rhode-Island College to Brown University in 1804. His younger brother Moses was a well-known Quaker & philanthropist, whilst his grand-nephew John Carter Brown founded the world-famous library of that name. John himself was merely a shrewd grasper dependent upon other people's taste. The really civilised member of the family was his elder brother Joseph, who in the 1750's, 1760's, & 1770's played a great part in bringing Providence up to the cultural level of Newport. Joseph was a scholar & man of taste, & the greatest architect in the town prior to the rise of John Holden Greene. With Stephen Hopkins he helped to found the Providence Library in 1753, & in 1769 he imported a telescope (now at the Ladd Observatory—I've seen it) to observe the transit of Venus in that year. He designed the John Brown house, as well as houses for himself & brother Nicholas—his own edifice (still standing in good condition) embodying original architectural ideas [cyma-curve pediment, &c.] destined to influence the Providence-Georgian tradition very strongly. To Joseph Brown are likewise due the plan of the Market House (1778—still intact), & the selection of the Gibbs design for the steeple of the First Baptist Church (1775). In later life he became Professor of Natural Philosophy at the college.

The house so well depicted in the leaflet may perhaps be regarded as his architectural masterpiece. He died in 1787, before its completion, but its splendid outlines survive as a memorial to his taste. The numerous French busts stuck around at various places are none of his doing. There is a legend that those on the gateposts turn & bow to each other at midnight—a phenomenon I have not personally witnessed!

The other house—of which I could secure no descriptive or pictorial matter—is the Edward Carrington mansion,[2] erected in 1809 & the work of John Holden Greene. This lacks the classic interior symmetry of the Brown house, but is extremely pleasing & homelike. It was recently presented to the R.I. School of Design—with all its original furniture & decorations to be kept intact for ever—by the last of the family, who resides in another colonial mansion inherited through another line. With its stables, coach-houses, cobblestoned courtyard, & extensive grounds & gardens, the Carrington house forms one of the most satisfying domestic units of the early-republic period now on exhibition. In its interior architecture it embodies a rather amusing hybridism seemingly peculiar to late 18th & early 19th century Providence—the use of rococo middle-18th-century architecture on the ground floor, & of the newer Adam-period design throughout the upper storeys. Some of the delicate Adam mantels upstairs are among the most exquisite I have ever seen. [#66 follows a simple form of the Adam tradition throughout.]

Glad to hear, by the way, that Detroit has begun to cherish such of its older buildings as remain. The moving of that steepled church must have been a prodigious feat. I understand that most of the really early buildings were wiped out by a fire in 1805 or so. Actually, Detroit is the very oldest of the towns of the Middle West—& older than many towns in New England & Virginia. Providence was only 65 years old when the original French post was established in 1701. I can picture the settlement in the days of Pontiac—with rows of French cottages with whitewashed walls & curved eaves like those seen in the Quebec region today.

In mid-July I took a boat trip to ancient Newport—rambling as usual around the venerable town with its 1726 church, 1739 colony-house, 1760 market-house, 1763 synagogue, 1749 library, & private houses extending back to 1675. I also did considerable writing on the high rocky cliffs—with nothing but the ocean betwixt me & the Iberian peninsula.

July 18–19 I had an enjoyable visit from my old friend Maurice W. Moe (poet-teacher . . . of Milwaukee) & his gifted son Robert (the latter the youth who was here with his car in the spring of '35). It was my first sight of M W M in 13 years, & I fancy he found me more changed in aspect than I found him. Bob brought him in the car, & we covered quite a bit of scenic & historic ground in the all-too-brief span of 2 days. We went to the quaint quondam fishing village of Pawtuxet (on a picturesque cove 6 m. S. of Providence's civic centre—now overtaken by the expanding network of city streets), ascended old Ft.

Independence (on the W. shore of the bay, with a magnificent view of the city skyline on the N. & of the blue water & green shores on the S.), wound through the foliage-shaded driveways of Roger Williams Park, traversed the deep woods & colonial farmlands north of the city, & as a climax repeated the Warren-Bristol drive which young Bob & I took in March of last year. This was much more enjoyable in July than in March, & the ancient seaport villages (E. shore of the bay) displayed their colonial doorways & giant elms to maximum advantage. We also took the seaside drive on Popasquash Neck—a sub-peninsula attached to the main Bristol peninsula. In Warren we had an all-ice-cream dinner at Maxfield's (that famous mecca of all our gang)—mine consisting of grape, pineapple, peach, raspberry, banana, & chocolate chip. Old Moe had to call a halt after 2½ pints, but his son finished 3 pints—with difficulty. I downed 3 pints with ease & avidity, & would have been good for 3 more. Weather favoured us greatly, for we had warmth & sun throughout—whereas the very next day was cold & rainy, with Grandpa E'ch-Pi-El heavily blanketed & shivering over an oil heater!

Glad to hear that the senior Searights had a glimpse of New England, & hope that you can follow in their footsteps. Maine has the fascinations—but the climate would keep me away! I fancy the Mass. shore north of Boston—especially the Magnolia region near Gloucester—could equal any scenic ruggedness possessed by its polar neighbour. For that matter, even Newport—in a relatively mild climate—is distinctly in the running. Those cliffs where I lounged during my recent trip were no pallid imitations—vide the enclosed card![3] Certainly, one ought to give the whole of ancient New England a good looking over before settling down in any particular spot!

I surely hope that the Mackinac–Houghton–Isle Royale trip may have constituted a pleasantly memorable event. I recall the interesting cards & descriptions of the Northern Peninsula (indeed, I still have them) which you sent a couple of years ago. Hope tourists & publicity haven't totally spoiled Isle Royale. I doubt whether I can manage any trips this year—at least, beyond 1-day & 2-day jaunts around New England. Even these I'll try to save for the very last of summer, so that the continuous period of hibernation may seem less extended. I'd like to get up around Salem, Marblehead, Newburyport, & Portsmouth, of whose multitudinous antiquities I never tire.

Sorry that small Marjorie had to endure so much surgery all at once—but the summer will doubtless bring her back to accustomed strength. I can imagine how you must have felt the strain—& hope that the diminutive heir-apparent can somehow escape a similar ordeal. After all, a fair percentage of mankind gets by without any of the customary extractions & modifications! Congratulations to the heir upon his early pedestrianism! Before long he'll be racing around like a blue streak & talking a mile a minute!

About glasses—I tried various pince-nez types 30 or so years ago, but they didn't show much affinity for my proboscis. The fact is, those that stayed on at all hurt my nose alone as badly as the average bows hurt nose & ears combined! If I have to resume the continuous use of specs, I shall certainly experiment with the newer types of snout-squeezers. Many thanks for the tip! So far I've let things rest—& my vision was vastly improved during the hot spell. I may compromise on specs for reading only—for the indistinctness of my distant vision never gives me dizziness or acute headaches as it used to do 15 or so years ago.

Had a prodigious file-cleaning around June 1st—spending 4 days in an effort to bring order out of chaos. I threw away about a couple of tons of junk, & once more know approximately where to find what I'm looking for. But my programme is still beyond control, & unperformed tasks tower high around me.

And mourning prevails in Kappa Alpha Tau circles. Alas—my best friends are no more, despite the late exemplary conduct & emergence from *local* peril of coal-black Mr. John Perkins! A month ago both Mr. Perkins & his younger brother the Earl of Minto (b. Oct. '35—black-&-white) succumbed to some malady which is afflicting all the local felidae—a thing which may be an obscure epidemic, yet which may reflect the malign activities of some contemptible poisoner.[4] The sad end of the brothers seemed connected with some digestive disorder, & recalled the equally sad fate of their bygone black brother—little Sam Perkins—in Sept. '34.[5] If this *is* the work of some wretched neo-Borgia, I hope to hell somebody feeds him a slow poison a thousandfold more painful than that with which he has subtly supplied his innocent furry victims! For a time it looked as if there would be no more kittens at the house across the garden, since a couple of months ago the white-&-black matriarch of the clan was given away to the psychological laboratory of Brown University, where it was expected she would round out her days in ease & luxury, being used (together with other felidae, canidae, &c.) in tests of instinct, intelligence, perception, &c., for the benefit of successive generations of students. Since the tragedy, however, old lady Perkins has been recalled from her academic career, & once more roams her accustomed gardens— serenaded by all the gallant swains of the Kappa Alpha Tau, including the night-black, rangy Mr. Perkins Sr. She called here the other day, & was duly regaled with catnip purchased for younger mouths!

Glad you liked "The Shadow Out of Time"—but when I came to correct my printed copies of that & the "Mts." I swore off (& at) Tremaine for good! Ædepol, what vandalism! Never again! To begin with, a crazy style-sheet, with "great god" changed to "great heavens", words (even *Moon* & *Moonlight*) wrongly capitalised, punctuation putrid & excessive, certain names changed to cumbrous scientific versions (*dinosaurs* to *Dinosauria* &c.), good spelling made bad (subterrene to subterrane &c.), & certain words capriciously & weakeningly replaced (*demoniac* to *demonic* &c.). Certain stupid changes in sentence-structure gave an effect of immaturity—& paragraphs were chopped up into small bits in imitation of the juvenile pulp "action" style—thus destroying original rhythm, emotional modulations, & minor climactic effects. The poor old "Mts. of Madness" got the worst deal—especially toward the end. I now consider the story as *unpublished.* Important passages were deleted—decreasing vitality & colour, & making the action mechanical. So many significant details & impressions are missing from the concluding parts that the effect is that of a flat ending. After all the adventure & detail *before* the encounter with the shoggoth in the abyss, the characters are shot up to the surface without any of the gradual experiences & emotions which make the reader *feel* their return to the world of man from the nighted, aeon-dead world of the *Others.* All sense of the *duration & difficulty* of the exhausted climb is lost when it is dismissed objectively in only a few words, with no adequate hint of the fugitives' responses to the scenes through which they pass. Among actual *plot* points omitted is one where the explorers notice (through a dropped battery) that the revived Old Ones have been pausing perplexedly before that ominous & grotesquely crude *palimpsest carving* in the passage to the sunken sea. With great difficulty I fixed up 3 copies each of the "Mts." & "Shadow"—joining broken paragraphs, & careting in missing passages written in fine pencil characters on the margins. I am lending a corrected copy of the "Mts." to all who have not seen the original MS. As for the "Shadow's" *illustrations*[6]—I did not like them as much as I liked those of the "Mts." In certain details & proportions they belied the text . . . . . for example, they shewed the narrator among the living Great Race *in his human body.*

 Crawford's "Innsmouth" book project still drags on incomplete—indeed, heaven only knows when he'll issue either that volume or his next *Marvel Tales!* Schwartz has a wild idea about getting some of my stuff reprinted in England (I'm sure it'll come to nothing), & in connexion with this matter I sent my two unsubmitted stories—"The Thing on the Doorstep" & "The Haunter of the Dark"—to W T in order to exhaust all cisatlantic possibilities first. I expected instant rejections—but to my surprise Wright took both items. The old boy must be hard up for MSS.—but I can certainly use the resultant 205 bucks . . . which will trickle fragmentarily in at some indefinite set of remote future dates.

 Glad you're encouraging the *Planeteer* boys—though I rather wish you'd saved the "Warder" for *Marvel Tales* or some other magazine about whose appearance we can make at least partial predictions. I haven't yet seen an issue of *The Planeteer,* though the youthful editors certainly seem in earnest. And so they wanted the full translated text of the Eltdown Shards! They also asked me for the complete Necronomicon to use as a serial, but I told them it would hardly be practicable to attempt anything of the sort. It is only by remaining unknown & indefinite that the old Necro can serve as a basis for such portentous allusions—for the *known* can never equal the *hidden* or *suggested* in potential horror. Besides, I've no time to devise & produce a ponderous tome! So I told the boys I'd have to limit myself to a few translated *extracts* at some indefinite future period. The case of the Shards is a precisely parallel one, & I fancy the same sort of solution is best for you also. A new "fan" magazine is now announced for September—*The Science-Fantasy Correspondent*, edited by one Willis Conover, Jr., of 27 High St., Cambridge, Maryland. Young Willis has very ambitious plans—& time will tell how fully they can materialise. Meanwhile *The Phantagraph* comes out monthly in miniature form. It will soon be joined by the companion (fiction) magazine *Fanciful Tales*. *Fantasy Magazine* plods along in a somewhat humble way—& Hill-Billy Crawford continues to promise. Young Hornig—of the lamented F F, & jobless since the transfer of *Wonder Stories* from Hugo the Rat to the Margulies group—has been in Los Angeles seeking his fortune. Good old Abe Merritt almost secured him a position on a San Francisco paper, but something went awry with that opening. After some searching in California, he is now back in Elizabeth, N.J.

Good luck with "Mists of Death"![7] Realistic characters & background are always a great asset to a story, & between your medical cousin & the Isle Royale setting you ought to have a good start. The unusual geographical impressions will of course be good for more than one story. At least two of my tales came directly from trips to unfamiliar regions—"Dunwich" from a Wilbraham, Mass. visit, & "The Whisperer in Darkness" from a fortnight in Vermont. More than that—"The Festival" really came directly from a Marblehead tour, "The Unnamable" from Salem, &c. &c. &c.

I come now to some bad news which I hate to record—but which you may by this time have heard from other sources. Robert Ervin Howard—good old Two-Gun Bob—is no more; having killed himself on June 11 after learning that his mother could not live more than 48 hours more. He sent a bullet through his brain at 8 a.m., & died 8 hours later without regaining consciousness. 30 hours after that his mother died without having known of her son's desperate act. The shock to his father, a veteran physician, must be appalling—wife & splendid only child gone at one stroke—but Dr. H. is bearing up like a true Texas pioneer. He has presented Robert's library to the latter's alma mater—Howard Payne College at Brownwood, Texas—as the nucleus of a Robert E. Howard Memorial Collection. Poor Two-Gun! Tough, hairy-chested, & eat-'em-alive as he seemed to be, he must have been highly emotional & morbidly sensitive at bottom. Most of us, despite the strongest filial affection, recognise the grim inevitability of the elder generation's passing & accept such bereavements philosophically. The tragedy is hard to understand—for although R E H had a moody side expressed in his resentment against civilisation (the basis of our perennial & voluminous epistolary debate), I always thought that this was a more or less *impersonal* sentiment—like Belknap's rage against the injustices of a capitalistic world. Obviously, the strain of melancholy must have run deeper than we ever suspected. He seemed pretty well adjusted to his environment—though for a year he had worried over his mother's pleural illness. Toward the last he had lost many nights of sleep watching at her bedside—& in the end the sombre phase of his temperament triumphed. To the gang this evil news is a staggering blow. E. Hoffmann Price—the only one of us ever to meet Two-Gun in person—says he feels "clubbed over the head",[8] & I can fully understand his sensation. He will prepare some reminiscences of R E H for the "fan" press—& perhaps devise an obituary for W T. I have prepared an obituary for *Fantasy Magazine*[9]—& Barlow has written a really touching elegiac sonnet which W T accepted at once.[10] This sonnet forms Ar-E'ch-Bei's first professional acceptance—& it is surely sad that his debut should have so tragic a background. The suddenness of the event makes it all the more devastating. Price & Wollheim had cheerful cards from R E H as late as June 3—& I had a long normal letter written May 13. My answer to that letter—a 32-page argumentative missive—undoubtedly reached Cross Plains too late to be read. Without question Two-Gun Bob had the last word in our 6-year-long debate—an advantage I won't begrudge him, poor chap, under the circumstances!

This is the worst blow weird magazine fiction has had since the passing of good old Whitehead in 1932. Nobody else in the gang had quite the driving zest & spontaneity of Two-Gun. It is hard to say just what made his stories stand out so, but the real secret is that *he was in every one of them himself.* Even when he made outward concessions to commercial critics & mammon-guided editors he had an inner force & sincerity which broke through the surface & put the imprint of his personality on everything he wrote. He was really even more gifted than appears from his published work; being an encyclopaedic student of southwestern history, & having a truly epical power of capturing the colour & repeating the annals of his beloved native region. His long, essay-like letters ought to see the light of print. Had he lived longer—he was 30 last January—he would almost undoubtedly have made his mark in serious literature as a regional author. But even his existing stories are distinctive enough. Never again will the pulp magazines get anything with such force & colour. R E H lived in & near Texas all his life, & was passionately devoted to its history & folkways. He came of old planter stock—largely Scotch-Irish—from Georgia & North Carolina. Celtic antiquities & ancient history in general claimed much of his attention—& no one could excel him in tales of barbaric or prehistoric life. He saw many phases of the disappearing frontier—from ranching to oil-drilling—& knocked about among all types of Texans. His first story was written at 15, & his first placement was with W T in 1924, at the age of 18. "Wolfshead", in the April 1926 issue of W T (a cover-design novelette), was the tale which first brought him general notice. Later came the "Solomon Kane", "Bran Mak Morn", "King Kull" & "Conan" yarns—plus the Oriental battle-tales, prize-fight stories, & humorously realistic "westerns" in other magazines. Two-Gun was nearly 6 feet tall, with the massive build of a pugilist. He was very dark except for Celtic blue eyes. A hearty liver &

heavy drinker, he always toted a gun & seemed a veritable embodiment of the wild west. Toward the last he changed a bit in aspect—getting stout & round-faced, & growing a large moustache which (in conjunction with a 10-gallon hat) made him look almost like a western cinema sheriff. 1936 surely has taken heavy toll! Deaths of weird writers outside the gang include those of Montague Rhodes James at 73, & of George Allan England at 59.

Among the phases of my attempted conquest of chaos has been a reading-up of recent issues of W T. In looking over the contents I am sadly impressed with the superiority of good old Two-Gun's work. By Crom & Mitra, how he could surround primal megalithic cities with an aura of aeon-old fear & necromancy! His "Hour of the Dragon" is certainly a great piece of work. "Black Canaan" is likewise magnificent in a more realistic way—reflecting a genuine regional background & giving a clutchingly powerful picture of the horror that stalks through the moss-hung, shadow-cursed, serpent-ridden swamps of the farther south. Of other material I was glad to see "The Brain in the Jar" once more—an old favourite which did not lose its charm on re-reading. Bloch's tales are all excellent according to average standards, while Derleth's "Telephone in the Library" could be a lot worse. The Quinn thing, as you said, *was* rather repulsive—besides being not weird, & containing an amusing reference to Petersburg & Alexandria about a half-century before either of those Virginia towns was founded. Hamilton & Burks are mediocre—though the former escapes his formula fairly well. M. J. Bardine's "Harbour of Ghosts" has promise & atmosphere. So has H. G. Shane's "Lethe." Klarkash-Ton & C L M dominate the July issue.[11]

Only one response so far to enquiries about the Cook's Tale. Here it is—& it need not be returned.[12] Kleiner evidently didn't get the exact drift of my question—not realising that the sets of Chaucer I had seen contained not even the fragmentary tale. He obviously thought I asked why the tale, in the editions where it occurs, is incomplete. But one thing is settled—the fragment *does* belong in the book. Indeed, since last writing you I've seen a (new illustrated) edition with it in. It must be through sheer coincidence that I had previously seen only editions lacking it. The explanation of its fragmentary condition is curious. Do you know anything about this "Cook's Tale of Gamelyn" which drove it into exile & caused the permanent loss of most of its text? I'll confess I don't![13] Every now & then I come up against some proof of how little I know. Kleiner's note seems to tell about all anybody could tell. Now that I realise how fully a part of the text the fragment is, I am doubly grateful for the copy which you so kindly furnished! Your admiration of old Geoff is surely well-founded—& you are fortunate in having found it easy to grasp his idiom.

Here is that list of words frequently mispronounced—the maximum form of it, which will doubtless be sliced down for the book.[14] It is hard to decide just what to include & what to exclude in such a list. In order to be eligible, a word must be mispronounced by enough different persons to make the error truly *typical.* Also, the slips must be characteristic of persons considerably above the crude stage. Obviously, a list of the errors of the frankly ignorant would be endless & basically futile. Narrowly *local* mispronunciations, too, must be counted out. The list as it stands contains both the author's original collection & my additions. Some of the original selections puzzle me, since I've never heard them mispronounced—but I presume the author has had wider experience. In certain cases more than one permissible pronunciation exists—but the word is included if one of the forms is decidedly to be preferred. In one or two cases prominent dictionary authority is defied in the interest of tradition, etymology, & observed good usage. Thus the superior correctness of *shŏn* (as opposed to *shōn*) as the pronunciation of *shone* is insisted on. In disputed cases like this the table ought to have notes—as it will in the book. Pronunciation is a much more elastic thing than spelling. Probably there is no one living who does not occasionally mispronounce many of the words on this list—as well as many not on it. I've rectified many of my own pronunciations late in life.

Hope "The Golem" won't disappoint you. There is nothing about the Chassidim in it—but the atmosphere is rich enough without 'em! Incidentally, I saw a new book on the Chassidim reviewed a fortnight or so ago in the *N Y Times.*[15]

My pile of unread borrowed books doesn't diminish as fast as it ought. Have just read biographies of Roger Williams by Emily M. Easton & James Ernst—the latter of whom emphasises R. W.'s influence on the revolution in England in the 1640's. Also finished Santayana's much advertised (but really good) "Last Puritan"—a truly remarkable dissection of the sterile genteel culture which dominated New England in the 19th century, & which is now in its death-throes.

Had an interesting view of Peltier's comet on July 22 at the Ladd Observatory—through a 12″ telescope. The object showed a small disc with a hazy, fan-like tail. I could have seen it through my own small telescope were the northern sky less cut off from the neighbourhood of 66.

All good wishes—Yrs sincerely
—H P L

[P.S.] Latest news—Barlow's in Providence for a stay of considerable length. Has taken quarters in the boarding-house across the garden from 66. Plenty of congenial conversation! Loan exhibit of Klarkash-Ton's weird carvings arrived simultaneously with Ar-E'ch-Bei. It includes some splendid stuff! I appreciated your postcard immensely. That fort is fascinating.

[P.P.S.] Old Adolphe de Castro—one-time friend of Bierce & later a revision client of mine—was in town early in August. He, Barlow, & I wrote rhymed acrostics to Poe while seated on a tomb in a local churchyard. Barlow & I went to Newport Aug. 15, & to ancient Salem & Marblehead Aug. 20.

Notes

1. See EHP 74n9.

2. Edward Carrington House (1810; 1812), 66 Williams Street. John Corliss built the original two-story part of the house in 1810. Margarethe Dwight, a descendant of Carrington, gave the house and many of its furnishings to the Museum of Art, Rhode Island School of Design as a museum showing the influence of the China trade in New England. It has been a private residence since 1931.

3. This card does not survive.

4. This, coincidentally, was the subject of HPL's "The Cats of Ulthar" (1920).

5. See HPL's "[Little Sam Perkins]" (EHP 42).

6. By Howard V. Brown, who also illustrated *At the Mountains of Madness*.

7. This story survives in two drafts, one of ten pages and the other of sixteen pages. The latter has as its prologue an extract from the Eltdown Shards nearly identical to that for "The Sealed Casket"; RFS, noting that Farnsworth Wright had omitted the extract from the latter tale, decided to reuse it in the new story.

8. EHP to HPL, [25 June 1936].

9. "In Memoriam: Robert Ervin Howard."

10. "R. E. H." (*WT*, October 1936).

11. HPL is discussing several issues of *WT*. May 1936: Arthur J. Burks, "The Room of Shadows"; Robert Bloch, "The Faceless God"; Seabury Quinn, "Strange Interval." June 1936: August Derleth, "The Telephone in the Library"; Robert Bloch, "The Grinning Ghoul"; Harold G. Shane, "Lethe"; M. J. Bardine, "The Harbor of Ghosts." July 1936: Edmond Hamilton, "When the World Slept"; C. L. Moore, "Lost Paradise"; CAS, "Necromancy in Naat."

12. This is a letter to HPL from Rheinhart Kleiner, 17 June 1936.

13. "The Tale of Gamelyn" is a text dating to c. 1350 but is not believed to be by Chaucer. The fragmentary "Cook's Tale" is sometimes printed as a "Prologue" to "The Tale of Gamelyn."

14. The chapter "Words Frequently Mispronounced" was wholly excised from *Well Bred Speech*.

15. David L. Meckler (1891–1976), *Miracle Men: Tales of the Chassidim* (New York: Covici, Friede, 1936), reviewed by Alfred Kazin in *New York Times Book Review* (19 July 1936): 8.

[34]　[ALS]

The Ancient Hill
—Novr. 19, 1936.

Dear Ar-Eph-Es:—

　　All too brief was the warm weather—but it at least gave

me enough life to last until another summer. I envy your father[1] his ability to get south—although I wouldn't particularly care to get *north* except for anti-quarian observation. It is never too warm for me anywhere, & I wish I might never be in a temperature of less than 85°! Glad you had some warm October weather. My outdoor sessions of reading & writing ended in early October, but I continued for a time to get out for occasional rural walks. This autumn I took to exploring a wooded hill—Neutaconkanut—on the western rim of the town (& visible from my window in the distance) whence a series of marvel-lous views of the outspread city & adjacent countryside & blue bay may be obtained. I had often ascended it before, but have only recently examined & appreciated the exquisitely mystical sylvan scenery—curious mounds, flower-starred meadows, & hushed hidden valleys—beyond the crest. Beginning next spring, it will become a favourite goal of mine!

Lamentations for good old Two-Gun's untimely end continue to re-sound. No doubt you've seen Barlow's elegiac sonnet in W T, & my mis-printed obituary in the anniversary F M. It surely was a grievous tragedy—& the loss to weird fiction is irreplaceable.

Glad the Brown house material proved of interest. Some day I surely hope to be able to show you this & other antiquarian shrines around New England. On my 46th birthday—August 20—Barlow, young Sterling & I made a tour of ancient Salem & Marblehead, during which the youngsters learned more about our *very earliest* type of houses—the 17th century sort with peaked gables & overhang—than they had ever known before. Detroit surely faces many problems in the matter of aesthetic development, & I hope she may be able to cope with them all successfully. The quick slumward drift of certain regions is typical of all metropolitan zones, no matter how assiduously fought through zoning. It is worst, of course, where great industries & vast masses of aliens exist. The survival of great trees in blighted areas must in-volve curious contrasts. Somehow or other, most of the slums in New Eng-land cities are repellently treeless—although I did notice some run-down districts with fine foliage in Richmond, Va.

The July Moe session was indeed a highly pleasant event—& as for ice cream . . . why, 3 pints is only a *beginning* for me! I like nothing better than an all-ice-cream dinner, & it makes no difference whether the flavour is homo-geneous or varied. We got different flavours down at Maxfield's simply be-cause they specialise in exotic varieties there.

Barlow was here from July 28 to Sept. 1, & became thoroughly initiated in the ways of Providence libraries, museums, & bookstalls. He had a room at the boarding-house across the garden, & was an incessant & congenial visitor at #66. He made himself very useful mending books & other objects, & I was able to help him quite a bit with his new fiction. We had an interesting time Aug. 6–10 when old Adolphe de Castro was here—& incidentally, that ses-sion of acrostic-writing in the hidden churchyard gave rise to an amusing series of echoes. Though it would never have occurred to Ar-Ech-Bei & me to submit our results for publication, our shrewd old colleague *did*—& secured an acceptance from Brother Farnsworth! After that, R H B & I did send our acrostics in—but they were turned down because Old 'Dolph's had already been taken. Now that the ball has started rolling, we'll probably let one or another of the now-innumerable "fan magazines" have our specimens. Meanwhile correspondents began to emulate. Young Kuttner has devised a splendidly poetic acrostic—best of them all because written at leisure. And Moe (who saw the churchyard in July) prepared a very clever academic variant—& is about to incorporate *all* the acrostics into a hectographed booklet for use in his English classes. Nor is that all. Derleth is editing a Wisconsin Poetry Anthology for that racketeering vanity-publisher Henry Harrison of N.Y., & having seen Moe's specimen, decided to include it in the volume. All this from Ar-Ech-Bei's idle notion of writing an acrostic (his original idea was to have each of us contribute parts to a single poem, but this soon proved impracticable) while seated on an ancient tomb on a summer's afternoon![2] Enclosed are the original three acrostics—which you might return some time. Well—Bob moved on Sept. 1st, & spent considerable time in N.Y. confabulating with Long, Koenig, Loveman, Howard Wandrei (Donald is back in St. Paul), &c. He then headed west (for the De Land home seems to be permanently dissolved), pausing in Indianapolis for a very congenial call on Miss Moore. He & his mother are now with an uncle in Kansas City—the address for the coming winter being % H. M. LANGWORTHY, 810 W. 57th ST. TERRACE, KANSAS CITY, MO.

My next social event was a visit from good old Jim Morton (Curator of the Paterson Museum), who was here Sept. 11–12–13. On the 12th we went down to Warren at noon & cleaned up *2 quarts apiece* of ice cream at Maxfield's—my flavours being orange, pineapple, raspberry, lemon, chocolate chip, banana, grape, & loganberry. We stopped eating not because we were full, but because our cash was running low. Later we had a big spaghetti dinner, & around midnight we consumed a pint more apiece of ice cream (coffee & vanilla) at a friend's where we spent the evening. That's what we call reducing! James Ferdinand was in his usual fine form, & radiant with the glow of the crossword-puzzle championship he had just won at the Boston convention of the Puzzlers' League. (They're sending him a big silver loving-cup duly inscribed with his name & prowess.) We had the usual round of arguments, after which J F M headed back to Massachusetts to shine at the Tercentenary celebration of his Alma Mater. Sterling, by the way, is now entering Harvard—being well recovered from last spring's operation.

The next event of the dying season was a visit from young Moe (the chap who downed 3 pints at Maxfield's last July when his father could manage only 2½)—whose presence in Prov. was largely for the purpose of calling on a brilliant young gentlewoman from his home town who is entering Brown as a graduate student of philosophy. He had his faithful 1928 Ford with him, & I showed the youngsters around considerably. All these visitors appreciated very much the loan-exhibit of Klarkash-Ton's grotesque miniature sculpture which remained here from Aug. 1 to Sept. 28. Meanwhile my programme became grievously tangled with excessive work, so that on one occasion I was obliged to labour 60 hours without sleep in order to meet the deadline of a rush revision job.

That job, by the way, was a later phase of the "Well-Bred English" enterprise at which I've been hammering since last winter in fits & starts, & out of which that list of mispronounced words was taken. Glad you found the list interesting & helpful. No need of returning it. I later expanded it considerably—only to have it cut down to about quarter-length by the "author" in the final version! I am, however, preserving my full list. A long table of words with parallel *permissible* pronunciations was *entirely eliminated* [but I have my rough draught], whilst a laboriously prepared *reading course* covering literature, history, philosophy, science, & the arts was reduced to inutile proportions. This reading course demanded a vast amount of research, & I'm keeping the MS. for possible future revision & publication in full.

Glad "The Golem" reached you at last. I was sure you'd appreciate it—for it is really a phenomenal triumph in its way. Few books indeed are capable of summoning up such a poignant & convincing pageant of mystical atmospheric impressions—& the absence of conventional "conflict" is all in its favour. I wish I owned it—but am told it is hard to get despite the relatively recent date (1928) of this translation. The original German novel, I believe, dates from the 1890's.[3] I wish I knew something of Meyrink, but have found almost nothing about him. The only thing of his besides "The Golem" that I've read are some rather mediocre short stories—one of which appeared in W T.[4] I believe he is still living—but doubt if he has written or ever will write anything to compare with this early tour de force.

Thanks for mentioning & describing *The Witches' Tales*. I haven't yet been able to locate a copy on the stands, but shall be on the lookout for it. Whether it will form any sort of market for my stuff remains to be seen. Undoubtedly it's the sort of thing to which the bright & adaptable young commercialists—Long, Wandrei, Bloch, Kuttner, &c. &c.—could readily contribute. I'm duly noting the address, & surely hope the thing survives. At present I've had no time to write anything new, & don't know when I ever shall have. I was glad to see your poem in the Nov. W T,[5] & to learn that some of your fiction is scheduled for the "fan" press.[6] Hope Oatmeal Addlepate Crime (who Bloch tells me is about to emulate his son & transfer his headquarters to N.Y.) will succeed in placing your northern tales. It is surely fortunate when one can secure a financial return from fiction without sacrificing any important part of his literary personality. Good luck with the novel if you ever attempt one! I've thought at times of attempting such a thing, but have never seemed to find quite the right opportunity.

Recent issues of W T show the usual ups & downs—mostly the latter. Sept. was an utter flop—containing nothing really first-rate. In Oct. the high spots were C L M's "Tree of Life" & Bloch's yarn—the Quick, Peirce, & Kuttner efforts deserving honourable mention.[7] In Nov. the fairish tales are those by R E H, McClusky, Bloch, & Whipple.[8] "Black Canaan" was certainly great stuff—&, as you point out, founded on a realistic regional condition. I had heard of this need of watching the niggers in the black belt before, & often wonder how much or little of it northern anti-lynching crusaders realise. It is, or course, confined to the *inner* south as distinguished from the ancient tidewater region.

Meanwhile the "fan" magazines are getting too numerous to keep track of! There must be 10 or 11 of them now—although most are heard of rather than actually seen. You've doubtless received the bulky anniversary F M, plus a couple of *Phantagraphs* from Shepherd & Wollheim. *Fanciful Tales* is slowly taking form, & Conover's *Correspondent* bids fair to be a rather ample venture despite its small page-size. This latter plans to continue the serialisation of my "Sup. Horr. in Lit.", left high & dry by the demise of the good old F F.[9] *Some* day Hill-Billy Crawford *may* git arount ter issuin' his long-postponed *Marvel Tales* & my "Innsmouth".

Thanks for the photographic glimpses of the younger generation—which I am returning, I hope, in better shape than a similar specimen a year or two ago! Both of the tender scions seem to be growing up with marvellous rapidity, & I am astonished at the mature aspect of the Crown Prince—whose generous shock of hair is anything but infantile. It seems only a day or two ago that I first heard of his advent—& now he is racing about like an athlete & on the point of bursting into eloquence! Glad that the summer has benefited his sister—who is now, I presume busy with the studies appropriate to the dignity of her six years. Hope they—& their elders—duly enjoyed the Houghton sojourn—& incidentally, I trust the Isle Royale excursion was successfully managed.

About Thomas Moore—nowadays his work is not extensively read (despite the perennial popularity of his Irish Melodies), but I feel sure he will last after a fashion. He is definitely a minor poet—not in the class with such contemporaries as Coleridge, Wordsworth, Byron, Shelley, & Keats—but I believe he comes far ahead of Campbell, Rogers,[10] & others of the period. Light & airy themes best suited him; & he will always be chiefly associated with his briefer lyrics, where the lilting music of a sprightly prosody & delicately managed tone-colour counts most heavily. One always thinks of *anapaests* in connexion with Moore—& it was not by chance that Dr. Holmes chose that measure in writing a tribute to him on the centennial of his birth. Today Moore's Anacreon translation holds its own as the best, though "Lalla Rookh" is regarded as a bit "dated"—overladen with ornament & extravagant sentiment. One can't, however, deny the occasionally fine colouring & imagery of L. R. "The Loves of the Angels" seems to have faded in reputation. "Alciphron"—either the prose version (called "The Epicurean") or the unfinished verse version—seems to be *forgotten* to a surprising extent. It is very hard to get hold of, & I am infinitely glad to have my tattered paper-bound copy of "The Epicurean". I suppose the *verse* version—"Alciphron"—occurs in many collected editions, hence is not quite so elusive. The future will remember Tom chiefly for Anacreon & the Irish Melodies.

The other night I attended a meeting of the local organisation of amateur astronomers—"The Skyscrapers", which functions more or less under the auspices of Brown U.—& was astonished at its degree of development. Some of the members are really serious scientific observers, & the society is contemplating the purchase of a well-known private observatory whose presiding genius recently died.[11] It has separate meteor, variable star, planet, &c. sections, which hold meetings of their own & report as units, & enjoys the use of the college observatory. At the recent meeting there was an address on early R.I. astronomy, & the reflecting telescope of Joseph Brown—used to observe the transit of Venus on June 3, 1769 & owned by the college since 1780—was exhibited.

I've been hearing recently from young Finlay, the new W T artist. Remarkable chap—only 22, but a proficient limner & very good *poet* to boot! Have also come in touch with a rather quaint egg in San Francisco—one Stuart Morton Boland, who seems to have occult leanings. He is a librarian, has travelled extensively, & has seen many of the real-life prototypes of the Necronomicon. He's just sent me a fine book on primal American civilisations, plus some of his photographs of Aztec-Maya ruins.[12]

Sorry to hear of the canine vicissitudes, & hope better luck in that direction looms ahead. ¶ With best wishes—
Yrs by the Red Hieroglyph
—Ech-Pi-El.

Notes

1. Benjamin Franklin Searight (1872–1937), who died about four months after HPL on 12 July.
2. The five acrostic poems are published in *Letters to Alfred Galpin and Others,* pp. 464–66.
3. In fact, *Der Golem* was first published in 1915.
4. "The Violet Death" (*WT,* July 1935). "The Man in the Bottle" appears in *The Lock and Key Library* (*LL* 428).
5. "The Wizard's Death."
6. It is not clear what works are being referred to. In a letter to RFS dated 12 March 1935, Charles D. Hornig states that he had passed on RFS's "The Haunted Relay" (accepted for *FF*) to Julius Schwartz for *Fantasy Magazine,* but it never appeared there.

7. C. L. Moore, "The Tree of Life"; Robert Bloch, "The Opener of the Way"; Dorothy Quick, "The Lost Door"; Earl Peirce, Jr., "Doom of the House of Duryea"; Henry Kuttner, "The Secret of Kralitz."

8. Robert E. Howard, "Black Hound of Death"; Thorp McClusky, "The Crawling Horror"; Robert Bloch, "The Dark Demon"; Chandler H. Whipple, "Brother Lucifer."

9. HPL had prepared a condensed summary of the installments that appeared in *FF* and made a few revisions to the remaining text for continuation in *Science-Fantasy Correspondent,* but it did not appear.

10. Thomas Campbell (1777–1844), Scottish poet; Samuel Rogers (1763–1855), English poet.

11. HPL refers to the Seagrave Observatory of Frank Evans Seagrave (1859–1934), headquarters of the Skyscrapers, a local astronomy club, now located at 47 Peeptoad Road, North Scituate, RI. Formerly it was located at 119 Benefit Street.

12. See Boland's memoir, "Interlude with Lovecraft," *Acolyte* 3, No. 3 (Summer 1945): 15–18.

[35]   [ALS]

66 College St.,
Providence, R.I.,
Feby. 14, 1937.

Dear Ar-Eph-Es:—

As I take my pen in hand to acknowledge yours of Jany. 12, the pages of the latter rest comfortably before me upon a wire lectern 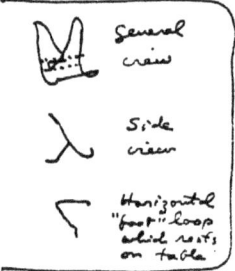 made according to the specifications you so kindly enclosed. Thanks endlessly for the tip! "Why didn't I ever think of such a thing before?" This sort of gadget is just what I've needed to hold MSS., open books, &c. during periods of copying, comparison, parallel consultation & research in general. I've made *two,* & may construct even a third—since I could advantageously use as many as my desk will accomodate. I have varied the pattern by very carefully bending the supporting hook so that the device will not easily sway from side to side—that is, have provided a "foot" which touches the table at more than one point. The accompanying views show my form of the device. The dotted lines in the top diagram indicate strings which cross the frame to hold small books at the bottom. No more useful innovation has dawned on my horizon in recent years, & you may be sure that I shall pass the idea along. Again, sincere thanks for mentioning it!

My sympathy with all the Sea-Brights anent grippe & kindred maladies is very sincere, since I am myself in rotten shape this winter. Not only have I my more or less accustomed hyemal ailment of badly swollen feet & ankles (I have to wear old shoes, cut & stretched), but a touch of the prevailing grippe seems to have descended upon me to complicate matters—manifesting itself very largely as intestinal indigestion & general weakness. This depletion of energy so reduces my speed of doing things that my programme is hopelessly congested . . . . tasks pouring in faster than I can perform them. Fortunately the warm weather (often 60°, 65°, & even 68°) has allowed me to get out-doors a bit for fresh air. I dread the coming of real cold—for that will make me a prisoner & aggravate all troubles. Unlike you, I don't associate warm win-ters with bad health. I'm for all the heat I can get whenever I can get it. Cold & death are to me synonymous—as witness my lines of 25 or so years ago:

> "It was in the cold season
>   It dawn'd on my gaze;
> The mad time of unreason,
>   The brain-numbing days
> When winter, white-sheeted & ghastly, stalks onward to torture & craze."[1]

If I had the cash to get to Florida or the West Indies each year, I'd never see snow, nor face any temperature much under 80°, again! Well—by this time I hope you[r] entire household is largely out of the woods.

I trust your Yuletide was pleasant, even though activity-harassed. Ours here was commendably festive—including a turkey dinner at the boarding-house across the garden, with a congenial cat meandering among the tables & finally jumping up on the window-seat for a nap. We had a tree in front of the hearth in the living-room—its verdant boughs thickly festooned with a tinsel imitation of Florida's best Spanish moss, & its outlines emphasised by a not ungraceful lighting system. Around its base were ranged the Saturnalian gifts—which included (on my side) a hassock tall enough to let me reach the top shelves of my bookcases, & (on my aunt's side) a cabinet of drawers for odds & ends, not unlike my own filing cabinets, but of more ladylike arrangement & aspect. Of outside gifts the most distinctive was perhaps that which came quite unexpectedly from young Conover, the editor of the new "fan mag" (which is, by the way, about to absorb Schwartz's *Fantasy*) in Cambridge, Maryland, down on the Eastern Shore. For lo! when I had removed numberless layers of corru-gated paper & excelsior, what should I find before me but the yellowed & crumbling fragments of *a long-interred human skull!* Verily, a fitting gift from a youthful ghoul to one of the hoary elders of the necropolitan clan! This sight-lessly staring monument of mortality came from an Indian mound not far from the sender's home—a place distinguished by many archaeological exploits on the part of the enterprising editor & his young friends. Its condition is such as to make its reassembling a somewhat ticklish task—so that I may reserve it for the ministrations of some expert mender like Barlow upon the occasion of a future visit. Viewing this shattered yield of the ossuary, the reflective fan-cy strives to evoke the image of him to whom it once belonged. Was it some feathered chieftain who in his day oft ululated in triumph as he counted the tufted scalps sliced from coppery or colonist foes? Or some crafty shaman who with mask & drum called forth from the Great Abyss those shadowy Things which were better left uncalled? This we may never know—unless perchance some incantation droned out of the pages of the Necronomicon, or from that most feared of the Eltdown Shards, will have power to draw strange emanations from the lifeless & centuried clay, & raise up amidst the cobwebs of my ancient study a shimmering mist not without power to speak. In such a case, the revelation might be such that no man hearing it could any longer live save as one of those hapless entities "who laugh, but smile no more."[2]

Your recent reading seems like a very interesting blend. It is long since I last read "Gulliver", but I never cease to relish the blunt force of Swift's style—a thing typical of the early 18th century. I've never read the prose of Eugene Field[3]—indeed, I've always slighted late 19th century authors. But I can well imagine the grace & urbanity of this material, as judged by such of the verse as I do know. My own reading has been almost nil of late, because of the constant demands of other things on my time. I did, though, get through a biography of Thomas Holley Chivers by my next-door (literally) neighbour S. Foster Damon,[4] who is now curator of the Harris Collection at the John Hay Library. This I found tremendously interesting, & my respect for Chivers has ascended soaringly since perusal. Previously the Georgia bard had seemed like a trivial, indeterminate figure somehow connected with Poe. After this interpretation, he stands out as a poet of genuine genius & originality despite the undeniable puerility of much of his work. I can sincerely recommend this volume to anyone wishing an increased understanding of the main stream of American literature. I've never met Prof. Damon (himself a poet of distinction) despite the closeness of the scene of his labours. I have, though, heard several interesting lectures & poetry readings of his.

Glad you like "The Thing on the Doorstep"—which I didn't realise you hadn't seen in MS. I've had no time to read either Jan. or Feb. W T, although I saw the MS. of Rimel's "Disinterment"[5] a year ago. I liked that story exceedingly. The slaying of the doctor & servant may seem abrupt, but I think that the narrator's mounting *fear* does much to explain it. Rimel will get somewhere if he plugs along steadily.

I envy you your sight of the Howard "Hamlet"—which I feel sure is not inferior to the current rival performance,[6] notwithstanding occasional press opinions. Both, I fancy, are excellent. The only Hamlets I've seen—all long ago—were E. H. Sothern, Robert Mantell, & Forbes-Robertson; in each case an old man rather at a disadvantage in portraying the youthful prince. Glad the entire Howard production is worthy of the star—& am interested in the accurate costuming. It is curious how recent the idea of accurate costume is. Garrick often played Macbeth in an 18th century officer's uniform, with well-powdered bag-wig!

Congratulations on inclusion in the anthology![7] I don't know anything concerning Tumasel, but it's to his credit that he doesn't charge his contributors for space. Some anthologies have become a veritable racket preying on poetic vanity. Congrats also on the sale to *Witches Tales*.[8] If you think the pay is bad, pray be informed that Hugo the Rat often parallelled it in the old days, & that according to some reports *Amazing Stories* now does little better! I haven't yet been able to locate a copy of the new venture.

Still more congratulations on the new feline member of the household—who may, I trust, grow up to be as revered a matriarch as Mrs. Spotty Perkins (mother of my late friends Samuel & John Perkins, & the Earl of Minto) at the boarding-house across the garden. Glad the newcomer gets along well with the younger generation—& imagine that the latter will take much delight in her presence. As for the matter of *demonstrativeness*—I've never given it much attention, since the most I ask of a feline colleague is just to be around & look graceful. However, I fancy most cats become more or less visibly attached to those who pay them attention & treat them with scrupulous consideration. I am so fond of cats that I can't help making a great deal of them, & they usually seem to recognise me as a sort of natural friend. I always play with them extensively—usually with a long, slender branch, or a spool or piece of paper on the end of a string. A hassock is a great aid to feline sport—using it as a screen or barrier behind which to draw . . . slowly & tantalisingly . . . the spool on which one's furry playmate's eyes are interestedly centred. Cats also enjoy *tunnels* formed of rugs or newspapers. One favourite pastime of theirs is to leap at anything which moves or bulges mysteriously beneath a covering—as a hand creeping under a rug & forming a curious moving mountain. Considerate attention always pleases a cat. I never evict one from a chair, or disturb his slumbers or repose. People have compared me to Mohammed, who once cut off the loose part of one of his sleeves rather than disturb the cat who had curled up to sleep on it. Tones of voice are likewise influential. I always talk to cats individually, & in accents of such obvious friendliness that they seem to recognise me as a fraternity-brother. And I always acknowledge gestures of consideration on their part—talking pleasantly, stroking them, or scratching them gently under the chin when they jump up in my lap, rub around my ankles, or otherwise express esteem. I am also generous with catnip, keeping a supply always on hand for the regaling of my favourite callers. I generally scatter it on an outspread newspaper in a certain spot on the floor—& my friends have come to know the old gentleman so well that they always make for that spot without delay upon entering Grandpa's study. In the end, an average kittie will always be notably friendly toward any person whom he can remember as always speaking & acting considerately, & never speaking or acting harshly. When I moved to #66 there was a fine old neighbour cat (now, alas, moved away) whose fear of strangers was notorious. However—beginning with friendly discourse at a distance I had the old fellow in three months so that he would roll over on my approach & play like a kitten! Good old Peter Randall! I certainly miss him now that I no longer see him & his brother sprawled on the shed roof beneath my window!

I feel rather well repaid for that 60-hour job, despite the cuts, because of the favourable manner in which the book was received. The "author" tells me that it was recently praised over the radio in a review by the critic of the *Milwaukee Journal*. Did I tell you of the appearance of the volume? It is gratifyingly well-printed & bound, & fills me with envy as I contrast it with the lousy mess which Hill-Billy Crawford made of my poor old "Innsmouth".

About the placing of adverbs with verbs in future, perfect, pluperfect or future-perfect tenses—my own instinctive custom & preference seems to be the direct opposite of your own. In the absence of any barrier against the separation of auxiliary & principal verbs (the absence, that is, of any rule corresponding to that of the split infinitive), I tend to say "I have always been" rather than "I always have been". Just why I do this, I cannot be certain. It merely seems to me a trifle more natural & idiomatic as judged by common usage down the centuries. Somehow it seems to me in most cases to make a better sentence rhythm. Certainly, it is typical enough of the 18th century, which has influenced my style enormously, & whose prose I believe to be the most graceful & perspicuous ever written. In prose as well as verse I lay great stress on *rhythm*—including a kind of rhythm bound up inextricably with the meaning & closely dependent upon the latter's turns & modulations. But in all these finer points one can do no more than observe & emulate the best literary models. I may add that even the pedantic Woolley, in his extravagantly prim "Handbook of Composition", has no objection to offer to the splitting of a verb & its auxiliary.

About my woodland walks—no, far from being on the outskirts, #66 is on a hill which plunges straight down to the central business district! The secret of the country's accessibility is the irregular shape of the city—which puts open fields within about three miles of the civic centre in two directions. In youth I *did* live near what was *then* the edge of the compact section, & as a result have always preserved something of our ancestral rural outlook toward nature.

Congratulations on the newly-discovered chess-player! I am indifferent toward all games—including chess—but if I *were* to enjoy any, it would surely be something as flexible & traditional as this ancient & thoughtful pastime. Glad you have your grandfather's set of men, which adds to the interest. We have several old sets, including a Japanese one which might interest antiquarians. That Egyptian set you describe must be fascinating.

About Klarkash-Ton's carvings—I can do better than merely *describe* them. Under separate cover you'll find some of his own drawings of several. Sorry these don't include the most bizarre & picturesque. He expects to have an exhibition of them in Sacramento soon. The drawings are for return at your leisure.

Glad the younger generation is active mentally & physically despite the season's maladies. The Crown Prince's human fly proclivities must have their disconcerting side (sympathy anent the lamp!), but they form such a sign of healthy activity that I fancy one hates to discourage them!

All good wishes—

     Yrs most sincerely—

       Ech-Pi-El

P.S. Old de Castro has gone to California & is visiting young Kuttner.

Notes

1. "The City" (1919), ll. 6–10 (the first line, however, reads "I remember the season").

2. This passage is nearly identical to that in HPL's letters to Robert Bloch, August Derleth, Henry Kuttner, James F. Morton, CAS, and others.

3. The only volume by Field owned by RFS was *Child Verses*.

4. S[amuel] Foster Damon (1893–1971), Harvard graduate who since 1927 was a professor of English at Brown University. For many years he was the curator of the Harris Collection of American Poetry and Plays at the John Hay Library. He accepted HPL's papers from RHB.

5. The stories by Rimel and HPL appeared in *WT*, January 1937.

6. In 1936, Leslie Howard (1893–1943) directed, produced, and starred in *Hamlet* on Broadway. In early 1937, Lawrence Olivier starred in the leading role.

7. "The Road" by RFS, included in *In the Realm of Poesy: An Anthology of Modern Verse*, ed. Charles Leon Tumasel (New York: Charles Leon Tumasel, 1937), 16.

8. *Witch's Tales* accepted RFS's "The Formula," but the magazine lasted for only two issues (November and December 1936), neither of which contained RFS's story.

Appendix

E. Hoffmann Price

[A Curry Recipe]

[from EHP to HPL, TLS
Postmarked 10 March 1933]

East Indian Curry: a dish prepared perfectly in[ ]but 2 places: holy Shamballah, and the Throne Room.

Directions: Into a small pot put a tablespoon of butter, brown a finely minced, small onion, *then* a finely minced clove of garlic; add sliced mutton (raw or roasted) veal, chicken, as you wish; add suitable amount of curry powder (conglomerate of from 5 to 10 spices--coriander, turmeric, ginger, cardamon [*sic*], cloves, pepper, god knows what, including fenugreek) and sauté the meat (if raw, until done; if previously cooked or roasted, until permeated with the fragrance of spices) then add 4 cloves, a cup of soup stock, let simmer 20–30 minutes, then add cup of cream of *evaporated* milk, thickened with spoonful dissolved cornstarch; stirr [*sic*] smooth, and when well wobbled around, you are ready to serve, by dumping the tawny, golden curry into the center of a fortress of cooked rice, which forms a parapet about the edge of a platter. May be garnished with sliced, cooked eggs.

Curry may be made, substituting cooked eggs for meat.

A glass of sherry may be added just before serving. Optional.

Lemon rind may be grated into the simmering hell brew. Optional.

It is a dish for gods and demons, and for men also. Oh, divine Curry! It is the peer of dishes, and withal simple.

Robert Ervin Howard

Gentlemen, this is the hand that shook the hand of Robert E. Howard! Line forms on the right, quit shoving, and don't step on the women and children. My claim to be the only writer who ever met Robert E. Howard, face to face, in the heart of the post oak belt of Texas, has not thus far been refuted.

Get your road maps. Cross Plains is thirty-two miles from Cisco, which town is where highways U.S. 80 and 283 intersect. From whatever direction you approach Cross Plains, you have a piece of driving to do. I say it was worth doing.

He was broad and towering, with a bluff, tanned face and a big, hearty hand, and a voice which was surprisingly soft and easy, not at all the bull-bellow one might expect of the creator of Conan and those other sabre-hackers. I should like to speak of Howard's parents, with whom he lived, and to whose home he welcomed me, but I must stick to telling of the man who made Cross Plains famous.

For the next few days, I was busy trying to combine two images: that of the actual man, and that of the one who loomed up in those stirring yarns, and in those salty letters I'd been getting from him since 1928. The synthesis was never effected. As a matter of fact, writers rarely do resemble the fan-image!

Howard's expression was boyish, not having yet squared off into angles; his blue eyes, somewhat prominent, had a wide-openness which did not suggest anything of the man's keen wit and agile fancy. That first picture persists: a powerful, solid, round-faced fellow, kindly and somewhat stolid. At times, I got the fantastic notion that the father rather than the son must have been the author. I cannot remember ever having met another man who had eyes as penetrating as Dr. Howard's; clear, ice-blue, vibrant with expression, seconding his voice and gestures. White haired, shaggy browed, a face marked in rugged lines: the father's speech and spirit seemed an outward expression of the inner something which made the son a writer.

The post oak belt, so called because of the stunted trees of the region, does not have the New England literary tradition. A writer, I gathered, is regarded as a harmless freak. That Howard earned considerable sums, right from the start, when he was fifteen, and eventually better than doubled the figure set forth as the average income of a pulp fictioneer, merely made him conspicuous. He must always have felt himself to be, whether he wanted to or not, someone and something apart from the standard model Texan. While guiding me from the house to the barbershop, he said, abruptly, "Ed, I am God damn proud to have you visit me."

He meant precisely what he said, and he said exactly what he meant, no more, no less. Since I was a fellow freak, he didn't have to mince around. I said, "I've looked forward to this a long time, but I fail to see what you have to be proud about!"

"It's this way," he explained. "Nobody thinks I amount to much, so I am glad to have a chance to show these sons of ——s that a successful writer will drive a thousand miles to hell and gone out of his way to see me."

As a matter of fact, I'd spent a year starving. I'd even quit writing and tried making expenses by repairing Fords for the Osage Indians, up in Oklahoma. But since Howard had predicted two years previously that I'd make a go of it, he considered the issue settled: I was a successful writer!

To this day, I do not know how seriously he underrated his standing in Cross Plains. I do however know that on the day of his death, the local paper published as a reprint from a magazine, one of his last yarns. Between that 6000 word piece, and the obituary, Robert E. Howard got more space than any other citizen of Cross Plains ever got, before or after. Yet, during his life, he did undoubtedly feel that the townsmen wondered why the son of a man as esteemed and solid as Dr. I. M. Howard fooled around writing for magazines.

In the sense I have implied, Robert Howard was without a doubt a lonely person. This feeling of isolation often revealed itself. Once he asked, with characteristic abruptness, "Ed, have you any enemies?"

His tone told me that he had lots of them, that he expected my answer to be yes, and that purely rhetorical query was to start me off on a subject vital to him. In many a letter he had told me of the post oak region, a land of hard working, hard fighting, hard hating people, a land of feuds which, even in his time, might well have equaled the heights of the Hatfield-McCoy tradition. So when I answered, "Not that I know of," Howard was stumped.

It was plain that he accepted my statement on faith, rather than plausibility.

Howard lived in a realm of wonder and fantasy. After hearing my reasons for considering certain early yarns, such as "Kings of the Night," "Mirrors of Tuzun Thune," "Shadow Kingdom," and the "Brule the Spear Slayer" epoch, far superior to the Conan series, he agreed and said, "I dreamed them, so they're naturally more realistic than those I deliberately wrote."

He composed instinctively, without any conscious attention to form. He told me, "Of every three stories, I scrap two and offer the third; it's easier than trying for conscious technique which would give me perhaps only a third as many stories, all of which would sell. What in hell's the difference, I like to write!"

Howard's westerns are superior to all but his few outstanding fantasy yarns, and because characters like Buckner J. Grimes were drawn from life, and not cooked up from fancy. Those characters, for all their Paul Bunyanish extravagance, are real, speaking the speech of the country. Dr. Howard and his son often garnished their conversation with quips and phrases which I had already, or would later read in a published western.

The news of Howard's death hit me between the eyes; but when I picked up the newspaper which contained his last published story, I forgot that the author was dead. For the time of my reading, he lived, and I was able to laugh, and right down to my ankles. Gentlemen, when you write copy which can do that for your friends, you are really writing!

It was a first person story; Buckner J. Grimes, and Robert E. Howard were for the time one and the same person. For a little while, the author had come back from the dead. Chaw on that for a moment.

During his thirty years of life, he lived in two worlds. The transition from one plane to the other must have seemed far more natural to him than to the ordinary person.

He loved the whopping story; and he said of Sir Richard Burton, "Ten to one he was a damn liar in a lot of respects which is what makes a good story teller!"

Howard once told me that whenever, as a boy, he ran out of fiction, he'd saddle up his horse, and ride out to raid the skimpy libraries of country schoolhouses; he'd jimmy a window, make his selection, stuff it into a gunny sack, and gallop home. Maybe this was one of his whoppers, but if it isn't true, it ought to be.

Though he drank beer, he refused to smoke, and the explanation he offered me, very solemnly, was this: "The most contemptible son of a —— I know of smokes, so I won't!" Then he added, "Well, I'm not any too consistent; I breathe, and so does that dirty —!"

And now I must re-read "Man-Eating Jeopard," for to read it is to hear Robert E. Howard. The trouble is, I can't answer back, I can't tell him that within a few weeks after his death, I sold my first adventure story, and to one of the magazines in which he had been a top flight contributor, and that a month or two later, I started a series of westerns, inspired largely by his inimitable characters. These were not imitations, because Howard couldn't be imitated, yet they follow the pattern: and the hero, Simon Bolivar Grimes, is my version of Buckner Jeopardy Grimes of Knife River, Texas, who as everyone who reads the story and knew the author must know, was Robert Howard as burlesqued by himself.

My series of western burlesques has an unusual vitality: in seven years, I have sold twenty-four of the sequence without a rejection, and since we all know that no imitation could be so durable, I leave it to you to draw your own inferences as to the source of this character's appeal. Robert Ervin Howard encouraged me during the tough days of my start, and he has been contributing ever since; with Texas stubbornness he still lives.

Correspondence Regarding "Through the Gates of the Silver Key"

[1]   [TLS] [EHP to FW]

Irvington, New York.
August 7, 1933.

Dear Plato:

I am sending you a story entitled THROUGH THE GATES OF THE SILVER KEY, 14,000 words. My name on the by-line is there mainly on account of HPL's uncompromising New England conscience. I did suggest the story, and did write a tentative draft; but Lovecraft's changes were so sweeping (and warranted in every respect) and have introduced such a complete Lovecraft atmosphere—as indeed the work demanded, a fact that became painfully apparent to me early in the tentative draft—that were it not for my more flexible conscience, I would have to quarrel with him about my appearing on the by-line at all.

Some of the spatial and dimensional concepts are mine, and two or three passages of the original have been incorporated into the present text almost unchanged; yet, after all, it is so much a Lovecraft story, and so little mine that it seems of all things the most natural to sit here and tell you that in my opinion this is one of the most self consistent, carefully worked out pictures of the cosmos and hyperspace that I have ever read. My first reading of the completed job was in HPL's utterly inimitable script—yet despite that severe handicap, I found its fascination become more and more compelling. I find no loopholes; and the entire fantasy world of Randolph Carter is now completed. That strange, charming character who has from time to time wandered through Weird Tales, and was left in an ambiguous position in THE SILVER KEY, has now a more rounded history; and, as I said before, despite my apparent position as collaborator, the work is really so little of mine that I can with all propriety sit along the side lines and applaud the performance, commend it to your attention.

The caravan marches on or about September first, to dig in down South, where expenses will be low enough to permit me to weather the shellacking this rash eastern trip has administered. A month's rent is paid up in advance—unconsumed rent, *c'est á dire*—and a bale of rare & costly Persian carpets which may in a pinch be converted into ham sandwiches unless Otis comes to the rescue with one of his every-so-often miracles. Later in the season, however, when & if things pick up, I hope to take a jaunt to Chicago; but at present I must deny myself the long anticipated reunion with the Pious Companions, [of the Prophet—ED.] and look forward to the bounty of Allah. Despite my efforts, production since leaving New Orleans has been much less than it should have been—and I was about sold out when I left New Orleans—so I'm put in the position of having to replenish Kline's stock of fiction, and hope that Allah, the Generous, sees fit to offer a lakh of rupees in lieu of the present lack.

In the meanwhile, my salaam to the Royal Family, & the Pious Companions, One & All.   S.S.S. Q. B.S.M.—*

مهدي طاولس

[P.S.] This may properly belong to your file on G. of S.K. Keep it—or return it—it is immaterial. But one of us should keep it as a record until the matter is settled. I hope the story sells.

---

*Su somiso servidor que besa sus manos, or your obedient servant who kisses your hands.—ED.

[2]   [TLS]   [FW to HPL]

[Weird Tales . . .]

Aug. 17, 1933

Mr. H. P. Lovecraft
66 College St.
Providence, R.I.

Dear Mr. Lovecraft:

I have carefully read THROUGH THE GATES OF THE SILVER KEY and am almost overwhelmed by the colossal scope of the story. It is cyclopean in its daring and titanic in its execution (though not bungled as were the affairs of the Cyclops and the Titans).

But I am afraid to offer it to our readers. Many there would be, without any doubt whatever, who would go into raptures of esthetic delight while reading the story; but just as certainly there would be a great many—probably a clear majority—of our readers who would be unable to wade through it. These would find the descriptions and discussions of polydimensional space poison to their enjoyment of the tale. The story is so much more than a piece of fiction, and so far transcends not only the experiences of the readers, but even their wildest dreams, that they would have no point of contact with the ideas and thoughts presented in this opus.

I know only of two possibly markets for this story, other than WEIRD TALES; and it may be worth submitting it to them, on the slim chance that they might buy it. These are the two new magazines of weird fiction. One is the old ASTOUNDING STORIES, which has been sold to Street & Smith by T. R. Foley who bought it at the auction of the Clayton publications. Street & Smith are going to use weird fiction, as well as pseudo-scientific stories. The other new weird magazine has not yet been named, but it is to be put out by American Fiction Magazines, 205 E. 42nd St., New York

It may seem strange that I reject a story which arouses my admiration as much as THROUGH THE GATES OF THE SILVER KEY; but with business as poor as it is now, I feel that we cannot risk discouraging so many readers from buying the magazine, merely by printing a story that is so utterly alien to even their wildest dreams and reveries that they are incapable of comprehending it—let alone appreciating it.

I am returning this story under separate cover by express collect; and I assure you that never have I turned down a story with more regret than in this case.

Best regards.

Sincerely yours,
F. W.
Wright.

FW:RG

[3]   [TLS] [EHP to FW]

Irvington on Hudson, New York.

Aug. 19th.

Dear Plato:

Sorry you can't use Gates of Silver Key. Your praise of Lovecraft's work is certainly gratifying. I myself was overwhelmed when I read what he had done with my start, a 6000 word job that was hardly more than a mathematical treatise, setting forth the thesis of hyper-dimensions. I know I was stumped; knew I could never put it into acceptable or even interesting form, and so turned it over to him, carte blanche.

It returned to me in the[ ]form you saw, except it was handwritten. Though I was technically a "collaborator", I touched not a line. I knew he had made such a worthy job of a thing that was but a plot-germ, virtually a mathematical theorem minus the +- signs and x's, that it could not stand and did not need any collaboration.

As for other markets—which you so generously suggest—I am sure now, without even second thought, that they would not and could not consider it. It is not "snappy" enough, not enough synthetic "horror". Maybe he will want to try it; but that's his business. When I typed it, I did mine.

I fancy that perhaps when business improves, and you are in a position to gamble, you may want to try it out. Cthul[h]u made a bit hit; and other monumental tales—was it Whisperer in the [*sic*] Darkness? Well, several have had a cosmic sweep. I am inclined to think that when the story business has regained its footing—which surely it will, else I am hopelessly damned & doomed—Lovecraft's epic might justify your risking the space, however much I am forced to agree with your contentions as to present conditions. I am also inclined to think that should you later feel able to use the story, it will be available—as you have thus far led the field in daring fiction of the Lovecraft type, as distinguished from the conventional ghost–vampire–black magic line.

The richness of praise is rightfully Lovecraft's—for after all, anyone can fictionize a differential equation to put one asleep as rapidly as the unfictionized, whereas he is the only one I know who could even remotely approach the job as it stands. Maybe Clark Ashton Smith could have done it; probably he could. And there the list ends. Still, I bask in my own private spotlight: I conceived the basic idea (though devoid of all that marvellous REALISM which so effectively supports the[ ]fantasy) and secondly, had the wisdom to know I was utterly incompetent to finish the task. Thus, but for Lovecraft, a real piece of literature would not have been produced or every attempted—but I did prod him to[ ]the task—so I'll take a bow as an accessory before the fact, and express my appreciation of your kind words.

[. . .]

In the meanwhile, best wishes and pious salutations[.]

[illegible]

A linoleum cut of Price

A proof made by Rimel, which Lovecraft modified. On verso, Lovecraft has written "would not a thickening of the neck to this extent make a better proportioned figure?" See p. 203.

Alvin Earl Perry

A Biographical Sketch of E. Hoffmann Price

Picture, if you will, a man five feet seven inches tall; with grayish eyes that vary in color according to the weather; dark hair; and an olive complexion inclined to be ruddy. Add a moustache and a prominent nose, and you see E. Hoffmann Price in person. Mr. Price insists that, while the above nasal organ is perhaps smaller insofar as sheer bulk is concerned than Edmond Hamilton's it certainly has the more unique and classical curves. This matter of noses is the source of an intense rivalry between these two fantasy favorites.

In 1898, in the town of Fowler, California, E. Hoffmann Price was born. He remained in the sun-shiny state for the next 19 years, going to school, delivering newspapers, working as an usher in a movie theater, jerking soda in a candy store, and trying his hand at numerous other methods of turning a few pennies.

He joined the Fifteenth Cavalry in June, 1917; and in 1919, while attending the colorful but unheard-of AEF University—an institution founded after the Armistice more to keep the soldiers away from cognac and the ladies of France than to improve their minds—he passed the entrance examinations for West Point. Four years later, in '23, he was graduated from the academy on the Hudson.

Commissioned in the coast artillery, Price was there when he began writing. His first story? Well, he wrote two tales concurrently, a page or two of one, and a few pages of the other, finally finishing both first drafts and revising them alternately. Thus both were begun and completed at about the same time. "Triangle with Variations" (*Droll Stories*, May, 1924) was the first to sell—for $24—and its running mate, "Rajah's Gift," was published a short time later, in *Weird Tales*. So Price's first yarn seems to have been two yarns—Siamese twins, you might say.

He continued with the coast artillery until a fine offer came his way in the form of a position as Superintendent of an Acetylene plant. He took it.

Then, upon losing this job in 1932, he entered the writing field for the first time as a true professional, and has been at it ever since.

Mr. Price has a passion for motoring, planning extensive trips months before it is possible to undertake them. During these jaunts, he has met, among others, H. P. Lovecraft, Frank B. Long, Seabury Quinn, Harold Ward, Edmond Hamilton, Jack Williamson, Kirk Mashburn, Otis A. Kline, S. Gordon Gurwitt, Robert E. Howard, Clark Ashton Smith, Robert S. Carr, and Farnsworth Wright.

Around 500,000 words come from Price's pen—or Dictaphone—each year, and his ambition is to raise that to a million. He has had tales in *Droll Stories*, *Weird Tales*, England's *Sovereign Magazine*, *Oriental Stories*, *Magic Carpet*, *All Detective*, *Detective Fiction Weekly*, *Nickel Detective*, *Real Detective*, *Popular Detective*, *Spicy Mystery*, *New Detective*, *True Gang Life*, *Five Novels*, *Ten Detective Aces*, *Strange Detective Stories*, *Clues*, *Super Detective*, *Alibi*, *Udderworld*, *Spicy Adventure*, *Spicy Detective*, *Terror Tales*, *Spy Stories*, *Spy Novels*, and *Thrilling Mystery*.

Mr. Price has seen most of the things on this old globe worth seeing; some time ago, he sailed from San Francisco to Honolulu, thence to Guam and Manila. Later he moved up the China Sea along the coast of Formosa; then north to Japan. Besides serving in the Fifteenth Cavalry in France, he was with this unit in the Phillipines and on the Mexican Border. He has seen the ballerinas of Manila, the geisha girls of Japan, Waikiki Beach, the leper island, the Arizona desert, the fortified city of Bayonne, and all the Pyrenees country in Southern France.

He picks chilli con carne, East Indian curry, sheeshkabab, pilaf, and Creole gumbo as his favorite foods. And he likes Turk Brandy, Bacardi Rum, Jerez de la Frontera sherry, Burgundy, and Chablis. A big beer with a New Orleans poor boy sandwich is just about the "nerts" in his opinion. As to smoking, he enjoys cigars, Bull Durham, and the Turkish water pipe. And he can drink Turkish coffee any time, day or night.

Writing is work to Mr. Price; and hard work at that. For this reason he can't say which story he most enjoyed setting down, tho he does mention "The Girl from Samarkand", "Pale Hands", "Saladin's Throne Rug", "Tarbis of the Lake", "Million Dollar Legs", and "Plunder from Kurdistan" as being his own favorites among his yarns. He also got a big kick out of writing "Makeda's Cousin" wherein Pierre d'Artois, Ismeddin the Darvish, and Glenn Farrell are featured in a bedroom scene in the Arabian desert. What an imagination this man must have!

He used to take part in fencing competitions, with the dueling sword as well as being on various pistol teams; but because of the voluminous writing he is doing now, active participation in these sports has become impossible. As a spectator, he enjoys polo and football.

While he isn't especially an avid fan, he believes that Clark Gable and Claudette Colbert are his movie favorites. No particular author stands out his literary idol, because he likes so many, each in his own field.

Concerning the merits of his own works, this famous soldier of fortune says: "I'm sure that none of my stories have any literary value. If anyone were to remember them a century from now, then I would be convinced that they did have literary value. Time, I believe, is the only test of literary merit. Passing favor and criticism mean very little. Anyway, my endeavor is to entertain. While of course I wish my stories did have literary value, I am quite content that they are entertaining. Or maybe they aren't entertaining. Anyway, editors buy them, and somebody probably reads them."

Versatility would be Mr. Price's middle name if Hoffmann wasn't. He can and does write anything from weird fiction to sex stuff and has a different style for each type. He admits, tho, that it's becoming harder and harder each year for him to write first class fantastic tales; in fact, to quote him , ". . . in another year, I probably will be as extinct as the dodo, as far as weird fiction is concerned . . . I do at times still write them [fantastic yarns], but they won't sell anymore I guess tastes in weird fiction are changing, or the fans have booted me in the pants." That shows you how modest he is; the fans booted him in the pants, indeed! That, he may rest assured, will never happen to him—he is as popular as ever!

Long may E. Hoffmann Price, West Point graduate, write stories for our enjoyment!

Richard F. Searight

Winds

The North Wind blares a gelid, lee-born roar,
Down from the arctic wastes where sit the ghosts
Of one-eyed Odin, bloody-handed Thor,
In frost-bound silence with their warrior hosts.

The East Wind murmurs softly through the night
Of dank and noisome things, and evil lore,
Old in the days when Atlar rose to might,
And Chaldic magic ruled a world of gore.

The South Wind breathes a pestilential dirge.
It whispers of corruption and the tomb;
Of life in death, and mankind's biting urge
To gain the secrets hidden in Time's womb.

The West Wind keens a warning cry of hate,
As, from the boundless voids of sea and sky,
It sweeps upon a race bowed low by fate,
Yet striving still to gain the heights or die.

The Dead World

I dreamed I stood atop a craggy verge
And scanned long miles of dreary, jumbled waste
That stretched, sharp-etched in airless, frozen surge
Beneath the sable, star-strewn vault it faced.

Black empty mouths of craters, grim and cold,
Yawned bottomless, abysmal pits of slag
Amid the desert stretching fold on fold
To distant jagged peak and sharp-thrust crag.

The desolation flooded through my soul—
No living thing relieved the dismal rifts
Of long-past cataclysms; the bleak roll
Of upflung ridge and tangled lava drifts.

It was as if a Titan band had played
With this dead world when it was young and fair,
And tired of the sport when they had made
A ruin and a wreckage past repair.

The cold of outer voids lay like a blight
Of cosmic hate across the planet's face;
And from the riven features I took flight
To seek relief in fairer realms of space.

Impressions of the Planets—Venus

I dreamed I stood upon a rockbound shore,
Drenched by a ceaseless spume of bitter sprays
High flung from nameless seas beneath, which roar
Against the ribbed fangs of stone always.

An acrid, sulphide fog hung close, and bound
The shallow sea and spongy grey terrain;
The moaning breakers voiced the only sound
To join the endless drip of falling rain.

A mist-wrapped world where life is yet to rise
In dim and distant aeons far in Time,
When heat shall wane and clouds desert the skies,
And destiny achieve its goal sublime.

The Wizard's Death

The end draws near, and weakness weights my limbs;
My step is leaden, and my keen eye dims.
No longer may my arts contrive a way
To hold the demon from his tryst with me—
Aye, soon will come the fiend to claim his fee:
The price I pledged him on a long-past day.

Is there no way I may evade this doom?
Evade, and pass in quiet to my tomb,
And in the saving arms of death sink down?
Ah, must I pay the frightful toll I swore,
'Mid ghastly rites of hideous primal lore,
Should be the price of sorcerous renown?

Nay, come! Rise up from grim Plutonian deep,
Ye lesser Forms of Evil. Rise and creep
Before my presence. Say there is a way. . . .
Ye will not speak? Ye smirk and mock at me,
And gibbering, titter with disloyal glee?
Then, go! I'll gain my grave as best I may. . . .

The final bitter dark begins to close;
My waning vigor fades and fails, and those,
    My hasty plans, are rendered null. Now life,
As sweet to wizards as to common men,
Unversed in that dark ill beyond their ken,
    Must vanish, with its victories and strife.

My breath grows short, and like a sable pall
The horror-ridden shadows spread and fall;
Now through the whispering blackness stirs a stray
    And vagrant icy breath, and crimson eyes
Glare close and closer. Lo! I strive to rise—
The taloned paws have seized me—*aye, I pay!*

The Road

Beneath the summer stars' wan light,
Beneath the towering leaf-bent elms,
The road lies broad and shining white—
A mystic path to faery realms.

There winds' caressing fingers play
A leafy, rustling song serene,
And calm and sweet contentment lay
A benediction on the scene.

Small dwellings nestle near the side,
Set back beyond dense-foliaged walls,
And from the windows, opened wide,
Float cheery words and laughing calls.

And strains of music, sweetly faint,
Breathe through the aromatic night
Where bowered seats and arbors quaint
Shrink shyly from the roamer's sight.

Along the roadway, winding far
Amongst the ancient, whispering trees,
There stands a faery door ajar:
There doubt and pain and sorrow cease.

Glossary of Frequently Mentioned Names

Anger, William Frederick (1921–1982), weird fiction fan and late correspondent of HPL. For HPL's letters to him, see *Letters to Robert Bloch and Others* (2015).

Baldwin, F[ranklin] Lee (1913–1987), weird fiction fan and late associate of HPL. He wrote columns for the *Fantasy Fan* and wrote a biographical sketch of HPL for *Fantasy Magazine* (April 1935). For HPL's letters to him, see *Letters to F. Lee Baldwin, Duane W. Rimel, and Nils Frome* (2016).

Barlow, R[obert] H[ayward] (1918–1951), author and collector. As a teenager he corresponded with HPL and acted as his host during two long visits in the summers of 1934 and 1935. In the 1930s he wrote several works of weird and fantasy fiction, some in collaboration with HPL. HPL appointed him his literary executor. He assisted August Derleth and Donald Wandrei in preparing the early HPL volumes for Arkham House. In the 1940s he went to Mexico and became a distinguished anthropologist. For HPL's letters to him, see *O Fortunate Floridian* (2007).

Bates, Hiram Gilmore ("Harry") III (1900–1981), editor of *Strange Tales* and *Astounding Stories*, author of "Farewell to the Master," the basis of the movie *The Day the Earth Stood Still* (1951).

Binder, Eando, pen-name of science fiction authors and brothers, **Earl Andrew Binder** (1904–1965) and **Otto Binder** (1911–1974).

Blackwood, Algernon (1869–1951), prolific British author of weird and fantasy tales whose work HPL greatly admired when he read it in 1924.

Bloch, Robert (1917–1994), author of weird and suspense fiction who came into correspondence with HPL in 1933. HPL tutored him in the craft of writing during their four-year association. For HPL's letters to him, see *Letters to Robert Bloch and Others* (2015).

Brobst, Harry K[ern] (1909–2010), late associate of HPL who moved to Providence in 1932 and saw HPL regularly thereafter.

Burks, Arthur J. (1898–1974), voluminous contributor to *WT* and other pulp magazines.

Coates, Walter J[ohn] (1880–1941), amateur journalist, printer, editor of *Driftwind,* and staunch advocate of the literature of Vermont.

Cole, Edward H[arold] (1892–1966), longtime amateur associate of HPL, living in the Boston area; editor of the *Olympian.*

Conover, Willis, Jr. (1920–1996), weird fiction fan who edited the *Science-Fantasy Correspondent* (1936–37, 1975) and was a late correspondent of HPL.

He later wrote the poignant memoir *Lovecraft at Last* (1975). For HPL's letters to him, see *Letters to Robert Bloch and Others* (2015).

Cook, W. Paul (1880–1948), publisher of the *Monadnock Monthly*, the *Vagrant*, and other amateur journals; a longtime amateur journalist, printer, and lifelong friend of HPL. He first visited HPL in 1917, and it was he who urged HPL to resume writing fiction after a hiatus of nine years. In 1927 Cook published the *Recluse*, containing HPL's "Supernatural Horror in Literature."

Crawford, William L[evy] (1911–1984), editor of *Marvel Tales* and *Unusual Stories* and publisher of the Visionary Publishing Company, which issued HPL's *The Shadow over Innsmouth* (1936).

de Castro, Adolphe [Danziger] (1859–1959), dentist, diplomat, author, co-translator with Ambrose Bierce of Richard Voss's *The Monk and the Hangman's Daughter*, and correspondent of HPL. HPL revised his "The Last Test" and "The Electric Executioner." For HPL's letters to him, see *Letters to Alfred Galpin and Others* (2020).

Derleth, August W[illiam] (1909–1971), author of weird tales and also a long series of regional and historical works set in his native Wisconsin. After HPL's death, he and Donald Wandrei founded the publishing firm of Arkham House to preserve HPL's work in book form. For HPL's letters to him, see *Essential Solitude* (2008).

Dunsany, Lord (Edward John Moreton Drax Plunkett) (1878–1957), Anglo-Irish writer of fantasy tales whose work notably influenced HPL after HPL read it in 1919.

Dwyer, Bernard Austin (1897–1943), weird fiction fan and would-be writer and artist, living in West Shokan, NY; correspondent of HPL. For HPL's letters to him, see *Letters to Maurice W. Moe and Others* (2018).

Edkins, Ernest A[rthur] (1867–1946), longtime amateur journalist with whom HPL began corresponding in 1932. HPL persuaded him to rejoin the amateur journalism movement, and Edkins subsequently edited several issues of the journal *Causerie.*

Finlay, Virgil (1914–1971), one of the great weird artists of his time and a prolific contributor of artwork to the pulps; late correspondent of HPL.

Gamwell, Annie E[meline] P[hillips] (1866–1941), HPL's younger maternal aunt, living with him at 66 College Street (1933–37). For HPL's letters to her, see *Letters to Family and Family Friends* (2020).

Greene, Marc Tiffany (1885–1966), reporter who covered the Far East, wrote some fiction. Regular contributor to *Quarterly Review.*

Hall, Desmond W[inter] (1911–1992) assistant editor (1931–33) of *Strange Tales* and associate editor of *Astounding Stories.*

Hodgson, William Hope (1877–1918), British author of weird fiction whose work had fallen into obscurity until it was rediscovered in the 1930s, largely through the efforts of H. C. Koenig.

Hornig, Charles D[erwin] (1916–1999), editor of the *Fantasy Fan* (1933–35) and associate editor of *Wonder Stories*.

Howard, Robert E[rvin] (1906–1936), prolific Texas author of weird and adventure tales for *Weird Tales* and other pulp magazines; creator of the adventure hero Conan of Cimmeria. He and HPL corresponded voluminously from 1930 to 1936. He committed suicide when he heard of his mother's impending death. For their joint correspondence, see *A Means to Freedom* (2009).

James, M[ontague] R[hodes] (1862–1936), celebrated British writer of ghost stories much admired by HPL. His *Collected Ghost Stories* appeared in 1931.

Kirk, George (1898–1962), member of the Kalem Club. He published *Twenty-one Letters of Ambrose Bierce* (1922), ran the Chelsea Bookshop in New York, and was a member of the Kalem Club.

Kline, Otis Adelbert (1891–1946), prolific writer for *WT* and other pulp magazines, literary agent for Robert E. Howard and others, amateur orientalist, and songwriter.

Koenig, H[erman] C[harles] (1893–1959), late associate of HPL who spearheaded the rediscovery of the work of William Hope Hodgson. He also published HPL's *Charleston* (1936).

Kuttner, Henry (1915–1958), prolific author of science fiction and horror tales for the pulp magazines, and a late correspondent of HPL (1936–37). HPL introduced him to C. L. Moore (1911–1987), whom he would later marry. For HPL's letters to him, see *Letters to C. L. Moore and Others* (2017).

Leeds, Arthur (1882–1952?), an associate of HPL in New York and member of the Kalem Club. He was the author (with J. Berg Esenwein) of *Writing the Photoplay* (Springfield, MA: The Home Correspondence School, 1913; rev. ed. 1919). For HPL's letters to him, see *Letters to Rheinhart Kleiner and Others* (2020).

Lenniger, August (1906–1989), literary agent for E. Hoffmann Price and others.

Long, Frank Belknap (1901–1994), fiction writer, poet, member of the Kalem Club, and one of HPL's closest friends and correspondents. For a time he was the literary agent for Zealia Bishop, and he also did revisory work for Adolphe de Castro.

Loveman, Samuel (1887–1976), poet and longtime friend of HPL, Ambrose Bierce, Hart Crane, George Sterling, and Clark Ashton Smith. He wrote

The Hermaphrodite (1926) and other works; member of the Kalem Club. For HPL's letters to him, see *Letters to Maurice W. Moe and Others* (2018).

Lumley, William (1880–1960), eccentric late associate of HPL for whom HPL revised "The Diary of Alonzo Typer" (1935).

Machen, Arthur (1863–1947), Welsh author of weird fiction much admired by HPL.

Merritt, A[braham] (1884–1943), writer of fantasy and horror tales for the pulps. His work was much admired by HPL in spite of its concessions to pulp formulae. His late novel, *Dwellers in the Mirage* (1932), may have been influenced by HPL.

Miniter, Edith (1867–1934), amateur journalist who also professionally published a novel, *Our Natupski Neighbors* (1916), and many short stories. HPL was guest at her home in Wilbraham, MA, in the summer of 1928.

Moe, Maurice W[inter] (1882–1940), amateur journalist, English teacher, and longtime friend and correspondent of HPL. He lived successively in Appleton and Milwaukee, WI. For HPL's letters to him, see *Letters to Maurice W. Moe and Others* (2018).

Moe, Robert Ellis (1912–1992), one of Maurice W. Moe's two sons, who began corresponding with HPL in 1934 and met him on several occasions. For HPL's letters to him, see *Letters to Maurice W. Moe and Others* (2018).

Moore, C[atherine] L[ucile] (1911–1987), late associate of HPL who later married Henry Kuttner and became a leading figure in science fiction and fantasy. For their joint correspondence, see *Letters to C. L. Moore and Others* (2017).

Morton, James Ferdinand (1870–1941), amateur journalist, author of many tracts on race prejudice, free thought, and taxation; longtime friend of HPL and member of the Kalem Club. In 1925 he became the curator of the Paterson (NJ) Museum. For HPL's letters to him, see *Letters to James F. Morton* (2011).

Munn, H[arold] Warner (1903–1981), prolific contributor to the pulp magazines, living near W. Paul Cook in Athol, MA.

Petaja, Emil (1915–2000), science fiction fan and late associate of HPL; later a prolific author and editor. For HPL's letters to him, see *Letters with Donald and Howard Wandrei and to Emil Petaja* (2019).

Quinn, Seabury (1889–1969), prolific author of weird and detective tales for the pulps, notably a series of tales involving the psychic detective Jules de Grandin. Editor of *Casket and Sunnyside* beginning in 1925.

Rimel, Duane W[eldon] (1915–1996), weird fiction fan and late correspondent of HPL, who revised some of his early tales. For HPL's letters to him, see *Letters to F. Lee Baldwin, Duane W. Rimel, and Nils Frome* (2016).

Ruppert, Conrad H. (1912–1997), printer of such fan publications as *Science Fiction Digest, Fantasy,* and *Fantasy Fan,* and *The Black Flame* by Stanley G. Weinbaum.

Schwartz, Julius (1915–2004), editor of *Fantasy Magazine* who acted as HPL's agent in marketing *At the Mountains of Madness* to *Astounding Stories.*

Shepherd, Wilson (1917–1985), amateur printer and publisher of the *Phantagraph, Fanciful Tales,* and HPL's *A History of the Necronomicon* (Rebel Press, 1937). For HPL's letters to him, see *Letters to Robert Bloch and Others* (2015).

Smith, Clark Ashton (1893–1961), prolific California poet and writer of fantasy tales. He received a "fan" letter from HPL in 1922 and corresponded with him until HPL's death. For their joint correspondence, see *Dawnward Spire, Lonely Hill* (2017).

Smith, Louis Clay (1914–1975), a weird fiction fan from California who planned to publish an edition of HPL's *Fungi from Yuggoth* and an "index" (actually an accumulation of tables of contents) of *WT.* Neither saw print.

Sterling, Kenneth (1920–1995), young science fiction fan who came into contact with HPL in 1934. He later became a distinguished physician. For HPL's letters to him, see *Letters to Robert Bloch and Others* (2015).

Strauch, Carl Ferdinand (1908–1989), friend of Harry Brobst and correspondent of HPL. He later became a distinguished professor and critic. For HPL's letters to him, see *Letters to J. Vernon Shea, Carl F. Strauch, and Lee McBride White* (2016).

Talman, Wilfred Blanch (1904–1986), correspondent of HPL and late member of the Kalem Club. HPL assisted Talman on his story "Two Black Bottles" (1926) and wrote "Some Dutch Footprints in New England" for Talman to publish in *De Halve Maen,* the journal of the Holland Society of New York. Late in life he wrote the memoir *The Normal Lovecraft* (1973). For HPL's letters to him, see *Letters to Wilfred B. Talman and Helen V. and Genevieve Sully* (2019).

Tremaine, F[rederick] Orlin (1899–1956), editor of various magazines, including *Astounding Stories* (1933–37). He enraged HPL for allowing *At the Mountains of Madness* to be copy-edited carelessly for publication. As editor at Bartholomew House, he edited and published the first paperbacks of HPL's fiction: *The Weird Shadow Over Innsmouth* (1944) and *The Dunwich Horror* (1945).

Utpatel, Frank (1905–1980), illustrator and late correspondent of HPL (1936–37). He produced several illustrations for the Visionary Press edition of HPL's *The Shadow over Innsmouth* (1936). He later illustrated a number of books published by Arkham House.

Wandrei, Donald (1908–1987), poet and author of weird fiction, science fiction, and detective tales. He corresponded with HPL from 1926 to 1937, visited HPL in Providence in 1927 and 1932, and met HPL occasionally in New York during the 1930s. He helped HPL get "The Shadow out of Time" published in *Astounding Stories*. For their joint correspondence, see *Letters with Donald and Howard Wandrei and to Emil Petaja* (2019).

Wandrei, Howard (1909–1956), younger brother of Donald Wandrei, premier weird artist and prolific author of weird fiction, science fiction, and detective stories; correspondent of HPL. For their joint correspondence, see *Letters with Donald and Howard Wandrei and to Emil Petaja* (2019).

Whitehead, Henry S[t. Clair] (1882–1932), deacon in the Episcopal church, author of weird and adventure tales, many of them set in the Virgin Islands. HPL once described him as "Musician, artist, athlete, traveller, cleric, liturgiologist, author, boys' camp leader, psychologist, civic leader, anthropologist" as well as an alienist and psychiatrist. HPL corresponded with him and visited him in Florida in 1931. HPL wrote a brief eulogy of Whitehead for *WT*.

Wollheim, Donald A[llen] (1914–1990), editor of the *Phantagraph* and *Fanciful Tales*, became prolific author and editor in the science fiction field. For HPL's letters to him, see *Letters to Robert Bloch and Others* (2015).

Wright, Farnsworth (1888–1940), editor of *Weird Tales* (1924–40). He often rejected HPL's work of the 1930s, only to publish some of it after HPL's death upon submittal by AWD.

Bibliography

A. Works by H. P. Lovecraft

Books

The Ancient Track: Complete Poetical Works. 2nd ed. Edited by S. T. Joshi. New York: Hippocampus Press, 2013.

The Cats of Ulthar. Cassia, FL: Dragon-Fly Press, Christmas 1935 (*LL* 585).

Collected Essays. Edited by S. T. Joshi. New York: Hippocampus Press, 2004–06. 5 vols. [*CE*]

Collected Fiction. Edited by S. T. Joshi. New York: Hippocampus Press, 2015–17. 4 vols. [*CF*]

Dawnward Spire, Lonely Hill: The Letters of H. P. Lovecraft and Clark Ashton Smith. Edited by David E. Schultz and S. T. Joshi. New York: Hippocampus Press, 2017.

Essential Solitude: The Letters of H. P. Lovecraft and August Derleth. Edited by David E. Schultz and S. T. Joshi. New York: Hippocampus Press, 2008. 2 vols.

Letters to Alfred Galpin and Others. Edited by S. T. Joshi and David E. Schultz. New York: Hippocampus Press, 2020.

Letters to C. L. Moore and Others. Edited by David E. Schultz and S. T. Joshi. New York: Hippocampus Press, 2017.

Letters to Elizabeth Toldridge and Anne Tillery Renshaw. Edited by David E. Schultz and S. T. Joshi. New York: Hippocampus Press, 2014.

Letters to F. Lee Baldwin, Duane W. Rimel, and Nils Frome. Edited by David E. Schultz and S. T. Joshi. New York: Hippocampus Press, 2016.

Letters to Family and Family Friends. Edited by S. T. Joshi and David E. Schultz. New York: Hippocampus Press, 2020.

Letters to J. Vernon Shea, Carl F. Strauch, and Lee McBride White. Edited by S. T. Joshi and David E. Schultz. New York: Hippocampus Press, 2016.

Letters to James F. Morton. Edited by David E. Schultz and S. T. Joshi. New York: Hippocampus Press, 2011.

Letters to Maurice W. Moe and Others. Edited by David E. Schultz and S. T. Joshi. New York: Hippocampus Press, 2018.

Letters to Rheinhart Kleiner and Others. Edited by S. T. Joshi and David E. Schultz. New York: Hippocampus Press, 2020.

Letters to Richard F. Searight. Edited by David E. Schultz and S. T. Joshi, with Franklyn Searight. West Warwick, RI: Necronomicon Press, 1992.

Letters to Robert Bloch and Others. Edited by David E. Schultz and S. T. Joshi. New York: Hippocampus Press, 2015.

Letters to Wilfred B. Talman and Helen V. and Genevieve Sully. Edited by David E. Schultz and S. T. Joshi. New York: Hippocampus Press, 2019.

Letters with Donald and Howard Wandrei and to Emil Petaja. Edited by S. T. Joshi and David E. Schultz. New York: Hippocampus Press, 2019.

Marginalia. Edited by August Derleth and Donald Wandrei. Sauk City, WI: Arkham House, 1944.

A Means to Freedom: The Letters of H. P. Lovecraft and Robert E. Howard. Edited by S. T. Joshi, David E. Schultz, and Rusty Burke. New York: Hippocampus Press, 2011.

O Fortunate Floridian: H. P. Lovecraft's Letters to R. H. Barlow. Edited by S. T. Joshi and David E. Schultz. Tampa: University of Tampa Press, 2007.

Selected Letters. Edited by August Derleth, Donald Wandrei, and James Turner. Sauk City, WI: Arkham House, 1965–76. 5 vols. [*SL*]

The Shadow over Innsmouth. Everett, PA: Visionary Press, 1936. (*LL* 591)

The Shunned House. Athol, MA: Recluse Press, 1928 (printed but not bound or distributed until 1959–61). (*LL* 592) Text in *CF* 1.

Fiction

At the Mountains of Madness. Astounding Stories 16, No. 6 (February 1936): 8–32; 17, No. 1 (March 1936): 125–55; 17, No. 2 (April 1936): 132–50. In *CF* 3.

"Beyond the Wall of Sleep." *Pine Cones* 1, No. 6 (October 1919): 2–10. *FF* 2, No. 2 (October 1934): 25–32. In *CF* 1.

"The Call of Cthulhu." *WT* 11, No. 2 (February 1928): 159–78, 287. In *Beware After Dark! The World's Most Stupendous Tales of Mystery, Horror, Thrills and Terror,* ed. T. Everett Harré. New York: Macaulay, 1929. 223–59. In *CF* 2.

The Case of Charles Dexter Ward. In *CF* 2.

"The Cats of Ulthar." *Tryout* 6, No. 11 (November 1920): [3–9]. *WT* 7, No. 3 (February 1926): 252–54. *WT* 21, No. 2 (February 1933): 259–61. In *CF* 1.

"Celephaïs." *Rainbow* No. 2 (May 1922): 10–12. *Marvel Tales* 1, No. 1 (May 1934): 26, 28–32. In *CF* 1.

"The Colour out of Space." *Amazing Stories* 2, No. 6 (September 1927): 557–67. In *CF* 2.

"Dagon." *Vagrant* No. 11 (November 1919): 23–29. *WT* 2, No. 3 (October 1923): 23–25. In *CF* 1.

"The Doom That Came to Sarnath." *Scot* No. 44 (June 1920): 90–98. *Marvel Tales of Science and Fantasy* 1, No. 4 (March–April 1935): 157–63. In *CF* 1.

The Dream-Quest of Unknown Kadath. In *CF* 2.

"The Dreams in the Witch House." *WT* 22, No. 1 (July 1933): 86–111. In *CF* 3.

"Facts concerning the Late Arthur Jermyn and His Family." *Wolverine* No. 9 (March 1921): 3–11; No. 10 (June 1921): 6–11. *WT* 3, No. 4 (April 1924): 15–18 (as "The White Ape"). *WT* 25, No. 5 (May 1935): 642–48 (as "Arthur Jermyn"). In *CF* 1.

"The Festival." *WT* 5, No. 1 (January 1925): 169–74. *WT* 22, No. 4 (October 1933): 519–20, 522–28. In *CF* 1.

"From Beyond." *FF* 1, No. 10 (June 1934): 147–51, 160. In *CF* 1.

"The Haunter of the Dark." *WT* 28, No. 5 (December 1936): 538–53. In *CF* 3.

"Herbert West—Reanimator" (as "Grewsome Tales"). *Home Brew* 1, No. 1 (February 1922): 84–88 ("From the Dark"); 1, No. 2 (March 1922): 45–50 ("The Plague Demon"); 1, No. 3 (April 1922): 21–26 ("Six Shots by Moonlight"); 1, No. 4 (May 1922): 53–58 ("The Scream of the Dead"); 1, No. 5 (June 1922): 45–50 ("The Horror from the Shadows,"); 1, No. 6 (July 1922): 57–62 ("The Tomb-Legions"). In *CF* 1.

"History of the 'Necronomicon.'" Oakman, AL: Wilson H. Shepherd/The Rebel Press, [1937] (as *A History of the Necronomicon*). In *CF* 2.

"The Horror at Red Hook." *WT* 9, No. 1 (January 1927): 59–73. In *You'll Need a Night Light,* ed. Christine Campbell Thomson. London: Selwyn & Blount, 1927. 228–54. In *Not at Night!,* ed. Herbert Asbury. New York: Macy-Masius (The Vanguard Press), November 1928. 27–52. In *CF* 1.

"The Hound." *WT* 3, No. 2 (February 1924): 50–52, 78. *WT* 14, No. 3 (September 1929): 421–25, 432. In *CF* 1.

"Hypnos." *National Amateur* 45, No. 5 (May 1923): 1–3. *WT* 4, No. 2 (May–June–July 1924): 33–35. In *CF* 1.

"In the Vault." *Tryout* 10, No. 6 (November 1925): [3–17]. *WT* 19, No. 4 (April 1932): 459–65. In *CF* 1.

"The Music of Erich Zann." *National Amateur* 44, No. 4 (March 1922): 38–40. *WT* 5, No. 5 (May 1925): 219–34. In *Creeps by Night: Chills and Thrills,* ed. Dashiell Hammett. New York: John Day Co., 1931. 347–63. In *Modern Tales of Horror,* ed. Dashiell Hammett. London: Victor Gollancz, 1932. 301–17. *Evening Standard* (London) (24 October 1932): 20–21. *WT* 24, No. 5 (November 1934): 644–48, 655–56. In *CF* 1.

"The Nameless City." *Wolverine* No. 11 (November 1921): 3–15. *Fanciful Tales* 1, No. 1 (Fall 1936): 5–18. In *CF* 1.

"The Other Gods." *Fantasy Fan* 1, No. 3 (November 1933): 35–38. *Weird Tales* 32, No. 4 (October 1938): 489–92. In *CF* 1.

"The Outsider." *WT* 7, No. 4 (April 1926): 449–53. *WT* 17, No. 4 (June–July 1931): 566–71. In *CF* 1.

"Pickman's Model." *WT* 10, No. 4 (October 1927): 505–14. In *By Daylight Only,* ed. Christine Campbell Thomson. London: Selwyn & Blount, 1929. 37–52. *WT* 28, No. 4 (November 1936): 495–505. In *The "Not at Night" Omnibus,* ed. Christine Campbell Thomson. London: Selwyn & Blount, [1937]. 279–307. In *CF* 2.

"The Picture in the House." *National Amateur* 41, No. 6 (July 1919 [*sic*]): 246–49. *WT* 3, No. 1 (January 1924): 40–42. *WT* 29, No. 3 (March 1937): 370–73. In *CF* 1.

"Polaris." *Philosopher* 1, No. 1 (December 1920): 3–5. *National Amateur* 48, No. 5 (May 1926): 48–49. *Fantasy Fan* 1, No. 6 (February 1934): 83–85. In *CF* 1.

"The Quest of Iranon." *Galleon* 1, No. 5 (July–August 1935): 12–20. In *CF* 1.

"The Rats in the Walls." *WT* 3, No. 3 (March 1924): 25–31. *WT* 15, No. 6 (June 1930): 841–53. In *Switch On the Light*, ed. Christine Campbell Thomson. London: Selwyn & Blount, 1931. 141–65. In *CF* 1.

"The Shadow out of Time."*Astounding Stories* 17, No. 4 (June 1936): 110–54. In *CF* 3.

"The Shadow over Innsmouth." In *CF* 3.

"The Shunned House." In *CF* 1.

"The Silver Key." *WT* 13, No. 1 (January 1929): 41–49, 144. In *CF* 2.

"The Statement of Randolph Carter." *Vagrant* No. 13 (May 1920): 41–48. *WT* 5, No. 2 (February 1925): 149–53. In *CF* 1.

"The Strange High House in the Mist." *WT* 18, No. 3 (October 1931): 394–400. In *CF* 2.

"The Temple." *WT* 6, No. 3 (September 1925): 329–36, 429, 431. *WT* 27, No. 2 (February 1936): 239–44, 246–49. In *CF* 1.

"The Terrible Old Man." *Tryout* 7, No. 4 (July 1921): [10–14]. *WT* 8, No. 2 (August 1926): 191–92. In *CF* 1.

"The Thing on the Doorstep." *WT* 29, No. 1 (January 1937): 52–70. In *CF* 3.

"The Tree." *Tryout* 7, No. 7 (October 1921): [3–10]. In *CF* 1.

"The Unnamable." *WT* 6, No. 1 (July 1925): 78–82. In *CF* 1.

"The Whisperer in Darkness." *WT* 18, No. 1 (August 1931): 32–73. In *CF* 3.

"The White Ship." *United Amateur* 19, No. 2 (November 1919): 30–33. *WT* 9, No. 3 (March 1927): 386–89. In *CF* 1.

Revisions and Collaborations (all items in *CF* 4 save where noted)
Barlow, R. H. "The Battle That Ended the Century." [De Land, FL: R. H. Barlow, 1934.]

de Castro, Adolphe. "The Electric Executioner." *WT* 16, No. 2 (August 1930): 223–36.

———. "The Last Test." *WT* 12, No. 5 (November 1928): 625–56. In *CF* 4.

Heald, Hazel. "The Horror in the Museum." *WT* 22, No. 1 (July 1933): 49–68. In *Terror by Night*, ed. Christine Campbell Thomson. London: Selwyn & Blount, (1934). 111–41. In. *The "Not at Night" Omnibus*, ed. Christine Campbell Thomson. London: Selwyn & Blount, [1937]. 279–307.

———. "Out of the Aeons." *WT* 25, No. 4 (April 1935): 478–96.

Houdini, Harry. "Under the Pyramids." *WT* 4, No. 2 (May–June–July 1924): 3–12 (as "Imprisoned with the Pharaohs"). In *CF* 1.

Lumley, William. "The Diary of Alonzo Typer." *WT* 31, No. 2 (February 1938): 152–66.

Moore, C. L.; Merritt, A.; Howard, Robert E.; and Long, Frank Belknap. "The Challenge from Beyond." *Fantasy Magazine* 5, No. 4 (September 1935): 221–29 (HPL portion on 223–27).

Price, E. Hoffmann. "Through the Gates of the Silver Key." *WT* 24, No. 1 (July 1934): 60–85. In *CF* 3.

Nonfiction

Antarctic Atlas. Juvenilia, nonextant.

"[Biographical Notice]." *The Best Short Stories of 1928 and the Yearbook of the American Short Story*. New York: Dodd, Mead, 1928. 324. In *CE* 5.

"Cats and Dogs." *Leaves* No. 1 (Summer 1937): 25–34. In *CE* 5.

"Commonplace Book." In *CE* 5.

"European Glimpses." In *CE* 4.

"Homes and Shrines of Poe." *Californian* 2, No. 3 (Winter 1934): 8–10. In *CE* 4.

"In Memoriam: Henry S. Whitehead." *WT* 21, No. 3 (March 1933): 391 (unsigned). In *CE* 2.

"In Memoriam: Robert Ervin Howard." *Fantasy Magazine* No. 38 (September 1936): 29–31 (Lovecraft's portion only). In *CE* 5.

"The Literature of Rome." *United Amateur* 18, No. 2 (November 1918): 17–21, 35–38]. In *CE* 2.

"A Living Heritage: Roman Architecture in Today's America." *Californian* 3, No. 1 (Summer 1935): 23–28 (abridged; as "Heritage or Modernism: Common Sense in Art Forms"). In *CE* 5.

Letter to Duane W. Rimel (28 September 1935). *Phantagraph* 5, No. 5 (February 1937): 4–8 (as "What's the Trouble with Weird Fiction?"; unsigned).

Letter to E. Hoffmann Price, (15 February 1933). *Arkham Sampler* 1, No. 3 (Summer 1948): 36–40 (as "A Letter to E. Hoffmann Price").

"Letters to Farnsworth Wright," edited by S. T. Joshi and David E. Schultz. *Lovecraft Annual* No. (2014): 5–59.

"Notes on Verse Technique." Published as *Further Criticism of Poetry*. Louisville, KY: George G. Fetter, 1932. In *CE* 1.

"Report of the Bureau of Critics." *National Amateur* 57, No. 3 (March 1935): 1. In *CE* 1.

"Robert Ervin Howard: 1906–1936." *Phantagraph* 4, No. 5 (August 1936): 4–5.

"Some Dutch Footprints in New England." *De Halve Maen* 9, No. 1 (18 October 1933): 2, 4.

"Some Notes on Interplanetary Fiction." *Californian* 3, No. 3 (Winter 1935): 39–42. In *CE* 2.

"[Suggestions for a Reading Guide]." In *CF* 2.

"Supernatural Horror in Literature." *Recluse* No. 1 (1927): 23–59. Rev. ed. in *FF* (October 1933–February 1935). In *CE* 2.

"The Unknown City in the Ocean." *Perspective Review* (Winter 1934 [Fourth Anniversary Number]): 4–8. In *CE* 4.

"Unpublished parts of Well-Bred Speech as written by H. P. Lovecraft." In *Letters to Elizabeth Toldridge and Anne Tillery Renshaw.*
"What Belongs in Verse." *Perspective Review* (Spring 1935): 10–11. In *CE* 1.

Poetry [all poems are in *AT*]
"[Anthem of the Kappa Alpha Tau]."
"The City." *Vagrant* No. 10 (October 1919): 6–7 (as by "Ward Phillips"). *WT* 42, No. 5 (July 1950): 48–49.
Fungi from Yuggoth.
  "III. The Key." *FF* 2, No. 5 (January 1935): 72.
  "V. Homecoming." *FF* 2, No. 5 (January 1935): 72.
"In a Sequester'd Providence Churchyard Where Once Poe Walk'd." In *Four Acrostic Sonnets on Edgar Allan Poe.* [Milwaukee, WI: Maurice W. Moe, 1936.] *Science-Fantasy Correspondent* 1, No. 3 (March–April 1937): 16–17 (as "In a Sequestered Churchyard Where Once Poe Walked"). WT 31, No. 5 (May 1938): 578 (as "Where Poe Once Walked: An Acrostic Sonnet").
"[Little Sam Perkins.]" *Olympian* No. 35 (Autumn 1940): 36.
"To Clark Ashton Smith, Esq., upon His Phantastick Tales, Verses, Pictures, and Sculptures." *WT* 31, No. 5 (April 1938): 392 (as "To Clark Ashton Smith").

B. Works by E. Hoffmann Price

The Book of the Dead: Friends of Yesteryear—Fictioneers and Others (Memories of the Pulp Fiction Era). Sauk City, WI: Arkham House, 2001.
E. Hoffmann Price's Fables of Ismeddin MEGAPACK. Cabin John, MD: Wildside Press, 2016.
E. Hoffmann Price's Pierre d'Artois: Occult Detective & Associates MEGAPACK. Cabin John, MD: Wildside Press, 2017.
Far Lands, Other Days. Chapel Hill, NC: Carcosa, 1975.
Strange Gateways. Sauk City, WI: Arkham House, 1967.

Fiction
"Agents of the Iron Claw." *Spy Novels Magazine* 1, No. 1 (February 1935): 10–32.
"Assassin's Gallery." *All Detective Magazine* 2, No. 6 (April 1933): 69–76 (as by "Hamlin Daly").
"The Breath of Doom." *Super Detective Stories* 2 No. 2 (November 1934): 42–67.
"The Bride of the Peacock." [Pierre d'Artois] *WT* 20, No. 2 (August 1932): 152–183.
"The Cat Goddess." *Terror Tales* 2, No. 3 (March 1935): 36–47. In *FL* (as "Kiss of Sekhmet").
"The Claw of Iblis." [Pâwang Ali] *Clues Detective Stories* 34, No. 2 (July 1935): 8–40.
"The Corpse without a Face." See "The Headless Corpse."
"The Crooked Square." *Strange Detective Stories* 5, No. 3 (February 1934): 132–42.

"Cyclops of Xoatl." With Otis Adelbert Kline. *WT* 28, No. 5 (December 1936): 570–96.

"The Daughter of the Dancer." First title of "Queen of the Lilin."

"The Dead Return." First title of "Spirit Madness."

"Death Rides an Elephant." [Pâwang Ali] *Clues Detective Stories* 34, No. 4 (September 1935): 6–36.

"The Devil's Crypt." [Pierre d'Artois] *Strange Detective Stories* 5, No. 2 (January 1934): 40–58.

"The Dragon's Shadow." [Pâwang Ali] *Clues Detective Stories* 33, No. 5 (April 1935): 76–115 (as by E. Hoffman Price).

"The Dreamer of Atlânaat." [Ismeddin] *WT* 8, No. 1 (July 1926): 91–100. In *FL*. (The first Ismeddin story.)

"Each Slew a Slayer." [Pâwang Ali] *Clues Detective Stories* 35, No. 4 (March 1936): 44–75.

"The Fifty Grand Murder." *Super-Detective Stories* 1, No. 1 (March 1934): 4–42. [Possibly identical to "Master of Assassins."]

"The Forgotten of Allah." [Ismeddin] *Magic Carpet Magazine* 3, No. 3 (July 1933): 342–62. In *FL*.

"The Girl from Samarcand." *WT* 13, No. 5 (May 1929): 636–44. *WT* 31, No. 3 (March 1938): 367–77. In *SG*.

"Gray Sphinx." First title of "Devil's Crypt." In *FL*.

"Grimes, Outlaw." [Simon Bolivar Grimes] *Spicy Western Stories* 1, No. 3 (January 1937): 42–53.

"The Hand of Hassan." *All Detective Magazine* 4, No. 11 (September 1933): 58–85 (as by "E. Hoffman Price").

"The Hand of Subramanya." [Pâwang Ali] *Clues Detective Stories* 35, No. 2 (January 1936): 8–39.

"The Hand of Wrath." *WT* 26, No. 5 (November 1935): 572–86.

"Headless Corpse." [Cliff Cragin] *Spicy Detective Stories* 6, No. 6 (April 1937): 28–39. [Possibly identical to "The Corpse without a Face."]

"In the Darkroom." *Detective Fiction Weekly* 76, No. 4 (27 May 1933): 59–69.

"A Jest and a Vengeance." *WT* 14, No. 3 (September 1929): 397–406.

"The Infidel's Daughter." [Ismeddin] *WT* 10, No. 6 (December 1927): 731–42. In *FL*.

"Ismeddin and the Holy Carpet." [Ismeddin] *Magic Carpet Magazine* 3, No. 1 (January 1933): 74–94. In *The Complete Magic Carpet Magazine*. Mississauga, ON: Girasol Collectables, 2008.

"Kiss of Sekhmet." First title of "The Cat Goddess."

"Libations for the Dead." Unpublished?

"The Lord of Illusion." *Ashes and Others by H. P. Lovecraft and Divers Hands* (*Crypt of Cthulhu* No. 10) (Yuletide 1982): 47–56.

"Lord of the Fourth Axis." [Pierre d'Artois] *WT* 22, No. 5 (November 1933): 571–93.

"Master of Assassins." First title of "Spotted Satan"?

"Million Dollar Doom." *Super-Detective Stories* 1, No. 6 (August 1934): 36–72.

"Naga's Kiss." *Spicy Mystery Stories* 1, No. 4 (August 1935): 44–55.

"Pale Hands." *Magic Carpet Magazine* 3, No. 4 (October 1933): 494–501. In *SG*.

"The Pâwang Moves." [Pâwang Ali] *Clues Detective Stories* 36, No. 1 (June 1936): 31–62.

"Prayer for My Enemy." *Real Detective* 28 No. 3, (May 1933): 28–31; 28, No. 4 (June 1933): 63–65.

"Queen of the Lilin." [Pierre d'Artois/Glenn Farrell] *WT* 24, No. 5 (November 1934): 530–51. In *FL*.

"Queen of the Morning." Unpublished, nonextant.

"Queen of Zemargad." Later titled "Queen of the Lilin."

"The Return of Balkis." [Pierre d'Artois] *WT* 21, No. 4 (April 1933): 438–60.

"Satan's Garden." [Pierre d'Artois/Glenn Farrell] *WT* 23, No. 4 (April 1934) 402–23; 23, No. 5 (May 1934): 601–24. In *FL*.

"Satan's Prayer Rug." First title of "Lord of the Fourth Axis."

"Satan's Prayer Rug." Second version, first title of "Who Killed Gilbert Foster?"

"Shaykh Ahmad and the Pious Companions." *Oriental Stories* 1, No. 5 (Summer 1931): 694–705.

"Silver Peacock." [Glenn Farrell] *All Detective Magazine* 3, No. 7 (May 1933): 6–34. (The first Glenn Farrell story.)

"The Sower of Swords." *Spy Stories* 2, No. 3 (March 1935): 12–42.

"Spirit Madness." [Harrison P. Steele] *Strange Detective Stories* 4, No. 6 (November 1933): 39–48.

"Spotted Satan." *WT* 35, No. 1 (January 1940): 7–31.

"The Stranger from Kurdistan." *WT* 6, No. 1 (July 1925): 95–98; 14, No. 6 (December 1929): 48–51. In *SG*.

"The Sultan's Jest." *WT* 6, No. 3 (September 1925): 324–328.

"Triangle with Variations." *Droll Stories* 3, No. 4 (June 1924): 99–102.

"Tarbis of the Lake." *WT* 23, No. 2 (February 1934): 208–17. In *SG*.

"Tenderfoot." *Spicy Western Stories* 1, No. 1 (November 1936): 4–15.

"Tong War" (with Ralph Milne Farley). *True Gang Life* 1, No. 5 (May 1935): 4–79.

"Treason's Kiss." *Spicy Western Stories* 1, No. 2 (December 1936): 66–77.

"Unfit for Command." *Short Stories* 176, No. 6 (25 September 1941): 65–86.

"When Winners Lose." *Nickel Detective* 4, No. 5 (August 1933): 24–32.

"Who Killed Gilbert Foster?" (with Ralph Milne Farley). *Five-Novels Monthly* 33, No. 1 (January 1936): 36–65.

"The Widow's Mite." [Don Cragston] *Spicy-Adventure Stories* 1, No. 5 (February 1935): 60–71.

"The Word of Bentley." *WT* 21, No. 5 (May 1933): 635–40.

"The Word of Santiago" *WT* 7, No. 2 (February 1926): 193–99. In *FL*.

Nonfiction

"The Book of the Dead: Farnsworth Wright." *Ghost* No. 2 (July 1944): 5–17; *Etchings and Odysseys* No. 3 (1983): 53–60, 62–66.

"Clark Ashton Smith: A Memoir." In Clark Ashton Smith, *Tales of Science and Sorcery*. Sauk City, WI: Arkham House, 1964. pp. 3–17.

"Flashes from the Readers." "In the Darkroom." *Detective Fiction Weekly* 76, No. 4 (27 May 1933): 140–41?.

"HPL: An Astrological Analysis." In *HPL*, ed. Meade Frierson III and Penny Frierson. [Birmingham, AL: The Editors, 1972, 1977.] 12–16 (as by "E. Hoffman Price").

"H. P. Lovecraft the Man." *Diversifier* 2, No. 5 (May 1976): 7–9.

"In Memoriam: Robert E. Howard." *Fantasy Magazine* No. 38 (September 1936): 31–32 (Prices's portion only).

"The Man Who Was Lovecraft." In H. P. Lovecraft et al. *Something about Cats and Other Pieces*. Sauk City, WI: Arkham House, 1949. 278–90.

"Reminiscences of HPL." In *HPL*, ed. Meade Frierson III and Penny Frierson. [Birmingham, AL: The Editors, 1972, 1977.] 16–17 (as by "E. Hoffman Price").

"Robert Ervin Howard." *Diablerie* No. 4 (May 1944): 4–6; rpt *Howard Collector* 1, No. 1 (Summer 1961): 7–13.

"The Sage of College Street." *Amateur Correspondent* 2, No. 1 (May–June 1937): 6–7.

C. Works by Richard F. Searight

The Brain in the Jar and Others: Collected Stories and Poems One. West Warwick, RI: Necronomicon Press, 1992.

The Sealed Casket and Others: Collected Stories and Poems Two. West Warwick, RI: Necronomicon Press, 1996.

The Cosmic Horror and Others. n.p.: JnJ Publications, 2013.

Wild Empire: A Copper Rush Adventure. Laurium, MI: Iroquis Press, 1994.

"The Brain in the Jar" (with Norman Elwood Hamerstrom [1899–1970]). *WT* 4, No. 3 (November 1924): 31–35, 183–88. 190. *WT* 27, No. 6 (June 1936): 750–56, 758–59.

"The Cavern of the Dragon." In *The Brain in the Jar*.

"The Cosmic Horror." *Wonder Stories* 5, No. 2 (August 1933): 120–127, 185.

"The Dead World." [v] *FF* 2, No. 5 (January 1935): 77.

"Guardian of the Cairn." In *The Sealed Casket and Others*.

"Impressions of the Planets—Venus." [v] *Wonder Stories* 5, No. 6 (January 1934): 656.

"The New World." [v] *WT* 25, No. 4 (April 1935): 477.

"The Road." [v] *In the Realm of Poesy: An Anthology of Modern Verse*, ed. Charles Leon Tumasel. New York: Charles Leon Tumasel, 1937. 16.

"The Sealed Casket." *WT* 25, No. 3 (March 1935): 375–79.

"The Warder of Knowledge." In *Tales of the Lovecraft Mythos*, ed. Robert M. Price. Minneapolis: Fedogan & Bremer, 1992. 153–66. In *The Yith Cycle: Lovecraftian Tales of the Great Race and Time Travel*, ed. Robert M. Price. n.p.: Chaosium, 2010. 220–232.

"Winds." [v] *FF* 1, No. 6 (February 1934): 88.

"The Wizard's Death." [v] *WT* 28, No. 4 (November 1936): 488.

D. Works by Others

Airne, C[lement] W[allace] (1889–?). *Britain's Story Told in Pictures*. Manchester: Sankey, Hudson & Co., [1935]. (*LL* 18)

———. *Our Empire's Story Told in Pictures*. Manchester: Sankey, Hudson & Co., [1934].

———. *The Story of Hanoverian and Modern Britain Told in Pictures*. Manchester: Sankey, Hudson & Co., 1935. (*LL* 19)

———. *The Story of Mediaeval Britain Told in Pictures*. Manchester: Sankey, Hudson & Co., 1935. (*LL* 20)

———. *The Story of Prehistoric & Roman Britain Told in Pictures*. Manchester: Sankey, Hudson & Co., [1935]. (*LL* 21)

———. *Story of Saxon and Norman Britain Told in Pictures*. Manchester: Sankey, Hudson & Co. [1935]. (*LL* 22)

———. *The Story of Tudor and Stuart Britain Told in Pictures*. Manchester: Sankey, & Hudson & Co., 1935. (*LL* 23)

Allen, Hervey (1889–1949). *Israfel: The Life and Times of Edgar Allan Poe*. New York: George H. Doran Co., 1927. 2 vols. (*LL* 27)

Anger, William F., and Louis C. Smith. "An Interview with E. Hoffman [*sic*] Price." *Fantasy Fan* 2, No. 4 (December 1934): 60–61; rpt. in HPL, *Letters to Robert Bloch and Others* pp. 461–42.

Asquith, Lady Cynthia (1887–1960) [et al.]. *My Grimmest Nightmare*. [Edited by Cecil Madden.] London: George Allen & Unwin, 1935. (*LL* 55)

Bacon, Edgar Mayhew (1855-1935). *Historic Pilgrimages in New England*. New York: Silver, Burdett & Co., 1898.

———. *Narragansett Bay: Its Historic and Romantic Associations and Picturesque Setting*. New York: G. P. Putnam's Sons, 1904). (*LL* 59)

Baldwin, F. Lee. "H. P. Lovecraft: A Biographical Sketch." *Fantasy Magazine* 4, No. 5 (April 1935): 108–10, 132. In *Letters to F. Lee Baldwin, Duane W. Rimel, and Nils Frome*.

Baudelaire, Charles Pierre (1821–1867). *Lettres 1841–1866*. Paris: Société de 28 Mercure de France, 1907. (*LL* 79)

Beckford, William (1759–1844). *The History of the Caliph Vathek.* <1786> Printed Verbatim from the First Edition, with the Original Prefaces and Notes by [Samuel] Henley. New York: W. L. Allinson, [1868?] or [188-?]. (*LL* 84)

Benson, E. F. (1867–1940). *Visible and Invisible.* New York: George H. Doran, 1923 or 1924. (*LL* 90)

Berkeley, George (1685–1753). *Alciphron; or, The Minute Philosopher.* London: Printed for J. Tonson, 1732.

The Holy Bible: Containing the Old and New Testaments. Translated out of the Original Tongues, and with the Former Translations Diligently Compared and Revised, by His Majesty's Special Command. Edinburgh: M. & C. Kell, 1795. (*LL* 96)

Bierce, Ambrose (1842–1914?). *Can Such Things Be?* <1893> New York: Boni & Liveright (Modern Library), 1918. (*LL* 98)

——. *In the Midst of Life: Tales of Soldiers and Civilians.* <1891> Introduction by George Sterling. New York: Modern Library, [1927]. (*LL* 99)

——. *The Monk and the Hangman's Daughter; Fantastic Fables; [etc.].* New York: Albert & Charles Boni, 1925. (*LL* 100)

——. *Write It Right: A Little Blacklist of Literary Faults.* New York: Neale Publishing Co., 1909.

Birch, A. G. *The Moon Terror. And Stories by Anthony M. Rud, Vincent Starrett, and Farnsworth Wright.* Indianapolis: Popular Fiction Publishing Co., [1927]. (*LL* 104)

Birkhead, Edith (1889–1951). *The Tale of Terror: A Study of the Gothic Romance.* New York: E. P. Dutton, 1921. (*LL* 105)

Biss, Gerald (1876–1922). *The Door of the Unreal.* New York: G. P. Putnam's Sons, 1920.

Blackwood, Algernon (1869–1951). *The Centaur.* London: Macmillan, 1911.

——. *Incredible Adventures.* London: Macmillan, 1914. New York: Macmillan, 1914; rpt. New York: Hippocampus Press, 2004. (*LL* 1079)

——. *Jimbo: A Fantasy.* New York: Macmillan, 1909. (*LL* 106)

——. *John Silence—Physician Extraordinary.* London: Eveleigh Nash, 1908. (*LL* 107)

——. *John Silence—Physician Extraordinary.* New York: E. P. Dutton, [1920] or [1929]. (*LL* 108)

——. *Julius LeVallon: An Episode.* London: Cassell, 1916. New York: E. P. Dutton, 1916. (*LL* 109)

——. *The Lost Valley and Other Stories.* London: Eveleigh Nash, 1910. (*LL* 110)

——. "The Willows." In *The Listener and Other Stories.* London: Eveleigh Nash, 1907. In *The Best Ghost Stories*, ed. John Gilbert Bohun Lynch. Boston: Small, Maynard, 1924. (*LL* 603)

Blavatsky, Helena Petrovna (1831–1891). *The Secret Doctrine.* London: Theosophical Publishing Co., 1888.

Boguet, Henri (d. 1619). *An Examen of Witches.* Tr. E. Allen Ashwin, ed. Montague Summers. [Bungay, UK]: John Rodker, 1929. [Translation of *Discours execrable des sorciers* (1606).]

The Book of Knowledge. New York: Grolier Society, 1928; 20 vols.

The Book of the Dead. An English Translation of the Chapters, Hymns, etc. of the Theban Recension, with Introduction, Notes, etc., by Sir E. A. Wallis Budge (1857–1934). 2nd ed., rev. & enl. London: Kegan Paul, Trench, Trübner & Co.; New York: E. P. Dutton, 1923. 3 vols. in 1. (*LL* 121)

Brewer, Ebenezer Cobham (1810–1897). *Dictionary of Phrase and Fable.* London: Cassell, Petter & Galpin, 1870.

Brown, J. Macmillan (1846–1935). *The Riddle of the Pacific.* London: T. Fisher Unwin, 1924.

Bulfinch, Thomas (1796–1867). *The Age of Fable; or, Beauties of Mythology* <1855>. Rev. ed., by J. Loughran Scott (Philadelphia: D. McKay, [1898]. (*LL* 132)

Butler, Samuel (1613–1680). *Hudibras.* <1663–78> With Notes and a Literary Memoir by the Rev. T. R. Nash. New-York: D. Appleton & Co., 1864. (*LL* 158)

Casey, Brigadier General Silas (1807–1882). *Infantry Tactics, for the Instruction, Exercise, and Manœuvres of the Soldier, a Company, Line of Skirmishers, Battalion, Brigade, or Corps d'Armée.* New York: D. Van Nostrand, 1862; 3 vols.

Chambers's Encyclopædia: A Dictionary of Universal Knowledge. London: W. & R. Chambers, 1860–68. 10 vols. Philadelphia: J. B. Lippincott Co., 1860–69. 10 vols. [Rev. eds. up to 1935.] (*LL* 185)

Chaucer, Geoffrey (1343?–1400). *The Canterbury Tales.* New York: Modern Library, 1929.

———. *The Canterbury Tales.* Rendered into Modern English by John Urban Nicholson. Illustrated by Rockwell Kent. Garden City, NY: Garden City Publ. Co., 1934.

Church, Alfred J[ohn] (1829–1912). *Stories from Homer.* New York: Harper & Brothers, 1878.

———. *Stories from Livy.* With illustrations from designs by Pinelli. New York: Dodd, Mead, 1883. (*LL* 191)

———. *Stories from the Greek Tragedians.* New York: Dodd, Mead, [1879].

Coleridge, Samuel Taylor (1772–1834). *The Rime of the Ancient Mariner.* Illustrated by Gustave Doré. New York: Harper & Brothers, 1876.

The Colonnade. Volume XIV: 1919–22. New York, 1922. [Part II contains *The Poetical Works of John Trumbull* (1750–1831) reprinted from the original edition of 1820.] (*LL* 211)

Cowan, Frank (1844–1905). *Revi-Lona: A Romance of Love in a Marvellous Land.* [Greenburg, PA: Tribune Press Publishing Co., 188-?.] (*LL* 217)

Crawford, F. Marion (1854–1909). *The Witch of Prague: A Fantastic Tale.* London: Macmillan, 1891.

Damon, S. Foster (1893–1971). *Thomas Holley Chivers, Friend of Poe, with Selections from His Poems: A Strange Chapter in American Literary History.* New York: Harper & Brothers, 1930.

Dark, Sidney (1874–1947). *London.* London: Macmillan & Co., 1924. (*LL* 234)

———. *London Town.* New York: Farrar & Rinehart, [1934]. (*LL* 235)

David-Néel, Alexandra (1868–1969). *Magic and Mystery in Tibet.* New York: Claude Kendall, 1932.

de Castro, Adolphe [Danziger] (1859–1959). *Portrait of Ambrose Bierce.* New York; London: Century Co., 1929.

De Mille, James (1833–1880). *A Strange Manuscript Found in a Copper Cylinder* <1888> New York: Harper & Brothers, 1900. (*LL* 245)

Derleth, August (1909–1971). *Evening in Spring.* New York: Charles Scribner's Sons, 1941.

———. *The Man on All Fours: A Judge Peck Mystery Story.* New York: Loring & Mussey, 1934. (*LL* 249)

———. *Place of Hawks.* New York: Loring & Mussey, 1935. (*LL* 250)

———. *Sign of Fear: A Judge Peck Mystery.* New York: Loring & Mussey, 1935. (*LL* 251)

———. *Three Who Died: A Judge Peck Mystery.* New York: Loring & Mussey, 1935. (*LL* 253)

Disraeli, Benjamin (1804–1881). *Alroy.* <1833> (*LL* 268)

Drake, Samuel Adams (1833–1905). *A Book of New England Legends and Folk Lore in Prose and Poetry.* Boston: Roberts Brothers, 1884. (*LL* 280)

———. *Nooks and Corners of the New England Coast.* New York: Harper & Brothers, 1876. (*LL* 281)

Dreiser, Theodore (1871–1945). *An American Tragedy.* New York: Boni & Liveright, 1925. 2 vols.

Dryden, John (1631–1700). *The Wild Gallant: A Comedy.* London: Printed by T. Warren for Henry Herringman, 1694. (*LL* 284)

Dunsany, Edward John Moreton Drax Plunkett, 18th Baron (1878–1957). *The Book of Wonder* (1912) [with *Time and the Gods* (1906)]. New York: Boni & Liveright (Modern Library), [1918]. (*LL* 288)

———. *The Curse of the Wise Woman.* London: William Heinemann, 1933. New York: Longmans, Green, 1933.

———. *A Dreamer's Tales and Other Stories.* New York: Boni & Liveright [Modern Library], [1917], [1919], or [1921]. [Contains *The Sword of Welleran.*] (*LL* 290)

Easton, Emily M. *Roger Williams, Prophet and Pioneer.* Boston: Houghton, Mifflin, 1930.

Eddison, E. R. (1882–1945). *The Worm Ouroboros: A Romance.* Illustrated by Keith Henderson. New York: A. & C. Boni, 1926. (*LL* 309)

Ernst, James. *Roger Williams, New England Firebrand.* New York: Macmillan, 1932.

Field, Eugene (1850–1895). *Child Verses.* Akron, OH: Saalfield Publishing Co., 1927.

Field, John (1520/1530–1587). *Ephemeris anni. 1557. Currentis iuxta Copernici et Reinhaldi canones fideliter per Ioannem Feild Anglum, supputata ac examinata ad meredianum Londinensem qui occidentalior esse indicatur a Reinhaldo quam sit Regij Montis, per horam. 1. Scr. 50. Adiecta est etiam breuis quædam epistola Ioannis Dee, qua vulgares istos ephemeridum fictores merito reprehendit. Tabella denìq[ue], pro coelesti themate erigendo iuxta modum vulgariter rationalem dictum, per eundem Ioannem Feild confecta, Londinensis poli altitundini inseruiens exactissime.* Londini: [In ædibus Thomæ Marshe], M.D.LVI. [1556] Septembris. XII.

Grimm, Jakob Ludwig Karl (1785–1863), and Wilhelm Grimm (1786–1859). *Fairy Tales.* <1812–15> (*LL* 405)

Harré, T. Everett (1884–1948), ed. *Beware After Dark! The World's Most Stupendous Tales of Mystery, Horror, Thrills and Terror.* New York: Macaulay, 1929. (*LL* 425)

Hawthorne, Nathaniel (1804–1864). *Grandfather's Chair: A History for Youth* <1841> Philadelphia, H. Altemus, 1898 (*LL* 429)

———. *Tanglewood Tales for Girls and Boys: Being a Second Wonder-Book* <1853> New York: A. L. Burt, [189-?] or [1907]. (*LL* 435)

———. *A Wonder Book for Boys and Girls, Comprising Stories of Classical Fables* <1852> New York: A. L. Burt, [n.d.]. (*LL* 437)

Heyward, Du Bose (1885–1940). *Peter Ashley.* New York: Farrar & Rinehart, 1932.

Hodgson, William Hope (1877–1918). *The Boats of the "Glen Carrig."* London: Chapman & Hall, 1907.

———. *Carnacki the Ghost-Finder.* London: Eveleigh Nash, 1913.

———. *The Ghost Pirates.* London: Stanley Paul, 1909.

———. *The House on the Borderland.* London: Chapman & Hall, 1908.

Homer (fl. c. 750 B.C.E.?). *The Complete Works of Homer.* Tr. Andrew Lang. New York: Modern Library, 1935.

———. *The Iliad of Homer.* Tr. Alexander Pope <1715–20>, with notes and intro. by Theodore Alois Buckley. New York: A. L. Burt, [1902]. (*LL* 435)

———. *The Iliad of Homer.* Done into English Prose by Andrew Lang, Walter Leaf, and Ernest Myers. London: Macmillan, 1883.

———. *The Odyssey: To Which Is Added The Battle of the Frogs and Mice.* Tr. Alexander Pope <1725–26>. London: Printed for G. B. Whittaker, 1827. (*LL* 436)

———. *The Odyssey of Homer.* Done into English Prose by S. H. Butcher and Andrew Lang. London: Macmillan, 1879.

Hooker, Edward (1822–1903). *The Descendants of Rev. Thomas Hooker: Hartford, Connecticut: 1586–1908.* Rochester, NY: Printed for Margaret Huntington Hooker, 1909. (*LL* 1084)

Howard, Robert E. (1906–1936). *The Hyborian Age* [with *A Probable Outline of Conan's Career* by P. Schuyler Miller and John D. Clark, Ph.D.]. Los Angeles: LANY Coöperative Publications, 1938. Rpt. in Robert E. Howard, *The Coming of Conan*. New York: Gnome Press, 1953.

Huysmans, Joris-Karl (1848–1907). *Against the Grain*. Tr. John Howard. New York: A. & C. Boni, 1930. (*LL* 483) [Translation of *A Rebours* (1884).]

James, M. R. (1862–1936). *The Collected Ghost Stories of M. R. James*. London: Edward Arnold, 1931.

———. *Ghost-Stories of an Antiquary*. London: Edward Arnold, 1904. (*LL* 499) [Contains "Black Magnus."]

———. *More Ghost Stories of an Antiquary*. London: Edward Arnold, 1911. (*LL* 500)

———. *A Thin Ghost and Others*. London: Edward Arnold, 1919. (*LL* 501)

———. *A Warning to the Curious*. London: Edward Arnold, 1925. (*LL* 502)

Jenks, William (1778–1866), ed. *The Comprehensive Commentary on the Holy Bible*. Brattleboro, VT: Fessenden & Co., 1835–39. 5 vols. (*LL* 505)

Joshi, S. T., with David E. Schultz. *Lovecraft's Library: A Catalogue*. 4th ed. New York: Hippocampus Press, 2017.

Juvenal (D. Junius Juvenalis, 1st–2nd c. C.E.). *The Satires of Decimus Junius Juvenalis*. Translated into English Verse by Mr. [John] Dryden and Several Other Eminent Hands. London: Printed for Jacob Tonson, 1693.

Juvenal [et al.]. *The Satires of Juvenal, Persius, Sulpicia, and Lucilius, Literally Translated into English Prose by the Rev. Lewis Evans*. To Which Is Added the Metrical Version of Juvenal and Persius by the Late William Gifford <1802>. London: George Bell & Sons, 1910. (*LL* 523)

Kingsley, Charles (1819–1875). *The Heroes; or, Greek Fairy Tales for My Children*. <1856> Philadelphia: H. Altemus, 1895. (*LL* 534)

Kremer, Heinrich (1430–1505), and Jakob Sprenger (1436?–1495). *Malleus Maleficarum*. Tr. Montague Summers. London: J. Rodker, 1928.

Krutch, Joseph Wood (1893–1970). *Edgar Allan Poe: A Study in Genius*. New York: Knopf, 1926.

———. *The Modern Temper: A Study and a Confession*. New York: Harcourt, Brace, 1929.

Lamb, Charles (1775–1834), and Mary Lamb (1764–1847). *Tales from Shakespeare*. <1807> Ed., with an introduction by the Rev. Alfred Ainger. New York: Thomas Y. Crowell Co. 1895. (*LL* 548)

Lewis, Matthew Gregory (1775–1818). *The Monk: A Romance*. <1796> London: Brentano's, [1924]. 3 vols. in 1. (*LL* 567)

Loveman, Samuel (1887–1976). *The Hermaphrodite and Other Poems*. Caldwell, ID: Caxton Printers, 1936. (*LL* 594)

Lowell, James Russell (1819–1891). *My Study Windows*. <1871> Boston: Houghton Mifflin, 1886. (*LL* 596)

Lucan (M. Annaeus Lucanus, 39–65). *Lucan's Pharsalia*. Translated into English verse by Nicolas Rowe. London: Printed for T. Johnson, 1720.

Machen, Arthur (1863–1947). *The Canning Wonder*. New York: Alfred A. Knopf, 1926. (*LL* 614)

————. *Far Off Things*. New York: Alfred A. Knopf, 1923. (*LL* 615)

————. *Hieroglyphics: A Note upon Ecstasy in Literature*. London: Grant Richards, 1902. (*LL* 616)

————. *The Hill of Dreams*. London: E. Grant Richards, 1907. New York: Alfred A. Knopf, 1923. (*LL* 617)

————. *The House of Souls*. <1906> New York: Alfred A. Knopf, 1923. (*LL* 618)

————. *The London Adventure: An Essay in Wandering*. New York: Alfred A. Knopf, 1924. (*LL* 619)

————. *The Secret Glory*. London: Martin Secker, 1922. New York: Alfred A. Knopf, 1922. (*LL* 620)

————. *The Shining Pyramid*. London: Martin Secker, 1925. (*LL* 621)

————. *The Terror*. London: Duckworth, 1917. New York: McBride, 1917.

————. *Things Near and Far*. New York: Alfred A. Knopf, 1923. (*LL* 622)

————. *The Three Impostors*. <1895> New York: Alfred A. Knopf, 1930. (*LL* 623)

Mather, Cotton (1663–1728). *Magnalia Christi Americana; or, The Ecclesiastical History of New-England, from Its First Planting in the Year 1620, unto the Year of Our Lord, 1698*. London: Printed for T. Parkhurst, 1702. (*LL* 645)

Maturin, Charles Robert (1782–1824). *Melmoth the Wanderer*. <1820> London: Richard Bentley & Son, 1892. 3 vols. (*LL* 646)

Mawson, Christopher Orlando Sylvester (1870–1938). *The Dictionary Companion: Being a Supplement to the Dictionary and the Thesaurus*. Garden City, NY: Garden City Pub. Co., 1932.

Merritt, A. (1884–1943). *The Metal Monster*. *Argosy* (7 August–25 September 1920). New York: Hippocampus Press, 2002.

Meyrink, Gustav (1868–1932). *The Golem*. <1915> Tr. Madge Pemberton. London: Gollancz; Boston: Houghton Mifflin, 1928.

Miller, P. Schuyler (1912–1974), and John D[rury] Clark (1907–1988). *A Probable Outline of Conan's Career*. Los Angeles: LANY Cooperative Publications, 1938.

The Modern Encyclopedia: A New Library of World Knowledge. Ed. A. H. McDannald. New York: Grosset & Dunlap, 1935. (*LL* 668)

Monaghan, Frank (1904-1969). *Ambrose Bierce and the Authorship of "The Monk and the Hangman's Daughter*. [n.p.]: [n.p.], 1931.

Moore, Thomas (1779–1852). *The Epicurean: A Tale*. <1827> (*LL* 674)

————. *The Poetical Works of Thomas Moore*. Philadelphia: Carey & Hart, 1844. (*LL* 675)

O'Brien, Edward J. (1890–1941). *The Dance of the Machines: The American Short Story and the Industrial Age*. New York: Macaulay Co., 1929. (*LL* 714)

Ovid (P. Ovidius Naso, 43 B.C.E.–17 C.E.). *Ovid*. Tr. by Dryden, Pope, Congreve, Addison, and others. New York: Harper & Brothers, 1837. 2 vols. (*LL* 728) [Contains the translation of Ovid's *Metamorphoses* (1708) edited by Samuel Garth.]

———. *The Heroycall Epistles of the Learned Poet Publius Ouidius Naso, in English Verse*. Set Out and Translated by George Tuberuile. London: Henry Denham, 1567. (*LL* 725)

Palgrave, Francis T. (1824–1897), ed. *The Golden Treasury: Selected from the Best Songs and Lyrical Poems in the English Language*. London: Macmillan, 1861. (*LL* 736)

Peck, Harry Thurston (1856–1914), ed. *Harper's Dictionary of Classical Literature and Antiquities*. New York: American Book Co., 1896. (*LL* 746)

People's Cyclopedia: A Complete Library of Reference Containing the Exact Knowledge of the World. Under the Chief Editorship of Charles Leonard-Stuart and George J. Hagar. New York: Syndicate Publishing Co., [1914]. 5 vols. (*LL* 750)

Perutz, Leo (1884–1957). *The Master of the Day of Judgment*. Tr. Hedwig Singer. London: Elkin Mathews & Marrot, 1929. New York: Charles Boni, 1930. (*LL* 753) [Translation of *Der Meister des Jüngsten Tages* (1923).]

People's Cyclopedia: A Complete Library of Reference Containing the Exact Knowledge of the World. Under the Chief Editorship of Charles Leonard-Stuart and George J. Hagar. New York: Syndicate Publishing Co., [1914]. 5 vols. (*LL* 750)

Pierce, Frederick Clifton (1855–1904). *Field Genealogy*. Chicago: W. B. Conkey Co., 1901.

Radcliffe, Ann (1764–1823). *The Mysteries of Udolpho*. <1794> London: George Routledge & Sons, [1882]–[192-]. (*LL* 787)

Railo, Eino (1884–1948). *The Haunted Castle: A Study of the Elements of English Romanticism*. New York: E. P. Dutton, 1927.

Reeve, Clara (1729–1807). *The Old English Baron*. <1777/1778> (*LL* 793)

Remy, Nicholas (1525–1612). *Demonolatry*. Translation of *La démonolâtrie* by E. A. Ashwin. Edited with introduction and notes by Montague Summers. London: John Rodker, 1930.

Renshaw, Anne Tillery (1890–c. 1945). *Well Bred Speech: A Brief, Intensive Aid for English Students*. [Washington, DC: Standard Press, 1936.] (*LL* 796)

Reynolds, George W. M. (1814–1879). *Faust: A Romance of the Secret Tribunals*. London: Vickers, 1847. New York: Hurst, n.d. (as *Faust and the Demon*).

———. *Wagner, the Wehr-Wolf*. London: J. Dicks, 1848, 1857, 1872.

Richardson, Leon Burr (1878–1951). *History of Dartmouth College*. Hanover, NH: The Stephen Daye Press, 1932. 2 vols.

Robertson, Morgan (1861–1915). *Over the Border*. [New York]: McClure's Magazine and Metropolitan Magazine, [1898?].

Roget, Peter Mark (1779–1869). *Thesaurus of English Words and Phrases.* New York: Grosset & Dunlap, 1933.

Ruber, Peter (1940–2014). "Edgar Hoffmann Price." In Peter Ruber, ed. *Arkham's Masters of Horror. A 60th Anniversary Anthology Retrospective of the First 30 Years of Arkham House.* Sauk City, WI: Arkham House, 2000. 195–200.

Russell, W. Clark (1844–1911). *The Frozen Pirate.* <1887> (*LL* 821)

Safford, Henry Barnard (1883–1956). *That Bennington Mob.* New York: Messner, 1935.

Santayana, George (1863–1952). *The Last Puritan: A Memoir in the Form of a Novel.* London: Constable, 1935. New York: Charles Scribner's Sons, 1936.

Savile, Frank Mackenzie (1865–1950). *Beyond the Great South Wall: The Secret of the Antarctic.* <1899> New York: Grosset & Dunlap, 1901. (*LL* 828)

Schultz, David E. "'Whaddya Make Them Eyes at Me For?': Lovecraft and Book Publishers." *Lovecraft Annual* No. 12 (2018): 51–65.

Shakespeare, William. *A Midsummer Night's Dream.* Illustrated by Virgil Finlay. Chicago: Popular Fiction Pub. Co., 1935. (*LL* 1091)

Shiel, M. P. (1865–1947). *The Pale Ape and Other Pulses.* London: T. Werner Laurie, 1911.

Smith, Clark Ashton (1893–1961). *The Double Shadow and Other Fantasies.* [Auburn, CA: Clark Ashton Smith, 1933.] (*LL* 880)

———, and David H. Keller. *The White Sibyl* [by Smith] *and Men of Avalon* [by Keller]. Everett, PA: Fantasy Publications, 1934. (*LL* 885)

Smith, G. Elliot (1871–1937), and Warren R. Dawson (1888–1968). *Egyptian Mummies.* London: George Allen & Unwin, 1924.

Spengler, Oswald (1880–1936). *Der Untergang des Abendlandes.* <1918–22> Tr. by Charles Francis Atkinson as *The Decline of the West.* London: George Allen & Unwin, 1922–26. 2 vols.

Statius (P. Papinius Statius, 40?–96?). *The Thebaid.* Translated into English verse [by William Lillington Lewis]. Oxford: Clarendon Press, 1767.

Stevenson, Robert Louis (1850–1894). *A Child's Garden of Verses.* London, Longmans, 1890.

Stormonth, James (1824–1882). *A Dictionary of the English Language.* The Pronunciation Carefully Revised by the Rev. P. H. Help. <1871> New York: Harper & Brothers, 1885. (*LL* 928)

Syntax, Doctor [pseud. of William Combe, 1742–1823]. *The Life of Napoleon: A Hudibrastic Poem in Fifteen Cantos.* Embellished with thirty engravings by G. Cruikshank. London: T. Tegg, 1815.

———. *The Tour of Doctor Syntax in Search of the Picturesque.* <1812> Illustrated by Thomas Rowlandson. New ed. New York: D. Appleton & Co, 1903. (*LL* 941)

Tacitus (P. Cornelius Tacitus, 55?–117?). *The Works of Cornelius Tacitus*. With an Essay on His History and Genius, Notes, Supplements, &c., by Arthur Murphy. <1793> New ed. New York: Bangs, Brother & Co., 1855. (*LL* 942)

Thompson, Judge D. P. (1795–1868). *The Green Mountain Boys: A Historical Tale of the Early Settlement of Vermont*. Boston: Lothrop, Lee & Shepard, 1839.

Van Loon, Hendrik (1882–1944). *The Story of Mankind*. New York: Boni & Liveright, 1921.

———. *The Story of the Bible*. New York: Boni & Liveright, 1923.

Vaughan, L. Brent (1873–1950), comp. *Hill's Spanish-English and English-Spanish Dictionary*. Chicago: G. M. Hill Co., [1898]. (*LL* 992)

Velázquez de la Cavena, Mariano (1778–1860), and T. Simmone. *Ollendorff's New Method of Learning to Read, Write, and Speak the Spanish Language*. New York: D. Appleton & Co., 1850. (*LL* 993).

Virgil (P. Vergilius Maro, 70–19 B.C.E.). *The Æneid of Virgil*. Translated into English Verse by John Conington. London: Longmans, Green, 1866.

———. *The Works of Virgil*. Tr. John Dryden <1697>. London: Henry Frowde/Oxford University Press, World's Classics, 1903–06. (*LL* 1002)

———. *The Works of Virgil*. Literally Translated into English Prose, with Notes, by Davidson. A new ed., rev., with additional notes by Theodore Alois Buckley. London: H. G. Bohn, 1855.

[Walpole, Horace (1717–1797).] *Jeffery's Edition of the Castle of Otranto, a Gothic Story*. <1764> London: Printed by W. Blackader ... for the Publisher [Edward Jeffery], 1800. (*LL* 1007)

Wandrei, Donald (1908–1987). *Dead Titans, Waken!/Invisible Sun*. Ed. S. T. Joshi. Lakewood CO: Centipede Press, 2011.

Wanostrocht, Nicholas (1745–1812). *Recueil choisi de traits historiques, et de contes moraux*. <1785> Baltimore: S. Jefferis, 1810. (*LL* 1011)

Webster, Noah (1758–1834). *An American Dictionary of the English Language*. Rev. & enl. by Chauncey A. Goodrich and Noah Porter. Springfield, MA: G. & C. Merriam, 1864. (*LL* 1022)

———. *Webster's International Dictionary of the English Language*. Now Thoroughly Revised and Enlarged under the Supervision of Noah Porter. Springfield, MA: G. & C. Merriam, 1891. (*LL* 1024)

Weigall, Arthur (1880–1934), *Wanderings in Roman Britain*. London: T. Butterworth, [1926]. (*LL* 1025)

Wells, H. G. (1866–1946). *The Outline of History*. London: Newnes, 1920 (2 vols.). Garden City, NY: Garden City Publishing Co., [1920?]–[1931]. (*LL* 1028)

———. *The Outline of History* (abridged). Garden City, NY: Star Books, 1931.

———. *A Short History of the World*. New York: Macmillan Co., 1922. (*LL* 1029)

————. *The War of the Worlds.* London: Heinemann, 1898. New York: Harper & Brothers, 1898.

————, Julian Huxley (1887–1975), and G. P. Wells (1901–1985). *The Science of Life: A Summary of Contemporary Knowledge about Life and Its Possibilities.* London: Amalgamated Press, 1930. 2 vols. New York: Doubleday, 1931. 4 vols.

Williams, Blanche Colton (1879–1944), ed. *O. Henry Memorial Award Prize Stories.* Garden City, NY: Doubleday, 1932.

Wittie, Robert (1613?–1684) *ΟΥΡΟΝΟΣΚΟΠΙΑ; or, A Survey of the Heavens: A Plain Description of the Admirable Fabrick and Motions of the Heavenly Bodies, to Which Is Added the Gout-Raptures, Augmented & Improved.* In English, Latine, and Greek Lyrick Verse (London: Printed by J. M. for the Author, 1681. (*LL* 1062)

Woolley, Edwin Campbell (1878–1916). *Handbook of Composition.* Boston: D. C. Heath, 1907.

Index